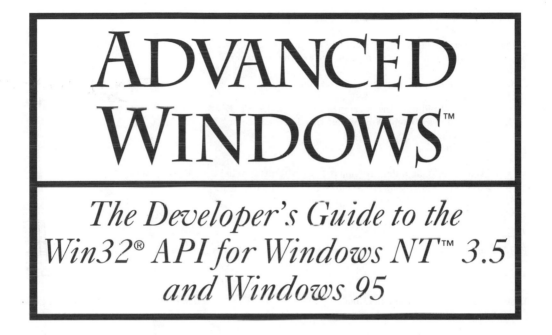

ADVANCED WINDOWS™

The Developer's Guide to the Win32® API for Windows NT™ 3.5 and Windows 95

JEFFREY RICHTER

Microsoft® *Press*

PUBLISHED BY
Microsoft Press
A Division of Microsoft Corporation
One Microsoft Way
Redmond, Washington 98052-6399

Library of Congress Cataloging-in-Publication Data
Richter, Jeffrey.
      Advanced Windows : the developer's guide to the Win32
   API for Windows NT and Windows 95 / by Jeffrey Richter.
            p.   cm.
      Includes index.
      ISBN 1-55615-677-4
      1. Windows (Computer programs)   2. Microsoft Win32.   3. Microsoft
   Windows NT.   4. Microsoft Windows 95.   I. Title.
   QA76.76.W56R52   1995
   005.26--dc20   94-47264
                                                                        CIP

Printed and bound in the United States of America.

1 2 3 4 5 6 7 8 9   QBP   0 9 8 7 6 5

Distributed to the book trade in Canada by Macmillan of Canada, a division of Canada Publishing Corporation.

A CIP catalogue record for this book is available from the British Library.

Microsoft Press books are available through booksellers and distributors worldwide. For further information about international editions, contact your local Microsoft Corporation office. Or contact Microsoft Press International directly at fax (206) 936-7329.

Acquisitions Editor: Dean Holmes
Project Editor: Rebecca Gleason
Technical Editor: Jim Fuchs

To my mother, Arlene, for her bravery and courage through the most difficult and trying of times. Your love and support have shaped me into the person I am. You're with me wherever I go.
—With all my love, Jeff

To Susan "Q-bert" Ramee, for showing me that computers are not at the center of the Universe with all of the planets circling around.
—J "BBB" R

CONTENTS SUMMARY

CHAPTER ONE

THE WIN32 API AND PLATFORMS THAT SUPPORT IT **1**

▶ This chapter explains Microsoft's various APIs and operating system platforms; clarifies the latest catchwords *(Win32, Win32s, Windows 95,* and *Windows NT);* and discusses Microsoft's goals for each of them. By the end of the chapter, you will understand why I believe this is a very exciting time for software developers and why the Win32 API is the area in which software engineers should be concentrating their development efforts.

CHAPTER TWO

PROCESSES **9**

▶ Under Windows 95 and Windows NT, an instance of an executing application is a process. This chapter explains how a new process is invoked, how it initializes, and how it is destroyed. Various attributes associated with a process are also explained. For example, in Win32 each process has its own address space, which means that one process cannot adversely affect another process—this is not true in 16-bit Windows. This chapter also introduces Win32 Kernel objects, which are the basis for all kernel-related tasks in both Windows 95 and Windows NT. A solid understanding of Kernel objects is required for any serious Win32 developer.

CHAPTER THREE

THREADS **51**

▶ Threads are at the heart of Windows 95's and Windows NT's multitasking abilities. In order for a Win32 process to actually do anything, it must have threads that execute the code and manipulate the data contained in the process. All Win32 processes contain at least one thread, but both Windows 95 and Windows NT allow a process to contain several threads that are scheduled and preemptively multitasked by the operating system. This chapter explains how threads are created, scheduled, and destroyed.

▶ Advanced operating systems such as Windows 95 and Windows NT require sophisticated memory architectures. This chapter explains how the system manages the computer's RAM and paging files on the hard disk in order to give each process a full 4 GB of virtual address space. The chapter also covers how each process's address space is partitioned and discusses the implementation differences between Windows 95 and Windows NT. One of the features that make the Win32 memory architecture unique is that Win32 separates the task of reserving regions of address space from the task of committing physical storage to these regions. This chapter explains how these two tasks are accomplished as well as how protection attributes can be assigned to pages of committed physical storage.

▶ This chapter builds on the information presented in Chapter 4. The chapter introduces various Win32 functions that allow you to explore the system's memory configuration and the contents (code and data) of a process's address space.

▶ This chapter shows how to use virtual memory management techniques in your own applications. Topics include how to reserve regions in a process's address space and techniques for knowing when to commit physical storage to these regions. These techniques allow an application to use physical storage more efficiently than it could under most other operating systems.

CHAPTER SEVEN

MEMORY-MAPPED FILES **207**

▶ Windows 95 and Windows NT use memory-mapped files to implement virtual memory management. All of a process's code and data are backed by a file on disk—a memory-mapped file. This chapter demonstrates how memory-mapped files make manipulation of disk files almost trivially simple. The chapter also shows how to use memory-mapped files to share code and data among multiple processes.

CHAPTER EIGHT

HEAPS **261**

▶ Heaps are the third and last memory management technique offered by the Win32 API. This chapter shows how to create multiple heaps within a single process and explains why a developer might want to do this. This chapter also discusses how the 16-bit Windows heap functions are emulated by the Win32 API under Windows 95 and Windows NT in order to make it easier for developers to port existing 16-bit Windows source code.

CHAPTER NINE

THREAD SYNCHRONIZATION **283**

▶ Whenever multiple threads are executing simultaneously or are being preemptively interrupted, an application will often need to suspend a thread in order to prevent data corruption. Windows 95 and Windows NT offer several objects for performing thread synchronization; this chapter discusses these objects and describes techniques for using them.

CHAPTER TEN

WINDOW MESSAGES
AND ASYNCHRONOUS INPUT **417**

▶ One of the biggest problems with 16-bit Windows is that it is too easy for a single application to hang all running applications. Robust operating systems such as Windows 95 and Windows NT do not allow applications to compromise the smooth execution of other processes in the system. In order to create a robust environment, window messages and hardware input are handled differently in Win32 than in 16-bit Windows.

These changes may break some source code originally written for 16-bit Windows. This chapter explains how window messages are processed in both Windows 95 and Windows NT.

▶ Dynamic-link libraries (DLLs) have always been the cornerstone of all Windows applications—and they continue to be in Windows 95 and Windows NT. However, DLLs are managed quite differently under Win32 than under 16-bit Windows. This chapter explains how a DLL is mapped into a process's address space and how to appropriately initialize a DLL. In addition, this chapter demonstrates how a DLL can be used to export both functions and data.

CHAPTER TWELVE

▶ In an environment in which multiple threads are running concurrently, it's important to associate data objects and variables with the individual threads of a process. This chapter describes how to use both dynamic and static thread-local storage techniques in order to associate data with specific threads.

▶ This chapter discusses how an application can manipulate the many file systems offered by Windows 95 and Windows NT: FAT, CDFS, HPFS, and NTFS. It also discusses how to manipulate directories, files, and the data contained in the files. Also discussed are some additional techniques for manipulating the file system, such as directory tree walking and file system change notifications. Finally, this chapter presents methods for using asynchronous file I/O, alertable file I/O, and file change notification.

CHAPTER FOURTEEN

▶ Structured exception handling (SEH) is a new mechanism that allows application developers to write more robust and reliable applications.

SEH consists of two components that work together: exception handling and termination handling. Exception handling is a mechanism that allows an application to catch both hardware and software exceptions (for example, invalid memory accesses). Termination handling guarantees that clean-up tasks are performed even if an exception occurs.

CHAPTER FIFTEEN

▶ Software developers are finding a huge potential for software distribution in international markets. To help developers, Microsoft built full Unicode support into Windows NT and limited Unicode support into Windows 95. Unicode is a 16-bit character set that lets developers easily manipulate characters and strings for different languages and writing systems. This chapter discusses how you can best take advantage of Win32's Unicode facilities to help localize your development projects.

▶ The robust nature of the Windows 95 and Windows NT environments makes it much more difficult to manipulate other processes in the system. While it is not normal for processes to alter one another, some processes, such as debuggers and other tools, require intimate knowledge of other processes in order to be useful to the software developer. This chapter demonstrates three techniques that allow a process to inject a DLL into another process's address space. These techniques require a knowledge of processes, threads, virtual memory, thread synchronization, window messages, DLLs, structured exception handling, and Unicode.

▶ Most Windows programmers have never heard of message crackers, even though these programming aids exist for both 16-bit Windows and Win32. This appendix explains how to use message crackers to help you write, read, and maintain your source code. In addition, message crackers make it much easier to port 16-bit Windows source code to Win32 and vice versa.

TABLE OF CONTENTS

CHAPTER THREE

THREADS **51**

CHAPTER FOUR

WIN32 MEMORY ARCHITECTURE **93**

CHAPTER FIVE

EXPLORING VIRTUAL MEMORY **127**

CHAPTER SIX

USING VIRTUAL MEMORY
IN YOUR OWN APPLICATIONS **169**

CHAPTER SEVEN

MEMORY-MAPPED FILES **207**

CHAPTER EIGHT

HEAPS **261**

CHAPTER NINE

THREAD SYNCHRONIZATION **283**

CHAPTER TWELVE

THREAD-LOCAL STORAGE **535**

CHAPTER THIRTEEN

FILE SYSTEMS AND FILE I/O **569**

CHAPTER FOURTEEN

STRUCTURED EXCEPTION HANDLING **683**

ACKNOWLEDGMENTS

Although my name appears alone on the cover of this book, many people have contributed in some form or another to the book's creation. In many cases, these people are good friends of mine (that is, we occasionally go to movies or out to dinner together); and in other cases, I have never met the individuals and have conversed with them only on the phone or by electronic mail. I could not have completed this book without the assistance or support of each of the following—I thank you all.

Susan "Q" Ramee gave me her love and support throughout the entire process. Sue also proofread chapters and helped me come up with some ideas for the sample programs. And, of course, it would not be right to thank Sue without also thanking her two cats, Natt and Cato. Often, late at night, when I could not sleep and decided to write, Natt and Cato would keep me company. They would frequently shed on my notes and walk across the keyboard as I typed. Any typos you sea in thid boot are duw too Natt amd Cato, knot me, I assure you.

Jim Harkins is one of my best friends. Whenever I think of Jim, I can hear him saying, "When was the last time you put chlorine in the Jacuzzi?" And, although it's not publicly known, Jim is the creator of the very popular and hilariously outrageous game "Guess What The Plant Said?" His direct contribution to this book can be found in the Directory Walker, Alertable File I/O, and File Change sample programs. In addition, Jim also helped me think through many of the thread synchronization issues in the book and the CPU-independent version of *InjectLib*.

Scott Ludwig and Valerie Horvath have become my closest friends. Our favorite pastime is going to movies that have lots of explosions and destruction in them. Scott and Valerie have also been initiating me into the world of professional basketball. (You mean the Harlem Globetrotters?) Scott was a lead developer at Microsoft for the first version of Windows NT. When I was writing the first edition of this book, Scott was extremely patient with me and answered all of my questions. Through the discussions we have had, Scott has earned my utmost respect and admiration.

Lucy Gooding added spice and spices (mostly garlic) to my life. She deserves a medal for putting up with my busy schedule. Now that the book is done, we can spend more time with Me-yow-zer and Chirrp-per.

Jeff Cooperstein is a friend with a keen sense of how to muck with a system and make it do things that it was specifically designed *not* to do. Jeff devised several ways to circumvent Windows NT security (all of which have been fixed in Windows NT 3.5) and was also about to start work on his Virus Developer's Kit (VDK). He is also known for saying, "Just disconnect the network cable, the machine won't receive the broadcast packet, plug the cable back in and you're set!"

Jonathan Locke and I share a common interest in music, but for some reason, he prefers 386/25MHz machines to MIPS machines. Jonathan helped with proofing many of the chapters and made several recommendations to mangle my text and alter its meaning. Many of his suggestions opened up either a ball of worms or a can of wax. However, we managed to incorporate them into the book before it went to press.

Lou Perazzoli, Steve Wood, and Marc Lucovsky of the Windows NT development team reviewed a number of chapters and answered many questions related to threads and memory management.

Brian Smith, Jon Thomason, and Michael Toutonghi of the Windows 95 development team answered several questions having to do with Windows 95 memory and thread management.

Asmus Freytag (aka Dr. Unicode) reviewed the Unicode chapter and gave me some last-minute suggestions over dinner at Red Robin one very rainy Seattle evening.

Dave Hart of the Windows NT NTVDM development team spent a lot of time with me in person and via e-mail while I asked numerous questions about running 16-bit MS-DOS and Windows applications under Windows NT's NTVDM layer. While very little of this information appears in the book, Dave gave me a good deal more insight into the workings of Windows NT.

Chuck Mitchell, Steve Salisbury, and Jonathan Mark of the Win32 Visual C++ team answered my questions about structured exception handling, thread-local storage, the C run-time library, and linking.

I would also like to thank/mention Mark Durley and Cezary Marcjan, who found bugs in the first edition and provided me with numerous ideas and stimulating conversations about Win32 programming.

I would also like to thank/mention several additional developers on the Visual C++ team I had the opportunity to work with: Byron Dazey, Eric Lang ("Do they sell milk at the Crest of London?"), Dan Spalding, Matthew Tebbs ("Thanks for brunch!"), Bruce Johnson, Jon Jorstad ("How's this for a better thing to say?"), Dave Henderson, and T.K. Brackman.

Bernie McIlroy helped me test the sample applications on a DEC Alpha machine. Bernie thinks that all introductions should begin with "In the beginning..." and is also well known for his philosophy on life: "Life is a heck of a thing."

Numerous developers at Microsoft helped fill in the gaps for me: Mark Cliggett, Cameron Ferroni, Eric Fogelin, Randy Kath, and Steve Sinofsky.

Rebecca Gleason was my editor at Microsoft Press for the second edition of the book. I still owe her a big favor for putting all the RC files back into the book at the last moment. Rebecca was on top of everything and always had an answer to my questions—even though her answer was frequently, "It's a style thing." I'm still trying to recover from the 10-alarm barbecue lunch we had from Dixie's BBQ/Porter's Automotive Service shop.

Jim Fuchs was my technical editor at Microsoft Press for the second edition. Jim worked incredibly hard on proofing my source code and resource files. He was absolutely indefatigable while dealing with code changes as he and I worked on the source code at the same time.

Nancy Siadek, my editor for the first edition of this book, deserves an award for the amount of effort and dedication she gave to me. I'm sure she had no idea what she was getting into. Nancy taught me more about writing in the short time I spent with her than I learned in all my years.

Jeff Carey, my technical editor for the first edition of this book, was a big help in letting me off the hook by answering many of Nancy's questions, which allowed me to rewrite some of the material.

I also want to thank the rest of the Microsoft Press team. Many of them I have never met, but I do appreciate all their efforts. For the second edition: Shawn Peck, John Sugg, Jim Kramer, Michael Victor, Kim Eggleston, David Holter, Penelope West, Richard Carter, Elisabeth Thebaud, Peggy Herman, and Barbara Remmele. And those of the first edition: Erin O'Connor, Laura Sackerman, Deborah Long, Peggy Herman, Lisa Iversen, and Barb Runyan.

Thanks also to:

Dan Horn at Borland International, for his suggestions and comments on several chapters and for giving an apple to the teacher.

Jim Lane, Tom Van Baak, Rich Peterson, and Bill Baxter, for their assistance with the DEC Alpha compiler.

Dean Holmes, acquisitions director at Microsoft Press, for signing me and for putting up with delays in the first edition while I purchased my new house.

Gretchen Bilson and everyone at *Microsoft Systems Journal,* for encouraging me to continue writing.

Charles Petzold, for introducing me to Microsoft Press and hot and sour soup.

Carlos Richardson, for helping me get TJ-Net (my home network) up and running in my new house.

Donna Murray, for her love, support, and friendship over the years. I admire you for always pursuing your dreams.

My brother, Ron, for trying to find me a copy of Patrick Moraz's "Salamander." Even though you never found it, I know you tried. I'll ask Peter Gabriel to autograph your golf clubs the next time he's in town. Here's hoping you win the contest and that we and Velveeta-Clear–loving Maria take a trip to Bath, England.

My mom and dad, Arlene and Sylvan, for their love and support over the years. Both of you are welcome to visit me anytime you want. I'll keep the Jacuzzi hot and a bag of popcorn by the TV, and I'll order another set of contour pillows.

INTRODUCTION

I have really enjoyed writing this book. There is nothing I like more than being at the forefront of technology and learning new things. Windows 95 and Windows NT are definitely at the forefront of technology, and boy, is there a lot of new stuff to learn. But don't let the amount of new stuff scare you. If you are already a 16-bit Windows programmer, you will find that you can start writing Win32 applications after learning just a few simple techniques for porting your existing code. However, these ported programs will not be taking advantage of the new, powerful, and exciting features that the Win32 environments of Windows 95 and Windows NT offer.

After you have started working with Win32, you can begin incorporating more and more of these features into your applications. Many of the Win32 features make it much easier to write programs. And, as I soon discovered when porting some of my own code, I was able to delete large sections of code from my existing programs and replace them with calls to facilities offered by Win32.

The new features are such a pleasure to use and work with that I now do Win32 programming exclusively and frequently speak at companies and conferences explaining how developers can effectively write Win32 applications.

This book is the result of my experiences in working with Windows 95 and Windows NT. I have learned a lot since the first edition of this book; for this edition, I have rewritten almost all of the chapters and have greatly expanded the depth to which I cover the more advanced Win32 features. I have also reorganized the material and present it in what I believe is a much clearer fashion.

There is no doubt in my mind that the Win32 API will become a standard API for both minicomputers and mainframe computers (with Windows NT) and for personal computer systems (with Windows 95 and Windows NT). This book should help you get ready for developing applications for an environment that is destined to be the industry standard.

What I Expect from You

This book is for the Windows developer who already has some experience writing programs for 16-bit Windows. However, an extensive knowledge of 16-bit Windows is not necessary—you need only know the basics of Windows programming, including window procedures, window messages, and dialog boxes. This book covers new features that have been introduced in the Win32 API as it runs under the Windows 95 and Windows NT operating systems. No attempt will be made to teach introductory Windows programming. This book also covers the types of issues you should expect when porting 16-bit Windows applications to the Win32 API.

About the Sample Applications

The purpose of the sample applications is to demonstrate with real code how to use the advanced features of Win32. You could never read enough text to replace the knowledge and experience that you gain by writing your own applications. I know that this has certainly been true of my experience with Win32. Many of the sample applications presented throughout this book are direct descendants of experimental programs that I created myself in an effort to understand how the Win32 functions behave.

Programs Written in C

When it came time to decide on a language for the sample applications, I was torn between C and C++. For large projects, I always use C++—but the fact of the matter is that most Windows programmers are not using C++ yet, and I didn't want to alienate my largest potential audience.

Message Cracker Macros

If you are not writing your Win32 application using C++ and a Windows class library (such as Microsoft's Foundation Classes), I highly recommend that you use the message cracker macros defined in the WINDOWSX.H header file. These macros make your programs easier to write, read, and maintain. I feel so strongly about the message cracker macros that I have included Appendix A in this book to explain why message crackers exist and how to use them effectively.

Knowledge of 16-Bit Windows Programming

None of the programs presented rely on extensive knowledge of 16-bit Windows programs, although experience with 16-bit Windows programming is definitely a plus. The sample programs do assume that you are familiar with the creation and manipulation of dialog boxes and their child controls. Very little knowledge of GDI and Kernel functions is required.

When presenting various topics in this book, I do make behavior comparisons between 16-bit Windows and Win32. If you already understand how 16-bit Windows behaves, you should have an easier time understanding how behaviors have changed in Win32.

Running the Sample Applications Under Windows 95

Windows 95 is targeted to run on machines that have only 4 MB of RAM. In order to accomplish this, Microsoft had to cut some corners when creating Windows 95. For the software developer, this means that some Win32 functions do not have full implementations on Windows 95. With respect to my sample applications, this means that some of the applications have additional functionality when run under Windows NT.

In addition, at the time I was working on this book Windows 95 was still under development. All the sample programs were tested with Windows 95 build 275, but there was no way to check the sample programs with the final release of Windows 95. At the time I finished the book, the following programs did not run under Windows 95 build 275: ALTERTIO.EXE (Chapter 13) and TINJLIB.EXE (Chapter 16)—for reasons that I explain when I introduce them in their respective chapters.

For up-to-the-minute changes in information about Windows 95, I recommend that you periodically visit the WIN_NEWS forum, which you can find at the following locations:

On CompuServe:	*GO WINNEWS*
On the Internet:	*ftp://ftp.microsoft.com/peropsys/Win_News*
	http://www.microsoft.com
On AOL:	keyword *WINNEWS*
On Prodigy:	jumpword *WINNEWS*
On Genie:	*WINNEWS* file area on Windows RTC

You can also subscribe to Microsoft's electronic newsletter, *WinNews*. To subscribe, send Internet e-mail to *enews@microsoft.nwnet.com* and put the words *SUBSCRIBE WINNEWS* in the text of the e-mail.

Unrelated Code

I wanted to remove any code from the sample programs that was not directly related to the techniques I wanted to demonstrate. Unfortunately, this is not possible when writing any Windows program. For example, most Windows programming books repeat the code for registering window classes in every application presented in the book. I have done my best to reduce this type of nonrelevant code.

One way that I reduce nonrelevant code is by using techniques that are not always obvious to Windows programmers. For example, the user interface for most of the sample programs is a dialog box. In fact, most of the sample programs have a single line of code in *WinMain* that simply calls the *DialogBox* function. As a result, none of the sample programs initialize a WNDCLASS structure or call the *RegisterClass* function. In addition, only one sample application—FileChng in Chapter 13—has a message loop in it.

Independent Sample Applications

I have tried to keep the sample applications independent from one another. For example, the memory-mapped files chapter is the only chapter containing memory-mapped file sample programs. Because I have structured the sample programs so that they are independent, feel free to skip earlier chapters and proceed to later chapters.

Occasionally you'll find a sample program that uses techniques or information presented in earlier chapters. For example, the SEHExcpt sample application, presented in Chapter 14, "Structured Exception Handling," demonstrates how to manipulate virtual memory. I decided to mix these two topics in a single sample program because structured exception handling (SEH) is a very useful mechanism for manipulating virtual memory. In order to fully understand this sample application, you should read Chapters 4, 5, and 6 prior to examining the SEHExcpt sample application.

There is one sample application, however, that has a little bit of everything: TInjLib, presented in Chapter 16. To fully understand this application, you must have a good understanding of kernel objects, virtual memory, processes, threads, thread synchronization, dynamic-link libraries, structured exception handling, and Unicode. I would say that understanding the TInjLib application qualifies you to go on an interview and say that you really understand Win32 programming.

STRICT Compliance

All of the sample programs have been compiled with the STRICT identifier defined, which catches frequent coding errors. For example, with the STRICT identifier defined, the passing of an incorrect handle type to a function is caught during compilation instead of at run time. For more information about using the STRICT identifier, refer to the *Programming Techniques* documentation included in the Win32 SDK.

Error Checking

Error checking should be a big part of any software project. Unfortunately, proper error checking can make the size and complexity of a software project grow exponentially. In order to make the sample applications more understandable and less cluttered, I have not put very much error-checking code into them. If you use any of my code fragments and incorporate them into your own production code, I strongly encourage you to examine my code closely and add any appropriate error checking.

Bug Free

I would love to say that all of the sample programs are bug free. But, as with all software, it's only bug free until someone finds a bug. Of course, I have given my own code several walk-throughs in the hope of catching everything. If you do find a bug, I would appreciate your reporting it to me via my Internet address: *v-jeffrr@microsoft.com*.

Tested Platforms and Environments

The bulk of my research and development for this book has been on a machine with only one Intel 486 CPU. I have also recompiled and tested all the sample programs on a MIPS machine and on a DEC Alpha machine, using the compilers and linkers that come with Visual C++ 2.0 for these platforms. All of the programs have been tested under both Windows 95 and Windows NT.

For most of the sample programs, I use no vendor-specific compiler extensions. These programs should compile and link regardless of the machine on which you are running and regardless of which tools you are using to compile and link the sample programs.

However, several of the sample programs do take advantage of compiler-specific features:

- Named data sections using the following syntax:

```
#pragma data_seg (...)
```

- Static thread-local storage using the following syntax:

```
__declspec(thread)
```

- Structured exception handling using the following keywords:

```
__try, __leave, __finally, and __except
```

Because most compiler vendors will be modifying their compilers to recognize these four new keywords, it is unlikely that you will have to modify the structured exception handling sample programs at all.

- Compiler-assisted function importing and exporting using the following syntax:

```
__declspec(dllimport) and __declspec(dllexport)
```

If you are using tools other than those included in Visual C++ 2.0, you will need to discover how your vendor exposes these features and modify the sample programs accordingly.

Important

There is a problem with the Microsoft Visual C++ 2.0 Setup program. If you turn off MFC support when installing Visual C++, the Setup program does not copy the WINRES.H file to the \MSVC20\MFC\INCLUDE directory. If WINRES.H is missing from this directory, you will not be able to compile the resource files that come with this book. There are two ways to fix this problem. First, you can reinstall Visual C++ with the MFC option turned on. Second, you can manually copy the WINRES.H file from the Visual C++ CD-ROM to the \MSVC20\MFC\INCLUDE directory on your hard disk.

Unicode

Originally I wrote all the sample programs so that they could compile natively using the ANSI character set only. Then, when I started writing the Unicode chapter, I became a very strong believer in Unicode and tried desperately to come up with a sample program for the Unicode chapter. Then the answer came to me: convert all the sample applications in the book so that they demonstrate Unicode. This conversion effort took only four hours and allows you to compile all the sample applications natively for both ANSI and Unicode.

The disadvantage in doing this is that you might see calls to unfamiliar functions that manipulate characters and strings within the sample applications. For the most part, you should be able to guess what that function does if you are familiar with the standard C run-time library functions for manipulating characters and strings. However, if you get stuck, you should refer to Chapter 15. This chapter explains in much greater detail what I have done in the sample programs. It is my hope that you not be confused by the new character and string functions and that you see how easy it is to write your application code using Unicode.

Installing the Sample Programs

The companion CD-ROM contains the source code for all the sample applications presented throughout this book. In addition, the EXE and DLL files for the x86, MIPS, and Alpha AXP versions of the sample programs are included. Because none of the files on the CD-ROM are compressed, you can simply insert the CD-ROM and load the source code files; you can also run the sample applications directly from the CD-ROM.

On the CD-ROM, the root directory contains the installation software and the ADVWIN32.H header file discussed in Appendix B. The root directory also contains several subdirectories. Three of these subdirectories are called X86.BIN, MIPS.BIN, and ALPHA.BIN. These subdirectories contain the EXE and the DLL files for their respective CPU platforms. If you are running Windows NT on a platform other than an x86, MIPS, or Alpha, you can still access the source code files but you will not be able to execute any of the sample applications without building them yourself. This means you will need to install the source code files on your hard disk. The section "Windows NT" later in this Introduction discusses how to perform this installation.

The remaining subdirectories contain the source code files for the sample applications. Each sample application is in its very own subdirectory. The eight-letter name of each subdirectory contains the name of the sample program, and the subdirectory's extension indicates the chapter in the book where the program is presented. For example, the subdirectory FILECHNG.09 identifies the File Change sample application presented in Chapter 9.

If you are interested only in examining the source code or running the sample applications, you do not have to copy anything to your hard disk. However, if you want to modify, compile, or debug the sample applications, you will need to copy the files to your hard disk. The next two sections explain how to access the sample application files depending on whether you are running Windows 95 or Windows NT.

Windows 95

When you insert a CD-ROM into your CD-ROM drive, Windows 95 detects the disc and can automatically execute a Setup program contained on that CD-ROM. The CD-ROM supplied with this book has been prepared to take advantage of this feature. When you insert the CD-ROM, the following dialog box appears:

If you click on the Copy Source Code, EXEs, And DLLs To The Hard Disk button, the Setup program supplied on the CD-ROM executes and allows you to type in the directory path where you would like the files copied. When the Setup program is complete, a new menu item will be created for the Programs menu of the system's task bar. You can execute any of the sample applications by selecting the desired application from the task bar's Programs menu.

If you select the Explore The Sample Applications On The CD-ROM button, the Windows 95 Explorer will display the icons for all the sample applications, as shown below. Double-click on an icon to run the associated application.

Windows NT

Under Windows NT, you must manually invoke the SETUP.BAT batch file located in the root directory of the CD-ROM. This batch file determines which type of CPU platform you are running Windows NT on and invokes the correct Setup application for your platform (ISETUP.EXE for *x*86, MSETUP.EXE for MIPS, and ASETUP.EXE for Alpha). The Setup program then prompts you to type in a destination directory and, after you have done so, copies all the source code files and binary files to your hard drive. After all the files have been copied, a new Program Manager group is created and all the sample programs arc added to this group, as shown on the next page.

If you are running Windows NT on a platform other than *x*86, MIPS, or Alpha, you must invoke SETUP.BAT and specify a location at which the files should be installed. For example, the following line assumes that the CD-ROM is in drive H and that you want to install the source code files in the ADVWIN32 directory on drive C. (This directory will be created if it doesn't exist.)

```
C:\>H:\SETUP C:\ADVWIN32
```

Of course, the Setup batch file cannot create a Program Manager group because no EXE files are installed. You will have to create your own Program Manager group, compile each of the sample applications, and manually add each application to the newly created Program Manager group.

CHAPTER ONE

THE WIN32 API AND PLATFORMS THAT SUPPORT IT

I am a frequent speaker at industry events, where I am often asked, "What is the difference between Win32, Win32s, Windows NT, and Windows 95?" In this chapter, I will attempt to clarify these differences once and for all. I will also explain why I chose to focus exclusively on Windows 95 and Windows NT when writing this book.

To Dream: The Win32 API

Win32 is the name of an application programming interface (API), that's all—no more, no less. So a set of functions that are available to call from your source code is contained in the Win32 API. When you write a Win32 program, you are doing so because you are calling functions in the Win32 API.

The Win32 API defines a set of functions that an application may call and also defines how these functions behave. Some of the areas covered by the API's functions are listed in Figure 1-1 on the next page.

The Win32 API is implemented on three platforms: Win32s,[1] Windows NT, and Windows 95. Microsoft's plan is to have *all* the Win32 functions implemented in *every* platform that supports the Win32 API. This is a major win for software developers like you and me, as well as for Microsoft. For us it means we can write the code for our application just once and then package it for the different platforms and ship it off to

---

1. It is unfortunate that the Win32s platform has *Win32* in its name, because this only adds to the confusion.

our customers. For Microsoft it means existing applications can run on all their operating system platforms.

Atoms	Networks
Child controls	Pipes and mailslots
Clipboard manipulations	Printing
Communications	Processes and threads
Consoles	Registry database manipulation
Debugging	Resources
Dynamic-link libraries	Security
Event logging	Services
Files	Structured exception handling
Graphics drawing primitives	System information
Keyboard and mouse input	Tape backup
Memory management	Time
Multimedia services	Window management

Figure 1-1.
Some areas covered by the Win32 API.

Of course, you may be asking yourself, Why do we need to have different Win32 platforms? Wouldn't it make more sense to have a single Win32 platform and make this one platform pervasive?

Well, if this were a perfect world, the answer to the second question would be "yes." However, this is the real world—and in the real world, one Win32 platform just doesn't cut it. I'll explain why in the next three sections, which introduce the three Win32 platforms and describe where each one fits into Microsoft's operating system strategy.

Win32s

The Win32s platform was the very first shipping platform capable of running Win32 applications. Win32s consists of a set of dynamic-link libraries (DLLs) and a virtual-device driver that add the Win32 API to the 16-bit Windows 3.*x* system. Win32s is not much more than a 32-bit to 16-bit mapping layer sitting on top of 16-bit Windows 3.*x*. This mapping layer uses thunking to convert the 32-bit function parameters to 16-bit parameters and to call the corresponding 16-bit Windows function.

Because Win32s does not extend the operating system's capabilities, most of the Win32 functions are implemented as small stub functions that simply return, indicating failure. For example, because 16-bit Windows does not support threads, the *CreateThread* function does nothing but return a NULL handle. All of the Win32 functions that create kernel objects such as mutexes and events return NULL handles. The Win32s platform does add a few new capabilities, however, such as structured exception handling and limited implementations of memory-mapped files.

Microsoft created Win32s to allow developers to begin writing 32-bit code immediately. Microsoft hoped this would help spark interest in Win32 programming so that when Windows NT shipped, some 32-bit applications would already be available. Unfortunately, Win32s did not take off too well, and I personally know of no software development effort that has specifically targeted the Win32s platform.

Windows NT

Windows NT, Microsoft's high-end operating system, is the second Win32 platform to ship from the company. Windows NT is a relatively new operating system that has no MS-DOS heritage. Microsoft expects this new design and architecture to take the company's operating systems into the future. However, Windows NT requires substantial memory and hard disk space. This means the average end user probably needs to purchase additional memory and hard disk space in order to run the system. As many software companies have discovered over the years, getting users to buy hardware to run software is very difficult.

And so, to date, Windows NT has had less than spectacular sales. But, in my opinion, we will all be running Windows NT someday—it just may take a few more years. Why is Windows NT the operating system of the future? I'm glad you asked. I explain in detail below.

First, Windows NT native applications are Win32 applications, giving them the power, robustness, and speed provided by the API. In addition, Windows NT is capable of running several different types of applications simultaneously. For example, Windows NT can run OS/2 1.*x* character applications, POSIX applications, Presentation Manager 2.*x* applications, MS-DOS applications, and 16-bit Windows applications.

Second, Windows NT is a portable operating system. This means that Windows NT is capable of running on machines that have different CPUs. Most of Windows NT itself is written in C or C++. So if Microsoft wants Windows NT to run on a MIPS R4000, a DEC Alpha, or Motorola's PowerPC, Microsoft needs only to recompile the operating system source code using the target CPU's native compiler and voilà—a version of Windows NT for another platform. Of course, porting the operating system to another CPU architecture is not quite this easy. Two very low level components of the Windows NT Executive, called the Kernel and the Hardware Abstraction Layer (HAL), need to be written to support the target architecture. Much of the Kernel and the HAL is written in native assembly language and is quite specific to the target machine architecture.

After Microsoft finishes porting Windows NT to a new architecture, all you need to do is recompile your Win32 application and voilà again—your application now runs on a new machine architecture. This actually *is* as simple as it sounds! I have compiled and tested all of the sample applications in this book for the following three Windows NT platforms: *x*86, MIPS, and Alpha. The first time I did this, I was amazed at how simple it was. Now I just take it for granted.

You should note that Windows NT is the only Win32 platform for machine architectures based on CPUs other than the *x*86. In other words, if you want to run Win32 applications on a MIPS, Alpha, or PowerPC machine, you will have to use the Windows NT platform. If you have an *x*86 machine, you can choose from three platforms: Win32s, Windows NT, or Windows 95. Windows NT is the most competent of these operating systems but does require the additional hardware.

The third big feature of Windows NT is that it supports machines with multiple CPUs. So if you are running Windows NT on a machine that contains 30 CPUs, the operating system is capable of letting 30 threads run simultaneously. This means the machine can perform 30 tasks in the time that it takes to perform one task. This is an incredibly powerful capability, but, as you might expect, a machine with several CPUs costs significantly more than a single-CPU machine.

Windows 95

Windows 95 is Microsoft's most recent Win32 platform, and the long-awaited successor to 16-bit Windows 3.*x*. Because Windows 95 replaces Windows 3.*x*, the Win32s platform is now considered obsolete. So this leaves two Win32 platforms worthy of your consideration: Windows 95 and Windows NT.

Windows 95 is a much better implementation of the Win32 API than its predecessor, Win32s. However, Windows 95 does not contain the full implementation of the Win32 API as found in Windows NT. Windows 95 fills a very large and strategic marketing gap: users with 386 (or better) machines with 4 MB (or more) of RAM. The number of machines that fall into this category is staggering—and it's expected to grow significantly over the next couple of years. Because the Windows NT hardware requirements are too demanding to address this market, Microsoft produced the Windows 95 platform.

In order for Windows 95 to fit in a 4-MB machine, Microsoft was forced to cut back on some of the Win32 API's functionality. As a result, Windows 95 does not fully support some of Win32's asynchronous file I/O functions, debugging functions, registry functions, security functions, and event logging functions (just to name a few)—the functions exist, but they have restricted implementations. Surprisingly, however, Microsoft was able to shoehorn quite a bit of the Win32 API set into Windows 95, making it a very feasible and powerful operating system. So powerful, in fact, that it is expected to be the most purchased and used Win32 platform in the near future.

The Reality: The Win32 API

The Win32s, Windows NT, and Windows 95 platforms all contain implementations of all the Win32 functions, which means you can call any of the functions in the Win32 API regardless of which platform you are running on. However, there is implementation and there is *implementation*. When Microsoft says that every Win32 function will be implemented on every platform, what it really means is that every Win32 function will *exist* on every platform. For example, the *CreateRemoteThread* function exists on all three platforms: Win32s, Windows NT, and Windows 95. However, the function doesn't actually create a remote thread unless the application calling the function is running on the Windows NT platform. If a process running on Win32s or Windows 95 calls *CreateRemoteThread*, the function does nothing and simply returns NULL, indicating that a new thread of execution could not be created.

The reason for this limitation on Win32s is that Win32s is really just an extension to 16-bit Windows 3.*x* that implements most of the Win32

API by thunking calls to 16-bit Windows functions. Because 16-bit Windows does not support the creation of new threads of execution, Win32s does not support this feature. But remember, Win32s implements all of the Win32 functions, although some of the implementations are limited. On Windows 95, a new thread of execution cannot be created because Microsoft didn't feel that the function was useful enough to warrant the additional memory overhead required to make Windows 95 run in a 4-MB machine.

Because this is a Win32 programming book, you might think that you can compile all the sample programs you find here and run them on all three Win32 platforms. This is true; however, most of the features that I discuss in this book (for example, multithreaded programming, virtual memory, and memory-mapped files) have full implementations on the Windows 95 and Windows NT platforms but only limited implementations on the Win32s platform. Because of this, you must run the sample programs under the Windows 95 or the Windows NT platform to see them in all their glory.

In fact, because the Win32s platform is so limited in its capabilities, I have given no thought whatsoever to the Win32s platform in this book. Everything I have written applies to the Windows 95 and Windows NT platforms only—if something I say happens to be true for the Win32s platform, I assure you it is purely coincidental.

I'd like to make one more point: With the introduction of the Windows 95 platform, Microsoft has added a new wrinkle to the Win32 story. Windows 95 has added new functions to the Win32 API in order to support image color matching, modems, and other services. The functions that support these new services will not exist on the Windows NT implementation of the Win32 API until Microsoft ships a future, post-3.5 version of Windows NT. This means that there are some Win32 functions that exist on one platform and not on another. And I don't just mean that the Windows NT implementation of these functions is limited—I mean the Windows NT version of the Win32 API doesn't include these functions *at all*. This is terrible—Windows NT is always supposed to have the complete implementation of the Win32 API.

Finally, while writing this book I have tried to pay particular attention to differences between the Windows 95 and Windows NT implementations of the Win32 API. Where appropriate, I have placed boxes with icons, as shown on the facing page, in the text to draw attention to implementation details specific to one platform or the other.

This is an implementation detail specific to the Windows 95 platform.

This is an implementation detail specific to the Windows NT platform.

I have also used boxes with icons to include information helpful to programmers porting from 16-bit Windows to Win32, and for important notes—both shown below.

This is important information to help programmers porting from 16-bit Windows to Win32.

This is an important note.

CHAPTER TWO

PROCESSES

This chapter discusses how the system manages all of the running applications. I'll begin by defining what a process is and how the system creates a process kernel object to manage each process. Special attention will be paid to kernel objects because a solid understanding of kernel objects is critical to becoming a proficient Win32 software developer. Kernel objects are used by the system and the applications we write to manage numerous resources such as processes, threads, and files (to name just a few).

After this short departure to discuss kernel objects, I'll return to processes and show how to manipulate a process using its associated kernel object. Then I'll discuss the various attributes or properties of a process as well as several functions that are available for querying and changing these properties. I'll also examine the functions that allow you to create or spawn additional processes in the system. And of course, no discussion of processes would be complete without an in-depth look at how they terminate. OK, let's begin.

A process is usually defined as an instance of a running program. In Win32, a process owns a 4-GB address space. Unlike their counterparts in MS-DOS and 16-bit Windows operating systems, Win32 processes are inert. That is, a Win32 process executes nothing—it simply owns a 4-GB address space containing the code and data for an application's EXE file. Any DLLs required by the EXE also have their code and data loaded into the process's address space. In addition to an address space, a process owns certain resources such as files, dynamic memory allocations, and threads. The various resources created during a process's life are destroyed when the process is terminated—*guaranteed*.

As I said, processes are inert. In order for a process to accomplish anything, the process must own a thread; it is this thread that is responsible for executing the code contained in the process's address space. In fact, a single process might contain several threads, all of them executing code "simultaneously" in the process's address space. In order to do this, each thread has its very own set of CPU registers and its own stack. Every process has at least one thread executing code contained in the process's address space. If there were no threads executing code in the process's address space, there would be no reason for the process to continue to exist and the system would automatically destroy the process and its address space.

In order for all of these threads to run, the operating system schedules some CPU time for each individual thread. The operating system gives the illusion that all the threads are running concurrently by offering time slices (called *quantums*) to the threads in a round-robin fashion, as shown in Figure 2-1.

When a Win32 process is created, its first thread, called the primary thread, is automatically created by the system. This primary thread can then create additional threads, and these additional threads can create even more threads.

Windows NT is capable of utilizing machines that contain several CPUs. For example, Sequent sells a computer system that includes 30 Intel CPUs. Windows NT is able to assign a CPU to each thread so that 30 threads are actually running simultaneously. The Windows NT Kernel handles all the management and scheduling of threads on this type of system. You do not need to do anything special in your code in order to gain the advantages offered by a multiprocessor machine.

Kernel Objects

Before getting knee-deep into processes and threads, it is extremely important to understand kernel objects and how the system manages them. This information is not only important for manipulating processes and threads; it is also critical to understanding how much of the Win32 system operates. As a Win32 software developer, you will be creating, opening, and otherwise manipulating kernel objects on a regular basis. The system creates and manipulates several types of kernel objects, including:

Event objects	MailSlot objects	Process objects
File-mapping objects	Mutex objects	Semaphore objects
File objects	Pipe objects	Thread objects

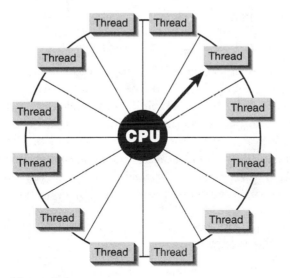

Figure 2-1.
Individual threads are scheduled time quantums by the operating system in a round-robin fashion.

These objects are created by calling various Win32 functions. For example, the *CreateFileMapping* function causes the system to create a file-mapping object. When an object is created, the system allocates a block of memory for the object, initializes the memory with some management information, and returns a handle to your application identifying the object. Your application can then pass the handle to other Win32 functions in order to manipulate the object.

Your application might also use other types of objects, such as menus, windows, mouse cursors, brushes, and fonts. These objects are User or Graphics Device Interface (GDI) objects, not kernel objects.

When you first start programming for Win32, you might be confused when trying to differentiate a User or GDI object from a kernel object. For example, is an icon a User object or a kernel object? The easiest way to determine whether an object is a kernel object or not is by examining the Win32 function that creates the object. All functions that create kernel objects have a parameter that allows you to specify security attribute information. For example, the *CreateMutex* function:

```
HANDLE CreateMutex(LPSECURITY_ATTRIBUTES lpsa,
    BOOL fInitialOwner, LPCTSTR lpszMutexName);
```

has, as its first parameter, a pointer to a SECURITY_ATTRIBUTES structure. The *CreateIcon* function, shown on the next page, does not have a parameter allowing you to specify security attributes.

```
HICON CreateIcon(HINSTANCE hinst, int nWidth, int nHeight,
   BYTE cPlanes, BYTE cBitsPixel,
   CONST BYTE *lpbANDbits, CONST BYTE *lpbXORbits);
```

Once a kernel object exists, any application can open the object (subject to security checks). For example, one application might create a mutex object, which is then available for another application to open. This capability allows the two applications to manipulate the same mutex object. When an application opens a kernel object, the system does not create another block of memory for the object. Instead, the system increments a usage count associated with the already existing object and returns a handle, identifying the existing object, to the thread opening the object.

When a thread no longer needs to manipulate a kernel object, it should call the *CloseHandle* function:

```
BOOL CloseHandle(HANDLE hObject);
```

This function causes the system to decrement the usage count for the object, and if the usage count reaches 0, the system frees the memory allocated to manage the object.

To help make the system more robust and secure, a handle to a kernel object is process-relative—that is, it is meaningful only to the process that called the create or open function. If a thread calls *CreateMutex*, the system might return the handle value 0x22222222. If a thread in another process opens the same mutex object, the system might return the handle value 0x12345678. Both handles identify the same mutex object even though the values are different.

Because handles for kernel objects are process-relative, a thread cannot successfully get a handle to an object and give or pass that handle to a thread in another process through some form of interprocess communication (such as sending a window message). When the thread in the receiving process attempts to use the handle, one of two things happens: the handle value does not identify an object accessible to the thread, or the handle identifies a different object created or opened by another thread in the process. In either case, an error will most likely result when the handle is used.

Contrast this to the User or GDI objects, which use the same handle value across processes. For example, if a window is identified with a handle value of 0x34343434, all processes use this same value to refer to the window.

Writing Your First Win32 Application

Win32 supports two types of applications: graphical user interface (GUI)-based and console-based. A GUI-based application has a graphical front end. GUI applications create windows, have menus, interact with the user via dialog boxes, and use all the standard "Windowsy" stuff. Almost all the accessory applications that ship with Windows (Notepad, Calculator, and Clock, for instance) are typical examples of GUI-based applications. Console-based applications more closely resemble MS-DOS text applications: their output is text-based, they don't create windows or process messages, and they don't require a graphical user interface. Although console-based applications are contained within a window on the screen, the window contains only text. The command shells, CMD .EXE (for Windows NT) and COMMAND.COM (for Windows 95), are typical examples of console-based applications.

Although there are two types of applications, the line between them is very fuzzy. It is possible to create console-based applications that display dialog boxes. For example, the command shell could have a special command that causes it to display a graphical dialog box, allowing you to select the command you want to execute instead of having to remember the various commands supported by the shell. You could also create a GUI-based application that outputs text strings to a console window. I have frequently created a GUI-based application that creates a console window where I can send debugging information as the application executes. Of the two application types, you are certainly encouraged to use a graphical user interface in your applications instead of using the old-fashioned character interface. It has been proven time and time again that GUI-based applications are much more user friendly.

The real difference between the two applications is how your code starts executing. If you are writing a GUI-based application, the process's primary thread will execute your code starting with its *WinMain* function. (See Chapter 3 for more details.) However, a console-based application's primary thread begins execution with a *main* function. Because the system passes more information to a GUI application's *WinMain* function than to a console-based application's *main* function, I encourage you to write GUI-based applications that begin with *WinMain*.

In this chapter, my discussion of the mechanics of creating processes applies to both GUI-based and console-based applications, but I emphasize GUI-based applications and don't discuss some of the finer details of creating console-based applications. If you want more information on creating console-based applications, please refer to the *Microsoft Win32 Programmer's Reference*.

All Win32 GUI-based applications must have a *WinMain* function that you implement in your source code. The function must have the following prototype:

```
int WINAPI WinMain(HINSTANCE hinstExe, HINSTANCE hinstPrev,
   LPSTR lpszCmdLine, int nCmdShow);
```

This function is not actually called by the operating system. Instead, the operating system calls the C/C++ run-time's startup function. The Visual C++ linker knows that the name of this function is *_WinMainCRT-Startup*, but you can override this using the linker's /ENTRY switch. The *_WinMainCRTStartup* function is responsible for performing the following actions:

1. Retrieves a pointer to the new process's full command line.

2. Retrieves a pointer to the new process's environment variables.

3. Initializes the C run-time's global variables accessible from your code by including STDLIB.H. Figure 2-2 shows the list of variables available.

4. Initializes the heap used by the C run-time memory allocation functions (that is, *malloc* and *calloc*) and other low-level input/ output routines.

5. Calls your *WinMain* function as follows:

   ```
   GetStartupInfoA(&StartupInfo);

   int nMainRetVal = WinMain(GetModuleHandle(NULL), NULL,
      lpszCommandLine,
      (StartupInfo.dwFlags & STARTF_USESHOWWINDOW)  ?
         StartupInfo.wShowWindow : SW_SHOWDEFAULT);
   ```

6. When *WinMain* returns, the startup code calls the C run-time's *exit* function, passing it *WinMain*'s return value (*nMainRetVal*). The *exit* function performs some cleanup and then calls the Win32 *ExitProcess* function, passing it *WinMain*'s return value.

The remainder of this section discusses the various attributes that are "bestowed" upon a new process.

Variable Name	Type	Description
_osver	unsigned int	Build version of the operating system. For example, Windows NT 3.5 was build 807. Thus _osver has a value of 807. As of this writing, the most recent build of Windows 95 is 275.
_winmajor	unsigned int	Major version of Windows in hexadecimal notation. For Windows NT 3.5, the value is 0x03.
_winminor	unsigned int	Minor version of Windows in hexadecimal notation. For Windows NT 3.5, the value is 0x32.
_winver	unsigned int	$(\_winmajor << 8) + \_winminor$
__argc	unsigned int	The number of arguments passed on the command line.
__argv	char **	An array of __argc pointers to ANSI strings. Each array entry points to a command-line argument.
_environ	char **	An array of pointers to ANSI strings. Each array entry points to an environment string.

Figure 2-2.
The C run-time global variables available to your programs.

A Process's Instance Handle

Every EXE or DLL loaded into a process's address space is assigned a unique *instance handle*. Your process is passed its instance value as *Win-Main*'s first parameter, *hinstExe*. The handle's value is typically needed for calls that load resources. For example, to load an icon resource from the EXE file's image, you will need to call:

```
HICON LoadIcon(HINSTANCE hinst, LPCTSTR lpszIcon);
```

The first parameter to *LoadIcon* indicates which file (EXE or DLL) contains the resource that you want to load. Many applications save *WinMain*'s *hinstExe* parameter in a global variable so that it is easily accessible to all of the EXE file's code.

The Win32 documentation states that some Win32 functions require a parameter of the type HMODULE. An example is the *GetModuleFile-Name* function, shown on the next page.

```
DWORD GetModuleFileName(HMODULE hinstModule, LPTSTR lpszPath,
    DWORD cchPath);
```

However, the Win32 API makes no distinction between a process's HMODULE and HINSTANCE values—they are one and the same. Wherever the Win32 documentation for a function indicates that HMODULE is required, you can pass HINSTANCE.

The actual value of *WinMain*'s *hinstExe* parameter is the base memory address indicating where the system loaded the EXE file's image into the process's address space. For example, if the system opens the executable file and loads its contents at address 0x00400000, *WinMain*'s *hinstExe* parameter will have a value of 0x00400000. This "definition" of the *hinstExe* parameter is documented and can be relied on for future versions of Win32 implementations.

The base address where an application loads is determined by the linker. Different linkers can use different default base addresses. The Visual C++ linker uses a default base address of 0x00400000 because this is the lowest address an executable file image can load to when you are running Windows 95. Some older linkers use a default base address of 0x00010000 because this is the lowest address an executable file image can load to when running under Windows NT. You can change the base address that your application loads to by using the /BASE: *address* linker switch for Microsoft's linker.

If you attempt to load an executable that has a base address below 0x00400000 on Windows 95, the Windows 95 loader must relocate the executable to a different address. This increases the loading time of the application, but at least the application can run. If you are developing an application intended to run on both Windows 95 and Windows NT, you should make sure that the application's base address is at 0x00400000 or above.

The *GetModuleHandle* function:

```
HMODULE GetModuleHandle(LPCTSTR lpszModule);
```

returns the handle/base address indicating where an EXE or DLL file loaded in the process's address space. When calling this function, you pass a zero-terminated string that specifies the name of an EXE or DLL file loaded into the calling process's address space. If the system finds the specified EXE or DLL name, *GetModuleHandle* returns the base address at which that EXE or DLL's file image is loaded. The system returns NULL if it cannot find the specified file. You can also call *GetModule-Handle*, passing NULL for the *lpszModule* parameter. When you do this, *GetModuleHandle* returns the EXE file's base address. This is what the C run-time startup code does when it calls your *WinMain* function, as discussed in step 5 on page 14.

There are two important things to note about the *GetModuleHandle* function. First, *GetModuleHandle* examines only the calling process's address space. If the calling process does not use any GDI functions, calling *GetModuleHandle* and passing it "GDI32" will cause NULL to be returned even though GDI32.DLL is probably loaded into other processes' address spaces. Second, calling *GetModuleHandle* and passing a value of NULL returns the base address of the EXE file in the process's address space. So even if you call *GetModuleHandle(NULL)* from code that is contained inside a DLL, the value returned is the EXE file's base address—not the DLL file's base address. This is different from how the *GetModuleHandle* function works under 16-bit Windows.

In 16-bit Windows, a task's *hModule* indicates the module database (a block of information used internally by the system to manage the module) for an EXE or a DLL. Even if 200 instances of Notepad are running, there is only one module database for Notepad and therefore only one *hmodExe* value shared by all the instances. There can be one and only one instance of a DLL loaded in 16-bit Windows, so only one *hmodExe* value exists for each loaded DLL.

In 16-bit Windows, each running instance of a task receives its very own *hinstExe* value. This value identifies the task's default data segment. If 200 instances of Notepad are running, there are 200 *hinstExe* values— one for each running instance. Because DLLs also have a default data segment, each loaded DLL also receives its very own *hinstExe* value. You might think that because a DLL can be loaded only once, 16-bit Windows could use the same value for a DLL's *hmodExe* and *hinstExe*. This is not the case, however, because *hmodExe* identifies the DLL's module database, while *hinstExe* identifies the DLL's default data segment.

(continued)

continued

In Win32, each process gets its own address space, which means each process thinks it is the only process running in the system. One process cannot easily see another process. For this reason, no distinction is made between a process's *hinstExe* and its *hmodExe*—they are one and the same. For historical reasons, the two terms continue to exist throughout the Win32 documentation.

As stated in the previous section, an application's *hinstExe* actually identifies the base memory address where the system loaded the EXE file's code into the process's address space. Because of this, it is extremely likely that many processes will have the same *hinstExe* value. For example, invoking NOTEPAD.EXE causes the system to create a 4-GB process address space and load Notepad's code and data into this address space. The code and data might load at memory address 0x00400000. If we now invoke a second instance of NOTEPAD.EXE, the system will create a new 4-GB address space for this process and again load Notepad's code and data at memory address 0x00400000. Because an application's *hinstExe* value is the same as the base memory address where the system loaded the EXE's code, the *hinstExe* value for both of these processes is 0x00400000.

In 16-bit Windows, it is possible to call the *DialogBox* function and pass it an *hinstExe* value that belongs to a task other than your own:

```
int DialogBox(HINSTANCE hInstance, LPCTSTR lpszTemplate,
   HWND hwndOwner, DLGPROC dlgprc);
```

This causes 16-bit Windows to load the dialog box template from the other application's resources. Of course, this is a questionable action to take anyway, but in Win32 it's no longer possible to do this. When you make a call to a function that expects an *hinstExe* value, Win32 interprets the call to mean that you are requesting information from the EXE or DLL loaded into your own process's address space at the address indicated by the *hinstExe* parameter.

A Process's Previous Instance Handle

As noted earlier, the C run-time's startup code always passes NULL to *WinMain*'s *hinstPrev* parameter. This parameter exists for backward compatibility and has no meaning to Win32 applications.

In a 16-bit Windows application, the *hinstPrev* parameter specifies the handle of another instance of the same application. If no other instances of the application are running, *hinstPrev* is passed as NULL. A 16-bit Windows application frequently examines this value for two reasons:

- To determine whether another instance of the same application is already running and, if so, to terminate the newly invoked instance. This termination occurs if a program such as the Print Manager wants to allow only a single instance of itself to run at a time.

- To determine whether window classes need to be registered. In 16-bit Windows, window classes need to be registered only once per module. These classes are then shared among all instances of the same application. If a second instance attempts to register the same window classes a second time, the call to *RegisterClass* fails. In Win32, each instance of an application must register its own window classes because window classes aren't shared among all instances of the same application.

To ease the porting of a 16-bit Windows application to the Win32 API, Microsoft decided to always pass NULL in the *hinstPrev* parameter of *WinMain*. Because many 16-bit Windows applications examine this parameter when registering window classes, all instances see that *hinstPrev* is NULL and automatically reregister their window classes.

While this decision eases the job of porting your applications, it also means that applications cannot use the value of *hinstPrev* to prevent a second instance from running. An application must use alternative methods to determine whether other instances of itself are already running. In one method, the application calls *FindWindow* and looks for a particular window class or caption that uniquely identifies that application. If *FindWindow* returns NULL, the application knows that it's the only instance of itself running. In Chapter 11, I present another method for determining whether multiple instances of an application are running.

A Process's Command Line

When a new process is created, it is passed a command line. The command line is almost never blank; at the very least, the name of the executable file used to create the new process is the first token on the command line. However, as you'll see later when we discuss the *CreateProcess* function, it is possible that a process can receive a command line that consists of a single character: the string-terminating zero. When the C run-time's startup code begins executing, it retrieves the process's command line, skips over the executable file's name, and passes a pointer to the remainder of the command line to *WinMain*'s *lpszCmdLine* parameter.

It's important to note that the *lpszCmdLine* parameter always points to an ANSI string. Because the system doesn't know whether you are interested in using ANSI or Unicode, Microsoft chose to always pass an ANSI string. Microsoft chose ANSI to help with porting 16-bit Windows code to Win32, because 16-bit Windows applications expect an ANSI string. I discuss Unicode in detail in Chapter 16.

An application can parse and interpret the ANSI string any way it chooses. Because the *lpszCmdLine* is an LPSTR instead of an LPCSTR, feel free to write to the buffer that it points to—but you should not, under any circumstances, write beyond the end of the buffer. Personally, I always consider this a read-only buffer. If I want to make changes to the command line, I first copy the command-line buffer to a local buffer in my application; then I modify my local buffer.

You can also obtain a pointer to your process's complete command line by calling the *GetCommandLine* function:

```
LPTSTR GetCommandLine(VOID);
```

This function returns a pointer to a buffer containing the full command line, including the full pathname of the executed file. Probably the most compelling reason to use the *GetCommandLine* function instead of the *lpszCmdLine* parameter is that both Unicode and ANSI versions of *GetCommandLine* exist in the Win32 API, whereas the *lpszCmdLine* parameter always points to a buffer containing an ANSI character string.

Many applications would prefer to have the command line parsed into its separate tokens. An application can gain access to the command line's individual components by using the global __argc and __argv variables. But again, the __argv variable is an array of character pointers to

ANSI strings, not Unicode strings. Win32 offers a function that separates any string into its separate tokens, *CommandLineToArgvW:*[1]

```
LPWSTR *CommandLineToArgvW(LPWSTR lpCmdLine, LPINT pArgc);
```

As the *W* at the end of the function name implies, this function exists in a Unicode version only. (The *W* stands for *wide*.) The first parameter, *lpCmdLine*, points to a command-line string. This is usually the return value from an earlier call to *GetCommandLine*. The *pArgc* parameter is the address of an integer; the integer will be set to the number of arguments that are in the command line. *CommandLineToArgvW* returns the address to an array of Unicode string pointers.

A Process's Environment Variables

Every process has an environment block associated with it. An environment block is a block of memory allocated within the process's address space. Each block contains a set of strings with the following appearance:

```
VarName1=VarValue1\0
VarName2=VarValue2\0
VarName3=VarValue3\0
  .
  .
  .
VarNameX=VarValueX\0
\0
```

The first part of each string is the name of an environment variable. This name is followed by an equal sign, which is followed by the value you want to assign to the variable. All strings in the environment block must be sorted alphabetically by environment variable name.

Because the equal sign is used to separate the name from the value, an equal sign cannot be part of the name. Also, spaces are significant. For example, if you declare these two variables:

```
XYZ= Win32        (Notice the space after the equal sign.)
ABC=Win32
```

and then compare the value of *XYZ* with the value of *ABC*, the system will report that the two variables are different. This is because any white

---

1. This function was added in Windows NT 3.5; it does not exist in Windows NT 3.1.

space that appears immediately before or after the equal sign is taken into account. For example, if you were to add these two strings to the environment block:

```
XYZ =Home          (Notice the space before the equal sign.)
XYZ=Work
```

the environment variable "*XYZ* " would contain "*Home*" and another environment variable "*XYZ*" would contain "*Work.*" Finally, an additional 0 byte must be placed at the end of all the environment variables to mark the end of the block.

In order to create an initial set of environment variables for Windows 95, you must modify the system's AUTOEXEC.BAT file by placing a series of SET lines in the file. Each line must be of the following form:

```
SET VarName=VarValue
```

When you reboot your system, the contents of the AUTOEXEC .BAT file are parsed, and any environment variables you have set will be available to any processes you invoke during your Windows 95 session.

When a user logs on to Windows NT, the system creates the shell process and associates a set of environment strings with it. The system obtains the initial set of environment strings by examining two keys in the Registry. The first key:

```
HKEY_LOCAL_MACHINE\SYSTEM\CurrentControlSet\Control\
   SessionManager\Environment
```

contains the list of all environment variables that apply to the system, while the second key:

```
HKEY_CURRENT_USER\Environment
```

contains the list of all environment variables that apply to the user currently logged on.

A user may add, delete, or change any of these entries by double-clicking on the System option in the Control Panel. This presents the following dialog box:

(continued)

Windows NT

continued

```
┌─────────────────────────────────────────────────────────┐
│ ─                         System                          │
│ Computer Name:  RINCEWIND            ┌──────────────┐     │
│ ┌─Operating System─────────────────┐ │      OK      │     │
│ │                                  │ └──────────────┘     │
│ │                                  │ ┌──────────────┐     │
│ │ Startup: "Windows NT Workstation Version 3.5" ▼│ │   Cancel   │ │
│ │                                  │ ┌──────────────┐     │
│ │ Show list for 10 ▲ seconds       │ │ Virtual Memory...│ │
│ │                                  │ └──────────────┘     │
│ └──────────────────────────────────┘ ┌──────────────┐    │
│                                       │   Recovery   │    │
│                                       └──────────────┘    │
│ System Environment Variables:        ┌──────────────┐     │
│                                       │   Tasking... │    │
│ ComSpec = D:\NT35\system32\cmd.exe   └──────────────┘     │
│ Os2LibPath = D:\NT35\system32\os2\dll;┌──────────────┐    │
│ Path = D:\NT35\system32;D:\NT35\windows\system;d:\batch   │
│ windir = D:\NT35                      │     Help     │    │
│                                       └──────────────┘     │
│                                                           │
│ User Environment Variables for jimf                       │
│ include = d:\msvc20\include;d:\msvc20\mfc\include          │
│ init = D:\MSVC20                                          │
│ lib = d:\msvc20\lib;d:\msvc20\mfc\lib                      │
│ path = D:\MSVC20\BIN                                      │
│ temp = D:\temp                                           │
│ tmp = D:\temp                                            │
│                                                           │
│ Variable: [                              ]  ┌────────┐    │
│                                              │   Set  │    │
│ Value:    [                              ]  ┌────────┐    │
│                                              │ Delete │    │
└─────────────────────────────────────────────────────────┘
```

Only a user who has administrator privileges can alter the variables contained in the System Environment Variables list.

Your application can use the various Registry functions to modify these Registry entries as well. However, in order for the changes to take effect, the user must log off and then log back on. Some applications, such as Program Manager, Task Manager, and the Control Panel, can update their environment block with the new Registry entries when their main windows receive a WM_WININICHANGE message. For example, if you update the Registry entries and want to have the interested applications update their environment blocks, you can make the following call:

```
SendMessage(HWND_BROADCAST, WM_WININICHANGE,
    0L, (LPARAM) "Environment");
```

Normally, a child process inherits a set of environment variables that are exactly the same as its parent process's. However, the parent process can control what environment variables a child inherits, as I'll show later when we discuss the *CreateProcess* function. By inherit, I mean that the child process gets its own copy of the parent's environment block, not that the child and parent share the same block. This means that a child process can add, delete, or modify a variable in its block and the change will not be reflected in the parent's block.

Environment variables are usually used by applications to allow the user to fine-tune the application's behavior. The user creates an environment variable and initializes it. Then, when the user invokes the application, the application examines the environment block for the variable. If the application finds the variable, the application parses the value of the variable and adjusts its behavior.

The problem with environment variables is that they are not easily set or understood by users. Users need to spell variable names correctly, and they must also know the exact syntax expected of the variable's value. Most (if not all) graphical applications, on the other hand, allow users to fine-tune an application's behavior using dialog boxes. This approach is far more user friendly and is very strongly encouraged.

If you still wish to continue using environment variables, Win32 offers a few functions that your applications can call. The *GetEnvironmentVariable* function allows you to determine the existence and value of an environment variable:

```
DWORD GetEnvironmentVariable(LPCTSTR lpszName,
    LPTSTR lpszValue, DWORD cchValue);
```

When calling *GetEnvironmentVariable*, *lpszName* points to the desired variable name, *lpszValue* points to the buffer that will hold the variable's value, and *cchValue* indicates the size of this buffer in characters. The function returns either the number of characters copied into the buffer or 0 if the variable name cannot be found in the environment.

The *SetEnvironmentVariable* function allows you to add a variable, delete a variable, or modify a variable's value:

```
BOOL SetEnvironmentVariable(LPCTSTR lpszName, LPCTSTR lpszValue);
```

This function sets the variable identified by the *lpszName* parameter to the value identified by the *lpszValue* parameter. If a variable with the specified name already exists, *SetEnvironmentVariable* modifies the value. If the specified variable doesn't exist, the variable is added and, if *lpszValue* is NULL, the variable is deleted from the environment block.

You should always use these functions for manipulating your process's environment block. As I said at the beginning of this section, the strings in an environment block must be sorted alphabetically by variable name. This means that *GetEnvironmentVariable* can locate strings faster; it also means that the *SetEnvironmentVariable* function is smart enough to keep the environment variables in sorted order.

A Process's Error Mode

Associated with each process is a set of flags that tells the system how the process should respond to serious errors. Serious errors include disk media failures, unhandled exceptions, file-find failures, and data misalignment. A process can tell the system how to handle each of these errors by calling the *SetErrorMode* function:

```
UINT SetErrorMode(UINT fuErrorMode);
```

The *fuErrorMode* parameter is a combination of any of the following flags bitwise ORed together:

Note that a child process inherits the error mode flags of its parent. In other words, if a process currently has the SEM_NOGPFAULT-ERRORBOX flag turned on and then spawns a child process, the child process will also have this flag turned on. However, the child process is not notified of this and might not have been written to handle GP fault errors itself. If a GP fault does occur in one of the child's threads, the child application might terminate without notifying the user.

Flag	Description
SEM_FAILCRITICALERRORS	The system does not display the critical-error-handler message box and returns the error to the calling process.
SEM_NOGPFAULTERRORBOX	The system does not display the general-protection-fault message box. This flag should be set only by debugging applications that handle general protection (GP) faults themselves with an exception handler.
SEM_NOOPENFILEERRORBOX	The system does not display a message box when it fails to find a file.
SEM_NOALIGNMENTFAULTEXCEPT	The system automatically fixes memory alignment faults and makes them invisible to the application. This flag has no effect on *x*86 or Alpha processors.

A Process's Current Drive and Directory

The current directory of the current drive is where the various Win32 functions look for files and directories when full pathnames are not supplied. For example, if a thread in a process calls *CreateFile* to open a file (without specifying a full pathname), the system will look for the file in the current drive and directory.

The system keeps track of a process's current drive and directory internally. Because this information is maintained on a per-process basis, a thread in the process that changes the current drive or directory changes this information for all the threads in the process.

A thread can obtain and set its process's current drive and directory by calling the following two functions:

```
DWORD GetCurrentDirectory(DWORD cchCurDir, LPTSTR lpszCurDir);
BOOL SetCurrentDirectory(LPCTSTR lpszCurDir);
```

I discuss these functions in more detail in Chapter 13.

A Process's Current Directories

Notice that the system keeps track of the process's current drive and directory but does *not* keep track of the current directory for each and every drive. However, there is some operating system support for handling current directories for multiple drives. This support is offered by using the process's environment strings. For example, a process can have two environment variables such as:

```
=C:=C:\UTILITY\BIN
=D:=D:\PROJECTS\ADVWIN32\CODE
```

These variables indicate that the process's current directory for drive C is \UTILITY\BIN and that its current directory for drive D is \PROJECTS\ ADVWIN32\CODE.

If you call a Win32 function, passing a drive-qualified name indicating a drive that is not the current drive, then the system looks in the process's environment block for the variable associated with the specified drive letter. If the variable for the drive exists, the system uses the variable's value as the current directory. If the variable does not exist, the system assumes that the current directory for the specified drive is its root directory.

For example, if your process's current directory is C:\UTILITY\ BIN, and you call *CreateFile* to open D:README.TXT, the system looks up the environment variable =D:. Because the =D: variable exists, the system attempts to open the README.TXT file from the D:\PROJECTS\ ADVWIN32\CODE directory. If the =D: variable did not exist, the system would attempt to open the README.TXT file from the root directory of drive D. The Win32 file functions never add or change a drive-letter environment variable—they only read the variables.

Important

You can use the C run-time function _chdir instead of the Win32 *SetCurrentDirectory* function to change the current directory. The _chdir function calls *SetCurrentDirectory* internally, but _chdir also adds or modifies the environment variables so that the current directory of different drives is preserved.

If a parent process creates an environment block that it wants to pass to a child process, the child's environment block will *not* automatically inherit the parent process's current directories. Instead, the child process's current directories will default to the root directory of every drive. If you want the child process to inherit the parent's current directories, the parent process must create these drive-letter environment variables and add them to the environment block before spawning the child process. The parent process can obtain its current directories by calling *GetFullPathName*:

```
DWORD GetFullPathName(LPCTSTR lpszFile, DWORD cchPath,
   LPTSTR lpszPath, LPTSTR *ppszFilePart);
```

For example, to get the current directory for drive C, you would call *GetFullPathName* as follows:

```
TCHAR szCurDir[MAX_PATH];
DWORD GetFullPathName(__TEXT("C:"), MAX_PATH, szCurDir, NULL);
```

Note that a process's environment variables must always be kept in alphabetical order. Because of this, the drive letter environment variables will usually need to be placed at the beginning of the environment block.

A Process's Inherited Kernel Objects

When a parent process creates a child process, one of the parameters indicates whether the parent wants the child process to inherit the parent's inheritable kernel objects. If the child is to inherit the parent's kernel objects, the system cycles through all of the parent's inheritable objects and increments each object's usage count by 1. The system then assigns handles to these kernel objects relative to the newly created child process. This makes the kernel objects accessible to the child process.

For example, let's say that a process creates an inheritable mutex object and the system returns a handle value of 0x44442222 that identifies the object. Then this same process creates a child process and tells the system that the child is to inherit all inheritable kernel objects. When the system creates the new child process, the system increments the usage count of the mutex from 1 to 2. The system also assigns a handle, relative to the child process, that identifies the same mutex object. In fact, the system will assign the same exact handle value for this object that the parent process has—0x44442222.

You can use this handle value to manipulate the mutex object as soon as the primary thread in the child process begins executing. Since the usage count of the mutex object is 2, both the parent and the child process will have to close their handles to the object before the usage count decrements to 0 and the system can free the kernel object from its memory.

How to Make a Kernel Object Inheritable

Remember, I said earlier that the Win32 functions that create kernel objects all accept a pointer to a SECURITY_ATTRIBUTES structure as a parameter. When a kernel object is created, you have the option of creating one of these structures, initializing its members, and passing the address of the structure to the function to create the appropriate security attributes—or you can simply pass NULL.

If you pass NULL for this parameter, the created kernel object will not be inheritable by any child processes spawned by your process. However, you can have the system create an inheritable kernel object by initializing the SECURITY_ATTRIBUTES structure and passing this structure to one of the create functions. The example below shows how to create an inheritable mutex object:

```
HANDLE hMutex;
SECURITY_ATTRIBUTES sa;
sa.nLength = sizeof(sa);
sa.lpSecurityDescriptor = NULL;
sa.bInheritHandle = TRUE;          // Makes object inheritable

// Call CreateMutex passing the address of the sa variable.
hMutex = CreateMutex(&sa, FALSE, NULL);
```

When the system creates the kernel object, the system will know that this object is inheritable. This does not automatically mean that any and all child processes spawned later by this process will automatically inherit the kernel object. When a process spawns a child process, the parent gets the opportunity to tell the system whether it wants the child to inherit all of the inheritable kernel objects. If the *bInheritHandle* member of the SECURITY_ATTRIBUTES structure is not set to TRUE when a kernel object is created, the system will not allow a child process to inherit the kernel object at all.

In addition, a process can also open a handle to an existing kernel object. For example, the function to open a mutex object is *OpenMutex*:

```
HANDLE OpenMutex(DWORD fdwAccess, BOOL fInherit,
    LPCTSTR lpszMutexName);
```

This function does not accept a parameter that points to a SECURITY_ATTRIBUTES structure because the security attributes for a kernel object must be set when the object is created. However, this function's second parameter, *fInherit*, does allow a process to open a kernel object and tell the system that the opened object is inheritable by any child processes created in the future.

The system performs the exact same actions when creating a child process regardless of whether the parent process created the kernel object or opened an existing kernel object—that is, the system increments the object's usage count by 1 and assigns the exact same handle value to the object relative to the child process.

I will discuss later in this chapter how a parent tells the system that a child process should inherit the parent's inheritable kernel objects.

Telling a Child About Its Inherited Kernel Objects

The problem with inheritance is that the child process is not made aware of the kernel objects it inherits. The objects are opened for the child and the handle values are set, but somehow the parent process must explicitly tell the child the values of the inherited object handles.

Several techniques can be employed here. The simplest is for the parent process to create the child process, convert the handle value to a string, and pass it as part of the child process's command line. The child process will then, as it initializes, parse the command line and retrieve the handle values of any objects it has inherited.

Another technique is for the parent to wait for the child to complete initialization (using the *WaitForInputIdle* function discussed in Chapter 9);

then the parent can send or post a message to a window created by a thread in the child process.

A third technique is for the parent process to add an environment variable to its environment block. The variable name would be something that the child process knows to look for and the variable's value would be the handle value of the kernel object to be inherited. Then, when the parent spawns the child process, the child process inherits the parent's environment variables and can easily call *GetEnvironmentVariable* to obtain the inherited object's handle value. This is an excellent approach if the child process is going to spawn another child process because the environment variables can be inherited again.

The System Version

Frequently an application needs to determine which version of Windows the user is running the application on. This might be required for several reasons. For example, an application might take advantage of security features by calling the Win32 security functions. However, these functions are fully implemented only on Windows NT.

For as long as I can remember, the Windows API has had a *GetVersion* function:

```
DWORD GetVersion(VOID);
```

This simple function has quite a history behind it. It was first designed for 16-bit Windows. The idea was a simple one: return the MS-DOS version number in the high-word and return the Windows version number in the low-word. For each word, the high-byte would represent the major version number and the low-byte would represent the minor version number.

Unfortunately, the programmer who wrote this code made a small mistake, coding the function so that the Windows version numbers were reversed—the major version number was in the low-byte and the minor number was in the high-byte. Since many programmers had already started using this function, Microsoft was forced to leave the function as is and change the documentation to reflect the mistake.

This was not the end of the problem, however, because now many programmers misunderstood how to use and compare the version information returned from *GetVersion,* and they frequently wrote code that was incorrect as a result. Sure, their programs functioned correctly on Windows 3.1, but when Microsoft started working on Windows 95 and tested many of the existing applications on that system, they soon discovered that the applications were failing simply because they incorrectly compared version numbers. For this reason, the *GetVersion* function is forever hard-coded to return version 3.95 in all future versions of Windows 95 and Windows NT.

This, of course, is simply not a good enough solution. Programs require an effective and accurate method for determining the version number of the system they're running on. So Microsoft added a new function to the Win32 API, *GetVersionEx*:

```
BOOL GetVersionEx(LPOSVERSIONINFO lpVersionInformation);
```

This function requires you to allocate an OSVERSIONINFO structure in your application and pass the structure's address to *GetVersionEx*. The OSVERSIONINFO structure is shown below:

```
typedef struct {
    DWORD dwOSVersionInfoSize;
    DWORD dwMajorVersion;
    DWORD dwMinorVersion;
    DWORD dwBuildNumber;
    DWORD dwPlatformId;
    TCHAR szCSDVersion[128];
} OSVERSIONINFO, *LPOSVERSIONINFO;
```

Notice that the structure has different members for each of the individual components of the system's version number. This was done purposely so that programmers would not have to bother with extracting low-words, high-words, low-bytes, and high-bytes; it should make things much easier for applications to compare their expected version number with the host system's version number. The table below describes the OSVERSIONINFO structure's members:

Member	Description
dwOSVersionInfoSize	Must be set to *sizeof(OSVERSIONINFO)* prior to calling the *GetVersionEx* function.
dwMajorVersion	Major version number of the host system.
dwMinorVersion	Minor version number of the host system.
dwBuildNumber	Build number of the current system.

(continued)

continued

Member	Description
dwPlatformId	Identifies the platform supported by the current system. This can be VER_PLATFORM_WIN32s (Win32s on Windows 3.1), VER_PLATFORM_WIN32_WINDOWS (Win32 on Windows 95), or VER_PLATFORM_WIN32_NT (Windows NT).
szCSDVersion	This field contains additional text that provides further information about the installed operating system.

The *CreateProcess* Function

A process is created when your application calls the *CreateProcess* function:

```
BOOL CreateProcess(
   LPCTSTR lpszImageName,
   LPCTSTR lpszCommandLine,
   LPSECURITY_ATTRIBUTES lpsaProcess,
   LPSECURITY_ATTRIBUTES lpsaThread,
   BOOL fInheritHandles,
   DWORD fdwCreate,
   LPVOID lpvEnvironment,
   LPTSTR lpszCurDir,
   LPSTARTUPINFO lpsiStartInfo,
   LPPROCESS_INFORMATION lppiProcInfo);
```

When a thread in your application calls *CreateProcess*, the system creates a process kernel object with an initial usage count of 1. This process kernel object is not the process itself but rather a small data structure that the operating system uses to manage the process—think of the process kernel object as a small data structure that consists of statistical information about the process. The system then creates a virtual 4-GB address space for the new process and loads the code and data for the executable file and any required dynamic-link libraries into the process's 4-GB address space.

The system then creates a thread kernel object (with a usage count of 1) for the new process's primary thread. Like the process kernel object, the thread kernel object is a small data structure that the operating system uses to manage the thread. This primary thread will begin by executing the C run-time startup code, which will eventually call your *WinMain* function (or *main* function if your application is console-based). If the system successfully creates the new process and primary thread, *Create-Process* returns TRUE.

OK, that's the broad overview. The following sections dissect each of *CreateProcess*'s parameters.

If you are familiar with the two 16-bit Windows functions for creating a process, *WinExec* and *LoadModule*, you can see by comparing the number of parameters for these two functions with the new *CreateProcess* function that *CreateProcess* offers much more control over process creation. Both the *WinExec* and *LoadModule* functions are implemented internally as calls to the *CreateProcess* function. And because these functions are supplied only for backward compatibility with 16-bit Windows, no Unicode versions of these functions exist—you can call these functions only by passing ANSI strings.

lpszImageName and *lpszCommandLine*

The *lpszImageName* and *lpszCommandLine* parameters specify both the name of the executable file the new process will use and the command-line string that will be passed to the new process. Let's talk about the *lpszCommandLine* parameter first.

The *lpszCommandLine* parameter allows you to specify a complete command line that *CreateProcess* uses to create the new process. When *CreateProcess* parses the *lpszCommandLine* string, it examines the first token in the string and assumes that this token is the name of the executable file you want to run. If the executable file's name does not have an extension, an EXE extension is assumed. *CreateProcess* will also search for the executable in the following order:

1. The directory containing the EXE file of the calling process

2. The current directory of the calling process

3. The Windows system directory

4. The Windows directory

5. The directories listed in the PATH environment variable

Of course, if the filename includes a full path, the system looks for the executable using the full path and does not search the directories. If the system finds the executable file, it creates a new process and maps the executable's code and data into the new process's address space. The system then calls the C run-time startup routine. As noted earlier in this chapter, the C run-time startup routine examines the process's command line and passes the address to the first argument after the executable file's name as *WinMain*'s *lpszCmdLine* parameter.

What I have just described is what happens as long as the *lpszImageName* parameter is NULL. Instead of passing NULL, you can pass the address to a string containing the name of the executable file you want to run in the *lpszImageName* parameter. Note that you must specify the file's extension; the system will not automatically assume that the filename ends with an EXE extension. *CreateProcess* assumes the file is in the current directory unless a path is specified preceding the filename. If the file can't be found in the current directory, *CreateProcess* does not look for the file in any other directory—*CreateProcess* simply fails.

However, even if you specify a filename in the *lpszImageName* parameter, *CreateProcess* passes the contents of the *lpszCommandLine* parameter to the new process as its command line. For example, say that you call *CreateProcess* like this:

```
CreateProcess("C:\\WINNT\\SYSTEM32\\NOTEPAD.EXE",
    "WRITE README.TXT", ...);
```

The system invokes the Notepad application, but Notepad's command line is "WRITE README.TXT". This is certainly a little strange, but that's how *CreateProcess* works.

lpsaProcess, *lpsaThread*, and *fInheritHandles*

In order to create a new process, the system must create a process object and a thread object (for the process's primary thread). Because these are kernel objects, the parent process gets the opportunity to associate security attributes with these two objects. The *lpsaProcess* and *lpsaThread* parameters allow you to specify the desired security for the process object and the thread object, respectively. You can pass NULL for these parameters, in which case the system gives these objects default security descriptors. Or you can allocate and initialize two SECURITY_ATTRIBUTES structures to create and assign your own security privileges to the process and thread objects.

Another reason to use SECURITY_ATTRIBUTES structures for the *lpsaProcess* and *lpsaThread* parameters is if you want either of these two objects to be inheritable by any child processes.

Figure 2-3 is a short program that demonstrates kernel inheritance. Let's say that Process A creates Process B by calling *CreateProcess* and passing the address of a SECURITY_ATTRIBUTES structure for the *lpsaProcess* parameter in which the *bInheritHandle* member is set to TRUE. In this same call, the *lpsaThread* parameter points to another SECURITY_ATTRIBUTES structure in which its *bInheritHandles* member is set to FALSE.

When the system creates Process B, it allocates both a process kernel object and a thread kernel object and returns handles back to Process A in the structure pointed to by the *lppiProcInfo* parameter (discussed shortly). Process A can now manipulate the newly created process object and thread object by using these handles.

Now let's say that Process A is going to call *CreateProcess* a second time to create Process C. Process A can decide whether to grant Process C inheritance privileges. The *fInheritHandles* parameter is used for this purpose. If *fInheritHandles* is set to TRUE, the system causes Process C to inherit any inheritable handles. In this case, the handle to Process B's process object is inheritable. The handle to Process B's primary thread object is not inheritable no matter what the value of the *fInheritHandles* parameter to *CreateProcess* is. Also, if Process A calls *CreateProcess*, passing FALSE for the *fInheritHandles* parameter, Process C will not inherit any of the handles currently in use by Process A.

INHERIT.C

```
/***************************************************************
Module name: Inherit.C
Notices: Copyright (c) 1995 Jeffrey Richter
***************************************************************/


#include <windows.h>


int WINAPI WinMain (HINSTANCE hinstExe, HINSTANCE hinstPrev,
   LPSTR lpszCmdLine, int nCmdShow) {

   STARTUPINFO si;
   SECURITY_ATTRIBUTES saProcess, saThread;
   PROCESS_INFORMATION piProcessB, piProcessC;
```

Figure 2-3.

An inheritance example.

(continued)

Figure 2-3. *continued*

```
// Prepare a STARTUPINFO structure for spawning processes.
ZeroMemory(&si, sizeof(si));
si.cb = sizeof(si);

// Prepare to spawn Process B from Process A.
// The handle identifying the new process
// object should be inheritable.
saProcess.nLength = sizeof(saProcess);
saProcess.lpSecurityDescriptor = NULL;
saProcess.bInheritHandle = TRUE;

// The handle identifying the new thread
// object should NOT be inheritable.
saThread.nLength = sizeof(saThread);
saThread.lpSecurityDescriptor = NULL;
saThread.bInheritHandle = FALSE;

// Spawn Process B
CreateProcess(NULL, "ProcessB", &saProcess, &saThread,
    FALSE, 0, NULL, NULL, &si, &piProcessB);

// The pi structure contains two handles
// relative to Process A:
// hProcess, which identifies Process B's process
// object and is inheritable; and hThread, which identifies
// Process B's primary thread object and is NOT inheritable.

// Prepare to spawn Process C from Process A.
// Since NULL is passed for the lpsaProcess and lpsaThread
// parameters, the handles to Process C's process and
// primary thread objects default to "noninheritable."

// If Process A were to spawn another process, this new
// process would NOT inherit handles to Process C's process
// and thread objects.

// Because TRUE is passed for the fInheritHandles parameter,
// Process C will inherit the handle that identifies Process
// B's process object but will not inherit a handle to
// Process B's primary thread object.
CreateProcess(NULL, "ProcessC", NULL, NULL,
    TRUE, 0, NULL, NULL, &si, &piProcessC);

return(0);
}
```

fdwCreate

The *fdwCreate* parameter identifies flags that affect how the new process is created. Multiple flags can be specified when combined with the Boolean OR operator.

The DEBUG_PROCESS flag tells the system that the parent process wants to debug the child process and any processes created by the child process in the future. This flag instructs the system to notify the parent process (now the debugger) when certain events occur in any of the child processes (debuggees).

The DEBUG_ONLY_THIS_PROCESS flag is similar to the DEBUG-_PROCESS flag except that the debugger is notified of special events occurring only in the immediate child process. If the child process creates any additional processes, the debugger is not notified of events in these additional processes.

The CREATE_SUSPENDED flag causes the new process to be created, but its primary thread is suspended. A debugger provides a good example for using this flag. When a debugger is told to load a debuggee, it must have the system initialize the process and primary thread, but the debugger does not want to allow the primary thread to begin execution yet. Using this flag, the user debugging the application can set various breakpoints throughout the program in case there are special events that need trapping. Once all the breakpoints have been set, the user can tell the debugger that the primary thread can begin execution.

The DETACHED_PROCESS flag blocks a console-based process's access to its parent's console window and tells the system to send its output to a new console window. If a console-based process is created by another console-based process, the new process will, by default, use the parent's console window. (When you run the C compiler from the command shell, a new console window isn't created; the output is simply appended to the bottom of the window.) By specifying this flag, the new process will send its output to a new console window.

The CREATE_NEW_CONSOLE flag tells the system to create a new console window for the new process. It is an error to specify both the CREATE_NEW_CONSOLE and DETACHED_PROCESS flags.

The CREATE_NEW_PROCESS_GROUP flag is used to modify the list of processes that get notified when the user presses the Ctrl+C or Ctrl+Break keys. If you have several console-based processes running when the user presses one of these key combinations, the system notifies all the processes in a process group that the user wants to break out of the current operation. By specifying this flag when creating a new console-based process, you are creating a new process group. If the user presses Ctrl+C or Ctrl+Break while a process in this new process group is active, the system notifies only processes in this group of the user's request.

The CREATE_DEFAULT_ERROR_MODE flag tells the system that the new process is not to inherit the error mode used by the parent process. (See the *SetErrorMode* function discussed earlier in this chapter.)

The CREATE_SEPARATE_WOW_VDM flag is useful only when you are invoking a 16-bit Windows application. If the flag is specified, the system will create a separate Virtual DOS Machine (VDM) and run the 16-bit Windows application in this VDM. By default, all 16-bit Windows applications execute in a single, shared VDM. The advantage of running an application in a separate VDM is that if the application crashes it kills only the single VDM; any other programs running in distinct VDMs continue to function normally. Also, 16-bit Windows applications that are run in separate VDMs have separate input queues. That means that if one application hangs momentarily, applications in separate VDMs continue to receive input. The disadvantage of running multiple VDMs is that each VDM consumes a significant amount of physical storage.

The CREATE_UNICODE_ENVIRONMENT flag tells the system that the child process's environment block should contain Unicode characters. By default, a process's environment block contains ANSI strings.

You can also specify a priority class when you're creating a new process. However, you don't have to specify a priority class, and for most applications it is recommended that you don't; the system will assign a default priority class to the new process. The table below shows the possible priority classes.

Priority Class	Flag Identifier
Idle	IDLE_PRIORITY_CLASS
Normal	NORMAL_PRIORITY_CLASS
High	HIGH_PRIORITY_CLASS
Realtime	REALTIME_PRIORITY_CLASS

These priority classes affect how the threads contained within the process are scheduled with respect to other processes' threads. See the section "How the System Schedules Threads" in Chapter 3 for more information.

lpvEnvironment

The *lpvEnvironment* parameter points to a block of memory containing environment strings that the new process will use. Most of the time NULL is passed for this parameter, causing the child process to inherit the set of environment strings that its parent is using. Or you can use the *GetEnvironmentStrings* function:

```
LPVOID GetEnvironmentStrings(VOID);
```

This function gets the address of the environment string data block that the calling process is using. You can use the address returned by this function as the *lpvEnvironment* parameter of *CreateProcess*. This is exactly what *CreateProcess* does if you pass NULL for the *lpvEnvironment* parameter.

lpszCurDir

The *lpszCurDir* parameter allows the parent process to set the child process's current drive and directory. If this parameter is NULL, the new process's working directory will be the same as that of the application spawning the new process. If this parameter is not NULL, *lpszCurDir* must point to a zero-terminated string containing the desired working drive and directory. Notice that you must specify a drive letter in the path.

lpsiStartInfo

The *lpsiStartInfo* parameter points to a STARTUPINFO structure:

```
typedef struct _STARTUPINFO {
    DWORD   cb;
    LPSTR   lpReserved;
    LPSTR   lpDesktop;
    LPSTR   lpTitle;
    DWORD   dwX;
    DWORD   dwY;
    DWORD   dwXSize;
    DWORD   dwYSize;
    DWORD   dwXCountChars;
    DWORD   dwYCountChars;
    DWORD   dwFillAttribute;
    DWORD   dwFlags;
    WORD    wShowWindow;
    WORD    cbReserved2;
    LPBYTE  lpReserved2;
    HANDLE  hStdInput;
    HANDLE  hStdOutput;
    HANDLE  hStdError;
} STARTUPINFO, *LPSTARTUPINFO;
```

Win32 uses the members of this structure when it creates the new process. We'll discuss each member in turn. Some members are meaningful only if the child application creates an overlapped window, while others are meaningful only if the child performs console-based input and output. Figure 2-4 indicates the usefulness of each member:

Member	Window, Console, or Both	Purpose
cb	Both	Contains the number of bytes in the STARTUPINFO structure. Acts as a version control in case Microsoft expands this structure in a future version of Win32. Your application must initialize *cb* to *sizeof(STARTUPINFO)*:
lpReserved	Both	Reserved. Must be initialized to NULL.
lpDesktop	Both	Identifies the name of the desktop in which to start the application. If the desktop exists, the new process is associated with the specified desktop. If the desktop does not exist, a desktop with default attributes will be created with the specified name for the new process. If *lpDesktop* is NULL (which is most common), the process is associated with the current desktop. Currently there are no implementations of Win32 that allow you to create multiple desktops. Microsoft plans to add this feature in future versions.
lpTitle	Console	Specifies the window title for a console window. If *lpTitle* is NULL, the name of the executable file is used as the window title.
dwX *dwY*	Both	Specify the *x*- and *y*-coordinates (in pixels) of the location where the application's window should be placed on the screen. These coordinates are used only if the child process creates its first overlapped window with CW_USEDEFAULT as the *x* parameter of *CreateWindow*. For applications that create console windows, these members indicate the upper left corner of the console window.

Figure 2-4.   *(continued)*

The members of the STARTUPINFO structure.

Figure 2-4. *continued*

Member	Window, Console, or Both	Purpose
dwXSize *dwYSize*	Both	Specify the width and height (in pixels) of an application's window. These values are used only if the child process creates its first overlapped window with CW_USEDEFAULT as the *nWidth* parameter of *CreateWindow*. For applications that create console windows, these members indicate the width and height of the console window.
dwXCountChars *dwYCountChars*	Console	Specify the width and height (in characters) of a child's console windows.
dwFillAttribute	Console	Specifies the text and background colors used by a child's console window.
dwFlags	Both	See below and the table on page 42.
wShowWindow	Window	Specifies how the child's first overlapped window should appear if the application's first call to *ShowWindow* passes SW_SHOWDEFAULT as the *nCmdShow* parameter. This member can be any of the SW_* identifiers normally used with the *ShowWindow* function.
cbReserved2	Both	Reserved. Must be initialized to 0.
lpReserved2	Both	Reserved. Must be initialized to NULL.
hStdInput *hStdOutput* *hStdError*	Console	Specify handles to buffers for console input and output. By default, the *hStdInput* identifies a keyboard buffer, whereas *hStdOutput* and *hStdError* identify a console window's buffer.

Now, as promised, I'll discuss the *dwFlags* member. This member contains a set of flags that modify how the child process is to be created. Most of the flags simply tell *CreateProcess* whether other members of the STARTUPINFO structure contain useful information, or whether some of the members should be ignored. The table on page 42 shows the list of possible flags and their meanings.

Flag	Meaning
STARTF_USESIZE	Use the *dwXSize* and *dwYSize* members.
STARTF_USESHOWWINDOW	Use the *wShowWindow* member.
STARTF_USEPOSITION	Use the *dwX* and *dwY* members.
STARTF_USECOUNTCHARS	Use the *dwXCountChars* and *dwYCountChars* members.
STARTF_USEFILLATTRIBUTE	Use the *dwFillAttribute* member.
STARTF_USESTDHANDLES	Use the *hStdInput*, *hStdOutput*, and *hStdError* members.

Two additional flags, STARTF_FORCEONFEEDBACK and STARTF-_FORCEOFFFEEDBACK, give you control over the mouse cursor when invoking a new process. Because Windows 95 and Windows NT support true preemptive multitasking, it is possible to invoke an application and, while the process is initializing, use another program. To give visual feedback to the user, *CreateProcess* temporarily changes the system's mouse cursor to a new cursor called a start glass:

This cursor indicates that you can wait for something to happen or you can continue to use the system. In the very early beta releases of Windows NT this cursor didn't exist—*CreateProcess* did not change the appearance of the cursor at all. This was confusing; often, when I ran a program from the Program Manager, the program's windows would not appear immediately and the cursor would still appear as the normal arrow. So I would click on the program icon again in the Program Manager, which I thought wasn't acknowledging my request. Soon the program I wanted would pop up on the screen, followed by another, and another, and another. Now I had to close all the additional instances of the program. It is amazing how big a difference changing the cursor can make. The problem was compounded, of course, because 16-bit Windows does change the cursor to an hourglass when an application is being initialized. Because I was expecting this, I thought that Windows NT wasn't working properly. Old habits are hard to break.

The *CreateProcess* function gives you more control over the cursor when invoking another process. When you specify the STARTF_FORCE-OFFFEEDBACK flag, *CreateProcess* does not change the cursor into the start glass, leaving it as the normal arrow.

Specifying STARTF_FORCEONFEEDBACK causes *CreateProcess* to monitor the new process's initialization and to alter the cursor based on the result. When *CreateProcess* is called with this flag, the cursor changes into the start glass. If, after 2 seconds, the new process does not make a GUI call, *CreateProcess* resets the cursor to an arrow.

If the process does make a GUI call within 2 seconds, *CreateProcess* waits for the application to show a window. This must occur within 5 seconds after the process makes the GUI call. If a window is not displayed, *CreateProcess* resets the cursor. If a window is displayed, *CreateProcess* keeps the start glass cursor on for another 5 seconds. If at any time the application calls the *GetMessage* function, indicating that it is finished initializing, *CreateProcess* immediately resets the cursor and stops monitoring the new process.

The final flag to discuss is STARTF_SCREENSAVER. This flag tells the system that the application is a screen-saver application, which causes the system to initialize the application in a very special way. When the process begins executing, the system allows the process to initialize at the foreground priority of the class that was specified in the call to *CreateProcess*. As soon as the process makes a call to either *GetMessage* or *PeekMessage*, the system automatically changes the process's priority to the idle priority class.

If the screen-saver application is active and the user presses a key or moves the mouse, the system automatically boosts the priority class of the screen-saver application back to the foreground priority of the class flag passed to *CreateProcess*.

To start a screen-saver application, you should call *CreateProcess* using the NORMAL_PRIORITY_CLASS flag. Doing so has the following two effects:

- The system allows the screen-saver application to initialize before making it run idle. If the screen-saver application ran 100 percent of its time at idle priority, normal and realtime processes would preempt it, and the screen-saver application would never get a chance to initialize.

- The system allows the screen-saver application to terminate. Usually a screen saver terminates because the user starts using an application. This application is probably running at normal priority, which would cause the threads in the screen-saver application to be preempted again, and the screen saver would never be able to terminate.

Before leaving this section, I'd like to say a word about START-UPINFO's *wShowWindow* member. You initialize this member to the value that is passed to *WinMain*'s last parameter, *nCmdShow*. This value indicates how you would like the main window of your application shown. The value is one of the identifiers that can be passed to the *ShowWindow* function. Usually *nCmdShow*'s value is either SW_SHOWNORMAL or SW_SHOWMINNOACTIVE. However, the value can sometimes be SW_SHOWDEFAULT.

When you invoke an application from the Program Manager by double-clicking, the application's *WinMain* function is called with SW-_SHOWNORMAL passed as the *nCmdShow* parameter. If you hold down the Shift key while double-clicking, your application is invoked passing SW_SHOWMINNOACTIVE as the *nCmdShow* parameter. In this way, the user can easily start an application with its main window showing in either the normal state or the minimized state.

lppiProcInfo

The *lppiProcInfo* parameter points to a PROCESS_INFORMATION structure that you must allocate; *CreateProcess* will initialize the members of this structure before it returns. The structure appears as follows:

```
typedef struct _PROCESS_INFORMATION {
    HANDLE hProcess;
    HANDLE hThread;
    DWORD  dwProcessId;
    DWORD  dwThreadId;
} PROCESS_INFORMATION;
```

As already mentioned, creating a new process causes the system to create a process kernel object and a thread kernel object. At creation time, the system gives each object an initial usage count of 1. Then, just before *CreateProcess* returns, the function opens the process object and the thread object and places the process-relative handles for each in the *hProcess* and *hThread* members of the PROCESS_INFORMATION structure. When *CreateProcess* opens these objects, the usage count for each increments to 2.

This means that before the system can free the process object, the process must terminate (decrementing the usage count to 1) and the parent process must call *CloseHandle* (decrementing the usage count to 0). Similarly, to free the thread object, the thread must terminate and the parent process must close the handle to the thread object.

Important

Don't forget to close these handles. Failure to close handles is one of the most common mistakes developers make and results in a system memory leak until the process that called *CreateProcess* terminates.

When a process is created, the system assigns the process a unique identifier; no other process running in the system will have the same ID number. The same is true for threads. When a thread is created, the thread is also assigned a unique, systemwide ID number. Before *CreateProcess* returns, it fills the *dwProcessId* and *dwThreadId* members of the PROCESS_INFORMATION structure with these IDs. The parent process can use these two IDs to communicate with the child process.

It is extremely important to note that the system reuses process and thread IDs. For example, let's say that when a process is created, the system allocates a process object and assigns it the ID value 0x22222222. If a new process object is created, the system doesn't assign the same ID number. However, if the first process object is freed, the system might assign 0x22222222 to the next process object created.

This is important to know so that you avoid writing code that references an incorrect process object (or thread). It's easy to acquire a process ID and save the ID, but the next thing you know, the process identified by the ID is freed and a new process is created and given the same ID. When you use the saved process ID, you end up manipulating the new process, not the process you originally acquired the handle to.

You can easily guarantee this doesn't happen by making sure you have an outstanding lock on the process object. In other words, make sure that you have incremented the usage count for the process object. The system will never free the process object while it has a usage count greater than 0. In most situations, you will already have incremented the usage count. For example, the call to *CreateProcess* returns after incrementing the usage count for the process object.

With the usage count incremented, you can feel free to use the process ID to your heart's content. When you no longer need the process ID, call *CloseHandle* to decrement the process object's usage count. Simply make sure that you don't use that process ID after you have called *CloseHandle*.

Terminating a Process

A process can be terminated in two ways: by calling the *ExitProcess* function, which is the most common method, or by calling the *Terminate-Process* function, which is a method that should be reserved as a last resort. This section discusses both methods for terminating a process and describes what actually happens when a process ends.

The *ExitProcess* Function

A process terminates when one of the threads in the process calls *ExitProcess*:

```
VOID ExitProcess(UINT fuExitCode);
```

This function terminates the process and sets the exit code of the process to *fuExitCode*. *ExitProcess* doesn't return a value because the process has terminated. If you include any code following the call to the *ExitProcess* function, that code will never execute.

This is the most common method for terminating a process because *ExitProcess* is called when *WinMain* returns to the C run-time's startup code. The startup code calls *ExitProcess*, passing it the value returned from *WinMain*. Any other threads running in the process terminate along with the process.

Note that the Win32 documentation states that a process does not terminate until all its threads terminate. The C run-time's startup code ensures that the process terminates by calling *ExitProcess*. However, if you call *ExitThread* in your *WinMain* function instead of calling *ExitProcess* or simply returning, the primary thread for your application will stop executing, but the process will not terminate if at least one other thread in the process is still running.

The *TerminateProcess* Function

A call to *TerminateProcess* also ends a process:

```
BOOL TerminateProcess(HANDLE hProcess, UINT fuExitCode);
```

This function is different from *ExitProcess* in one major way: any thread can call *TerminateProcess* to terminate another process or its own process. The *hProcess* parameter identifies the handle of the process to be terminated. When the process terminates, its exit code becomes the value you passed as the *fuExitCode* parameter.

Note that using *TerminateProcess* is discouraged; use it only if you can't force a process to exit by using another method. Normally, when a process ends the system notifies any DLLs attached to the process that the process is ending. If you call *TerminateProcess*, however, the system doesn't notify any DLLs attached to the process, which can mean that the process won't close down correctly. For example, a DLL might be written to flush data to a disk file when the process detaches from the DLL. Detachment usually occurs when an application unloads the DLL by calling *FreeLibrary*. Because the DLL isn't notified about the detachment when you use *TerminateProcess*, the DLL can't perform its normal cleanup. The system does notify the DLL when a process ends normally or when *ExitProcess* is called. (See Chapter 11 for more information about DLLs.)

Although it's possible that the DLL won't have a chance to clean up its data, the system guarantees that all allocated memory is freed, all opened files are closed, all kernel objects have their usage counts decremented, and all User or GDI objects are freed regardless of how the process terminates.

What Happens When a Process Terminates

When a process terminates, the following actions are set in motion:

1. All the threads in the process are halted.

2. All the User and GDI objects allocated by the process are freed, and all the kernel objects are closed.

3. The process kernel object status becomes signaled. (See Chapter 9 for more information about signaling.) Other threads in the system can suspend themselves until the process is terminated.

4. The process's exit code changes from STILL_ACTIVE to the code passed to *ExitProcess* or *TerminateProcess*.

5. The process kernel object's usage count is decremented by 1.

When a process terminates, its associated process kernel object isn't freed until all outstanding references to the object are closed. Also, terminating a process does not cause any of its child processes to terminate.

When a process terminates, the code for the process and any resources that the process allocated are removed from memory. However, the private memory that the system allocated for the process kernel object is not freed until the process object's usage count reaches 0. This can happen only if all other processes that have created or opened handles to the now-defunct process notify the system that they no longer need to reference the process. These processes notify the system by calling *CloseHandle*.

After a process is no longer running, the parent process can't do much with the process handle. However, it can call *GetExitCodeProcess* to check whether the process identified by *hProcess* has terminated and, if so, determine its exit code.

```
BOOL GetExitCodeProcess(HANDLE hProcess, LPDWORD lpdwExitCode);
```

The exit code value is returned in the DWORD pointed to by *lpdwExitCode*. If the process hasn't terminated when *GetExitCodeProcess* is called, the function fills the DWORD with the STILL_ACTIVE identifier (defined as 0x103). If the function is successful, TRUE is returned. Using the child process's handle to determine when the child process has terminated is discussed further in Chapter 9.

Child Processes

When you design an application, situations might arise in which you want another block of code to perform work. You assign work like this all the time by calling functions or subroutines. When you call a function, your code cannot continue processing until the function has returned. And in many situations, this single-tasking synchronization is needed.

An alternative way to have another block of code perform work is to create a new thread within your process and have it help with the processing. This allows your code to continue processing while the other thread performs the work you requested. This technique is useful, but it creates synchronization problems when your thread needs to see the results of the new thread.

Another approach is to spawn off a new process—a child process—to help with the work. Let's say that the work you need to do is pretty complex. To process the work, you decide to simply create a new thread within the same process. You write some code, test it, and get some incorrect results. You might have an error in your algorithm, or maybe you dereferenced something incorrectly and accidentally overwrote something important in your address space. One way to protect your address space while having the work processed is to have a new process perform the work. You could then wait for the new process to terminate before continuing on with your own work, or you could continue working while the new process works.

Unfortunately, the new process probably would need to perform operations on data contained in your address space. In this case, it might be a good idea to have the process run in its own address space and simply give it access to the relevant data contained in the parent process's address space, thus protecting all the data not relevant to the job. Win32 gives you several different methods for transferring data between different processes: Dynamic Data Exchange (DDE), OLE, Pipes, MailSlots, and so on. One of the most convenient ways to share the data is to use memory-mapped files. (See Chapter 7 for a detailed discussion of memory-mapped files.)

If you want to create a new process, have it do some work, and wait for the result, you can use code similar to the following:

```
PROCESS_INFORMATION ProcessInformation;
DWORD dwExitCode;

BOOL fSuccess = CreateProcess(..., &ProcessInformation);
if (fSuccess) {
    HANDLE hProcess = ProcessInformation.hProcess;

    // Close the thread handle as soon as it is no longer needed!
    CloseHandle(ProcessInformation.hThread);

    if (WaitForSingleObject(hProcess, INFINITE) != WAIT_FAILED) {
        // The process terminated.
        GetExitCodeProcess(hProcess, &dwExitCode);
    }

    // Close the process handle as soon as it is no longer needed.
    CloseHandle(hProcess);
}
```

In the code fragment above you create the new process and, if successful, call the *WaitForSingleObject* function:

```
DWORD WaitForSingleObject(HANDLE hObject, DWORD dwTimeout);
```

We'll discuss the *WaitForSingleObject* function exhaustively in Chapter 9. For now, all you need to know is that it waits until the object identified by the *hObject* parameter becomes *signaled*. Process objects become signaled when they terminate. So the call to *WaitForSingleObject* suspends the parent's thread until the child process terminates. After *WaitForSingleObject* returns, you can get the exit code of the child process by calling *GetExitCodeProcess*.

The calls to *CloseHandle* in the code fragment above cause the system to decrement the usage count for the thread and process objects to 0, allowing the objects' memory to be freed.

You'll notice that in the code fragment I close the handle to the child process's primary thread kernel object immediately after *CreateProcess* returns. This does *not* cause the child's primary thread to terminate—it simply decrements the usage count of the child's primary thread object. Here's why this is a good practice: Suppose the child process's primary thread spawns off another thread and then the primary thread terminates. At this point, the system can free the child's primary thread object from its memory if the parent process doesn't have an outstanding handle to this thread object. But if the parent process does have a handle to the child's thread object, the system can't free the object until the parent process closes the handle.

Running Detached Child Processes

Most of the time, an application starts another process as a *detached process*. This means that after the process is created and executing, the parent process doesn't need to communicate with the new process or doesn't require that the child process complete its work before the parent process continues. This is how the Program Manager and Explorer work. After the Program Manager or Explorer creates a new process for the user, it doesn't care whether that process continues to live or whether the user terminates it.

To give up all ties to the child process, the Program Manager or Explorer must close its handles to the new process and its primary thread by calling *CloseHandle*. The code sample below shows how to create a new process and how to let it run detached:

```
PROCESS_INFORMATION ProcessInformation;
BOOL fSuccess = CreateProcess(..., &ProcessInformation);
if (fSuccess) {
   CloseHandle(ProcessInformation.hThread);
   CloseHandle(ProcessInformation.hProcess);
}
```

CHAPTER THREE

THREADS

In this chapter, I'll discuss the concept of a thread and describe how the system uses threads to execute your application's code. Like processes, threads have properties associated with them, and I'll discuss some of the functions available for querying and changing these properties. I'll also examine the functions that allow you to create or spawn additional threads in the system. And finally, I'll discuss how threads terminate.

When to Create a Thread

A thread describes a path of execution within a process. Every time a process is initialized, the system creates a primary thread. This thread starts at the C run-time's startup code, which in turn calls your *WinMain* function and continues executing until the *WinMain* function returns and the C run-time's startup code calls *ExitProcess*. For many applications, this primary thread is the only thread that the application requires. However, processes can create additional threads to help them do their work. The whole idea behind creating additional threads is to utilize the CPU's time as much as possible.

For example, a spreadsheet program needs to perform recalculations as the data entries in the cells are changed by the user. Because recalculations of a complex spreadsheet might require several seconds to complete, a well-designed application should not recalculate the spreadsheet after each change made by the user. Instead, the spreadsheet's recalculation function should be executed as a separate thread with a lower priority than that of the primary thread. This way, if the user is typing the primary thread is running, which means that the system won't schedule any time to the recalculation thread. When the user stops typing, the primary thread is suspended, waiting for input, and the recalculation thread is scheduled time. As soon as the user starts typing again, the primary thread, having a higher priority, preempts the recalculation thread. Creating an additional thread makes the program very responsive to the user. It is also rather easy to implement this type of design.

In a similar example, you can create an additional thread for a repagination function in a word processor that needs to repaginate the document as the user enters text into the document. Microsoft Word for Windows, for example, must simulate multithreaded behavior in 16-bit Windows but could easily spawn a thread dedicated to repaginating the document for the Win32 version. The primary thread would be responsible for processing the user's input, and a background thread would be responsible for locating the page breaks.

It's also useful to create a separate thread to handle any printing tasks in an application. In this way the user can continue to use the application while it's printing. In addition, when performing a long task many applications display a dialog box that allows the user to abort the task. For example, when the File Manager copies files, it displays a dialog box that, besides listing the names of the source file and the destination file, also contains a Cancel button. If you click on the Cancel button while the files are being copied, you abort the operation.

In 16-bit Windows, implementing this type of functionality requires periodic calls to *PeekMessage* inside the File Copy loop. And calls to *PeekMessage* can be made only between file reading and writing. If a large data block is being read, the response to the button click doesn't occur until after the block has been read. If the file is being read from a floppy disk, this can take several seconds. Because the response is so sluggish, I have frequently clicked on the button several times, thinking that the system didn't know I'd canceled the operation.

By putting the File Copy code in a different thread, you don't need to sprinkle calls to the *PeekMessage* function throughout your code—your user interface thread operates independently. This means that a click on the Cancel button results in an immediate response.

You can also use threads for creating applications that simulate real-world events. In Chapter 9 I show a simulation of a supermarket. Because each shopper is represented by his or her own thread, theoretically each shopper is independent of any other shopper and can enter, shop, check out, and exit as he or she sees fit. The simulation can monitor these activities to determine how well the supermarket functions.

Although simulations can be performed, potential problems lurk. First, you would ideally want each shopper thread to be executed by its very own CPU. Because it is not practical to expect a CPU for every shopper thread, the solution is to incur a time overhead when the operating system preempts 1 thread and schedules another. For example, if your simulation has 2 threads and your machine has eight CPUs, the system can assign 1 thread to each CPU. However, if your simulation has 1000 threads, the system will have to assign and reassign the 1000 threads among the eight CPUs over and over again. And some overhead results when the operating system schedules a large number of threads among a few CPUs. If your simulation lasts a long time, this overhead has a relatively small impact on the simulation. However, if the simulation is short, the overhead of the operating system can take a larger percentage of the simulation's total execution time.

Second, the system itself requires threads to run while other processes might be executing. All these processes' threads need to be scheduled for CPU time as well, which almost certainly affects the outcome of the simulation.

And third, the simulation is useful only if you keep track of its progress. For example, the supermarket simulation in Chapter 9 adds entries to a list box as the shoppers progress through the store; adding entries to the list box takes time away from the simulation. The Heisenberg Uncertainty Principle states that a more accurate determination of one quantity results in a less precise measurement of the other.[1] This is most definitely true here.

When Not to Create a Thread

The first time many programmers are given access to an environment that supports multiple threads, they're ecstatic. If only they had had threads sooner, their applications would have been so simple to write. And, for some unknown reason, these programmers start dividing an application into individual pieces, each of which can execute as its own thread. This is not the way to go about developing an application.

Threads are incredibly useful and have a place, but when you use threads you can potentially create new problems while trying to solve the old ones. For example, let's say you're developing a word processing

---

1. Werner Heisenberg actually developed the theory with respect to quantum mechanics, not computer science.

application and want to allow the printing function to run as its own thread. This sounds like a good idea because the user can immediately go back and start editing the document while it is printing. But wait—this means that the data in the document might be changed *while* the document is printing. This is a whole new type of problem you'll need to address. Maybe it would be best not to have the printing take place in its own thread, but this seems a bit drastic. How about if you let the user edit another document but lock the printing document so that it can't be modified until the printing has been completed? Or here's a third idea: Copy the document to a temporary file, print the contents of the temporary file, and let the user modify the original. When the temporary file containing the document has finished printing, delete the temporary file.

As you can see, threads help solve some problems at the risk of creating new ones. Another common misuse of threads can arise in the development of an application's user interface. In most applications, all the user interface components (windows) should be sharing the same thread. If you're producing a dialog box, for example, it wouldn't make much sense for a list box to be created by one thread and a button to be created by another.

Let's take this a step further and say that you have your own list box control that sorts data every time an element is added or deleted. The sorting operation might take several seconds, so you decide to assign this control to its very own thread. In this way, the user can continue to work with other controls while the list box control's thread continues sorting.

Doing this wouldn't be a very good idea. First, every thread that creates a window must also contain a *GetMessage* loop. Second, because the list box thread contains its own *GetMessage* loop, you potentially open yourself up to some synchronization problems among the threads. You can solve these problems by assigning to the list box control a dedicated thread whose sole purpose is to sort elements in the background.

For Windows NT, a third reason exists. The Windows NT Win32 subsystem is like a parallel universe in that, for every thread you create that creates a window, the subsystem creates a complementary thread for itself. This adds unnecessary overhead in your application.

Now, having said all this, let me take some of it back. In rare situations, assigning individual threads to user interface objects is useful. In the system, each process has its own separate thread controlling its own user interface. For example, the Calculator application has one thread that creates and manipulates all the application's windows, and the Paintbrush application has its own thread that creates and manipulates Paintbrush's own windows. These separate threads were assigned for protection and robustness. If Calculator's thread enters an infinite loop, the resulting problem has no effect on Paintbrush's thread. This is quite different from the behavior we see in 16-bit Windows. In 16-bit Windows, if one application hangs, the entire system hangs. The Win32-based systems allow you to switch away from Calculator (even though it is hung) and start using Paintbrush. See Chapter 10 for more details.

Another use for multiple threads in GUI components is in multiple document interface (MDI) applications in which each MDI child window is running on its own thread. If one of the MDI child threads enters an infinite loop or starts a time-consuming procedure, the user can switch to another MDI child window and begin working with it while the other MDI child thread continues to chug along. This can be so useful, in fact, that Win32 offers a special function, shown below, whose result is similar to creating an MDI child window by sending the WM-_MDICREATE message to an MDIClient window.

```
HWND CreateMDIWindow(LPTSTR lpszClassName, LPTSTR lpszWindowName,
   DWORD dwStyle, int x, int y, int nWidth, int nHeight,
   HWND hwndParent, HINSTANCE hinst, LONG lParam);
```

The only difference is that the *CreateMDIWindow* function allows the MDI child to be created with its own thread.

The moral of the story is that multiple threads should be used judiciously. Don't use them only because you can. You can still write many useful and powerful applications using nothing more than the primary thread assigned to the process. If after reading all this you're convinced you have a valid need for threads, read on.

Writing Your First Thread Function

All threads begin executing at a function that you must specify. The function must have the following prototype:

```
DWORD WINAPI YourThreadFunc(LPVOID lpvThreadParm);
```

Like *WinMain*, this function is not actually called by the operating system. Instead, the operating system calls an internal function, not part of the C run-time, contained in KERNEL32.DLL. I call this function

StartOfThread; the actual internal name is not important. Below is what *StartOfThread* looks like:

```
void StartOfThread (LPTHREAD_START_ROUTINE lpStartAddr,
   LPVOID lpvThreadParm) {

   __try {
      DWORD dwThreadExitCode = lpStartAddr(lpvThreadParm);
      ExitThread(dwThreadExitCode);
   }
   __except(UnhandledExceptionFilter(GetExceptionInformation())) {
      ExitProcess(GetExceptionCode());
   }
}
```

The *StartOfThread* function sets into motion the following actions:

1. Sets up a structured exception handling (SEH) frame around your thread function so that any exceptions raised while your thread executes will get some default handling by the system. See Chapter 14 for more information about structured exception handling.

2. The system calls your thread function, passing it the 32-bit *lpvThreadParm* parameter that you passed to the *CreateThread* function (discussed shortly).

3. When your thread function returns, the *StartOfThread* function calls *ExitThread*, passing it your thread function's return value. The thread kernel object's usage count is decremented, and the thread stops executing.

4. If your thread raises an exception that is not handled, the SEH frame set up by the *StartOfThread* function will handle the exception. Usually, this means that a message box is presented to the user and that, when the user dismisses the message box, *StartOfThread* calls *ExitProcess* to terminate the entire process, not just the offending thread.

Although I left it out of the earlier discussion, a process's primary thread actually begins by executing the system's *StartOfThread* function. The *StartOfThread* function then calls the C run-time's startup code, which calls your *WinMain* function. The C run-time's startup code, however, does not ever return back to the *StartOfThread* function because the startup code explicitly calls *ExitProcess*.

The remainder of this section discusses the various attributes that are "bestowed" upon a new thread.

A Thread's Stack

Each thread is allocated its very own stack from the owning process's 4-GB address space. When you use static and global variables, multiple threads can access the variables at the same time, potentially corrupting the variables' contents. However, local and automatic variables are created on the thread's stack and are therefore far less likely to be corrupted by another thread. For this reason, you should always try to use local or automatic variables when writing your functions and avoid the use of static and global variables.

The actual size of a thread's stack, and how the operating system and compiler manage the stack, are very complex subjects—I postpone discussing these details until Chapter 6.

A Thread's CONTEXT Structure

Each thread has its own set of CPU registers, called the thread's *context*. This CONTEXT structure reflects the state of the thread's CPU registers when the thread was last executing. The CONTEXT structure is the only CPU-specific Win32 data structure. In fact, the Win32 help file doesn't show the contents of this structure at all. If you want to see the members of this structure, you must look in the WINNT.H file, where you will find this structure defined several times: once for x86, once for MIPS, and once for Alpha. The compiler selects the appropriate version of this structure depending on the target CPU type for your EXE or DLL.

When a thread is scheduled CPU time, the system initializes the CPU's registers with the thread's context. Of course, one of the CPU registers is an instruction pointer that identifies the address of the next CPU instruction for the thread to execute. The CPU registers also include a stack pointer that identifies the address of the thread's stack.

A Thread's Execution Times

In a multithreaded environment, it becomes much more difficult to time how long it takes your process to perform various tasks. This is because your process might have a thread that is busy recalculating some complex algorithm while threads in other processes are all competing for the same CPU. Since your recalc thread is constantly being preempted, you can't simply write code to time your algorithm as shown on the next page.

```
DWORD dwStartTime = GetTickCount();
// Perform complex algorithm
DWORD dwElapsedTime = GetTickCount() - dwStartTime;
```

What is needed here is a function that returns the amount of time that the CPU has been assigned to this thread. Fortunately, in Win32 there is a function that returns this information:

```
BOOL GetThreadTimes(HANDLE hThread, LPFILETIME lpCreationTime,
    LPFILETIME lpExitTime, LPFILETIME lpKernelTime,
    LPFILETIME lpUserTime);
```

GetThreadTimes returns four different time values, as shown in the table below:

Time Value	Meaning
Creation time	The time when the thread was created.
Exit time	The time when the thread exited. If the thread is still running, the exit time is undefined.
Kernel time	The amount of time that the thread has spent executing operating system code.
User time	The amount of time that the thread has spent executing application code.

Using this function, you can determine the amount of time necessary to execute a complex algorithm by using code such as this:

```
__int64 FileTimeToQuadWord (PFILETIME pFileTime) {
    __int64 qw;
    qw = pFileTime->dwHighDateTime;
    qw <<= 32;
    qw |= pFileTime->dwLowDateTime;
    return(qw);
}

PFILETIME QuadWordToFileTime (__int64 qw, PFILETIME pFileTime) {
    pFileTime->dwHighDateTime = (DWORD) (qw >> 32);
    pFileTime->dwLowDateTime  = (DWORD) (qw & 0xFFFFFFFF);
    return(pFileTime);
}


void Recalc () {
    FILETIME ftKernelTimeStart, ftKernelTimeEnd;
```

```
FILETIME ftUserTimeStart, ftUserTimeEnd;
FILETIME ftDummy, ftTotalTimeElapsed;
__int64 qwKernelTimeElapsed, qwUserTimeElapsed,
   qwTotalTimeElapsed;

// Get starting times.
GetThreadTimes(GetCurrentThread(), &ftDummy, &ftDummy,
   &ftKernelTimeStart, &ftUserTimeStart);

// Perform complex algorithm here.
   .
   .
   .
// Get ending times.
GetThreadTimes(GetCurrentThread(),&ftDummy, &ftDummy,
   &ftKernelTimeEnd, &ftUserTimeEnd);

// Get the elapsed kernel and user times by converting the start
// and end times from FILETIMEs to quad words, and then subtract
// the start times from the end times.
qwKernelTimeElapsed = FileTimeToQuadWord(&ftKernelTimeEnd) -
   FileTimeToQuadWord(&ftKernelTimeStart);
qwUserTimeElapsed = FileTimeToQuadWord(&ftUserTimeEnd) -
   FileTimeToQuadWord(&ftUserTimeStart);

// Get total time duration by adding the kernel and user times.
qwTotalTimeElapsed = qwKernelTimeElapsed + qwUserTimeElapsed;

// Convert resultant quad word to FILETIME.
QuadWordToFileTime(qwTotalTimeElapsed, &ftTotalTimeElapsed);

// The total elapsed time is in qwTotalElapsedTime and in
// ftTotalTimeElapsed. You can use either form.
   .
   .
   .
}
```

Let me also point out here that there is a function similar to *Get-ThreadTimes* that applies to all of the threads in a process:

```
BOOL GetProcessTimes (HANDLE hProcess, LPFILETIME lpCreationTime,
   LPFILETIME lpExitTime, LPFILETIME lpKernelTime,
   LPFILETIME lpUserTime);
```

GetProcessTimes returns times that apply to all the threads in a specified process. For example, the kernel time returned will be the sum of all the elapsed times that all of the process's threads have spent in kernel code.

Unfortunately, the *GetThreadTimes* and *GetProcessTimes* functions are not functional in Windows 95. If you call either of these functions in Windows 95, they return FALSE. A subsequent call to *GetLastError* returns a value of 120 (ERROR_CALL_NOT_IMPLEMENTED), which indicates that these functions are valid only in Windows NT.

There is no reliable mechanism for an application to determine how much CPU time a thread or process has used under Windows 95.

The *CreateThread* Function

We've already discussed how a process's primary thread comes into being when *CreateProcess* is called. However, if you want a primary thread to create additional threads, you can have it call *CreateThread*:

```
HANDLE CreateThread(
    LPSECURITY_ATTRIBUTES lpsa,
    DWORD cbStack,
    LPTHREAD_START_ROUTINE lpStartAddr,
    LPVOID lpvThreadParm,
    DWORD fdwCreate,
    LPDWORD lpIDThread);
```

For every call to *CreateThread*, the system must perform the following steps:

1. Allocate a thread kernel object to identify and manage the newly created thread. This object holds much of the system information to manage the thread. A handle to this object is the value returned from the *CreateThread* function.

2. Initialize the thread's exit code (maintained in the thread kernel object) to STILL_ACTIVE and set the thread's suspend count (also maintained in the thread kernel object) to 1.

3. Allocate a CONTEXT structure for the new thread.

4. Prepare the thread's stack by reserving a region of address space, committing 2 pages of physical storage to the region, setting the protection of the committed storage to PAGE_READWRITE, and setting the PAGE_GUARD attribute on the second-to-top page. See Chapter 6 for more information about a thread's stack.

5. Initialize the stack pointer register in the thread's CONTEXT structure to point to the top of the stack; initialize the instruction pointer register to point to the internal *StartOfThread* function.

OK, that's the broad overview. The following sections dissect each of *CreateThread*'s parameters.

lpsa

The *lpsa* parameter is a pointer to a SECURITY_ATTRIBUTES structure. You can also pass NULL if you want the default security attributes for the object. If you want any child processes to be able to inherit a handle to this thread object, you must specify a SECURITY_ATTRIBUTES structure whose *bInheritHandle* member is initialized to TRUE.

cbStack

The *cbStack* parameter specifies how much address space the thread is allowed to use for its own stack. Every thread owns its very own stack. When *CreateProcess* starts an application, it calls *CreateThread* to initialize the process's primary thread. For the *cbStack* parameter, *CreateProcess* uses the value stored inside the executable file. You can control this value using the linker's /STACK switch:

```
/STACK:[reserve] [,commit]
```

The *reserve* argument sets the amount of memory the system should reserve in the address space for the thread's stack. The default is 1 MB. The *commit* argument specifies the amount of reserved address space that should initially be committed to the stack. The default is 1 page. (See Chapter 6 for a discussion of reserving and committing memory.) As the code in your thread executes, it is quite possible that you'll require more than 1 page of memory. When your thread overflows its stack, an exception is generated. (See Chapter 14 for detailed information about handling exceptions.) The system catches the exception and commits another page (or whatever you specified for the *commit* argument) to the reserved space, which allows your thread's stacks to grow dynamically as needed.

When calling *CreateThread* you can pass 0 to the *cbStack* parameter. In this case, *CreateThread* creates a stack for the new thread using the *commit* argument embedded in the EXE file by the linker. The amount of reserved space is always 1 MB. The system sets a limit of 1 MB to stop functions that recurse endlessly.

For example, let's say that you are writing a function that calls itself recursively. This function also has a bug that causes endless recursion. Every time the function calls itself, a new stack frame is created on the stack. If the system didn't set a maximum limit on the stack size, the recursive function would never stop calling itself. All of the process's address space would be allocated, and enormous amounts of physical storage would be committed to the stack. By setting a stack limit, you prevent your application from using up enormous amounts of physical storage, and you'll also know much sooner when a bug exists in your program. The SEHSum sample application in Chapter 14 shows how you can trap and handle stack overflows in your application.

lpStartAddr and lpvThreadParm

The *lpStartAddr* parameter indicates the address of the thread function that you want the new thread to execute. It is perfectly legal and actually quite useful to create multiple threads that all have the same function address as their starting point. For example, you might create an MDI application in which all the child windows behave similarly but each operates on its own thread. The thread function you write must have the same function prototype as this function:

```
DWORD WINAPI ThreadFunc(LPVOID lpvThreadParm) {
    DWORD dwResult = 0;
    :
    :
    return(dwResult);
}
```

The thread function's *lpvThreadParm* parameter is the same as the *lpvThreadParm* parameter that you originally passed to *CreateThread*. *CreateThread* does nothing with this parameter except pass it on to the thread function when the thread starts executing. This parameter provides a way to pass an initialization value to the thread function. This initialization data can be either a 32-bit value or a 32-bit pointer to a data structure that contains additional information.

fdwCreate

The *fdwCreate* parameter specifies additional flags that control the creation of the thread. It can be one of two values. If the value is 0, the thread starts executing immediately. If the value is CREATE_SUSPENDED, the system creates the thread, creates the thread's stack, initializes the CPU register members in the thread's CONTEXT structure, and gets ready to execute the first instruction of the thread function but suspends the thread so that it doesn't start executing.

Immediately before *CreateThread* returns, and while the thread that called it continues to execute, the new thread is also executing—that is, as long as the CREATE_SUSPENDED flag wasn't specified.[2] Because the new thread is running simultaneously, the possibility of problems exists. Watch out for code like this:

```
DWORD WINAPI FirstThread (LPVOID lpvThreadParm) {
    int x = 0;
    DWORD dwResult = 0, dwThreadId;
    HANDLE hThread;

    hThread = CreateThread(NULL, 0, SecondThread, (LPVOID) &x,
        0, &dwThreadId);
    CloseHandle(hThread);

    return(dwResult);
}


DWORD WINAPI SecondThread (LPVOID lpvThreadParm) {
    DWORD dwResult = 0;

    // Do some lengthy processing here.
    :
    :
    * ((int *) lpvThreadParm) = 5;
    :
    :
    return(dwResult);
}
```

In the code above, it is very likely that *FirstThread* will finish its work before *SecondThread* assigns 5 to *FirstThread*'s *x*. If this happens, *SecondThread* won't know that *FirstThread* no longer exists and will attempt to change the contents of what is now an invalid address. This is certain to cause *SecondThread* to raise an access violation because *FirstThread*'s stack is destroyed when *FirstThread* terminates. One way to solve the problem is to declare *x* as a static variable. In this way, the compiler will create a storage area for *x* in the application's data section rather than on the stack.

---

2. Actually, on a single-CPU machine threads execute one at a time, but it's best to think of them as all executing simultaneously. Also, the new thread's execution is subject to the priority levels of all other threads.

However, this makes the function non-reentrant. In other words, you couldn't create two threads that execute the same function because the static variable would be shared between the two threads.

Another way to solve this problem, as well as its more complex variations, is to use synchronization objects, which I discuss in Chapter 9.

lpIDThread

The last parameter of *CreateThread*, *lpIDThread*, must be a valid address of a DWORD in which *CreateThread* will store the ID that the system assigns to the new thread. Under Windows NT, this parameter cannot be NULL even if you are not interested in the thread's ID; passing NULL causes an access violation.

I personally believe that you should be able to pass NULL for the *lpIDThread* parameter because more often than not the thread's unique ID number is not that useful. Apparently, some of the developers on Microsoft's Windows 95 team felt as I did because Windows 95 does allow you to pass NULL for the *lpIDThread* parameter, in which case the function does not raise an access violation and you don't get the thread's ID back. This is a small but nice feature of Windows 95.

Of course, this inconsistency between Windows 95 and Windows NT can cause problems for software developers. For example, let's say you develop and test an application on Windows 95 that takes advantage of the fact that *CreateThread* will accept NULL for the *lpIDThread* parameter. Now, when you later run your application on Windows NT, your program will fail. This means that you *must* thoroughly test your applications on both Windows 95 and Windows NT.

Terminating a Thread

Like a process, a thread can be terminated in two ways: by calling the *ExitThread* function, which is the most common method, or by calling the *TerminateThread* function, which you should reserve as a last resort. This section discusses both methods for terminating a thread and describes what actually happens when a thread ends.

The *ExitThread* Function

A thread terminates when it calls *ExitThread*:

```
VOID ExitThread(UINT fuExitCode);
```

This function terminates the thread and sets the thread's exit code to *fuExitCode. ExitThread* doesn't return a value because the thread has terminated.

This method is the most common because *ExitThread* is called when the thread function returns to the system's internal *StartOfThread* function. The *StartOfThread* function calls *ExitThread*, passing it the value returned from your thread function.

The *TerminateThread* Function

A call to *TerminateThread* also ends a thread:

```
BOOL TerminateThread(HANDLE hThread, DWORD dwExitCode);
```

The function ends the thread identified by the *hThread* parameter and sets its exit code to *dwExitCode.* The *TerminateThread* function exists so you can terminate a thread when it no longer responds. You should use it only as a last resort.

Under Windows NT, when a thread dies by calling *ExitThread,* the stack for the thread is destroyed. However, if the thread is terminated by *TerminateThread,* the system does not destroy the stack until the process that owns the thread terminates because other threads might still be using pointers that reference data contained on the terminated thread's stack. If these other threads attempted to access the stack, an access violation would occur.

Under Windows 95, the *TerminateThread* function does destroy the stack of the thread that's being terminated.

When a thread ends, the system notifies any DLLs attached to the process owning the thread that the thread is ending. If you call *TerminateThread,* however, the system doesn't notify any DLLs attached to the process, which can mean that the process won't be closed down correctly. For example, a DLL might be written to flush data to a disk file when the thread detaches from the DLL. Because the DLL isn't notified about the detachment when you use *TerminateThread*, the DLL cannot perform its normal cleanup.

The *ExitProcess* and *TerminateProcess* functions discussed in Chapter 2 also terminate threads. The difference is that these functions terminate all the threads contained in the process being terminated.

What Happens When a Thread Terminates

The following actions occur when a thread terminates:

1. All User object handles owned by the thread are freed. In Win32, most objects are owned by the process containing the thread that creates the objects. However, there are a few objects (mostly User objects such as windows, accelerators, and hooks) that can be owned by a thread. When the threads that create these objects die, the system automatically destroys the objects.

2. The state of the thread kernel object becomes signaled.

3. The thread's exit code changes from STILL_ACTIVE to the code passed to *ExitThread* or *TerminateThread*.

4. If the thread is the last active thread in the process, the process ends.

5. The thread kernel object's usage count is decremented by 1.

When a thread terminates, its associated thread kernel object doesn't automatically become freed until all the outstanding references to the object are closed.

Once a thread is no longer running, there isn't much any other thread in the system can do with the thread's handle. However, these other threads can call *GetExitCodeThread* to check whether the thread identified by *hThread* has terminated and, if it has, determine its exit code.

```
BOOL GetExitCodeThread(HANDLE hThread, LPDWORD lpdwExitCode);
```

The exit code value is returned in the DWORD pointed to by *lpdwExitCode*. If the thread hasn't terminated when *GetExitCodeThread* is called, the function fills the DWORD with the STILL_ACTIVE identifier (defined as 0x103). If the function is successful, TRUE is returned. Using the thread's handle to determine when the thread has terminated is discussed further in Chapter 9.

Gaining a Sense of One's Own Identity

Several Win32 functions require a process handle as a parameter. A thread can get the handle of the process it is running in by calling *GetCurrentProcess*:

```
HANDLE GetCurrentProcess(VOID);
```

This function returns a pseudo-handle to the process; it doesn't create a new handle, and it doesn't increment the process object's usage count. If you call *CloseHandle* and pass this pseudo-handle as the parameter, *CloseHandle* simply ignores the call and does nothing but return.

You can use pseudo-handles in calls to functions that require a process handle. For example, the line below changes the priority class of the calling process to HIGH_PRIORITY_CLASS:

```
SetPriorityClass(GetCurrentProcess(), HIGH_PRIORITY_CLASS);
```

The Win32 API also includes a few functions that require a process ID. A thread can acquire the ID of the process it is running in by calling *GetCurrentProcessId*:

```
DWORD GetCurrentProcessId(VOID);
```

This function returns the unique, systemwide ID that identifies the process.

When you call *CreateThread*, the handle of the newly created thread is returned to the thread making the call, but the new thread does not know what its own handle is. For a thread to acquire a handle to itself, it must call:

```
HANDLE GetCurrentThread(VOID);
```

Like *GetCurrentProcess*, *GetCurrentThread* returns a pseudo-handle that is meaningful only when used in the context of the current thread. The thread object's usage count is not incremented, and calls to *CloseHandle* passing the pseudo-handle have no effect.

A thread acquires its ID by calling:

```
DWORD GetCurrentThreadId(VOID);
```

Sometimes you might need to acquire a "real" handle to a thread instead of a pseudo-handle. By "real," I mean a handle that unambiguously identifies a unique thread. Examine the following code:

```
DWORD WINAPI ParentThread (LPVOID lpvThreadParm) {
   DWORD IDThread;
```

(continued)

67

```
      HANDLE hThreadParent = GetCurrentThread();
      CreateThread(NULL, 0, ChildThread, (LPVOID) hThreadParent, 0,
         &IDThread);
      // Function continues...
}

DWORD WINAPI ChildThread (LPVOID lpvThreadParm) {
      HANDLE hThreadParent = (HANDLE) lpvThreadParm;
      SetThreadPriority(hThreadParent, THREAD_PRIORITY_NORMAL);
      // Function continues...
}
```

Can you see the problem with this code fragment? The idea is to have the parent thread pass to the child thread a thread handle that identifies the parent thread. However, the parent thread is passing a pseudo-handle, not a "real" handle. When the child thread begins execution, it passes the pseudo-handle to the *SetThreadPriority* function, which causes the child thread—not the parent thread—to change priority. This happens because a thread pseudo-handle is a handle to the current thread—that is, a handle to whichever thread is making the function call.

To fix this code, we must turn the pseudo-handle into a "real" handle. This can be done by using the *DuplicateHandle* function:

```
BOOL DuplicateHandle(
    HANDLE hSourceProcess,
    HANDLE hSource,
    HANDLE hTargetProcess,
    LPHANDLE lphTarget,
    DWORD fdwAccess,
    BOOL fInherit,
    DWORD fdwOptions);
```

Usually this function is used to create a new process-relative handle from a kernel object handle that is relative to another process. The first parameter, *hSourceProcess*, identifies the process that has access to the object to be duplicated. The handle value of *hSourceProcess* must be relative to the process that is making the call to *DuplicateHandle*. The third parameter, *hTargetProcess*, identifies the process to be granted access to the same object. Again, this handle value must be relative to the process that is making the call to *DuplicateHandle*.

The second parameter, *hSource*, identifies the existing object. This handle value must be relative to the process identified by the *hSourceProcess* parameter. The fourth parameter, *lphTarget*, is the address to a HANDLE variable that *DuplicateHandle* will fill with the duplicated handle's value. This new handle value identifies the same object that the *hSource* parameter identifies, but the new handle is relative to the process identified by the *hTargetProcess* parameter. In other words, only threads in the process identified by the *hSourceProcess* parameter can use the object identified by the *hSource* parameter, and only threads in the process identified by the *hTargetProcess* parameter can use the object identified by the *lphTarget* parameter. The remaining three parameters allow you to specify how the new handle can be accessed, whether the new handle is inheritable by child processes spawned by the target process, and whether the original object should be closed automatically. (See the *Microsoft Win32 Programmer's Reference* for more information about the *DuplicateHandle* function.)

We can use the *DuplicateHandle* function in an unusual way to correct the code fragment discussed earlier. The corrected code fragment is as follows:

```
DWORD WINAPI ParentThread (LPVOID lpvThreadParm) {
   DWORD IDThread;
   HANDLE hThreadParent;

   DuplicateHandle(
      GetCurrentProcess(),     // Handle of process that thread
                               // pseudo-handle is relative to
      GetCurrentThread(),      // Parent thread's pseudo-handle
      GetCurrentProcess(),     // Handle of process that the new,
                               // "real," thread handle is
                               // relative to
      &hThreadParent           // Will receive the new,
                               // "real," handle identifying
                               // the parent thread
      0,                       // Ignored because of
                               // DUPLICATE_SAME_ACCESS
      FALSE,                   // New thread handle is not
                               // inheritable
      DUPLICATE_SAME_ACCESS);  // New thread handle has same
                               // access as pseudo-handle

   CreateThread(NULL, 0, ChildThread, (LPVOID) hThreadParent, 0,
      &IDThread);
   // Function continues...
}

DWORD WINAPI ChildThread (LPVOID lpvThreadParm) {
   HANDLE hThreadParent = (HANDLE) lpvThreadParm;
```

(continued)

```
        SetThreadPriority(hThreadParent, THREAD_PRIORITY_NORMAL);
        CloseHandle(hThreadParent);
        // Function continues...
}
```

Now when the parent thread executes, it converts the ambiguous pseudo-handle identifying the parent thread to a new, "real," handle that unambiguously identifies the parent thread, and it passes this "real" handle to *CreateThread*. When the child thread starts executing, its *lpv-ThreadParm* parameter contains the "real" thread handle. Any calls to functions, passing this handle, will now affect the parent thread, not the child thread.

Because *DuplicateHandle* does increment the usage count of the specified kernel object, it is very important to remember to decrement the object's usage count by passing the target handle to *CloseHandle* when you are finished using the duplicated object handle. This is demonstrated in the code fragment on the previous page. Immediately after the call to *SetThreadPriority*, the child thread calls *CloseHandle* to decrement the parent thread object's usage count. In the previous code fragment, I assumed that the child thread would not call any other functions using this handle. If other functions are to be called passing the parent thread's handle, the call to *CloseHandle* should not be made until the handle is no longer required by the child thread.

I should also point out that the *DuplicateHandle* function can be used to convert a pseudo-handle for a process to a "real" process handle as follows:

```
HANDLE hProcess;
DuplicateHandle(
    GetCurrentProcess(),     // Handle of process that the process
                             // pseudo-handle is relative to
    GetCurrentProcess(),     // Process's pseudo-handle
    GetCurrentProcess(),     // Handle of process that the new,
                             // "real," process handle is
                             // relative to
    &hProcess,               // Will receive the new, "real,"
                             // handle identifying the process
    0,                       // Ignored because of
                             // DUPLICATE_SAME_ACCESS
    FALSE,                   // New thread handle is not
                             // inheritable
    DUPLICATE_SAME_ACCESS);  // New process handle has same
                             // access as pseudo-handle
    :
    :
```

How the System Schedules Threads

The system schedules all active threads based on their priority levels. Each thread in the system is assigned a priority level. Priority levels range from 0, the lowest, to 31, the highest. Priority level 0 is assigned to a special thread in the system called the *zero page* thread. The zero page thread is responsible for zeroing any free pages in the system when there are no other threads that need to perform work in the system. It is not possible for any other thread to have a priority level of 0.

When the system assigns a CPU to a thread, it treats all threads of the same priority as equal. That is, the system simply assigns the first thread of priority 31 to a CPU, and after that thread's time slice is finished, the system assigns the next priority 31 thread to the CPU. When all the priority 31 threads have had a time slice, the system assigns the first priority 31 thread back to the CPU. Note that if you always have at least one priority 31 thread for each CPU, other threads having priorities less than 31 will never be assigned to a CPU and will therefore never execute. This is called *starvation*. Starvation occurs when some threads use so much of the CPU's time that other threads are never able to execute.

When no priority 31 threads need to run, the system will begin assigning the CPU to priority 30 threads. When no priority 31 and no priority 30 threads need to run, the system assigns the CPU to priority 29 threads, and so on.

At first, you might think that low priority threads (like the zero page thread) will never get a chance to run in a system designed like this. But as it turns out, threads frequently do not have a reason to run. For example, if your process's primary thread calls *GetMessage* and the system sees that there are no messages pending, the system suspends your process's thread, relinquishes the remainder of the thread's time slice, and immediately assigns the CPU to another, waiting, thread.

If no messages show up for *GetMessage* to retrieve, the process's thread stays suspended, and the CPU is never assigned to it. However, when a message is placed in the thread's queue, the system knows that the thread should no longer be suspended and will assign the CPU to the thread as long as no higher-priority threads need to execute.

Let me point out another issue here. If a priority 5 thread is running, and the system determines that a higher-priority thread is ready to run, the system will immediately suspend the lower-priority thread (even if it's in the middle of its time slice) and assign the CPU to the higher-priority thread, which gets a full time slice. Higher-priority threads always preempt lower-priority threads regardless of what the lower-priority threads are executing.

How Priority Levels Are Assigned Using the Win32 API

When you create threads, you don't assign them priority levels using numbers. Instead, the system determines the thread's priority level using a two-step process. The first step is to assign a priority class to a process. A process's priority class tells the system the priority required by the process compared to other running processes. The second step is to assign relative priority levels to threads owned by the process. The following sections discuss both steps.

Process Priority Classes

Win32 supports four different priority classes: idle, normal, high, and realtime. You assign a priority class to a process by ORing one of the *CreateProcess* flags listed in the table below with the other *fdwCreate* flags when calling *CreateProcess*. The table below shows the priority level associated with each priority class:

Class	*CreateProcess* Flag	Level
Idle	IDLE_PRIORITY_CLASS	4
Normal	NORMAL_PRIORITY_CLASS	7–9
High	HIGH_PRIORITY_CLASS	13
Realtime	REALTIME_PRIORITY_CLASS	24

This means that any thread created in a process whose priority class is idle has the priority level 4.

I can't stress enough how important it is to select a priority class for your process carefully. When calling *CreateProcess*, most applications should either not specify a priority class or use the NORMAL_PRIORITY_CLASS flag. When you don't specify a priority class, the system assumes normal priority class unless the parent process has an idle priority class. In this case, the child process is also of the idle priority class.

Processes of the normal priority class behave a little differently than processes using other priority classes. Most applications a user runs are of the normal priority class. When the user is working with a process, that process is said to be the foreground process and all other processes are called background processes. When a normal process is brought to the foreground, Windows NT automatically boosts all of that process's threads by 2. Windows 95 boosts all that process's threads by 1.

The reason for this boosting is to make the foreground process react faster to the user's input. If the process's threads weren't boosted, a normal process printing in the background and a normal process accepting user input in the foreground would be competing equally for the CPU's time. The user, of course, would see that text was not appearing smoothly in the foreground application. But because the system boosts the foreground process's threads, the foreground process's threads always preempt threads in background normal processes.

When running Windows NT, the user can control the system's boosting of normal foreground processes by double-clicking on the System option in the Control Panel and then clicking on the Tasking button. This presents the following dialog box:

Tasking
┌ Foreground/Background Responsiveness ───────────────────
⦿ Best Foreground Application Response Time
◯ Foreground Application More Responsive than Background
◯ Foreground and Background Applications Equally Responsive
OK   Cancel   Help

The Best Foreground Application Response Time option means that normal processes in the foreground have a priority level of 9, the Foreground Application More Responsive Than Background option means that normal processes in the foreground have a priority level of 8, and the Foreground And Background Applications Equally Responsive option means that normal processes in the foreground have a priority level of 7.

This feature is not offered in Windows 95 because Windows 95 is not designed to be run on a dedicated server machine. Windows NT server machines are frequently installed in a room where no user will operate them directly. When Windows NT machines are set up as dedicated servers, the administrator should select the Foreground And Background Applications Equally Responsive option so that all processes compete equally for the CPU.

Idle priority is perfect for system-monitoring applications. For example, you might write an application that periodically displays the amount of free RAM in the system. Because you would not want this application to interfere with the performance of other applications, you would set this process's priority class to IDLE_PRIORITY_CLASS.

Another good example of an application that can use idle priority is a screen saver. Most of the time a screen saver simply monitors actions from the user. When the user is idle for a specified period of time, the screen saver activates itself. There is no reason to have the screen saver monitoring the user's actions at a very high priority, so the perfect priority for this process is idle priority.

High priority class should be used only when absolutely necessary. You might not guess this, but the Windows NT Task Manager runs at high priority. Most of the time the Task Manager's thread is suspended, waiting to be awakened when the user presses Ctrl+Esc. While the Task Manager's thread is suspended, the system doesn't assign a CPU to the thread, which allows lower-priority threads to execute. However, once the user does press Ctrl+Esc, the system wakes up the Task Manager's thread. If any lower-priority threads are executing, the system preempts those threads immediately and allows the Task Manager to run. The Task Manager responds by displaying a dialog box that lists all the running applications. Microsoft designed the Task Manager this way because users expect the Task Manager to be extremely responsive, regardless of what else is going on in the system. In fact, the Task Manager's window can be displayed even when lower-priority threads are hung in infinite loops. Because the Task Manager's thread has a higher priority level, the thread executing the infinite loop is preempted, and the Task Manager allows the user to terminate the hung process.

The Task Manager is very well behaved. Most of the time it simply sits idle, not requiring any CPU time at all. If this were not the case, the whole system would perform much more slowly, and many applications would not respond.

The fourth priority flag, REALTIME_PRIORITY_CLASS, should almost never be used. In fact, earlier betas of the Win32 API did not expose this priority class to applications even though the operating system supported it. Realtime priority is extremely high, and because most threads in the system (including system management threads) execute at a lower priority, they will be affected by a process of this class. In fact, the threads in the system that control the mouse and the keyboard, background disk flushing, and Ctrl+Alt+Del trapping all operate at a lower priority class than realtime priority. If the user is moving the mouse, the thread responding to the mouse's movement will be preempted by a realtime thread. This affects the movement of the mouse, causing it to move jerkily rather than smoothly. Even more serious consequences can occur, such as loss of data.

You might use the realtime priority class if you are writing an application that talks directly to hardware, or if you need to perform some short-lived task and want to be pretty sure it will not be interrupted.

A process cannot run in the realtime priority class unless the user logged on to the system has Increase Scheduling Priority permission. Any user designated an administrator or a power user has this permission by default. You can give this permission to other users and groups by using the Windows NT User Manager application.

Altering a Process's Priority Class

It might seem odd to you that the process that creates a child process chooses the priority class at which the child process runs. Let's consider the Explorer or the Program Manager as an example. When you run an application from either of these applications, the new process runs at normal priority. The Explorer or the Program Manager has no idea what the process does or how quickly it needs to operate. However, once the child process is running, it can change its own priority class by calling *SetPriorityClass*:

```
BOOL SetPriorityClass(HANDLE hProcess, DWORD fdwPriority);
```

This function changes the priority class identified by *hProcess* to the value specified in the *fdwPriority* parameter. The *fdwPriority* parameter can be one of the following: IDLE_PRIORITY_CLASS, NORMAL_PRIORITY_CLASS, HIGH_PRIORITY_CLASS, or REALTIME_PRIORITY_CLASS. If the function succeeds, the return value is TRUE; otherwise, it's FALSE. Because this function takes a process handle, you can alter the priority class of any process running in the system as long as you have a handle to it and ample access privileges.

The complementary function used to retrieve the priority class of a process is:

```
DWORD GetPriorityClass(HANDLE hProcess);
```

As you might expect, this function returns one of the *CreateProcess* flags listed previously.

When you invoke a program using the command shell instead of the Explorer or the Program Manager, the program's starting priority is normal. However, if you invoke the program using the START command, you can use a switch to specify the starting priority of the application. For example, the following command entered at the command shell causes the system to invoke the Calculator and initially run it at low priority:

```
C:\>START /LOW CALC.EXE
```

The START command also recognizes the /NORMAL, /HIGH, and /REALTIME switches to start executing an application at normal priority (also the default), high priority, and realtime priority, respectively. Of course, once an application starts executing, it can call *SetPriorityClass* to alter its own priority to whatever it chooses.

The Windows 95 START command does not support the /LOW, /NOR-MAL, /HIGH, and /REALTIME switches. Processes started from the Windows 95 command shell always run using the normal priority class.

Setting a Thread's Relative Priority

When a thread is first created, its priority level is that of the process's priority class. For example, the primary thread of a HIGH_PRIORITY-_CLASS process is assigned an initial priority level value of 13. However, it is possible to raise or lower the priority of an individual thread. A thread's priority is always relative to the priority class of the process that owns it.

You can change a thread's relative priority within a single process by calling *SetThreadPriority*:

```
BOOL SetThreadPriority(HANDLE hThread, int nPriority);
```

The first parameter, *hThread*, is the handle to the thread whose priority class you're changing. The *nPriority* parameter can be one of the values shown in the following table.

Identifier	Meaning
THREAD_PRIORITY_LOWEST	The thread's priority should be 2 less than the process's priority class.
THREAD_PRIORITY_BELOW_NORMAL	The thread's priority should be 1 less than the process's priority class.
THREAD_PRIORITY_NORMAL	The thread's priority should be the same as the process's priority class.
THREAD_PRIORITY_ABOVE_NORMAL	The thread's priority should be 1 more than the process's priority class.
THREAD_PRIORITY_HIGHEST	The thread's priority should be 2 more than the process's priority class.

When a thread is first created, its initial relative priority value is THREAD_PRIORITY_NORMAL. The rules for threads within a process are similar to the rules for threads across processes. You should set a thread's priority to THREAD_PRIORITY_HIGHEST only when it is absolutely necessary in order for the thread to execute correctly. The scheduler will starve lower-priority threads if higher-priority threads require execution.

In addition to the above flags, two special flags can be passed to *SetThreadPriority*: THREAD_PRIORITY_IDLE and THREAD_PRIORITY_TIME_CRITICAL. Specifying THREAD_PRIORITY_IDLE causes the thread's priority level to be set to 1 regardless of whether the priority class for the process is idle, normal, or high. However, if the priority class for the process is realtime, THREAD_PRIORITY_IDLE sets the thread's priority level to 16. Specifying THREAD_PRIORITY_TIME_CRITICAL causes the thread's priority level to be set to 15 regardless of whether the priority class for the process is idle, normal, or high. However, if the priority class for the process is realtime, THREAD_PRIORITY_TIME-_CRITICAL sets the thread's priority level to 31. Figure 3-1 on the next page shows how the system combines a process's priority class with a thread's relative priority to determine a thread's base priority level.

	Process Priority Class					
Relative Thread Priority	Idle	Normal, in Background	Normal, in Foreground (Boost +1)	Normal, in Foreground (Boost +2)	High	Realtime
Time critical	15	15	15	15	15	31
Highest	6	9	10	11	15	26
Above normal	5	8	9	10	14	25
Normal	4	7	8	9	13	24
Below normal	3	6	7	8	12	23
Lowest	2	5	6	7	11	22
Idle	1	1	1	1	1	16

Figure 3-1.
How the system determines a thread's base priority level.

The complementary function to *SetThreadPriority*, *GetThreadPriority*, can be used to query a thread's relative priority:

```
int GetThreadPriority(HANDLE hThread);
```

The return value is one of the identifiers listed above or THREAD_PRIORITY_ERROR_RETURN if an error occurs.

Changing a process's priority class has no effect on any of its threads' relative priorities. Also note that the effects of calling *SetThreadPriority* are not cumulative. For example, if a thread is created in a process of the high priority class and you execute the following two lines:

```
SetThreadPriority(hThread, THREAD_PRIORITY_LOWEST);
SetThreadPriority(hThread, THREAD_PRIORITY_LOWEST);
```

the thread will have a priority level of 11, not a priority level of 9.

Dynamic Boosting of Thread Priority Levels

The priority level determined by combining a thread's relative priority with the priority class of the process containing the thread is called a thread's *base priority level*. Occasionally, the system boosts the priority level of a thread. This usually happens in response to a window message. For example, a thread having a relative priority of normal and running in a normal priority class process has a base priority of 9 (assuming that the process is in the foreground).

If the user presses a key, the system places a WM_KEYDOWN message in the thread's queue. Because a message has appeared in the thread's queue, the system assigns the CPU to the thread so that the thread can process the message. The system also temporarily boosts the priority level of the thread from 9 to 11. (The actual value may vary.) This new thread priority level is called a thread's *dynamic priority*. The CPU executes the thread for a complete time slice, and when the time slice is over, the system reduces the thread's priority by 1 so that it is now 10. The CPU is again assigned to the thread for another time slice, and at the end of this time slice, the system again reduces the thread's priority by 1. The thread's dynamic priority is now back to the thread's base priority level. The system never allows a thread's dynamic priority to drop below the thread's base priority level.

Microsoft is always fine-tuning the dynamic boosts of the system in order to determine the best overall results. All of this is in an effort to keep the system behaving very responsively to the end user. By the way, threads that have a base priority level in the realtime range (between 16 and 31) are never boosted by the system. The system boosts only threads that are in the dynamic range (between 0 and 15). In addition, the system will never boost a thread's priority into the realtime range (greater than 15).

Suspending and Resuming Threads

Earlier I mentioned that a thread can be created in a suspended state (by passing the CREATE_SUSPENDED flag to *CreateProcess* or *CreateThread*). When you do this, the system creates the kernel object identifying the thread, creates the thread's stack, and initializes the thread's CPU register members in the CONTEXT structure. However, the thread object is given an initial suspend count of 1, which means the system will never assign a CPU to execute the thread. To allow the thread to begin execution, another thread must call *ResumeThread* and pass it the thread handle returned by the call to *CreateThread* (or the thread handle from the structure pointed to by the *lppiProcInfo* parameter passed to *CreateProcess*):

```
DWORD ResumeThread(HANDLE hThread);
```

If *ResumeThread* is successful, it returns the thread's previous suspend count; otherwise, it returns 0xFFFFFFFF.

A single thread can be suspended several times. If a thread is suspended three times, the thread must be resumed three times before it is eligible for assignment to a CPU. Aside from using the CREATE_SUS-PENDED flag when creating a thread, you can suspend a thread by calling *SuspendThread*:

```
DWORD SuspendThread(HANDLE hThread);
```

Any thread can call this function to suspend another thread. It goes without saying (but I'll say it anyway) that a thread can suspend itself but it cannot resume itself. Like *ResumeThread*, *SuspendThread* returns the thread's previous suspend count. A thread can be suspended as many as MAXIMUM_SUSPEND_COUNT times (defined as 127 in WINNT.H).

What's Going On in the System

You can use two utilities that ship with Visual C++ 2.0—PSTAT.EXE and PVIEW.EXE—to find out which processes are loaded in the system and which threads exist in each process. At the time of this writing, neither of these tools runs under Windows 95. Figure 3-2 shows a dump from the PSTAT.EXE application. It lists all the processes and threads currently running in the system. The *pid* field shows the process ID for each process. For example, the process ID for the Program Manager (PROG-MAN.EXE) is 0xA0. The *pri* field to the right of the process ID shows the priority class value for the process. The Program Manager's priority value is 13, indicating that it has high priority.

Under each process is a list of threads owned by that process. The Event Log (EVENTLOG.EXE) has four threads. For each thread, the *tid* field shows the ID of the thread. The *pri* field indicates the priority number of the thread. The *cs* field shows the number of context switches for the thread. The status of the thread is shown at the end of the line. The word *Wait* indicates that the thread is suspended and is waiting for an event to occur before it can resume execution. The reason for the wait is also included.

```
Pstat version 0.2:  memory: 20032 kb  uptime:  0  2:30:10.575

PageFile: \DosDevices\F:\pagefile.sys
   Current Size: 32768 kb Total Used: 8764 kb  Peak Used 9680 kb

pid:  0 pri: 0 (null)
   tid:  0 pri:16 cs: 188262 Running
```

Figure 3-2.
Output from the PSTAT.EXE application.

(continued)

Figure 3-2. *continued*

```
pid:  7 pri: 8 (null)
   tid:  8 pri: 0 cs:       433 Wait:FreePage
   tid:  6 pri:16 cs:       579 Wait:Executive
   tid:  5 pri:12 cs:       656 Wait:Executive
   tid:  4 pri:16 cs:       624 Wait:Executive
   tid:  3 pri:12 cs:       531 Wait:Executive
   tid:  2 pri:16 cs:       613 Wait:Executive
   tid:  1 pri:12 cs:       488 Wait:Executive
   tid: 28 pri:16 cs:       598 Wait:Executive
   tid: 27 pri:12 cs:       540 Wait:Executive
   tid: 26 pri:16 cs:       556 Wait:Executive
   tid: 25 pri:12 cs:       546 Wait:Executive
   tid: 24 pri:18 cs:       260 Wait:VirtualMemory
   tid: 23 pri:17 cs:       212 Wait:FreePage
   tid: 22 pri:16 cs:      8992 Wait:Executive
   tid: 21 pri:16 cs:     16814 Wait:Executive
   tid: 20 pri:16 cs:         1 Wait:Executive
   tid: 1f pri:16 cs:         1 Wait:UserRequest
   tid: 1e pri:16 cs:         1 Wait:UserRequest
   tid: 1d pri:11 cs:         5 Wait:LpcReceive
   tid: 17 pri:17 cs:         1 Wait:VirtualMemory
   tid: 7c pri:16 cs:        20 Wait:Executive

pid: 1b pri:11 SMSS.EXE
   tid: 1c pri:13 cs:       344 Wait:UserRequest
   tid: 1a pri:13 cs:         7 Wait:LpcReceive
   tid: 19 pri:12 cs:         5 Wait:LpcReceive
   tid: 18 pri:13 cs:        13 Wait:Executive
   tid: 16 pri:12 cs:         5 Wait:LpcReceive
   tid: 15 pri:12 cs:         5 Wait:Executive
   tid: 14 pri:12 cs:         5 Wait:LpcReceive
   tid: 13 pri:13 cs:         6 Wait:Executive
   tid: 12 pri:12 cs:         5 Wait:LpcReceive

pid: 10 pri:11 CSRSS.EXE
   tid:  f pri:20 cs:      5765 Wait:UserRequest
   tid:  e pri:12 cs:        22 Wait:UserRequest
   tid:  d pri:11 cs:        34 Wait:Executive
   tid:  c pri:12 cs:       300 Wait:LpcReceive
   tid:  b pri:12 cs:       325 Wait:LpcReceive
   tid:  a pri:12 cs:       314 Wait:LpcReceive
   tid:  9 pri:12 cs:       292 Wait:LpcReceive
   tid: 48 pri:12 cs:         5 Wait:LpcReceive
```

(continued)

Figure 3-2. *continued*

```
    tid: 47 pri:12 cs:       7 Wait:LpcReceive
    tid: 38 pri:13 cs:     946 Wait:UserRequest
    tid: 37 pri:19 cs: 168639 Wait:UserRequest
    tid: 36 pri:12 cs:       9 Wait:UserRequest
    tid: 35 pri:31 cs:     903 Wait:UserRequest
    tid: 31 pri:12 cs:      12 Wait:EventPairLow
    tid: 53 pri:13 cs:      48 Wait:UserRequest
    tid: 4c pri:12 cs:      52 Wait:UserRequest
    tid: a6 pri:13 cs:      44 Wait:UserRequest
    tid: 6e pri:12 cs:      65 Wait:UserRequest
    tid: 6d pri:11 cs:     474 Wait:UserRequest
    tid: 9d pri:14 cs:   13863 Wait:UserRequest
    tid: 9c pri:12 cs:      98 Wait:UserRequest
    tid: a5 pri:12 cs:       6 Wait:EventPairLow
    tid: 69 pri:12 cs:       7 Wait:EventPairLow
    tid: a4 pri:12 cs:4574710 Wait:UserRequest
    tid: 97 pri:13 cs:   46430 Wait:UserRequest

pid: 45 pri: 8 OS2SS.EXE
    tid: 44 pri: 9 cs:       5 Wait:LpcReceive

pid: 42 pri: 8 PSXSS.EXE
    tid: 41 pri:10 cs:       6 Wait:LpcReceive
    tid: 40 pri:10 cs:       6 Wait:Executive
    tid: 3f pri:10 cs:       6 Wait:LpcReceive
    tid: 3e pri:10 cs:       6 Wait:Executive
    tid: 3d pri: 9 cs:       5 Wait:LpcReceive
    tid: 3c pri: 9 cs:       7 Wait:UserRequest

pid: 3a pri:13 WINLOGON.EXE
    tid: 3b pri:15 cs:     907 Wait:EventPairHigh
    tid: 39 pri:15 cs:       6 Wait:UserRequest

pid: 33 pri: 7 SCREG.EXE
    tid: 34 pri: 8 cs:     313 Wait:UserRequest
    tid: 32 pri: 8 cs:      17 Wait:DelayExecution
    tid: 30 pri: 8 cs:       8 Wait:UserRequest
    tid: 5d pri: 8 cs:     213 Wait:UserRequest

pid: 2e pri: 8 LSASS.EXE
    tid: 29 pri:10 cs:       6 Wait:LpcReceive
    tid: 2d pri:10 cs:     120 Wait:UserRequest
    tid: 68 pri:10 cs:      15 Wait:Executive
    tid: 67 pri: 9 cs:      18 Wait:LpcReceive
```

(continued)

Figure 3-2. *continued*

```
    tid: 66 pri: 9 cs:      34 Wait:LpcReceive
    tid: 65 pri:10 cs:      14 Wait:Executive
    tid: 63 pri:10 cs:      22 Wait:UserRequest

pid: 2c pri: 8 SPOOLSS.EXE
    tid: 2a pri: 7 cs:      58 Wait:DelayExecution
    tid: 71 pri: 8 cs:      12 Wait:UserRequest
    tid: 70 pri: 8 cs:      11 Wait:UserRequest
    tid: 99 pri:10 cs:      66 Wait:UserRequest

pid: 60 pri: 8 EVENTLOG.EXE
    tid: 61 pri:10 cs:      21 Wait:Executive
    tid: 5c pri:11 cs:      94 Wait:UserRequest
    tid: 5b pri:10 cs:       7 Wait:Executive
    tid: 5a pri:10 cs:      15 Wait:UserRequest

pid: 58 pri: 8 NETDDE.EXE
    tid: 59 pri:10 cs:      34 Wait:Executive
    tid: 5e pri: 9 cs:      18 Wait:UserRequest
    tid: 57 pri: 9 cs:       7 Wait:UserRequest
    tid: 56 pri:10 cs:      17 Wait:UserRequest
    tid: 55 pri:10 cs:      14 Wait:UserRequest
    tid: 54 pri: 9 cs:      79 Wait:EventPairHigh
    tid: 5f pri:11 cs:       7 Wait:UserRequest

pid: 51 pri: 8 (null)
    tid: 52 pri:15 cs:      49 Wait:UserRequest
    tid: 86 pri: 9 cs:       1 Wait:UserRequest
    tid: 85 pri: 9 cs:       1 Wait:UserRequest
    tid: 84 pri: 9 cs:       1 Wait:UserRequest
    tid: 83 pri: 9 cs:       1 Wait:UserRequest
    tid: 82 pri: 9 cs:       1 Wait:UserRequest
    tid: 81 pri: 9 cs:     300 Wait:UserRequest
    tid: 80 pri:11 cs:      31 Wait:FreePage

pid: 4f pri: 8 CLIPSRV.EXE
    tid: 50 pri:10 cs:      23 Wait:Executive
    tid: 4e pri: 9 cs:      77 Wait:EventPairHigh

pid: 4a pri: 8 LMSVCS.EXE
    tid: 4b pri:10 cs:      27 Wait:Executive
    tid: 49 pri:11 cs:     154 Wait:UserRequest
    tid: 88 pri:10 cs:      60 Wait:UserRequest
    tid: 7f pri:10 cs:       6 Wait:LpcReceive
```

(continued)

Figure 3-2. *continued*

```
    tid: 7e pri:10 cs:         6 Wait:LpcReceive
    tid: 7d pri:10 cs:         6 Wait:LpcReceive
    tid: 7b pri:10 cs:        22 Wait:UserRequest
    tid: 7a pri:10 cs:        57 Wait:UserRequest
    tid: 79 pri:10 cs:        83 Wait:UserRequest
    tid: 87 pri: 9 cs:         5 Wait:UserRequest
    tid: 6f pri:10 cs:         7 Wait:UserRequest

pid: 77 pri: 8 MSGSVC.EXE
    tid: 78 pri:10 cs:        22 Wait:Executive
    tid: 76 pri:10 cs:        51 Wait:UserRequest
    tid: 75 pri:10 cs:         7 Wait:UserRequest
    tid: 74 pri:10 cs:         6 Wait:UserRequest
    tid: 73 pri:10 cs:        11 Wait:UserRequest
    tid: 72 pri:11 cs:        11 Wait:UserRequest

pid: a7 pri: 8 NDDEAGNT.EXE
    tid: a8 pri:10 cs:        60 Wait:EventPairHigh

pid: a2 pri:13 TASKMAN.EXE
    tid: a3 pri:15 cs:        77 Wait:EventPairHigh

pid: a0 pri:13 PROGMAN.EXE
    tid: a1 pri:14 cs:     16233 Wait:EventPairHigh

pid: 9e pri: 7 NTVDM.EXE
    tid: 9f pri: 7 cs:       450 Wait:EventPairHigh
    tid: 9b pri: 7 cs:        21 Wait:UserRequest
    tid: 9a pri: 7 cs:    248664 Ready
    tid: 4d pri: 9 cs:        13 Wait:UserRequest
    tid: 64 pri:12 cs:   4587766 Wait:EventPairHigh

pid: 2b pri: 7 WINHLP32.EXE
    tid: 98 pri: 8 cs:     45151 Wait:EventPairHigh

pid: 90 pri: 9 CMD.EXE
    tid: 8e pri:11 cs:       282 Wait:UserRequest

pid: 8d pri: 9 PSTAT.EXE
    tid: 8f pri:12 cs:         6 Running
```

Figure 3-3 shows how the PVIEW utility appears when you first
execute it. The Process list box lists all the processes running in the system. Listed to the right of each process is the amount of CPU time the
process has used since it was started and the percentage of that time

spent in privileged mode (the Windows NT Executive's code) vs. user mode (the application's code). When you select a process, PVIEW updates the Priority group's radio buttons and fills the Thread(s) list box with a list of all the threads owned by the selected process, the amount of CPU time used by each thread, and the percentage of time each thread has spent in privileged mode vs. user mode. When you select a thread, PVIEW updates the Thread Priority group's radio buttons.

Figure 3-3.
The PVIEW utility.

Important

You might notice that PVIEW's window has radio buttons to indicate whether a process priority class is very high, normal, or idle but that there is no radio button to indicate whether the process is running in the realtime priority class. PVIEW was written before the realtime priority class was exposed to the Win32 API, and no one at Microsoft has seen fit to update this extremely useful utility.

You might also notice that the Thread Priority radio buttons do not include radio buttons to indicate the time-critical priority and the lowest priority.

Ideally, someday Microsoft will update PVIEW to add support for these flags and will also fix PVIEW so that it runs under Windows 95.

Processes, Threads, and the C Run-Time Library

Microsoft ships three C run-time libraries with Visual C++ 2.0. The table below lists the names of the libraries and their descriptions:

Library Name	Description
LIBC.LIB	Statically linked library for single-threaded applications.
LIBCMT.LIB	Statically linked library for multithreaded applications.
MSVCRT.LIB	Import library for dynamically linking the MSVCRT20.DLL library. This library supports both single-threaded and multithreaded applications.

The first question you're probably asking yourself is, "Why do I need one library for single-threaded applications and an additional library for multithreaded applications?" The reason is that the standard C run-time library was invented around 1970, long before threads became available. The inventors of the library didn't consider the problems of using the C run-time library with multithreaded applications.

Consider, for example, the standard C run-time global variable *errno*. Some functions set this variable when an error occurs. Let's say you have the following code fragment:

```
BOOL fFailure = (system("NOTEPAD.EXE README.TXT") == -1);

if (fFailure) {
   switch (errno) {
   case E2BIG:     // Argument list or environment too big
      break;

   case ENOENT:    // Command interpreter cannot be found
      break;

   case ENOEXEC:   // Command interpreter has bad format
      break;

   case ENOMEM:    // Insufficient memory to run command
      break;
   }
}
```

Now let's imagine that the thread executing the code above is interrupted after the call to the *system* function and before the *if* statement.

Let's further imagine that the thread is being interrupted to allow a second thread in the same process to execute and that this new thread will execute another C run-time function that sets the global variable *errno*. When the CPU is later assigned back to the first thread, the value of *errno* no longer reflects the proper error code for the call to *system* on the previous page. To solve this problem, you need to assign each thread its very own *errno* variable.

This is only one example of how the standard C run-time library was not designed for multithreaded applications. Some of the C run-time variables and functions that have problems in multithreaded environments are *errno, _doserrno, strtok, _wcstok, strerror, _strerror, tmpnam, tmpfile, asctime, _wasctime, gmtime, _ecvt,* and *_fcvt*—just to name a few.

In order for multithreaded C and C++ programs that use the C run-time library to work properly, a data structure must be created and associated with each thread that uses C run-time library functions. To do this, you create threads using the C run-time's *_beginthreadex* function instead of the Win32 *CreateThread* function:

```
unsigned long _beginthreadex(void *security, unsigned stack_size,
   unsigned (*start_address)(void *), void *arglist,
   unsigned initflag, unsigned *thrdaddr);
```

Parameter-wise, *_beginthreadex* has the same exact parameter list as the *CreateThread* function, although the parameter names and types are not exactly the same. The *_beginthreadex* function also returns the handle of the newly created thread just like *CreateThread*. However, if you define STRICT when you compile the Windows.H file, you will need to cast *_beginthreadex*'s return value to a HANDLE.

When you call *_beginthreadex*, it performs the following actions:

1. Allocates an undocumented, internal data structure that contains the per-thread instance data. For example, the single thread's *errno* variable and a pointer to the thread's *strtok* buffer is maintained in this data structure. This data structure also contains two members that are initialized to contain the *start_address* and *arglist* parameters that you passed to *_beginthreadex*.

2. Calls the Win32 *CreateThread* function to create the new thread. *CreateThread* is called as follows:

```
hThread = CreateThread(security, stack_size, _threadstart,
   &PerThreadData, initflag, thrdaddr);
```

3. Returns the handle of the newly created thread, or returns 0 if an error occurred.

You'll notice that the new thread is instructed to start at a function called *_threadstart* instead of at the function that you passed to *_beginthreadex*. The *_threadstart* function is a function inside the C run-time library that performs the following tasks:

1. Associates the memory address of the per-thread instance data block with the thread using dynamic thread-local storage. (For more information on thread-local storage, see Chapter 12.) The *_threadstart* function is passed this data block's address as its parameter.

2. Initializes the C run-time's floating-point support for the new thread.

3. Enters a structured exception handling frame in order to support the C run-time's *signal* function.

4. Retrieves the address of your thread function and the parameter you want passed to it from the per-thread instance data block members. The *_threadstart* function then uses these values to call your thread function, passing it the 32-bit value you want.

5. Calls another C run-time function named *_endthreadex* when your thread function returns; passes *_endthreadex* the value that your thread function returns.

The *_endthreadex* function then terminates a thread created by the *_beginthreadex* function; its prototype is as follows:

```
void _endthreadex(unsigned retval);
```

The *retval* parameter is the thread's exit code. The *_endthreadex* function performs the following actions:

1. Terminates floating-point support for the thread

2. Gets the address of the per-thread instance data block associated with the thread

3. Frees the per-thread instance data block

4. Terminates the thread by calling the Win32 *ExitThread* function, passing it the value that was passed as *_endthreadex*'s *retval* parameter

Note that you can call the _endthreadex_ function explicitly if you want. Just be aware that if your thread function returns, the C run-time's _threadstart_ function calls _endthreadex_ on your behalf.

By now you should understand why the C run-time library's functions need a separate data block for each thread created, and you should also see how calling _beginthreadex_ allocates, initializes, and associates this data block with the newly created thread. You should also be able to see how the _endthreadex_ function frees the data block when the thread terminates.

Once this data block is initialized and associated with the thread, any C run-time library functions the thread calls that require per-thread instance data can easily retrieve the address to the calling thread's data block and manipulate the thread's data. This is fine for functions, but you might be wondering how this works for a global variable such as _errno_. Well, _errno_ is defined in the standard C headers like this:

```
#if defined(_MT) || defined(_DLL)
extern int * __cdecl _errno(void);
#define errno     (*_errno())
#else    /* ndef _MT && ndef _DLL */
extern int errno;
#endif    /* _MT || _DLL */
```

If you're creating a multithreaded application, you'll need to specify the /MT (multithreaded application) or /MD (multithreaded DLL) switch on the compiler's command line. This causes the compiler to define the _MT identifier. Then, whenever you reference _errno_, you are actually making a call to the internal C run-time library function _errno_. This function returns the address to the _errno_ data member in the calling thread's associated data block. You'll notice that the _errno_ macro is defined as taking the contents of this address. This is necessary because it's possible to write code like this:

```
int *p = &errno;
if (*p == ENOMEM) {
   :
   :
}
```

If the internal _errno_ function simply returned the value of _errno_, the above code wouldn't compile.

The multithreaded version of the C run-time library also places synchronization primitives around certain functions. For example, if two threads simultaneously call *malloc*, the heap could possibly become corrupted. The multithreaded version of the C run-time library prevents two threads from allocating memory from the heap at the same time. It does this by making the second thread wait until the first has returned from *malloc*. Then the second thread is allowed to enter. Thread synchronization is discussed in more detail in Chapter 9.

Obviously, the performance of the multithreaded version of the C run-time library is impacted by all this additional work. This is why Microsoft supplies the single-threaded version of the statically linked C run-time library in addition to the multithreaded version.

The dynamically linked version of the C run-time library was written to be generic so that it could be shared by any and all running applications and DLLs using the C run-time library functions. For this reason, the library exists only in a multithreaded version. Because the C run-time library is supplied in a DLL, applications (EXE files) and DLLs don't need to include the code for the C run-time library function and are smaller as a result. Also, if Microsoft fixes a bug in the C run-time library DLL, applications will automatically gain the fix as well.

You might be wondering what would happen if you created your new threads by calling the Win32 *CreateThread* function instead of the C run-time's *_beginthreadex* function. Well, here is what happens if a thread created with *CreateThread* calls a C run-time library function that requires the per-thread instance data block:

1. The C run-time function first attempts to get the address of the thread's data block.

2. If the address is NULL, the C run-time library allocates a data block for the thread, initializes, and then associates the block's address with the thread using thread-local storage. (See Chapter 12 for more information on thread-local storage.)

3. The function can now execute successfully because it has the address of the thread's data block.

There are a couple of problems, however. First, if the thread uses the C run-time's *signal* function, the entire process will terminate because the structured exception handling frame has not been prepared. Second, if the thread terminates without calling *_endthreadex*, the data block cannot be destroyed and a memory leak occurs. There is a caveat to this second problem: if the application is using the dynamic-link library version of the C run-time library, the DLL is notified when the thread terminates and the DLL will destroy the thread's data block. Only if the application uses the static-link versions of the C run-time does this memory leak occur. As a rule, you should always use the C run-time's *_beginthreadex/_endthreadex* functions instead of the Win32 *CreateThread/ ExitThread* functions.

As you might expect, the C run-time's startup code allocates and initializes a data block for your application's primary thread. This allows the primary thread to safely call any of the C run-time functions. When your primary thread returns from *WinMain*, the C run-time frees the associated data block. In addition, the startup code sets up the proper structured exception handling code so that the primary thread can successfully call the C run-time's *signal* function.

C Run-Time Functions to Avoid

The C run-time library also contains two other functions:

```
unsigned long _beginthread(void (__cdecl *start_address)(void *),
    unsigned stack_size, void *arglist);
```

and

```
void _endthread(void);
```

These two functions were originally created to do the work of the new *_beginthreadex* and *_endthreadex* functions, respectively. However, as you can see, the *_beginthread* function has fewer parameters and is therefore more limited than the full-featured *_beginthreadex* function. For example, if you use *_beginthread*, you cannot create the new thread with security attributes, you cannot create the thread suspended, and you cannot obtain the thread's ID value. The *_endthread* function has a similar story: it takes no parameters, which means you can't give your thread an exit value when it terminates.

There is a major problem with the *_endthread* function that you can't see, however. Just before *_endthread* calls *ExitThread*, it calls *Close-Handle*, passing the handle of the new thread. To see why this is a problem, examine the following code:

```
DWORD dwExitCode;
HANDLE hThread = _beginthread(...);
GetExitCodeThread(hThread, &dwExitCode);
CloseHandle(hThread);
```

It is quite possible that the newly created thread will execute, return, and terminate before the first thread can call *GetExitCodeThread*. If this happens, the value in *hThread* is invalid because *_endthread* has closed the new thread's handle. Needless to say, the call to *CloseHandle* will also fail for the same reason.

The new *_endthreadex* function does *not* close the thread's handle, and therefore the code fragment on the previous page will work correctly if we replace the call to *_beginthread* with a call to *_beginthreadex*. Remember that *_beginthreadex* calls *_endthreadex* when your thread function returns, whereas *_beginthread* calls *_endthread* when your thread function returns.

CHAPTER FOUR

WIN32 MEMORY ARCHITECTURE

The memory architecture used by an operating system is the most important key to understanding how the operating system does what it does. When you start working with a new operating system, many questions come to mind, such as "How do I share data between two applications?" "Where does the system store the information I'm looking for?" and "How can I make my program run more efficiently?" just to name a few.

I have found that, more often than not, a good understanding of how the system manages memory can help determine the answers to these questions quickly and accurately. So this chapter explores the memory architecture used by the various implementations of Win32.

CPUs I Have Known

It's both interesting and exciting to watch advances in microcomputer architecture. The first microcomputer I ever owned was Tandy/Radio Shack's TRS-80 Model I. This computer was designed around the Z80 microprocessor and came standard with 4 KB of RAM, although the machine could actually address up to 64 KB of memory. I can still remember how happy I was when I had earned enough money duplicating disks so that I could upgrade my machine to 16 KB of RAM.

When IBM introduced the IBM PC, it had no idea of the impact the machine would have on the microcomputer industry. In fact, IBM was so skeptical of how well its PC would be received that the company decided to minimize its risk by utilizing hardware that was readily available instead of designing and manufacturing custom hardware. Because of this decision, IBM has been plagued almost from the beginning by many competitors making PC clones. If IBM could easily get the parts for the machines, anyone could.

The PC was a big step forward because it used Intel's 8088 CPU. This 16-bit CPU allowed the processor to access as much as 1 MB of memory. But soon applications required even more than 1 MB of memory. This need to access more memory became so great a problem that several companies responded by offering various solutions.

Most of these solutions shared a common theme: to make different memory objects available in the same memory location at different times. The first of these solutions, which became known as the Expanded Memory Specification (EMS), was developed by a Lotus, Intel, and Microsoft collaboration. EMS allowed you to place a hardware card with, say, 2 MB of memory on it in your computer. The card would then be given instructions to swap various sections of the EMS memory into and out of a fixed 64-KB section of the CPU's addressable address space.

Another solution added overlay technology to applications' code segments. If segments of code had not been executed in a while, an overlay manager could overlay the code segment with another code segment from the same application. Both Borland and Microsoft offer this support today in their respective C/C++ compilers. Borland calls it VROOMM (Virtual Runtime Object-Oriented Memory Manager), and Microsoft calls it MOVE (Microsoft Overlay Virtual Environment).

In 1982 Intel introduced a new microprocessor, the 80286, which was capable of addressing up to 16 MB of memory. Unfortunately, the upper 15 MB of memory could be accessed only when the processor was set to a special mode called *protected mode* (used by Windows 3.*x*). Protected mode also enabled additional features, such as virtual memory and support for the separation of tasks in a multitasking environment. For backward compatibility, the 80286 also contained *real mode,* the default mode of the processor, which allowed applications written for the 8086 to run. For years following, the 80286 was considered to be not much more than a fast 8086 because no software was developed to take advantage of its advanced features.

But the need to access more memory continued, and Microsoft soon introduced a technology that allowed applications running in real mode to access the additional memory that could be installed on 80286 machines. This technology was called the Extended Memory Specification (XMS). Applications running in real mode on an 80286 could access up to 15 MB of extended memory by making calls to functions contained in a device driver. Microsoft's implementation of this device driver is called HIMEM.SYS and is still used by 16-bit Windows today.

Once we had reached the point where the hardware and software could gain access to 16 MB of memory, it became practical to run several applications at once. This, in turn, further drove up the demand for memory—16 MB may have been plenty for one application but not for six or seven applications running simultaneously. For this we needed a more powerful CPU with a more sophisticated memory architecture than the 80286's.

Enter the 32-bit 80386. The 80386 offered several advantages over the 80286. In addition to supporting the 8086 real mode and the 16-bit protected mode of the 80286, the 80386 also offered a 32-bit protected mode and a virtual 8086 mode. The virtual 8086 mode enabled the operating system to create the illusion that several 8086 CPUs were available on the system. When in 32-bit protected mode, the operating system could instruct the 80386 to create virtual 8086 machines. Each of these virtual machines could support MS-DOS running an MS-DOS application. In fact, these applications could be preemptively multitasked by the 80386. The virtual 8086 mode was extremely important because it allowed a migration path for users. They could use the added benefits of 32-bit protected mode without having to give up all their current MS-DOS applications. Plus, they had the advantage of being able to run multiple MS-DOS applications concurrently.

I have neglected to say how much memory can be addressed by the 80386 in 32-bit protected mode (the mode used by Win32 applications). The answer is a whopping 4 GB. Not only is it 4 GB, but each application running in this mode has its own 4-GB address space, which should be more than enough memory for even the most demanding of applications. The only problem is that memory isn't free. To purchase 4 GB of memory would cost approximately $140,800 at the time I'm writing this.

Most of you probably can't afford to walk up to your nearest computer store, lay this kind of money down on the counter, and push a wheelbarrow full of RAM back to your house. Besides, even if you could buy all this RAM, where would you put it? It certainly wouldn't fit in any 80386-based computer I've ever seen!

Instead, the 80386 was designed to support a technique called *page swapping,* which Microsoft has implemented in 16-bit Windows, Windows NT, and Windows 95. Page swapping allows portions of the hard disk to simulate RAM. Of course, the CPU needs to work on data that is actually in memory. But if some of the data hasn't been accessed in a while, the operating system can step in and copy some of that data to a location on the hard disk. After the information has been copied, the RAM that was occupied by that data can be reallocated to data required for another application. When the CPU needs to access the old data, the operating system again steps in, copies another application's data to the hard disk, and pulls the earlier data back into memory. The CPU can then do its stuff.

In 1989 Intel introduced the 80486. Having satisfied the demand for addressable memory with the 80386, Intel made no major improvements to the 80486's memory architecture. Instead, the most notable feature of the 80486 was improved execution speed. When I was writing the first edition of this book, Intel released Pentium, its next-generation CPU. Again, there are no major changes to the memory management capabilities of the chip, but execution speed is improved.

A Virtual Address Space

In Win32, every process's virtual address space is 4 GB. A 32-bit pointer can have any value from 0x00000000 through 0xFFFFFFFF. This allows a pointer to have one of 4,294,967,296 values, which covers a process's 4-GB range.

In MS-DOS and 16-bit Windows, all processes share a single address space. This means that any process can read from and write to memory belonging to any other process, including the operating system itself. Of course, this leaves every process at the mercy of every other running process. If Process A accidentally overwrites data belonging to Process B, Process B may become very unstable and will probably crash. A robust operating system and environment should not allow this to occur.

In the Win32 environment, this problem is solved because each Win32 process is given its very own private address space. When a thread in a process is running, that thread can access only memory that belongs to its process. The memory that belongs to all other processes is hidden and inaccessible to the running thread.

Important

In Windows NT, the memory belonging to the operating system itself is also hidden from the running thread. This means that the operating system's data cannot be accidentally accessed by the thread.

(continued)

Important

continued

In Windows 95, the memory belonging to the operating system is not hidden from the running thread. It is therefore possible that the running thread could accidentally access the operating system's data and corrupt the operating system. It is *not* possible in Windows 95 for one process's thread to access memory belonging to another process. This makes the system much more robust than 16-bit versions of Windows but still leaves the operating system open to potential crashes.

As I said, every process has its own private address space. This means that Process A can have a data structure stored in its address space at address 0x12345678 while Process B has a totally different data structure stored in *its* address space at address 0x12345678. When threads running in Process A access memory at address 0x12345678, these threads are accessing Process A's data structure. When threads running in Process B access memory at address 0x12345678, these threads are accessing Process B's data structure. Threads running in Process A cannot access the data structure in Process B's address space, and vice versa.

Now, before you get all excited about having so much address space for your application, keep in mind that this is *virtual* address space—not physical storage. This address space is simply a range of memory addresses. Physical storage needs to be assigned or mapped to portions of the address space before you can successfully access data without raising access violations. We will discuss how this is done later in this chapter.

Different implementations of Win32 partition a process's 4-GB virtual address space in slightly different ways. The next two sections describe how Windows 95 and Windows NT partition a process's address space.

Partitions in a Process's Address Space

Figure 4-1 on the following page shows how the Windows 95 implementation of Win32 partitions a process's address space.

The Partition from 0x00000000 through 0x003FFFFF

This 4-MB region at the bottom of the process's address space is required by Windows 95 in order to maintain compatibility with MS-DOS and 16-bit Windows. From our Win32 applications, we should not attempt to read from or write to this region. Ideally, the CPU should raise an access violation if a thread in our process touches this memory, but, for technical reasons, Microsoft was unable to guard this 4 MB of address space. However, Microsoft was able to guard the bottom 4 KB. If a thread in your process attempts to read or write to a memory address between

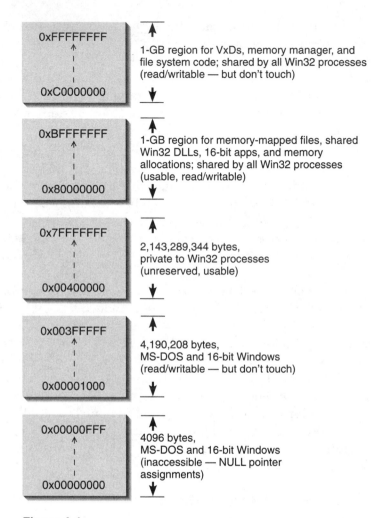

0xFFFFFFFF

0xC0000000

1-GB region for VxDs, memory manager, and file system code; shared by all Win32 processes (read/writable — but don't touch)

0xBFFFFFFF

0x80000000

1-GB region for memory-mapped files, shared Win32 DLLs, 16-bit apps, and memory allocations; shared by all Win32 processes (usable, read/writable)

0x7FFFFFFF

0x00400000

2,143,289,344 bytes, private to Win32 processes (unreserved, usable)

0x003FFFFF

0x00001000

4,190,208 bytes, MS-DOS and 16-bit Windows (read/writable — but don't touch)

0x00000FFF

0x00000000

4096 bytes, MS-DOS and 16-bit Windows (inaccessible — NULL pointer assignments)

Figure 4-1.
Win32 partitions in Windows 95.

0x00000000 and 0x00000FFF, the CPU will catch this and raise an access violation. Protecting this 4-KB region is incredibly useful in helping to detect NULL-pointer assignments.

It is quite common that error checking is not religiously performed in C programs. For example, the following code performs no error checking:

```
int *pnSomeInteger;
pnSomeInteger = malloc(sizeof(int));
*pnSomeInteger = 5;
```

If *malloc* cannot find enough memory to satisfy the request, it returns NULL. However, the foregoing code doesn't check for this possibility—it assumes that the allocation was successful and proceeds to access memory at address 0x00000000. Because the bottom 4 KB of the address space is off-limits, a memory access violation occurs and the process is terminated. This feature helps developers find bugs in their applications.

The Partition from 0x00400000 through 0x7FFFFFFF

This 2,143,289,344-byte (2 GB minus 4 MB) partition is where the process's private (unshared) address space resides. One Win32 process cannot read from, write to, or in any way access another process's data residing in this partition.[1] For all Win32 applications, this partition is where the bulk of the process's data is maintained. Because each process gets its own private, unshared partition for data, Win32 applications are far less likely to be corrupted by other applications, making the whole system more robust.

The Partition from 0x80000000 through 0xBFFFFFFF

This 1-GB partition is where the system stores data that is shared among all Win32 processes. For example, the system dynamic-link libraries, KERNEL32.DLL, USER32.DLL, GDI32.DLL, and ADVAPI32.DLL, are all loaded in this address space partition. This makes these four DLLs easily available to all Win32 processes simultaneously. It also means that these DLLs are loaded at the same memory address for every Win32 process. The system also maps all memory-mapped files in this partition. I will discuss memory-mapped files in more detail in Chapter 7.

The Partition from 0xC0000000 through 0xFFFFFFFF

This 1-GB partition is where the operating system's code is located, including the system's virtual device drivers (VxDs), low-level memory management code, and file system code. As with the preceding partition, all the code in this partition is shared among all Win32 processes. Unfortunately, the data in this partition is not protected—any Win32 application may read from or write to this section, potentially corrupting the operating system.

---

1. Win32 does offer special functions (*ReadProcessMemory* and *WriteProcessMemory*) that do allow one process to read from or write to data in another process's address space, but these functions are usually called by debuggers.

How Windows NT Partitions a Process's Address Space

Figure 4-2 shows how the Windows NT implementation of Win32 partitions a process's address space:

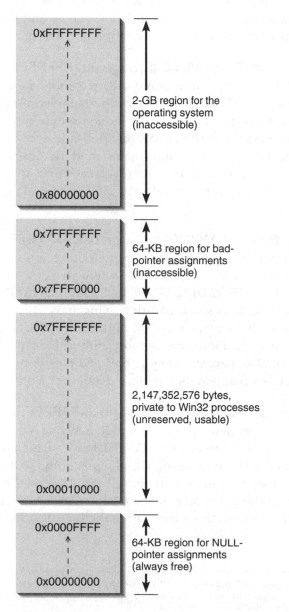

Figure 4-2.
Win32 partitions in Windows NT.

The Partition from 0x00000000 through 0x0000FFFF

This 64-KB range at the bottom of the process's address space is set aside by Windows NT to help programmers catch NULL-pointer assignments—just like the bottommost 4 KB under Windows 95. Any attempts to read from or write to memory addresses in this partition cause an access violation.

The Partition from 0x00010000 through 0x7FFEFFFF

This 2,147,352,576-byte (2 GB minus 64 KB minus 64 KB) partition is where the process's private (unshared) address space resides. This partition is like the 0x00400000 through 0x7FFFFFFF partition under Windows 95.

When a Win32 process loads, it will require access to the system dynamic-link libraries, KERNEL32.DLL, USER32.DLL, GDI32.DLL, and ADVAPI32.DLL. The code for these DLLs as well as for any other DLLs is loaded into this partition. Each process may load these DLLs at a different address within this partition (although this is very unlikely). The system also maps all memory-mapped files accessible to this process within this partition.

The Partition from 0x7FFF0000 through 0x7FFFFFFF

This 64-KB partition just below the 2-GB line is similar to the 0x00000000 through 0x0000FFFF partition. That is, the operating system sets this partition aside to catch invalid-pointer assignments in this range. Any attempts to read from or write to addresses in this range always result in an access violation.

The Partition from 0x80000000 through 0xFFFFFFFF

This 2-GB partition is where the Windows NT Executive, Kernel, and device drivers are loaded. Unlike with Windows 95, the Windows NT operating system components are completely protected. If you attempt to access memory addresses in this partition, your thread will raise an access violation, causing the system to display a message box to the user and causing Windows NT to terminate your application. See Chapter 14 for more information about access violations and how to handle them.

You're probably thinking that it seems a little unreasonable that Windows NT should steal 2 GB of your address space, and I'd have to agree. However, the MIPS R4000 CPUs require that this range be reserved. Microsoft could have implemented the Windows NT version of Win32 differently on different CPU platforms but decided that developers could port their applications more easily if the top 2 GB were reserved on every Windows NT implementation of Win32.

Regions in an Address Space

When a process is created and given its address space, the bulk of this usable address space is *free,* or unallocated. In order to use portions of this address space, you must allocate regions within it by calling the Win32 *VirtualAlloc* function (discussed in Chapter 6). The act of allocating a region is called *reserving.*

Whenever you reserve a region of address space, the system ensures that the region begins on an even *allocation granularity* boundary. The allocation granularity may vary from one CPU platform to another. However, as of this writing, all the CPU platforms (*x*86, MIPS, Alpha, and PowerPC) use the same allocation granularity of 64 KB. The system uses the allocation granularity to more easily manage its internal record keeping of the reserved regions in your address space, and to reduce the amount of address space region fragmentation that can occur in your address space.

When you reserve a region of address space, the system ensures that the size of the region is an even multiple of the system's *page* size. A page is a unit of memory that the system uses in managing memory. Like the allocation granularity, the page size can vary from one CPU to another. The *x*86, MIPS, and PowerPC implementations of Win32 use a 4-KB page size, whereas the DEC Alpha implementation uses an 8-KB page size.

If you attempt to reserve a 10-KB region of address space, the system will automatically round up your request and reserve a region whose size is an even multiple of the page size. This means that on an *x*86, a MIPS, or a PowerPC, the system will actually reserve a region that is 12 KB, and on an Alpha, the system will reserve a 16-KB region.

When your program's algorithms no longer need to access a reserved region of address space, the region should be freed. This is called *releasing* the region of address space and is accomplished by calling the *VirtualFree* function.

> **Important**
>
> Sometimes the system reserves regions of address space on behalf of your process. For example, the system allocates a region of address space in order to store a *process environment block* (PEB). A PEB is a small data structure created, manipulated, and destroyed entirely by the system. When a process is created, the system allocates a region of address space for the PEB.
>
> The system also needs to create *thread environment blocks* (TEBs) to help manage all the threads that currently exist in the process. The regions for these TEBs will be reserved and released as threads in the process are created and destroyed.
>
> Although the system demands that any of your requests to reserve address space regions begin on an even allocation granularity boundary (64 KB), the system itself is not subjected to the same limitation. It is extremely likely that the region reserved for your process's PEB and TEBs will not start on an even 64-KB boundary. However, these reserved regions will still have to be an even multiple of the CPU's page size.

Committing Physical Storage Within a Region

To actually use a reserved region of address space, you must allocate physical storage and then map this storage to the reserved region. This process is called *committing* physical storage. Physical storage is always committed in pages. To commit physical storage to a reserved region, you again call the *VirtualAlloc* function.

When you commit physical storage to regions, you do not have to commit physical storage to the entire region. For example, you can reserve a region that is 64 KB and then commit physical storage to the second and fourth pages within the region. Figure 4-3 on the following page shows what a process's address space might look like. Note that the address space is different depending on which CPU platform you're running on. The address space on the left shows what happens on an *x*86, a MIPS, or a PowerPC machine (all of which have 4-KB pages), and the address space on the right shows what happens on an Alpha machine (which has 8-KB pages).

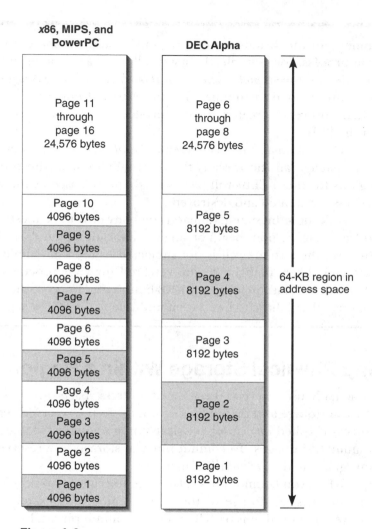

Figure 4-3.
Example process address spaces for different CPUs.

When your program's algorithms no longer need to access committed physical storage in the reserved region, the physical storage should be freed. This is called *decommitting* the physical storage and is accomplished by calling the *VirtualFree* function.

Physical Storage

In 16-bit Windows 3.1, physical storage was considered to be the amount of RAM that you had in your machine. In other words, if you had 16 MB of RAM in your machine you could load and run applications that used up to 16 MB of RAM. To help conserve memory, 16-bit Windows had lots of memory optimizations. For example, if you wanted to run two or more instances of an application, 16-bit Windows created a new data segment for each instance but all instances shared the program's code. This significantly reduced the amount of RAM needed to run multiple instances of an application.

Also, in 16-bit Windows 3.1 Microsoft added support for virtual memory in the form of hard disk swap files. But an operating system can use swap files only if the CPU directly supports them. For this reason, 16-bit Windows was able to use swap files only when running on a computer driven by a 386 or later CPU. From an application's perspective, a swap file transparently increases the amount of RAM (or storage) that the application can use. If you have 16 MB of RAM in your machine and also have a 20-MB swap file on your hard disk, the applications you're running believe that your machine has a grand total of 36 MB of RAM.

Of course, you don't actually have 36 MB of RAM. Instead, the operating system, in coordination with the CPU, saves portions of RAM to the swap file and loads portions of the swap file back into RAM as the running applications need them. Because a swap file increases the apparent amount of RAM available for applications, the use of a swap file in 16-bit Windows is optional. If you don't have a swap file, the system just thinks that there is less RAM available for applications to use.

The Windows 95 and Windows NT implementations of memory management are drastically different from the Windows 3.1 implementation. In these Win32 systems, the amount of RAM in the computer is completely managed by the operating system, and no application has any direct control over this memory.

With Win32 systems, it is best to think of physical storage as data stored in a paging file on a disk drive (usually a hard disk drive). So when an application commits physical storage to a region of address space by calling the *VirtualAlloc* function, space is actually allocated from a file on the hard disk. The size of the system's paging file is the most important factor in determining how much physical storage is available to applications; the amount of RAM you have has very little effect.

Now, when a thread in your process attempts to access a block of data in the process's address space, one of two things can happen, as shown in the flowchart in Figure 4-4.

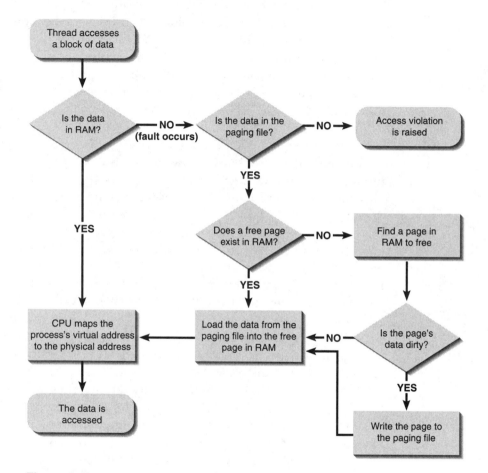

Figure 4-4.
How data is accessed.

In the first possibility, the data that the thread is attempting to access is in RAM. In this case, the CPU maps the data's virtual memory address to the physical address in RAM, and the desired access is performed.

In the second possibility, the data that the thread is attempting to access is not in RAM but is contained somewhere in the paging file. In this case, the attempted access is called a page fault and the CPU notifies the operating system of the attempted access. The operating system then locates a free page of memory in RAM; if a free page cannot be found, the system must free one. If a page has not been modified, the system can simply free the page. But if the system needs to free a page that was modified, it must first copy the page from RAM to the paging file. Next the system goes to the paging file, locates the block of data that needs to be accessed, and loads the data into the free page of memory. The operating system then maps the data's virtual memory address to the appropriate physical memory address in RAM.

The more often the system needs to copy pages of memory to the paging file and vice versa, the more your hard disk thrashes and the slower the system runs. (*Thrashing* means that the operating system spends all its time swapping pages in and out of memory instead of running programs.) So by adding more RAM to your computer, you reduce the amount of thrashing necessary to run your applications; this will, of course, greatly improve the performance of the system.

Windows NT requires a paging file. The system will automatically create one at boot time if one doesn't exist. In addition, Windows NT is capable of using multiple paging files. If multiple paging files exist on different physical hard drives, the system can perform much faster because it can write to the multiple drives simultaneously. You can add and remove paging files by opening the Control Panel, double-clicking on the System icon, and then choosing the Virtual Memory button.

Physical Storage Not Maintained in the Paging File

After reading the previous section, you must be thinking the paging file can get pretty large if many programs are all running at once—especially if you're thinking that every time you run a program the system must reserve regions of address space for the process's code and data, commit physical storage to these regions, and then copy the code and data from the program's file on the hard disk to the committed physical storage in the paging file.

The system does not do what I describe above; if it did, it would take a very long time to load a program and start it running. Instead, when you invoke an application the system opens the application's EXE file and determines the size of the application's code and data. Then the system reserves a region of address space and notes that the physical storage associated with this region is the EXE file itself. That's right—instead of allocating space from the paging file, the system uses the actual contents or *image* of the EXE file as the program's reserved region of address space. This, of course, makes loading an application very fast and reduces the size of the paging file.

When a program's file image (that is, an EXE or a DLL file) on the hard disk is used as the physical storage for a region of address space, it is called a *memory-mapped file*. When an EXE or a DLL is loaded, the system automatically reserves a region of address space and maps the file's image to this region. However, the system also offers a set of Win32 functions that allow you to map data files to a region of address space. We will talk about memory-mapped files much more in Chapter 7.

Important

When an EXE or a DLL file is loaded from a floppy disk, both Windows 95 and Windows NT allocate storage for the entire file from the system's paging file. The system then copies the file from the floppy into the system's RAM and the system's paging file; the paging file is said to *back* the RAM. This is how setup programs operate.

Often a setup program begins with one floppy, which the user removes from the drive in order to insert another floppy. If the system needs to go back to the first floppy to load some of the EXE's or the DLL's code, it is of course no longer in the floppy drive. However, because the system copied the file to RAM and the paging file, it will have no trouble accessing the setup program. When the setup program terminates, the system frees the RAM and the storage in the paging file.

Protection Attributes

Individual pages of physical storage allocated by the *VirtualAlloc* function can be assigned different protection attributes. The Win32 protection attributes are shown in the following table:

Protection Attribute	Description
PAGE_NOACCESS	Attempts to read, write, or execute memory in this region cause an access violation.
PAGE_READONLY	Attempts to write or execute memory in this region cause an access violation.
PAGE_READWRITE	Attempts to execute memory in this region cause an access violation.
PAGE_EXECUTE	Attempts to read or write memory in this region cause an access violation.
PAGE_EXECUTE_READ	Attempts to write to memory in this region cause an access violation.
PAGE_EXECUTE_READWRITE	There is nothing you can do to this region to cause an access violation.
PAGE_WRITECOPY	Attempts to execute memory in this region cause an access violation. Attempts to write to memory in this region cause the system to give the process its own private copy of the page of physical storage.
PAGE_EXECUTE_WRITECOPY	There is nothing you can do to this region to cause an access violation. Attempts to write to memory in this region cause the system to give the process its own private copy of the page of physical storage.

The *x*86, MIPS, PowerPC, and Alpha platforms do not support the execute protection attribute, although this attribute is supported in the Win32 operating system software. These hardware platforms treat read access as execute access. This means that if you assign PAGE_EXECUTE protection to memory, that memory will also have read privileges. Of course, you should not rely on this behavior because Windows NT implementations on other CPUs may very well treat execute protection as execute-only protection.

Windows 95 assigns only the PAGE_NOACCESS, PAGE_READONLY, and PAGE_READWRITE protection attributes to pages of physical storage.

Copy-On-Write Access

The protection attributes listed in the table on the previous page should all be pretty self-explanatory except the last two: PAGE_WRITECOPY and PAGE_EXECUTE_WRITECOPY. These attributes exist in order to conserve RAM usage and space in the paging file. Win32 supports a mechanism that allows two or more processes to share a single block of data. There is usually no problem doing this as long as the processes all consider the block of data to be read-only or execute-only and do not attempt to write to it. If threads in different processes all wrote to the same block of data, there would be total chaos.

In order to prevent this chaos, *copy-on-write* protection is assigned to shared data by the operating system. When a thread in one process attempts to write to a shared block of data, the system intervenes and performs the following actions:

1. The system allocates a page of physical storage from the paging file.

2. The system finds a free page of memory in RAM.

3. The system copies the page containing the data that the thread attempted to write to a shared block of data to the free page of RAM obtained in step 2.

4. The system then maps the process's virtual memory address for this page to the new page of RAM.

After the system has performed these steps, the process is able to access its very own private instance of this page of data. I will talk about sharing memory and copy-on-write protection in much more detail in Chapter 7.

In addition, you should not pass either PAGE_WRITECOPY or PAGE_EXECUTE_WRITECOPY when you are reserving address space or committing physical storage using the *VirtualAlloc* function. Doing so will cause the call to *VirtualAlloc* to fail; calling *GetLastError* returns ERROR_INVALID_PARAMETER. These two attributes are used by the operating system when it maps EXE and DLL file images.

Windows 95 does not support copy-on-write protection. When Windows 95 sees that copy-on-write protection has been requested, it immediately makes copies of the data instead of waiting for the attempted memory write.

Special Access Protection Attribute Flags

In addition to the protection attributes already discussed, there are also two protection attribute flags: PAGE_NOCACHE and PAGE_GUARD. You use these two flags by bitwise ORing them with any of the protection attributes except PAGE_NOACCESS.

The first of these protection attribute flags, PAGE_NOCACHE, disables caching of the committed pages. This flag is not recommended for general use; it exists mostly for hardware device driver developers who need to manipulate memory buffers.

The second of these protection attribute flags, PAGE_GUARD, is also not recommended for general use. Windows NT uses this flag when it creates a thread's stack. See the section "A Thread's Stack" in Chapter 6 for more information about this flag.

Windows 95 ignores the PAGE_NOCACHE and PAGE_GUARD protection attribute flags.

Bringing It All Home

In this section we'll bring address spaces, partitions, regions, blocks, and pages all together. The best way to start is by examining a virtual memory map that shows all the regions of address space within a single process. The process happens to be the VMMAP.EXE sample application, presented in Chapter 5. To fully understand the process's address space, we'll begin by discussing the address space as it appears when VMMap is running under Windows NT. A sample address space map is shown in Figure 4-5 on the following page. Later I'll discuss the differences between the Windows NT and Windows 95 address spaces.

Base Address	Type	Size	Blocks	Protection Attribute(s)	Description
00000000	Free	65536			
00010000	Private	4096	1	-RW-	
00011000	Free	61440			
00020000	Private	4096	1	-RW-	
00021000	Free	61440			
00030000	Private	1048576	3	-RW-	Thread Stack
00130000	Private	4096	1	-RW-	
00131000	Free	61440			
00140000	Private	1048576	2	-RW-	Default Process Heap
00240000	Mapped	65536	2	-RW-	
00250000	Mapped	36864	1	-R--	
00259000	Free	28672			
00260000	Mapped	57344	1	-R--	
0026E000	Free	8192			
00270000	Mapped	266240	1	-R--	
002B1000	Free	61440			
002C0000	Mapped	4096	1	-R--	
002C1000	Free	61440			
002D0000	Private	4096	1	-RW-	
002D1000	Free	61440			
002E0000	Private	1048576	2	-RW-	
003E0000	Private	4096	1	-RW-	
003E1000	Free	126976			
00400000	Image	36864	6	ERWC	C:\AdvWin32\VMMap.05\Dbg_x86\VMMap.EXE
00409000	Free	28672			
00410000	Mapped	65536	1	-RW-	
00420000	Free	265158656			
10100000	Image	270336	8	ERWC	F:\WINNT35\System32\MSVCRT20.dll
10142000	Free	1740562432			
77D30000	Image	126976	7	ERWC	F:\WINNT35\System32\WINSPOOL.DRV
77D4F000	Free	659456			
77DF0000	Image	208896	6	ERWC	F:\WINNT35\system32\ADVAPI32.dll
77E23000	Free	118784			
77E40000	Image	225280	6	ERWC	F:\WINNT35\system32\RPCRT4.dll
77E77000	Free	36864			
77E80000	Image	229376	7	ERWC	F:\WINNT35\system32\USER32.dll
77EB8000	Free	32768			
77EC0000	Image	208896	6	ERWC	F:\WINNT35\system32\GDI32.dll
77EF3000	Free	53248			
77F00000	Image	405504	7	ERWC	F:\WINNT35\system32\KERNEL32.dll
77F63000	Free	53248			
77F70000	Image	286720	10	FRWC	F:\WINNT35\System32\ntdll.dll

Figure 4-5.

A sample address space map showing regions under Windows NT.

(continued)

Figure 4-5. *continued*

Base Address	Type	Size	Blocks	Protection Attribute(s)	Description
77FB6000	Free	122920960			
7F4F0000	Mapped	524288	2	ER--	
7F570000	Free	524288			
7F5F0000	Mapped	2097152	4	ER--	
7F7F0000	Free	7864320			
7FF70000	Private	262144	2	-RW-	
7FFB0000	Mapped	147456	1	-R--	
7FFD4000	Free	40960			
7FFDE000	Private	4096	1	-RW-	
7FFDF000	Private	4096	1	-RW-	
7FFE0000	Private	65536	2	-R--	

The address space map in Figure 4-5 shows the various regions in the process's address space. There is one region shown per line, and each line contains six fields.

The first, or leftmost, field shows the region's base address. You'll notice that we start walking the process's address space starting with the region at address 0x00000000 and ending with the last region of usable address space, which begins at address 0x7FFE0000. All regions are contiguous. You'll also notice that almost all of the base addresses for nonfree regions start on an even multiple of 64 KB. This is because of the allocation granularity of address space reservation imposed by the system. A region that does not start on an even allocation granularity boundary represents a region that was allocated by operating system code on your process's behalf.

The second field shows the region's type, which is one of the four values—free, private, image, or mapped—described in the following table.

Type	Description
Free	The region of address space is not reserved, and the application may reserve a region either at the shown base address or anywhere within the free region.
Private	The region contains physical storage residing in the system's paging file.

(continued)

continued

Type	Description
Image	The region contains physical storage residing in a memory-mapped EXE or DLL file.
Mapped	The region contains physical storage residing in a memory-mapped data file.

The way that my VMMap application calculates this field may lead to misleading results. When the region is not free, the VMMAP.EXE sample application guesses at which of the three remaining values applies—there is no Win32 function we can call to request this region's exact usage. The way that I calculate this field's value is by scanning all of the blocks within the region and taking an educated guess. You should examine my code in Chapter 5 to understand this better.

The third field shows the number of bytes that were reserved for the region. For example, the system mapped the image of USER32.DLL at memory address 0x77E80000. When the system reserved address space for this image, it needed to reserve 229,376 bytes. The number in the third field will always be an even multiple of the CPU's page size (4096 bytes for an $x86$).

The fourth field shows the number of blocks within the reserved region. A block is a set of contiguous pages that all have the same protection attributes and that are all backed by the same type of physical storage—I'll talk more about this in the next section of this chapter. For free regions, this value will always be 0 because there can be no physical storage committed within a free region. (Nothing is displayed in the third column for a free region.) For the nonfree regions, this value can be anywhere from 1 to a maximum number of (region size / page size). For example, the region that begins at memory address 0x77E80000 has a region size of 229,376 bytes. Because this process is running on an $x86$, for which the page size is 4096 bytes, the maximum number of different committed blocks is 56 (229,376 / 4096); the map shows that there are 7 blocks in the region.

The fifth field on the line shows the region's protection attributes. The individual letters represent the following: E = execute, R = read, W = write, C = copy-on-write. If the region does not show any of these protection attributes, the region has no access protection. The free regions show no protection attributes since unreserved regions do not have protection attributes associated with them. Neither the guard protection attribute flag nor the no cache protection attribute flag will ever appear here; these flags have meaning only when associated with physical storage, not reserved address space. Protection attributes are given to a region for the sake of efficiency only and are always overridden by protection attributes assigned to physical storage.

The sixth and last field shows a text description of what's in the region. For free regions, this field will always be blank; for private regions, it will usually be blank because VMMAP.EXE has no way of knowing why the application reserved this private region of address space. However, VMMAP.EXE can identify two types of private regions: thread stacks and the process's default heap. VMMAP.EXE can usually detect thread stacks because they will commonly have a block of physical storage within them with the guard protection attribute. However, when a thread's stack is full it will not have a block with the guard protection attribute, and VMMAP.EXE will be unable to detect it. VMMAP.EXE can detect the process's default heap (discussed in Chapter 8) by obtaining the region's base address and comparing it with the value returned by the *GetProcessHeap* function.

For image regions, I can display the full pathname of the file that is mapped into the region. VMMAP.EXE obtains this information by calling *GetModuleFileName*. For mapped regions, nothing is displayed because VMMAP.EXE has no way of determining what data file the process has mapped to the region.

Inside the Regions

It's possible to break down the regions even further than shown in Figure 4-5. Figure 4-6 shows the same address space map as Figure 4-5, but the blocks contained inside each region are also displayed.

Base Address	Type	Size	Blocks	Protection Attribute(s)	Description
00000000	Free	65536			
00010000	Private	4096	1	-RW-	
00010000	Private	4096		-RW- --	
00011000	Free	61440			
00020000	Private	4096	1	-RW-	
00020000	Private	4096		-RW- --	

Figure 4-6. *(continued)*

A sample address space map showing blocks within regions under Windows NT.

Figure 4-6. *continued*

Base Address	Type	Size	Blocks	Protection Attribute(s)	Description
00021000	Free	61440			
00030000	Private	1048576	3	-RW-	Thread Stack
00030000	Reserve	1036288		-RW- --	
0012D000	Private	4096		-RW- G-	
0012E000	Private	8192		-RW- --	
00130000	Private	4096	1	-RW-	
00130000	Private	4096		-RW- --	
00131000	Free	61440			
00140000	Private	1048576	2	-RW-	Default Process Heap
00140000	Private	8192		-RW- --	
00142000	Reserve	1040384		-RW- --	
00240000	Mapped	65536	2	-RW-	
00240000	Mapped	4096		-RW- --	
00241000	Reserve	61440		-RW- --	
00250000	Mapped	36864	1	-R--	
00250000	Mapped	36864		-R-- --	
00259000	Free	28672			
00260000	Mapped	57344	1	-R--	
00260000	Mapped	57344		-R-- --	
0026E000	Free	8192			
00270000	Mapped	266240	1	-R--	
00270000	Mapped	266240		-R-- --	
002B1000	Free	61440			
002C0000	Mapped	4096	1	-R--	
002C0000	Mapped	4096		-R-- --	
002C1000	Free	61440			
002D0000	Private	4096	1	-RW-	
002D0000	Private	4096		-RW- --	
002D1000	Free	61440			
002E0000	Private	1048576	2	-RW-	
002E0000	Private	65536		-RW- --	
002F0000	Reserve	983040		-RW- --	
003E0000	Private	4096	1	-RW-	
003E0000	Private	4096		-RW- --	
003E1000	Free	126976			
00400000	Image	36864	6	ERWC	C:\AdvWin32\VMMap.05\Dbg_x86\VMMap.EXE
00400000	Image	4096		-R-- --	
00401000	Image	8192		ER-- --	
00403000	Image	4096		-RW- --	
00404000	Image	4096		-R-- --	
00405000	Image	8192		-RW- --	
00407000	Image	8192		-R-- --	
00409000	Free	28672			

(continued)

Figure 4-6. *continued*

Base Address	Type	Size	Blocks	Protection Attribute(s)	Description
00410000	Mapped	65536	1	-RW-	
00410000	Mapped	65536		-RW- --	
00420000	Free	265158656			
10100000	Image	270336	8	ERWC	F:\WINNT35\System32\MSVCRT20.dll
10100000	Image	4096		-R-- --	
10101000	Image	172032		ER-- --	
1012B000	Image	8192		-RW- --	
1012D000	Image	4096		-R-- --	
1012E000	Image	12288		-RW- --	
10131000	Image	20480		-RWC --	
10136000	Image	4096		-RW- --	
10137000	Image	45056		-R-- --	
10142000	Free	1740562432			
77D30000	Image	126976	7	ERWC	F:\WINNT35\System32\WINSPOOL.DRV
77D30000	Image	4096		-R-- --	
77D31000	Image	73728		ER --	
77D43000	Image	4096		-RW- --	
77D44000	Image	8192		-R-- --	
77D46000	Image	8192		-RW- --	
77D48000	Image	4096		-RWC -	
77D49000	Image	24576		-R-- --	
77D4F000	Free	659456			
77DF0000	Image	208896	6	ERWC	F:\WINNT35\system32\ADVAPI32.dll
77DF0000	Image	4096		-R-- --	
77DF1000	Image	131072		ER-- --	
77E11000	Image	4096		-RW- --	
77E12000	Image	12288		-R-- --	
77E15000	Image	20480		-RWC --	
77E1A000	Image	36864		-R-- --	
77E23000	Free	118784			
77E40000	Image	225280	6	ERWC	F:\WINNT35\system32\RPCRT4.dll
77E40000	Image	4096		-R-- --	
77E41000	Image	180224		ER-- --	
77E6D000	Image	4096		-RW- --	
77E6E000	Image	4096		-R-- --	
77E6F000	Image	4096		-RWC --	
77E70000	Image	28672		-R-- --	
77E77000	Free	36864			
77E80000	Image	229376	7	ERWC	F:\WINNT35\system32\USER32.dll
77E80000	Image	4096		-R-- --	
77E81000	Image	172032		ER-- --	
77EAB000	Image	4096		-RW- --	
77EAC000	Image	4096		-R-- --	

(continued)

Figure 4-6. *continued*

Base Address	Type	Size	Blocks	Protection Attribute(s)	Description
77EAD000	Image	4096		-RW- --	
77EAE000	Image	4096		-RWC --	
77EAF000	Image	36864		-R-- --	
77EB8000	Free	32768			
77EC0000	Image	208896	6	ERWC	F:\WINNT35\system32\GDI32.dll
77EC0000	Image	4096		-R-- --	
77EC1000	Image	167936		ER-- --	
77EEA000	Image	4096		-RW- --	
77EEB000	Image	4096		-R-- --	
77EEC000	Image	4096		-RW- --	
77EED000	Image	24576		-R-- --	
77EF3000	Free	53248			
77F00000	Image	405504	7	ERWC	F:\WINNT35\system32\KERNEL32.dll
77F00000	Image	4096		-R-- --	
77F01000	Image	229376		ER-- --	
77F39000	Image	8192		-RW- --	
77F3B000	Image	4096		-R-- --	
77F3C000	Image	8192		-RW- --	
77F3E000	Image	4096		-RWC --	
77F3F000	Image	147456		-R-- --	
77F63000	Free	53248			
77F70000	Image	286720	10	ERWC	F:\WINNT35\System32\ntdll.dll
77F70000	Image	4096		-R-- --	
77F71000	Image	155648		ER-- --	
77F97000	Image	4096		-RW- --	
77F98000	Image	4096		-R-- --	
77F99000	Image	4096		-RWC --	
77F9A000	Image	4096		-RW- --	
77F9B000	Image	4096		-RWC --	
77F9C000	Image	28672		-R-- --	
77FA3000	Image	4096		-RWC --	
77FA4000	Image	73728		-R-- --	
77FB6000	Free	122920960			
7F4F0000	Mapped	524288	2	ER--	
7F4F0000	Mapped	126976		ER-- --	
7F50F000	Reserve	397312		ER-- --	
7F570000	Free	524288			
7F5F0000	Mapped	2097152	4	ER--	
7F5F0000	Mapped	8192		ER-- --	
7F5F2000	Reserve	1040384		ER-- --	
7F6F0000	Mapped	20480		ER-- --	
7F6F5000	Reserve	1028096		ER-- --	

(continued)

Figure 4-6. *continued*

Base Address	Type	Size	Blocks	Protection Attribute(s)	Description
7F7F0000	Free	7864320			
7FF70000	Private	262144	2	-RW-	
7FF70000	Private	4096		-RW- --	
7FF71000	Reserve	258048		-RW- --	
7FFB0000	Mapped	147456	1	-R--	
7FFB0000	Mapped	147456		-R-- --	
7FFD4000	Free	40960			
7FFDE000	Private	4096	1	-RW-	
7FFDE000	Private	4096		-RW- --	
7FFDF000	Private	4096	1	-RW-	
7FFDF000	Private	4096		-RW- --	
7FFE0000	Private	65536	2	-R--	
7FFE0000	Private	4096		-R-- --	
7FFE1000	Reserve	61440		-R-- --	

Of course, free regions do not expand at all because they have no committed pages of storage within them. Each block line shows four fields as explained below.

The first field shows the address of a set of pages all having the same state and protection attributes. For example, there is a single page (4096 bytes) of memory with read protection committed at address 0x10100000. At address 0x10101000, there is a block of 42 pages (172,032 bytes) of committed storage that has execute and read protection. If both of these blocks had the same protection attributes, the two would be combined and would appear as a single 43-page (176,128-byte) entry in the memory map.

The second field shows what type of physical storage is backing the block within the reserved region. One of four possible values can appear in this field: private, mapped, image, or reserve. A value of private, mapped, or image indicates that the block is backed by physical storage in the paging file, a data file, or a loaded EXE or DLL file, respectively. If the value is reserve, the block is not backed by any physical storage at all, but the system may commit physical storage to it later.

For the most part, all the committed blocks within a single region are backed by the same type of physical storage. However, it is possible for different committed blocks within a single region to be backed by different types of physical storage. For example, a memory-mapped file image will be backed by an EXE or a DLL file. If you were to write to a

119

single page in this region that had PAGE_WRITECOPY or PAGE_EXE-CUTE_WRITECOPY, the system would make your process a private copy of the page backed by the paging file instead of the file image. This new page would have the same attributes as the original page without the copy-on-write protection attribute.

The third field shows the size of the block. All blocks are contiguous within a region—there will not be any gaps.

The fourth field shows the protection attributes and protection attribute flags of the block. A block's protection attributes override the protection attributes of the region that contains the block. The possible protection attributes are identical to those that can be specified for a region; however, the two protection attribute flags, PAGE_GUARD and PAGE_NOCACHE, which are never associated with a region, may be associated with a block.

Address Space Differences for Windows 95

Figure 4-7 shows the address space map when the same VMMAP.EXE program is executed under Windows 95.

Base Address	Type	Size	Blocks	Protection Attribute(s)	Description
00000000	Free	4194304			
00400000	Private	65536	6	----	C:\ADVWIN32\VMMAP.05\REL_X86\VMMAP.EXE
00400000	Private	8192		-R-- --	
00402000	Private	4096		-RW- --	
00403000	Private	4096		-R-- --	
00404000	Private	8192		-RW- --	
00406000	Private	8192		-R-- --	
00408000	Reserve	32768		---- --	
00410000	Private	1114112	4	----	Default Process Heap
00410000	Private	4096		-RW- --	
00411000	Reserve	1044480		---- --	
00510000	Private	4096		-RW- --	
00511000	Reserve	61440		---- --	
00520000	Private	65536	2	-RW-	
00520000	Private	4096		-RW- --	
00521000	Reserve	61440		-RW- --	

Figure 4-7.   *(continued)*

A sample address space map showing blocks within regions under Windows 95.

Figure 4-7. *continued*

Base Address	Type	Size	Blocks	Protection Attribute(s)	Description
00530000	Private	1179648	6	----	Thread Stack
00530000	Reserve	1077248		---- --	
00637000	Private	4096		-RW- --	
00638000	Reserve	24576		---- --	
0063E000	Private	4096		---- --	
0063F000	Private	4096		RW- --	
00640000	Reserve	65536		---- --	
00650000	Private	1048576	2	-RW-	
00650000	Private	65536		-RW- --	
00660000	Reserve	983040		-RW- --	
00750000	Private	65536	2	-RW-	
00750000	Private	4096		-RW- --	
00751000	Reserve	61440		-RW- --	
00760000	Free	261750784			
10100000	Private	327680	6	----	C:\WINDOWS\SYSTEM\MSVCRT20.DLL
10100000	Private	176128		-R-- --	
1012B000	Private	8192		-RW- --	
1012D000	Private	4096		-R-- --	
1012E000	Private	36864		-RW- --	
10137000	Private	45056		-R-- --	
10142000	Reserve	57344		---- --	
10150000	Free	1877671936			
80000000	Private	4096	1	----	
80000000	Reserve	4096		---- --	
80001000	Private	4096	1	----	
80001000	Private	4096		-RW- --	
80002000	Private	4096	1	----	
80002000	Private	4096		-RW- --	
80003000	Private	4096	1	----	
80003000	Private	4096		-RW- --	
80004000	Private	622592	1	----	
80004000	Private	622592		-RW- --	
8009C000	Private	65536	2	----	
8009C000	Private	16384		-RW- --	
800A0000	Reserve	49152		---- --	
800AC000	Private	4096	1	----	
800AC000	Private	4096		-RW- --	
800AD000	Private	516096	1	----	
800AD000	Private	516096		-RW- --	

(continued)

Figure 4-7. *continued*

Base Address	Type	Size	Blocks	Protection Attribute(s)	Description
8012B000	Private	196608	1	- - - -	
8012B000	Private	196608		-RW- - -	
:					
:					
81A81000	Private	16384	3	- - - -	
81A81000	Private	4096		-RW- - -	
81A82000	Reserve	8192		- - - - - -	
81A84000	Private	4096		-RW- - -	
81A85000	Private	12288	1	- - - -	
81A85000	Private	12288		-R- - - -	
81A88000	Private	12288	1	- - - -	
81A88000	Private	12288		-R- - - -	
81A8B000	Private	94208	1	- - - -	
81A8B000	Private	94208		-R- - - -	
81AA2000	Private	24576	1	- - - -	
81AA2000	Private	24576		-R- - - -	
81AA8000	Private	4096	1	- - - -	
81AA8000	Private	4096		-RW- - -	
81AA9000	Private	2228224	7	-RW-	
81AA9000	Private	69632		-RW- - -	
81ABA000	Reserve	61440		-RW- - -	
81AC9000	Private	24576		-RW- - -	
81ACF000	Reserve	8192		-RW- - -	
81AD1000	Private	8192		-RW- - -	
81AD3000	Reserve	2052096		-RW- - -	
81CC8000	Private	4096		-RW- - -	
81CC9000	Private	4096	1	- - - -	
81CC9000	Private	4096		-RW- - -	
81CCA000	Private	524288	3	- - - -	
81CCA000	Private	12288		-RW- - -	
81CCD000	Reserve	507904		- - - - - -	
81D49000	Private	4096		-RW- - -	
81D4A000	Private	4096	1	- - - -	
81D4A000	Private	4096		-RW- - -	
81D4B000	Private	4096	1	- - - -	
81D4B000	Private	4096		-RW- - -	
81D4C000	Private	4096	1	- - - -	
81D4C000	Private	4096		-RW- - -	
81D4D000	Private	4096	1	- - - -	
81D4D000	Private	4096		-RW- - -	

(continued)

Figure 4-7. *continued*

Base Address	Type	Size	Blocks	Protection Attribute(s)	Description
81D4E000	Private	2228224	5	-RW-	
81D4E000	Private	69632		-RW- --	
81D5F000	Reserve	61440		-RW- --	
81D6E000	Private	8192		-RW- --	
81D70000	Reserve	2084864		-RW- --	
81F6D000	Private	4096		-RW- --	
81F6E000	Private	2162688	11	-RW-	
81F6E000	Private	4096		-RW- --	
81F6F000	Reserve	61440		-RW- --	
81F7E000	Private	8192		-RW- --	
81F80000	Reserve	4096		-RW- --	
81F81000	Private	24576		-RW- --	
81F87000	Reserve	4096		-RW- --	
81F88000	Private	4096		-RW- --	
81F89000	Reserve	24576		-RW- --	
81F8F000	Private	4096		-RW- --	
81F90000	Reserve	2019328		-RW- --	
8217D000	Private	4096		-RW- --	
8217E000	Private	4096	1		
8217E000	Private	4096		-RW- --	
8217F000	Private	12288	1	----	
8217F000	Private	12288		-R-- --	
82182000	Private	4096	1	----	
82182000	Private	4096		-RW- --	
82183000	Private	4096	1	----	
82183000	Private	4096		-RW- --	
82184000	Private	2097152	3	----	
82184000	Private	4096		-RW- --	
82185000	Reserve	2088960		---- --	
82383000	Private	4096		-RW- --	
82384000	Private	4096	1	----	
82384000	Private	4096		-RW- --	
82385000	Free	16384			
82389000	Private	4096	1	----	
82389000	Private	4096		-RW- --	
8238A000	Free	12288			
8238D000	Private	4096	1	----	
8238D000	Private	4096		-RW- --	
8238E000	Free	24576			

(continued)

Figure 4-7. *continued*

Base Address	Type	Size	Blocks	Protection Attribute(s)	Description
82394000	Private	4096	1	- - - -	
82394000	Private	4096		-RW- - -	
82395000	Free	4096			
82396000	Private	4096	1	- - - -	
82396000	Private	4096		-RW- - -	
82397000	Private	16384	2	-RW-	
82397000	Private	4096		-RW- - -	
82398000	Reserve	12288		-RW- - -	
8239B000	Free	4096			
8239C000	Private	4096	1	- - - -	
8239C000	Private	4096		-RW- - -	
8239D000	Free	16384			
823A1000	Private	73728	1	- - - -	
823A1000	Private	73728		-R-- - -	
823B3000	Free	20480			
823B8000	Private	4096	1	- - - -	
823B8000	Private	4096		-RW- - -	
823B9000	Private	2097152	5	- - - -	
823B9000	Private	49152		-RW- - -	
823C5000	Reserve	4096		- - - - - -	
823C6000	Private	8192		-RW- - -	
823C8000	Reserve	2031616		- - - - - -	
825B8000	Private	4096		-RW- - -	
825B9000	Private	1056768	3	- - - -	
825B9000	Private	4096		-RW- - -	
825BA000	Reserve	1048576		- - - - - -	
826BA000	Private	4096		-RW- - -	
826BB000	Private	1052672	3	- - - -	
826BB000	Private	4096		-RW- - -	
826BC000	Reserve	1044480		- - - - - -	
827BB000	Private	4096		-RW- - -	
827BC000	Private	94208	1	-RW-	
827BC000	Private	94208		-RW- - -	
827D3000	Private	24576	1	-RW-	
827D3000	Private	24576		-RW- - -	
827D9000	Free	2039808			
829CB000	Private	163840	1	- - - -	
829CB000	Private	163840		-R-- - -	
829F3000	Private	73728	1	- - - -	
829F3000	Private	73728		-R-- - -	

(continued)

Figure 4-7. *continued*

Base Address	Type	Size	Blocks	Protection Attribute(s)	Description
82A05000	Free	1027649536			
BFE10000	Private	73728	5	- - - -	
BFE10000	Private	40960		-R-- --	
BFE1A000	Private	4096		-RW- --	
BFE1B000	Private	4096		-R-- --	
BFE1C000	Private	4096		-RW- --	
BFE1D000	Private	20480		-R-- --	
BFE22000	Free	712704			
BFED0000	Private	32768	3	- - - -	C:\WINDOWS\SYSTEM\ADVAPI32.DLL
BFED0000	Private	8192		-R-- --	
BFED2000	Private	4096		-RW- --	
BFED3000	Private	20480		-R-- --	
BFED8000	Free	98304			
BFEF0000	Private	200704	3	- - - -	
BFEF0000	Private	143360		-R-- --	
BFF13000	Private	4096		-RW- --	
BFF14000	Private	53248		-R-- --	
BFF21000	Free	61440			
BFF30000	Private	147456	5	- - - -	C:\WINDOWS\SYSTEM\GDI32.DLL
BFF30000	Private	106496		-R-- --	
BFF4A000	Private	8192		-RW- --	
BFF4C000	Private	16384		-R-- --	
BFF50000	Private	4096		-RW- --	
BFF51000	Private	12288		-R-- --	
BFF54000	Free	49152			
BFF60000	Private	57344	3	- - - -	C:\WINDOWS\SYSTEM\USER32.DLL
BFF60000	Private	24576		-R-- --	
BFF66000	Private	4096		-RW- --	
BFF67000	Private	28672		-R-- --	
BFF6E000	Free	8192			
BFF70000	Private	524288	8	- - - -	C:\WINDOWS\SYSTEM\KERNEL32.DLL
BFF70000	Private	278528		-R-- --	
BFFB4000	Reserve	8192		- - - - --	
BFFB6000	Private	12288		-R-- --	
BFFB9000	Private	16384		-RW- --	
BFFBD000	Private	24576		-R-- --	
BFFC3000	Private	12288		-RW- --	
BFFC6000	Private	73728		-R-- --	
BFFD8000	Reserve	98304		- - - - --	
BFFF0000	Free	65536			

The biggest difference between the two address space maps is the lack of information offered under Windows 95. For example, each region and block will reflect whether the area of address space is free, reserve, or private. You will never see mapped or image because Windows 95 does not offer the additional information indicating whether the physical storage backing the region is a memory-mapped file or is contained in an EXE or a DLL's file image.

You'll notice that most of the region sizes are exact multiples of the allocation granularity (64 KB). If the sizes of the blocks contained within a region do not add up to a multiple of the allocation granularity, there is frequently a block of reserved address space at the end of the region. This block is whatever size is necessary to bring the region to an even 64 KB. For example, the region starting at address 0x00520000 consists of 2 blocks: a 4-KB committed block of storage and a reserved block that occupies a 60-KB range of memory addresses.

Finally, the protection flags never reflect execute or copy-on-write access because Windows 95 does not support these flags. The two protection attribute flags, no cache and guard, are also not supported. Because the guard flag is not supported, VMMAP.EXE uses a more complicated technique to determine whether a region of address space is reserved for a thread's stack.

You will notice that, unlike under Windows NT, under Windows 95 the region of address space between 0x80000000 and 0xBFFFFFFF can be examined. This is the partition that contains the address space shared by all Win32 applications. As you can see, the four system DLLs are loaded into this region of address space and are therefore available to all Win32 processes.

CHAPTER FIVE

EXPLORING VIRTUAL MEMORY

In the last chapter, we discussed how the system manages virtual memory, how each process receives its very own private address space, and what a process's address space looks like. In this chapter, we move away from the abstract and examine some of the Win32 functions that give us information about the system's memory management and about the virtual address space in a process.

System Information

To understand how Win32 uses virtual memory, you need to know how the current Win32 implementation works. The *GetSystemInfo* function retrieves information (including virtual memory information) about the current Win32 implementation:

```
VOID GetSystemInfo (LPSYSTEM_INFO lpSystemInfo);
```

You must pass the address of a SYSTEM_INFO structure to this function. The function will initialize the structure's members and return. Here is what the SYSTEM_INFO data structure looks like:

```
typedef struct _SYSTEM_INFO {
    DWORD   dwOemId;
    DWORD   dwPageSize;
    LPVOID  lpMinimumApplicationAddress;
    LPVOID  lpMaximumApplicationAddress;
    DWORD   dwActiveProcessorMask;
    DWORD   dwNumberOfProcessors;
    DWORD   dwProcessorType;
    DWORD   dwAllocationGranularity;
    DWORD   dwReserved;
} SYSTEM_INFO;
```

When the system boots, it determines what the values of these members should be; for a given system the values will always be the same. *GetSystemInfo* exists so that an application can query these values at run time. Of all the members in the structure, only four of them have anything to do with memory. These four members are explained in the table below:

Member Name	Description
dwPageSize	Shows the size of a memory page. On *x*86, MIPS, and PowerPC CPUs, this value is 4 KB. On Alpha CPUs, this value is 8 KB.
lpMinimumApplicationAddress	Gives the minimum memory address of every process's usable address space. On Windows 95, this value is 4,194,304, or 0x00400000, because the bottom 4 MB of every process's address space is inaccessible. On Windows NT, this value is 65,536, or 0x00010000, because the first 64 KB of every process's address space is reserved.
lpMaximumApplicationAddress	Gives the maximum memory address of every process's usable private address space. On Windows 95, this address is 2,147,483,647, or 0x7FFFFFFF, because the shared memory-mapped file region and the shared operating system code are contained in the top 2-GB partition. On Windows NT, this address is 2,147,418,111, or 0x7FFEFFFF, because unusable address space begins just 64 KB below the 2-GB line and extends to the end of the process's address space.
dwAllocationGranularity	Shows the granularity of a reserved region of address space. As of this writing, this value is 65,536 because all implementations of Win32 reserve address space on even 64-KB boundaries.

The System Information Sample Application

The SysInfo application (SYSINFO.EXE), listed in Figure 5-1 beginning on page 130, is a very simple program that calls *GetSystemInfo* and displays the information returned in the SYSTEM_INFO structure. The source code files, resource files, and make file for the application are in the

SYSINFO.05 directory on the companion disc. The dialog boxes below show the results of running the SysInfo application on several different platforms.

Windows 95 on Intel x86.

Windows NT on Intel x86.

Windows NT on MIPS R4000.

Windows NT on DEC Alpha.

SysInfo.ico

SYSINFO.C

```
/************************************************************
Module name: SysInfo.C
Notices: Copyright (c) 1995 Jeffrey Richter
************************************************************/


#include "..\AdvWin32.H"    /* See Appendix B for details. */
#include <windows.h>
#include <windowsx.h>

#pragma warning(disable: 4001)      /* Single-line comment */

#include <tchar.h>
#include <stdio.h>
#include "Resource.H"


///////////////////////////////////////////////////////////


typedef struct {
   const DWORD dwValue;
   LPCTSTR szText;
} LONGDATA;

LONGDATA CPUFlags[] = {
   { PROCESSOR_INTEL_386,     __TEXT("Intel 386")      },
   { PROCESSOR_INTEL_486,     __TEXT("Intel 486")      },
   { PROCESSOR_INTEL_PENTIUM, __TEXT("Intel Pentium")  },
   { PROCESSOR_INTEL_860,     __TEXT("Intel 860")      },
   { PROCESSOR_MIPS_R2000,    __TEXT("MIPS R2000")     },
   { PROCESSOR_MIPS_R3000,    __TEXT("MIPS R3000")     },
   { PROCESSOR_MIPS_R4000,    __TEXT("MIPS R4000")     },
   { PROCESSOR_ALPHA_21064,   __TEXT("DEC Alpha 21064") },
#ifdef PROCESSOR_PPC_601
   { PROCESSOR_PPC_601,       __TEXT("PowerPC 601")    },
   { PROCESSOR_PPC_603,       __TEXT("PowerPC 603")    },
   { PROCESSOR_PPC_604,       __TEXT("PowerPC 604")    },
   { PROCESSOR_PPC_620,       __TEXT("PowerPC 620")    },
#endif
   { 0, NULL }
};
```

Figure 5-1.   *(continued)*
The SysInfo application.

Figure 5-1. *continued*

```
/////////////////////////////////////////////////////////////


LPCTSTR GetFlagStr (DWORD dwFlag, LONGDATA FlagList[],
   LPTSTR pszBuf) {

   int x;

   for (x = 0; FlagList[x].dwValue != 0; x++) {
      if (FlagList[x].dwValue == dwFlag)
         return(FlagList[x].szText);
   }

   _stprintf(pszBuf, __TEXT("Unknown (%d)"), dwFlag);
   return(pszBuf);
}


/////////////////////////////////////////////////////////////


// This function accepts a number and converts it to a
// string, inserting commas where appropriate.
LPTSTR BigNumToString (LONG lNum, LPTSTR szBuf) {
   WORD wNumDigits = 0, wNumChars = 0;

   do {
      // Put the last digit of the string
      // in the character buffer.
      szBuf[wNumChars++] = (TCHAR) (lNum % 10 + __TEXT('0'));

      // Increment the number of digits
      // that we put in the string.
      wNumDigits++;

      // For every three digits put in
      // the string, add a comma (,).
      if (wNumDigits % 3 == 0)
         szBuf[wNumChars++] = __TEXT(',');

      // Divide the number by 10, and repeat the process.
      lNum /= 10;
```

(continued)

131

Figure 5-1. *continued*

```
        // Continue adding digits to the
        // string until the number is zero.
    } while (lNum != 0);

    // If the last character added to
    // the string was a comma, truncate it.
    if (szBuf[wNumChars - 1] == __TEXT(','))
        szBuf[wNumChars - 1] = 0;

    // Ensure that the string is zero-terminated.
    szBuf[wNumChars] = 0;

    // We added all the characters to the string in
    // reverse order. We must reverse the contents
    // of the string.
    _tcsrev(szBuf);

    // Returns the address of the string. This is the same
    // value that was passed to us initially. Returning it
    // here makes it easier for the calling function to
    // use the string.
    return(szBuf);
}


///////////////////////////////////////////////////////////////


BOOL Dlg_OnInitDialog (HWND hwnd, HWND hwndFocus,
    LPARAM lParam) {

    TCHAR szBuf[50];
    SYSTEM_INFO si;

    // Associate an icon with the dialog box.
    SetClassLong(hwnd, GCL_HICON, (LONG)
        LoadIcon((HINSTANCE) GetWindowLong(hwnd, GWL_HINSTANCE),
            __TEXT("SysInfo")));

    GetSystemInfo(&si);

    // Fill the static controls in the
    // list box with the appropriate number.
```

(continued)

Figure 5-1. *continued*

```
      SetDlgItemText(hwnd, IDC_OEMID,
         BigNumToString(si.dwOemId, szBuf));

      SetDlgItemText(hwnd, IDC_PAGESIZE,
         BigNumToString(si.dwPageSize, szBuf));

      SetDlgItemText(hwnd, IDC_MINAPPADDR,
         BigNumToString((LONG) si.lpMinimumApplicationAddress,
         szBuf));

      SetDlgItemText(hwnd, IDC_MAXAPPADDR,
         BigNumToString((LONG) si.lpMaximumApplicationAddress,
         szBuf));

      _stprintf(szBuf, __TEXT("0x%08X"),
         si.dwActiveProcessorMask);
      SetDlgItemText(hwnd, IDC_ACTIVEPROCMASK, szBuf);

      SetDlgItemText(hwnd, IDC_NUMOFPROCS,
         BigNumToString(si.dwNumberOfProcessors, szBuf));

      SetDlgItemText(hwnd, IDC_PROCTYPE,
         GetFlagStr(si.dwProcessorType, CPUFlags, szBuf));

      SetDlgItemText(hwnd, IDC_ALLOCGRAN,
         BigNumToString(si.dwAllocationGranularity, szBuf));

      return(TRUE);
}


///////////////////////////////////////////////////////////


void Dlg_OnCommand (HWND hwnd, int id, HWND hwndCtl,
   UINT codeNotify) {

   switch (id) {
      case IDCANCEL:
         EndDialog(hwnd, id);
         break;
   }
}
```

(continued)

133

Figure 5-1. *continued*

```
//////////////////////////////////////////////////////////


BOOL CALLBACK Dlg_Proc (HWND hDlg, UINT uMsg,
   WPARAM wParam, LPARAM lParam) {

   BOOL fProcessed = TRUE;

   switch (uMsg) {
      HANDLE_MSG(hDlg, WM_INITDIALOG, Dlg_OnInitDialog);
      HANDLE_MSG(hDlg, WM_COMMAND, Dlg_OnCommand);

      default:
         fProcessed = FALSE;
         break;
   }
   return(fProcessed);
}



//////////////////////////////////////////////////////////


int WINAPI WinMain (HINSTANCE hinstExe,
   HINSTANCE hinstPrev, LPSTR lpszCmdLine, int nCmdShow) {

   DialogBox(hinstExe, MAKEINTRESOURCE(IDD_SYSINFO),
      NULL, Dlg_Proc);

   return(0);
}


/////////////////////// End Of File ///////////////////////
```

SYSINFO.RC

```
//Microsoft Visual C++ generated resource script.
//
#include "Resource.h"

#define APSTUDIO_READONLY_SYMBOLS
```

(continued)

Figure 5-1. *continued*

```
///////////////////////////////////////////////////////////////
//
// Generated from the TEXTINCLUDE 2 resource.
//
#include "afxres.h"


///////////////////////////////////////////////////////////////
#undef APSTUDIO_READONLY_SYMBOLS


#ifdef APSTUDIO_INVOKED
///////////////////////////////////////////////////////////////
//
// TEXTINCLUDE
//

1 TEXTINCLUDE DISCARDABLE
BEGIN
    "Resource.h\0"
END

2 TEXTINCLUDE DISCARDABLE
BEGIN
    "#include ""afxres.h""\r\n"
    "\0"
END

3 TEXTINCLUDE DISCARDABLE
BEGIN
    "\r\n"
    "\0"
END


///////////////////////////////////////////////////////////////
#endif    // APSTUDIO_INVOKED


///////////////////////////////////////////////////////////////
//
// Dialog
//

IDD_SYSINFO DIALOG DISCARDABLE  18, 18, 170, 103
```

(continued)

Figure 5-1. *continued*

```
STYLE WS_MINIMIZEBOX ¦ WS_POPUP ¦ WS_VISIBLE ¦ WS_CAPTION
    ¦ WS_SYSMENU
CAPTION "System Information"
FONT 8, "System"
BEGIN
    RTEXT           "OEM ID:",IDC_STATIC,4,4,88,8,SS_NOPREFIX
    RTEXT           "ID_OEMID",IDC_OEMID,96,4,68,8,
                    SS_NOPREFIX
    RTEXT           "Page size:",IDC_STATIC,4,16,88,8,
                    SS_NOPREFIX
    RTEXT           "ID_PAGESIZE",IDC_PAGESIZE,96,16,68,8,
                    SS_NOPREFIX
    RTEXT           "Minimum app. address:",IDC_STATIC,4,28,
                    88,8,SS_NOPREFIX
    RTEXT           "ID_MINAPPADDR",IDC_MINAPPADDR,96,28,68,
                    8,SS_NOPREFIX
    RTEXT           "Maximum app. address:",IDC_STATIC,4,40,88,
                    8,SS_NOPREFIX
    RTEXT           "ID_MAXAPPADDR",IDC_MAXAPPADDR,96,40,68,8,
                    SS_NOPREFIX
    RTEXT           "Active processor mask:",IDC_STATIC,4,52,88,
                    8,SS_NOPREFIX
    RTEXT           "ID_ACTIVEPROCMASK",IDC_ACTIVEPROCMASK,
                    96,52,68,8,SS_NOPREFIX
    RTEXT           "Number of processors:",IDC_STATIC,4,64,88,
                    8,SS_NOPREFIX
    RTEXT           "ID_NUMOFPROCS",IDC_NUMOFPROCS,96,64,68,8,
                    SS_NOPREFIX
    RTEXT           "Processor type:",IDC_STATIC,4,76,88,8,
                    SS_NOPREFIX
    RTEXT           "ID_PROCTYPE",IDC_PROCTYPE,96,76,68,8,
                    SS_NOPREFIX
    RTEXT           "Allocation granularity:",IDC_STATIC,4,88,
                    88,8,SS_NOPREFIX
    RTEXT           "ID_ALLOCGRAN",IDC_ALLOCGRAN,96,88,68,8,
                    SS_NOPREFIX
END


/////////////////////////////////////////////////////////////
//
// Icon
//
```

(continued)

Figure 5-1. *continued*

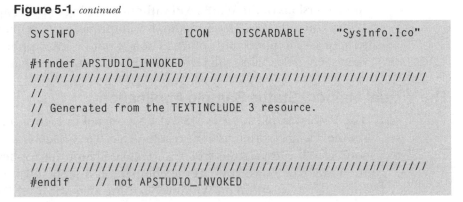

```
SYSINFO                   ICON    DISCARDABLE      "SysInfo.Ico"

#ifndef APSTUDIO_INVOKED
/////////////////////////////////////////////////////////////////
//
// Generated from the TEXTINCLUDE 3 resource.
//


/////////////////////////////////////////////////////////////////
#endif    // not APSTUDIO_INVOKED
```

Virtual Memory Status

There is a Win32 function called *GlobalMemoryStatus* that retrieves dynamic information about the current state of memory:

```
VOID GlobalMemoryStatus (LPMEMORYSTATUS lpmstMemStat);
```

I think that this function is very poorly named—*GlobalMemoryStatus* implies that the function is somehow related to the global heaps in 16-bit Windows. Win32 does not have a global heap but does offer the old global heap functions such as *GlobalAlloc* purely to ease the burden of porting a 16-bit Windows application to Win32. I think that *Global-MemoryStatus* should have been called something like *VirtualMemory-Status* instead.

When you call *GlobalMemoryStatus,* you must pass the address of a MEMORYSTATUS structure. Here is what the MEMORYSTATUS data structure looks like:

```
typedef struct _MEMORYSTATUS {
   DWORD dwLength;
   DWORD dwMemoryLoad;
   DWORD dwTotalPhys;
   DWORD dwAvailPhys;
   DWORD dwTotalPageFile;
   DWORD dwAvailPageFile;
   DWORD dwTotalVirtual;
   DWORD dwAvailVirtual:
} MEMORYSTATUS, *LPMEMORYSTATUS;
```

Before calling *GlobalMemoryStatus,* you must initialize the *dwLength* member to the size of the structure in bytes—that is, sizeof(MEMO-RYSTATUS). This allows Microsoft to add members to this structure in future versions of the Win32 API without breaking existing applications. When you call *GlobalMemoryStatus*, it will initialize the remainder of the structure's members and return. The VMStat sample application in the next section describes the various members and their meanings.

The Virtual Memory Status Sample Application

The VMStat application (VMSTAT.EXE), listed in Figure 5-2, displays a simple dialog box that lists the results of a call to *GlobalMemoryStatus*. The source code files, resource files, and make file for the application are in the VMSTAT.05 directory on the companion disc. Below is the result of running this program on Windows 95 using an 8-MB Intel 486 machine:

Virtual Memory Status			
Memory load:			61
TotalPhys:		6,983,680	
AvailPhys:		4,096	
TotalPageFile:		58,777,600	
AvailPageFile:		57,204,736	
TotalVirtual:		2,143,289,344	
AvailVirtual:		2,139,422,720	

The *dwMemoryLoad* member (shown as Memory Load) gives a rough estimate of how busy the memory management system is. This number can be anywhere from 0 to 100. The exact algorithm used to calculate this value varies between Windows 95 and Windows NT. In addition, the algorithm is subject to change in future versions of the operating system. In practice, the value reported by this member variable is all but useless.

The *dwTotalPhys* member (shown as TotalPhys) indicates the total number of bytes of physical memory (RAM) that exist. On this 8-MB 486 machine, this value is 6,983,680, which is just over 6.6 MB. This value is the exact amount of memory, including any holes in the address space between the low 640 KB and 1 MB of physical memory. The *dwAvailPhys* member (shown as AvailPhys) indicates the total number of bytes of physical memory available for allocation.

The *dwTotalPageFile* member (shown as TotalPageFile) indicates the maximum number of bytes that can be contained in the paging file(s) on your hard disk(s). Although VMStat reported that the paging file is currently 58,777,600 bytes, the system can expand and shrink the paging file as it sees fit. The *dwAvailPageFile* member (shown as AvailPageFile) indicates that 57,204,736 bytes in the paging file(s) are not committed to any process and are currently available should a process decide to commit any private storage.

The *dwTotalVirtual* member (shown as TotalVirtual) indicates the total number of bytes that are private in each process's address space. The value 2,143,289,344 is 4 MB short of being exactly 2 GB. The bottom 4 MB of inaccessible address space accounts for the 4-MB difference. If you run VMStat under Windows NT, you'll see that *dwTotalVirtual* comes back with a value of 2,147,352,576, which is just 128 KB short of being exactly 2 GB. The 128-KB difference exists because the system never lets an application gain access to the 64 KB at the beginning or the 64 KB at the end of a 2-GB mark of address space.

The last member, *dwAvailVirtual* (shown as AvailVirtual), is the only member of the structure specific to the process calling *GlobalMemoryStatus*—all the other members apply to the system and would be the same regardless of which process was calling *GlobalMemoryStatus*. To calculate this value, *GlobalMemoryStatus* adds up all of the free regions in the calling process's address space. The *dwAvailVirtual* value 2,139,422,720 indicates the amount of free address space that is available for VMStat to do with what it wants. If you subtract the *dwAvailVirtual* member from the *dwTotalVirtual* member, you'll see that VMStat has 3,866,624 bytes reserved in its virtual address space.

There is no member that indicates the amount of physical storage currently in use by the process.

VMStat.ico

VMSTAT.C

```
/*****************************************************************
Module name: VMStat.C
Notices: Copyright (c) 1995 Jeffrey Richter
*****************************************************************/


#include "..\AdvWin32.H"    /* See Appendix B for details. */
#include <windows.h>
#include <windowsx.h>

#pragma warning(disable: 4001)      /* Single-line comment */

#include <tchar.h>
#include "Resource.H"
```

Figure 5-2.   *(continued)*
The VMStat application.

Figure 5-2. *continued*

```
/////////////////////////////////////////////////////////////////

// This function accepts a number and converts it to a string.
// inserting commas where appropriate.
LPTSTR WINAPI BigNumToString (LONG lNum, LPTSTR szBuf) {
   WORD wNumDigits = 0, wNumChars = 0;

   do {
      // Put the last digit of the string
      // in the character buffer.
      szBuf[wNumChars++] = (TCHAR) (lNum % 10 + __TEXT('0'));

      // Increment the number of digits
      // that we put in the string.
      wNumDigits++;

      // For every three digits put in
      // the string, add a comma (,).
      if (wNumDigits % 3 == 0)
         szBuf[wNumChars++] = __TEXT(',');

      // Divide the number by 10, and repeat the process.
      lNum /= 10;
      // Continue adding digits to
      // the string until the number is zero.
   } while (lNum != 0);

   // If the last character added to
   // the string was a comma, truncate it.
   if (szBuf[wNumChars - 1] == __TEXT(','))
      szBuf[wNumChars - 1] = 0;

   // Ensure that the string is zero-terminated.
   szBuf[wNumChars] = 0;

   // We added all the characters to the string in reverse
   // order. We must reverse the contents of the string.
   _tcsrev(szBuf);

   // Returns the address of the string. This is the same
   // value that was passed to us initially. Returning it
   // here makes it easier for the calling function
   // to use the string.
   return(szBuf);
}
```

(continued)

Figure 5-2. *continued*

```
///////////////////////////////////////////////////////////

BOOL Dlg_OnInitDialog (HWND hwnd, HWND hwndFocus,
   LPARAM lParam) {

   TCHAR szBuf[50];
   MEMORYSTATUS ms;

   // Associate an icon with the dialog box.
   SetClassLong(hwnd, GCL_HICON, (LONG)
      LoadIcon((HINSTANCE) GetWindowLong(hwnd, GWL_HINSTANCE),
      (LPCTSTR) __TEXT("VMStat")));

   // Initialize the structure length before
   // calling GlobalMemoryStatus.
   ms.dwLength = sizeof(ms);
   GlobalMemoryStatus(&ms);

   // Fill the static controls in the
   // list box with the appropriate number.
   SetDlgItemText(hwnd, IDC_MEMLOAD,
      BigNumToString(ms.dwMemoryLoad, szBuf));

   SetDlgItemText(hwnd, IDC_TOTALPHYS,
      BigNumToString(ms.dwTotalPhys, szBuf));

   SetDlgItemText(hwnd, IDC_AVAILPHYS,
      BigNumToString(ms.dwAvailPhys, szBuf));

   SetDlgItemText(hwnd, IDC_TOTALPAGEFILE,
      BigNumToString(ms.dwTotalPageFile, szBuf));

   SetDlgItemText(hwnd, IDC_AVAILPAGEFILE,
      BigNumToString(ms.dwAvailPageFile, szBuf));

   SetDlgItemText(hwnd, IDC_TOTALVIRTUAL,
      BigNumToString(ms.dwTotalVirtual, szBuf));

   SetDlgItemText(hwnd, IDC_AVAILVIRTUAL,
      BigNumToString(ms.dwAvailVirtual, szBuf));

   return(TRUE);
}
```

(continued)

Figure 5-2. *continued*

```
//////////////////////////////////////////////////////////

void Dlg_OnCommand (HWND hwnd, int id, HWND hwndCtl,
   UINT codeNotify) {

   switch (id) {
      case IDCANCEL:
         EndDialog(hwnd, id);
         break;
   }
}


//////////////////////////////////////////////////////////

BOOL CALLBACK Dlg_Proc (HWND hDlg, UINT uMsg,
   WPARAM wParam, LPARAM lParam) {

   BOOL fProcessed = TRUE;

   switch (uMsg) {
      HANDLE_MSG(hDlg, WM_INITDIALOG, Dlg_OnInitDialog);
      HANDLE_MSG(hDlg, WM_COMMAND, Dlg_OnCommand);

      default:
         fProcessed = FALSE;
         break;
   }
   return(fProcessed);
}


//////////////////////////////////////////////////////////

int WINAPI WinMain (HINSTANCE hinstExe,
   HINSTANCE hinstPrev, LPSTR lpszCmdLine, int nCmdShow) {

   DialogBox(hinstExe, MAKEINTRESOURCE(IDD_VMSTAT),
      NULL, Dlg_Proc);

   return(0);
}


/////////////////////// End Of File ///////////////////////
```

(continued)

Figure 5-2. *continued*

```
VMSTAT.RC
//Microsoft Visual C++ generated resource script.
//
#include "Resource.h"

#define APSTUDIO_READONLY_SYMBOLS
/////////////////////////////////////////////////////////////////////
//
// Generated from the TEXTINCLUDE 2 resource.
//
#include "afxres.h"


/////////////////////////////////////////////////////////////////////
#undef APSTUDIO_READONLY_SYMBOLS


#ifdef APSTUDIO_INVOKED
/////////////////////////////////////////////////////////////////////
//
// TEXTINCLUDE
//

1 TEXTINCLUDE DISCARDABLE
BEGIN
    "Resource.h\0"
END

2 TEXTINCLUDE DISCARDABLE
BEGIN
    "#include ""afxres.h""\r\n"
    "\0"
END

3 TEXTINCLUDE DISCARDABLE
BEGIN
    "\r\n"
    "\0"
END


/////////////////////////////////////////////////////////////////////
#endif    // APSTUDIO_INVOKED
```

(continued)

143

Figure 5-2. *continued*

```
/////////////////////////////////////////////////////////////////
//
// Dialog
//


IDD_VMSTAT DIALOG DISCARDABLE  60, 27, 129, 101
STYLE WS_MINIMIZEBOX ¦ WS_POPUP ¦ WS_VISIBLE ¦ WS_CAPTION
     ¦ WS_SYSMENU
CAPTION "Virtual Memory Status"
FONT 8, "System"
BEGIN
    RTEXT           "Memory load:",IDC_STATIC,4,4,52,8
    RTEXT           "Text",IDC_MEMLOAD,60,4,60,8
    RTEXT           "TotalPhys:",IDC_STATIC,4,20,52,8
    RTEXT           "Text",IDC_TOTALPHYS,60,20,60,8
    RTEXT           "AvailPhys:",IDC_STATIC,4,32,52,8
    RTEXT           "Text",IDC_AVAILPHYS,60,32,60,8
    RTEXT           "TotalPageFile:",IDC_STATIC,4,48,52,8
    RTEXT           "Text",IDC_TOTALPAGEFILE,60,48,60,8
    RTEXT           "AvailPageFile:",IDC_STATIC,4,60,52,8
    RTEXT           "Text",IDC_AVAILPAGEFILE,60,60,60,8
    RTEXT           "TotalVirtual:",IDC_STATIC,4,76,52,8
    RTEXT           "Text",IDC_TOTALVIRTUAL,60,76,60,8
    RTEXT           "AvailVirtual:",IDC_STATIC,4,88,52,8
    RTEXT           "Text",IDC_AVAILVIRTUAL,60,88,60,8
END




/////////////////////////////////////////////////////////////////
//
// Icon
//


VMStat                  ICON    DISCARDABLE     "VMStat.Ico"

#ifndef APSTUDIO_INVOKED
/////////////////////////////////////////////////////////////////
//
// Generated from the TEXTINCLUDE 3 resource.
//



/////////////////////////////////////////////////////////////////
#endif    // not APSTUDIO_INVOKED
```

Determining the State of an Address Space

Win32 offers a function that lets you query certain information (for example, size, storage type, and protection attributes) about a memory address in your address space. In fact, the VMMap sample application shown later in this chapter uses this function to produce the virtual memory map dumps that appeared in Chapter 4. This Win32 function is called *VirtualQuery*:

```
DWORD VirtualQuery(LPVOID lpAddress,
   PMEMORY_BASIC_INFORMATION lpBuffer,
   DWORD dwLength);
```

When you call *VirtualQuery*, the first parameter, *lpAddress*, must contain the virtual memory address that you want information about. The *lpBuffer* parameter is the address to a MEMORY_BASIC_INFORMATION structure that you must allocate. This structure is defined in WINNT.H as follows:

```
typedef struct _MEMORY_BASIC_INFORMATION {
   PVOID BaseAddress;
   PVOID AllocationBase;
   DWORD AllocationProtect;
   DWORD RegionSize;
   DWORD State;
   DWORD Protect;
   DWORD Type;
} MEMORY_BASIC_INFORMATION, *PMEMORY_BASIC_INFORMATION;
```

The last parameter, *dwLength*, specifies the size of a MEMORY_BASIC_INFORMATION structure. *VirtualQuery* returns the number of bytes copied into the buffer.

Based on the address that you pass in the *lpAddress* parameter, *VirtualQuery* fills the MEMORY_BASIC_INFORMATION structure with information about the range of adjoining pages that share the same state, protection attributes, and type. See the table on the following page for a description of the structure's members.

Member Name	Description
BaseAddress	This is the same value as the *lpAddress* parameter rounded down to an even page boundary.
AllocationBase	Identifies the base address of the region containing the address specified in the *lpAddress* parameter.
AllocationProtect	Identifies the protection attribute assigned to the region when it was initially reserved.
RegionSize	Identifies the size, in bytes, for all pages starting at *BaseAddress* that have the same protection attributes, state, and type as the page containing the address specified in the *lpAddress* parameter.
State	Identifies the state (MEM_FREE, MEM_RESERVE, or MEM_COMMIT) for all adjoining pages that have the same protection attributes, state, and type as the page containing the address specified in the *lpAddress* parameter. If the state is free, the *AllocationBase*, *AllocationProtect*, *Protect*, and *Type* members are undefined. If the state is reserve, the *Protect* member is undefined.
Protect	Identifies the protection attribute (PAGE_*) for all adjoining pages that have the same protection attributes, state, and type as the page containing the address specified in the *lpAddress* parameter.
Type	Identifies the type of physical storage (MEM_IMAGE, MEM_MAPPED, or MEM_PRIVATE) that is backing all adjoining pages that have the same protection attributes, state, and type as the page containing the address specified in the *lpAddress* parameter. For Windows 95, this member will always indicate MEM_PRIVATE.

The *VMQuery* Function

When I was first learning how the Win32 memory architecture is designed, I used *VirtualQuery* as my guide. In fact, if you examine the first edition of this book, you'll see that the VMMAP.EXE program was much simpler than the new version I present in the next section. In the old version, I had a very simple loop that called *VirtualQuery* repeatedly, and for each call, I simply constructed a single line containing the members of the MEMORY_BASIC_INFORMATION structure. I studied this dump and tried to piece the Win32 memory management architecture together while referring to the Windows NT 3.1 SDK documentation (which was rather poor at the time). Well, I've come a long way, baby—I now know that the *VirtualQuery* function and the MEMORY_BASIC_INFORMA-TION structure are not good for creating a process's virtual address space memory map.

The problem is that the MEMORY_BASIC_INFORMATION structure does not return all of the information that the system has stored internally. If you have a memory address and want to obtain some simple information about it, *VirtualQuery* is great. If you just want to know whether there is committed physical storage to an address or whether a memory address can be read from or written to, *VirtualQuery* works fine. But if you want to know the total size of a reserved region or the number of blocks in a region, or whether a region contains a thread's stack, a single call to *VirtualQuery* is just not going to give you the information you're looking for.

In order to obtain much more complete memory information, I have created my own function, named *VMQuery*:

```
BOOL VMQuery (PVOID pvAddress, PVMQUERY pVMQ);
```

This function is similar to *VirtualQuery* in that it takes a memory address specified by the *pvAddress* parameter and a pointer to a structure that is to be filled, specified by the *pVMQ* parameter. This structure is a VMQUERY structure that I have also defined:

```
typedef struct {
    // Region information
    PVOID pvRgnBaseAddress;
    DWORD dwRgnProtection;    // PAGE_*
    DWORD dwRgnSize;
    DWORD dwRgnStorage;       // MEM_*: Free, Image,
                              //       Mapped, Private
    DWORD dwRgnBlocks;
    DWORD dwRgnGuardBlks;     // If > 0, region contains thread stack
    BOOL  fRgnIsAStack;       // TRUE if region contains thread stack

    // Block information
    PVOID pvBlkBaseAddress;
    DWORD dwBlkProtection;    // PAGE_*
    DWORD dwBlkSize;
    DWORD dwBlkStorage;       // MEM_*: Free, Reserve, Image,
                              //       Mapped, Private
} VMQUERY, *PVMQUERY;
```

As you can see from just a quick glance, my VMQUERY structure contains much more information than *VirtualQuery*'s MEMORY_BASIC-_INFORMATION structure. My structure is divided into two distinct parts: region information and block information. The region portion describes information about the region, and the block portion contains information about the block containing the address specified by the *pvAddress* parameter. The table below describes all the members:

Member Name	Description
pvRgnBaseAddress	Identifies the base address of the virtual address space region containing the address specified in the *pvAddress* parameter.
dwRgnProtection	Identifies the protection attribute that was assigned to the region of address space when it was initially reserved.
dwRgnSize	Identifies the size, in bytes, of the region that was reserved.
dwRgnStorage	Identifies the type of physical storage that is used for the bulk of the blocks in the region. The value is one of the following: MEM_FREE, MEM_IMAGE, MEM_MAPPED, or MEM_PRIVATE. Windows 95 doesn't distinguish between different storage types, so this member will always be MEM_FREE or MEM_PRIVATE under Windows 95.
dwRgnBlocks	Identifies the number of blocks contained within the region.
dwRgnGuardBlks	Identifies the number of blocks that have the PAGE_GUARD protection attribute flag turned on. This value will usually be either 0 or 1. If it's 1, that's a good indicator that the region was reserved to contain a thread's stack. Under Windows 95, this member will always be 0.
fRgnIsAStack	Identifies whether the region contains a thread's stack. This value is determined by taking a "best guess" because it is impossible to be 100 percent sure whether a region contains a stack.
pvBlkBaseAddress	Identifies the base address of the block that contains the address specified in the *pvAddress* parameter.
dwBlkProtection	Identifies the protection attribute for the block that contains the address specified in the *pvAddress* parameter.
dwBlkSize	Identifies the size, in bytes, of the block that contains the address specified in the *pvAddress* parameter.

(continued)

continued

Member Name	Description
dwBlkStorage	Identifies the content of the block that contains the address specified in the *pvAddress* parameter. The value is one of the following: MEM_FREE, MEM_RESERVE, MEM_IMAGE, MEM_MAPPED, or MEM_PRIVATE. Under Windows 95, this member will never be MEM_IMAGE or MEM_MAPPED.

There is no doubt that *VMQuery* must do a significant amount of processing, including many calls to *VirtualQuery*, in order to obtain all this information—which means it executes much more slowly than *VirtualQuery*. For this reason, you should think carefully when deciding which of these two functions to call. If you do not need the extra information obtained by *VMQuery*, call *VirtualQuery*.

The VMQUERY.C file, listed in Figure 5-3, shows how I obtain and massage all the information needed to set the members of the VMQUERY structure. The VMQUERY.C and VMQUERY.H files are in the VMMAP.05 directory on the companion disc. Rather than go into detail in the text about how I process this data, I'll let my comments (sprinkled liberally throughout the code) speak for themselves.

VMQUERY.C

```
/*************************************************************
Module name: VMQuery.C
Notices: Copyright (c) 1995 Jeffrey Richter
*************************************************************/


#include "..\AdvWin32.H"      /* See Appendix B for details.*/
#include <windows.h>
#include <windowsx.h>

#pragma warning(disable: 4001)      /* Single-line comment */

#include "VMQuery.H"


/////////////////////////////////////////////////////////////
```

Figure 5-3.
The VMQuery listings.

(continued)

Figure 5-3. *continued*

```
typedef struct {
   DWORD dwRgnSize;
   DWORD dwRgnStorage;       // MEM_*: Free, Image,
                             //        Mapped, Private
   DWORD dwRgnBlocks;
   DWORD dwRgnGuardBlks;     // If > 0, region contains
                             // thread stack
   BOOL  fRgnIsAStack;       // TRUE if region contains
                             // thread stack
} VMQUERY_HELP;

// Global-static variable that holds the
// allocation granularity value for this CPU platform. This
// variable is initialized the first time VMQuery is called.
static DWORD gs_dwAllocGran = 0;


////////////////////////////////////////////////////////////


// When NTBUG_VIRTUALQUERY is defined, the code below
// compensates for a bug in Windows NT's implementation of
// the VirtualQuery function.
#define NTBUG_VIRTUALQUERY

#ifdef NTBUG_VIRTUALQUERY
DWORD NTBug_VirtualQuery (LPVOID lpvAddress,
   PMEMORY_BASIC_INFORMATION pmbiBuffer, DWORD cbLength) {

   DWORD dwRetVal = VirtualQuery(lpvAddress,
      pmbiBuffer, cbLength);

   if (dwRetVal == cbLength) {
      // If successful, correct the MBI structure's values.

      if (((DWORD) pmbiBuffer->AllocationBase % 0x1000)
         == 0xFFF) {
         // If the AllocationBase member ends with 0xFFF,
         // the address is 1 byte off.
         pmbiBuffer->AllocationBase = (PVOID)
            ((PBYTE) pmbiBuffer->AllocationBase + 1);
      }
```

(continued)

Figure 5-3. *continued*

```
      if ((pmbiBuffer->RegionSize % 0x1000) == 0xFFF) {
         // If the RegionSize member ends with 0xFFF,
         // the size is 1 byte off.
         pmbiBuffer->RegionSize++;
      }

      if ((pmbiBuffer->State != MEM_FREE) &&
          (pmbiBuffer->AllocationProtect == 0)) {
         // If the the region is not free and the
         // AllocationProtect member is 0, AllocationProtect
         // should be PAGE_READONLY.
         pmbiBuffer->AllocationProtect = PAGE_READONLY;
      }
   }
   return(dwRetVal);
}


#define VirtualQuery NTBug_VirtualQuery
#endif


///////////////////////////////////////////////////////////////////


// This function iterates through all the blocks in a
// region and initializes a structure with its findings.
static BOOL VMQueryHelp (PVOID pvAddress,
   VMQUERY_HELP *pVMQHelp) {

   MEMORY_BASIC_INFORMATION MBI;
   PVOID pvRgnBaseAddress, pvAddressBlk;
   BOOL fOk;
   DWORD dwProtectBlock[4] = { 0 };
      // 0 = reserved, PAGE_NOACCESS, PAGE_READWRITE

   // Zero the contents of the structure.
   memset(pVMQHelp, 0, sizeof(*pVMQHelp));

   // From the passed memory address, obtain the
   // base address of the region that contains it.
   fOk = (VirtualQuery(pvAddress,
      &MBI, sizeof(MBI)) == sizeof(MBI));
```

(continued)

Figure 5-3. *continued*

```
if (!fOk) {
   // If we can't get any information about the passed
   // address, return FALSE, indicating an error.
   // GetLastError() will report the actual problem.
   return(fOk);
}


// pvRgnBaseAddress identifies the region's
// base address and will never change.
pvRgnBaseAddress = MBI.AllocationBase;

// pvAddress identifies the address of the first block
// and will change as we iterate through the blocks.
pvAddressBlk = pvRgnBaseAddress;

// Save the memory type of the physical storage block.
pVMQHelp->dwRgnStorage = MBI.Type;

for (;;) {
   // Get info about the current block.
   fOk = VirtualQuery(pvAddressBlk, &MBI, sizeof(MBI));
   if (!fOk) {
      // Couldn't get the information, end loop.
      break;
   }

   // Check to see whether the block we got info for is
   // contained in the requested region.
   if (MBI.AllocationBase != pvRgnBaseAddress) {
      // Found a block in the next region; end loop.
      break;
   }


   // We have found a block contained
   // in the requested region.


   // The following if statement is for detecting stacks in
   // Windows 95. Windows 95 stacks are in a region wherein
   // the last 4 blocks have the following attributes:
   // reserved block, PAGE_NOACCESS, PAGE_READWRITE,
   // and another reserved block.
   if (pVMQHelp->dwRgnBlocks < 4) {
      // If this is the 0th through 3rd block, make
      // a note of the block's protection in our array.
```

(continued)

Figure 5-3. *continued*

```
            dwProtectBlock[pVMQHelp->dwRgnBlocks] =
                (MBI.State == MEM_RESERVE) ? 0 : MBI.Protect;
        } else {
            // We have already seen 4 blocks in this region.
            // Shift the protection values down in the array.
            MoveMemory(&dwProtectBlock[0], &dwProtectBlock[1],
                sizeof(dwProtectBlock) - sizeof(DWORD));

            // Add the new protection value to the end
            // of the array.
            dwProtectBlock[3] =
                (MBI.State == MEM_RESERVE) ? 0 : MBI.Protect;
        }


        // Add 1 to the number of blocks in the region.
        pVMQHelp->dwRgnBlocks++;

        // Add the block's size to the reserved region size.
        pVMQHelp->dwRgnSize += MBI.RegionSize;

        // If the block has the PAGE_GUARD protection attribute
        // flag, add 1 to the number of blocks with this flag.
        if (MBI.Protect & PAGE_GUARD) {
            pVMQHelp->dwRgnGuardBlks++;
        }


        // Take a best guess as to the type of physical storage
        // committed to the block. This is a guess because some
        // blocks can convert from MEM_IMAGE to MEM_PRIVATE or
        // from MEM_MAPPED to MEM_PRIVATE; MEM_PRIVATE can
        // always be overridden by MEM_IMAGE or MEM_MAPPED.
        if (pVMQHelp->dwRgnStorage == MEM_PRIVATE) {
            pVMQHelp->dwRgnStorage = MBI.Type;
        }


        // Get the address of the next block.
        pvAddressBlk = (PVOID)
            ((PBYTE) pvAddressBlk + MBI.RegionSize);
    }

    // After examining the region, check to see whether it is
    // a thread stack.
    // Windows NT: Assume a thread stack if the region contains
    //             at least 1 block with the PAGE_GUARD flag.
```

(continued)

153

Figure 5-3. *continued*

```
    // Windows 95: Assume a thread stack if the region contains
    //             at least 4 blocks wherein the last 4 blocks
    //             have the following attributes:
    //             3rd block from end: reserved
    //             2nd block from end: PAGE_NOACCESS
    //             1st block from end: PAGE_READWRITE
    //             block at end: another reserved block.
    pVMQHelp->fRgnIsAStack =
        (pVMQHelp->dwRgnGuardBlks > 0) ||
        ((pVMQHelp->dwRgnBlocks >= 4) &&
        (dwProtectBlock[0] == 0) &&
        (dwProtectBlock[1] == PAGE_NOACCESS) &&
        (dwProtectBlock[2] == PAGE_READWRITE) &&
        (dwProtectBlock[3] == 0));


    // Return that the function completed successfully.
    return(TRUE);
}


///////////////////////////////////////////////////////////////////


BOOL VMQuery (PVOID pvAddress, PVMQUERY pVMQ) {

    MEMORY_BASIC_INFORMATION MBI;
    VMQUERY_HELP VMQHelp;
    BOOL fOk;

    if (gs_dwAllocGran == 0) {
        // If this is the very first time a thread in this
        // application is calling us, we must obtain the size
        // of a page used on this system and save this value
        // in a global-static variable.
        SYSTEM_INFO SI;
        GetSystemInfo(&SI);
        gs_dwAllocGran = SI.dwAllocationGranularity;
    }


    // Zero the contents of the structure.
    memset(pVMQ, 0, sizeof(*pVMQ));

    // Get the MEMORY_BASIC_INFORMATION for the passed address.
    fOk = VirtualQuery(pvAddress,
        &MBI, sizeof(MBI)) == sizeof(MBI);
```

(continued)

Figure 5-3. *continued*

```
if (!fOk) {
    // If we can't get any information about the passed
    // address, return FALSE, indicating an error.
    // GetLastError() will report the actual problem.
    return(fOk);
}


// The MEMORY_BASIC_INFORMATION structure contains valid
// information. Time to start setting the members
// of our own VMQUERY structure.

// First, fill in the block members. We'll get the
// data for the region containing the block later.
switch (MBI.State) {
    case MEM_FREE:
        // We have a block of free address space that
        // has not been reserved.
        pVMQ->pvBlkBaseAddress = NULL;
        pVMQ->dwBlkSize = 0;
        pVMQ->dwBlkProtection = 0;
        pVMQ->dwBlkStorage = MEM_FREE;
        break;


    case MEM_RESERVE:
        // We have a block of reserved address space that
        // does NOT have physical storage committed to it.
        pVMQ->pvBlkBaseAddress = MBI.BaseAddress;
        pVMQ->dwBlkSize = MBI.RegionSize;

        // For an uncommitted block, MBI.Protect is invalid.
        // So we will show that the reserved block inherits
        // the protection attribute of the region in which it
        // is contained.
        pVMQ->dwBlkProtection = MBI.AllocationProtect;
        pVMQ->dwBlkStorage = MEM_RESERVE;
        break;

    case MEM_COMMIT:
        // We have a block of reserved address space that
        // DOES have physical storage committed to it.
        pVMQ->pvBlkBaseAddress = MBI.BaseAddress;
        pVMQ->dwBlkSize = MBI.RegionSize;
        pVMQ->dwBlkProtection = MBI.Protect;
        pVMQ->dwBlkStorage = MBI.Type;
        break;
}
```

(continued)

Figure 5-3. *continued*

```
// Second, fill in the region members now that we have
// used the MBI data obtained from the first call to
// VirtualQuery. We might have to call VirtualQuery again
// to obtain complete region information.
switch (MBI.State) {
   case MEM_FREE:
      // We have a block of address space
      // that has not been reserved.
      pVMQ->pvRgnBaseAddress = MBI.BaseAddress;
      pVMQ->dwRgnProtection = MBI.AllocationProtect;
      pVMQ->dwRgnSize = MBI.RegionSize;
      pVMQ->dwRgnStorage = MEM_FREE;
      pVMQ->dwRgnBlocks = 0;
      pVMQ->dwRgnGuardBlks = 0;
      pVMQ->fRgnIsAStack = FALSE;
      break;

   case MEM_RESERVE:
      // We have a reserved region that does NOT have
      // physical storage committed to it.
      pVMQ->pvRgnBaseAddress = MBI.AllocationBase;
      pVMQ->dwRgnProtection = MBI.AllocationProtect;

      // To get complete information about the region, we
      // must iterate through all the region's blocks.
      VMQueryHelp(pvAddress, &VMQHelp);

      pVMQ->dwRgnSize = VMQHelp.dwRgnSize;
      pVMQ->dwRgnStorage = VMQHelp.dwRgnStorage;
      pVMQ->dwRgnBlocks = VMQHelp.dwRgnBlocks;
      pVMQ->dwRgnGuardBlks = VMQHelp.dwRgnGuardBlks;
      pVMQ->fRgnIsAStack = VMQHelp.fRgnIsAStack;
      break;

   case MEM_COMMIT:
      // We have a reserved region that DOES have
      // physical storage committed to it.
      pVMQ->pvRgnBaseAddress = MBI.AllocationBase;
      pVMQ->dwRgnProtection = MBI.AllocationProtect;

      // To get complete information about the region, we
      // must iterate through all the region's blocks.
      VMQueryHelp(pvAddress, &VMQHelp);
```

(continued)

Figure 5-3. *continued*

```
        pVMQ->dwRgnSize = VMQHelp.dwRgnSize;
        pVMQ->dwRgnStorage = VMQHelp.dwRgnStorage;
        pVMQ->dwRgnBlocks = VMQHelp.dwRgnBlocks;
        pVMQ->dwRgnGuardBlks = VMQHelp.dwRgnGuardBlks;
        pVMQ->fRgnIsAStack = VMQHelp.fRgnIsAStack;
        break;
    }

    // Return that the function completed successfully.
    return(fOk);
}


///////////////////////// End Of File /////////////////////////
```

VMQUERY.H

```
/***********************************************************
Module name: VMQuery.H
Notices: Copyright (c) 1995 Jeffrey Richter
***********************************************************/


typedef struct {
    // Region information
    PVOID pvRgnBaseAddress;
    DWORD dwRgnProtection;   // PAGE_*
    DWORD dwRgnSize;
    DWORD dwRgnStorage;      // MEM_*: Free, Image,
                             //        Mapped, Private
    DWORD dwRgnBlocks;
    DWORD dwRgnGuardBlks;    // If > 0, region contains
                             // thread stack
    BOOL  fRgnIsAStack;      // TRUE if region contains
                             // thread stack


    // Block information
    PVOID pvBlkBaseAddress;
    DWORD dwBlkProtection;   // PAGE_*
    DWORD dwBlkSize;
    DWORD dwBlkStorage;      // MEM_*: Free, Reserve, Image,
                             //        Mapped, Private
} VMQUERY, *PVMQUERY;
```

(continued)

Figure 5-3. *continued*

```
///////////////////////////////////////////////////////////////


BOOL VMQuery (PVOID pvAddress, PVMQUERY pVMQ);


///////////////////////// End Of File /////////////////////////
```

The Virtual Memory Map Sample Application

The VMMap application (VMMAP.EXE), listed in Figure 5-4 beginning on page 160, walks its own address space and shows the regions and the blocks within regions. The source code files, resource files, and make file for the application are in the VMMAP.05 directory on the companion disc. When you start the program, the following window appears:

The contents of this application's list box were used to produce the virtual memory map dumps presented in Figure 4-5 on page 112, Figure 4-6 on page 115, and Figure 4-7 on page 120 in Chapter 4.

Each entry in the list box shows the result of information obtained by calling my *VMQuery* function. The main loop looks like this:

```
PVOID pvAddress = 0x00000000;
BOOL fOk = TRUE;
VMQUERY VMQ;
    :
    :
```

```
        while (fOk) {
            fOk = VMQuery(pvAddress, &VMQ);

            if (fOk) {
                // Construct the line to be displayed, and
                // add it to the list box.
                ConstructRgnInfoLine(&VMQ, szLine, sizeof(szLine));
                ListBox_AddString(hWndLB, szLine);

#if 1
                // Change the 1 above to a 0 if you do not want
                // to see the blocks contained within the region.

                for (dwBlock = 0; fOk && (dwBlock < VMQ.dwRgnBlocks);
                    dwBlock++) {

                    ConstructBlkInfoLine(&VMQ, szLine, sizeof(szLine));
                    ListBox_AddString(hWndLB, szLine);

                    // Get the address of the next region to test.
                    pvAddress = ((BYTE *) pvAddress + VMQ.dwBlkSize);
                    if (dwBlock < VMQ.dwRgnBlocks - 1) {
                        // Don't query the memory info after
                        // the last block.
                        fOk = VMQuery(pvAddress, &VMQ);
                    }
                }
#endif

                // Get the address of the next region to test.
                pvAddress = ((BYTE *) VMQ.pvRgnBaseAddress +
                    VMQ.dwRgnSize);
            }
        }
```

This loop starts walking from virtual address 0x00000000 and ends when *VMQuery* returns FALSE, indicating that it can no longer walk the process's address space. With each iteration of the loop, there is a call to *ConstructRgnInfoLine*; this function fills a character buffer with information about the region. Then this information is appended to the list.

Within this main loop, there is a nested loop that iterates through each of the blocks in the region. Each iteration of this loop calls *ConstructBlkInfoLine* to fill a character buffer with information about the region's blocks. Then the information is appended to the list box. It's very easy to walk the process's address space using the *VMQuery* function.

VMMap.ico

VMMAP.C

```
/***************************************************************
Module name: VMMap.C
Notices: Copyright (c) 1995 Jeffrey Richter
***************************************************************/


#include "..\AdvWin32.H"     /* See Appendix B for details. */
#include <windows.h>
#include <windowsx.h>

#pragma warning(disable: 4001)      /* Single-line comment */
#include <tchar.h>
#include <stdio.h>                // For sprintf
#include <string.h>               // For strchr
#include "Resource.H"
#include "VMQuery.H"



///////////////////////////////////////////////////////////////


// Set COPYTOCLIPBOARD to TRUE if you want the
// memory map to be copied to the clipboard.
#define COPYTOCLIPBOARD     FALSE


#if COPYTOCLIPBOARD
// Function to copy the contents of a list box to the clipboard.
// I used this function to obtain the memory map dumps
// for the figures in this book.


void CopyControlToClipboard (HWND hwnd) {
   int nCount, nNum;
   TCHAR szClipData[20000] = { 0 };
   HGLOBAL hClipData;
   LPTSTR lpClipData;
   BOOL fOk;

   nCount = ListBox_GetCount(hwnd);
   for (nNum = 0; nNum < nCount; nNum++) {
      TCHAR szLine[1000];
      ListBox_GetText(hwnd, nNum, szLine);
```

Figure 5-4.
The VMMap application.

(continued)

Figure 5-4. *continued*

```
        _tcscat(szClipData, szLine);
        _tcscat(szClipData, __TEXT("\r\n"));
    }

    OpenClipboard(NULL);
    EmptyClipboard();

    // Clipboard accepts only data that is in a block allocated
    // with GlobalAlloc using the GMEM_MOVEABLE and
    // GMEM_DDESHARE flags.
    hClipData = GlobalAlloc(GMEM_MOVEABLE | GMEM_DDESHARE,
        sizeof(TCHAR) * (_tcslen(szClipData) + 1));
    lpClipData = (LPTSTR) GlobalLock(hClipData);

    _tcscpy(lpClipData, szClipData);

#ifdef UNICODE
    fOk = (SetClipboardData(CF_UNICODETEXT, hClipData)
        == hClipData);
#else
    fOk = (SetClipboardData(CF_TEXT, hClipData) == hClipData);
#endif
    CloseClipboard();

    if (!fOk) {
        GlobalFree(hClipData);
        MessageBox(GetFocus(),
            __TEXT("Error putting text on the clipboard"),
            NULL, MB_OK | MB_ICONINFORMATION);
    }
}

#endif


//////////////////////////////////////////////////////////////


LPCTSTR GetMemStorageText (DWORD dwStorage) {
    LPCTSTR p = __TEXT("Unknown");
    switch (dwStorage) {
        case MEM_FREE:    p = __TEXT("Free   "); break;
        case MEM_RESERVE: p = __TEXT("Reserve"); break;
        case MEM_IMAGE:   p = __TEXT("Image  "); break;
```

(continued)

Figure 5-4. *continued*

```
        case MEM_MAPPED:  p = __TEXT("Mapped "); break;
        case MEM_PRIVATE: p = __TEXT("Private"); break;
    }
    return(p);
}


//////////////////////////////////////////////////////////////////

LPTSTR GetProtectText (DWORD dwProtect, LPTSTR szBuf,
    BOOL fShowFlags) {
    LPCTSTR p = __TEXT("Unknown");
    switch (dwProtect & ~(PAGE_GUARD | PAGE_NOCACHE)) {
        case PAGE_READONLY:           p = __TEXT("-R--"); break;
        case PAGE_READWRITE:          p = __TEXT("-RW-"); break;
        case PAGE_WRITECOPY:          p = __TEXT("-RWC"); break;
        case PAGE_EXECUTE:            p = __TEXT("E---"); break;
        case PAGE_EXECUTE_READ:       p = __TEXT("ER--"); break;
        case PAGE_EXECUTE_READWRITE:  p = __TEXT("ERW-"); break;
        case PAGE_EXECUTE_WRITECOPY:  p = __TEXT("ERWC"); break;
        case PAGE_NOACCESS:           p = __TEXT("----"); break;
    }
    _tcscpy(szBuf, p);
    if (fShowFlags) {
        _tcscat(szBuf, __TEXT(" "));
        _tcscat(szBuf, (dwProtect & PAGE_GUARD)   ?
            __TEXT("G") : __TEXT("-"));
        _tcscat(szBuf, (dwProtect & PAGE_NOCACHE) ?
            __TEXT("N") : __TEXT("-"));
    }
    return(szBuf);
}


//////////////////////////////////////////////////////////////////

void ConstructRgnInfoLine (PVMQUERY pVMQ,
    LPTSTR szLine, int nMaxLen) {

    int nLen;

    _stprintf(szLine, __TEXT("%08X    %s %10u  "),
        pVMQ->pvRgnBaseAddress,
        GetMemStorageText(pVMQ->dwRgnStorage),
        pVMQ->dwRgnSize);
```

(continued)

Figure 5-4. *continued*

```
    if (pVMQ->dwRgnStorage != MEM_FREE) {
        _stprintf(_tcschr(szLine, 0), __TEXT("%5u  "),
            pVMQ->dwRgnBlocks);
        GetProtectText(pVMQ->dwRgnProtection,
            _tcschr(szLine, 0), FALSE);
    }


    _tcscat(szLine, __TEXT("      "));

    // Try to obtain the module pathname for this region.
    nLen = _tcslen(szLine);
    if (pVMQ->pvRgnBaseAddress != NULL)
        GetModuleFileName((HINSTANCE) pVMQ->pvRgnBaseAddress,
            szLine + nLen, nMaxLen - nLen);

    if (pVMQ->pvRgnBaseAddress == GetProcessHeap()) {
        _tcscat(szLine, __TEXT("Default Process Heap"));
    }

    if (pVMQ->fRgnIsAStack) {
        _tcscat(szLine, __TEXT("Thread Stack"));
    }
}


///////////////////////////////////////////////////////////////

void ConstructBlkInfoLine (PVMQUERY pVMQ,
    LPTSTR szLine, int nMaxLen) {

    _stprintf(szLine, __TEXT("   %08X  %s %10u        "),
        pVMQ->pvBlkBaseAddress,
        GetMemStorageText(pVMQ->dwBlkStorage),
        pVMQ->dwBlkSize);

    if (pVMQ->dwBlkStorage != MEM_FREE) {
        GetProtectText(pVMQ->dwBlkProtection,
            _tcschr(szLine, 0), TRUE);
    }
}
```

(continued)

163

Figure 5-4. *continued*

```
//////////////////////////////////////////////////////////////


void Dlg_OnSize (HWND hwnd, UINT state, int cx, int cy) {
   SetWindowPos(GetDlgItem(hwnd, IDC_LISTBOX), NULL, 0, 0,
      cx, cy, SWP_NOZORDER);
}


//////////////////////////////////////////////////////////////


BOOL Dlg_OnInitDialog (HWND hwnd, HWND hwndFocus,
   LPARAM lParam) {

   HWND hWndLB = GetDlgItem(hwnd, IDC_LISTBOX);
   PVOID pvAddress = 0x00000000;
   TCHAR szLine[200];
   RECT rc;
   DWORD dwBlock;
   VMQUERY VMQ;
   BOOL fOk = TRUE;

     // Associate an icon with the dialog box.
   SetClassLong(hwnd, GCL_HICON, (LONG)
      LoadIcon((HINSTANCE) GetWindowLong(hwnd, GWL_HINSTANCE),
      __TEXT("VMMap")));

   // Make a horizontal scroll bar appear in the list box.
   ListBox_SetHorizontalExtent(hWndLB,
      150 * LOWORD(GetDialogBaseUnits()));

   // The list box must be sized first because the system
   // doesn't send a WM_SIZE message to the dialog box when
   // it's first created.
   GetClientRect(hwnd, &rc);
   SetWindowPos(hWndLB, NULL, 0, 0, rc.right, rc.bottom,
      SWP_NOZORDER);

   // Walk the virtual address space, adding
   // entries to the list box.
   while (fOk) {
      fOk = VMQuery(pvAddress, &VMQ);
```

(continued)

Figure 5-4. *continued*

```
        if (fOk) {
            // Construct the line to be displayed, and
            // add it to the list box.
            ConstructRgnInfoLine(&VMQ, szLine, sizeof(szLine));
            ListBox_AddString(hWndLB, szLine);

#if 1

            // Change the 1 above to a 0 if you do not want
            // to see the blocks contained within the region.

            for (dwBlock = 0; fOk && (dwBlock < VMQ.dwRgnBlocks);
                dwBlock++) {

                ConstructBlkInfoLine(&VMQ, szLine, sizeof(szLine));
                ListBox_AddString(hWndLB, szLine);

                // Get the address of the next region to test.
                pvAddress = ((BYTE *) pvAddress + VMQ.dwBlkSize);
                if (dwBlock < VMQ.dwRgnBlocks - 1) {
                    // Don't query the memory info after
                    // the last block.
                    fOk = VMQuery(pvAddress, &VMQ);
                }
            }
#endif

            // Get the address of the next region to test.
            pvAddress = ((BYTE *) VMQ.pvRgnBaseAddress +
                VMQ.dwRgnSize);
        }
    }

#if COPYTOCLIPBOARD
    CopyControlToClipboard(hWndLB);
#endif
    return(TRUE);
}


//////////////////////////////////////////////////////////////////


void Dlg_OnCommand (HWND hwnd, int id, HWND hwndCtl,
    UINT codeNotify) {
```

(continued)

Figure 5-4. *continued*

```
    switch (id) {
       case IDCANCEL:
          EndDialog(hwnd, id);
          break;
    }
}


//////////////////////////////////////////////////////////////////


BOOL CALLBACK Dlg_Proc (HWND hDlg, UINT uMsg,
   WPARAM wParam, LPARAM lParam) {

   BOOL fProcessed = TRUE;
   switch (uMsg) {
      HANDLE_MSG(hDlg, WM_INITDIALOG, Dlg_OnInitDialog);
      HANDLE_MSG(hDlg, WM_COMMAND, Dlg_OnCommand);
      HANDLE_MSG(hDlg, WM_SIZE, Dlg_OnSize);

      default:
         fProcessed = FALSE;
         break;
   }
   return(fProcessed);
}


//////////////////////////////////////////////////////////////////


int WINAPI WinMain (HINSTANCE hinstExe,
   HINSTANCE hinstPrev, LPSTR lpszCmdLine, int nCmdShow) {

   DialogBox(hinstExe, MAKEINTRESOURCE(IDD_VMMAP),
      NULL, Dlg_Proc);
   return(0);
}


///////////////////////// End Of File /////////////////////////
```

(continued)

Figure 5-4. *continued*

```
VMMAP.RC
//Microsoft Visual C++ generated resource script.
//
#include "Resource.h"

#define APSTUDIO_READONLY_SYMBOLS

/////////////////////////////////////////////////////////////////////////
//
// Generated from the TEXTINCLUDE 2 resource.
//
#include "afxres.h"

/////////////////////////////////////////////////////////////////////////
#undef APSTUDIO_READONLY_SYMBOLS

#ifdef APSTUDIO_INVOKED
/////////////////////////////////////////////////////////////////////////
//
// TEXTINCLUDE
//

1 TEXTINCLUDE DISCARDABLE
BEGIN
    "Resource.h\0"
END

2 TEXTINCLUDE DISCARDABLE
BEGIN
    "#include ""afxres.h""\r\n"
    "\0"
END

3 TEXTINCLUDE DISCARDABLE
BEGIN
    "\r\n"
    "\0"
END

/////////////////////////////////////////////////////////////////////////
#endif    // APSTUDIO_INVOKED
```

(continued)

Figure 5-4. *continued*

```
////////////////////////////////////////////////////////////
//
// Dialog
//


IDD_VMMAP DIALOG DISCARDABLE  10, 18, 250, 250
STYLE WS_MINIMIZEBOX : WS_MAXIMIZEBOX : WS_POPUP : WS_VISIBLE
    : WS_CAPTION : WS_SYSMENU : WS_THICKFRAME
CAPTION "Virtual Memory Map"
FONT 8, "Courier"
BEGIN
    LISTBOX             IDC_LISTBOX,0,0,0,0,NOT LBS_NOTIFY
                        : LBS_NOINTEGRALHEIGHT : NOT WS_BORDER
                        : WS_VSCROLL : WS_HSCROLL : WS_GROUP
                        : WS_TABSTOP
END



////////////////////////////////////////////////////////////
//
// Icon
//


VMMap                  ICON    DISCARDABLE    "VMMap.Ico"

#ifndef APSTUDIO_INVOKED
////////////////////////////////////////////////////////////
//
// Generated from the TEXTINCLUDE 3 resource.
//



////////////////////////////////////////////////////////////
#endif    // not APSTUDIO_INVOKED
```

USING VIRTUAL MEMORY IN YOUR OWN APPLICATIONS

Win32 offers the following three mechanisms for manipulating memory:

- Virtual memory, which is best for managing large arrays of objects or structures

- Memory-mapped files, which are best for managing large streams of data (usually from files) and for sharing data between multiple processes

- Heaps, which are best for managing large numbers of small objects

In this chapter, we discuss the first method, virtual memory. The other two methods, memory-mapped files and heaps, are discussed in Chapter 7 and Chapter 8, respectively.

The Win32 functions for manipulating virtual memory allow you to directly reserve a region of address space, commit physical storage (from the paging file) to the region, and set your own protection attributes.

Reserving a Region in an Address Space

You reserve a region in your process's address space by calling *VirtualAlloc*:

```
LPVOID VirtualAlloc(LPVOID lpAddress, DWORD cbSize,
    DWORD fdwAllocationType, DWORD fdwProtect);
```

The first parameter, *lpAddress*, contains a memory address specifying where you would like the system to reserve the address space. Most of the time, you'll pass NULL as the *lpAddress* parameter. This tells *VirtualAlloc* that the system, which keeps a record of free address ranges, should reserve the region wherever it sees fit. The system can reserve a region from anywhere in your process's address space—there are no guarantees that the system will allocate regions from the bottom of your address space up or vice versa. However, you can have some say over this by using the MEM_TOP_DOWN flag, discussed later.

For most programmers, the ability to choose a specific memory address where a region will be reserved is a new concept. When you allocated memory in the past, the operating system simply found a block of memory large enough to satisfy the request, allocated the block, and returned its address. But because each Win32 process has its own address space, you can actually specify the base memory address where you would like the operating system to reserve the region.

For example, say that you want to allocate a region starting 50 MB into your process's address space. In this case, you will pass 52,428,800 (50 × 1024 × 1024) as the *lpAddress* parameter. If there is a free region large enough to satisfy your request at this memory address, the system will reserve the desired region and return. If a free region does not exist at the specified address, or if the free region is not large enough, the system cannot satisfy your request and *VirtualAlloc* returns NULL.

Under Windows 95, you can attempt to reserve a region only in the 0x00400000 through 0x7FFFFFFF partition of a process's address space. An attempt to reserve a region in any other partition will fail, causing *VirtualAlloc* to return NULL.

Under Windows NT, you can attempt to reserve a region only in the 0x00010000 through 0x7FFEFFFF partition of a process's address space. An attempt to reserve a region in any other partition will fail, causing *VirtualAlloc* to return NULL.

As mentioned in Chapter 4, regions are always reserved on an allocation granularity boundary (64 KB for all implementations of Win32 to date). So if you attempt to reserve a region starting at address 19,668,992 (300 × 65,536 + 8192) in your process's address space, the system rounds that address down to an even multiple of 64 KB and will actually reserve the region starting at address 19,660,800 (300 × 65,536).

If *VirtualAlloc* can satisfy your request, it returns a value indicating the base address of the reserved region. If you passed a specific address as *VirtualAlloc*'s *lpAddress* parameter, this return value is the same value that you passed to *VirtualAlloc* rounded down (if necessary) to an even 64-KB boundary.

VirtualAlloc's second parameter, *cbSize*, specifies the size of the region you want to reserve in bytes. Because the system must always reserve regions in multiples of the CPU's page size, an attempt to reserve a region that spans 79 KB will actually result in reserving a region that spans 80 KB on machines that use either 4-KB or 8-KB pages.

VirtualAlloc's third parameter, *fdwAllocationType*, tells the system whether you want to reserve a region or commit physical storage. (This distinction is necessary because *VirtualAlloc* is also used to commit physical storage.) To reserve a region of address space, you must pass the MEM_RESERVE identifier as the value for the *fdwAllocationType* parameter.

If you're going to reserve a region that you don't expect to release for a long time, you might want to reserve the region at the highest memory address possible. That way, the region does not get reserved from the middle of your process's address space, where it can potentially cause fragmentation. If you want the system to reserve a region at the highest possible memory address, you must pass NULL for the *lpAddress* parameter and you must also bitwise OR the MEM_TOP_DOWN flag with the MEM_RESERVE flag when calling *VirtualAlloc*.

> Under Windows 95, the MEM_TOP_DOWN flag is ignored.

The last parameter, *fdwProtect*, indicates the protection attribute that should be assigned to the region. The protection attribute associated with the region has no effect on the committed storage mapped to the region. Regardless of the protection attribute assigned to a region, if no physical storage is committed, any attempt to access a memory address in the range will cause the thread to raise an access violation. This is identical to what happens if you reserve and commit storage to a region using the PAGE_NOACCESS flag.

When reserving a region, assign the protection attribute that will be used most often with the storage committed to the region. For example, if you intend to commit physical storage with a protection attribute of PAGE_READWRITE, you should reserve the region with PAGE_READWRITE. The internal record keeping of the system behaves more efficiently when the region's protection attribute matches the committed storage's protection attribute.

You can use any of the following protection attributes: PAGE-_NOACCESS, PAGE_READWRITE, PAGE_READONLY, PAGE_EXE-CUTE, PAGE_EXECUTE_READ, or PAGE_EXECUTE_READWRITE. However, you cannot specify either the PAGE_WRITECOPY or the PAGE_EXECUTE_WRITECOPY attribute. If you do so, *VirtualAlloc* will not reserve the region and will return NULL. Also, you cannot use either of the protection attribute flags PAGE_GUARD or PAGE_NOCACHE when reserving regions—they can be used only with committed storage.

Windows 95 supports only the PAGE_NOACCESS, PAGE_READONLY, and PAGE_READWRITE protection attributes. Attempting to reserve a region using PAGE_EXECUTE or PAGE_EXECUTE_READ results in a region with PAGE_READONLY protection. Likewise, reserving a region using PAGE_EXECUTE_READWRITE results in a region with PAGE_READWRITE protection.

Committing Storage in a Reserved Region

After you have reserved a region, you will need to commit physical storage to the region before you can access the memory addresses contained within it. The system allocates physical storage committed to a region from the system's paging file on your hard disk. Physical storage is committed on page boundaries and in page-size chunks.

To commit physical storage, you must call *VirtualAlloc* again. This time, however, you'll pass the MEM_COMMIT identifier instead of the MEM_RESERVE identifier for the *fdwAllocationType* parameter. You usually pass the same page protection attribute that was used when *VirtualAlloc* was called to reserve the region, although you can specify a different protection attribute.

From within the reserved region, you must tell *VirtualAlloc* where you want to commit physical storage and how much physical storage to commit. You do this by specifying the desired memory address in the *lpAddress* parameter and the amount of physical storage, in bytes, in the *cbSize* parameter. Note that you don't have to commit physical storage to the entire region at one time.

Let's look at an example of how to commit memory. Say your application is running on an Intel *x86* CPU and the application reserves a 512-KB region starting at address 5,242,880. Now you would like your application to commit storage to the 6-KB portion of the reserved region starting 2 KB into the reserved region's address space. To do this, call *VirtualAlloc* using the MEM_COMMIT flag as follows:

```
VirtualAlloc(5242880 + (2 * 1024), 6 * 1024,
   MEM_COMMIT, PAGE_READWRITE);
```

In this case, the system must commit 8 KB of physical storage, spanning the address range 5,242,880 through 5,251,072 (5,242,880 + 8 KB). Both of these committed pages have a protection attribute of PAGE_READWRITE. Protection attributes are assigned on a whole-page basis only. It is not possible to use different protection attributes for portions of the same page of storage. However, it is possible for one page in a region to have one protection attribute (such as PAGE_READWRITE) and for another page in the same region to have a different protection attribute (such as PAGE_READONLY).

Reserving a Region and Committing Storage Simultaneously

There will be times when you'll want to reserve a region and commit storage to it simultaneously. You can do this by placing a single call to *VirtualAlloc* as follows:

```
PVOID pvMem = VirtualAlloc(NULL, 99 * 1024,
   MEM_RESERVE | MEM_COMMIT, PAGE_READWRITE);
```

This call is a request to reserve a 99-KB region and commit 99 KB of physical storage to the region. When the system processes this call, it first searches your process's address space to find a contiguous area of unreserved address space large enough to hold 100 KB (on a 4-KB page machine) or 104 KB (on an 8-KB page machine).

The system searches the address space because you specified NULL as the *lpAddress* parameter. If you had specified a memory address for *lpAddress*, the system would see whether there was enough unreserved address space at that memory address. If the system could not find enough unreserved address space, *VirtualAlloc* would return NULL.

If a suitable region can be reserved, the system then commits 100 KB (on a 4-KB page machine) or 104 KB (on an 8-KB page machine) of physical storage to the region. Both the region and the committed storage will be assigned PAGE_READWRITE protection.

Finally, *VirtualAlloc* returns the virtual address of the reserved and committed region, which is then saved in the *pvMem* variable. If the system couldn't find a large enough address space or commit the physical storage, *VirtualAlloc* returns NULL.

It is certainly possible when reserving a region and committing physical storage this way to pass a specific address as the *lpvAddress* parameter to *VirtualAlloc*. Or you might need to have the system select a suitable region toward the top of your process's address space by ORing the MEM_TOP_DOWN flag to the *fdwAllocationType* parameter and passing NULL for the *lpAddress* parameter.

When to Commit Physical Storage

Let's pretend you're implementing a spreadsheet application that supports 200 rows by 256 columns. For each cell, you need a CELLDATA structure that describes the contents of the cell. The easiest way for you to manipulate the two-dimensional matrix of cells would be to declare the following variable in your application:

```
CELLDATA CellData[200][256];
```

If the size of a CELLDATA structure were 128 bytes, it would require 6,553,600 ($200 \times 256 \times 128$) bytes of physical storage. That's a lot of physical storage to allocate from the paging file right up front for a spreadsheet, especially when you consider that most users put information into only a few spreadsheet cells, leaving the majority unused. The matrix would be very inefficient.

So, historically, spreadsheets have been implemented using other data structure techniques, such as linked lists. With the linked-list approach, CELLDATA structures have to be created only for the cells in the spreadsheet that actually contain data. Since most cells in a spreadsheet go unused, this method saves a tremendous amount of storage. However, this technique makes it much more difficult to obtain the contents of a cell. If you want to know the contents of the cell in row 5, column 10, you must walk through linked lists in order to find the desired cell, which makes the linked-list method slower than the declared-matrix method.

Virtual memory offers a compromise between declaring the two-dimensional matrix up front and implementing linked lists. With virtual memory, you get the fast, easy access offered by the declared-matrix technique combined with the superior storage savings offered by the linked-list technique.

For you to obtain the advantages of the virtual memory technique, your program needs to do the following:

1. Reserve a region large enough to contain the entire matrix of CELLDATA structures. Reserving a region requires no physical storage at all.

2. When the user enters data into a cell, locate the memory address in the reserved region where the CELLDATA structure should go. There is, of course, no physical storage mapped to this address yet, so any attempts to access memory at this address will raise an access violation.

3. Commit just enough physical storage to the memory address located in step 2 for a CELLDATA structure. (You can tell the system to commit physical storage to specific parts of the reserved region—a region can contain both parts that are mapped to physical storage and parts that are not.)

4. Set the members of the new CELLDATA structure.

Now that physical storage is mapped to the proper location, your program can access the storage without raising an access violation. This virtual memory technique is excellent because physical storage is committed only as the user enters data into the spreadsheet's cells. Because most of the cells in a spreadsheet are empty, most of the reserved region will not have physical storage committed to it.

The one problem with the virtual memory technique is that you must determine when physical storage needs to be committed. If the user enters data into a cell and then simply edits or changes that data, there is no need to commit physical storage—the storage for the cell's CELLDATA structure was committed the first time data was entered.

Also, the system always commits physical storage with page granularity (4 KB on $x86$, MIPS, and PowerPC; 8 KB on Alpha). So when you attempt to commit physical storage for a single CELLDATA structure (as in step 2 on the previous page), the system is actually committing a full page of storage. This is not as wasteful as it sounds: committing storage for a single CELLDATA structure has the effect of committing storage for other nearby CELLDATA structures. If the user then enters data into a neighboring cell, which is frequently the case, you might not need to commit additional physical storage.

There are four methods for determining whether to commit physical storage to a portion of a region:

- Always attempt to commit physical storage. Instead of checking to see whether physical storage is mapped to a portion of the region, have your program try to commit storage every time it calls *VirtualAlloc*. The system first checks to see whether storage has already been committed and, if so, does not commit additional physical storage. This is the easiest approach but has the disadvantage of making an additional function call every time a CELLDATA structure is altered, which makes your program perform more slowly.

- Determine (using the *VirtualQuery* function) whether physical storage has already been committed to the address space containing the CELLDATA structure. If it has, do nothing else; if it hasn't, call *VirtualAlloc* to commit the memory. This is actually worse than the first method; it both increases the size of your code and slows down your program because of the additional call to *VirtualQuery*.

- Keep a record of which pages have been committed and which haven't. Doing so makes your application run faster: you avoid the call to *VirtualAlloc*, and your code can determine more quickly than the system whether storage has already been committed. The disadvantage is that you must keep track of the page commit information somehow, which could be either very simple or very difficult depending on your specific situation.

- The best method takes advantage of structured exception handling (SEH). SEH is a Win32 feature that causes the system to notify your application when certain situations occur. Essentially, you set up your application with an exception handler, and then, whenever an attempt is made to access uncommitted memory, the system notifies your application of the problem. Your application then commits the memory and tells the system to retry the instruction that caused the exception. This time, the memory access succeeds, and the program continues running as though there had never been a problem. This is the best method because it requires the least amount of work from you (meaning less code) and because your program will run at full speed. A complete discussion of the SEH mechanism is saved for Chapter 14 in this book.

Decommitting Physical Storage and Releasing a Region

To decommit physical storage mapped to a region or release an entire region of address space, call the *VirtualFree* function:

```
BOOL VirtualFree(LPVOID lpAddress, DWORD cbSize,
    DWORD fdwFreeType);
```

Let's examine the simple case of calling *VirtualFree* first to release a reserved region. When your process will no longer be accessing the physical storage within a region, you can release the reserved region, and all the physical storage committed to the region, by making a single call to *VirtualFree*.

For this call, the *lpAddress* parameter must be the base address of the region. This would be the same address that *VirtualAlloc* returned when the region was reserved. The system knows the size of the region at the specified memory address, so you can pass 0 for the *cbSize* parameter. In fact, you must pass 0 for the *cbSize* parameter, or the call to *VirtualFree* will fail. For the third parameter, *fdwFreeType*, you must pass MEM_RE-LEASE to tell the system to decommit all physical storage mapped to the region and to release the region. When releasing a region, you must release all the address space that was reserved by the region. For example, you cannot reserve a 500-MB region and then decide to release only 200 MB of it. All 500 MB must be released.

When you want to decommit some physical storage from the region without releasing the region, you also call *VirtualFree*. To decommit some physical storage, you must pass the memory address that identifies the first page to be decommitted in *VirtualFree*'s *lpAddress* parameter. You must also specify the number of bytes to free in the *cbSize* parameter and the MEM_DECOMMIT identifier in the *fdwFreeType* parameter.

Like committing, decommitting is done with page granularity. That is, specifying a memory address in the middle of a page decommits the entire page. And, of course, if *lpAddress* + *cbSize* falls in the middle of a page, the whole page that contains this address is decommitted as well. So all pages that fall within the range of *lpAddress* to *lpAddress* + *cbSize* are decommitted.

If *cbSize* is 0 and *lpAddress* is the base address for the allocated region, *VirtualFree* will decommit the complete range of allocated pages. After the pages of physical storage have been decommitted, the freed physical storage is available to any other process in the system; any attempt to access the decommitted memory results in an access violation.

When to Decommit Physical Storage

In practice, knowing when it's OK to decommit memory is a very tricky thing. Consider the spreadsheet example again. If your application is running on an Intel *x*86 machine, each page of storage is 4 KB and can hold 32 (4096 / 128) CELLDATA structures. If the user deletes the contents of *CellData[0][1]*, you might be able to decommit the page of storage as long as cells *CellData[0][0]* through *CellData[0][31]* are also not in use. But how do you know? There are many different ways to tackle this problem.

- Without a doubt, the easiest solution is to design a CELLDATA structure that is exactly 1 page in size. Then, because there is always one structure per page, you can simply decommit the page of physical storage when you don't need the data in the structure any longer. Even if your data structures were multiples of a page, say, 8 KB or 12 KB for Intel CPUs (these would be unusually large structures), decommitting memory would still be pretty easy. Of course, to use this method you must define your data structures to meet the page size of the CPU you're targeting—not how we usually write our programs.

- A more practical solution is to keep a record of which structures are in use. To save memory, you might use a bitmap. So if you have an array of 100 structures, you also maintain an array of 100 bits. Initially, all the bits are set to 0, indicating that no structures are in use. As you use the structures, you set the corresponding bits to 1. Then, whenever you don't need a structure and change its bit back to 0, you check the bits of the adjacent structures that fall into the same page of memory. If none of the adjacent structures is in use, you can decommit the page.

■ The last solution implements a garbage collection function. This scheme relies on the fact that the system sets all the bytes in a page to 0 when physical storage is first committed. To use this scheme, you must first set aside a BOOL (perhaps called *fInUse*) in your structure. Then, every time you put a structure in committed memory, you need to ensure that *fInUse* is set to TRUE.

As your application runs, you'll want to call the garbage collection function periodically. This function should traverse all the potential data structures. For each structure, the function first determines whether storage is committed for the structure; if so, the function checks the *fInUse* member to see whether it is 0. A value of 0 means that the structure is not in use, while a value of TRUE means that it is in use. After the garbage collection function has checked all the structures that fall within a given page, it calls *VirtualFree* to decommit the storage if all the structures are not in use.

You can call the garbage collection function immediately after a structure is no longer considered in use, but doing so might take more time than you want to spend because the function cycles through all the possible structures. An excellent way to implement this function is to have it run as part of a lower-priority thread. In this way, you don't take time away from the thread executing the main application. Whenever the main application is idle or the main application's thread is performing file I/O, the system can schedule time to the garbage collection function.

Of all the methods listed above, the first two are my personal favorites. However, if your structures are not big (less than a page), I recommend using the last method.

The Virtual Memory Allocation Sample Application

The VMAlloc application (VMALLOC.EXE), listed in Figure 6-1 beginning on page 182, demonstrates how to use virtual memory techniques for manipulating an array of structures. The source code files, resource files, and make file for the application are in the VMALLOC.06 directory on the companion disc. When you start the program, the following window appears:

Initially, no region of address space has been reserved for the array, and all the address space that would be reserved for it is free, as shown by the memory map. When you click the Reserve A Region For 50 Structures, 2 KB Each button, VMAlloc calls *VirtualAlloc* to reserve the region, and the memory map is updated to reflect this. After *VirtualAlloc* reserves the region, the remaining buttons become active.

You can now type an index into the edit control or use the scroll bar to select an index, and then click on the Use button. This has the effect of committing physical storage to the memory address where the array element is to be placed. When a page of storage is committed, the memory map is redrawn to reflect the state of the reserved region for the entire array. So if, after reserving the region, you use the Use button to mark array elements 7 and 46 as *in use*, the window will look like the window on the facing page (when you are running the program on a 4-KB page machine).

Any element that is marked as *in use* can be cleared by clicking on the Clear button. But doing so does not decommit the physical storage mapped to the array element. This is because each page contains room for multiple structures—just because one is clear doesn't mean the others are too. If the memory was decommitted, the data in the other structures would be lost. Because selecting Clear doesn't affect the region's physical storage, the memory map is not updated when an array element is cleared.

However, when a structure is cleared, its *fInUse* member is set to FALSE. This is necessary so that the garbage collection routine can make its pass over all the structures and decommit storage that's no longer in use. If you haven't guessed it by now, the Garbage Collect button tells VMAlloc to execute its garbage collection routine. To keep things simple, I have not implemented the garbage collection function as its own thread.

To demonstrate the garbage collection function, clear the array element at index 46. Notice that the memory map does not change. Now click on the Garbage Collect button. The program decommits the page of storage containing element 46, and the memory map is updated to reflect this:

Finally, even though there is no visual display to inform you, all the committed memory is decommitted and the reserved region is freed when the window is destroyed.

There is another element to this program that I haven't described yet. The program needs to determine the state of memory in the region's address space in three places:

■ After changing the index, the program needs to enable the Use button and disable the Clear button or vice versa.

■ In the garbage collection function, the program needs to see whether storage is committed before actually testing to see whether the *fInUse* flag is set.

■ When updating the memory map, the program needs to know which pages are free, reserved, and committed.

VMAlloc performs all these tests by calling the *VirtualQuery* function, discussed in the previous chapter.

VMAlloc.ico

```
VMALLOC.C
/************************************************************
Module name: VMAlloc.C
Notices: Copyright (c) 1995 Jeffrey Richter
*************************************************************/


#include "..\AdvWin32.H"        /* See Appendix B for details.*/
#include <windows.h>
#include <windowsx.h>

#pragma warning(disable: 4001)         /* Single-line comment */

#include <tchar.h>
#include <stdio.h>                  // For sprintf
#include "Resource.H"



///////////////////////////////////////////////////////////////


UINT g_uPageSize = 0;
```

Figure 6-1. *(continued)*
The VMAlloc sample application.

Figure 6-1. *continued*

```
typedef struct {
   BOOL fAllocated;
   BYTE bOtherData[2048 - sizeof(BOOL)];
} SOMEDATA, *PSOMEDATA;

#define MAX_SOMEDATA    (50)
PSOMEDATA g_pSomeData = NULL;

RECT g_rcMemMap;


///////////////////////////////////////////////////////////////////


BOOL Dlg_OnInitDialog (HWND hwnd, HWND hwndFocus,
   LPARAM lParam) {

   TCHAR szBuf[10];

   // Associate an icon with the dialog box.
   SetClassLong(hwnd, GCL_HICON, (LONG)
      LoadIcon((HINSTANCE) GetWindowLong(hwnd, GWL_HINSTANCE),
      __TEXT("VMAlloc")));

   // Initialize the dialog box by disabling all
   // the nonsetup controls.
   EnableWindow(GetDlgItem(hwnd, IDC_INDEXTEXT), FALSE);
   EnableWindow(GetDlgItem(hwnd, IDC_INDEX), FALSE);
   ScrollBar_SetRange(GetDlgItem(hwnd, IDC_INDEXSCRL),
      0, MAX_SOMEDATA - 1, FALSE);
   ScrollBar_SetPos(GetDlgItem(hwnd, IDC_INDEXSCRL), 0,TRUE);
   EnableWindow(GetDlgItem(hwnd, IDC_INDEXSCRL), FALSE);
   EnableWindow(GetDlgItem(hwnd, IDC_USE), FALSE);
   EnableWindow(GetDlgItem(hwnd, IDC_CLEAR), FALSE);
   EnableWindow(GetDlgItem(hwnd, IDC_GARBAGECOLLECT), FALSE);

   // Get the coordinates of the memory map display.
   GetWindowRect(GetDlgItem(hwnd, IDC_MEMMAP), &g_rcMemMap);
   MapWindowPoints(NULL, hwnd, (LPPOINT) &g_rcMemMap, 2);

   // Destroy the temporary window that identifies the
   // location of the memory map display.
   DestroyWindow(GetDlgItem(hwnd, IDC_MEMMAP));
```

(continued)

183

Figure 6-1. *continued*

```
        // Put the page size in the dialog box
        // for the user's information.
        _stprintf(szBuf, __TEXT("%dKB"), g_uPageSize / 1024);
        SetDlgItemText(hwnd, IDC_PAGESIZE, szBuf);

        // Initialize the edit control.
        SetDlgItemInt(hwnd, IDC_INDEX, 0, FALSE);

        return(TRUE);
}


///////////////////////////////////////////////////////////////


void Dlg_OnDestroy (HWND hwnd) {
    if (g_pSomeData != NULL)
        VirtualFree(g_pSomeData, 0, MEM_RELEASE);
}


///////////////////////////////////////////////////////////////


void Dlg_OnCommand (HWND hwnd, int id, HWND hwndCtl,
    UINT codeNotify) {

    UINT uIndex, uIndexLast, uPage, uMaxPages;
    BOOL fTranslated, fOk, fAnyAllocs;
    MEMORY_BASIC_INFORMATION MemoryBasicInfo;

    switch (id) {
        case IDC_RESERVE:
            // Reserve enough address space to hold MAX_SOMEDATA
            // SOMEDATA structures.
            g_pSomeData = (PSOMEDATA) VirtualAlloc(NULL,
                MAX_SOMEDATA * sizeof(SOMEDATA), MEM_RESERVE,
                PAGE_READWRITE);

            // Disable the Reserve button and
            // enable all the other controls.
            EnableWindow(GetDlgItem(hwnd, IDC_RESERVE), FALSE);
            EnableWindow(GetDlgItem(hwnd, IDC_INDEXTEXT), TRUE);
            EnableWindow(GetDlgItem(hwnd, IDC_INDEX), TRUE);
```

(continued)

Figure 6-1. *continued*

```
      EnableWindow(GetDlgItem(hwnd, IDC_INDEXSCRL), TRUE);
      EnableWindow(GetDlgItem(hwnd, IDC_USE), TRUE);
      EnableWindow(GetDlgItem(hwnd, IDC_GARBAGECOLLECT),
         TRUE);

      // Force the index edit control to have the focus.
      SetFocus(GetDlgItem(hwnd, IDC_INDEX));

      // Invalidate the memory map display.
      InvalidateRect(hwnd, &g_rcMemMap, FALSE);
      break;

   case IDC_INDEX:
      if (codeNotify != EN_CHANGE)
         break;

      uIndex = GetDlgItemInt(hwnd, id, &fTranslated,
         FALSE);
      if ((g_pSomeData == NULL) ||
         (uIndex >= MAX_SOMEDATA)) {
         // If the index is out of range, assume the
         // translation was unsuccessful.
         fTranslated = FALSE;
      }

      if (fTranslated) {
         VirtualQuery(&g_pSomeData[uIndex],
            &MemoryBasicInfo, sizeof(MemoryBasicInfo));
         fOk = (MemoryBasicInfo.State == MEM_COMMIT);
         if (fOk)
            fOk = g_pSomeData[uIndex].fAllocated;

         EnableWindow(GetDlgItem(hwnd, IDC_USE),  !fOk);
         EnableWindow(GetDlgItem(hwnd, IDC_CLEAR), fOk);
         ScrollBar_SetPos(GetDlgItem(hwnd, IDC_INDEXSCRL),
            uIndex, TRUE);

      } else {
         EnableWindow(GetDlgItem(hwnd, IDC_USE,   FALSE);
         EnableWindow(GetDlgItem(hwnd, IDC_CLEAR, FALSE);
      }
      break;
```

(continued)

Figure 6-1. *continued*

```
case IDC_USE:
    uIndex = GetDlgItemInt(hwnd, IDC_INDEX, &fTranslated,
        FALSE);

    if (uIndex >= MAX_SOMEDATA) {
        // If the index is out of range, assume the
        // translation was unsuccessful.
        fTranslated = FALSE;
    }

    if (fTranslated) {
        VirtualAlloc(&g_pSomeData[uIndex],
            sizeof(SOMEDATA), MEM_COMMIT, PAGE_READWRITE);

        // When pages are committed, Windows NT ensures
        // that they are zeroed.
        g_pSomeData[uIndex].fAllocated = TRUE;

        EnableWindow(GetDlgItem(hwnd, IDC_USE),   FALSE);
        EnableWindow(GetDlgItem(hwnd, IDC_CLEAR), TRUE);

        // Force the Clear button control to
        // have the focus.
        SetFocus(GetDlgItem(hwnd, IDC_CLEAR));

        // Invalidate the memory map display.
        InvalidateRect(hwnd, &g_rcMemMap, FALSE);
    }
    break;

case IDC_CLEAR:
    uIndex = GetDlgItemInt(hwnd, IDC_INDEX, &fTranslated,
        FALSE);

    if (uIndex >= MAX_SOMEDATA) {
        // If the index is out of range, assume the
        // translation was unsuccessful.
        fTranslated = FALSE;
    }

    if (fTranslated) {
        g_pSomeData[uIndex].fAllocated = FALSE;
        EnableWindow(GetDlgItem(hwnd, IDC_USE),   TRUE);
        EnableWindow(GetDlgItem(hwnd, IDC_CLEAR), FALSE);
```

(continued)

Figure 6-1. *continued*

```
            // Force the Use button control to have the focus.
            SetFocus(GetDlgItem(hwnd, IDC_USE));
        }
        break;

    case IDC_GARBAGECOLLECT:
        uMaxPages = MAX_SOMEDATA * sizeof(SOMEDATA) /
            g_uPageSize;

        for (uPage = 0; uPage < uMaxPages; uPage++) {
            fAnyAllocs = FALSE;

            uIndex = uPage * g_uPageSize / sizeof(SOMEDATA);

            uIndexLast = uIndex + g_uPageSize /
                sizeof(SOMEDATA);

            for (; uIndex < uIndexLast; uIndex++) {
                VirtualQuery(&g_pSomeData[uIndex],
                    &MemoryBasicInfo, sizeof(MemoryBasicInfo));

                if ((MemoryBasicInfo.State == MEM_COMMIT) &&
                    g_pSomeData[uIndex].fAllocated) {

                    fAnyAllocs = TRUE;
                    break;
                }
            }

            if (!fAnyAllocs) {
                // No allocated structures exist in the page.
                // We can safely decommit it.
                VirtualFree(&g_pSomeData[uIndexLast - 1],
                    sizeof(SOMEDATA), MEM_DECOMMIT);
            }
        }

        // Invalidate the memory map display.
        InvalidateRect(hwnd, &g_rcMemMap, FALSE);
        break;

    case IDCANCEL:
        EndDialog(hwnd, id);
        break;
    }
}
```

(continued)

Figure 6-1. *continued*

```
///////////////////////////////////////////////////////////////

void Dlg_OnHScroll (HWND hwnd, HWND hwndCtl,
   UINT code, int pos) {

   INT nScrlPos;
   if (hwndCtl != GetDlgItem(hwnd, IDC_INDEXSCRL))
      return;

   nScrlPos = ScrollBar_GetPos(hwndCtl);
   switch (code) {
      case SB_LINELEFT:
         nScrlPos--;
         break;

      case SB_LINERIGHT:
         nScrlPos++;
         break;

      case SB_PAGELEFT:
         nScrlPos -= g_uPageSize / sizeof(SOMEDATA);
         break;

      case SB_PAGERIGHT:
         nScrlPos += g_uPageSize / sizeof(SOMEDATA);
         break;

      case SB_THUMBTRACK:
         nScrlPos = pos;
         break;

      case SB_LEFT:
         nScrlPos = 0;
         break;

      case SB_RIGHT:
         nScrlPos = MAX_SOMEDATA - 1;
         break;
   }

   if (nScrlPos < 0)
      nScrlPos = 0;
```

(continued)

Figure 6-1. *continued*

```
    if (nScrlPos >= MAX_SOMEDATA)
        nScrlPos = MAX_SOMEDATA - 1;

    ScrollBar_SetPos(hwndCtl, nScrlPos, TRUE);
    SetDlgItemInt(hwnd, IDC_INDEX, nScrlPos, TRUE);
}


///////////////////////////////////////////////////////////////


void Dlg_OnPaint (HWND hwnd) {
    UINT uPage, uIndex, uIndexLast, uMemMapWidth;
    UINT uMaxPages = MAX_SOMEDATA * sizeof(SOMEDATA) /
        g_uPageSize;

    MEMORY_BASIC_INFORMATION MemoryBasicInfo;
    PAINTSTRUCT ps;

    BeginPaint(hwnd, &ps);

    if (g_pSomeData == NULL) {
        // The memory has yet to be reserved.
        Rectangle(ps.hdc, g_rcMemMap.left, g_rcMemMap.top,
            g_rcMemMap.right, g_rcMemMap.bottom);
    }

    // Walk the virtual address space, adding
    // entries to the list box.
    uPage = 0;
    while ((g_pSomeData != NULL) && uPage < uMaxPages) {

        uIndex = uPage * g_uPageSize / sizeof(SOMEDATA);

        uIndexLast = uIndex + g_uPageSize / sizeof(SOMEDATA);

        for (; uIndex < uIndexLast; uIndex++) {

            VirtualQuery(&g_pSomeData[uIndex], &MemoryBasicInfo,
                sizeof(MemoryBasicInfo));
```

(continued)

Figure 6-1. *continued*

```
        switch (MemoryBasicInfo.State) {
            case MEM_FREE:
                SelectObject(ps.hdc,
                    GetStockObject(WHITE_BRUSH));
                break;

            case MEM_RESERVE:
                SelectObject(ps.hdc,
                    GetStockObject(GRAY_BRUSH));
                break;

            case MEM_COMMIT:
                SelectObject(ps.hdc,
                    GetStockObject(BLACK_BRUSH));
                break;
        }

        uMemMapWidth = g_rcMemMap.right - g_rcMemMap.left;
        Rectangle(ps.hdc,
            g_rcMemMap.left +
                uMemMapWidth / uMaxPages * uPage,
            g_rcMemMap.top,
            g_rcMemMap.left +
                uMemMapWidth / uMaxPages * (uPage + 1),
            g_rcMemMap.bottom);

        }

        uPage++;
    }

    EndPaint(hwnd, &ps);
}


//////////////////////////////////////////////////////////////


BOOL CALLBACK Dlg_Proc (HWND hDlg, UINT uMsg,
    WPARAM wParam, LPARAM lParam) {

    BOOL fProcessed = TRUE;
```

(continued)

Figure 6-1. *continued*

```
    switch (uMsg) {
        HANDLE_MSG(hDlg, WM_INITDIALOG,  Dlg_OnInitDialog);
        HANDLE_MSG(hDlg, WM_COMMAND,  Dlg_OnCommand);
        HANDLE_MSG(hDlg, WM_HSCROLL,  Dlg_OnHScroll);
        HANDLE_MSG(hDlg, WM_PAINT,    Dlg_OnPaint);
        HANDLE_MSG(hDlg, WM_DESTROY,  Dlg_OnDestroy);

        default:
           fProcessed = FALSE;
           break;
    }
    return(fProcessed);
}


///////////////////////////////////////////////////////////////


int WINAPI WinMain (HINSTANCE hinstExe,
    HINSTANCE hinstPrev, LPSTR lpszCmdLine, int nCmdShow) {

    SYSTEM_INFO SystemInfo;

    // Get the page size used on this CPU.
    GetSystemInfo(&SystemInfo);
    g_uPageSize = SystemInfo.dwPageSize;

    DialogBox(hinstExe, MAKEINTRESOURCE(IDD_VMALLOC),
        NULL, Dlg_Proc);
    return(0);
}


/////////////////////// End Of File ///////////////////////
```

VMALLOC.RC
```
//Microsoft Visual C++ generated resource script.
//
#include "Resource.h"

#define APSTUDIO_READONLY_SYMBOLS
```

(continued)

Figure 6-1. *continued*

```
///////////////////////////////////////////////////////////
//
// Generated from the TEXTINCLUDE 2 resource.
//
#include "afxres.h"


///////////////////////////////////////////////////////////
#undef APSTUDIO_READONLY_SYMBOLS


#ifdef APSTUDIO_INVOKED
///////////////////////////////////////////////////////////
//
// TEXTINCLUDE
//

1 TEXTINCLUDE DISCARDABLE
BEGIN
    "Resource.h\0"
END

2 TEXTINCLUDE DISCARDABLE
BEGIN
    "#include ""afxres.h""\r\n"
    "\0"
END

3 TEXTINCLUDE DISCARDABLE
BEGIN
    "\r\n"
    "\0"
END


///////////////////////////////////////////////////////////
#endif    // APSTUDIO_INVOKED


///////////////////////////////////////////////////////////
//
// Dialog
//

IDD_VMALLOC DIALOG DISCARDABLE  15, 24, 243, 120
STYLE WS_MINIMIZEBOX | WS_POPUP | WS_VISIBLE | WS_CAPTION
    | WS_SYSMENU
```

(continued)

Figure 6-1. *continued*

```
CAPTION "Virtual Memory Allocator"
FONT 8, "System"
BEGIN
    LTEXT           "CPU page size:",IDC_STATIC,4,4,51,8
    CONTROL         "16 KB",IDC_PAGESIZE,"Static",
                    SS_LEFTNOWORDWRAP | SS_NOPREFIX |
                    WS_GROUP,60,4,32,8
    DEFPUSHBUTTON   "&Reserve a region for 50 structures, 2 KB\
each",
                    IDC_RESERVE,32,16,180,14,WS_GROUP
    LTEXT           "&Index (0 - 49):",IDC_INDEXTEXT,4,38,
                    45,8
    EDITTEXT        IDC_INDEX,56,36,16,12
    SCROLLBAR       IDC_INDEXSCRL,80,38,160,9,WS_TABSTOP
    PUSHBUTTON      "&Use",IDC_USE,4,52,40,14
    PUSHBUTTON      "&Clear",IDC_CLEAR,48,52,40,14
    PUSHBUTTON      "&Garbage collect",IDC_GARBAGECOLLECT,
                    160,52,80,14
    GROUPBOX        "Memory map",IDC_STATIC,4,66,236,52
    CONTROL         "",IDC_MEMMAP,"Static",SS_BLACKRECT,8,82,
                    228,16
    LTEXT           "Free: White",IDC_STATIC,8,104,39,8
    CTEXT           "Reserved: Gray",IDC_STATIC,88,104,52,8
    RTEXT           "Committed: Black",IDC_STATIC,176,104,
                    58,8
END


/////////////////////////////////////////////////////////////
// Icon
//


VMALLOC               ICON    DISCARDABLE    "VMAlloc.Ico"

#ifndef APSTUDIO_INVOKED
/////////////////////////////////////////////////////////////
//
// Generated from the TEXTINCLUDE 3 resource.
//



/////////////////////////////////////////////////////////////
#endif    // not APSTUDIO_INVOKED
```

Changing Protection Attributes

Although it is a very uncommon practice, it is possible to change the protection attributes associated with a page or pages of committed physical storage. For example, say you've developed code to manage a linked list, the nodes of which you are keeping in a reserved region. You could design the functions that process the linked list so that they change the protection attributes of the committed storage to PAGE_READWRITE at the start of each function and then back to PAGE_NOACCESS just before each function terminates.

By doing this, you protect your linked-list data from other bugs hiding in your program. If any other code in your process has a stray pointer that attempts to access your linked-list data, an access violation is raised. This can be incredibly useful when you're trying to locate hard-to-find bugs in your application.

You can alter the protection rights of a page of memory by calling *VirtualProtect*:

```
BOOL VirtualProtect(LPVOID lpAddress, DWORD dwSize,
    DWORD flNewProtect, PDWORD lpflOldProtect);
```

Here *lpAddress* points to the base address of the memory, *dwSize* indicates the number of bytes for which you want to change the protection attribute, and *flNewProtect* can represent any one of the PAGE_* protection attribute identifiers except PAGE_WRITECOPY and PAGE_EXECUTE_WRITECOPY.

The last parameter, *lpflOldProtect*, is the address of a DWORD that *VirtualProtect* will fill in with the old protection attributes for the storage. You must pass a valid address for this parameter, or the function will raise an access violation. If you are changing the protection attribute of more than one page, the DWORD pointed to by *lpflOldProtect* will receive the old protection attribute for the first page only. *VirtualProtect* returns TRUE if it's successful.

Of course, protection attributes are associated with entire pages of storage and cannot be assigned to individual bytes. So if you were to call *VirtualProtect* on a 4-KB page machine as follows:

```
VirtualProtect(lpRgnBase + (3 * 1024), 2 * 1024,
    PAGE_NOACCESS, &flOldProtect);
```

You would end up assigning the PAGE_NOACCESS protection attribute to 2 pages of storage.

The TInjLib sample application, shown in Chapter 16, demonstrates how to use *VirtualProtect* to alter protection attributes on committed storage.

Windows 95 supports only the PAGE_NOACCESS, PAGE_READONLY, and PAGE_READWRITE protection attributes. If you attempt to change a page's protection to PAGE_EXECUTE or PAGE_EXECUTE_READ, the page receives PAGE_READONLY protection. Likewise, if you change a page's protection to PAGE_EXECUTE_READWRITE, the page receives PAGE_READWRITE protection.

Locking Physical Storage in RAM

Remember that committing physical storage is really a matter of allocating space from the system's paging file. However, for your program to actually access its data, the system must locate your program's physical storage in the paging file and load it into RAM. The system has been finely tuned and optimized to perform this page swapping so that applications run very efficiently. However, there are two Win32 functions that allow you to override this process: *VirtualLock* and *VirtualUnlock*.

The *VirtualLock* function tells the system that you want to lock a set of pages in RAM. However, the system guarantees that the pages are locked in RAM only while a thread in your process is running. When the system preempts all the threads in your process, the system is free to unlock the pages and swap them to the physical storage in the paging file. When the system is ready to reschedule a thread in your process, it loads all of the pages that you wanted locked back into RAM. When the locked pages are back in RAM, the system allows the rescheduled thread to continue executing. In this situation, your process takes an immediate performance hit whenever a thread is being rescheduled.

When the system is not running any threads in your process, it does not immediately swap the locked pages to the paging file. Instead, the system tries to keep locked pages in RAM as long as possible. If threads in another process do not make heavy use of the RAM, the system will not need to swap your process's locked pages. In this case, when the system reschedules threads in your process, the locked pages will already be loaded in RAM and the system will not have to access the paging file.

> **Important**
>
> The locking of physical storage into RAM is a feature that Win32 offers for special purposes. For example, many device drivers must respond to events very quickly and cannot afford to wait for the system's paging mechanism to load the physical storage on demand. You are much better off allowing the system to perform the page swapping rather than getting involved with it yourself. After all, only the operating system knows how other applications are behaving and what toll they are taking on the system's memory. The operating system's memory management routines have been fine-tuned for this—let them do their job.
>
> In addition, the locking of physical storage into RAM cannot be used to make your application in any way "realtime" because you cannot lock down all the pages—for system DLLs, device drivers, stack pages, heaps, and so forth—that the system might access while your thread is running. If the system is doing any paging at all, having your application process lock down some of the pages that it knows about will probably make your application *less* realtime by forcing pages of storage that might be accessed even more often out of RAM.

If you still want to lock physical storage in RAM, you need to call *VirtualLock*:

```
BOOL VirtualLock(LPVOID lpvMem, DWORD cbMem);
```

This function locks the *cbMem* bytes starting at address *lpvMem* in RAM. If it is successful, TRUE is returned. It is important to note that all the pages you attempt to lock must be committed physical storage. In addition, *VirtualLock* cannot be used to lock memory allocated with a PAGE_NOACCESS protection attribute. Also, the system will not allow a single process to lock more than approximately 30 pages of storage. This number may seem rather small to you—on an *x*86, this comes to only 122,880 bytes. The reason for this small number is to prevent a single process from greatly affecting the overall performance of the system.

When it is no longer necessary for your application to keep the memory locked, you can unlock it with *VirtualUnlock*:

```
BOOL VirtualUnlock(LPVOID lpvMem, DWORD cbMem);
```

This function unlocks the *cbMem* bytes of memory starting at address *lpvMem*. When you're unlocking memory, it is not necessary to unlock the exact amount that was locked with *VirtualLock*. If the range of memory is unlocked successfully, *VirtualUnlock* returns TRUE.

As with all of the virtual functions, operations are performed on a page basis. So if you lock a range of bytes that straddles a series of pages, all pages affected by the range are locked or unlocked.

> Under Windows 95, the *VirtualLock* and *VirtualUnlock* functions have no useful implementation and simply return FALSE; calling *GetLastError* returns ERROR_CALL_NOT_IMPLEMENTED.

A Thread's Stack

Sometimes the system reserves regions in your own process's address space. I mentioned that this happened for process and thread environment blocks in Chapter 4. Another time that the system does this is for a thread's stack.

Whenever a thread is created in your process, the system reserves a region of address space for the thread's stack (each thread gets its very own stack) and also commits some physical storage to this reserved region. By default, the system reserves 1 MB of address space and commits 2 pages of storage. However, these defaults can be changed by specifying the /STACK option to the linker when you link your application:

```
/STACK:reserve[,commit]
```

When a thread's stack is created, the system reserves a region of address space indicated by the linker's /STACK switch. However, you can override the amount of storage that is initially committed when you call the *CreateThread* or the *_beginthreadex* function. Both functions have a parameter that allows you to override the storage that is initially committed to the stack's address space region. If you specify 0 for this parameter, the system uses the commit size indicated by the /STACK switch. For the remainder of this discussion, I will assume we're using the default stack sizes: 1 MB of reserved region with storage committed in single pages.

Figure 6-2 on the following page shows what a stack region (reserved starting at address 0x08000000) might look like on a machine whose page size is 4 KB. The stack's region and all of the physical storage committed to it have a page protection of PAGE_READWRITE.

Memory Address	State of Page
0x080FF000	Top of stack: committed page
0x080FE000	Committed page with guard protection attribute flag
0x080FD000	Reserved page
0x08003000	Reserved page
0x08002000	Reserved page
0x08001000	Reserved page
0x08000000	Bottom of stack: reserved page

Figure 6-2.
What a thread's stack region looks like when it is first created.

After reserving this region, the system commits physical storage to the top 2 pages of the region. Just before allowing the thread to begin execution, the system sets the thread's stack pointer register to point to the end of the top page of the stack region (an address very close to 0x08100000). This page is where the thread will begin using its stack. The second page from the top is called the guard page. As the thread increases its call tree by calling more functions, the thread needs more stack space.

Whenever the thread attempts to access storage in the guard page, the system is notified. In response, the system commits another page of storage just below the guard page. Then the system removes the guard page protection flag from the current guard page and assigns the guard page protection flag to the newly committed page of storage. This technique allows the stack storage to increase only as the thread requires it. Eventually, if the thread's call tree continues to expand, the stack region will look like Figure 6-3.

Memory Address	State of Page
0x080FF000	Top of stack: committed page
0x080FE000	Committed page
0x080FD000	Committed page
0x08003000	Committed page
0x08002000	Committed page with guard protection attribute flag
0x08001000	Reserved page
0x08000000	Bottom of stack: reserved page

Figure 6-3.
A nearly full thread's stack region.

Referring to Figure 6-3, assume that the thread's call tree is very deep and that the stack pointer CPU register points to the stack memory address 0x08003004. Now, when the thread calls another function, the system has to commit more physical storage. However, when the system commits physical storage to the page at address 0x08001000, it does not do exactly what it did when committing physical storage to the rest of the stack's memory region. Figure 6-4 on the following page shows what the stack's reserved memory region looks like.

Memory Address	State of Page
0x080FF000	Top of stack: committed page
0x080FE000	Committed page
0x080FD000	Committed page
0x08003000	Committed page
0x08002000	Committed page
0x08001000	Committed page
0x08000000	Bottom of stack: reserved page

Figure 6-4.
A full thread stack region.

As you'd expect, the page starting at address 0x08002000 has the guard attribute removed, and physical storage is committed to the page starting at 0x08001000. The difference is that the system does not apply the guard attribute to the new page of physical storage (0x08001000). This means that the stack's reserved address space region contains all the physical storage that it can ever contain. The bottommost page is always reserved and never gets committed. I will explain the reason for this shortly.

The system performs one more action when it commits physical storage to the page at address 0x08001000—it raises an EXCEPTION-_STACK_OVERFLOW exception (defined as 0xC00000FD in WINNT.H). By using Win32 structured exception handling (SEH), your program will be notified of this condition and can recover gracefully. For more information on SEH, see Chapter 14, including the SEHSum application.

If the thread continues to use the stack after the stack overflow exception is raised, all the memory in the page at 0x08001000 will be used and the thread will attempt to access memory in the page starting at 0x08000000. When the thread attempts to access this reserved (uncommitted) memory, the system raises an access violation exception. If this access violation exception is raised while the thread is attempting to access the stack, the thread is in very deep trouble. The system takes control at this point and terminates the process—not just the thread, but the whole process. The system doesn't even show a message box to the user; the whole process just disappears!

Now I will explain why the bottommost page of a stack's region is always reserved. Doing so protects against accidental overwriting of other data being used by the process. You see, it's possible that at address 0x07FFF000 (1 page below 0x08000000), another region of address space has committed physical storage. If the page at 0x08000000 contained physical storage, the system would not catch attempts by the thread to access the reserved stack region. If the stack were to dip below the reserved stack region, the code in your thread would overwrite other data in your process's address space—a very, very difficult bug to catch.

A Thread's Stack Under Windows 95

Under Windows 95, stacks behave similarly to their Windows NT counterparts. However, there are some significant differences.

Figure 6-5 on the following page shows what a stack region (reserved starting at address 0x00530000) might look like for a 1-MB stack when running under Windows 95.

Memory Address	Size	State of Page
0x00640000	16 pages (65,536 bytes)	Top of stack: reserved for stack underflow
0x0063F000	1 page (4096 bytes)	Committed page with PAGE_READWRITE protection; stack in use
0x0063E000	1 page (4096 bytes)	PAGE_NOACCESS page to simulate PAGE_GUARD flag
0x00638000	6 pages (24,576 bytes)	Reserved pages for stack overflow
0x00637000	1 page (4096 bytes)	Committed page with PAGE_READWRITE protection for 16-bit component compatibility
0x00540000	247 pages (1,011,712 bytes)	Reserved pages to allow stack to grow
0x00530000	16 pages (65,536 bytes)	Bottom of stack: reserved for stack overflow

Figure 6-5.
*What a thread's stack region looks like when it is first created under
Windows 95.*

First, note that the region is actually 1 MB plus 128 KB in size, even
though we wanted only to create a stack that was up to 1 MB in size. In
Windows 95, whenever a region is reserved for a stack, the system actually reserves a region that is 128 KB larger than the requested size. The
stack is in the middle of this region, with a 64-KB block before the stack
and another 64-KB block after the stack.

The 64 KB at the beginning of the stack are there to catch stack
overflow conditions, while the 64 KB at the end of the stack are there to
catch stack underflow conditions. To see why stack underflow detection
is useful, examine the following code fragment:

```
int WINAPI WinMain (HINSTANCE hinstExe, HINSTANCE hinstPrev,
    LPSTR lpszCmdLine, int nCmdShow) {

    char szBuf[100];
    szBuf[10000] = 0;     // Stack underflow

    return(0);
}
```

When this function's assignment statement is executed, an attempt is made to access beyond the end of the thread's stack. Of course, the compiler and the linker will not catch the bug in the code on the previous page, but if your application is running under Windows 95, an access violation will be raised when the statement executes. This is a nice feature of Windows 95 that is not offered by Windows NT. On Windows NT, it is possible to have another region immediately after your thread's stack. If this happens and you attempt to access memory beyond your stack, you might corrupt memory related to another part of your process—and the system will *not* detect this corruption.

Second, note that there are no pages with the PAGE_GUARD protection attribute flag. Since Windows 95 does not support this flag, it uses a slightly different technique in order to expand a thread's stack. Windows 95 marks the committed page immediately below the stack with the PAGE_NOACCESS protection attribute (address 0x0063E000 in Figure 6-5). Then, when the thread touches the page below the read/write pages, an access violation occurs. The system catches this, changes the no access page to a read/write page, and commits a new "guard" page just below the previous guard page.

Third, note the single page of PAGE_READWRITE storage at address 0x00637000 in Figure 6-5. This page exists for 16-bit Windows compatibility. Although Microsoft never documented it, developers found out that the 16 bytes at the beginning of a 16-bit application's stack segment contains information about the 16-bit application's stack, local heap, and local atom table. Because Win32 applications running on Windows 95 frequently call 16-bit DLL components, and some of these 16-bit components assume that this information is available at the beginning of the stack segment, Microsoft was forced to simulate these bytes in Windows 95. When 32-bit code thunks to 16-bit code, Windows 95 maps a 16-bit CPU selector to the 32-bit stack and sets the stack segment (SS) register to point to the page at address 0x00637000. The 16-bit code can now access the 16 bytes at the beginning of the stack segment and continue executing without any problems.

Now, as Windows 95 grows the thread's stack, it continues to grow the block at address 0x0063F000; it also keeps moving the guard page down until 1 MB of stack storage is committed, and then the guard page disappears just as it does under Windows NT. The system also continues to move the page for 16-bit Windows component compatibility down, and eventually this page goes into the 64-KB block at the beginning of the stack region. So a fully committed stack on Windows 95 looks like Figure 6-6:

Memory Address	Size	State of Page
0x00640000	16 pages (65,536 bytes)	Top of stack: reserved for stack underflow
0x00540000	256 pages (1 MB)	Committed pages with PAGE_READWRITE protection; stack in use
0x00539000	7 pages (28,672 bytes)	Reserved pages for stack overflow
0x00538000	1 page (4096 bytes)	Committed page with PAGE_READWRITE protection for 16-bit component compatibility
0x00530000	8 pages (32,768 bytes)	Bottom of stack: reserved for stack overflow

Figure 6-6.
A full thread stack region under Windows 95.

The C Run-Time's Stack Checking Function

MS-DOS and 16-bit Windows applications run in a system that doesn't take advantage of the CPU's ability to assign memory protections to regions of memory. So when your application uses its stack, the CPU can't detect when a stack overflow occurs. Because this can be a very difficult bug to detect in these 16-bit environments, many C/C++ compiler vendors offer a compiler switch that causes the compiler to add a call to an internal function (provided in the C run-time library) that verifies the stack hasn't overflowed. This compiler switch is optional because adding the call to the stack checking function both increases the size of your EXE file and makes your application run more slowly.

In the Win32 environment, the CPU can automatically detect when a thread overflows its stack, so there's no need for additional function calls that would make your code bigger and slower.

The 32-bit C/C++ compilers still offer a stack checking function, but the purpose of the function has changed totally. Now the 32-bit stack checking function makes sure that pages are committed to your thread's stack appropriately. Let's look at an example; here's a small function that requires a lot of memory for its local variables:

```
void SomeFunction () {
   int nValues[4000];

   // Do some processing with the array.
   nValues[0] = 0;       // Some assignment
}
```

This function will require at least 16,000 bytes (4000 × sizeof(int); each integer is 4 bytes) of stack space to accommodate the array of integers. Usually, the code generated by a compiler to allocate this stack space simply decrements the CPU's stack pointer by 16,000 bytes. However, the system does not commit physical storage to this lower area of the stack's region until an attempt is made to access the memory address.

On a system with a 4-KB or 8-KB page size, this could cause a problem. If the first access to the stack is at an address that is below the guard page (as shown on the assignment line in the code above), the thread will be accessing reserved memory and the system will raise an access violation. To ensure that you can successfully write functions like the one shown above, the compiler inserts calls to the C run-time's stack checking function.

When compiling your program, the compiler knows the page size for the CPU system you are targeting. If you are compiling your application for the x86, MIPS, or PowerPC, the x86, MIPS, and PowerPC compilers all know that the page size for these platforms is 4 KB. If you are compiling for the Alpha, the Alpha compiler knows that the page size is 8 KB. As the compiler encounters each function in your program, it determines the amount of stack space required for the function; if the function requires more stack space than the target system's page size, the compiler inserts a call to the C run-time's stack checking function. You do not need to specify any compiler switches—the compiler inserts this function automatically as needed.

The pseudo-code on the next page shows what the stack checking function does. I say *pseudo-code* because this function is usually implemented in assembly language by the compiler vendors.

```
// The C run-time knows the page size for the target system.
#ifdef _M_ALPHA
#define PAGESIZE    (8 * 1024)    // 8-KB page
#else
#define PAGESIZE    (4 * 1024)    // 4-KB page
#endif


void StackCheck (int nBytesNeededFromStack) {
   // Get the stack pointer position.
   // At this point, the stack pointer has NOT been decremented
   // to account for the function's local variables.
   PBYTE pbStackPtr = (CPU's stack pointer);

   while (nBytesNeededFromStack >= PAGESIZE) {
      // Move down a page on the stack--should be a guard page.
      pbStackPtr -= PAGESIZE;

      // Access a byte on the guard page--forces new page to be
      // committed and guard page to move down a page.
      pbStackPtr[0] = 0;

      // Reduce the number of bytes needed from the stack.
      nBytesNeededFromStack -= PAGESIZE;
   }

   // Before returning, the StackCheck function sets the CPU's
   // stack pointer to the address below the function's
   // local variables.
}
```

Visual C++ does offer a compiler switch that allows you to control the page-size threshold that the compiler uses to determine when to add the automatic call to *StackCheck*. This compiler switch should be used only if you know exactly what you are doing and have a special need for it. For 99.99999 percent of all applications and DLLs written, this switch should not be used.

CHAPTER SEVEN

MEMORY-MAPPED FILES

Working with files is something almost every application must do, and it's always a hassle. Should your application open the file, read it, and close the file, or should it open the file and use a buffering algorithm to read from and write to different portions of the file? Win32 offers the best of both worlds: memory-mapped files.

Like virtual memory, memory-mapped files allow you to reserve a region of address space and commit physical storage to the region. The difference is that the physical storage comes from a file that is already on the disk instead of the system's paging file. Once the file has been mapped, you can access it as if the whole file were loaded in memory.

Memory-mapped files are used for three different purposes:

- The system uses memory-mapped files to load and execute EXE and DLL files. This greatly conserves both paging file space and the time required for an application to begin executing.

- You can use memory-mapped files to access a data file on disk. This shelters you from performing file I/O operations on the file and from buffering the file's contents.

- You can use memory-mapped files to allow multiple processes running on the same machine to share data with each other. (Win32 does offer other methods for communicating data among processes—but these other methods are implemented using memory-mapped files.)

In this chapter, we will examine each of these uses for memory-mapped files.

Memory-Mapped EXEs and DLLs

When a thread calls *CreateProcess*, the system performs the following steps:

1. The system locates the EXE file specified in the call to *CreateProcess*. If the EXE file cannot be found, the process is not created and *CreateProcess* returns NULL.

2. The system creates a new process kernel object with a usage count of 1.

3. The system creates a 4-GB address space for this new process.

4. The system reserves a region of address space large enough to contain the EXE file. The desired location of this region is specified inside the EXE file itself. By default, an EXE file's base address is 0x00400000. However, you can override this when you create your application's EXE file by using the linker's /BASE option when you link your application.

5. The system notes that the physical storage backing the reserved region is in the EXE file on disk instead of the system's paging file.

After the EXE file has been mapped into the process's address space, the system accesses a section of the EXE file that lists the DLLs containing functions that the code in the EXE calls. The system then calls *LoadLibrary* for each of these DLLs and, if any of the DLLs require additional DLLs, the system calls *LoadLibrary* to load those DLLs as well. Every time *LoadLibrary* is called to load a DLL, the system performs steps similar to steps 4 and 5 above:

1. The system reserves a region of address space large enough to contain the DLL file. The desired location of this region is specified inside the DLL file itself. By default, Visual C++ 2.0 makes the DLL's base address 0x10000000. However, you can override this when you build your DLL by using the linker's /BASE option. All the standard system DLLs that ship with Windows NT and Windows 95 have different base addresses.

2. If the system is unable to reserve a region at the DLL's preferred base address, either because the region is occupied by another DLL or EXE or because the region just isn't big enough, the system will then try to find another region of address space to reserve for the DLL. It is unfortunate when a DLL cannot load at its preferred base address, for two reasons. First, the

system might not be able to load the DLL at all if it does not have fixup information. (You can remove fixup information from a DLL when it is created by using the linker's /FIXED switch. This makes the DLL file smaller, but it also means that the DLL *must* load at its preferred address.) Second, the system must perform some relocations within the DLL. On Windows 95, the system can fix the relocations as pages are swapped into RAM. On Windows NT, these relocations require additional storage from the system's paging file; they also increase the amount of time needed to load the DLL.

3. The system notes that the physical storage backing the reserved region is in the DLL file on disk instead of in the system's paging file. If Windows NT has to perform relocations because the DLL could not load at its preferred base address, the system also notes that some of the physical storage for the DLL is mapped to the paging file.

If for some reason the system is unable to map the EXE and all the required DLLs, the system displays a message box to the user and frees the process's address space and the process object. *CreateProcess* will return NULL to its caller; the caller can call *GetLastError* to get a better idea of why the process could not be created.

After all the EXE and DLL files have been mapped into the process's address space, the system can begin executing the EXE file's startup code. After the EXE file has been mapped, the system takes care of all the paging, buffering, and caching. For example, if there is code in the EXE that causes it to jump to the address of an instruction that isn't loaded into memory, a fault will occur. The system detects the fault and automatically loads the page of code from the file's image into a page of RAM. Then the system maps the page of RAM to the proper location in the process's address space and allows the thread to continue executing as though the page of code were loaded all along. Of course, all this is invisible to the application. This process is repeated each time any thread in the process attempts to access code or data that is not loaded into RAM.

Static Data Is Not Shared by Multiple Instances of an EXE or a DLL

When you create a new process for an application that is already running, the system simply opens another memory-mapped view of the file-mapping object that identifies the executable file's image and creates a new process object and a new thread object (for the primary thread). The system also assigns new process and thread IDs to these objects. By using memory-mapped files, multiple running instances of the same application can share the same code and data in RAM.

Note one small problem here. Win32 processes use a flat, 4-GB address space. When you compile and link your program, all the code and data are thrown together as one large entity. The data is separated from the code but only to the extent that it follows the code in the EXE file.[1] The illustration below shows a simplified view of how the code and data for an application are loaded into virtual memory and then mapped into an application's address space.

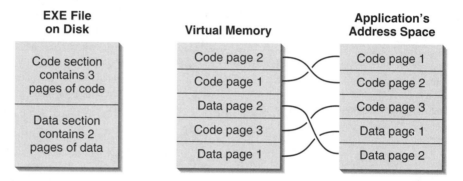

As an example, let's say that a second instance of an application is run. The system simply maps the pages of virtual memory containing the file's code and data into the second application's address space, as shown here:

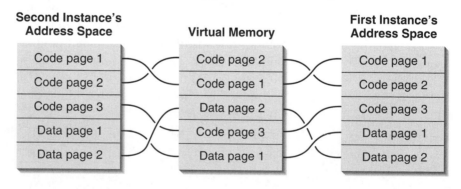

---

1. Actually, the contents of a file are broken down into sections. The code is in one section, and the global variables are in another section. Sections are aligned on page boundaries. Pages are 4 KB on x86, MIPS, and PowerPC CPUs, and 8 KB on the DEC Alpha CPU. An application can determine the page size being used by calling *GetSystemInfo*. In the EXE or DLL file, the code section usually precedes the data section.

If one instance of the application alters some global variables residing in a data page, the memory contents for all instances of the application change. This type of change could cause disastrous effects and must not be allowed.

The system prohibits this by using the copy-on-write feature of the memory management system. Any time an application attempts to write to its memory-mapped file, the system catches the attempt, allocates a new block of memory for the page containing the memory the application is trying to be write to, copies the contents of the page, and allows the application to write to this newly allocated memory block. As a result, no other instances of the same application are affected. The illustration below shows what happens when the first instance of an application attempts to change a global variable in data page 2.

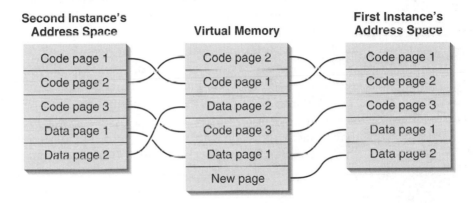

The system allocated a new page of virtual memory and copied the contents of data page 2 into it. The first instance's address space is changed so that the new data page is mapped into the address space at the same location as the original address page. Now the system can let the process alter the global variable without fear of altering the data for another instance of the same application.

A similar sequence of events occurs when an application is being debugged. Let's say that you're running multiple instances of an application and want to debug only one instance. You access your debugger and set a breakpoint in a line of source code. The debugger actually modifies your code by changing one of your assembly language instructions to an instruction that causes the debugger to activate itself. So we have the same problem again. When the debugger modifies the code, it causes all instances of the application to activate the debugger when the changed assembly instruction is executed. To fix this situation, the system again uses copy-on-write memory. When the system senses that the debugger is attempting to change the code, it allocates a new block of memory, copies the page containing the instruction into the new page, and allows the debugger to modify the code in the page copy.[2]

When a process is loaded, the system examines all the file image's pages. The system commits storage in the page file immediately for those pages that would normally be protected with the copy-on-write attribute. These pages are simply committed; they are not touched in any way. When a page in the file image is accessed, the system loads the appropriate page. If that page is never modified, it can be discarded from memory and reloaded when necessary. However, if the file's page is modified, the system swaps the modified page to one of the previously committed pages in the paging file.

The only difference in behavior between Windows NT and Windows 95 occurs when you have two copies of a module loaded and the writable data hasn't been modified. In this case, processes running under Windows NT share the data, while under Windows 95 each process receives its own copy of the data. Windows NT and Windows 95 behave exactly the same if there is only one copy of the module loaded or if the writable data has been modified (which is normally the case).

Memory-Mapped Data Files

The operating system automatically uses the technique described in the previous section whenever an EXE or a DLL file is loaded. However, it is also possible to memory map a data file into your process's address space. This makes it very convenient to manipulate large streams of data.

---

2. Note that you can create global variables in an EXE or a DLL file and share them among all instances of the file. Briefly, this method requires placing the variables you want to share in their own section by using the *#pragma data_seg()* compiler directive. Then you must use the /SECTION:*name, attributes* switch to tell the linker that you want the data in the section to be shared for all instances or mappings of the file. The *name* argument identifies the name of the section containing the data variables you want to share, and the *attributes* argument specifies the attributes of data in this section. To share variables, you'll need to use RSW for read, shared, and write. See Chapter 11 for more information about sharing global variables among multiple instances of a DLL.

To understand the power of using memory-mapped files this way, let's look at four possible methods of implementing a program to reverse the order of all the bytes in a file.

Method 1: One File, One Buffer

The first and theoretically simplest method involves allocating a block of memory large enough to hold the entire file. The file is opened, its contents are read into the memory block, and the file is closed. With the contents in memory, we can now reverse all the bytes by swapping the first byte with the last, the second byte with the second-to-last, and so on. This swapping continues until you swap the two middle bytes in the file. After all the bytes have been swapped, you reopen the file and overwrite its contents with the contents of the memory block.

This method is pretty easy to implement but has two major drawbacks. First, a memory block the size of the file must be allocated. This might not be too bad if the file is small, but if the file is huge—say, 2 GB—the system will not allow the application to commit a block of physical storage that large. Large files require a different method.

Second, if the process is interrupted in the middle, while the reversed bytes are being written back out to the file, the contents of the file will be corrupted. The simplest way to guard against this is to make a copy of the original file before reversing its contents. If the whole process succeeds, you can delete the copy of the file. Unfortunately, this safeguard requires additional disk space.

Method 2: Two Files, One Buffer

In the second method, you open the existing file and create a new file of 0 length on the disk. Then you allocate a small internal buffer—say, 8 KB. You seek to the end of the original file minus 8 KB, read the last 8 KB into the buffer, reverse the bytes, and write the buffer's contents to the newly created file. The process of seeking, reading, reversing, and writing repeats until you reach the beginning of the original file. Some special handling is required if the file's length is not an exact multiple of 8 KB, but it's not extensive. After the original file is fully processed, both files are closed and the original file is deleted.

This method is a bit more complicated to implement than the first one. It uses memory much more efficiently because only an 8-KB chunk is ever allocated, but there are two big problems. First, the processing is slower than in the first method because on each iteration you must perform a seek on the original file before performing a read. Second, this method can potentially use an enormous amount of hard disk space. If the original file is 400 MB, the new file will grow to be 400 MB as the process continues. Just before the original file is deleted, the two files will occupy 800 MB of disk space. This is 400 MB more than should be required—which leads us to the next method.

Method 3: One File, Two Buffers

For this method, let's say the program initializes by allocating two separate 8-KB buffers. The program reads the first 8 KB of the file into one buffer and the last 8 KB of the file into the other buffer. The process then reverses the contents of both buffers and writes the contents of the first buffer back to the end of the file, and the contents of the second buffer back to the beginning of the same file. Each iteration continues by moving blocks from the front and back of the file in 8-KB chunks. Some special handling is required if the file's length is not an exact multiple of 16 KB and the two 8-KB chunks overlap. This special handling is more complex than the special handling in the previous method, but it's nothing that should scare off a seasoned programmer.

Compared with the previous two methods, this method is better at conserving hard disk space. Because everything is read from and written to the same file, no additional disk space is required. As for memory use, this method is also not too bad, using only 16 KB. Of course, this is probably the most difficult method to implement. Like the first method, this method can result in corruption of the data file if the process is somehow interrupted.

Now let's take a look at how this process might be accomplished using memory-mapped files.

Method 4: One File, Zero Buffers

When using memory-mapped files to reverse the contents of a file, you open the file and then tell the system to reserve a region of virtual address space. You tell the system to map the first byte of the file to the first byte of this reserved region. You can then access the region of virtual memory as though it actually contained the file. In fact, if there were a single 0 byte at the end of the file, you could simply call the C run-time function _strrev to reverse the data in the file.

This method's great advantage is that the system manages all the file caching for you. You don't have to allocate any memory, load file data into memory, write data back to the file, or free any memory blocks at all. Unfortunately, the possibility that an interruption such as a power failure could corrupt data still exists with memory-mapped files.

214

Using Memory-Mapped Files

There are three steps that you must perform in order to use a memory-mapped file:

1. Create or open a file kernel object that identifies the file on disk that you want to use as a memory-mapped file.

2. Create a file-mapping kernel object that tells the system the size of the file and how you intend to access the file.

3. Tell the system to map all or part of the file-mapping object into your process's address space.

When you are finished using the memory-mapped file, there are three steps you must perform in order to clean up:

1. Tell the system to unmap the file-mapping kernel object from your process's address space.

2. Close the file-mapping kernel object.

3. Close the file kernel object.

The next five sections discuss all these steps in more detail.

Step 1: Creating or Opening a File Kernel Object

To create or open a file kernel object, you always call the *CreateFile* function:

```
HANDLE CreateFile(LPCSTR lpFileName, DWORD dwDesiredAccess,
    DWORD dwShareMode, LPSECURITY_ATTRIBUTES lpSecurityAttributes,
    DWORD dwCreationDisposition, DWORD dwFlagsAndAttributes,
    HANDLE hTemplateFile);
```

Although its name does not suggest it, *CreateFile* is also the function you should use to open an existing file. The 16-bit Windows *OpenFile* function still exists in the Win32 API, but it is supplied for backward compatibility only. New applications should avoid the *OpenFile* function and always use the new *CreateFile* function.

The *CreateFile* function takes quite a few parameters. For this discussion, I'll concentrate only on the first three: *lpFileName*, *dwDesiredAccess*, and *dwShareMode. CreateFile* is discussed in more detail in Chapter 13 of this book.

As you might guess, the first parameter, *lpFileName*, identifies the name (including an optional path) of the file that you want to create or open. The second parameter, *dwDesiredAccess*, specifies how you intend to access the contents of the file. You can specify one of the four following values here:

Value	Meaning
0	You cannot read from or write to the file's contents. Specify 0 when you just want to get a file's attributes.
GENERIC_READ	You can read from the file.
GENERIC_WRITE	You can write to the file.
GENERIC_READ ¦ GENERIC_WRITE	You can read from the file and write to the file.

When creating or opening a file for use as a memory-mapped file, select the access flag or flags that make the most sense for how you intend to access the file's data. For memory-mapped files, you must open the file for read-only access or read-write access, so you'll want to specify either GENERIC_READ or GENERIC_READ ¦ GENERIC_WRITE respectively.

The third parameter, *dwShareMode*, tells the system how you want to share this file. You can specify one of the four following values for *dwShareMode*:

Value	Meaning
0	Any other attempts to open the file fail.
FILE_SHARE_READ	Other attempts to open the file using GENERIC_WRITE fail.
FILE_SHARE_WRITE	Other attempts to open the file using GENERIC_READ fail.
FILE_SHARE_READ ¦ FILE_SHARE_WRITE	Other attempts to open the file succeed.

If *CreateFile* successfully creates or opens the specified file, a file handle is returned; otherwise, INVALID_HANDLE_VALUE is returned.

Important

Most Win32 functions that return a handle return NULL when they are unsuccessful. *CreateFile*, however, returns INVALID_HANDLE_VALUE, which is defined as 0xFFFFFFFF.

Step 2: Creating a File-Mapping Kernel Object

In order to map a file's data, you must create a file-mapping kernel object by calling *CreateFileMapping*:

```
HANDLE CreateFileMapping(HANDLE hFile, LPSECURITY_ATTRIBUTES lpsa,
    DWORD fdwProtect, DWORD dwMaximumSizeHigh,
    DWORD dwMaximumSizeLow, LPSTR lpszMapName);
```

A file-mapping object describes several important pieces of information that the operating system requires while managing a memory-mapped file.

The first parameter, *hFile*, identifies the handle of the file you want mapped into the process's address space. This handle is returned by the previous call to *CreateFile*. The *lpsa* parameter is a pointer to a SECURITY_ATTRIBUTES structure, usually NULL.

As I pointed out at the beginning of this chapter, creating a memory-mapped file is just like reserving a region of address space and then committing physical storage to the region. It's just that the physical storage for a memory-mapped file comes from a file on a disk rather than from space allocated from the system's paging file. When you create a file-mapping object, the system does not reserve a region of address space and map the file's storage to the region. (I'll describe how to do this in the next section.) However, when the system does map the storage to the process's address space, the system must know what protection attribute to assign to the pages of physical storage. *CreateFileMapping*'s *fdwProtect* parameter allows you to specify the desired protection attributes. For the most part, you will specify one of the protection attributes shown on the following page.

Protection Attribute	Meaning
PAGE_READONLY	When the file-mapping object is mapped, you can read the file's data. You must have passed GENERIC_READ to *CreateFile*.
PAGE_READWRITE	When the file-mapping object is mapped, you can read and write the file's data. You must have passed GENERIC_READ ¦ GENERIC_WRITE to *CreateFile*.
PAGE_WRITECOPY	When the file-mapping object is mapped, you can read and write the file's data. Writing causes a private copy of the page to be created. You must have passed either GENERIC_READ or GENERIC_READ ¦ GENERIC_WRITE to *CreateFile*.

Under Windows 95, you can pass the PAGE_WRITECOPY flag to *CreateFileMapping*; this tells the system to commit storage from the paging file. This paging file storage is reserved for a copy of the data file's data; only modified pages are actually written to the paging file. Any changes you make to the file's data are not propagated back to the original data file. The end result is that the PAGE_WRITECOPY flag has the same effect on both Windows NT and Windows 95.

In addition to the above page protections, there are four section attributes that you may bitwise OR in the *CreateFileMapping* function's *fdwProtect* parameter. A section is just another word for a memory mapping.

The first of these attributes, SEC_NOCACHE, tells the system that none of the file's memory-mapped pages are to be cached. So as you write data to the file, the system will update the file's data on the disk more often than it normally would. This flag, like the PAGE_NOCACHE protection attribute, exists for the device driver developer and is not usually used by applications.

Windows 95 ignores the SEC_NOCACHE flag.

The second section attribute, SEC_IMAGE, tells the system that the file you are mapping is a Win32 portable executable (PE) file. When the system maps this file into your process's address space, the system examines the file's contents to determine which protection attributes to assign to the various pages of the mapped image. For example, a PE file's code section is usually mapped with PAGE_EXECUTE_READ attributes, whereas the PE file's data is usually mapped with PAGE_READWRITE attributes. Specifying the SEC_IMAGE attribute tells the system to map the file's image and automatically set the appropriate page protections.

Windows 95 ignores the SEC_IMAGE flag.

The last two attributes, SEC_RESERVE and SEC_COMMIT, are mutually exclusive and do not apply when you are using a memory-mapped data file. These two flags will be discussed in the section "Using Memory-Mapped Files to Share Data Among Processes" later in this chapter. When creating a memory-mapped data file, you should not specify either of these flags. *CreateFileMapping* will ignore them.

CreateFileMapping's next two parameters, *dwMaximumSizeHigh* and *dwMaximumSizeLow*, tell the system the maximum size of the file in bytes. Two 32-bit values are required because Win32 supports file sizes that can be expressed using a 64-bit value; the *dwMaximumSizeHigh* parameter specifies the high 32 bits, and the *dwMaximumSizeLow* parameter specifies the low 32 bits. For files that are 4 GB or less, *dwMaximumSizeHigh* will always be 0.

Using a 64-bit value means that Win32 can process files as large as 18 exabytes. (An exabyte, which is abbreviated EB, is 1 quintillion, or 1,152,921,504,606,846,976, bytes.) If you want to create the file-mapping object so that it reflects the current size of the file, you can pass 0 for both parameters. If you intend only to read from the file or to access the file without changing its size, this is what you should do. If you intend to append data to the file, you will want to choose a maximum file size that leaves you some breathing room.

If you have been paying attention so far, you must be thinking that there is something terribly wrong here. It's nice that Win32 supports files and file-mapping objects that can be anywhere up to 18 EB, but how are you ever going to map a file that big into your process's address space, which has a maximum limit of 4 GB? I'll explain how this is accomplished in the next section.

If you call *CreateFileMapping*, passing the PAGE_READWRITE flag, the system will check to make sure that the associated data file on the disk is at least the same size as the size specified in the *dwMaximum-SizeHigh* and *dwMaximumSizeLow* parameters. If the file is smaller than the specified size, *CreateFileMapping* will make the file on the disk larger by extending its size. This is required so that the physical storage will already exist when the file is used as a memory-mapped file later. If the file-mapping object is being created with the PAGE_READONLY or the PAGE_WRITECOPY flag, the size specified to *CreateFileMapping* must be no larger than the physical size of the disk file. This is because you will not be able to append any data to the file.

CreateFileMapping's last parameter, *lpszMapName*, is a zero-terminated string that assigns a name to this file-mapping object. The name is used to share the object with another process and is discussed later in this chapter. A memory-mapped data file usually doesn't need to be shared; therefore, this parameter is usually NULL.

The system creates the file-mapping object and returns a handle identifying the object back to the calling thread. If the system cannot create the file-mapping object, a NULL handle value is returned. Again, please note that this is different from *CreateFile*'s invalid handle value of INVALID_HANDLE_VALUE (defined as 0xFFFFFFFF).

Step 3: Mapping the File's Data into the Process's Address Space

After you have created a file-mapping object, you still need to have the system reserve a region of address space for the file's data and commit the file's data as the physical storage that is mapped to the region. This is done by calling *MapViewOfFile*:

```
LPVOID MapViewOfFile(HANDLE hFileMappingObject,
   DWORD dwDesiredAccess, DWORD dwFileOffsetHigh,
   DWORD dwFileOffsetLow, DWORD dwNumberOfBytesToMap);
```

The *hFileMappingObject* parameter identifies the handle of the file-mapping object, which was returned by the previous call to either *CreateFileMapping* or *OpenFileMapping* (discussed later in this chapter). The *dwDesiredAccess* parameter identifies how the data can be accessed. That's right, we must again specify how we intend to access the file's data. You can specify one of four possible values:

Value	Meaning
FILE_MAP_WRITE	You can read and write file data. *CreateFileMapping* had to be called by passing PAGE_READWRITE.
FILE_MAP_READ	You can read file data. *CreateFileMapping* could be called with any of the protection attributes: PAGE_READONLY, PAGE_READWRITE, or PAGE_WRITECOPY.
FILE_MAP_ALL_ACCESS	Same as FILE_MAP_WRITE.
FILE_MAP_COPY	You can read and write file data. Writing causes a private copy of the page to be created. *CreateFileMapping* could be called with any of the protection attributes: PAGE_READONLY, PAGE_READWRITE, or PAGE_WRITECOPY.

It certainly seems strange and annoying that Win32 requires all these protection attributes to be set over and over again. I assume this was done to give an application as much control over data protection as possible.

The remaining three parameters have to do with reserving the region of address space and mapping the physical storage to the region. When you map a file into your process's address space, you do not have to map the entire file at once. Instead, you can map only a small portion of the file into the address space. A portion of a file that is mapped to your process's address space is called a *view*, which explains how *MapViewOfFile* got its name.

When you map a view of a file into your process's address space, you must specify two things. First, you must tell the system which byte in the data file should be mapped as the first byte in the view. This is done using the *dwFileOffsetHigh* and *dwFileOffsetLow* parameters. Because Win32 supports files that can be up to 18 EB, you must specify this byte-offset using a 64-bit value of which the high 32 bits are passed in the *dwFileOffsetHigh* parameter and the low 32 bits are passed in the *dwFileOffsetLow* parameter. Note that the offset in the file must be an even multiple of the system's allocation granularity. (To date, all implementations of Win32 have an allocation granularity of 64 KB.) The section "System Information" in Chapter 5 shows how to obtain the allocation granularity value for a given system.

Second, you must tell the system how much of the data file to map into the address space. This is the same thing as specifying how large a region of address space to reserve. You specify this size using the *dwNumberOfBytesToMap* parameter. You'll notice that this parameter is a single 32-bit value because it could never be larger than 4 GB. If you specify a size of 0, the system will attempt to map a view consisting of the entire file.

Under Windows 95, if *MapViewOfFile* cannot find a region large enough to contain the entire file-mapping object, *MapViewOfFile* returns NULL regardless of the size of the view requested.

Under Windows NT, *MapViewOfFile* needs only to find a region large enough for the view requested, regardless of the size of the entire file-mapping object.

If you specify the FILE_MAP_COPY flag when calling *MapView-OfFile*, the system commits physical storage from the system's paging file. The amount of space committed is determined by the *dwNumberOfBytes-ToMap* parameter. As long as you do nothing more than read from the file's mapped view, the system will never use these committed pages in the paging file. However, the first time any thread in your process writes to any memory address within the file's mapped view, the system will grab one of the committed pages from the paging file, copy the page of original data to this paging-file page, and then map this copied page into your process's address space. From this point on, the threads in your process are accessing a local copy of the data and cannot read or modify the original data.

When the system makes the copy of the original page, the system changes the protection of the page from PAGE_WRITECOPY to PAGE_READWRITE. The following code fragment explains it all:

```
HANDLE hFile, hFileMapping;
BYTE bSomeByte, *pbFile;
    .
    .
    .

// Open the file that we want to map.
hFile = CreateFile(lpszName, GENERIC_READ | GENERIC_WRITE, 0, NULL,
    OPEN_ALWAYS, FILE_ATTRIBUTE_NORMAL, NULL);
```

```
// Create a file-mapping object for the file.
hFileMapping = CreateFileMapping(hFile, NULL, PAGE_WRITECOPY, 0, 0,
   NULL);

// Map a copy-on-write view of the file; the system will commit
// enough physical storage from the paging file to accommodate
// the entire file. All pages in the view will initially have
// PAGE_WRITECOPY access.
pbFile = (PBYTE) MapViewOfFile(hFileMapping, FILE_MAP_COPY, 0, 0,
   0);

// Read a byte from the mapped view.
bSomeByte = pbFile[0];
// When reading, the system does not touch the committed pages in
// the paging file. The page keeps its PAGE_WRITECOPY attribute.

// Write a byte to the mapped view.
pbFile[0] = 0;
// When writing for the first time, the system grabs a committed
// page from the paging file, copies the original contents of the
// page at the accessed memory address, and maps the new page
// (the copy) into the process's address space. The new page has
// a PAGE_READWRITE attribute.

// Write another byte to the mapped view.
pbFile[1] = 0;
// Because this byte is now in a PAGE_READWRITE page, the system
// simply writes the byte to the page (backed by the paging file).

// When finished using the file's mapped view, unmap it.
// UnmapViewOfFile is discussed in the next section.
UnmapViewOfFile(pbFile);
// The system decommits the physical storage from the paging file.
// Any writes to the pages are lost.

// Clean up after ourselves.
CloseHandle(hFileMapping);
CloseHandle(hFile);
```

As mentioned earlier, Windows 95 must commit storage in the paging file for the memory-mapped file up front. However, it will write modified pages to the paging file only as necessary.

Step 4: Unmapping the File's Data
from the Process's Address Space

When you no longer need to keep a file's data mapped to a region of your process's address space, you can release the region by calling:

```
BOOL UnmapViewOfFile(LPVOID lpBaseAddress);
```

The only parameter, *lpBaseAddress*, specifies the base address of the returned region. This value must be the same value returned from a call to *MapViewOfFile*. It is important to remember to call *UnmapViewOfFile*. If you do not call this function, the reserved region won't be released until your process terminates. Whenever you call *MapViewOfFile*, the system always reserves a new region within your process's address space—any previously reserved regions are *not* released.

In the interest of speed, the system buffers the pages of the file's data and doesn't update the disk image of the file immediately while working with the file's mapped view. However, when you are finished with the view and call *UnmapViewOfFile*, the system forces all the modified data in memory to be written back to the disk image. If you need to ensure that your updates have been written to disk, you can force the system to write all the modified data back to the disk image by calling *FlushViewOfFile*:

```
BOOL FlushViewOfFile(LPVOID lpBaseAddress,
    DWORD dwNumberOfBytesToFlush);
```

This function requires the address of the mapped view as returned by the previous call to *MapViewOfFile* and also requires the number of bytes you want to write to disk. If you call *FlushViewOfFile* and none of the data has been changed, the function simply returns without writing anything to the disk.

For a memory-mapped file whose storage is over a network, *Flush-ViewOfFile* guarantees that the file's data has been written from the workstation. However, *FlushViewOfFile* cannot guarantee that the server machine that is sharing the file has written the data to the remote disk drive because the server might be caching the file's data. To ensure that the server writes the file's data, you should pass the FILE_FLAG_WRITE-_THROUGH flag to the *CreateFile* function whenever you create a file-mapping object for the file and then map the view of the file-mapping object. If the file is opened using this flag, *FlushViewOfFile* will return when all of the file's data has been stored on the server's disk drive.

There is one special note about the *UnmapViewOfFile* function. If the view was originally mapped using the FILE_MAP_COPY flag, any changes that you made to the file's data were actually made to a copy of the file's data stored in the system's paging file. In this case, if you call *Unmap-ViewOfFile* the function has nothing to update on the disk file and simply causes the pages in the paging file to be decommitted. The data contained in the pages is lost.

If you want to preserve the changed data, you must take additional measures yourself. For example, you might want to create another file-mapping object (using PAGE_READWRITE) from the same file and map this new file-mapping object into your process's address space using the FILE_MAP_WRITE flag. Then you could scan the first view looking for pages with the PAGE_READWRITE protection attribute. Whenever you found a page with this attribute, you could examine its contents and decide whether to write the changed data to the file. If you do not want to update the file with the new data, keep scanning the remaining pages in the view until you reach the end. However, if you do want to save the changed page of data, just call *MoveMemory* to copy the page of data from the first view to the second view. Because the second view is mapped with PAGE_READWRITE protection, the *MoveMemory* function will be updating the actual contents of the file on the disk. You can use this method to determine changes and preserve your file's data.

Windows 95 does not support the copy-on-write protection attribute, so you cannot test for pages marked with the PAGE_READWRITE flag when scanning the first view of the memory-mapped file. You will have to devise a method of your own for determining which pages in the first view you have actually modified.

Steps 5 and 6: Closing the File-Mapping Object and the File Object

It goes without saying that you should always close any kernel objects you open. Forgetting to do so will cause a resource leak in your process. Of course, when your process terminates, the system automatically closes any objects your process opened but forgot to close. But if your process does not terminate for a while, you will accumulate resource handles. You should always write clean, "proper" code that closes any objects you have opened. In order to close the file-mapping object and the file object, you simply need to call the *CloseHandle* function twice—once for each handle.

Let's look at this a little closer. The pseudo-code below shows an example of memory-mapping a file:

```
HANDLE hFile, hFileMapping;
PVOID pFile;

hFile = CreateFile(...);
hFileMapping = CreateFileMapping(hFile, ...);
pFile = MapViewOfFile(hFileMapping, ...);

// Use the memory-mapped file.

UnmapViewOfFile(pFile);
CloseHandle(hFileMapping);
CloseHandle(hFile);
```

The code above shows the "expected" method for manipulating memory-mapped files. However, what it does not show is that the system increments the usage counts of the file object and the file-mapping object when you call *MapViewOfFile*. This side effect is significant because it means that we could rewrite the code fragment above as follows:

```
HANDLE hFile, hFileMapping;
PVOID pFile;

hFile = CreateFile(...);
hFileMapping = CreateFileMapping(hFile, ...);
CloseHandle(hFile);
pFile = MapViewOfFile(hFileMapping, ...);
CloseHandle(hFileMapping);

// Use the memory-mapped file.

UnmapViewOfFile(pFile);
```

In working with memory-mapped files, it is quite common to open the file, create the file-mapping object, and then use the file-mapping object to map a view of the file's data into the process's address space. Because the system increments the internal usage counts of the file object and the file-mapping object, you can close these objects at the beginning of your code and eliminate potential resource leaks.

If you will be creating additional file-mapping objects from the same file or mapping multiple views of the same file-mapping object, you cannot call *CloseHandle* early—you'll need the handles later to make the additional calls to *CreateFileMapping* and *MapViewOfFile*, respectively.

Processing a Big File Using Memory-Mapped Files

In an earlier section, I said I would tell you how to map an 18-EB file into a 4-GB address space. Well, you can't. Instead, you must map a view of the file that contains only a small portion of the file's data. You should start by mapping a view of the very beginning of the file. When you've finished accessing the first view of the file, you can unmap it and then map a new view starting at an offset deeper within the file. You'll need to repeat this process until you access the complete file. This certainly makes dealing with large memory-mapped files less convenient, but the good news is that most files are well under 4 GB in size.

Let's look at an example using an 8-GB file. Here is a routine that counts all the *J* characters (one of my favorites) in this ASCII file in several steps:

```
__int64 WINAPI CountJs (void) {

   HANDLE hFile, hFileMapping;
   PBYTE pbFile;
   SYSTEM_INFO si;
   __int64 qwFileSize, qwFileOffset = 0, qwNumOfJs = 0;
   DWORD dwFileSizeHigh;
   DWORD dwByte, dwBytesInBlock;
   DWORD dwErr;

   // We need the allocation granularity value for this system
   // because views must always begin with an offset in the data
   // file that is a multiple of the allocation granularity value.
   GetSystemInfo(&si);

   // Open the data file.
   hFile = CreateFile("c:\\HugeFile.Big", GENERIC_READ,
      FILE_SHARE_READ, NULL, OPEN_EXISTING,
      FILE_FLAG_SEQUENTIAL_SCAN, NULL);

   if (hFile == INVALID_HANDLE_VALUE)
      return(0);

   // Create the file-mapping object.
   hFileMapping = CreateFileMapping(hFile, NULL, PAGE_READONLY,
      0, 0, NULL);

   if (hFileMapping == NULL) {
      CloseHandle(hFile);
      return(0);
   }
```

(continued)

227

```
qwFileSize = GetFileSize(hFile, &dwFileSizeHigh);
qwFileSize += (((__int64) dwFileSizeHigh) << 32);

// We no longer need access to the file object's handle.
CloseHandle(hFile);

while (qwFileSize > 0) {

    // Determine the number of bytes to be mapped.
    if (qwFileSize < si.dwAllocationGranularity)
        dwBytesInBlock = (DWORD) qwFileSize;
    else
        dwBytesInBlock = si.dwAllocationGranularity;

    pbFile = MapViewOfFile(hFileMapping,
        FILE_MAP_READ,                       // Desired access
        (DWORD) (qwFileOffset >> 32),        // Starting byte
        (DWORD) (qwFileOffset & 0xFFFFFFFF),//   in file
        dwBytesInBlock);                     // # of bytes to map

    // Count the number of Js in this block.
    for (dwByte = 0; dwByte < dwBytesInBlock; dwByte++) {
        if (pbFile[dwByte] == 'J')
            qwNumOfJs++;
    }

    // Unmap the view so that we don't get multiple
    // views in our address space.
    UnmapViewOfFile(pbFile);

    // Skip to the next set of bytes in the file.
    qwFileOffset += dwBytesInBlock;
    qwFileSize -= dwBytesInBlock;
}

CloseHandle(hFileMapping);
return(qwNumOfJs);
}
```

This algorithm maps views of 64 KB (the allocation granularity size) or less. Also, remember that *MapViewOfFile* requires that the file offset parameters be an even multiple of the allocation granularity size. As each view is mapped into the address space, the scanning for *J*s continues. After each 64-KB chunk of the file has been mapped and scanned, it's time to tidy up by closing the file-mapping object.

Memory-Mapped Files and Coherence

The system allows you to map multiple views of the same data of a file. For example, you can map the first 10 KB of a file into a view and then map the first 4 KB of that same file into a separate view. As long as you are mapping the same file-mapping object, the system ensures that the viewed data is *coherent*. For example, if your application alters the contents of the file in one view, the data in the other view is updated to reflect the changes. This is because, although the page is mapped into the process's virtual address space more than once, the system really has the data in only a single page of RAM. If multiple processes are mapping views of a single data file, the data is still coherent because there is still only one instance of each page of RAM within the data file—it's just that the pages of RAM are mapped into multiple process address spaces.

Important

Win32 allows you to create several file-mapping objects that are backed by a single data file. Win32 does *not* guarantee that views of these different file-mapping objects will be coherent. It guarantees only that multiple views of a single file-mapping object will be coherent.

When we're working with files, however, there is no reason why another application can't call *CreateFile* to open the same file that another process has mapped. This new process can then read from and write to the file using the *ReadFile* and *WriteFile* functions. Of course, whenever a process makes these calls, it must be either reading file data from or writing file data to a memory buffer. This memory buffer must be one the process itself created, *not* the memory that is being used by the mapped files. There can be problems when two applications have opened the same file: one process can call *ReadFile* to read a portion of a file, modify the data, and write it back out using *WriteFile* without the file-mapping object of the second process being aware of the first process's actions. For this reason, it is recommended that when you call *CreateFile* for files that will be memory mapped, you specify 0 as the value of the *fdwShareMode* parameter. Doing so tells the system that you want exclusive access to the file and that no other process can open it.

Windows 95 is not able to maintain file coherence as well as Windows NT. For example, examine the following code fragment:

```
BYTE bBuf[1];
DWORD dwNumBytesRead;
HANDLE hFile = CreateFile(...);
HANDLE hFileMap = CreateFileMapping(hFile, ...);
PBYTE pbData = MapViewOfFile(hFileMap, ...);

// Change first byte of file to a capital "X."
pbData[0] = 'X';

// Read the first byte of the file into a buffer.
ReadFile(hFile, bBuf, 1, &dwNumBytesRead, NULL);

// Test to see whether the first byte of the file
// matches the byte read into the buffer.
if (pbData[0] == bBuf[0]) {
    // OS may or may not be Windows 95.
} else {
    // OS is Windows 95.
}
```

This code fragment modifies the first byte of the memory-mapped file and then reads the supposedly modified byte back into a buffer. Windows NT guarantees that the file is coherent, while Windows 95 does not. For this reason, you should not write to a file using both memory-mapped file techniques and buffer write techniques. Of course, if the file is opened in read-only mode, you'll have no problem accessing it using either technique. The problem occurs only if you attempt to write to the file.

By the way, when the file above is closed, Windows NT guarantees that the X will be the first byte of the file, while Windows 95 does not.

Read-only files do not have coherence problems, which makes them good candidates for memory-mapped files. Memory-mapped files should never be used to share writable files over a network because the system cannot guarantee coherent views of the data. If someone's computer updates the contents of the file, someone else's computer with the original data in memory will not know that the information has changed.

The File Reverse Sample Application

The FileRev application (FILEREV.EXE), listed in Figure 7-1 beginning on page 233, demonstrates how to use memory-mapped files to reverse the contents of an ANSI or a Unicode text file. The source code files, resource files, and make file for the application are in the FILEREV.07 directory on the companion disc. FileRev doesn't create any windows or do anything visual, and it won't work correctly for binary files. FileRev determines whether the text file is ANSI or Unicode by calling the *IsTextUnicode* function (discussed in Chapter 15). This function is new with Windows NT 3.5, and you will have to edit the source code and recompile if you want the program to run correctly on Windows NT 3.1.

Under Windows 95, the *IsTextUnicode* function has no useful implementation and simply returns FALSE; calling *GetLastError* returns ERROR-_CALL_NOT_IMPLEMENTED. This means that the FileRev sample application always thinks that it is manipulating an ANSI text file when it is run under Windows 95.

When *WinMain* begins executing, it takes whatever filename was specified on FileRev's command line and makes a copy of that file called FILEREV.DAT. It does this so that the original file won't become unusable because its contents have been reversed. Next FileRev calls the *CreateFile* function, opening FILEREV.DAT for reading and writing.

As I said earlier, the easiest way to reverse the contents of the file is to call the C run-time function *_strrev*. As with all C strings, the last character of the string must be a zero terminator. Because text files do not end with a zero character, FileRev must append one to the file. It does so by first calling *GetFileSize*:

```
dwFileSize = GetFileSize(hFile, NULL);
```

Now that you're armed with the length of the file, you can create the file-mapping object by calling *CreateFileMapping*. The file-mapping object is created with a length of *dwFileSize* plus the size of a wide character (for the zero character). If there is a bug in FileRev that overwrites the address space occupied by the file-mapping object, an access violation will occur. After the file-mapping object is created, a view of the object is mapped into FileRev's address space. The *lpvFile* variable contains the return value from *MapViewOfFile* and points to the first byte of the text file.

The next step is to write a zero character at the end of the file and to reverse the string:

```
((LPSTR) lpvFile)[dwFileSize] = 0;
_strrev(lpvFile);
```

In a text file, every line is terminated by a return character ('\r') followed by a newline character ('\n'). Unfortunately, when we call _strrev to reverse the file, these characters also get reversed. So that the reversed text file can be loaded into a text editor, every occurrence of the "\n\r" pair needs to be converted back to its original "\r\n" order. This is the job of the following loop:

```
// Find first occurrence of '\n'.
lpch = strchr(lpvFile, '\n');

while (lpch != NULL) {
   *lpch++ = '\r';   // Change the '\n' to '\r'.
   *lpch++ = '\n';   // Change the '\r' to '\n'.

   // Find the next occurrence.
   lpch = strchr(lpch, '\n');
}
```

When you examine simple code like this, it is easy to forget that you are actually manipulating the contents of a file on the hard disk, which shows you how powerful memory-mapped files are.

After the file has been adjusted, FileRev must clean up by unmapping the view of the file-mapping object and closing all the kernel object handles. In addition, FileRev must also remove the zero character added to the end of the file (remember that _strrev doesn't reverse the position of the terminating zero character). If you don't remove the zero character, the reversed file would be 1 character larger, and calling FileRev again would not reverse the file back to its original form. To remove the trailing zero character, you need to drop back a level and use the file-management functions instead of manipulating the file through memory mapping.

Forcing the reversed file to end at a specific location requires positioning the file pointer at the desired location (the end of the original file) and calling the *SetEndOfFile* function:

```
SetFilePointer(hFile, dwFileSize, NULL, FILE_BEGIN);
SetEndOfFile(hFile);
```

> **Important**
>
> Note that *SetEndOfFile* must be called after the view is unmapped and the file-mapping object is closed; otherwise, an ERROR_USER_MAPPED-_FILE will occur. This error indicates that the end-of-file operation cannot be performed on a file that is associated with a file-mapping object.

The last thing FileRev does is spawn an instance of Notepad so that you can look at the reversed file. Below is the result of running FileRev on its own FILEREV.C file:

```
/////////////////////// eliF fO dnE ///////////////////////


}
;)0(nruter

}
;)ssecorPh.ip(eldnaHesolC
;)daernih.ip(eldnaHesolC

{ ))ip& ,is& ,LLUN ,LLUN ,0 ,ESLAF ,LLUN ,LLUN
,EMANELIF )" EXE.DAPETON"(TXET_ ,LLUN(ssecorPetaerC(
;WODNIWWOHSESU_FTRATS = sgalFwd.is
;WOHS_WS = wodniWwohSw.is
;)is(Foezis = bc.is
.srobal ruo fo stiurf eht ees ot dapetoN nwapS //


;)eliFh(eldnaHesolC
;)eliFh(eliFFOdnEteS
.desolc si tcejbo lenrek gnippam-elif //
```

FileRev.ico

FILEREV.C

```c
/*******************************************************************
Module name: FileRev.C
Notices: Copyright (c) 1995 Jeffrey Richter
********************************************************************/



#include "..\AdvWin32.H"        /* See Appendix B for details. */
#include <windows.h>
#include <windowsx.h>

#pragma warning(disable: 4001)       /* Single-line comment */
```

Figure 7-1. *(continued)*

The FileRev Application.

Figure 7-1. *continued*

```
#include <tchar.h>
#include <string.h>                   // For _strrev
#include "Resource.H"


///////////////////////////////////////////////////////////////


#define FILENAME  __TEXT("FILEREV.DAT")


///////////////////////////////////////////////////////////////


int WINAPI WinMain (HINSTANCE hinstExe,
   HINSTANCE hinstPrev, LPSTR lpszCmdLine, int nCmdShow) {

   HANDLE hFile, hFileMap;
   LPVOID lpvFile;
   LPSTR lpchANSI;         // Always ANSI
   LPWSTR lpchUnicode;     // Always Unicode
   BOOL fIsTextUnicode = FALSE;
   DWORD dwFileSize;
   LPTSTR lpszCmdLineT;

   STARTUPINFO si = { 0 };
   PROCESS_INFORMATION pi;

   // Get the name of the file the user wants to reverse.
   // We must use GetCommandLine here instead of WinMain's
   // lpszCmdLine parameter because lpszCmdLine is always an
   // ANSI string, never a Unicode string. GetCommandLine
   // returns ANSI or Unicode depending
   // on how we've compiled.
   lpszCmdLineT = _tcschr(GetCommandLine(), __TEXT(' '));

   if (lpszCmdLineT != NULL) {
      // We found a space after the executable file's name.
      // Now let's skip over any white space to get to
      // the first argument.
      while (*lpszCmdLineT == __TEXT(' '))
         lpszCmdLineT++;
   }
```

(continued)

Figure 7-1. *continued*

```
if ((lpszCmdLineT == NULL) || (*lpszCmdLineT == 0)) {
   // If no space was found or there are no arguments
   // after the executable file's name, display an
   // error message.
   MessageBox(NULL,
       __TEXT("You must enter a filename on ")
       __TEXT("the command line."),
       __TEXT("FileRev"), MB_OK);
   return(0);
}


// Copy input file to FILEREV.DAT so that the original is
// not destroyed. We must use GetCommandLine here instead
// of lpszCmdLine because the lpszCmdLine passed to WinMain
// is always ANSI, never Unicode.
if (!CopyFile(lpszCmdLineT, FILENAME, FALSE)) {
   // Copy failed.
   MessageBox(NULL,
       __TEXT("New file could not be created."),
       __TEXT("FileRev"), MB_OK);
   return(0);
}


// Open the file for reading and writing.
hFile = CreateFile(FILENAME, GENERIC_WRITE | GENERIC_READ,
   0, NULL, OPEN_EXISTING, FILE_ATTRIBUTE_NORMAL, NULL);

if (hFile == INVALID_HANDLE_VALUE) {
   // File open failed.
   MessageBox(NULL, __TEXT("File could not be opened."),
       __TEXT("FileRev"), MB_OK);
   return(0);
}


// Get the size of the file. I am assuming here that the
// file is smaller than 4 GB.
dwFileSize = GetFileSize(hFile, NULL);


// Create the file-mapping object. The file-mapping object
// is 1 character bigger than the file size so that a zero
// character can be placed at the end of the file to
// terminate the string (file). Because I don't yet know if
// the file contains ANSI or Unicode characters, I assume
// worst case and add the size of a WCHAR instead of a CHAR.
```

(continued)

235

Figure 7-1. *continued*

```
hFileMap = CreateFileMapping(hFile, NULL, PAGE_READWRITE,
   0, dwFileSize + sizeof(WCHAR), NULL);

if (hFileMap == NULL) {
   // File-mapping open failed.
   MessageBox(NULL, __TEXT("File map could not be opened."),
      __TEXT("FileRev"), MB_OK);
   CloseHandle(hFile);
   return(0);
}

// Get the address where the first byte of the file
// is mapped into memory.
lpvFile = MapViewOfFile(hFileMap, FILE_MAP_WRITE, 0, 0, 0);

if (lpvFile == NULL) {
   // Map view of file failed.
   MessageBox(NULL, __TEXT("Could not map view of file."),
      __TEXT("FileRev"), MB_OK);
   CloseHandle(hFileMap);
   CloseHandle(hFile);
   return(0);
}


// If we are not running on Windows NT 3.10, check to see
// whether the text file is Unicode; otherwise, assume ANSI.
if (LOWORD(GetVersion()) != 0x0A03){
   // Take an educated guess as to whether the text file
   // contains ANSI or Unicode characters.
   fIsTextUnicode = IsTextUnicode(lpvFile, dwFileSize,
      NULL);
}

if (!fIsTextUnicode){
   // For all the file manipulations below, we explicitly
   // use ANSI functions instead of Unicode functions
   // because, although the application can be ANSI or
   // Unicode, it is processing an ANSI file.

   // Put a zero character at the very end of the file.
   lpchANSI = (LPSTR) lpvFile;
   lpchANSI[dwFileSize] = 0;
```

(continued)

Figure 7-1. *continued*

```
    // Reverse the contents of the file.
    _strrev(lpchANSI);

    // Convert all "\n\r" combinations back to "\r\n" to
    // preserve the normal end-of-line sequence.
    lpchANSI = strchr(lpchANSI, '\n'); // Find first '\n'.

    while (lpchANSI != NULL) {
        // We have found an occurrence....
        *lpchANSI++ = '\r';   // Change '\n' to '\r'.
        *lpchANSI++ = '\n';   // Change '\r' to '\n'.
        lpchANSI = strchr(lpchANSI, '\n'); // Find the next
                                           // occurrence.
    }

} else {
    // For all the file manipulations below, we explicitly
    // use Unicode functions instead of ANSI functions
    // because, although the application can be ANSI or
    // Unicode, it is processing a Unicode file.

    // Put a zero character at the very end of the file.
    lpchUnicode = (LPWSTR) lpvFile;
    lpchUnicode[dwFileSize] = 0;

    // Reverse the contents of the file.
    _wcsrev(lpchUnicode);

    // Convert all "\n\r" combinations back to "\r\n" to
    // preserve the normal end-of-line sequence.
    lpchUnicode = wcschr(lpchUnicode, L'\n'); // Find first
                                              // '\n'.

    while (lpchUnicode != NULL) {
        // We have found an occurrence....
        *lpchUnicode++ = L'\r';   // Change '\n' to '\r'.
        *lpchUnicode++ = L'\n';   // Change '\r' to '\n'.
        lpchUnicode = wcschr(lpchUnicode, L'\n'); // Find the
                                                  // next
                                                  //occurrence.
    }
}
```

(continued)

Figure 7-1. *continued*

```
    // Clean up everything before exiting.
    UnmapViewOfFile(lpvFile);
    CloseHandle(hFileMap);

    // Remove the trailing zero byte added earlier by
    // positioning the file pointer at the end of the file,
    // not including the zero byte, and setting
    // the end-of-file.
    SetFilePointer(hFile, dwFileSize, NULL, FILE_BEGIN);

    // SetEndOfFile must be called after the
    // file-mapping kernel object is closed.
    SetEndOfFile(hFile);
    CloseHandle(hFile);

    // Spawn Notepad to see the fruits of our labors.
    si.cb = sizeof(si);
    si.wShowWindow = SW_SHOW;
    si.dwFlags = STARTF_USESHOWWINDOW;
    if (CreateProcess(NULL, _TEXT("NOTEPAD.EXE ") FILENAME,
        NULL, NULL, FALSE, 0, NULL, NULL, &si, &pi)){

        CloseHandle(pi.hThread);
        CloseHandle(pi.hProcess);
    }

    return(0);
}


/////////////////////// End Of File ///////////////////////
```

FILEREV.RC

```
//Microsoft Visual C++ generated resource script.
//
#include "Resource.h"

#define APSTUDIO_READONLY_SYMBOLS
/////////////////////////////////////////////////////////////////
//
// Generated from the TEXTINCLUDE 2 resource
//
#include "afxres.h"
```

(continued)

Figure 7-1. *continued*

```
//////////////////////////////////////////////////////////////
#undef APSTUDIO_READONLY_SYMBOLS


//////////////////////////////////////////////////////////////
//
// Icon
//

FileRev                 ICON    DISCARDABLE     "FileRev.Ico"

#ifdef APSTUDIO_INVOKED
//////////////////////////////////////////////////////////////
//
// TEXTINCLUDE
//

1 TEXTINCLUDE DISCARDABLE
BEGIN
    "Resource.h\0"
END

2 TEXTINCLUDE DISCARDABLE
BEGIN
    "#include ""afxres.h""\r\n"
    "\0"
END

3 TEXTINCLUDE DISCARDABLE
BEGIN
    "\r\n"
    "\0"
END


//////////////////////////////////////////////////////////////
#endif    // APSTUDIO_INVOKED


#ifndef APSTUDIO_INVOKED
//////////////////////////////////////////////////////////////
//
// Generated from the TEXTINCLUDE 3 resource
//


//////////////////////////////////////////////////////////////
#endif    // not APSTUDIO_INVOKED
```

Specifying the Base Address of a Memory-Mapped File

Just as you can use the *VirtualAlloc* function to suggest an initial address to reserve address space, you can also use the *MapViewOfFileEx* function instead of the *MapViewOfFile* function to suggest that a file be mapped into a particular address.

```
LPVOID MapViewOfFileEx(HANDLE hFileMappingObject,
    DWORD dwDesiredAccess, DWORD dwFileOffsetHigh,
    DWORD dwFileOffsetLow, DWORD dwNumberOfBytesToMap,
    LPVOID lpBaseAddress);
```

All the parameters and the return value for this function are identical to those of the *MapViewOfFile* function with the single exception of the last parameter, *lpBaseAddress*. In this parameter, you specify a target address for the file you're mapping. As with *VirtualAlloc*, the target address you specify must be on an even allocation granularity boundary (usually 64 KB); otherwise, *MapViewOfFileEx* returns NULL, indicating an error.

If the system can't map the file at this location (usually because the file is too large and would overlap another reserved address space), the function fails and returns NULL. *MapViewOfFileEx* does not attempt to locate another address space that can accommodate the file. Of course, you can specify NULL as the *lpBaseAddress* parameter, in which case *MapViewOfFileEx* behaves exactly the same as *MapViewOfFile*.

MapViewOfFileEx is useful when you're using memory-mapped files to share data with other processes. As an example, you might need a memory-mapped file at a particular address when two or more applications are sharing a group of data structures containing pointers to other data structures. A linked list is a perfect example. In a linked list, each node, or element, of the list contains the memory address of another element in the list. To walk the list, you must know the address of the first element and then reference the member of the element that contains the address of the next element. This can be a problem when you're using memory-mapped files.

If one process prepares the linked list in a memory-mapped file and then shares this file with another process, it is possible that the other process will map the file into a completely different location in its address space. When the second process attempts to walk the linked list, it looks at the first element of the list, retrieves the memory address of the next element, and then tries to reference this next element. However, the address of the next element in the first node will be incorrect for this second process.

There are two ways to solve this problem. First, the second process can simply call *MapViewOfFileEx* instead of *MapViewOfFile* when it maps the memory-mapped file containing the linked list into its own address space. Of course, this requires that the second process know where the first process originally mapped the file when constructing the linked list. When the two applications have been designed to interact with each other—which is most likely the case—this isn't a problem: the address can be hard-coded into both, or one process can notify the other process using another form of interprocess communication, such as sending a message to a window.

The second method for solving the problem is for the process that creates the linked list to store in each node the offset from within the address space where the next node is located. This requires that the application add the offset to the base address of the memory-mapped file in order to access each node. This method is not great: it can be slow, it makes the program bigger (because of the additional code the compiler generates to perform all the calculations), and it can be quite error prone. However, this is certainly a viable method and the Microsoft compiler offers assistance for based-pointers using the __based keyword.

When calling *MapViewOfFileEx*, you must specify an address that is between 0x80000000 and 0xBFFFFFFF, or *MapViewOfFileEx* will return NULL.

When calling *MapViewOfFileEx*, you must specify an address that is between 0x00010000 and 0x7FFEFFFF, or *MapViewOfFileEx* will return NULL.

Memory-Mapped Files and Win32 Implementations

Windows 95 and Windows NT implement memory-mapped files differently. You need to be aware of these differences because they can affect the way that you write your code and the robustness of your data.

Under Windows 95, a view is always mapped in the address space partition that ranges from 0x80000000 to 0xBFFFFFFF. This means that all successful calls to *MapViewOfFile* will return an address within this range. You might recall that the data in this partition is shared by all Win32 processes. This means that if a process maps a view of a file-mapping object, the data of the file-mapping object is physically accessible to all Win32 processes whether they have mapped a view of the file-mapping object or not. If another process calls *MapViewOfFile* using the same file-mapping object, Windows 95 will return the same memory address to the second process that it did to the first process. The two processes are accessing the same data and the views are coherent.

In Windows 95, it is possible for one process to call *MapViewOfFile* and pass the returned memory address to another process's thread using some form of interprocess communication. Once this thread has received the memory address, there is nothing to stop the thread from successfully accessing the same view of the file-mapping object. However, you should not do this for two reasons:

- Your application will not run under Windows NT, for reasons that I'll describe shortly.

- If the first process calls *UnmapViewOfFile*, the address space region will revert to the free state; this means the second process's thread will raise an access violation when it attempts to access the memory where the view once was.

In order for the second process to access the view of the memory-mapped file, a thread in the second process should call *MapViewOfFile* on its own behalf. When the second process does this, the system increments a usage count for the memory-mapped view. So if the first process calls *UnmapViewOfFile*, the system will not release the region of address space occupied by the view until the second process also calls *UnmapViewOfFile*.

When the second process calls *MapViewOfFile*, the address returned will be the same address that was returned to the first process. This averts the need for the first process to send the memory address to the second process using interprocess communication.

The Windows NT implementation of memory-mapped files is better than the Windows 95 implementation because Windows NT *requires* a process to call *MapViewOfFile* before the file's data is accessible in the process's address space. If one process calls *MapViewOfFile*, the system reserves a region of address space for the view in the calling process's address space—no other process can see the view at all. If another process wants to access the data in the same file-mapping object, a thread in the second process must call *MapViewOfFile*, and the system will reserve a region for the view in the second process's address space.

It is very important to note that the memory address returned by the first process's call to *MapViewOfFile* will most likely *not* be the same memory address returned by the second process's call to *MapViewOfFile*. This is true even though both processes are mapping a view of the same file-mapping object. In Windows 95, the memory addresses returned from *MapViewOfFile* are the same—but you should absolutely not *count* on them being the same if you want your application to run under Windows NT!

Let's look at another implementation difference. Here is a small program that maps two views of a single file-mapping object:

```
#define STRICT
#include <Windows.h>

int WINAPI WinMain (HINSTANCE hinstExe, HINSTANCE hinstPrev,
   LPSTR lpCmdLine, int nCmdShow) {

   HANDLE hFile, hFileMapping;
   BYTE *pbFile, *pbFile2;

   // Open an existing file--it must be bigger than 64 KB.
   hFile = CreateFile(lpCmdLine, GENERIC_READ | GENERIC_WRITE, 0,
      NULL, OPEN_ALWAYS, FILE_ATTRIBUTE_NORMAL, NULL);

   // Create a file-mapping object backed by the data file.
   hFileMapping = CreateFileMapping(hFile, NULL, PAGE_READWRITE,
      0, 0, NULL);

   // Starting at offset 0, map a view of the file
   // into the process's address space.
   pbFile = (PBYTE) MapViewOfFile(hFileMapping, FILE_MAP_WRITE,
      0, 0, 0);

   // Starting at offset 65536, map another view of the file
   // into the process's address space.
   pbFile2 = (PBYTE) MapViewOfFile(hFileMapping, FILE_MAP_WRITE,
      0, 65536, 0);

   if (pbFile + 65536 == pbFile2) {
      // If the addresses overlap, there is one address
      // space region for both views: this must be Windows 95.
      MessageBox(NULL, "We are running under Windows 95",
         NULL, MB_OK);
   } else {
```

(continued)

243

```
    // If the addresses do not overlap, each view has its own
    // address space region: this must be Windows NT.
    MessageBox(NULL, "We are running under Windows NT",
        NULL, MB_OK);
}


UnmapViewOfFile(pbFile2);
UnmapViewOfFile(pbFile);
CloseHandle(hFileMapping);
CloseHandle(hFile);

return(0);
}
```

Under Windows 95, when a view of a file-mapping object is mapped, the system reserves enough address space for the entire file-mapping object. This happens even if *MapViewOfFile* is called with parameters that indicate that you want the system to map only a small portion of the file-mapping object. This means that you can't map a 1-GB file-mapping object to a view even if you specify that only a 64-KB portion of the object be mapped.

Whenever any process calls *MapViewOfFile*, the function returns an address within the address space region that was reserved for the *entire* file-mapping object. So in the code above, the first call to *MapViewOfFile* returns the base address of the region that contains the entire mapped file. The second call to *MapViewOfFile* returns an address that is 64 KB into the same address space region.

The Windows NT implementation is again quite different. The two calls to *MapViewOfFile* in the code above cause Windows NT to reserve two different address space regions. The size of the first region is the size of the file-mapping object, and the size of the second region is the size of the file-mapping object minus 64 KB. Even though there are two different regions, the data is guaranteed to be coherent because both views are made from the same file-mapping object. Under Windows 95, the views are coherent because it *is* the same memory.

Using Memory-Mapped Files to Share Data Among Processes

The ability to share data and information quickly and easily among processes is one of the most compelling reasons to use a Microsoft Windows environment over more restrictive environments such as MS-DOS. Win32 and 16-bit Windows both handle these sharing tasks in a number of ways. In 16-bit Windows, for example, there are several methods for sharing data. Probably the most common method is to call either *Send-Message* or *PostMessage* using a window belonging to another process. Unfortunately, in 16-bit Windows *SendMessage* and *PostMessage* allow only one 16-bit value and one 32-bit value to be passed to another process. You can also allocate a block of global memory (using the GMEM-_SHARE flag) and then pass the handle (as the *wParam* or *lParam* parameter) in a call to *SendMessage* or *PostMessage*. The receiver of this message then calls *GlobalLock* to get an address to the memory block and reads or writes the data.

This method doesn't work in Win32, however, because each process has its own address space and one process cannot easily probe the data in another process's address space. 16-bit Windows makes it almost too easy to share data—applications frequently manipulate data that doesn't belong to them, causing other applications to crash.

The Win32 system, on the other hand, allows multiple applications (running on the same machine) to share data using memory-mapped files. Memory-mapped files are, in fact, the only mechanism that offers this capability in the Win32 environment. Other techniques for sharing and transferring data, such as using *PostMessage* or *SendMessage* (including using *SendMessage* passing the new Win32 WM_COPYDATA window message), all use memory-mapped files internally.

This data sharing is accomplished by having two or more processes map views of the same file-mapping object, which means they are sharing the same pages of physical storage. As a result, when one process writes to data in a view of a shared file-mapping object, the other processes see the change instantly in their views. Note that for multiple processes to share a single file-mapping object, all processes must use exactly the same name for the file-mapping object.

Let's look at an example: starting an application. When an application starts, the system calls *CreateFile* to open the EXE file on the disk. Then the system calls *CreateFileMapping* to create a file-mapping object. Finally the system calls *MapViewOfFileEx* on behalf of the newly created process so that the EXE file is mapped into the process's address space. *MapViewOfFileEx* is called instead of *MapViewOfFile* so that the file's image is mapped to the base address stored in the EXE file's image. The system creates the process's initial thread, puts the address of the first byte of executable code of this mapped view in the thread's instruction pointer, and then lets the CPU start executing the code.

If the user runs a second instance of the same application, the system sees that a file-mapping object already exists for the desired EXE file and doesn't create a new file object or file-mapping object. Instead, the system maps a view of the file a second time, this time in the context of the newly created process's address space. What the system has done is map the identical file into two address spaces simultaneously. Obviously, this is a more efficient use of memory because both processes are sharing the same pages of physical storage containing portions of the code that are executing.

The next two sections discuss various techniques for sharing a file-mapping object among multiple processes.

CreateFileMapping and *OpenFileMapping*

Let's begin by again looking at the *CreateFileMapping* function:

```
HANDLE CreateFileMapping(HANDLE hFile, LPSECURITY_ATTRIBUTES lpsa,
    DWORD fdwProtect, DWORD dwMaximumSizeHigh,
    DWORD dwMaximumSizeLow, LPSTR lpName);
```

When you call this function to create a file-mapping object, you can give the object a name by passing a zero-terminated string as the *lpName* parameter. For example, one process might create a file-mapping object and assign it the name *MyFileMapObj*:

```
HANDLE hFileMap = CreateFileMapping(..., "MyFileMapObj");
```

When the code above executes, *CreateFileMapping* creates the file-mapping object and, if another file-mapping object with the specified name doesn't exist, stores the name with the new file-mapping object.

If a file-mapping object *does* exist with the specified name, however, *CreateFileMapping* does not create a new object. Instead, it increments the usage count for the object and returns a process-relative handle identifying the existing file-mapping object. Note that the system does not change the size of the existing file-mapping object.

You can determine whether a new file-mapping object was created by calling *GetLastError*. Usually, you would call *GetLastError* to determine why a function failed. However, in the case of *CreateFileMapping* you can call *GetLastError* if the function is successful. If *GetLastError* returns ERROR_ALREADY_EXISTS, *CreateFileMapping* has returned a handle to a previously existing object. If you don't want to use this existing object, you need to close the handle. The following code fragment guarantees that *CreateFileMapping* will create a new object or none at all:

```
HANDLE hFileMap = CreateFileMapping(...);
if ((hFileMap != NULL) &&
    (GetLastError() == ERROR_ALREADY_EXISTS)) {
    CloseHandle(hFileMap);
    hFileMap = NULL;
}
return(hFileMap);
```

Another way that multiple processes can share a file-mapping object is by calling *OpenFileMapping*:

```
HANDLE OpenFileMapping(DWORD dwDesiredAccess,
    BOOL bInheritHandle, LPSTR lpName);
```

This function is similar to *CreateFileMapping* except that it assumes that a file-mapping object already exists—and if the object does not exist, *OpenFileMapping* will not create a new one. So in order to share a file-mapping object using *OpenFileMapping*, one process must first create the object using *CreateFileMapping*; then the other processes can open the file-mapping object using *OpenFileMapping*. In keeping with my example, all processes but the first open the file-mapping object by calling *OpenFileMapping* and passing a zero-terminated string as the *lpName* parameter:

```
HANDLE hFileMap = OpenFileMapping(..., "MyFileMapObj");
```

OpenFileMapping's first parameter, *dwDesiredAccess*, specifies access rights, such as FILE_MAP_READ, FILE_MAP_WRITE, FILE_MAP_ALL_ACCESS, or FILE_MAP_COPY, and the second parameter, *bInheritHandle*, indicates whether child processes should automatically inherit the handle to this file-mapping object. The handle that *OpenFileMapping* returns identifies the process-relative handle to the file-mapping object created by the first process.

If *OpenFileMapping* cannot find a file-mapping object that has the passed name, NULL is returned. If a valid handle is returned, mapping the data into a process's own address space is simply a matter of calling *MapViewOfFile* or *MapViewOfFileEx*. Don't forget to call *CloseHandle* when you have finished using the opened file-mapping object.

Inheritance

A great way for two processes to share a file-mapping object is for one process to create an inheritable file-mapping object; a new child process then inherits the parent's file-mapping object. The child process's handle to the file-mapping object will be exactly the same as the parent's handle,

In order to create an inheritable file-mapping object, you must call *CreateFileMapping* and pass it the address of a SECURITY_ATTRIBUTES structure that is initialized as follows:

```
SECURITY_ATTRIBUTES sa;
sa.nLength = sizeof(sa);
sa.lpSecurityDescriptor = NULL;
sa.bInheritHandle = TRUE;
hFileMap = CreateFileMapping(hFile, &sa, ...);
```

(Alternatively, if the parent process is sharing a file-mapping object created by another process, the parent process can call *OpenFileMapping* and simply pass TRUE for the *bInheritHandle* parameter.)

Then, when the parent process is ready to create the child process, the parent must call the *CreateProcess* function and pass TRUE for the *fInheritHandle* parameter:

```
BOOL CreateProcess(LPCTSTR lpszImageName, LPCTSTR lpszCommandLine,
    LPSECURITY_ATTRIBUTES lpsaProcess,
    LPSECURITY_ATTRIBUTES lpsaThread,
    BOOL fInheritHandles, DWORD fdwCreate, LPVOID lpvEnvironment,
    LPCTSTR lpszCurDir, LPSTARTUPINFO lpsiStartInfo,
    LPPROCESS_INFORMATION lppiProcInfo);
```

This causes the usage count of the file-mapping object to increment; the new child process will be able to use the handle to the file-mapping object, but it will not know what the value of the handle is. You must have some other technique for passing the value of the handle to the child. You can do this by passing a command-line parameter to the child or by sending or posting a message to a window created by the child process.

Whatever method you use (and others exist), the child is responsible for closing its handle to the file-mapping object. Only after all the processes have closed their handles to the file-mapping object does the system delete the object and all of the physical storage that was committed from the paging file for the object.

Memory-Mapped Files Backed by the Paging File

So far I've been discussing techniques that allow you to map a view of a file that resides on a disk drive. Many applications create some data while they run and need to transfer the data or share it with another process. It would be terribly inconvenient if the applications had to create a data file on a disk drive and store the data there in order to share it.

Microsoft realized this and added the ability to create memory-mapped files that are backed by the system's paging file rather than a dedicated hard disk file. This method is almost identical to the method for creating a memory-mapped disk file except that it's even easier. First, there is no need to call *CreateFile* since you will not be creating or opening a dedicated file. Instead, you simply call *CreateFileMapping* as you would normally and pass (HANDLE) 0xFFFFFFFF as the *hFile* parameter. This tells the system that you are not creating a file-mapping object whose physical storage resides in a file on the disk; instead, you want the system to commit physical storage from the system's paging file. The amount of storage allocated is determined by *CreateFileMapping*'s *dwMaximumSizeHigh* and *dwMaximumSizeLow* parameters.

After you have created this file-mapping object and mapped a view of it into your process's address space, you can use it as you would any region of memory. If you want to share this data with other processes, call *CreateFileMapping* and pass a zero-terminated string as the *lpName* parameter. Then other processes that want to access the storage can call *CreateFileMapping* or *OpenFileMapping* and pass the same name.

When a process no longer needs access to the file-mapping object, that process should call *CloseHandle*. When all the handles are closed, the system will reclaim the committed storage from the system's paging file.

Important

Here is an interesting problem that has caught unsuspecting programmers by surprise. Can you guess what is wrong with the following code fragment:

```
HANDLE hFile = CreateFile(...);
HANDLE hMap = CreateFileMapping(hFile, ...);
if (hMap == NULL)
    return(GetLastError());
    :
    :
```

If the call to *CreateFile* above fails, it returns 0xFFFFFFFF (INVALID-_HANDLE_VALUE). However, the unsuspecting programmer who wrote the code above didn't test to check whether the file was created successfully. When *CreateFileMapping* is called, 0xFFFFFFFF is passed in the *hFile* parameter, which causes the system to create a file mapping using pages from the paging file instead of the intended disk file.

The Memory-Mapped File Sharing Sample Application

The MMFShare application (MMFSHARE.EXE), listed in Figure 7-2, demonstrates how to use memory-mapped files to transfer data among two or more separate processes. The source code files, resource files, and make file for the application are in the MMFSHARE.07 directory on the companion disc.

You're going to need to execute at least two instances of the MMFSHARE.EXE program. Each instance creates its own dialog box, shown below.

To transfer data from one instance of MMFShare to another, type the data to be transferred into the Data edit field. Then click on the Create Mapping Of Data button. When you do, MMFShare calls *CreateFile-Mapping* to create a 4-KB memory-mapped file object backed by the system's paging file and names the object *MMFSharedData*. If MMFShare sees that a file-mapping object with this name already exists, it displays a message box notifying you that it could not create the object. If, on the other hand, MMFShare succeeds in creating the object, it proceeds to map a view of the file into the process's address space and copies the data from the edit control into the memory-mapped file.

After the data has been copied, MMFShare unmaps the view of the file, disables the Create Mapping Of Data button, and enables the Close Mapping Of Data button. At this point, there is a memory-mapped file named *MMFSharedData* just sitting somewhere in the system. No processes have mapped a view to the data contained in the file.

If you now go to another instance of MMFShare and click on this instance's Open Mapping And Get Data button, MMFShare attempts to locate a file-mapping object called *MMFSharedData* by calling *OpenFile-Mapping*. If an object of this name cannot be found, MMFShare displays another message box notifying you. If MMFShare finds the object, it maps a view of the object into its process's address space and copies the data from the memory-mapped file into the edit control of the dialog box. Voilà! You have transferred data from one process to another.

The Close Mapping Of Data button in the dialog box is used to close the file-mapping object, which frees up the storage in the paging file. If no file-mapping object exists, no other instance of MMFShare will be able to open one and get data from it. Also, if one instance has created a memory-mapped file, no other instance is allowed to create one and overwrite the data contained within the file.

MMFShare.ico

MMFSHARE.C

```
/************************************************************
Module name: MMFShare.C
Notices: Copyright (c) 1995 Jeffrey Richter
************************************************************/


#include "..\AdvWin32.H"      /* See Appendix B for details. */
#include <windows.h>
#include <windowsx.h>

#pragma warning(disable: 4001)      /* Single-line comment */

#include "Resource.H"



///////////////////////////////////////////////////////////////


BOOL Dlg_OnInitDialog (HWND hwnd, HWND hwndFocus,
   LPARAM lParam) {

   // Associate an icon with the dialog box.
   SetClassLong(hwnd, GCL_HICON, (LONG)
      LoadIcon((HINSTANCE) GetWindowLong(hwnd, GWL_HINSTANCE),
      __TEXT("MMFShare")));

   // Initialize the edit control with some test data.
   Edit_SetText(GetDlgItem(hwnd, IDC_DATA),
      __TEXT("Some test data"));

   // Disable the Close button because the file can't
   // be closed if it was never created or opened.
   Button_Enable(GetDlgItem(hwnd, IDC_CLOSEFILE), FALSE);
   return(TRUE);
}
```

Figure 7-2. *(continued)*
The MMFShare application.

Figure 7-2. *continued*

```
///////////////////////////////////////////////////////////

void Dlg_OnCommand (HWND hwnd, int id, HWND hwndCtl,
    UINT codeNotify) {

    // Handle of the open memory-mapped file
    static HANDLE s_hFileMap = NULL;
    HANDLE hFileMapT;

    switch (id) {
        case IDC_CREATEFILE:
            if (codeNotify != BN_CLICKED)
                break;

            // Create an in-memory memory-mapped file that
            // contains the contents of the edit control. The
            // file is 4 KB at most and is named MMFSharedData.
            s_hFileMap = CreateFileMapping((HANDLE) 0xFFFFFFFF,
                NULL, PAGE_READWRITE, 0, 4 * 1024,
                __TEXT("MMFSharedData"));

            if (s_hFileMap != NULL) {

                if (GetLastError() == ERROR_ALREADY_EXISTS) {
                    MessageBox(hwnd,
                        __TEXT("Mapping already exists - ")
                        __TEXT("not created."),
                        NULL, MB_OK);
                    CloseHandle(s_hFileMap);

                } else {

                    // File mapping created successfully.

                    // Map a view of the file
                    // into the address space.
                    LPVOID lpView = MapViewOfFile(s_hFileMap,
                        FILE_MAP_READ | FILE_MAP_WRITE, 0, 0, 0);

                    if ((BYTE *) lpView != NULL) {
                        // View mapped successfully; put contents
                        // of edit control into the memory-mapped
                        // file.
```

(continued)

Figure 7-2. *continued*

```
                    Edit_GetText(GetDlgItem(hwnd, IDC_DATA),
                       (LPTSTR) lpView, 4 * 1024);

                    // Unmap the view. This protects the
                    // data from wayward pointers.
                    UnmapViewOfFile((LPVOID) lpView);

                    // The user can't create
                    // another file right now.
                    Button_Enable(hwndCtl, FALSE);

                    // The user closed the file.
                    Button_Enable(GetDlgItem(hwnd,
                       IDC_CLOSEFILE), TRUE);

                } else {
                    MessageBox(hwnd,
                       __TEXT("Can't map view of file."),
                       NULL, MB_OK);
                }
             }

         } else {
             MessageBox(hwnd,
                __TEXT("Can't create file mapping."),
                NULL, MB_OK);
         }
         break;

      case IDC_CLOSEFILE:
         if (codeNotify != BN_CLICKED)
             break;

         if (CloseHandle(s_hFileMap)) {
             // User closed the file. A new file can be
             // created, but the new file can't be closed.
             Button_Enable(GetDlgItem(hwnd, IDC_CREATEFILE),
                TRUE);
             Button_Enable(hwndCtl, FALSE);
         }
         break;

      case IDC_OPENFILE:
         if (codeNotify != BN_CLICKED)
             break;
```

(continued)

Figure 7-2. *continued*

```
        // See if a memory-mapped file named
        // MMFSharedData already exists.
        hFileMapT = OpenFileMapping(
           FILE_MAP_READ | FILE_MAP_WRITE,
           FALSE, __TEXT("MMFSharedData"));

        if (hFileMapT != NULL) {
           // Memory-mapped file does exist. Map a view
           // of it into the process's address space.
           LPVOID lpView = MapViewOfFile(hFileMapT,
              FILE_MAP_READ | FILE_MAP_WRITE, 0, 0, 0);

           if ((BYTE *) lpView != NULL) {

              // Put the contents of the
              // file into the edit control.
              Edit_SetText(GetDlgItem(hwnd, IDC_DATA),
                 (LPTSTR) lpView);
              UnmapViewOfFile((LPVOID) lpView);

           } else {
              MessageBox(hwnd,
                 __TEXT("Can't map view."), NULL, MB_OK);
           }

           CloseHandle(hFileMapT);

        } else {
           MessageBox(hwnd,
              __TEXT("Can't open mapping."), NULL, MB_OK);
        }
        break;

     case IDCANCEL:
        EndDialog(hwnd, id);
        break;
  }
}


/////////////////////////////////////////////////////////////


BOOL CALLBACK Dlg_Proc (HWND hDlg, UINT uMsg,
   WPARAM wParam, LPARAM lParam) {
```

(continued)

Figure 7-2. *continued*

```
BOOL fProcessed = TRUE;

    switch (uMsg) {
        HANDLE_MSG(hDlg, WM_INITDIALOG, Dlg_OnInitDialog);
        HANDLE_MSG(hDlg, WM_COMMAND, Dlg_OnCommand);

        default:
            fProcessed = FALSE;
            break;
    }
    return(fProcessed);
}



//////////////////////////////////////////////////////////////



int WINAPI WinMain (HINSTANCE hinstExe,
    HINSTANCE hinstPrev, LPSTR lpszCmdLine, int nCmdShow) {

    DialogBox(hinstExe, MAKEINTRESOURCE(IDD_MMFSHARE),
        NULL, Dlg_Proc);

    return(0);
}



////////////////////////// End Of File //////////////////////////
```

MMFSHARE.RC
```
//Microsoft Visual C++ generated resource script.
//
#include "Resource.h"

#define APSTUDIO_READONLY_SYMBOLS
//////////////////////////////////////////////////////////////
//
// Generated from the TEXTINCLUDE 2 resource.
//
#include "afxres.h"


//////////////////////////////////////////////////////////////
#undef APSTUDIO_READONLY_SYMBOLS
```

(continued)

Figure 7-2. *continued*

```
//////////////////////////////////////////////////////////////
//
// Dialog
//

IDD_MMFSHARE DIALOG DISCARDABLE  38, 36, 186, 61
STYLE WS_MINIMIZEBOX ¦ WS_POPUP ¦ WS_VISIBLE ¦ WS_CAPTION
    ¦ WS_SYSMENU
CAPTION "Memory-Mapped File Sharing Application"
FONT 8, "System"
BEGIN
    PUSHBUTTON      "&Create mapping of Data",IDC_CREATEFILE,
                    4,4,84,14,WS_GROUP
    PUSHBUTTON      "&Close mapping of Data",IDC_CLOSEFILE,
                    96,4,84,14
    LTEXT           "&Data:",IDC_STATIC,4,24,18,8
    EDITTEXT        IDC_DATA,28,24,153,12
    PUSHBUTTON      "&Open mapping and get Data",IDC_OPENFILE,
                    40,44,104,14,WS_GROUP
END


//////////////////////////////////////////////////////////////
//
// Icon
//

MMFSHARE                ICON    DISCARDABLE     "MMFShare.Ico"

#ifdef APSTUDIO_INVOKED
//////////////////////////////////////////////////////////////
//
// TEXTINCLUDE
//

1 TEXTINCLUDE DISCARDABLE
BEGIN
    "Resource.h\0"
END

2 TEXTINCLUDE DISCARDABLE
BEGIN
    "#include ""afxres.h""\r\n"
    "\0"
END
```

(continued)

Figure 7-2. *continued*

```
3 TEXTINCLUDE DISCARDABLE
BEGIN
    "\r\n"
    "\0"
END


/////////////////////////////////////////////////////////////
#endif     // APSTUDIO_INVOKED


#ifndef APSTUDIO_INVOKED
/////////////////////////////////////////////////////////////
//
// Generated from the TEXTINCLUDE 3 resource.
//


/////////////////////////////////////////////////////////////

#endif     // not APSTUDIO_INVOKED
```

Sparsely Committed Memory-Mapped Files

In all the discussion of memory-mapped files so far, we see that the system requires that all storage for the memory-mapped file be committed either in the data file on disk or in the paging file. This means that we can't use storage as efficiently as we might like. Let's return to the discussion of the spreadsheet from the section "When to Commit Physical Storage" in Chapter 6. Let's say that you want to share the entire spreadsheet with another process. If we were to use memory-mapped files, we would need to commit the physical storage for the entire spreadsheet:

```
CELLDATA CellData[200][256];
```

If a CELLDATA structure is 128 bytes, this array requires 6,553,600 ($200 \times 256 \times 128$) bytes of physical storage. As I said in Chapter 6, "That's a lot of physical storage to allocate from the paging file right up front for a spreadsheet, especially when you consider that most users put information into only a few spreadsheet cells, leaving the majority unused."

It should be obvious that we would prefer to share the spreadsheet as a file-mapping object without having to commit all of the physical storage up front. *CreateFileMapping* offers a way to do this by specifying either the SEC_RESERVE or the SEC_COMMIT flag in the *fdwProtect* parameter.

These flags are meaningful only if you're creating a file-mapping object that is backed by the system's paging file. The SEC_COMMIT flag causes *CreateFileMapping* to commit storage from the system's paging file. This is also the result if you specify neither flag.

When you call *CreateFileMapping* and pass the SEC_RESERVE flag, the system does not commit physical storage from the system's paging file; it just returns a handle to the file-mapping object. You can now call *MapViewOfFile* or *MapViewOfFileEx* to create a view of this file-mapping object. *MapViewOfFile* and *MapViewOfFileEx* will reserve a region of address space and will not commit any physical storage to back the region. Any attempts to access a memory address in the reserved region will cause the thread to raise an access violation.

What we have here is a region of reserved address space and a handle to a file-mapping object that identifies the region. Other processes can use the same file-mapping object in order to map a view of the same region of address space. Physical storage is still not committed to the region, and if threads in other processes attempt to access a memory address of the view in their regions, these threads will raise access violations.

Now, here is where things get exciting. In order to commit physical storage to the shared region, all a thread has to do is call *VirtualAlloc*:

```
LPVOID VirtualAlloc(LPVOID lpvAddress, DWORD cbSize,
    DWORD fdwAllocationType, DWORD fdwProtect);
```

We already discussed this function in great detail in Chapter 6. Calling *VirtualAlloc* to commit physical storage to the memory-mapped view region is just like calling *VirtualAlloc* to commit storage to a region initially reserved by a simple call to *VirtualAlloc* using the MEM_RESERVE flag. And just as you can commit storage sparsely in a region reserved with *VirtualAlloc*, you can also commit storage sparsely within a region reserved by *MapViewOfFile* or *MapViewOfFileEx*. However, when you commit storage to a region reserved by *MapViewOfFile* or *MapViewOfFileEx*, all the processes that have mapped a view of the same file-mapping object can now successfully access the committed pages.

Using the SEC_RESERVE flag and *VirtualAlloc*, we can successfully share the spreadsheet application's *CellData* matrix with other processes—and use physical storage very efficiently.

Normally, *VirtualAlloc* will fail when you pass it a memory address outside 0x00400000 through 0x7FFFFFFF. However, when committing physical storage to a memory-mapped file created using the SEC_RESERVE flag, you have to call *VirtualAlloc,* passing a memory address that is between 0x80000000 and 0xBFFFFFFF. Windows 95 knows that you are committing storage to a reserved memory-mapped file and allows the call to succeed.

Important

Under Windows NT, you cannot use the *VirtualFree* function to decommit storage from a memory-mapped file that was reserved with the SEC-_RESERVE flag.

However, Windows 95 does allow you to call *VirtualFree* to decommit storage in this case.

CHAPTER EIGHT

HEAPS

The third and last mechanism for manipulating memory in Win32 is the use of heaps. Heaps are great for allocating lots of small blocks of data. For example, linked lists and trees are best managed using heaps rather than the virtual memory techniques discussed in Chapter 6 or the memory-mapped file techniques discussed in Chapter 7.

If you are coming from a 16-bit Windows programming background, you are familiar with the two different types of heaps: the local heap and the global heap. Each process and DLL in 16-bit Windows receives its very own local heap, and all processes share a single global heap.

In Win32, heap management is vastly different. Here is a list of some of the differences:

- There is just one type of heap. (It has no special name like "local" or "global" because there is only one type.)

- Heaps are always local to a process; the contents of a process's heap cannot be accessed by a thread in another process. Because many 16-bit Windows applications use the global heap as a method for sharing data between processes, this change to heaps is frequently the source of problems encountered in porting from 16-bit Windows to Win32.

- A single process can create several heaps within its address space and manipulate all of them.

- A DLL does not get its own heap; it uses heaps that are part of the process's address space. However, a DLL can create a heap in the process's address space for the DLL's own purposes. Because many 16-bit DLLs share data between processes using the DLLs' local heap, this change is also a frequent source of porting problems.

This chapter discusses Win32 heaps and the functions that are available to create them, manipulate them, and destroy them. For all new Win32 applications, these are the functions that you should be using. At the end of this chapter, I present a section that describes how Win32 implements the 16-bit Windows heap functions. Take note that the 16-bit Windows heap functions exist in the Win32 API for backward compatibility only. The functions are implemented on top of the new heap functions; they perform slowly and require additional memory. Use the 16-bit Windows global and local heap functions only if you must.

What Is a Win32 Heap?

A Win32 heap is a region of reserved address space. Initially, most of the pages within the reserved region are not committed with physical storage. As you make more allocations from the heap, the heap manager commits more physical storage to the heap. As allocations in the heap are freed, the heap manager decommits physical storage from the heap. Physical storage is committed to the heap in pages.

Every now and then someone asks me for the exact rules that the heap manager uses to decide when to commit or decommit physical storage. To be honest, I knew what the rules were once but I've forgotten them now. Also, different implementations and different versions of the Win32 API might use slightly different rules. Microsoft is constantly performing stress tests and running different scenarios to determine the rules that work best most of the time. As applications and the hardware that runs them change, these rules will change. If this knowledge is critical to your application, don't use heaps. Instead, use the virtual memory functions (that is, *VirtualAlloc* and *VirtualFree*) so that you can control these rules yourself.

A Process's Default Heap

When a Win32 process is initialized, the system creates a heap in the process's address space. This heap is called the process's default heap. By default, this heap's region of address space is 1 MB in size. However, the system can grow a process's default heap so that it becomes larger than 1 MB in size. The default region size of 1 MB can be changed using the /HEAP linker switch when you create an application. A DLL does not have a heap associated with it, and therefore you should not use the

/HEAP switch when you are linking a DLL. The heap switch has the following syntax:

`/HEAP:reserve[,commit]`

The process's default heap is required by many of the Win32 functions. For example, the core functions in Windows NT perform all of their operations using Unicode characters and strings. If you call an ANSI version of a Win32 function, this ANSI version must convert the ANSI strings to Unicode strings and then call the Unicode version of the same function. In order to convert the strings, the ANSI function needs to allocate a block of memory to hold the Unicode version of the string. This block of memory is allocated from your process's default heap. There are many other Win32 functions that require the use of temporary memory blocks; these blocks are allocated from the process's default heap. Also, the 16-bit Windows global and local heap functions make their memory allocations from the process's default heap.

Because the process's default heap is used by many of the Win32 functions and because your application has many threads calling the various Win32 functions simultaneously, access to the default heap is serialized. In other words, the system guarantees that only one thread at a time may allocate or free blocks of memory in the default heap at any given time. If two threads attempt to allocate a block of memory in the default heap simultaneously, only one thread will be able to allocate a block and the other thread will be forced to wait until the first thread's block is allocated. Once the first thread's block is allocated, the heap functions will allow the second thread to allocate a block. This serialized access causes a small performance hit. If your application has only one thread and you want to have the fastest possible access to a heap, you should create your own separate heap and not use the process's default heap. Unfortunately, you cannot tell the Win32 functions not to use the default heap, so their accesses to the heap are always serialized.

As I mentioned at the beginning of this chapter, a single process can have several heaps at once. These heaps can be created and destroyed during the lifetime of the process. The default heap, however, is created before the process begins execution and is destroyed automatically when the process terminates. You cannot destroy the process's default heap. Each heap is identified by its own heap handle, and all of the Win32 heap functions that allocate and free blocks within a heap require this heap handle as a parameter.

You can obtain the handle to your process's default heap by calling *GetProcessHeap*:

```
HANDLE GetProcessHeap(VOID);
```

Creating Your Own Win32 Heaps

In addition to the process's default heap, you can create additional heaps in your process's address space. Basically, there are three main reasons why you would want to create additional heaps in your own applications:

- Component protection
- More efficient memory management
- Local access

Let's look at each of these in detail.

Component Protection

For this discussion, imagine that your application needs to process two components: a linked list of NODE structures and a binary tree of BRANCH structures. You have two C files: LNKLST.C, which contains the functions that process the linked list of NODEs; and BINTREE.C, which contains the functions that process the binary tree of BRANCHes.

If the NODEs and the BRANCHes are stored together in a single heap, the combined heap might look like Figure 8-1. Now let's say that there's a bug in the linked-list code that causes the 8 bytes after NODE 1 to be accidentally overwritten. This causes the data in BRANCH 3 to be corrupted. When the code in BINTREE.C later attempts to traverse the binary tree, it will probably fail because of this memory corruption. This will, of course, lead you to believe that there is a bug in your binary-tree code when, in fact, the bug exists in the linked-list code. Because the different types of objects are mixed together in a single heap, it becomes significantly more difficult to track down and isolate bugs.

By creating two separate heaps, one for NODEs and the other for BRANCHes, you localize your problems. A small bug in your linked-list code does not compromise the integrity of your binary tree and vice versa. It is still possible to have a bug in your code that causes a wild memory write to another heap, but this is far less likely to happen.

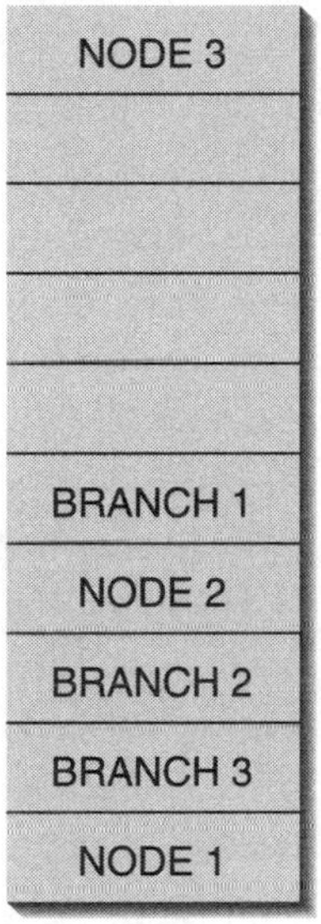

Figure 8-1.
A single heap that stores NODEs and BRANCHes together.

Efficient Memory Management

Heaps can be managed more efficiently by allocating objects of the same size within them. For example, let's say that every NODE structure requires 24 bytes and every BRANCH structure requires 32 bytes. All of these objects are allocated from a single heap. Figure 8-2 on the following page shows a fully occupied single heap with several NODE and BRANCH objects allocated within it. If NODE 2 and NODE 4 are freed, memory in the heap becomes fragmented. If you then attempt to allocate a BRANCH structure, the allocation will fail even though 48 bytes are available and a BRANCH needs only 32 bytes.

If each heap consisted only of objects that were the same size, freeing an object would guarantee that another object would fit perfectly into the freed object's space.

Local Access

The last reason to use separate heaps in your application is to provide local access. Giving applications a 4-GB address space when you're using a machine containing far less than 4 GB of physical memory requires that the operating system and the CPU work together. When the system

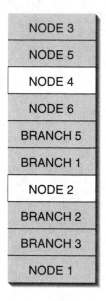

Figure 8-2.
A single fragmented heap that contains several NODE and
BRANCH objects.

swaps a page of RAM out to its paging file, it takes a performance hit. By the same token, another performance hit is taken when the system needs to swap a page of data back from the paging file into RAM. If you keep accesses to memory localized to a small range of addresses, it is less likely that the system will need to swap pages between RAM and the paging file.

So, in designing an application, it's a good idea to allocate things that will be accessed together close to each other. Returning to our linked list and binary tree example, traversing the linked list is not related in any way to traversing the binary tree. By keeping all the NODEs close together (in one heap), you can keep the NODEs in adjoining pages; in fact, it's likely that several NODEs will fit within a single page of physical memory. Traversing the linked list will not require that the CPU refer to several different pages of memory for each NODE access.

If you were to allocate both NODEs and BRANCHes in a single heap, the NODEs would not necessarily be close together. In the worst-case situation, you might be able to have one NODE only per page of memory, with the remainder of each page occupied by BRANCHes. In this case, traversing the linked list could cause page faults for each NODE, which would make the process extremely slow.

Creating Another Win32 Heap

You can create additional heaps in your process by having a thread call *HeapCreate*:

```
HANDLE HeapCreate(DWORD flOptions, DWORD dwInitialSize,
    DWORD cbMaximumSize);
```

The first parameter, *flOptions*, modifies how operations are performed on the heap. You can specify 0, HEAP_NO_SERIALIZE, HEAP_GENERATE_EXCEPTIONS, or a combination of the two flags.

By default, a heap will serialize access to itself so that multiple threads can allocate and free blocks from the heap without the danger of corrupting the heap. When an attempt is made to allocate a block of memory from the heap, the *HeapAlloc* function (discussed later) must do the following:

1. Traverse the linked list of allocated and freed memory blocks

2. Find the address of a free block

3. Allocate the new block by marking the free block as allocated

4. Add a new entry into the linked list of memory blocks

To illustrate how you might use the HEAP_NO_SERIALIZE flag, let's say that two threads are attempting to allocate blocks of memory from the same heap at the same time. The first thread executes steps 1 and 2 above and gets the address of a free memory block. However, before this thread can execute step 3, the thread is preempted and the second thread gets a chance to execute steps 1 and 2. Because the first thread has not executed step 3 yet, the second thread finds the address to the same free memory block.

With both threads having found what they believe to be a free memory block in the heap, Thread 1 updates the linked list, marking the new block as allocated. Thread 2 then also updates the linked list, marking the *same* block as allocated. Neither thread has detected a problem so far, but both threads receive an address to the exact same block of memory.

This type of bug can be very difficult to track down because it usually doesn't manifest itself immediately. Instead, the bug waits in the background until the most inopportune moment. The potential problems are listed on the following page.

- The linked list of memory blocks has been corrupted. This problem will not be discovered until an attempt to allocate or free a block is made.

- Both threads are sharing the same memory block. Thread 1 and Thread 2 might both write information to the same block. When Thread 1 examines the contents of the block, it will not recognize the data introduced by Thread 2.

- One thread might proceed to use the block and free it, causing the other thread to overwrite unallocated memory. This will corrupt the heap.

The solution to these problems is to allow a single thread exclusive access to the heap and its linked list until the thread has performed all the operations it needs to on the heap. The absence of the HEAP-_NO_SERIALIZE flag does exactly this. It is safe to use the HEAP_NO-_SERIALIZE flag only if one or more of the following conditions are true for your process:

- Your process uses only a single thread.

- Your process uses multiple threads, but the heap is accessed by only a single thread.

- Your process uses multiple threads but manages access to the heap itself by using other forms of mutual exclusion, such as mutexes and semaphores, as discussed in Chapter 9.

If you're not sure whether to use the HEAP_NO_SERIALIZE flag, don't use it. Not using it will cause your threads to take a slight performance hit whenever a heap manipulation function is called, but you won't risk corrupting your heap and its data.

The other flag, HEAP_GENERATE_EXCEPTIONS, causes the system to raise an exception whenever an attempt to allocate or reallocate a block of memory in the heap fails. An exception is just another way for the system to notify your application that an error has occurred. Sometimes it's easier to design your application to look for exceptions rather than to check for return values. Exceptions are discussed in Chapter 14.

The second parameter of *HeapCreate*, *dwInitialSize*, indicates the number of bytes initially committed to the heap. *HeapCreate* rounds this value up to an even multiple of the CPU's page size if necessary. The final parameter, *dwMaximumSize*, indicates the maximum size to which the heap can expand (the maximum amount of address space the system can reserve for the heap). If *dwMaximumSize* is 0, the system reserves a region (size determined by the system) for the heap and expands the region as needed until the region has reached its maximum size. If the heap is created successfully, *HeapCreate* returns a handle identifying the new heap. This handle is used by the other heap functions.

Allocating a Block of Memory from a Heap

Allocating a block of memory from a heap is simply a matter of calling *HeapAlloc*:

```
LPVOID HeapAlloc(HANDLE hHeap, DWORD dwFlags, DWORD dwBytes);
```

The first parameter, *hHeap*, identifies the handle of the heap from which an allocation should be made. This handle must be a handle that was returned by an earlier call to *HeapCreate* or *GetProcessHeap*. The *dwBytes* parameter specifies the number of bytes that are to be allocated from the heap. The middle parameter, *dwFlags*, allows you to specify flags that affect the allocation. Currently only three flags are supported: HEAP_ZERO_MEMORY, HEAP_GENERATE_EXCEPTIONS, and HEAP_NO_SERIALIZE.

The purpose of the HEAP_ZERO_MEMORY flag should be pretty obvious. This flag causes the contents of the block to be filled with zeros before *HeapAlloc* returns. The second flag, HEAP_GENERATE_EXCEPTIONS, causes the *HeapAlloc* function to raise a software exception if insufficient memory is available in the heap to satisfy the request. When creating a heap with *HeapCreate*, you can specify the HEAP_GENERATE_EXCEPTIONS flag, which tells the heap that an exception should be raised when a block cannot be allocated. If you specify this flag when calling *HeapCreate*, you don't need to specify it when calling *HeapAlloc*. On the other hand, you might want to create the heap without using this flag. In this case, specifying this flag to *HeapAlloc* affects only the single call to *HeapAlloc*, not every call to this function.

If *HeapAlloc* fails and then raises an exception, the exception raised will be one of the two shown in the table on the following page.

Identifier	Meaning
STATUS_NO_MEMORY	The allocation attempt failed because of insufficient memory.
STATUS_ACCESS_VIOLATION	The allocation attempt failed because of heap corruption or improper function parameters.

A block allocated with *HeapAlloc* is fixed and nondiscardable, so it is quite possible for the heap to become fragmented as the application allocates and frees various memory blocks. If the block has been successfully allocated, *HeapAlloc* returns the address of the block. If the memory could not be allocated and HEAP_GENERATE_EXCEPTIONS was not specified, *HeapAlloc* returns NULL.

The last flag, HEAP_NO_SERIALIZE, allows you to force this individual call to *HeapAlloc* to not be serialized with other threads that are accessing the same heap. You should use this flag with extreme caution because it is possible that the heap will become corrupted if other threads are manipulating the heap at the same time.

Changing the Size of a Block

Often it's necessary to alter the size of a memory block. Some applications initially allocate a larger than necessary block and then, after all the data has been placed into the block, resize the block to a smaller size. Some applications begin by allocating a small block of memory and then attempt to enlarge the block when more data needs to be copied into it. Resizing a memory block is accomplished by calling the *HeapReAlloc* function:

```
LPVOID HeapReAlloc(HANDLE hHeap, DWORD dwFlags,
    LPVOID lpMem, DWORD dwBytes);
```

As always, the *hHeap* parameter indicates the heap that contains the block you want to resize. The *dwFlags* parameter specifies the flags that *HeapReAlloc* should use when attempting to resize the block. The following four flags only are available: HEAP_GENERATE_EXCEPTIONS, HEAP_NO_SERIALIZE, HEAP_ZERO_MEMORY, and HEAP_REAL-LOC_IN_PLACE_ONLY.

The first two flags have the same meaning as when they are used with *HeapAlloc*. The HEAP_ZERO_MEMORY flag is useful only when you are resizing a block to make it larger. In this case, the additional bytes in the block will be zeroed. This flag has no effect if the block is being reduced.

The HEAP_REALLOC_IN_PLACE_ONLY flag tells *HeapReAlloc* that it is not allowed to move the memory block within the heap, which *HeapReAlloc* might attempt to do if the memory block were growing. If *HeapReAlloc* is able to enlarge the memory block without moving it, it will do so and return the original address of the memory block. On the other hand, if *HeapReAlloc* must move the contents of the block, the address of the new, larger block is returned. If the block is made smaller, *HeapReAlloc* returns the original address of the memory block. You would want to specify the HEAP_REALLOC_IN_PLACE_ONLY flag if the block were part of a linked list or tree. In this case, other nodes in the list or tree might have pointers to this node and relocating the node in the heap would corrupt the integrity of the linked list.

The remaining two parameters, *lpMem* and *dwBytes*, specify the current address of the block that you want to resize and the new size—in bytes—of the block. *HeapReAlloc* returns either the address of the new, resized block or NULL if the block cannot be resized.

Obtaining the Size of a Block

After a memory block has been allocated, the *HeapSize* function can be called to retrieve the actual size of the block:

```
DWORD HeapSize(HANDLE hHeap, DWORD dwFlags, LPCVOID lpMem);
```

The *hHeap* parameter (returned from an earlier call to either *HeapCreate* or *GetProcessHeap*) identifies the heap, and the *lpMem* parameter (returned from an earlier call to *HeapAlloc* or *HeapReAlloc*) indicates the address of the block. The *dwFlags* parameter can be either 0 or HEAP_NO-_SERIALIZE.

Freeing a Block

When you no longer need the memory block, you can free it by calling *HeapFree*:

```
BOOL HeapFree(HANDLE hHeap, DWORD dwFlags, LPVOID lpMem);
```

HeapFree frees the memory block and returns TRUE if successful. The *dwFlags* parameter can be either 0 or HEAP_NO_SERIALIZE. Calling this function may cause the heap manager to decommit some physical storage, but there are no guarantees.

Destroying a Win32 Heap

If your application no longer has a need for a heap that it created, you can destroy the heap by calling *HeapDestroy*:

```
BOOL HeapDestroy(HANDLE hHeap);
```

Calling *HeapDestroy* causes all the memory blocks contained within the heap to be freed and causes the physical storage and reserved address space region occupied by the heap to be released back to the system. If the function is successful, *HeapDestroy* returns TRUE. If you don't explicitly destroy the heap before your process terminates, the system will destroy it for you. However, a heap is destroyed only when a process terminates. If a thread creates a heap, the heap won't be destroyed when the thread terminates.

The system will not allow the process's default heap to be destroyed until the process completely terminates. If you pass the handle to the process's default heap to *HeapDestroy*, the system simply ignores the call.

Using Heaps with C++

One of the best ways to take advantage of Win32 heaps is to incorporate them into your existing C++ programs. In C++, class-object allocation is performed by calling the *new* operator instead of the normal C run-time routine *malloc*. Then, when we no longer need the class object, the *delete* operator is called instead of the normal C run-time routine *free*. For example, let's say that we have a class called CSomeClass and we want to allocate an instance of this class. To do this we would use syntax similar to the following:

```
CSomeClass* pCSomeClass = new CSomeClass;
```

When the C++ compiler examines this line, it first checks whether the CSomeClass class contains a member function for the *new* operator; if it does, the compiler generates code to call this function. If the compiler doesn't find a function overloading the *new* operator, the compiler generates code to call the standard C++ *new* operator function.

After you're done using the allocated object, you can destroy it by calling the *delete* operator:

```
delete pCSomeClass;
```

By overloading the *new* and *delete* operators for our C++ class, we can easily take advantage of the Win32 heap functions. To do this, let's define our CSomeClass class in a header file like this:

```
class CSomeClass {
   private:

   static HHEAP s_hHeap;
   static UINT s_uNumAllocsInHeap;

   // Other private data and member functions
   :
   :
   public:
   void* operator new (size_t size);
   void operator delete (void* p);
   // Other public data and member functions
   :
   :
};
```

In the code fragment above, I have declared two member variables, *s_hHeap* and *s_uNumAllocsInHeap,* as static variables. Because they are static, C++ will make all instances of CSomeClass share the same variables. That is, C++ will *not* allocate separate *s_hHeap* and *s_uNumAllocsIn-Heap* variables for each instance of the class that is created. This is very important to us because we want all of our instances of CSomeClass to be allocated within the same heap.

The *s_hHeap* variable will contain the handle to the heap within which CSomeClass objects should be allocated. The *s_uNumAllocsInHeap* variable is simply a counter of how many CSomeClass objects have been allocated within the heap. Every time a new CSomeClass object is allocated in the heap, *s_uNumAllocsInHeap* is incremented. Every time a CSomeClass object is destroyed, *s_uNumAllocsInHeap* is decremented. When *s_uNumAllocsInHeap* reaches 0, the heap is no longer necessary and is freed. The code to manipulate the heap should be included in a CPP file that looks like this:

```
HHEAP CSomeClass::s_hHeap = NULL;
UINT CSomeClass::s_uNumAllocsInHeap = 0;

void* CSomeClass::operator new (size_t size) {
   if (s_hHeap == NULL) {
      // Heap does not exist; create it.
      s_hHeap = HeapCreate(HEAP_NO_SERIALIZE, 0, 0);

      if (s_hHeap == NULL)
         return(NULL);
   }
```

(continued)

```
// The heap exists for CSomeClass objects.
void* p;
while ((p  = (void *) HeapAlloc(s_hHeap, 0, size)) == NULL) {
    // A CSomeClass object could not be allocated from the heap.
    if (_new_handler != NULL) {
        // Call the application-defined handler.
        (*_new_handler)();
    } else {
        // No application-defined handler exists; just return.
        break;
    }
}

if (p != NULL) {
    // Memory was allocated successfully; increment
    // the count of CSomeClass objects in the heap.
    s_uNumAllocsInHeap++;
}

// Return the address of the allocated CSomeClass object.
return(p);
}
```

You'll notice that I first defined the two static member variables, *s_hHeap* and *s_uNumAllocsInHeap*, at the top and initialized them as NULL and 0, respectively.

The C++ *new* operator receives one parameter—*size*. This parameter indicates the number of bytes required to hold a CSomeClass object. The first thing that our *new* operator function must do is create a heap if one hasn't been created already. This is simply a matter of checking the *s_hHeap* variable to see whether it is NULL. If it is, a new heap is created by calling *HeapCreate*, and the handle that *HeapCreate* returns is saved in *s_hHeap* so that the next call to the *new* operator will not create another heap but rather use the heap we have just created.

When I called the *HeapCreate* function above, I used the HEAP_NO_SERIALIZE flag because the remainder of the sample code is not multithread safe. In Chapter 9, I discuss features of Win32 that can be incorporated into the above code to make it multithread safe. The other two parameters in the call to *HeapCreate* indicate the initial size and the maximum size of the heap, respectively. I chose 0 and 0 here. The first 0 means that the heap has no initial size, whereas the second 0 means that the heap starts out small and expands as needed. You might want to change either or both of these values depending on your needs.

You might think it would be worthwhile to pass the *size* parameter to the *new* operator function as the second parameter to *HeapCreate*. In this way, you could initialize the heap so that it is large enough to contain one instance of the class. Then, the first time that *HeapAlloc* is called, it will execute faster because the heap won't have to resize itself to hold the class instance. Unfortunately, things don't always work the way you want them to. Because each allocated memory block within the heap has an overhead associated with it, the call to *HeapAlloc* will still have to resize the heap so that it is large enough to contain the one class instance and its associated overhead.

Once the heap has been created, new CSomeClass objects can be allocated from it using *HeapAlloc*. The first parameter is the handle to the heap, and the second parameter is the size of the CSomeClass object. *HeapAlloc* returns the address to the allocated block.

Once the allocation is performed successfully, I increment the *s_uNumAllocsInHeap* variable so that I know there is one more allocation in the heap. The last thing that the *new* operator does is return the address of the newly allocated CSomeClass object.

Well, that's it for creating a new CSomeClass object. Let's turn our attention now to destroying one when our application no longer needs it. This is the responsibility of the *delete* operator function, coded as follows:

```
void CSomeClass::operator delete (void* p) {
   if (HeapFree(s_hHeap, 0, p)) {
      // Object was deleted successfully.
      s_uNumAllocsInHeap--;
   }

   if (s_uNumAllocsInHeap == 0) {
      // If there are no more objects in the heap,
      // destroy the heap.
      if (HeapDestroy(s_hHeap)) {
         // Set the heap handle to NULL so that the new operator
         // will know to create a new heap if a new CSomeClass
         // object is created.
         s_hHeap = NULL;
      }
   }
}
```

The *delete* operator function receives only one parameter: the address of the object being deleted. The first thing that the function does is call *HeapFree*, passing it the handle of the heap and the address of the object to be freed. If the object is freed successfully, *s_uNumAllocsInHeap* is decremented, indicating that one fewer CSomeClass object is in the heap. Next the function checks whether *s_uNumAllocsInHeap* is 0, and, if it is, the function calls *HeapDestroy*, passing it the heap handle. If the heap is destroyed successfully, *s_hHeap* is set to NULL. This is extremely important because our program might attempt to allocate another CSomeClass object sometime in the future. When it does, the *new* operator will be called and will examine the *s_hHeap* variable to determine whether it should use an existing heap or create a new one.

This example demonstrates a very convenient scheme for using multiple heaps. It is easy to set up and can be incorporated into several of your classes. You will probably want to give some thought to inheritance, however. If you derive a new class using CSomeClass as a base class, the new class will inherit CSomeClass's *new* and *delete* operators. The new class will also inherit CSomeClass's heap, which means that when the *new* operator is applied to the derived class, the memory for the derived class object will be allocated from the same heap that CSomeClass is using. Depending on your situation, this may or may not be what you want. If the objects are very different in size, you might be setting yourself up for a situation in which the heap might fragment badly. You might also be making it harder to track down bugs in your code, as mentioned in the "Component Protection" and "Efficient Memory Management" sections earlier in this chapter.

If you want to use a separate heap for derived classes, all you need to do is duplicate what I did in the CSomeClass class. More specifically, include another set of *s_hHeap* and *s_uNumAllocsInHeap* variables, and copy the code over for the *new* and *delete* operators. When you compile, the compiler will see that you have overloaded the *new* and *delete* operators for the derived class and will make calls to those functions instead of to the ones in the base class.

The only advantage to not creating a heap for each class is that you won't need to devote overhead and memory to each heap. However, the amount of overhead and memory the heaps tie up is not great and is probably worth the potential gains. The compromise might be to have each class use its own heap and to let derived classes share the base class's heap when your application has been well tested and is close to shipping. But be aware that fragmentation might still be a problem.

The 16-Bit Windows Heap Functions

In this section, I'll discuss how the 16-bit Windows heap functions are implemented in the Win32 API. I'll cover all the global and local heap memory management functions, but I won't offer techniques for using them because I'm assuming that you're already familiar with 16-bit Windows programming techniques and because these functions should be avoided in new Win32 applications. Win32 supports the 16-bit Windows memory management functions solely for easy porting from one environment to another. If you are developing a new 32-bit application, and if you do not intend to compile the application natively for 16-bit Windows, I recommend that you don't use the global and local memory functions—they're slower and have more overhead than do the new Win32 heap functions.

In order to support the 16-bit Windows local and global heap functions, every Win32 process receives its very own default process heap and its very own handle table when initialized. The default process heap has already been discussed earlier in this chapter. This default heap is where the global and local memory allocations will be made.

The handle table exists so that Win32 can manage the local and global allocations. The handle table is an array of structures; each entry in the array points to a block of memory allocated from the default heap. When you call *GlobalAlloc*, the Win32 system allocates a block of memory from the process's default heap and locates an unused entry in the process's handle table. Then the system saves the address of the allocated block in the handle table and returns the address of the entry in the handle table. This returned value is the handle of the memory block. When you call *GlobalLock*, the system looks at the handle table and simply returns the address of the allocated block of memory in the default heap.

Initially Win32 allocates a small amount of storage to hold only a small number of handle table entries. As the application continues to make allocations from the handle table, additional handles might become necessary. When this happens, Win32 can increase the amount of storage used by the handle table, allowing additional handles to be allocated.

Because of this additional work required by the system to manage this handle table, it is easy to see why the new Win32 heap functions should be used instead of the old 16-bit Windows functions. However, if you want to continue to use the 16-bit Windows functions so that you can write code that can be natively compiled for both 16-bit Windows and Win32, or if you want to port your application to Win32 quickly, you should know that not all of the 16-bit Windows heap functions perform exactly as they did in 16-bit Windows. The remaining sections in this chapter explain what the 16-bit heap functions do in a Win32 environment.

16-Bit Windows Functions That Port to Win32

Figure 8-3 shows what the 16-bit Windows memory management functions do in Win32. For each entry, the two functions listed perform identical tasks on the heap. (Note that in Win32, both HGLOBAL and HLOCAL are typedefed as HANDLE.)

Of all the functions listed, only a few had semantic changes when they were ported to Win32. The following section covers these changes.

16-Bit Windows Memory Function	Meaning in Win32
HGLOBAL GlobalAlloc(UINT fuAlloc, DWORD cbAlloc); HLOCAL LocalAlloc(UINT fuAlloc, UINT cbAlloc);	Allocate a memory block.
HGLOBAL GlobalDiscard(HGLOBAL hglb); HLOCAL LocalDiscard(HLOCAL hlcl);	Discard a memory block. Macros defined as: GlobalReAlloc((hglb), 0, GMEM_MOVEABLE); LocalReAlloc((hglb), 0, LMEM_MOVEABLE);
UINT GlobalFlags(HGLOBAL hglb); UINT LocalFlags(HLOCAL hlcl);	Return flag information about a memory block.
HGLOBAL GlobalFree(HGLOBAL hglb); HLOCAL LocalFree(HLOCAL hlcl);	Free a memory block.
LPVOID GlobalLock(HGLOBAL hglb); LPVOID LocalLock(HLOCAL hlcl);	Lock a memory block.
BOOL GlobalUnlock(HGLOBAL hglb); BOOL LocalUnlock(HLOCAL hlcl);	Unlock a memory block.
HGLOBAL GlobalReAlloc(HGLOBAL hglb, DWORD cbNewSize, UINT fuAlloc); HLOCAL LocalReAlloc(HLOCAL hlcl, UINT cbAlloc, UINT fuAlloc);	Change the size and/or flags of a memory block.
DWORD GlobalSize(HGLOBAL hglb); UINT LocalSize(HLOCAL hlcl);	Return the size of a memory block.
HGLOBAL GlobalHandle(LPVOID lpvMem); HLOCAL LocalHandle(LPVOID lpvMem);	Return the handle of the memory block containing the passed address.

Figure 8-3.
Memory functions ported from 16-bit Windows to Win32.

Functions with Semantic Changes

Whenever an application calls *GlobalAlloc* or *LocalAlloc* to allocate non-fixed memory, the Win32 system must allocate a handle for the data as well as memory space for the data. When *GlobalAlloc* or *LocalAlloc* returns, it returns a handle—the address of an entry in the handle table. For example, let's say that these lines of code are executed:

```
HGLOBAL hglb = GlobalAlloc(GMEM_MOVEABLE, 10);
LPVOID lpv = GlobalLock(hglb);
```

The variable *hglb* is an address to a structure in the handle table. When *GlobalLock* is called, the entry in the handle table is examined to determine the address of the memory block. *GlobalLock* then returns this address.

Both *GlobalLock* and *LocalLock* return the address to the memory block that was allocated. Immediately preceding this block in memory is an internal data structure. This data structure contains some internal management information, such as the size of the allocated block and the handle of the block. When allocating fixed memory blocks, the system does not need to allocate a handle from the handle table. Instead, the system simply allocates the memory block and returns the address to this block when *GlobalAlloc* or *LocalAlloc* returns.

For *GlobalAlloc* and *LocalAlloc*, some of the flags' meanings have changed. Figure 8-4 shows all of the possible flags and what they mean in Win32.

Flag	Meaning in Win32
GHND	Defined as (GMEM_MOVEABLE ¦ GMEM_ZEROINIT)
LHND	Defined as (LMEM_MOVEABLE ¦ LMEM_ZEROINIT)
GPTR	Defined as (GMEM_FIXED ¦ GMEM_ZEROINIT)
LPTR	Defined as (LMEM_FIXED ¦ LMEM_ZEROINIT)
GMEM_DDESHARE, GMEM_SHARE	Win32 does not allow memory to be shared in this way. However, this flag may be used as a hint to the system about how to share memory in the future.

Figure 8-4. *(continued)*

Memory flags and their meanings in Win32.

279

Figure 8-4. *continued*

Flag	Meaning in Win32
GMEM_DISCARDABLE, LMEM_DISCARDABLE	Allocate block as discardable. Win32 ignores these flags.
GMEM_FIXED, LMEM_FIXED	Allocate block as fixed.
GMEM_LOWER, GMEM_NOT_BANKED, GMEM_NOCOMPACT, LMEM_NOCOMPACT, GMEM_NODISCARD, LMEM_NODISCARD, GMEM_NOTIFY, LMEM_NOTIFY	Ignored.
GMEM_MOVEABLE, LMEM_MOVEABLE	Allocate block as movable.
GMEM_ZEROINIT, LMEM_ZEROINIT	Zero contents of block after allocation.
NONZEROLHND	Defined as (LMEM_MOVEABLE)
NONZEROLPTR	Defined as (LMEM_FIXED)

It is incorrect to call *GlobalReAlloc* or *LocalReAlloc* specifying the GMEM_DISCARDABLE or LMEM_DISCARDABLE flag without also including the GMEM_MODIFY or LMEM_MODIFY flag.[1]

Functions That Should Be Avoided in Win32

Figure 8-5 shows 16-bit Windows memory allocation functions that have been kept in Win32 for easier porting between 16-bit Windows and Win32 applications but that are obsolete and should be avoided. Each of the functions existed for one or more of the following reasons:

- To allow applications to manipulate the shared global heap. In Win32, each application has its own address space and this type of functionality is no longer possible.

---

1. The GMEM_MODIFY flag and the LMEM_MODIFY flag do not appear in Figure 8-4 because they are used only in conjunction with the *GlobalReAlloc* and *LocalReAlloc* functions.

■ To help manage discardable memory. In Win32, memory blocks are never discarded by the system. They can be discarded if an application explicitly calls *GlobalDiscard* or *LocalDiscard*. Both functions really resize the blocks to 0 bytes anyway.

■ To help manage movable memory. In Win32, memory blocks are never moved or compacted by the system.

16 Bit Windows Memory Function	Meaning in Win32
BOOL DefineHandleTable(WORD w)	Macro defined as ((w), TRUE)
DWORD GetFreeSpace(UINT u)	Macro defined as (0x100000L)
DWORD GlobalCompact(DWORD);	Always returns 0x100000
void GlobalFix(HGLOBAL);	Same as calling GlobalLock
HGLOBAL GlobalLRUNewest (HGLOBAL h)	Macro defined as (HANDLE)(h)
HGLOBAL GlobalLRUOldest (HGLOBAL h)	Macro defined as (HANDLE)(h)
void GlobalUnfix(HGLOBAL);	Same as calling GlobalUnlock
BOOL GlobalUnWire(HGLOBAL);	Same as calling GlobalUnlock
void *GlobalWire(HGLOBAL);	Same as calling GlobalLock
void LimitEmsPages(DWORD)	Macro defined as nothing
UINT LocalCompact(UINT);	Always returns 0x100000
UINT LocalShrink (HLOCAL, UINT);	Always returns 0x100000
HGLOBAL LockSegment(UINT w)	Macro defined as GlobalFix((HANDLE)(w))
LONG SetSwapAreaSize (UINT w)	Macro defined as (w)
void UnlockSegment(UINT w)	Macro defined as GlobalUnfix((HANDLE)(w))

Figure 8-5.
These 16-bit Windows memory functions should be avoided in Win32.

Functions That Have Been Removed from Win32

The following list shows 16-bit Windows memory functions that have been removed from the Win32 API, mainly because they were Intel processor–specific functions. Win32 is a portable API designed to offer all of its functions on any and all CPU platforms to which Win32 is ported. Calling the following functions results in a compiler error because no prototype or macro exists for them:

AllocDStoCSAlias	*GlobalNotify*
AllocSelector	*GlobalPageLock*
ChangeSelector	*GlobalPageUnlock*
FreeSelector	*LocalInit*
GetCodeInfo	*SwitchStackBack*
GlobalDOSAlloc	*SwitchStackTo*
GlobalDOSFree	

CHAPTER NINE

THREAD SYNCHRONIZATION

In an environment in which several threads are running concurrently, it becomes important to be able to synchronize the activities of various threads. The Win32-based operating systems provide several synchronization objects that allow threads to synchronize their actions with one another. In this chapter, I'll concentrate on the four main synchronization objects: critical sections, mutexes, semaphores, and events. Other objects also exist for synchronization, and some of these are discussed and demonstrated in other chapters in this book.

This chapter offers numerous techniques for using the four main synchronization objects. For the most part, all the synchronization objects behave similarly. There are differences, however, which make one type of object more suitable for a particular task than another.

Of these four types of synchronization objects, all are kernel objects except critical sections. That is, a critical section is not managed by the low-level components of the operating system and is not manipulated using handles. A critical section is the easiest synchronization object to use and understand, and therefore, we'll discuss it before the other synchronization objects.

However, before we move directly on to critical sections, let's discuss the general concept of thread synchronization.

Thread Synchronization in a Nutshell

In general, a thread synchronizes itself with another thread by putting itself to sleep. When the thread is sleeping, it is no longer scheduled CPU time by the operating system and therefore stops executing. However, just before the thread puts itself to sleep, it tells the operating system what "special event" has to occur in order for the thread to resume execution.

The operating system remains aware of the thread's request and watches to see if and when this special event occurs. When it occurs, the thread is again eligible to be scheduled to a CPU. Eventually the thread will be scheduled and will continue its execution—the thread has now synchronized its execution with the occurrence of the special event.

As we discuss the various synchronization objects throughout this chapter, I'll show you how to specify a special event and how to put your thread to sleep after notifying the system to watch for the special event on your thread's behalf.

The Worst Thing You Can Do

Without synchronization objects and the operating system's ability to watch for special events, a thread would be forced to synchronize itself with special events by using the technique that I am about to demonstrate. However, because the operating system has built-in support for thread synchronization, you should *never* use this technique.

In this technique, one thread synchronizes itself with the completion of a task in another thread by continuously polling the state of a variable that is shared by or accessible to multiple threads. The code fragment below illustrates:

```
BOOL g_fFinishedCalculation = FALSE;

int WINAPI WinMain (...) {
   CreateThread(..., RecalcFunc, ...);
   :
   :

   // Wait for the recalculation to complete.
   while (!g_fFinishedCalculation)
      ;
   :
   :
}

DWORD WINAPI RecalcFunc (LPVOID lpvThreadParm) {
   // Perform the recalculation.
   :
   :

   g_fFinishedCalculation = TRUE;
   return(0);
}
```

As you can see, the primary thread (executing *WinMain*) doesn't put itself to sleep when it needs to synchronize itself with the completion of the *RecalcFunc* function. Because the primary thread does not sleep, it is being scheduled CPU time by the operating system. This takes precious time cycles away from other threads that could be executing code that does something more useful.

Another problem with the polling method as used in the previous code fragment is that the Boolean variable *g_fFinishedCalculation* might never be set to TRUE. This could happen if the primary thread has a higher priority than the thread executing the *RecalcFunc* function. In this case, the system never assigns any time slices to the *RecalcFunc* thread, which will never execute the statement that sets *g_fFinishedCalculation* to TRUE. If the thread executing the *WinMain* function were put to sleep instead of polling, it would not be scheduled time, and the system would have an opportunity to schedule time to lower-priority threads, such as the *RecalcFunc* thread, allowing them to execute.

I can't be any clearer than this: synchronize threads by putting them to sleep. Do not synchronize threads by having them continuously poll for special events.

Critical Sections

A critical section is a small section of code that requires exclusive access to some shared data before the code can execute. Of all the synchronization objects, critical sections are the simplest to use, but they can be used to synchronize threads only within a single process. Critical sections allow only one thread at a time to gain access to a region of data. Examine the following code fragment:

```
int    g_nIndex = 0;
const int MAX_TIMES = 1000;
DWORD g_dwTimes[MAX_TIMES];

DWORD WINAPI FirstThread (LPVOID lpvThreadParm) {
   BOOL fDone = FALSE;

   while (!fDone) {
      if (g_nIndex >= MAX_TIMES) {
         fDone = TRUE;
      } else {
         g_dwTimes[g_nIndex] = GetTickCount();
         g_nIndex++;
      }
   }
   return(0);
}
```

(continued)

```
DWORD WINAPI SecondThread (LPVOID lpvThreadParm) {
   BOOL fDone = FALSE;

   while (!fDone) {
      if (g_nIndex >= MAX_TIMES) {
         fDone = TRUE;
      } else {
         g_nIndex++;
         g_dwTimes[g_nIndex - 1] = GetTickCount();
      }
   }
   return(0);
}
```

Both of the thread functions here are supposed to produce the same result, although each is coded a bit differently. If the *FirstThread* function were running by itself, it would fill the *g_dwTimes* array with ascending values. The same is true if we were to run the *SecondThread* function by itself. Ideally, we would like to have both threads running concurrently and still have the *g_dwTimes* array produce ascending values. However, there is a problem with the code above: the *g_dwTimes* array won't be filled properly because the two thread functions are accessing the same global variables simultaneously. Here is an example of how this could happen.

Let's say that we have just started executing both threads on a system with one CPU. The operating system starts running *SecondThread* first (which could very well happen), and right after *SecondThread* increments *g_nIndex* to 1, the system preempts the thread and allows *FirstThread* to run. *FirstThread* then sets *g_dwTimes[1]* to the system time, and the system preempts the thread and gives time back to *SecondThread*. *SecondThread* now sets *g_dwTimes[1 – 1]* to the new system time. Because this operation occurred later, the new system time is a higher value than that of the time placed into *FirstThread*'s array. Also notice that index 1 of *g_dwTimes* was filled in before index 0. The data in the array is corrupted.

I admit that this example is a bit contrived. It is difficult to come up with a real-life example that doesn't require several pages of source code. However, you can easily see how this problem could extend itself to real-life examples. Consider the case of managing a linked list of objects. If access to the linked list was not synchronized, one thread could be adding an item to the list while another thread was simultaneously trying to search for an item in the list. The situation could become more chaotic if the two threads were adding items to the list at the same time. By using critical sections, you can ensure that access to the data structures is coordinated among threads.

Creating a Critical Section

To create a critical section, you must first allocate a CRITICAL_SECTION data structure in your own process. The allocation of the critical section structure must be global so that different threads can gain access to it. Usually, critical sections are simply global variables. Although the CRITICAL_SECTION structure and its members appear in WINNT.H,[1] you should think of the members of this structure as being off-limits. The Win32 functions that manipulate critical sections initialize and maintain all the members in the structure for you. You should not access or modify any of the members yourself.

After we've added critical sections to our example program, the code looks like this:

```
int   g_nIndex = 0:
const int MAX_TIMES = 1000:
DWORD g_dwTimes[MAX_TIMES];
CRITICAL_SECTION g_CriticalSection;

int WINAPI WinMain (...) {
   HANDLE hThreads[2];

   // Initialize the critical section before the threads so
   // that it is ready when the threads execute.
   InitializeCriticalSection(&g_CriticalSection);

   hThreads[0] = CreateThread(..., FirstThread ...);
   hThreads[1] = CreateThread(..., SecondThread ...);

   // Wait for both threads to terminate.
   // Don't worry about this line; it will be explained shortly.
   WaitForMultipleObjects(2, hThreads, TRUE, INFINITE);

   // Close the thread handles.
   CloseHandle(hThreads[0]);
   CloseHandle(hThreads[1]);

   // Delete the critical section.
   DeleteCriticalSection(&g_CriticalSection);
}
```

(continued)

1. CRITICAL_SECTION itself is in WINBASE.H as RTL_CRITICAL_SECTION. The RTL_CRITICAL_SECTION structure is typedefed in WINNT.H.

```
DWORD WINAPI FirstThread (LPVOID lpvThreadParm) {
   BOOL fDone = FALSE;

   while (!fDone) {
      EnterCriticalSection(&g_CriticalSection);
      if (g_nIndex >= MAX_TIMES) {
         fDone = TRUE;
      } else {
         g_dwTimes[g_nIndex] = GetTickCount();
         g_nIndex++;
      }
      LeaveCriticalSection(&g_CriticalSection);
   }
   return(0);
}

DWORD WINAPI SecondThread (LPVOID lpvThreadParm) {
   BOOL fDone = FALSE;

   while (!fDone) {
      EnterCriticalSection(&g_CriticalSection);
      if (g_nIndex >= MAX_TIMES) {
         fDone = TRUE;
      } else {
         g_nIndex++;
         g_dwTimes[g_nIndex - 1] = GetTickCount();
      }
      LeaveCriticalSection(&g_CriticalSection);
   }
   return(0);
}
```

Using a Critical Section

Before you can synchronize threads with a critical section, you must initialize the critical section by calling *InitializeCriticalSection*, passing the address to the CRITICAL_SECTION structure as the *lpCriticalSection* parameter:

```
VOID InitializeCriticalSection
   (LPCRITICAL_SECTION lpCriticalSection);
```

This initializes the members of the structure and must be done before *EnterCriticalSection* is called. The code above shows the critical section being initialized in *WinMain*. Both thread functions are expecting that the *g_CriticalSection* structure variable has been initialized by calling

288

InitializeCriticalSection before they begin executing. Let's see what happens next.

Referring again to our code example on the preceding pages, let's say that *SecondThread* executes first. It calls *EnterCriticalSection*, passing it the address to the *g_CriticalSection* structure variable:

```
VOID EnterCriticalSection(LPCRITICAL_SECTION lpCriticalSection);
```

EnterCriticalSection sees that this is the first time that *EnterCriticalSection* has been called for the *g_CriticalSection* variable, changes some members in the data structure, and lets the *g_nIndex++;* line execute. After this line executes, the system might preempt *SecondThread* and assign processor time to *FirstThread*. *FirstThread* calls *EnterCriticalSection*, passing the address of the same object that *SecondThread* used. This time, *EnterCriticalSection* sees that the *g_CriticalSection* structure variable is in use and puts *First-Thread* to sleep. Because *FirstThread* is asleep, the system can assign the remainder of its time slice to another thread. The system will stop trying to assign time slices to *FirstThread* until *FirstThread* is awakened.

Eventually *SecondThread* will be assigned another time slice. Then it will execute the following statement:

```
g_dwTimes[g_nIndex - 1] = GetTickCount();
```

This causes *g_dwTimes[0]* to be assigned the current system time. This is different from our first scenario, in which *g_dwTimes[1]* was assigned a lesser value than *g_dwTimes[0]*. At this point, if the system wants to preempt *SecondThread* it can do so, but it can't assign time to *FirstThread* because *FirstThread* is still waiting for the critical section to become available. Eventually *SecondThread* will be assigned a time slice again and will execute the following statement:

```
LeaveCriticalSection(&g_CriticalSection);
```

After this line executes, the *g_CriticalSection* variable indicates that the shared data structures are no longer protected and are available to any other thread that wants access to them. *FirstThread* was waiting on *g_CriticalSection*, so it can now be awakened. *FirstThread*'s call to *Enter-CriticalSection* sets ownership of *g_CriticalSection* to *FirstThread*, and then *EnterCriticalSection* returns so that *FirstThread* can continue execution.

As you can see, using critical sections allows access of data to only one thread at a time. In some cases, however, it is possible to have more than two threads requiring access to the same data at the same time.

When this happens, each thread must call *EnterCriticalSection* before it attempts to manipulate the data. If one of the threads already has ownership of the critical section, any thread waiting to gain access is put to sleep. When a thread relinquishes ownership by calling *LeaveCriticalSection*, the system wakes up only one of the waiting threads and gives that thread ownership. All the other sleeping threads continue to sleep.

Note that it is legal—and even useful—for a single thread to own a critical section several times. This can happen because calls to *EnterCriticalSection* from the thread owning the critical section increment a reference count. Before another thread can own the critical section, the thread currently owning it must call *LeaveCriticalSection* enough times so that the reference count drops back to 0. Let's see how this works using the following example:

```
int g_nNums[100];
CRITICAL_SECTION g_CriticalSection;
   :
   :

DWORD WINAPI Thread (LPVOID lpvParam) {
    int nIndex = (int) lpvParam;
    EnterCriticalSection(&g_CriticalSection);

    if (g_nNums[nIndex] < MIN_VAL)
       IncrementNum(nIndex);
    else
       g_nNums[nIndex] = MIN_VAL;

    LeaveCriticalSection(&g_CriticalSection);
    return(0);
}

void IncrementNum (int nIndex) {
    EnterCriticalSection(&g_CriticalSection);
    g_nNums[nIndex]++;
    LeaveCriticalSection(&g_CriticalSection);
}
```

In this code fragment, the *Thread* function acquires ownership of the critical section when it first begins executing. In this way, it can test *g_nNums[nIndex]*, knowing that no other thread can change *g_nNums[nIndex]* during the test. Then, if *g_nNums[nIndex]* contains a value less than MIN_VAL, the *IncrementNum* function is called.

IncrementNum is an independent function. It is implemented without any knowledge of what functions call it. Because the function will alter the *g_nNums* array, it requests access to the array by calling *EnterCriticalSection*. Because *IncrementNum* is executing under the thread that already owns the critical section, *EnterCriticalSection* increments only the reference count of the critical section and allows the thread to continue execution. If *IncrementNum* were called from another thread, the call to *EnterCriticalSection* would put that thread to sleep until the thread executing the *Thread* function called *LeaveCriticalSection.*

If you have several unrelated data structures in your application, you would create CRITICAL_SECTION variables for each of the data structures. Then your code would first have to call *InitializeCriticalSection* once for each of the CRITICAL_SECTION variables. Your threads would also need to call *EnterCriticalSection*, passing the address of the CRITICAL_SECTION variable that applies to the data structure(s) to which the thread wants access. Examine this code fragment:

```
int g_nNum[100];
char g_cChars[100];
CRITICAL_SECTION g_CriticalSection;
   :
   :
DWORD WINAPI ThreadFunc (LPVOID lpvParam) {
   int x;

   EnterCriticalSection(&g_CriticalSection);

   for (x = 0; x < 100; x++) {
      g_nNums[x] = 0;
      g_cChars[x] = 'X';
   }

   LeaveCriticalSection(&g_CriticalSection);
   return(0);
}
```

In this case, you enter a single critical section whose job it is to protect both the *g_nNums* array and the *g_cChars* array while they are being initialized. But the two arrays have nothing to do with one another. While this loop executes, no thread can gain access to either array. If the *ThreadFunc* function is implemented as shown on the next page, the two arrays are initialized separately.

```
DWORD WINAPI ThreadFunc (LPVOID lpvParam) {
   int x;

   EnterCriticalSection(&g_CriticalSection);

   for (x = 0; x < 100; x++)
      g_nNums[x] = 0;

   for (x = 0; x < 100; x++)
      g_cChars[x] = 'X';

   LeaveCriticalSection(&g_CriticalSection);
   return(0);
}
```

So, theoretically, after the *g_nNums* array has been initialized, a different thread that needs access only to the *g_nNums* array and not to the *g_cChars* array can begin executing while *ThreadFunc* continues to initialize the *g_cChars* array. But alas, this is not possible because both data structures are being protected by a single critical section. To fix this, you can create two critical sections, as follows:

```
int g_nNums[100];
char g_cChars[100];
CRITICAL_SECTION g_CriticalSectionForNums;
CRITICAL_SECTION g_CriticalSectionForChars;
   :
   :
DWORD WINAPI ThreadFunc (LPVOID lpvParam) {
   int x;

   EnterCriticalSection(&g_CriticalSectionForNums);

   for (x = 0; x < 100; x++)
      g_nNums[x] = 0;

   LeaveCriticalSection(&g_CriticalSectionForNums);


   EnterCriticalSection(&g_CriticalSectionForChars);

   for (x = 0; x < 100; x++)
      g_cChars[x] = 'X';

   LeaveCriticalSection(&g_CriticalSectionForChars);
   return(0);
}
```

Now this function has been implemented so that another thread can start using the *g_nNums* array as soon as *ThreadFunc* has finished initializing it. Sometimes you will need to access two data structures simultaneously. If this were a requirement of *ThreadFunc*, it would be implemented like this:

```
DWORD WINAPI ThreadFunc (LPVOID lpvParam) {
   int x;

   EnterCriticalSection(&g_CriticalSectionForNums);
   EnterCriticalSection(&g_CriticalSectionForChars);

   for (x = 0; x < 100; x++)
      g_nNums[x] = 0;

   for (x = 0; x < 100; x++)
      g_cChars[x] = 'X';

   LeaveCriticalSection(&g_CriticalSectionForChars);
   LeaveCriticalSection(&g_CriticalSectionForNums);
   return(0);
}
```

Suppose another thread in the process, written as follows, also requires access to the two arrays:

```
DWORD WINAPI OtherThreadFunc (LPVOID lpvParam) {
   int x;

   EnterCriticalSection(&g_CriticalSectionForChars);
   EnterCriticalSection(&g_CriticalSectionForNums);

   for (x = 0; x < 100; x++)
      g_nNums[x] = 0;

   for (x = 0; x < 100; x++)
      g_cChars[x] = 'X';

   LeaveCriticalSection(&g_CriticalSectionForNums);
   LeaveCriticalSection(&g_CriticalSectionForChars);
   return(0);
}
```

All I did in the function above was switch the order of the calls to *EnterCriticalSection* and *LeaveCriticalSection*. But because the two functions are written the way they are, there's a chance for *deadlock* to occur. Deadlock occurs when a thread will never execute because the resource

293

or resources it is waiting for (the critical sections, in this example) will never be available.

Suppose that *ThreadFunc* begins executing and gains ownership of the *g_CriticalSectionForNums* critical section. Then the thread executing the *OtherThreadFunc* function is given some CPU time and gains ownership of the *g_CriticalSectionForChars* critical section. Now you have a deadlock situation. When either *ThreadFunc* or *OtherThreadFunc* tries to continue executing, neither function will ever be able to gain ownership of the other critical section it requires.

In the example on the previous page, you can easily fix the problem by writing the functions so that they call *EnterCriticalSection* in the same order. This will keep one thread from locking the other one out of a needed resource.

Here is a technique you can use to minimize the time spent inside a critical section. The following code prevents other threads from changing the value in *g_nNums[3]* before the WM_SOMEMSG is sent to a window:

```
int g_nNums[100];
CRITICAL_SECTION g_CriticalSection;

DWORD WINAPI SomeThread (LPVOID lpvParam) {
    EnterCriticalSection(&g_CriticalSection);

    // Send a message to a window.
    SendMessage(hwndSomeWnd, WM_SOMEMSG, g_nNums[3], 0);

    LeaveCriticalSection(&g_CriticalSection);
    return(0);
}
```

It's impossible to tell how much time the window procedure requires to process the WM_SOMEMSG message—it could take a few microseconds or a few years.[2] During that time, no other threads can gain access to the *g_nNums* array. It would be much better to write the code as follows:

```
int g_nNums[100];
CRITICAL_SECTION g_CriticalSection;

DWORD WINAPI SomeThread (LPVOID lpvParam) {
    int nTemp;

    EnterCriticalSection(&g_CriticalSection);
```

---

2. Ideally, the window procedure is written a bit more efficiently than I suggest here and, at most, will not require more than a couple of seconds to run.

```
nTemp = g_nNums[3];

LeaveCriticalSection(&g_CriticalSection);

// Send a message to a window.
SendMessage(hwndSomeWnd, WM_SOMEMSG, nTemp, 0);
return(0);
}
```

This code saves the value in *g_nNums[3]* in a temporary integer variable *nTemp.* You can probably guess how long the CPU requires to execute this line—only a few CPU cycles. Immediately after saving the temporary variable, *LeaveCriticalSection* is called because the array no longer needs to be protected. This second implementation is much better than the first because other threads are stopped from using the *g_nNums* array for only a few CPU cycles instead of for an unknown amount of time.

When an application terminates, all the CRITICAL_SECTION variables should be cleaned up by calling *DeleteCriticalSection*:

```
VOID DeleteCriticalSection(LPCRITICAL_SECTION lpCriticalSection);
```

This function releases all the resources owned by the critical section. Naturally, you should not call *EnterCriticalSection* or *LeaveCriticalSection* using a deleted CRITICAL_SECTION variable unless it has been initialized again with *InitializeCriticalSection*. Also, be sure that you don't delete a critical section if a thread is waiting on a call to *EnterCriticalSection*.

The Critical Sections Sample Application

The CritSecs (CRITSECS.EXE) application, listed in Figure 9-1 beginning on page 300, demonstrates the importance of using critical sections in a multithreaded application. The source code files, resource files, and make file for the application are in the CRITSECS.09 directory on the companion disc.

When the program starts, *WinMain* invokes a modal dialog box. This dialog box serves as the interface to the application. When the dialog box function receives the WM_INITDIALOG message, the *Dlg_On-InitDialog* function initializes a global CRITICAL_SECTION structure, initializes all the child controls in the dialog box, and creates two threads—*CounterThread* and *DisplayThread*. At this point, three threads are running in this process: the primary thread that's handling the input to the dialog box and its controls, *CounterThread*, and *DisplayThread*.

Toward the top of CRITSECS.C, the following variable appears:

```
// The data that needs protecting
TCHAR g_szNumber[10] = __TEXT("0");
```

This is a character array that is initialized to a string containing the number 0. *CounterThread* converts the number in this character array to an integer, increments the integer by 1, and converts the integer back to a character array so that it can be stored in the *g_szNumber* array. *Display-Thread* reads the number in the *g_szNumber* array and appends the number to a list box control in the dialog box.

When CritSecs is invoked, its list box starts filling with numbers. The Critical Section Test Application dialog box appears as follows:

You might notice that the numbers in the list box don't appear in ascending order because CritSecs, by default, does not synchronize access to the *g_szNumber* array. While *CounterThread* is converting the array to an integer, incrementing it, and copying the number back, *DisplayThread* is reading the *g_szNumber* array and adding its contents to the list box.

To see what a big difference the critical sections make, click on the Synchronize check box. CritSecs immediately starts making use of the *g_CriticalSection* variable that guards access to the *g_szNumber* array. As a result, the list box now shows numbers that are in ascending order:

![Critical Section Test Application window showing Process priority class: Normal, Display thread priority: Normal, Counter thread priority: Normal, with Synchronize checked, Show counter thread and Pause unchecked, and a list box showing Dspy values from 125 to 157 in odd increments.]

I have added a few other capabilities to CritSecs. The Process Priority Class, Display Thread Priority, and Counter Thread Priority combo boxes let you fiddle with the priority class of the whole CritSecs application as well as the relative priorities of the two threads executing the *DisplayThread* and *CounterThread* functions.

The Pause check box demonstrates how to suspend the threads executing *CounterThread* and *DisplayThread* by calling the *SuspendThread* and *ResumeThread* functions.

The Show Counter Thread check box causes *CounterThread* to append the following line to the list box every time it completes its increment of the number and stores the digits of the number back in the *g_szNumber* array:

```
Cntr: Increment
```

When this check box is on, the list box appears as follows:

Now you can see that each iteration of *DisplayThread*'s loop executes faster than each iteration of *CounterThread*'s loop. In some cases, *Display-Thread*'s loop completes two iterations for just one iteration of *Counter-Thread*'s loop. This shows why you should get into the habit of anticipating how the system schedules time to threads. By altering the relative priorities of the two threads, you can alter the order and frequency of this behavior.

CritSecs might produce different results on your computer system depending on certain considerations, such as:

- The number of CPUs in your system (if you're running Windows NT)

- The speed of your system

- The number of threads created by other processes also running

- The priority class of other processes running

- The relative priorities of the threads running in these other processes

Two more features of the CritSecs program are worth noting. First, *CounterThread* calls the Win32 *Sleep* function after it stores the number back into the *g_szNumber* array. The prototype for the *Sleep* function is shown below:

```
VOID Sleep(DWORD cMilliseconds);
```

When a thread calls *Sleep*, it tells the system that it doesn't need any CPU time for the number of milliseconds specified by the *cMilliseconds* parameter. *CounterThread* calls *Sleep*, passing a value of 0 for *cMilliseconds*. This tells the system that the thread doesn't need any CPU time for the next 0 milliseconds. This might seem like a useless thing to do, but a side effect of the *Sleep* function exaggerates the results of CritSecs; *Sleep* also tells the system that the thread would like to voluntarily give up the remainder of its time slice. I put the call to *Sleep(0)* in *CounterThread* to dramatize the effect of unsynchronized threads in CritSecs. Without the call to *Sleep(0)*, CritSecs would still behave improperly and not synchronize the threads, but the problems would not be as pronounced.

The second note of interest in the CritSecs application is how it turns synchronization on and off. You'll see the following line at the beginning of both *CounterThread*'s and *DisplayThread*'s loop:

```
fSyncChecked = IsDlgButtonChecked(g_hwndDlg, ID_SYNCHRONIZE);
```

This line retrieves and saves the status of the Synchronize check box at the beginning of each loop's iteration. Elsewhere in the loop, I included code such as the following:

```
if (fSyncChecked) {
    EnterCriticalSection(&g_CriticalSection);
}
    .
    .
    .
if (fSyncChecked) {
    LeaveCriticalSection(&g_CriticalSection);
}
```

When I first developed CritSecs, the code above originally looked like this:

```
if (IsDlgButtonChecked(g_hwndDlg, ID_SYNCHRONIZE)) {
    EnterCriticalSection(&g_CriticalSection);
}
    .
    .
    .
if (IsDlgButtonChecked(g_hwndDlg, ID_SYNCHRONIZE)) {
    LeaveCriticalSection(&g_CriticalSection);
}
```

When CritSecs used the latter code fragment, a subtle bug was introduced that made some of the threads hang sometimes—but not every time. The *CounterThread* loop would start and see that the Synchronize check box was on. So *CounterThread* would call *EnterCriticalSection*. Then *DisplayThread*, seeing that the Synchronize check box was on, would also call *EnterCriticalSection*. But the system would not let *DisplayThread*'s call to *EnterCriticalSection* return because *CounterThread* currently had ownership of the critical section. While *CounterThread* was reading the number, I would turn off the Synchronize check box. When *CounterThread* made its call to *IsDlgButtonChecked*, it saw that the check box was off and would not call *LeaveCriticalSection*. As long as the check box remained off, *CounterThread* would never release the critical section and *DisplayThread* would stay forever hung, waiting for the critical section.

By saving the state of the check box in a variable and testing the variable before calling *EnterCriticalSection* or *LeaveCriticalSection*, I removed the possibility of executing unmatched *EnterCriticalSection* and *LeaveCriticalSection* calls. As you can see, you must be very careful when designing and implementing multithreaded applications.

CritSecs.ico

CRITSECS.C

```
/*********************************************************************
Module name: CritSecs.C
Notices: Copyright (c) 1995 Jeffrey Richter
*********************************************************************/


#include "..\AdvWin32.H"        /* See Appendix B for details. */
#include <windows.h>
#include <windowsx.h>


#pragma warning(disable: 4001)         /* Single-line comment */


#include <tchar.h>
#include <stdio.h>               // For sprintf
#include <process.h>             // For _beginthreadex
#include "Resource.H"



///////////////////////////////////////////////////////////////////



// Global variables
```

Figure 9-1.
The CritSecs application.

(continued)

Figure 9-1. *continued*

```
HWND      g_hwndDlg = NULL;
HANDLE    g_hThreadCntr = NULL;
HANDLE    g_hThreadDspy = NULL;

// The data that needs protecting
TCHAR     g_szNumber[10] = __TEXT("0");

// The critical section used to protect the data
CRITICAL_SECTION g_CriticalSection;


///////////////////////////////////////////////////////////////////


// Add a string to a list box.
void AddToListBox (LPCTSTR szBuffer) {
   HWND hwndDataBox = GetDlgItem(g_hwndDlg, IDC_DATABOX);

   int x = ListBox_AddString(hwndDataBox, szBuffer);
   ListBox_SetCurSel(hwndDataBox, x);

   if (ListBox_GetCount(hwndDataBox) > 100)
      ListBox_DeleteString(hwndDataBox, 0);
}


///////////////////////////////////////////////////////////////////


// Thread to increment the protected counter data
DWORD WINAPI CounterThread (LPVOID lpThreadParameter) {
   unsigned int nNumber, nDigit;
   BOOL fSyncChecked;

   for (;;) {
      // Get the status of the Synchronize check box
      // and save it.
      fSyncChecked =
         IsDlgButtonChecked(g_hwndDlg, IDC_SYNCHRONIZE);

      if (fSyncChecked) {
         // If the user wants us synchronized, do it.
         EnterCriticalSection(&g_CriticalSection);
      }
```

(continued)

301

Figure 9-1. *continued*

```
// Convert the string number to an integer and add 1.
_stscanf(g_szNumber, __TEXT("%d"), &nNumber);
nNumber++;

// Convert the new integer back to a string.
nDigit = 0;
while (nNumber != 0) {
   // Put a digit into the string.
   g_szNumber[nDigit++] = (TCHAR)
      (__TEXT('0') + (nNumber % 10));

   // A call to Sleep here tells the system that we want
   // to relinquish the remainder of our time slice to
   // another thread. This call is needed for
   // single-CPU systems so that the results of the
   // synchronization or lack thereof are obvious.
   // Normally, your programs would NOT call Sleep here.
   Sleep(0);

   // Get ready to get the next digit.
   nNumber /= 10;
}


// All digits converted to characters.
// Terminate the string.
g_szNumber[nDigit] = 0;

// Characters were generated in reverse order;
// reverse the string.
// Call _strrev if ANSI, Call _wcsrev if Unicode.
_tcsrev(g_szNumber);


if (fSyncChecked) {
   // If the user wants synchronization, do it.
   // In earlier versions of this program, I was calling
   // IsDlgButtonChecked as I did earlier instead of
   // using the fSyncChecked variable. This caused
   // problems because the user could check or uncheck
   // the Synchronize check box in between the calls to
   // EnterCriticalSection and LeaveCriticalSection.
   // This meant that my thread was sometimes leaving a
   // critical section that it had never entered. And my
   // thread was sometimes entering a critical section
   // that it had never left.
   LeaveCriticalSection(&g_CriticalSection);
}
```

(continued)

Figure 9-1. *continued*

```
        // If the user wants to display something
        // after each iteration, do it.
        if (IsDlgButtonChecked(g_hwndDlg, IDC_SHOWCNTRTHRD))
            AddToListBox(__TEXT("Cntr: Increment"));
    }
    return(0);  // We will never get here.
}


///////////////////////////////////////////////////////////////////


// Thread to add the current value of
// the counter (data) to the list box
DWORD WINAPI DisplayThread (LPVOID lpThreadParameter) {
    BOOL fSyncChecked;
    TCHAR szBuffer[50];

    for (;;) {

        // Determine whether the user wants the threads
        // to be synchronized.
        fSyncChecked =
            IsDlgButtonChecked(g_hwndDlg, IDC_SYNCHRONIZE);

        if (fSyncChecked)
            EnterCriticalSection(&g_CriticalSection);

        // Construct a string with the string form of the number.
        _stprintf(szBuffer, __TEXT("Dspy: %s"), g_szNumber);

        if (fSyncChecked)
            LeaveCriticalSection(&g_CriticalSection);

        // Add the string form of the number to the list box.
        AddToListBox(szBuffer);
    }
    return(0);  // We will never get here.
}
```

(continued)

Figure 9-1. *continued*

```
/////////////////////////////////////////////////////////////////

BOOL Dlg_OnInitDialog (HWND hwnd, HWND hwndFocus,
   LPARAM lParam) {
   HWND hWndCtl;
   DWORD dwThreadID;

   // Save the handle of the dialog box in a global so that
   // the threads can easily gain access to it. This must be
   // done before creating the threads.
   g_hwndDlg = hwnd;

   // Associate an icon with the dialog box.
   SetClassLong(hwnd, GCL_HICON, (LONG)
      LoadIcon((HINSTANCE) GetWindowLong(hwnd,
         GWL_HINSTANCE), __TEXT("CritSecs")));

   // Initialize the critical section. This must be
   // done before any threads try to use it.
   InitializeCriticalSection(&g_CriticalSection);

   // Create our counter thread and let it start running.
   g_hThreadCntr = BEGINTHREADEX(NULL, 0, CounterThread, NULL,
      0, &dwThreadID);

   // Create our display thread and let it start running.
   g_hThreadDspy = BEGINTHREADEX(NULL, 0, DisplayThread, NULL,
      0, &dwThreadID);


   // Fill the Process Priority Class combo box and select
   // Normal.
   hWndCtl = GetDlgItem(hwnd, IDC_PRIORITYCLASS);
   ComboBox_AddString(hWndCtl, __TEXT("Idle"));
   ComboBox_AddString(hWndCtl, __TEXT("Normal"));
   ComboBox_AddString(hWndCtl, __TEXT("High"));
   ComboBox_AddString(hWndCtl, __TEXT("Realtime"));
   ComboBox_SetCurSel(hWndCtl, 1);  // Normal

   // Fill the Display Thread Priority
   // combo box and select Normal.
   hWndCtl = GetDlgItem(hwnd, IDC_DSPYTHRDPRIORITY);
   ComboBox_AddString(hWndCtl, __TEXT("Idle"));
   ComboBox_AddString(hWndCtl, __TEXT("Lowest"));
   ComboBox_AddString(hWndCtl, __TEXT("Below normal"));
```

(continued)

Figure 9-1. *continued*

```
    ComboBox_AddString(hWndCtl, __TEXT("Normal"));
    ComboBox_AddString(hWndCtl, __TEXT("Above normal"));
    ComboBox_AddString(hWndCtl, __TEXT("Highest"));
    ComboBox_AddString(hWndCtl, __TEXT("Timecritical"));
    ComboBox_SetCurSel(hWndCtl, 3);  // Normal

    // Fill the Counter Thread Priority
    // combo box and select Normal.
    hWndCtl = GetDlgItem(hwnd, IDC_CNTRTHRDPRIORITY);
    ComboBox_AddString(hWndCtl, __TEXT("Idle"));
    ComboBox_AddString(hWndCtl, __TEXT("Lowest"));
    ComboBox_AddString(hWndCtl, __TEXT("Below normal"));
    ComboBox_AddString(hWndCtl, __TEXT("Normal"));
    ComboBox_AddString(hWndCtl, __TEXT("Above normal"));
    ComboBox_AddString(hWndCtl, __TEXT("Highest"));
    ComboBox_AddString(hWndCtl, __TEXT("Timecritical"));
    ComboBox_SetCurSel(hWndCtl, 3);  // Normal

    return(TRUE);
}


///////////////////////////////////////////////////////////


void Dlg_OnDestroy (HWND hwnd) {
    // When the dialog box is destroyed, terminate the
    // two threads and delete the critical section.
    TerminateThread(g_hThreadDspy, 0);
    TerminateThread(g_hThreadCntr, 0);
    DeleteCriticalSection(&g_CriticalSection);
}


///////////////////////////////////////////////////////////


void Dlg_OnCommand (HWND hwnd, int id, HWND hwndCtl,
    UINT codeNotify) {

    HANDLE hThread;
    DWORD dw;

    switch (id) {
```

(continued)

Figure 9-1. *continued*

```
    case IDCANCEL:
       EndDialog(hwnd, id);
       break;

    case IDC_PRIORITYCLASS:
       if (codeNotify != CBN_SELCHANGE)
          break;

       // User is changing priority class.
       switch (ComboBox_GetCurSel(hwndCtl)) {
          case 0:
             dw = IDLE_PRIORITY_CLASS;
             break;

          case 1:
          default:
             dw = NORMAL_PRIORITY_CLASS;
             break;

          case 2:
             dw = HIGH_PRIORITY_CLASS;
             break;

          case 3:
             dw = REALTIME_PRIORITY_CLASS;
             break;
       }
       SetPriorityClass(GetCurrentProcess(), dw);
       break;

    case IDC_DSPYTHRDPRIORITY:
    case IDC_CNTRTHRDPRIORITY:
       if (codeNotify != CBN_SELCHANGE)
          break;

       switch (ComboBox_GetCurSel(hwndCtl)) {
          case 0:
             dw = (DWORD) THREAD_PRIORITY_IDLE;
             break;

          case 1:
             dw = (DWORD) THREAD_PRIORITY_LOWEST;
             break;
```

(continued)

Figure 9-1. *continued*

```
            case 2:
                dw = (DWORD) THREAD_PRIORITY_BELOW_NORMAL;
                break;

            case 3:
            default:
                dw = (DWORD) THREAD_PRIORITY_NORMAL;
                break;

            case 4:
                dw = (DWORD) THREAD_PRIORITY_ABOVE_NORMAL;
                break;

            case 5:
                dw = (DWORD) THREAD_PRIORITY_HIGHEST;
                break;

            case 6:
                dw = (DWORD) THREAD_PRIORITY_TIME_CRITICAL;
                break;
            }
            // User is changing the relative priority
            // of one of the threads.
            hThread = (id == IDC_CNTRTHRDPRIORITY) ?
                g_hThreadCntr : g_hThreadDspy;

            SetThreadPriority(hThread, dw);
            break;

        case IDC_PAUSE:
            // User is pausing or resuming both threads.
            if (Button_GetCheck(hwndCtl)) {

                SuspendThread(g_hThreadCntr);
                SuspendThread(g_hThreadDspy);

            } else {

                ResumeThread(g_hThreadCntr);
                ResumeThread(g_hThreadDspy);

            }
            break;
    }
}
```

(continued)

Figure 9-1. *continued*

```
///////////////////////////////////////////////////////////////

BOOL CALLBACK Dlg_Proc (HWND hDlg, UINT uMsg,
   WPARAM wParam, LPARAM lParam) {

   BOOL fProcessed = TRUE;

   switch (uMsg) {
      HANDLE_MSG(hDlg, WM_INITDIALOG, Dlg_OnInitDialog);
      HANDLE_MSG(hDlg, WM_DESTROY, Dlg_OnDestroy);
      HANDLE_MSG(hDlg, WM_COMMAND, Dlg_OnCommand);

      default:
         fProcessed = FALSE;
         break;
   }
   return(fProcessed);
}


///////////////////////////////////////////////////////////////


int WINAPI WinMain (HINSTANCE hinstExe,
   HINSTANCE hinstPrev, LPSTR lpszCmdLine, int nCmdShow) {

   DialogBox(hinstExe, MAKEINTRESOURCE(IDD_CRITSECS),
      NULL, Dlg_Proc);

   return(0);
}


////////////////////////// End Of File //////////////////////////
```

CRITSECS.RC
```
//Microsoft Visual C++ generated resource script.
//
#include "Resource.h"

#define APSTUDIO_READONLY_SYMBOLS
```

(continued)

Figure 9-1. *continued*

```
////////////////////////////////////////////////////////////////
//
// Generated from the TEXTINCLUDE 2 resource.
//
#include "afxres.h"


////////////////////////////////////////////////////////////////
#undef APSTUDIO_READONLY_SYMBOLS



////////////////////////////////////////////////////////////////
//
// Icon
//


CritSecs                ICON    DISCARDABLE     "CritSecs.Ico"


////////////////////////////////////////////////////////////////
//
// Dialog
//


IDD_CRITSECS DIALOG DISCARDABLE  29, 28, 197, 208
STYLE WS_MINIMIZEBOX ¦ WS_POPUP ¦ WS_VISIBLE ¦ WS_CAPTION
    ¦ WS_SYSMENU
CAPTION "Critical Section Test Application"
FONT 8, "System"
BEGIN
    LTEXT           "&Process priority class:",IDC_STATIC,
                    4,4,74,8
    COMBOBOX        IDC_PRIORITYCLASS,88,4,64,48,
                    CBS_DROPDOWNLIST ¦ WS_GROUP ¦ WS_TABSTOP
    CONTROL         "&Display thread priority:",IDC_STATIC,
                    "Static",SS_LEFTNOWORDWRAP ¦ WS_GROUP
                    ¦ WS_TABSTOP,4,24,76,8
    COMBOBOX        IDC_DSPYTHRDPRIORITY,88,24,100,76,
                    CBS_DROPDOWNLIST ¦ WS_GROUP ¦ WS_TABSTOP
    CONTROL         "&Counter thread priority:",
                    IDC_STATIC,"Static",SS_LEFTNOWORDWRAP
                    ¦ WS_GROUP ¦ WS_TABSTOP,4,40,76,8
    COMBOBOX        IDC_CNTRTHRDPRIORITY,88,40,100,76,
                    CBS_DROPDOWNLIST ¦ WS_GROUP ¦ WS_TABSTOP
    CONTROL         "&Synchronize",IDC_SYNCHRONIZE,"Button",
                    BS_AUTOCHECKBOX ¦ WS_TABSTOP,4,60,52,10
```

(continued)

Figure 9-1. *continued*

```
      CONTROL          "S&how counter thread",IDC_SHOWCNTRTHRD,
                       "Button",BS_AUTOCHECKBOX | WS_TABSTOP,4,
                       72,77,10
      CONTROL          "P&ause",IDC_PAUSE,"Button",
                       BS_AUTOCHECKBOX | WS_TABSTOP,4,84,32,10
      LISTBOX          IDC_DATABOX,88,60,100,144,WS_VSCROLL
                       | WS_GROUP | WS_TABSTOP
END


#ifdef APSTUDIO_INVOKED
/////////////////////////////////////////////////////////////////
//
// TEXTINCLUDE
//

1 TEXTINCLUDE DISCARDABLE
BEGIN
    "Resource.h\0"
END

2 TEXTINCLUDE DISCARDABLE
BEGIN
    "#include ""afxres.h""\r\n"
    "\0"
END

3 TEXTINCLUDE DISCARDABLE
BEGIN
    "\r\n"
    "\0"
END


/////////////////////////////////////////////////////////////////
#endif    // APSTUDIO_INVOKED


#ifndef APSTUDIO_INVOKED
/////////////////////////////////////////////////////////////////
//
// Generated from the TEXTINCLUDE 3 resource.
//


/////////////////////////////////////////////////////////////////
#endif    // not APSTUDIO_INVOKED
```

Synchronizing Threads with Kernel Objects

Critical sections are great for serializing access to data within a process because they are very fast. However, you might want to synchronize some applications with other special events occurring in the machine or with operations being performed in other processes. For example, you might want to create a child process to help accomplish some work, and as a result, the parent process might need to wait until the child process completes before continuing.

The following kernel objects can be used to synchronize threads:

■ Processes

■ Threads

■ Files

■ Console input

■ File change notifications

■ Mutexes

■ Semaphores

■ Events (auto-reset and manual-reset events)

Each object can be in one of two states at any time: *signaled* or *nonsignaled*. Threads can be put to sleep until an object becomes signaled. If a thread in a parent process needs to wait for the child process to terminate, the parent's thread puts itself to sleep until the kernel object identifying the child process becomes signaled. You might recall from Chapter 2 that processes become signaled when they terminate. The same is true for thread objects. When a thread is created and running, its associated thread kernel object is nonsignaled. As soon as the thread terminates, its thread kernel object becomes signaled.

I like to think of the signaled state as a flag being raised. Threads sleep while the objects they are waiting for are nonsignaled (the flag is lowered). However, as soon as the object becomes signaled (the flag goes up), the sleeping thread sees the flag, wakes up, and resumes execution.

Of the kernel objects listed above, some exist for no other purpose than to help with the synchronization of threads. For example, if a thread has a handle to a process object, the thread can call various Win32 functions to change the priority class of the process or to get the exit code of the process. In addition, a thread can use the handle of a process object to synchronize itself with the termination of the process.

Thread handles also serve the same two purposes. You can use a thread handle to manipulate a thread, and you can use a handle of a thread object to synchronize a thread with the termination of another thread.

Like process handles and thread handles, file handles can also be used for two purposes: you can read from and write to a file using its handle, and you can set a thread to synchronize itself with the completion of an asynchronous file I/O operation. Asynchronous file I/O and this type of thread synchronization are discussed in Chapter 13.

The last type of kernel object that serves two purposes is the console input object. This object is very similar to a file, and, in fact, you call the *CreateFile* function to create a console input object. A console-based application can use a handle of this object to read input from the application's input buffer, and a thread can use this handle to put itself to sleep until input is available for processing.

The other kernel objects—file change notifications, mutexes, semaphores, and events—exist for the sole purpose of thread synchronization. Likewise, there are Win32 functions that exist to create these objects, open these objects, synchronize threads with these objects, and close these objects. No other operations can be performed with these kernel objects. This chapter discusses how to use mutexes, semaphores, and events; file change notification objects are discussed in Chapter 13.

Threads use two main functions to put themselves to sleep while waiting for kernel objects to become signaled:

```
DWORD WaitForSingleObject(HANDLE hObject, DWORD dwTimeout);
```

and

```
DWORD WaitForMultipleObjects(DWORD cObjects, LPHANDLE lpHandles,
    BOOL bWaitAll, DWORD dwTimeout);
```

The *WaitForSingleObject* function tells the system that the thread is waiting for the kernel object identified by the *hObject* parameter to be signaled. The *dwTimeout* parameter tells the system how long the thread is willing to wait in milliseconds. If the specified kernel object does not become signaled in the specified time, the system should wake the thread up and allow it to continue executing.

WaitForSingleObject returns one of the following values:

Return Value	Defined As	Meaning
WAIT_OBJECT_0	0x00000000	Object reached the signaled state.
WAIT_TIMEOUT	0x00000102	Object did not reach the signaled state in *dwTimeout* milliseconds.
WAIT_ABANDONED	0x00000080	The object was a mutex that reached the signaled state because it was abandoned. (See the section "Mutexes" later in this chapter.)
WAIT_FAILED	0xFFFFFFFF	An error occurred. Call *GetLastError* to get extended error information.

You can pass two special values as the *dwTimeout* parameter to *WaitForSingleObject*. Passing 0 tells the system that you don't want to wait at all and that the system should simply tell you if the object is signaled or nonsignaled. A return value of WAIT_OBJECT_0 indicates that the object is signaled, and a return value of WAIT_TIMEOUT indicates that the object is nonsignaled. Passing a value of INFINITE (defined as 0xFFFFFFFF) causes *WaitForSingleObject* to wait until the object reaches the signaled state. If the object never becomes signaled, the thread is never awakened and scheduled CPU time—the thread is forever hung.

The *WaitForMultipleObjects* function is similar to the *WaitForSingleObject* function except that it waits either for several objects to be signaled or for one object from a list of objects to be signaled. When calling this function, the *cObjects* parameter indicates the number of objects you want the function to check. This value cannot be larger than MAXIMUM_WAIT_OBJECTS, which is defined as 64. The *lpHandles* parameter is a pointer to an array of handles identifying these objects. An error occurs if the same object appears more than once in this list, even if the object is being identified by two different handle values.

The *bWaitAll* parameter indicates whether you want to wait for one of the objects in the list to become signaled or if you want all the objects in the list to become signaled. If *bWaitAll* is TRUE, *WaitForMultipleObjects* waits for all the objects to be signaled at the same time. If *bWaitAll* is FALSE, *WaitForMultipleObjects* waits until one of the objects becomes signaled. *WaitForMultipleObjects* scans the handle array from index 0 on up, and the first object that is signaled terminates the wait. The *dwTimeout* parameter is identical to the *dwTimeout* parameter for the *WaitForSingleObject* function. If multiple objects become signaled simultaneously, *WaitForMultipleObjects* returns the index of the first handle in the array identifying the object that became signaled.

WaitForMultipleObjects returns one of the following values:

Return Value	Defined As	Meaning
WAIT_OBJECT_0 to (WAIT_OBJECT_0 + cObjects – 1)	Start at 0x00000000	When waiting for all objects, this value indicates that the wait was completed successfully.
		When waiting for any object, this value indicates the index of the handle in the *lpHandles* array belonging to the object that satisfied the wait.
WAIT_TIMEOUT	0x00000102	The object or objects did not reach the signaled state in *dwTimeout* milliseconds.
WAIT_ABANDONED_0 to (WAIT_ABANDONED_0 + cObjects – 1)	Start at 0x00000080	When waiting for all objects, this value indicates that the wait was completed successfully and that at least one object was a mutex that became signaled because it was abandoned.
		When waiting for any object, this value indicates the index of the handle in the *lpHandles* array belonging to the mutex object that became signaled because it was abandoned.
WAIT_FAILED	0xFFFFFFFF	An error occurred. Call *GetLastError* to get extended error information.

The *WaitForSingleObject* and *WaitForMultipleObjects* functions have important side effects on certain kernel objects. For process and thread objects, there are no side effects. After process and thread objects become signaled, they stay signaled. Here's an example: if 10 threads are calling *WaitForSingleObject* and waiting for the same process object to become signaled, when the process terminates, the process object becomes signaled and all the waiting threads wake up to continue execution. The same is true for thread objects; once a thread object becomes signaled, it stays signaled.

For mutex, semaphore, and auto-reset event objects, the *WaitForSingleObject* and *WaitForMultipleObjects* functions change their states to nonsignaled. Once these objects become signaled and another thread is awakened, the object is immediately reset to its nonsignaled state. Because of this, only one thread waiting for a mutex or an auto-reset event will awaken; other waiting threads will continue to sleep. Semaphores behave a little differently in that they allow several threads to awaken simultaneously. These concepts will be made clearer as we go on and discuss each of these synchronization objects separately.

One more point regarding the *WaitForMultipleObjects* function: when *WaitForMultipleObjects* is called with *bWaitAll* passed as TRUE, none of the objects being waited for will be reset to their nonsignaled state until all the objects being waited for are signaled. In other words, the system periodically takes a snapshot of all the specified objects, and, if all of them are signaled, *WaitForMultipleObjects* resets any mutexes, semaphores, and auto-reset events back to their nonsignaled state. The system will not alter the state of any object unless all the specified objects are signaled simultaneously. The following discussion about *WaitForMultipleObjects* assumes that you understand the kernel synchronization objects. If you are new to thread synchronization, you might want to read the next section about mutexes and then return to these paragraphs.

Here is an example that demonstrates what I mean. Let's say that Thread 1 is waiting for two mutex objects: Mutex A and Mutex B. And let's say that Thread 2 is executing code and is just about to enter a wait for the Mutex A object that Thread 1 is also waiting for. If Mutex A now becomes signaled, Thread 1 has half of what it needs to stop waiting and continue execution—it still needs to wait for Mutex B. If Thread 2 now calls *WaitForSingleObject*, specifying Mutex A, the system will give ownership of Mutex A to Thread 2. Thread 1 must still wait for Mutex B to become available, but now it must also wait for Thread 2 to release Mutex A.

WaitForMultipleObjects does not take ownership of an object unless it can take ownership of all the specified objects. If *WaitForMultipleObjects* obtained ownership of the synchronization objects as they became available, it is very likely that a deadlock situation would occur. Here is what could happen: Let's say Thread 1 and Thread 2 are both suspended on a call to *WaitForMultipleObjects*, waiting for Mutex A and Mutex B to become signaled. Now a third thread releases Mutex A. The system detects this and gives ownership of Mutex A to Thread 1. The same third thread now releases Mutex B. The system detects this and gives Mutex B to Thread 2. At this point, both Thread 1 and Thread 2 are still suspended, waiting for the other mutex object to become signaled.

Now you see the problem: Thread 1 has ownership of Mutex A but can't resume itself, so Mutex A can never be released. This means that Thread 2 will never gain ownership of Mutex A and is also stuck in its suspended state. To avoid this deadlock situation, *WaitForMultipleObjects* doesn't reset any objects to their nonsignaled state unless all of the specified objects are signaled simultaneously.

Mutexes

Mutexes are very much like critical sections except that they can be used to synchronize data access across multiple processes. To use a mutex, one process must first create the mutex with the *CreateMutex* function:

```
HANDLE CreateMutex(LPSECURITY_ATTRIBUTES lpsa, BOOL fInitialOwner,
    LPTSTR lpszMutexName);
```

The *lpsa* parameter points to a SECURITY_ATTRIBUTES structure. The *fInitialOwner* parameter indicates whether the thread creating the mutex should be the initial owner of the mutex. The value TRUE means that the thread will own the mutex and therefore the mutex will be in the nonsignaled state. Any thread that waits on the mutex will be suspended until the thread that created the mutex releases it. Passing FALSE for the *fInitialOwner* parameter of *CreateMutex* means that the mutex is not owned by any thread and is therefore created in the signaled state. The first thread to wait for the mutex will immediately gain ownership of the mutex and continue execution.

The *lpszMutexName* parameter is either NULL or an address of a zero-terminated string that identifies the mutex. When an application calls *CreateMutex*, the system allocates a mutex kernel object and assigns it the name indicated by *lpszMutexName*. This name is used to share a mutex between processes. (I discuss this later in the chapter.) The

CreateMutex function returns a process-relative handle that identifies the new mutex object.

One of the big differences between mutexes and critical sections is that mutexes can be used to synchronize threads running in multiple processes. In order to do this, a thread in each process must have its own process-relative handle to a single mutex object. These handles can be obtained in several ways. The first and most common way is for one thread in each process to call *CreateMutex,* passing the identical string for the *lpszMutexName* parameter. The first thread to call *CreateMutex* will cause the system to create the mutex kernel object. As additional threads call *CreateMutex,* the system determines that a mutex with the specified name already exists; as a result, it does not create a new mutex object but returns a process-relative handle identifying the existing mutex object.

A thread can determine whether *CreateMutex* actually created a new mutex object by calling *GetLastError* immediately after the call to *Create-Mutex.* If *GetLastError* reports ERROR_ALREADY_EXISTS, a new mutex object was not created. If you are expecting to share this mutex with other processes, you can ignore this last step.

Another method for obtaining the handle of a mutex involves a call to the *OpenMutex* function:

```
HANDLE OpenMutex(DWORD fdwAccess, BOOL fInherit, LPTSTR lpszName);
```

The *fdwAccess* parameter can be either SYNCHRONIZE or MUTEX-_ALL_ACCESS. The *fInherit* parameter indicates whether any child process created by this process should inherit this handle to this mutex object. The *lpszName* parameter is the zero-terminated string name of the mutex object.

When the call to *OpenMutex* is made, the system scans all existing mutex objects to see if any of them have the name indicated by *lpszName.* If the system finds a mutex object with the specified name, it creates a process-relative handle identifying the mutex and returns the handle to the calling thread. Any thread in the calling process can now use this handle in any function that accepts a mutex handle. If a mutex with the specified name cannot be found, NULL is returned.

Both methods described above require that the mutex be named. Two other methods don't require naming the mutex—one involves the use of the *DuplicateHandle* function, and the other involves parent-child process inheritance.

Using Mutexes Instead of Critical Sections

Let's rewrite the critical section example shown on pages 287 and 288 using mutexes, and you will see how similar the code is:

```
int    g_nIndex = 0;
const int MAX_TIMES = 1000;
DWORD g_dwTimes[MAX_TIMES];
HANDLE g_hMutex = NULL;

int WinMain (...) {
   HANDLE hThreads[2];

   // Create the mutex before the threads so that it
   // exists when the threads execute.
   g_hMutex = CreateMutex(NULL, FALSE, NULL);

   // Save the handles of the threads in an array.
   hThreads[0] = CreateThread(..., FirstThread, ...);
   hThreads[1] = CreateThread(..., SecondThread, ...);

   // Wait for both threads to terminate.
   WaitForMultipleObjects(2, hThreads, TRUE, INFINITE);

   // Close the thread handles.
   CloseHandle(hThreads[0]);
   CloseHandle(hThreads[1]);

   // Close the mutex.
   CloseHandle(g_hMutex);
}

DWORD WINAPI FirstThread (LPVOID lpvThreadParm) {
   BOOL fDone = FALSE;
   DWORD dw;

   while (!fDone) {
      // Wait forever for the mutex to become signaled.
      dw = WaitForSingleObject(g_hMutex, INFINITE);

      if (dw == WAIT_OBJECT_0) {
         // Mutex became signaled.
         if (g_nIndex >= MAX_TIMES) {
            fDone = TRUE;
```

```
      } else {
         g_dwTimes[g_nIndex] = GetTickCount();
         g_nIndex++;
      }

      // Release the mutex.
      ReleaseMutex(g_hMutex);
   } else {

      // The mutex was abandoned.
      break;   // Exit the while loop.
   }
   }
   return(0);
}

DWORD WINAPI SecondThread (LPVOID lpvThreadParm) {
   BOOL fDone = FALSE;
   DWORD dw;

   while (!fDone) {
      // Wait forever for the mutex to become signaled.
      dw = WaitForSingleObject(g_hMutex, INFINITE);

      if (dw == WAIT_OBJECT_0) {
         // Mutex became signaled.
         if (g_nIndex >= MAX_TIMES) {
            fDone = TRUE;
         } else {
            g_nIndex++;
            g_dwTimes[g_nIndex - 1] = GetTickCount();
         }

         // Release the mutex.
         ReleaseMutex(g_hMutex);
      } else {
         // The mutex was abandoned.
         break;   // Exit the while loop.
      }
   }
   return(0);
}
```

Notice that I created the mutex before creating the threads. This is important because if it were done the other way around, the threads might attempt to call *WaitForSingleObject*, passing the handle NULL because the mutex had not been created yet. You can write the code differently so that you create the threads first. That code looks like this:

```
    :
    :
// Create both threads, but do not allow them to begin executing.
hThreads[0] = CreateThread(..., FirstThread, NULL,
    CREATE_SUSPENDED, ...);
hThreads[1] = CreateThread(..., SecondThread, NULL,
    CREATE_SUSPENDED, ...);

// Create the mutex.
g_hMutex = CreateMutex(NULL, FALSE, NULL);

// Allow the threads to run.
ResumeThread(hThreads[0]);
ResumeThread(hThreads[1]);
    :
    :
```

Here I create both threads, but they are suspended. They won't be scheduled any CPU time until they are resumed. Then I create the mutex and save its handle in the global *g_hMutex* variable. Now that I know this handle is not NULL, I resume both of the suspended threads by calling *ResumeThread* twice. The order here is very important. In my own work, I've forgotten to create objects before referencing them more often than I care to remember.

Back in *WinMain* in the code on pages 318 and 319, I showed how the process's primary thread waits for the two threads to terminate; it does this by calling *WaitForMultipleObjects*. In this call, the value 2 indicates that the primary thread is waiting for two objects to be signaled, *hThreads* identifies the array of handles, and TRUE means that the thread wants to wait until all the objects are signaled simultaneously—which will tell us that both threads have terminated. The inclusion of the INFINITE identifier means that the primary thread will wait forever for both threads to terminate. When *WaitForMultipleObjects* returns, *WinMain* calls *CloseHandle* so that the mutex object is destroyed.

Both thread functions have been modified to use mutex objects instead of critical sections. The calls to *EnterCriticalSection* have been replaced by calls to *WaitForSingleObject*. *WaitForSingleObject* can return WAIT_OBJECT_0, WAIT_ABANDONED, or WAIT_TIMEOUT. WAIT_TIMEOUT can never occur here because INFINITE was specified in the call. A return value of WAIT_OBJECT_0 means that the mutex was signaled and the thread can continue executing. When *WaitForSingle-Object* sees that the mutex has reached a signaled state, the thread immediately grabs ownership of the mutex, which places the mutex back into the nonsignaled state. The thread can then manipulate the data structure; when it no longer needs access to the structure, the thread calls the *ReleaseMutex* function:

```
BOOL ReleaseMutex(HANDLE hMutex);
```

ReleaseMutex is the function that changes the mutex from the non-signaled state to the signaled state just as the *LeaveCriticalSection* function does for critical sections. One important thing to note is that this function has an effect only if the thread that is calling *ReleaseMutex* also has ownership of the mutex. Immediately after this function is called, any thread that is waiting for the mutex can grab hold of it and begin executing. Of course, when the thread grabs the mutex, the mutex again becomes nonsignaled. If no threads are waiting on the mutex, the mutex remains in the signaled state, indicating that no thread is accessing the protected data. If a thread comes along and waits on the mutex, it will immediately be able to grab the mutex, locking other threads out if they try to wait on the mutex.

Let me reiterate that when working with any kind of synchronization object you always want to maintain ownership of that object for as short a time as possible. If other threads are waiting for the object, they are all sleeping and not doing their work.

Abandoned Mutexes

Mutex objects are different from all other synchronization kernel objects because mutex objects are owned by a thread. All other synchronization objects are either signaled or nonsignaled, period. Mutex objects, in addition to being signaled or nonsignaled, remember which thread owns them. A mutex is abandoned if a thread waits for a mutex object, grabs the object (putting it in the nonsignaled state), and then terminates. In this scenario, the mutex is nonsignaled and will never be signaled because no other thread can release the mutex by calling *ReleaseMutex*.

When the system sees that this has happened, it automatically sets the mutex back to the signaled state. Any threads that are currently waiting for the mutex with a call to *WaitForSingleObject* get awakened, and *WaitForSingleObject* returns WAIT_ABANDONED instead of WAIT_OB-JECT_0. In this way, a thread knows that the mutex has not been released gracefully. This is usually an indication that a bug exists in the source code. There is no way to know if the thread that previously owned the mutex finished what it was doing to the data before it terminated. (Remember that threads can be forcibly terminated by calling *ExitThread* or *TerminateThread*.)

In the code fragment on pages 318 and 319, I check to see whether the mutex has been abandoned, and if it has, I break out of the *while* loop, causing the thread to end. *WinMain* will eventually see that both threads have terminated, causing the mutex to be destroyed and the process to terminate. I could ignore the possibility that WAIT_ABANDONED can be returned from *WaitForSingleObject*, but I don't know what state the protected data might be in.

One last point about mutexes: mutexes have an ownership count associated with them. So if a thread calls *WaitForSingleObject* for a mutex object that the thread already owns, the call succeeds immediately every time because the system knows that this thread already owns the mutex. In addition, the reference count for the mutex is incremented each time. This means that the thread must call *ReleaseMutex* the same number of times before the mutex will be in the signaled state again. This is identical to the way that *EnterCriticalSection* and *LeaveCriticalSection* work for critical sections.

The Mutexes Sample Application

The Mutexes application (MUTEXES.EXE), listed in Figure 9-2, is simply the CritSecs program modified to use mutexes instead of critical sections. On the outside, the Mutexes program actually behaves identically to the CritSecs program. However, by using mutexes instead of critical sections, it would now be possible to put the *CounterThread* function in one process and the *DisplayThread* function in another process (although the sample does not demonstrate this). The source code files, resource files, and make file for the application are in the MUTEXES.09 directory on the companion disc.

Mutexes.ico

MUTEXES.C
```
/*********************************************************************
Module name: Mutexes.C
Notices: Copyright (c) 1995 Jeffrey Richter
*********************************************************************/
```

Figure 9-2. *(continued)*
The Mutexes application.

Figure 9-2. *continued*

```
#include "..\AdvWin32.H"        /* See Appendix B for details. */
#include <windows.h>
#include <windowsx.h>

#pragma warning(disable: 4001)          /* Single-line comment */

#include <tchar.h>
#include <stdio.h>                 // For sprintf
#include <process.h>               // For _beginthreadex
#include "Resource.H"


//////////////////////////////////////////////////////////////////


// Global variables
HWND     g_hwndDlg = NULL;
HANDLE   g_hThreadCntr = NULL;
HANDLE   g_hThreadDspy = NULL;


// The data that needs protecting
TCHAR    g_szNumber[10] = __TEXT("0");

// The mutex used to protect the data
HANDLE g_hMutex;


//////////////////////////////////////////////////////////////////

// Add a string to a list box.
void AddToListBox (LPCTSTR szBuffer) {
   HWND hwndDataBox = GetDlgItem(g_hwndDlg, IDC_DATABOX);

   int x = ListBox_AddString(hwndDataBox, szBuffer);
   ListBox_SetCurSel(hwndDataBox, x);

   if (ListBox_GetCount(hwndDataBox) > 100)
      ListBox_DeleteString(hwndDataBox, 0);
}


//////////////////////////////////////////////////////////////////

// Thread to increment the protected counter data
```

(continued)

Figure 9-2. *continued*

```
DWORD WINAPI CounterThread (LPVOID lpThreadParameter) {
   unsigned int nNumber, nDigit;
   BOOL fSyncChecked;

   for(;;) {

      // Get the status of the Synchronize
      // check box and save it.
      fSyncChecked =
         IsDlgButtonChecked(g_hwndDlg, IDC_SYNCHRONIZE);

      if (fSyncChecked) {
         // If the user wants us synchronized, do it.
         WaitForSingleObject(g_hMutex, INFINITE);
      }

      // Convert the string number to an integer and add 1.
      _stscanf(g_szNumber, __TEXT("%d"), &nNumber);
      nNumber++;

      // Convert the new integer back to a string.
      nDigit = 0;
      while (nNumber != 0) {
         // Put a digit into the string.
         g_szNumber[nDigit++] = (TCHAR) (__TEXT('0') +
            (nNumber % 10));
         // A call to Sleep here tells the system that we want
         // to relinquish the remainder of our time slice to
         // another thread. This call is needed for
         // single-CPU systems so that the results of the
         // synchronization or lack thereof are obvious.
         // Normally, your programs would NOT call Sleep here.
         Sleep(0);

         // Get ready to get the next digit.
         nNumber /= 10;
      }

      // All digits converted to characters.
      // Terminate the string.
      g_szNumber[nDigit] = 0;

      // Characters were generated in reverse order;
      // reverse the string.
```

(continued)

Figure 9-2. *continued*

```
        // Call _strrev if ANSI, call _wcsrev if Unicode.
        _tcsrev(g_szNumber);

        if (fSyncChecked) {
            // If the user wants synchronization, do it.
            ReleaseMutex(g_hMutex);
        }

        // If the user wants to display something
        // after each iteration, do it.
        if (IsDlgButtonChecked(g_hwndDlg, IDC_SHOWCNTRTHRD))
            AddToListBox(__TEXT("Cntr: Increment"));
    }
    return(0);  // We will never get here.
}


//////////////////////////////////////////////////////////////////

// Thread to add the current value of
// the counter (data) to the list box
DWORD WINAPI DisplayThread (LPVOID lpThreadParameter) {
    BOOL fSyncChecked;
    TCHAR szBuffer[50];

    for(;;) {

        // Determine whether the user wants the threads
        // to be synchronized.
        fSyncChecked =
            IsDlgButtonChecked(g_hwndDlg, IDC_SYNCHRONIZE);

        if (fSyncChecked)
            WaitForSingleObject(g_hMutex, INFINITE);

        // Construct a string with the string form of the number.
        _stprintf(szBuffer, __TEXT("Dspy: %s"), g_szNumber);

        if (fSyncChecked)
            ReleaseMutex(g_hMutex);
        // Add the string form of the number to the list box.
        AddToListBox(szBuffer);
    }
    return(0);  // We will never get here.
}
```

(continued)

Figure 9-2. *continued*

```
////////////////////////////////////////////////////////////////


BOOL Dlg_OnInitDialog (HWND hwnd, HWND hwndFocus,
   LPARAM lParam) {

   HWND hWndCtl;
   DWORD dwThreadId;

   // Save the handle of the dialog box in a global so that
   // the threads can easily gain access to it. This must be
   // done before creating the threads.
   g_hwndDlg = hwnd;

   // Associate an icon with the dialog box.
   SetClassLong(hwnd, GCL_HICON, (LONG)
      LoadIcon((HINSTANCE) GetWindowLong(hwnd, GWL_HINSTANCE),
      __TEXT("Mutexes")));

   // Initialize the mutex object. This must also be done
   // before any threads try to use it. There should be error
   // checking here.
   g_hMutex = CreateMutex(NULL, FALSE, NULL);

   // Create our counter thread and let it start running.
   g_hThreadCntr = BEGINTHREADEX(NULL, 0, CounterThread, NULL,
      0, &dwThreadId);

   // Create our display thread and let it start running.
   g_hThreadDspy = BEGINTHREADEX(NULL, 0, DisplayThread, NULL,
      0, &dwThreadId);


   // Fill the Process Priority Class combo box, and select
   // Normal.
   hWndCtl = GetDlgItem(hwnd, IDC_PRIORITYCLASS);
   ComboBox_AddString(hWndCtl, __TEXT("Idle"));
   ComboBox_AddString(hWndCtl, __TEXT("Normal"));
   ComboBox_AddString(hWndCtl, __TEXT("High"));
   ComboBox_AddString(hWndCtl, __TEXT("Realtime"));
   ComboBox_SetCurSel(hWndCtl, 1);   // Normal

   // Fill the Display Thread Priority
   // combo box, and select Normal.
   hWndCtl = GetDlgItem(hwnd, IDC_DSPYTHRDPRIORITY);
```

(continued)

Figure 9-2. *continued*

```
    ComboBox_AddString(hWndCtl, __TEXT("Idle"));
    ComboBox_AddString(hWndCtl, __TEXT("Lowest"));
    ComboBox_AddString(hWndCtl, __TEXT("Below normal"));
    ComboBox_AddString(hWndCtl, __TEXT("Normal"));
    ComboBox_AddString(hWndCtl, __TEXT("Above normal"));
    ComboBox_AddString(hWndCtl, __TEXT("Highest"));
    ComboBox_AddString(hWndCtl, __TEXT("Timecritical"));
    ComboBox_SetCurSel(hWndCtl, 3);  // Normal

    // Fill the Counter Thread Priority
    // combo box, and select Normal.
    hWndCtl = GetDlgItem(hwnd, IDC_CNTRTHRDPRIORITY);
    ComboBox_AddString(hWndCtl, __TEXT("Idle"));
    ComboBox_AddString(hWndCtl, __TEXT("Lowest"));
    ComboBox_AddString(hWndCtl, __TEXT("Below normal"));
    ComboBox_AddString(hWndCtl, __TEXT("Normal"));
    ComboBox_AddString(hWndCtl, __TEXT("Above normal"));
    ComboBox_AddString(hWndCtl, __TEXT("Highest"));
    ComboBox_AddString(hWndCtl, __TEXT("Timecritical"));
    ComboBox_SetCurSel(hWndCtl, 3);  // Normal

    return(TRUE);
}


///////////////////////////////////////////////////////////////


void Dlg_OnDestroy (HWND hwnd) {
    // When the dialog box is destroyed, terminate the
    // two threads and delete the mutex object.
    TerminateThread(g_hThreadDspy, 0);
    TerminateThread(g_hThreadCntr, 0);
    CloseHandle(g_hMutex);
}


///////////////////////////////////////////////////////////////


void Dlg_OnCommand (HWND hwnd, int id, HWND hwndCtl,
    UINT codeNotify) {

    HANDLE hThread;
    DWORD dw;
```

(continued)

Figure 9-2. *continued*

```
switch (id) {
   case IDCANCEL:
      EndDialog(hwnd, id);
      break;

   case IDC_PRIORITYCLASS:
      if (codeNotify != CBN_SELCHANGE)
         break;

      // User is changing priority class.
      switch (ComboBox_GetCurSel(hwndCtl)) {
         case 0:
            dw = IDLE_PRIORITY_CLASS;
            break;

         case 1:
         default:
            dw = NORMAL_PRIORITY_CLASS;
            break;

         case 2:
            dw = HIGH_PRIORITY_CLASS;
            break;

         case 3:
            dw = REALTIME_PRIORITY_CLASS;
            break;
      }
      SetPriorityClass(GetCurrentProcess(), dw);
      break;

   case IDC_DSPYTHRDPRIORITY:
   case IDC_CNTRTHRDPRIORITY:
      if (codeNotify != CBN_SELCHANGE)
         break;

      switch (ComboBox_GetCurSel(hwndCtl)) {
         case 0:
            dw = (DWORD) THREAD_PRIORITY_IDLE;
            break;

         case 1:
            dw = (DWORD) THREAD_PRIORITY_LOWEST;
            break;
```

(continued)

Figure 9-2. *continued*

```
            case 2:
               dw = (DWORD) THREAD_PRIORITY_BELOW_NORMAL;
               break;

            case 3:
            default:
               dw = (DWORD) THREAD_PRIORITY_NORMAL;
               break;

            case 4:
               dw = (DWORD) THREAD_PRIORITY_ABOVE_NORMAL;
               break;

            case 5:
               dw = (DWORD) THREAD_PRIORITY_HIGHEST;
               break;

            case 6:
               dw = (DWORD) THREAD_PRIORITY_TIME_CRITICAL;
               break;
         }
         // User is changing the relative priority
         // of one of the threads.
         hThread = (id == IDC_CNTRTHRDPRIORITY) ?
            g_hThreadCntr : g_hThreadDspy;

         SetThreadPriority(hThread, dw);
         break;

      case IDC_PAUSE:
         // User is pausing or resuming both threads.
         if (Button_GetCheck(hwndCtl)) {
            SuspendThread(g_hThreadCntr);
            SuspendThread(g_hThreadDspy);
         } else {
            ResumeThread(g_hThreadCntr);
            ResumeThread(g_hThreadDspy);
         }
         break;
   }
}
```

(continued)

Figure 9-2. *continued*

```
//////////////////////////////////////////////////////////////


BOOL CALLBACK Dlg_Proc (HWND hDlg, UINT uMsg,
   WPARAM wParam, LPARAM lParam) {

   BOOL fProcessed = TRUE;

   switch (uMsg) {
      HANDLE_MSG(hDlg, WM_INITDIALOG, Dlg_OnInitDialog);
      HANDLE_MSG(hDlg, WM_DESTROY, Dlg_OnDestroy);
      HANDLE_MSG(hDlg, WM_COMMAND, Dlg_OnCommand);

      default:
         fProcessed = FALSE;
         break;
   }
   return(fProcessed);
}



//////////////////////////////////////////////////////////////


int WINAPI WinMain (HINSTANCE hinstExe,
   HINSTANCE hinstPrev, LPSTR lpszCmdLine, int nCmdShow) {

   DialogBox(hinstExe, MAKEINTRESOURCE(IDD_MUTEXES),
      NULL, Dlg_Proc);

   return(0);
}



///////////////////////// End Of File /////////////////////////
```

MUTEXES.RC
```
//Microsoft Visual C++ generated resource script.
//
#include "Resource.h"

#define APSTUDIO_READONLY_SYMBOLS
```

(continued)

Figure 9-2. *continued*

```
///////////////////////////////////////////////////////////////
//
// Generated from the TEXTINCLUDE 2 resource.
//
#include "afxres.h"


///////////////////////////////////////////////////////////////
#undef APSTUDIO_READONLY_SYMBOLS


#ifdef APSTUDIO_INVOKED
///////////////////////////////////////////////////////////////
//
// TEXTINCLUDE
//

1 TEXTINCLUDE DISCARDABLE
BEGIN
    "Resource.h\0"
END

2 TEXTINCLUDE DISCARDABLE
BEGIN
    "#include ""afxres.h""\r\n"
    "\0"
END

3 TEXTINCLUDE DISCARDABLE
BEGIN
    "\r\n"
    "\0"
END


///////////////////////////////////////////////////////////////
#endif    // APSTUDIO_INVOKED


///////////////////////////////////////////////////////////////
//
// Dialog
//

IDD_MUTEXES DIALOG DISCARDABLE  29, 28, 197, 208
STYLE WS_MINIMIZEBOX | WS_POPUP | WS_VISIBLE | WS_CAPTION
    | WS_SYSMENU
```

(continued)

Figure 9-2. *continued*

```
CAPTION "Mutex Test Application"
FONT 8, "System"
BEGIN
    LTEXT          "&Process priority class:",IDC_STATIC,
                   4,4,74,8
    COMBOBOX       IDC_PRIORITYCLASS,88,4,64,48,
                   CBS_DROPDOWNLIST ¦ WS_GROUP ¦ WS_TABSTOP
    CONTROL        "&Display thread priority:",IDC_STATIC,
                   "Static",SS_LEFTNOWORDWRAP ¦ WS_GROUP
                   ¦ WS_TABSTOP,4,24,76,8
    COMBOBOX       IDC_DSPYTHRDPRIORITY,88,24,100,76,
                   CBS_DROPDOWNLIST ¦ WS_GROUP ¦ WS_TABSTOP
    CONTROL        "&Counter thread priority:",IDC_STATIC,
                   "Static",SS_LEFTNOWORDWRAP ¦ WS_GROUP
                   ¦ WS_TABSTOP,4,40,76,8
    COMBOBOX       IDC_CNTRTHRDPRIORITY,88,40,100,76,
                   CBS_DROPDOWNLIST ¦ WS_GROUP ¦ WS_TABSTOP
    CONTROL        "&Synchronize",IDC_SYNCHRONIZE,"Button",
                   BS_AUTOCHECKBOX ¦ WS_TABSTOP,4,60,52,10
    CONTROL        "S&how counter thread",IDC_SHOWCNTRTHRD,
                   "Button",BS_AUTOCHECKBOX ¦ WS_TABSTOP,4,
                   72,77,10
    CONTROL        "P&ause",IDC_PAUSE,"Button",
                   BS_AUTOCHECKBOX ¦ WS_TABSTOP,4,84,32,10
    LISTBOX        IDC_DATABOX,88,60,100,144,WS_VSCROLL
                   ¦ WS_GROUP ¦ WS_TABSTOP
END


/////////////////////////////////////////////////////////////////
//
// Icon
//

Mutexes                 ICON    DISCARDABLE     "Mutexes.Ico"

#ifndef APSTUDIO_INVOKED
/////////////////////////////////////////////////////////////////
//
// Generated from the TEXTINCLUDE 3 resource.
//


/////////////////////////////////////////////////////////////////
#endif    // not APSTUDIO_INVOKED
```

Semaphores

Semaphore kernel objects are used for resource counting. They offer a thread the ability to query the number of resources available; if one or more resources are available, the count of available resources is decremented. Semaphores perform this test-and-set operation atomically. That is, when you request a resource from a semaphore, the operating system checks whether the resource is available and decrements the count of available resources without letting another thread interfere. Only after the resource count has been decremented does the system allow another thread to request a resource.

For example, let's say that a computer has three serial ports. No more than three threads can use the serial ports at any given time; each port can be assigned to one thread. This situation provides a perfect opportunity to use a semaphore. To monitor serial port usage, you can create a semaphore with a count of 3—one for each port. A semaphore is signaled when its resource count is greater than 0 and is nonsignaled when the count is equal to 0. Every time a thread calls *WaitForSingleObject* and passes the handle of a semaphore, the system checks whether the resource count for the semaphore is greater than 0. If it is, the system decrements the resource count and wakes the thread. If the resource count is 0 when the thread calls *WaitForSingleObject*, the system puts the thread to sleep until another thread releases the semaphore (increments the resource count).

Because several threads can affect a semaphore's resource count, a semaphore, unlike a critical section or a mutex, is not considered to be owned by a thread. This means that it's possible for one thread to wait for the semaphore object (decrement the object's resource count) and another thread to release the object (increment the object's resource count).

You create a semaphore by calling the *CreateSemaphore* function:

```
HANDLE CreateSemaphore(LPSECURITY_ATTRIBUTE lpsa,
    LONG cSemInitial, LONG cSemMax, LPTSTR lpszSemName);
```

This function creates a semaphore that has a maximum resource count of *cSemMax*. So in the previous example, you would pass the value 3 to represent the three serial ports. The *cSemInitial* parameter lets you specify the starting resource count for the semaphore. When the system starts, all three serial ports are available, so you would set this value to 3 as well. When the operating system initializes, you might want it to indicate that there are three serial ports but that none are available. To do this, you would pass 0 as the *cSemInitial* parameter.

The last parameter of *CreateSemaphore*, *lpszSemName*, assigns a string name to the semaphore. You can use this string name in other processes to get the handle of the semaphore by calling *CreateSemaphore* or *OpenSemaphore*:

```
HANDLE OpenSemaphore(DWORD fdwAccess, BOOL fInherit,
    LPTSTR lpszName);
```

This function's semantics are identical to those of the *OpenMutex* function, discussed previously.

To release a semaphore (increment its resource count), you call the *ReleaseSemaphore* function:

```
BOOL ReleaseSemaphore(HANDLE hSemaphore, LONG cRelease,
    LPLONG lplPrevious);
```

This function is similar to the *ReleaseMutex* function, but there are a few differences. First, any thread can call this function at any time because semaphore objects are not owned by a single thread. Second, the *ReleaseSemaphore* function can be used to increment the resource count of the semaphore by more than 1. The *cRelease* parameter indicates by how much the semaphore should be released. For example, let's say that we have an application that copies data from one serial port to another. The application has to acquire the semaphore twice by calling *WaitForSingleObject* twice. However, it can release both resources with just a single call to *ReleaseSemaphore*. The code fragment below demonstrates:

```
// Get two serial ports.
WaitForSingleObject(g_hSemSerialPort, INFINITE);
WaitForSingleObject(g_hSemSerialPort, INFINITE);
    :
    :

// Use the serial ports to do the copy.
    :
    :

// Release the serial ports so that other applications
// can use them.
ReleaseSemaphore(g_hSemSerialPort, 2, NULL);
```

It would be nice if you could call *WaitForMultipleObjects* once instead of calling *WaitForSingleObject* twice. However, *WaitForMultipleObjects* does not allow the same handle to be used more than once in a single call. So although we must call *WaitForSingleObject* twice, it is convenient that we can call *ReleaseSemaphore* once at the end to increment the semaphore's count by 2.

ReleaseSemaphore's last parameter, *lplPrevious*, is a pointer to a long, which *ReleaseSemaphore* fills with the semaphore's resource count *before* adding *cRelease* back to it. If you are not interested in this value, you can simply pass NULL.

It would help if there were a Win32 function that determined the resource count of a semaphore without actually altering the semaphore's count. At first, I thought that calling *ReleaseSemaphore* and passing 0 for the second parameter might work by returning the actual count in the long pointed to by the *lplPrevious* parameter. But, unfortunately, this doesn't work; *ReleaseSemaphore* fills the long with 0. Next I tried passing a really big number as the second parameter, but *ReleaseSemaphore* still filled the long with 0. There is no way to get the count of a semaphore without altering it.

The Supermarket Sample Application

The SprMrkt (SPRMRKT.EXE) application, listed in Figure 9-4 beginning on page 348, demonstrates the use of mutexes and semaphores to control a supermarket simulation. The source code files, resource files, and make file for the application are in the SPRMRKT.09 directory on the companion disc. When you run SprMrkt, the following dialog box appears:

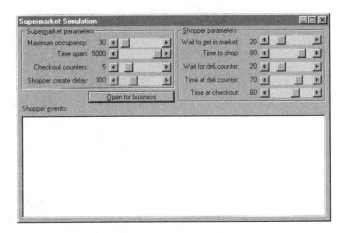

Using this dialog box, you can set up all the initial parameters before executing the simulation. When you have finished configuring the simulation parameters, click on the Open For Business button to create and start executing a thread that represents the supermarket. The function that identifies this thread is called *ThreadSuperMarket*.

The supermarket thread is responsible for:

1. Opening the supermarket

2. Creating threads that represent individual shoppers

3. Closing the front doors when the store closes so that no more shoppers can enter

4. Waiting until all the shoppers in the store have checked out their groceries before ending the simulation

5. Notifying the GUI thread (or primary thread) that the supermarket simulation has ended so that the dialog box can re-enable the simulation parameter controls and another simulation can be executed

As mentioned in number 2 above, each shopper is represented by his or her own thread. Every so often, the supermarket thread creates a new shopper thread by calling _beginthreadex:

```
hThread = (HANDLE) _beginthreadex (
   NULL,                    // Security attributes
   0,                       // Stack
   ThreadShopper,           // Thread function
   (LPVOID) ++nShopperNum,  // Shopper number as lpvParam
   0,                       // Flags
   &dwThreadId);            // Thread ID

CloseHandle(hThread);
```

The call to *CloseHandle* tells the system that the shopper thread isn't referenced directly from within the supermarket thread. After the supermarket thread creates a shopper thread, the shopper thread executes. When the shopper thread is finished shopping and exits the supermarket, the shopper thread terminates and its associated thread kernel object is destroyed with it.

I'm sure that by now you can guess what would happen if I forgot the call to *CloseHandle*: a resource leak would occur. Remember that the act of creating a thread causes the new thread object to have an initial usage count of 1. Then, because _beginthreadex returns a handle to the thread object, the thread object's usage count is incremented to 2. When the shopper thread leaves the supermarket (terminates), the thread object's usage count decrements to 1. If *CloseHandle* is not called, the object's usage count never decrements to 0 and the system won't free the thread object from its internal memory until the whole process is terminated. Because shoppers are created frequently and because the user can run the simulation several times in a row without exiting and restarting the program, the number of unfreed thread objects could really add up. So, as you can see, the call to *CloseHandle* is really quite necessary.

After the supermarket has created a shopper, it waits a random amount of time before creating another. The maximum duration of this wait is specified by the Shopper Create Delay setting in the dialog box.

By having the supermarket running as its own thread and each shopper also executing as his or her own thread, you create the feeling that every shopper can move around the supermarket at his or her own pace and that the supermarket itself is operating at its own pace.

Shoppers perform the following actions:

1. Wait to get into the store

2. Perform a random amount of shopping

3. Go to the deli counter to order luncheon meats

4. Stand in line at the checkout counter to pay for items

5. Spend a random amount of time at the checkout counter

6. Leave the checkout counter

7. Leave the supermarket

After a shopper thread leaves the supermarket, it terminates.

As the simulation progresses, the Shopper Events list box notifies you of the various events that are occurring in the supermarket. By examining this information, you can see where potential bottlenecks occur and how a change to the configuration parameters might alter the scenario for the next run. This information might be used by a manager to determine the best number of open checkout registers or the best number of workers attending the deli counters. Figure 9-3 beginning on the following page shows the results of a sample run using the parameter settings shown in the dialog box.

```
---> Opening the supermarket to shoppers.
0001: Waiting to get in store (11).
0002: Waiting to get in store (16).
0001: In supermarket, shopping for 46.
0002: In supermarket, shopping for 38.
0003: Waiting to get in store (17).
0003: In supermarket, shopping for 65.
0002: Not going to the deli counter.
0001: Waiting for service at deli counter (17).
0002: Waiting for an empty checkout counter.
0001: Being served at deli (49).
0002: Checking out (30).
0003: Waiting for service at deli counter (0).
0003: Tired of waiting at deli.
0004: Waiting to get in store (7).
0002: Leaving checkout counter.
0001: Waiting for an empty checkout counter.
0005: Waiting to get in store (3).
0003: Waiting for an empty checkout counter.
0004: In supermarket, shopping for 9.
0006: Waiting to get in store (8).
0002: Left the supermarket.
0001: Checking out (0).
0005: In supermarket, shopping for 0.
0003: Checking out (22).
0006: In supermarket, shopping for 42.
0004: Not going to the deli counter.
0001: Leaving checkout counter.
0005: Not going to the deli counter.
0003: Leaving checkout counter.
0004: Waiting for an empty checkout counter.
0001: Left the supermarket.
0005: Waiting for an empty checkout counter.
0004: Checking out (36).
0003: Left the supermarket.
0006: Waiting for service at deli counter (13).
0007: Waiting to get in store (7).
0005: Checking out (3).
0006: Being served at deli (42).
0004: Leaving checkout counter.
0007: In supermarket, shopping for 41.
0008: Waiting to get in store (16).
0005: Leaving checkout counter.
0006: Waiting for an empty checkout counter.
```

Figure 9-3.

(continued)

Simulation results using the dialog box settings.

Figure 9-3. *continued*

```
0005: Left the supermarket.
0004: Left the supermarket.
0008: In supermarket, shopping for 24.
0007: Not going to the deli counter.
0006: Checking out (43).
0007: Waiting for an empty checkout counter.
0008: Not going to the deli counter.
0007: Checking out (8).
0009: Waiting to get in store (10).
0008: Waiting for an empty checkout counter.
0008: Checking out (27).
0006: Leaving checkout counter.
0009: In supermarket, shopping for 18.
0007: Leaving checkout counter.
0006: Left the supermarket.
0007: Left the supermarket.
0009: Not going to the deli counter.
0008: Leaving checkout counter.
0008: Left the supermarket.
0009: Waiting for an empty checkout counter.
0009: Checking out (46).
0010: Waiting to get in store (16).
0010: In supermarket, shopping for 79.
0009: Leaving checkout counter.
0009: Left the supermarket.
0011: Waiting to get in store (12).
0011: In supermarket, shopping for 31.
0010: Waiting for service at deli counter (5).
0011: Not going to the deli counter.
0010: Being served at deli (1).
0011: Waiting for an empty checkout counter.
0010: Waiting for an empty checkout counter.
0010: Checking out (22).
0011: Checking out (5).
0012: Waiting to get in store (1).
0011: Leaving checkout counter.
0010: Leaving checkout counter.
0012: In supermarket, shopping for 0.
0011: Left the supermarket.
0010: Left the supermarket.
0012: Not going to the deli counter.
0013: Waiting to get in store (5).
0012: Waiting for an empty checkout counter.
0012: Checking out (35).
```

(continued)

Figure 9-3. *continued*

```
0013: In supermarket, shopping for 55.
0014: Waiting to get in store (14).
0014: In supermarket, shopping for 38.
0012: Leaving checkout counter.
0013: Waiting for service at deli counter (14).
0013: Being served at deli (32).
0012: Left the supermarket.
0014: Waiting for service at deli counter (18).
0013: Waiting for an empty checkout counter.
0014: Tired of waiting at deli.
0014: Waiting for an empty checkout counter.
0015: Waiting to get in store (2).
0013: Checking out (35).
0014: Checking out (23).
0015: In supermarket, shopping for 58.
0013: Leaving checkout counter.
0013: Left the supermarket.
0014: Leaving checkout counter.
0015: Not going to the deli counter.
0014: Left the supermarket.
0015: Waiting for an empty checkout counter.
0016: Waiting to get in store (7).
0015: Checking out (9).
0016: In supermarket, shopping for 18.
0015: Leaving checkout counter.
0015: Left the supermarket.
0016: Waiting for service at deli counter (16).
0016: Being served at deli (36).
0017: Waiting to get in store (15).
0016: Waiting for an empty checkout counter.
0017: In supermarket, shopping for 27.
0016: Checking out (10).
0017: Not going to the deli counter.
0016: Leaving checkout counter.
0017: Waiting for an empty checkout counter.
0017: Checking out (29).
0016: Left the supermarket.
0017: Leaving checkout counter.
0017: Left the supermarket.
0018: Waiting to get in store (13).
0018: In supermarket, shopping for 75.
0019: Waiting to get in store (2).
0019: In supermarket, shopping for 11.
0019: Not going to the deli counter.
```

(continued)

Figure 9-3. *continued*

```
0018: Not going to the deli counter.
0020: Waiting to get in store (8).
0019: Waiting for an empty checkout counter.
0018: Waiting for an empty checkout counter.
0019: Checking out (4).
0020: In supermarket, shopping for 54.
0021: Waiting to get in store (3).
0018: Checking out (52).
0019: leaving checkout counter.
0021: In supermarket, shopping for 65.
0019: Left the supermarket.
0020: Not going to the deli counter.
0020: Waiting for an empty checkout counter.
0018: Leaving checkout counter.
0021: Waiting for service at deli counter (3).
0020: Checking out (49).
0018: Left the supermarket.
0021: Being served at deli (35).
0022: Waiting to get in store (3).
0020: Leaving checkout counter.
0020: Left the supermarket.
0021: Waiting for an empty checkout counter.
0022: In supermarket, shopping for 58.
0023: Waiting to get in store (5).
0021: Checking out (34).
0023: In supermarket, shopping for 54.
0022: Not going to the deli counter.
0024: Waiting to get in store (9).
0021: Leaving checkout counter.
0023: Waiting for service at deli counter (7).
0022: Waiting for an empty checkout counter.
0024: In supermarket, shopping for 66.
0021: Left the supermarket.
0023: Being served at deli (2).
0022: Checking out (31).
0023: Waiting for an empty checkout counter.
0022: Leaving checkout counter.
0024: Not going to the deli counter.
0023: Checking out (56).
0025: Waiting to get in store (2).
0022: Left the supermarket.
0024: Waiting for an empty checkout counter.
0025: In supermarket, shopping for 73.
0024: Checking out (32).
```

(continued)

Figure 9-3. *continued*

```
0023: Leaving checkout counter.
0026: Waiting to get in store (9).
0023: Left the supermarket.
0025: Waiting for service at deli counter (16).
0024: Leaving checkout counter.
0026: In supermarket, shopping for 21.
0027: Waiting to get in store (9).
0025: Being served at deli (68).
0024: Left the supermarket.
0027: In supermarket, shopping for 45.
0028: Waiting to get in store (14).
0026: Waiting for service at deli counter (15).
0025: Waiting for an empty checkout counter.
0028: In supermarket, shopping for 67.
0026: Being served at deli (27).
0029: Waiting to get in store (17).
0027: Waiting for service at deli counter (19).
0025: Checking out (34).
0026: Waiting for an empty checkout counter.
0029: In supermarket, shopping for 4.
0028: Not going to the deli counter.
---> Waiting for shoppers to check out so store can close.
0027: Being served at deli (13).
0025: Leaving checkout counter.
0026: Checking out (50).
---> 0 shoppers NOT in store.
0028: Waiting for an empty checkout counter.
0029: Not going to the deli counter.
0027: Waiting for an empty checkout counter.
---> 1 shoppers NOT in store.
0025: Left the supermarket.
0028: Checking out (39).
0027: Checking out (11).
0029: Waiting for an empty checkout counter.
0026: Leaving checkout counter.
---> 2 shoppers NOT in store.
0027: Leaving checkout counter.
---> 3 shoppers NOT in store.
0029: Checking out (50).
0026: Left the supermarket.
0028: Leaving checkout counter.
0027: Left the supermarket.
---> 4 shoppers NOT in store.
0028: Left the supermarket.
```

(continued)

Figure 9-3. *continued*

```
0029: Leaving checkout counter.
---> 5 shoppers NOT in store.
0029: Left the supermarket.
---> 6 shoppers NOT in store.
---> 7 shoppers NOT in store.
---> 8 shoppers NOT in store.
---> 9 shoppers NOT in store.
---> 10 shoppers NOT in store.
---> 11 shoppers NOT in store.
---> 12 shoppers NOT in store.
---> 13 shoppers NOT in store.
---> 14 shoppers NOT in store.
---> 15 shoppers NOT in store.
---> 16 shoppers NOT in store.
---> 17 shoppers NOT in store.
---> 18 shoppers NOT in store.
---> 19 shoppers NOT in store.
---> 20 shoppers NOT in store.
---> 21 shoppers NOT in store.
---> 22 shoppers NOT in store.
---> 23 shoppers NOT in store.
---> 24 shoppers NOT in store.
---> 25 shoppers NOT in store.
---> 26 shoppers NOT in store.
---> 27 shoppers NOT in store.
---> 28 shoppers NOT in store.
---> 29 shoppers NOT in store.
---> Store closed--end of simulation.
```

Now let's imagine that this supermarket is open for business and inside several shoppers are going about their business. With so many things going on simultaneously, there must be some way to synchronize the actions of these executing threads. In this example, several forms of synchronization are being used.

When the supermarket thread starts executing, it immediately creates a semaphore object that is identified by the global *g_hSemEntrance* variable:

```
g_hSemEntrance = CreateSemaphore(
   NULL,                // Security attributes
   0,                   // Initial lock count
   g_nMaxOccupancy,     // Maximum people allowed in store
   NULL);               // Do not name the semaphore.
```

This object monitors the number of shoppers that are allowed into the supermarket at any one time. This maximum number of shoppers is identified by the Maximum Occupancy setting specified in the dialog box. For a brief moment after opening for business, the supermarket's doors are still closed, not allowing any shoppers into the store. This closed state is indicated by passing 0 as the initial lock count. When the store is ready to allow shoppers in, it calls:

```
ReleaseSemaphore(g_hSemEntrance, g_nMaxOccupancy, NULL);
```

When a new shopper thread is created, the first thing it does is call:

```
dwResult = WaitForSingleObject(g_hSemEntrance, nDuration);
```

This causes the shopper thread to suspend its execution if the store is already filled with shoppers to maximum occupancy. If the supermarket is not filled with shoppers, *WaitForSingleObject* returns immediately, granting the shopper admittance to the store. The count of the semaphore is also decremented so that one fewer shopper is allowed into the store.

You'll notice that I specified a duration value in the call in the code fragment above using the *nDuration* parameter. Shoppers will wait only so long to get into the supermarket before getting tired and going home. The maximum value of this duration can be set by using the Wait To Get In Market setting in the dialog box. If the shopper gets tired of waiting to enter the market, *WaitForSingleObject* returns WAIT_TIMEOUT. The shopper thread places the notification of this event into the Shopper Events list box and returns from the shopper thread, causing the thread to be terminated.

After the shopper has entered the store, some shopping must occur. The maximum duration of this shopping can be set by the Time To Shop setting in the dialog box. In the shopper thread, the action of shopping is performed by simply placing a call to the *Sleep* function and passing the value of the shopping duration.

After the shopper has picked up a few items (*Sleep* has returned), the shopper heads on over to the deli counter to buy roast beef (yummy— my favorite). Actually, as a friend pointed out to me, most people go to the market without stopping at the deli counter at all. So in the shopper thread, the shopper has only a one-in-three chance of going to the deli counter (which leaves more roast beef for me).

If, as luck would have it, the shopper does go to the deli counter, the shopper must be waited on. In the simulation, the deli counter is attended by only one worker. So the synchronization of shoppers with the deli counter is guarded by a mutex object. Only one shopper thread can own the mutex at any one time. If a shopper goes to the deli counter while another shopper is being waited on, the newly arriving shopper must wait until the first shopper completes his or her business at the counter. Completing his or her business means releasing the mutex so that another shopper can get waited on. A shopper thread spends time at the deli counter by calling *Sleep*, passing in a random duration whose maximum value is specified by the Time At Deli Counter setting in the dialog box.

It is also quite possible that the shopper currently being waited on is taking too long and a waiting shopper gets frustrated and leaves the deli counter. The maximum duration for waiting for service at the deli counter can be specified using the Wait For Deli Counter setting in the dialog box.

There are two problems with this part of the simulation. One, only one worker is attending the deli counter. You might want to add a simulation parameter in which the user controlling the simulation can specify the number of workers attending the deli counter. In this way, several shoppers could be served simultaneously. If you decide to do this, you could simply change the mutex object controlling the deli counter to a semaphore object in which the maximum count of the semaphore represents the number of people working at the deli counter. I chose not to do this because I wanted to show you another programming example using mutexes.

The second problem with this scheme is that shoppers are not necessarily waited on in the order in which they appear at the deli counter. In other words, let's say that Shopper 1 is currently being waited on when Shopper 2 appears, followed shortly by Shopper 3. When Shopper 1 leaves the counter, both Shopper 2 and Shopper 3 are still waiting to gain ownership of the mutex. The system makes no guarantee that it will give the mutex to Shopper 2 just because Shopper 2 was waiting for the mutex first. If you want to add this type of control for synchronizing threads, you'll have to add the logic yourself. The system and the Win32 API don't support any direct means of doing this automatically for you.

Regardless of how the shopper dealt with the deli counter, the next step is for the shopper to stand in line at the checkout counter. You can specify the number of checkout counters in the supermarket using the Checkout Counters setting in the dialog box.

Here is another place in which the simulation differs a little bit from reality. A standard pattern in all the supermarkets I've ever been in involves sauntering up to the checkout area and selecting a checkout line to stand in. This is usually a matter of examining what everyone else is buying to see which lines have the least number of items to be rung up before the cashier gets to your stuff. Then you see which lines contain people who have their checkbooks out—you know that these are the bad lines. And then, after you have used these factors to narrow down your decision, you take a quick glance to see which cashier looks friendliest and go with that line.

In the supermarket simulation, things are a little less detailed. Waiting for a checkout counter is more like raising your hand in class and hoping the teacher will call on you. When the teacher asks a question, all the students who think they know the answer raise their hands. But the teacher selects only one student (at random) to answer. In the supermarket simulation, there are a fixed number of checkout counters. These are guarded by a semaphore created by the supermarket thread, as shown below:

```
g_hSemCheckout = CreateSemaphore(
    NULL,                  // Security attributes
    g_nCheckoutRegisters,  // All registers are free.
    g_nCheckoutRegisters,  // The number of registers at the
                           // store
    NULL);                 // No name for the semaphore
```

When a shopper is ready to check out, the shopper thread waits for this semaphore. If a checkout counter is available, the shopper immediately starts checking out, and the semaphore is decremented. If all the checkout counters are in use, the shopper must wait. I designed the simulation so that a shopper cannot get tired of waiting for a checkout counter and leave the supermarket. Once a shopper thread begins waiting, it must continue waiting until it has checked out:

```
WaitForSingleObject(g_hSemCheckout, INFINITE);
```

After the shopper has gained access to a checkout counter, it takes some time for the cashier to ring up all his or her purchases. This time is determined by placing a call to *Sleep*, again passing it a random duration whose maximum value is specified by the Time At Checkout setting in the dialog box.

When all of the shopper's items have been totaled, the shopper leaves the checkout counter by releasing the *g_hSemCheckout* semaphore:

```
ReleaseSemaphore(g_hSemCheckout, 1, NULL);
```

This release allows another shopper waiting to check out to gain access to a checkout counter. The shopper that has checked out must exit the supermarket by releasing the *g_hSemEntrance* semaphore, as shown here:

```
ReleaseSemaphore(g_hSemEntrance, 1, NULL);
```

This release tells the semaphore controlling the admittance of shoppers into the market that one shopper has left and that another shopper can enter.

After the shopper has left the market, the shopper no longer has a reason for being and returns from the thread. Perhaps this is where the phrase "shop till you drop" comes from.

We have spent a good bit of time talking about the shopper threads. Let's return now to the supermarket thread. As mentioned at the beginning of this discussion, the supermarket thread is responsible for randomly creating shoppers. However, the supermarket also stays open for some amount of time and then closes. The amount of time that the supermarket stays open is set using the Time Open setting in the dialog box.

When the supermarket thread sees that the set amount of time has been reached, it stops creating shoppers. But the supermarket cannot close until all the existing shoppers have been served. The supermarket executes the following loop:

```
for (nMaxOccupancy = 0;
   nMaxOccupancy < g_nMaxOccupancy; nMaxOccupancy++) {

   WaitForSingleObject(g_hSemEntrance, INFINITE);
}
```

The loop simply calls *WaitForSingleObject* repeatedly until the supermarket has gained control of the entrance semaphore *g_nMaxOccupancy* times, which can happen only after every shopper has left the supermarket. You could have a problem here if a shopper thread was created just before the supermarket closed. In this case, both the supermarket and the shopper thread are waiting for the semaphore. The system makes no guarantee as to which thread will gain the semaphore when it becomes signaled. So it is possible that a waiting shopper can enter the supermarket even though the supermarket is closed.

It is also possible that the supermarket thread can gain all of the semaphore. In this case, any created shoppers that hadn't entered the store yet would just get tired of waiting and terminate themselves. In a real simulation, these areas would need to be cleaned up a bit.

It might be nice if the supermarket simply called *WaitForMultiple-Objects* once instead of calling *WaitForSingleObject* repeatedly in a loop. But this can't be done for two reasons. First, you can't pass a handle identifying a single object to *WaitForMultipleObjects* more than once. Second, *WaitForMultipleObjects* lets you wait for only MAXIMUM_WAIT_OBJECTS number of objects, which is currently defined as 64. Because we could set the maximum occupancy to be well over 64—maybe 500—calling *WaitForMultipleObjects* wouldn't work even if we could specify the handle to the semaphore more than once.

After the supermarket thread captures the *g_hSemEntrance* semaphore *g_nMaxOccupancy* number of times, it makes the following calls to be sure that all the synchronization objects are destroyed by the system:

```
CloseHandle(g_hSemCheckout);
CloseHandle(g_hMtxDeliCntr);
CloseHandle(g_hSemEntrance);
```

SprMrkt.ico

SPRMRKT.C

```
/***********************************************************
Module name: SprMrkt.C
Notices: Copyright (c) 1995 Jeffrey Richter
***********************************************************/


#include "..\AdvWin32.H"      /* See Appendix B for details. */
#include <windows.h>
#include <windowsx.h>


#pragma warning(disable: 4001)      /* Single-line comment */


#include <tchar.h>
#include <stdio.h>
#include <stdlib.h>                 // For random number stuff
#include <string.h>
#include <stdarg.h>
#include <process.h>                // For _beginthreadex
#include "Resource.H"



// This is the correction to a bug in windowsx.h:
#undef FORWARD_WM_HSCROLL
```

Figure 9-4.   *(continued)*
The SprMrkt application.

Figure 9-4. *continued*

```
#define FORWARD_WM_HSCROLL(hwnd, hwndCtl, code, pos, fn) \
    (void)(fn)((hwnd), WM_HSCROLL, \
        MAKEWPARAM((UINT)(code),(UINT)(pos)), \
        (LPARAM)(UINT)(hwndCtl))


///////////////////////////////////////////////////////////////


// Forward references to the supermarket
// and shopper thread functions.
DWORD WINAPI ThreadSuperMarket (LPVOID lpvParam);
DWORD WINAPI ThreadShopper (LPVOID lpvParam);


///////////////////////////////////////////////////////////////


// Global variables
HWND g_hwndLB = NULL;    // List box for shopper events

// User-settable simulation parameters
int g_nMaxOccupancy,
int g_nTimeOpen;
int g_nCheckoutCounters;
int g_nMaxDelayBetweenShopperCreation;
int g_nMaxWaitToGetInMarket;
int g_nMaxTimeShopping;
int g_nMaxWaitForDeliCntr;
int g_nMaxTimeSpentAtDeli;
int g_nMaxTimeAtCheckout;

// Synchronization objects used to control the simulation
HANDLE g_hSemEntrance;
HANDLE g_hMtxDeliCntr;
HANDLE g_hSemCheckout;


///////////////////////////////////////////////////////////////


// This function constructs a string using the format string
// passed and the variable number of arguments and adds the
// string to the shopper events list box identified by the
// global g_hwndLB variable.
```

(continued)

Figure 9-4. *continued*

```
void AddStr (LPCTSTR szFmt, ...) {
    TCHAR szBuf[150];
    int nIndex;
    va_list va_params;

    // Make va_params point to the first argument after szFmt.
    va_start(va_params, szFmt);

    // Build the string to be displayed.
    _vstprintf(szBuf, szFmt, va_params);
    do {
        // Add the string to the end of the list box.
        nIndex = ListBox_AddString(g_hwndLB, szBuf);

        // If the list box is full, delete the first item in it.
        if (nIndex == LB_ERR)
            ListBox_DeleteString(g_hwndLB, 0);

    } while (nIndex == LB_ERR);

    // Select the newly added item.
    ListBox_SetCurSel(g_hwndLB, nIndex);

    // Indicate that we are done referencing
    // the variable arguments.
    va_end(va_params);
}


///////////////////////////////////////////////////////////////


// This function returns a random number
// between 0 and nMaxValue, inclusive.
int Random (int nMaxValue) {
    return(((2 * rand() * nMaxValue + RAND_MAX) /
        RAND_MAX - 1) / 2);
}


///////////////////////////////////////////////////////////////


BOOL Dlg_OnInitDialog (HWND hwnd, HWND hwndFocus,
    LPARAM lParam) {
```

(continued)

Figure 9-4. *continued*

```
HWND hwndSB;

// Associate an icon with the dialog box.
SetClassLong(hwnd, GCL_HICON, (LONG)
   LoadIcon((HINSTANCE) GetWindowLong(hwnd, GWL_HINSTANCE),
   __TEXT("SprMrkt")));

// Save the window handle to the shopper events list box
// in a global variable so that the AddStr function has
// access to it.
g_hwndLB = GetDlgItem(hwnd, IDC_SHOPPEREVENTS);

// Set the scroll bar range and default positions for all of
// the simulation parameters.
hwndSB = GetDlgItem(hwnd, IDC_MAXOCCUPANCY);
ScrollBar_SetRange(hwndSB, 0, 500, TRUE);

// Set the initial value of the scroll bar.
FORWARD_WM_HSCROLL(hwnd, hwndSB, SB_THUMBTRACK,
   30, SendMessage);


hwndSB = GetDlgItem(hwnd, IDC_TIMEOPEN);
ScrollBar_SetRange(hwndSB, 0, 5000, TRUE);
FORWARD_WM_HSCROLL(hwnd, hwndSB, SB_THUMBTRACK,
   5000, SendMessage);

hwndSB = GetDlgItem(hwnd, IDC_NUMCOUNTERS);
ScrollBar_SetRange(hwndSB, 0, 30, TRUE);
FORWARD_WM_HSCROLL(hwnd, hwndSB, SB_THUMBTRACK,
   5, SendMessage);

hwndSB = GetDlgItem(hwnd, IDC_SHOPPERCREATIONDELAY);
ScrollBar_SetRange(hwndSB, 0, 1000, TRUE);
FORWARD_WM_HSCROLL(hwnd, hwndSB, SB_THUMBTRACK,
   300, SendMessage);

hwndSB = GetDlgItem(hwnd, IDC_DELAYTOGETIN);
ScrollBar_SetRange(hwndSB, 0, 100, TRUE);
FORWARD_WM_HSCROLL(hwnd, hwndSB, SB_THUMBTRACK,
   20, SendMessage);

hwndSB = GetDlgItem(hwnd, IDC_TIMETOSHOP);
ScrollBar_SetRange(hwndSB, 0, 100, TRUE);
```

(continued)

Figure 9-4. *continued*

```
   FORWARD_WM_HSCROLL(hwnd, hwndSB, SB_THUMBTRACK,
      80, SendMessage);

   hwndSB = GetDlgItem(hwnd, IDC_WAITDELICNTR);
   ScrollBar_SetRange(hwndSB, 0, 100, TRUE);
   FORWARD_WM_HSCROLL(hwnd, hwndSB, SB_THUMBTRACK,
      20, SendMessage);

   hwndSB = GetDlgItem(hwnd, IDC_TIMEATDELICNTR);
   ScrollBar_SetRange(hwndSB, 0, 100, TRUE);
   FORWARD_WM_HSCROLL(hwnd, hwndSB, SB_THUMBTRACK,
      70, SendMessage);

   hwndSB = GetDlgItem(hwnd, IDC_TIMEATCHECKOUT);
   ScrollBar_SetRange(hwndSB, 0, 100, TRUE);
   FORWARD_WM_HSCROLL(hwnd, hwndSB, SB_THUMBTRACK,
      60, SendMessage);

   return(TRUE);
}


//////////////////////////////////////////////////////////////////


void Dlg_OnHScroll(HWND hwnd, HWND hwndCtl,
   UINT code, int pos) {

   TCHAR szBuf[10];
   int nPosCrnt, nPosMin, nPosMax;

   // Get the current position and the legal range for the
   // scroll bar that the user is changing.
   nPosCrnt = ScrollBar_GetPos(hwndCtl);
   ScrollBar_GetRange(hwndCtl, &nPosMin, &nPosMax);

   switch (code) {
      case SB_LINELEFT:
         nPosCrnt--;
         break;

      case SB_LINERIGHT:
         nPosCrnt++;
         break;
```

(continued)

Figure 9-4. *continued*

```
      case SB_PAGELEFT:
         nPosCrnt -= (nPosMax - nPosMin + 1) / 10;
         break;

      case SB_PAGERIGHT:
         nPosCrnt += (nPosMax - nPosMin + 1) / 10;
         break;

      case SB_THUMBTRACK:
         nPosCrnt = pos;
         break;

      case SB_LEFT:
         nPosCrnt = nPosMin;
         break;

      case SB_RIGHT:
         nPosCrnt = nPosMax;
         break;
   }

   // Make sure that the new scroll bar position
   // is within the legal range.
   if (nPosCrnt < nPosMin)
      nPosCrnt = nPosMin;

   if (nPosCrnt > nPosMax)
      nPosCrnt = nPosMax;

   // Set the new scroll bar position.
   ScrollBar_SetPos(hwndCtl, nPosCrnt, TRUE);

   // Change the value displayed in the text box to
   // reflect the value in the scroll bar.
   _stprintf(szBuf, __TEXT("%d"), nPosCrnt);
   SetWindowText(GetPrevSibling(hwndCtl), szBuf);
}


///////////////////////////////////////////////////////////////


void Dlg_OnCommand (HWND hwnd, int id, HWND hwndCtl,
   UINT codeNotify) {
```

(continued)

Figure 9-4. *continued*

```
DWORD dwThreadId;
HANDLE hThread;

switch (id) {
   case IDOK:
      // Load the scroll bar settings into the global
      // variables so that they can be used
      // by the simulation.
      g_nMaxOccupancy = ScrollBar_GetPos(
         GetDlgItem(hwnd, IDC_MAXOCCUPANCY));

      g_nTimeOpen = ScrollBar_GetPos(
         GetDlgItem(hwnd, IDC_TIMEOPEN));

      g_nCheckoutCounters = ScrollBar_GetPos(
         GetDlgItem(hwnd, IDC_NUMCOUNTERS));

      g_nMaxDelayBetweenShopperCreation = ScrollBar_GetPos(
         GetDlgItem(hwnd, IDC_SHOPPERCREATIONDELAY));

      g_nMaxWaitToGetInMarket = ScrollBar_GetPos(
         GetDlgItem(hwnd, IDC_DELAYTOGETIN));

      g_nMaxTimeShopping = ScrollBar_GetPos(
         GetDlgItem(hwnd, IDC_TIMETOSHOP));

      g_nMaxWaitForDeliCntr = ScrollBar_GetPos(
         GetDlgItem(hwnd, IDC_WAITDELICNTR));

      g_nMaxTimeSpentAtDeli = ScrollBar_GetPos(
         GetDlgItem(hwnd, IDC_TIMEATDELICNTR));

      g_nMaxTimeAtCheckout = ScrollBar_GetPos(
         GetDlgItem(hwnd, IDC_TIMEATCHECKOUT));


      // Clear out everything in the list box.
      ListBox_ResetContent(
         GetDlgItem(hwnd, IDC_SHOPPEREVENTS));

      // Disable the Open For Business button
      // while simulation is in progress.

      EnableWindow(hwndCtl, FALSE);
```

(continued)

Figure 9-4. *continued*

```
        if (NULL == GetFocus()) {
            SetFocus(GetDlgItem(hwnd, IDC_MAXOCCUPANCY));
        }


        // The system overhead will cause the results
        // of the simulation to be skewed. To help
        // minimize this effect, we boost the priority class
        // of this process.
        SetPriorityClass(GetCurrentProcess(),
            HIGH_PRIORITY_CLASS);

        // Create the thread representing the supermarket.
        hThread = BEGINTHREADEX(
            NULL,               // Security attributes
            0,                  // Stack
            ThreadSuperMarket,  // Thread function
            (LPVOID) hwnd,      // Thread function parameter
            0,                  // Flags
            &dwThreadId);       // Thread ID

        // Since we are not interested in manipulating the
        // thread object from this function, we can close
        // our handle to it.
        CloseHandle(hThread);
        break;

    case IDCANCEL:
        EndDialog(hwnd, id);
        break;
    }
}


///////////////////////////////////////////////////////////////


BOOL CALLBACK Dlg_Proc (HWND hDlg, UINT uMsg,
    WPARAM wParam, LPARAM lParam) {

    BOOL fProcessed = TRUE;

    switch (uMsg) {
        HANDLE_MSG(hDlg, WM_INITDIALOG,  Dlg_OnInitDialog);
```

(continued)

Figure 9-4. *continued*

```
        HANDLE_MSG(hDlg, WM_COMMAND,  Dlg_OnCommand);
        HANDLE_MSG(hDlg, WM_HSCROLL,  Dlg_OnHScroll);

    case WM_USER:
        // This message is sent by the SuperMarketThread
        // function to notify us that the simulation
        // has completed.

        // Return the priority class of the simulation
        // back to normal.
        SetPriorityClass(GetCurrentProcess(),
            NORMAL_PRIORITY_CLASS);

        // Enable the Open For Business button so that
        // the user can run the simulation again with
        // new parameters.
        EnableWindow(GetDlgItem(hDlg, IDOK), TRUE);
        break;

    default:
        fProcessed = FALSE;
        break;
    }
    return(fProcessed);
}


//////////////////////////////////////////////////////////////////


int WINAPI WinMain (HINSTANCE hinstExe,
    HINSTANCE hinstPrev, LPSTR lpszCmdLine, int nCmdShow) {

    DialogBox(hinstExe, MAKEINTRESOURCE(IDD_SPRMRKT),
        NULL, Dlg_Proc);

    return(0);
}


//////////////////////////////////////////////////////////////////


DWORD WINAPI ThreadSuperMarket (LPVOID lpvParam) {
    DWORD dwCloseTime;
```

(continued)

Figure 9-4. *continued*

```
HANDLE hThread;
DWORD dwThreadId;
int nShopperNum = 0, nMaxOccupancy;

g_hSemEntrance = CreateSemaphore(
   NULL,                    // Security attributes
   0,                       // Initial lock count
   g_nMaxOccupancy,         // Maximum people allowed in store
   NULL);                   // Do not name the semaphore.

g_hMtxDeliCntr = CreateMutex(
   NULL,                    // Security attributes
   FALSE,                   // Initially no one is at the deli.
   NULL);                   // Do not name the mutex.

g_hSemCheckout = CreateSemaphore(
   NULL,                    // Security attributes
   g_nCheckoutCounters,     // All counters are free.
   g_nCheckoutCounters,     // The number of counters at the
                            // store
   NULL);                   // No name for the semaphore


// Open the store to the shoppers.
AddStr(__TEXT("---> Opening the supermarket to shoppers."));
ReleaseSemaphore(g_hSemEntrance, g_nMaxOccupancy, NULL);

// Get the time at which the store should
// stop creating shoppers.
dwCloseTime = GetTickCount() + g_nTimeOpen;

// Continue loop until the store closes.
while (GetTickCount() < dwCloseTime) {

   // Create the thread representing a shopper.
   hThread = BEGINTHREADEX(
      NULL,                    // Security attributes
      0,                       // Stack
      ThreadShopper,           // Thread function
      (LPVOID) ++nShopperNum,  // Shopper number as lpvParam
      0,                       // Flags
      &dwThreadId);            // Thread ID
```

(continued)

Figure 9-4. *continued*

```
        // Since we are not interested in manipulating the
        // thread object from this function, we can close
        // our handle to it.
        CloseHandle(hThread);

        // Wait until another shopper comes to the supermarket.
        Sleep(Random(g_nMaxDelayBetweenShopperCreation));
    }

    // The supermarket wants to close;
    // wait for all of the shoppers to leave.
    AddStr(__TEXT("---> Waiting for shoppers to check out ")
        __TEXT("so store can close."));

    nMaxOccupancy = 1;
    for (; nMaxOccupancy <= g_nMaxOccupancy; nMaxOccupancy++) {
        WaitForSingleObject(g_hSemEntrance, INFINITE);
        AddStr(__TEXT("---> %d shoppers NOT in store."),
        nMaxOccupancy);
    }

    AddStr(__TEXT("---> Store closed--end of simulation."));

    // Everybody has left the market--end of simulation.
    CloseHandle(g_hSemCheckout);
    CloseHandle(g_hMtxDeliCntr);
    CloseHandle(g_hSemEntrance);

    // Notify the GUI thread that the simulation has completed.
    // The window handle of the GUI thread's dialog box was
    // passed in the lpvParam parameter to this thread when
    // it was created.
    SendMessage((HWND) lpvParam, WM_USER, 0, 0);

    return(0);
}


///////////////////////////////////////////////////////////////////


DWORD WINAPI ThreadShopper (LPVOID lpvParam) {
    int nShopperNum = (int) lpvParam;
    DWORD dwResult;
    int nDuration;
```

(continued)

Figure 9-4. *continued*

```
// Wait till the shopper can enter the supermarket.
nDuration = Random(g_nMaxWaitToGetInMarket);
AddStr(__TEXT("%04lu: Waiting to get in store (%lu)."),
    nShopperNum, nDuration);

dwResult = WaitForSingleObject(g_hSemEntrance, nDuration);
if (dwResult == WAIT_TIMEOUT) {
    // The shopper got tired of
    // waiting to be let in and left.
    AddStr(__TEXT("%04lu: Tired of waiting; went home."),
    nShopperNum);
    return(0);
}



// Shopper entered the supermarket. Time to go shopping.
nDuration = Random(g_nMaxTimeShopping);
AddStr(__TEXT("%04lu: In supermarket, shopping for %lu."),
    nShopperNum, nDuration);
Sleep(nDuration);



// Done with initial shopping. Shopper has a one-in-three
// chance of going to the deli counter.
if (Random(2) == 0) {

    // Shopper going to deli counter
    nDuration = Random(g_nMaxWaitForDeliCntr);
    AddStr(
        __TEXT("%04lu: Waiting for service at ")
        __TEXT("deli counter (%lu)."),
        nShopperNum, nDuration);
    dwResult =
        WaitForSingleObject(g_hMtxDeliCntr, nDuration);

    if (dwResult == 0) {
        // Got attention at deli; order stuff.
        nDuration = Random(g_nMaxTimeSpentAtDeli);

        AddStr(__TEXT("%04lu: Being served at deli (%lu)."),
            nShopperNum, nDuration);
        Sleep(nDuration);

        // Leave the deli counter.
        ReleaseMutex(g_hMtxDeliCntr);
```

(continued)

Figure 9-4. *continued*

```
    } else {
        // Tired of waiting at deli counter;
        // leave and continue shopping.
        AddStr(__TEXT("%04lu: Tired of waiting at deli."),
            nShopperNum);
    }

} else {
    AddStr(__TEXT("%04lu: Not going to the deli counter."),
        nShopperNum);
}


// Waiting for a checkout counter
AddStr(
    __TEXT("%04lu: Waiting for an empty checkout counter."),
    nShopperNum);
WaitForSingleObject(g_hSemCheckout, INFINITE);

// Checking out
nDuration = Random(g_nMaxTimeAtCheckout);
AddStr(__TEXT("%04lu: Checking out (%lu)."),
    nShopperNum, nDuration);
Sleep(nDuration);

// Leaving the checkout counter
AddStr(__TEXT("%04lu: Leaving checkout counter."),
    nShopperNum);
ReleaseSemaphore(g_hSemCheckout, 1, NULL);

// Leaving the store
AddStr(__TEXT("%04lu: Left the supermarket."),
    nShopperNum);
ReleaseSemaphore(g_hSemEntrance, 1, NULL);

// Shopper shopped till he/she dropped. Shopper dead.
return(0);
}


/////////////////////// End Of File ///////////////////////
```

(continued)

360

Figure 9-4. *continued*

SPRMRKT.RC

```
//Microsoft Visual C++ generated resource script.
//
#include "Resource.h"

#define APSTUDIO_READONLY_SYMBOLS
/////////////////////////////////////////////////////////////////////
//
// Generated from the TEXTINCLUDE 2 resource.
//
#include "afxres.h"


/////////////////////////////////////////////////////////////////////
#undef APSTUDIO_READONLY_SYMBOLS


#ifdef APSTUDIO_INVOKED
/////////////////////////////////////////////////////////////////////
//
// TEXTINCLUDE
//

1 TEXTINCLUDE DISCARDABLE
BEGIN
    "Resource.h\0"
END

2 TEXTINCLUDE DISCARDABLE
BEGIN
    "#include ""afxres.h""\r\n"
    "\0"
END

3 TEXTINCLUDE DISCARDABLE
BEGIN
    "\r\n"
    "\0"
END

/////////////////////////////////////////////////////////////////////
#endif    // APSTUDIO_INVOKED
```

(continued)

Figure 9-4. *continued*

```
////////////////////////////////////////////////////////////////
//
// Dialog
//


IDD_SPRMRKT DIALOG DISCARDABLE  4, 58, 360, 206
STYLE WS_MINIMIZEBOX ¦ WS_POPUP ¦ WS_VISIBLE ¦ WS_CAPTION
     ¦ WS_SYSMENU
CAPTION "Supermarket Simulation"
FONT 8, "MS Sans Serif"
BEGIN
    GROUPBOX        "Super&market parameters",IDC_STATIC,
                    4,0,176,64,WS_GROUP
    RTEXT           "Maximum occupancy:",IDC_STATIC,8,12,72,
                    8,NOT WS_GROUP
    RTEXT           "MO",IDC_STATIC,84,12,16,8,SS_NOPREFIX
                    ¦ NOT WS_GROUP
    SCROLLBAR       IDC_MAXOCCUPANCY,104,12,72,10,WS_TABSTOP
    RTEXT           "Time open:",IDC_STATIC,8,24,72,8,
                    NOT WS_GROUP
    RTEXT           "TO",IDC_STATIC,84,24,16,8,SS_NOPREFIX
                    ¦ NOT WS_GROUP
    SCROLLBAR       IDC_TIMEOPEN,104,24,72,10,WS_TABSTOP
    RTEXT           "Checkout counters:",IDC_STATIC,8,38,72,
                    8,NOT WS_GROUP
    RTEXT           "CC",IDC_STATIC,84,38,16,8,SS_NOPREFIX
                    ¦ NOT WS_GROUP
    SCROLLBAR       IDC_NUMCOUNTERS,104,38,72,10,WS_TABSTOP
    RTEXT           "Shopper create delay:",IDC_STATIC,8,52,
                    72,8,NOT WS_GROUP
    RTEXT           "SC",IDC_STATIC,84,52,16,8,SS_NOPREFIX
                    ¦ NOT WS_GROUP
    SCROLLBAR       IDC_SHOPPERCREATIONDELAY,104,52,72,10,
                    WS_TABSTOP
    GROUPBOX        "&Shopper parameters",IDC_STATIC,184,0,
                    172,80,WS_GROUP
    RTEXT           "Wait to get in market:",IDC_STATIC,188,
                    12,72,8,NOT WS_GROUP
    RTEXT           "WTGI",IDC_STATIC,260,12,16,8,SS_NOPREFIX
                    ¦ NOT WS_GROUP
    SCROLLBAR       IDC_DELAYTOGETIN,280,10,72,10,WS_TABSTOP
    RTEXT           "Time to shop:",IDC_STATIC,188,24,72,
                    8,NOT WS_GROUP
```

(continued)

Figure 9-4. *continued*

```
    RTEXT              "TTS",IDC_STATIC,260,24,16,8,SS_NOPREFIX
                       | NOT WS_GROUP
    SCROLLBAR          IDC_TIMETOSHOP,280,24,72,10,WS_TABSTOP
    RTEXT              "Wait for deli counter:",IDC_STATIC,188,
                       38,72,8,NOT WS_GROUP
    RTEXT              "WFDC",IDC_STATIC,260,38,16,8,SS_NOPREFIX
                       | NOT WS_GROUP
    SCROLLBAR          IDC_WAITDELICNTR,280,38,72,10,WS_TABSTOP
    RTEXT              "Time at deli counter:",IDC_STATIC,188,52,
                       72,8,NOT WS_GROUP
    RTEXT              "TADC",IDC_STATIC,260,52,16,8,SS_NOPREFIX
                       | NOT WS_GROUP
    SCROLLBAR          IDC_TIMEATDELICNTR,280,52,72,10,WS_TABSTOP
    RTEXT              "Time at checkout:",IDC_STATIC,188,66,72,
                       8,NOT WS_GROUP
    RTEXT              "TAC",IDC_STATIC,260,66,16,8,SS_NOPREFIX
                       | NOT WS_GROUP
    SCROLLBAR          IDC_TIMEATCHECKOUT,280,66,72,10,WS_TABSTOP
    PUSHBUTTON         "&Open for business",IDOK,80,68,100,12,
                       WS_GROUP
    LTEXT              "Shopper &events:",IDC_STATIC,4,82,56,8
    LISTBOX            IDC_SHOPPEREVENTS,4,94,352,108,
                       LBS_NOINTEGRALHEIGHT | WS_VSCROLL
                       | WS_TABSTOP
END


/////////////////////////////////////////////////////////////////
//
// Icon
//

SprMrkt              ICON    DISCARDABLE    "SprMrkt.Ico"

#ifndef APSTUDIO_INVOKED
/////////////////////////////////////////////////////////////////
//
// Generated from the TEXTINCLUDE 3 resource.
//


/////////////////////////////////////////////////////////////////
#endif    // not APSTUDIO_INVOKED
```

Events

Event objects are the most primitive form of synchronization object and are quite different from mutexes and semaphores. Mutexes and semaphores are usually used to control access to data, but events are used to signal that some operation has completed. There are two different types of event objects: manual-reset events and auto-reset events. A manual-reset event is used to signal several threads simultaneously that an operation has completed, and an auto-reset event is used to signal a single thread that an operation has completed.

Events are most commonly used when one thread performs initialization work and then, when it completes, signals another thread to perform the remaining work. The initialization thread sets the event to the nonsignaled state and begins to perform the initialization. Then, after the initialization has completed, the thread sets the event to the signaled state. When the worker thread starts executing, it immediately suspends itself, waiting for the event to become signaled. When the initialization thread signals the event, the worker thread wakes up and performs the rest of the work necessary.

For example, a process might be running two threads. The first thread reads data from a file into a memory buffer. After the data has been read, the first thread signals the second thread that it can process the data. When the second thread finishes processing the data, it might need to signal the first thread again so that the first thread can read the next block of data from the file.

Let's start our discussion with how to create an event. The semantics for creating, opening, and closing events are identical to those for mutexes and semaphores. Events are created using the *CreateEvent* function:

```
HANDLE CreateEvent(LPSECURITY_ATTRIBUTES lpsa,
    BOOL fManualReset, BOOL fInitialState, LPTSTR lpszEventName);
```

The *fManualReset* parameter is a Boolean value that tells the system whether you want to create a manual-reset event (TRUE) or an auto-reset event (FALSE). The *fInitialState* parameter indicates whether the event should be initialized as signaled (TRUE) or nonsignaled (FALSE). After the system creates the event object, *CreateEvent* returns the process-relative handle to the event. Threads in other processes can gain access to the object by calling *CreateEvent* using the same value in the *lpszEventName* parameter; by using inheritance; by using the *DuplicateHandle* function; or by calling *OpenEvent* (shown on the facing page), specifying a name in the *lpszName* parameter that matches the name specified in the call to *CreateEvent*:

```
HANDLE OpenEvent(DWORD fdwAccess, BOOL fInherit, LPTSTR lpszName);
```

As always, events are closed by calling the very popular *CloseHandle* function.

Manual-Reset Events

Manual-reset events are not automatically reset to the nonsignaled state by the *WaitForSingleObject* and *WaitForMultipleObjects* functions. In the case of mutexes, when a thread calls *WaitForSingleObject* or *WaitForMultipleObjects*, the functions wait for the mutex to be signaled and then automatically reset the mutex to nonsignaled. This is important because it guarantees that no more than one thread waiting on the mutex will be able to wake up and continue executing. If threads were responsible for manually resetting the mutex back to the nonsignaled state, it would be possible for two or more threads to have their waits satisfied before each one reset the mutex to nonsignaled.

For manual-reset events, the story is quite different. You might have several threads, all of them waiting for the same event to occur. When the event does occur, each of the waiting threads might be able to perform its own processing. Let's go back to our file reading and processing example. It might be the case that one thread is responsible for reading data from a file into a buffer. After the data has been read, we might want to start nine other threads. Each of these nine threads might process the data in a slightly different way. Let's say the file contains a word processing document. The first thread could count characters, the second thread could count words, the third thread could count pages, the fourth thread could perform a spell check, the fifth thread could print the document, and so on. The one extremely important thing that all of these threads have in common is that none of them write to the data. All of them consider the data to be a read-only resource.

In this example, you most certainly would want to allow all the waiting threads to be satisfied when the event occurred. This is the reason for manual-reset events. When a manual-reset event is signaled, all threads waiting on the event are allowed to run. A thread sets an event object to the signaled state by calling:

```
BOOL SetEvent(HANDLE hEvent);
```

This function takes the handle to an event object and simply sets it to the signaled state. *SetEvent* returns TRUE if the function is successful. After the manual-reset event has been signaled, it remains signaled until one thread explicitly (or manually) resets the event by calling:

```
BOOL ResetEvent(HANDLE hEvent);
```

This function takes the handle to an event object and resets it to the non-signaled state. *ResetEvent* returns TRUE if the function is successful. See, I told you that events were the most primitive synchronization object.

For the file reading and processing example, the thread that reads the file data and puts it into the shared memory buffer would call *ResetEvent* just before reading the data into the buffer. It would then call *SetEvent* when the reading was completed.

I've left out one small issue: how does the file-read thread know when to read the next block of data? We know that it should read the next block of data when all the other threads have finished their work with the current block of data. But the other threads need a way to signal that they've finished. The best method is for each of the data processing threads to create their own event object. If all the handles for these event objects were stored in an array, the file-read thread could call *WaitForMultipleObjects*, indicating that it wanted to wait for all the event handles.

Because calling *SetEvent*, releasing waiting events, and immediately calling *ResetEvent* is quite common, Win32 offers another function that performs all three of these steps:

```
BOOL PulseEvent(HANDLE hEvent);
```

When *PulseEvent* returns, the event is left in the nonsignaled state. If the function is successful, TRUE is returned.

The Bucket of Balls Sample Application

A basic synchronization problem, commonly referred to as the classic multiple-readers/multiple-writers scenario, exists for many different applications. The problem involves an arbitrary number of threads that are attempting to access a global resource. Some of these threads (the writers) need to modify the contents of the global data, and some of the threads (the readers) need only to read the data. Synchronization is necessary because of the following rules:

1. When one thread is writing to the data, no other thread can write to the data.

2. When one thread is writing to the data, no other thread can read from the data.

3. When one thread is reading from the data, no other thread can write to the data.

4. When one thread is reading from the data, other threads can also read from the data.

Let's look at this problem in the context of a database application. Let's say we have five end users, all working on the same database: two employees are entering records into the database, and three employees are retrieving records from the database.

In this scenario, rule 1 is necessary because we certainly can't have both Employee 1 and Employee 2 updating record 3457 at the same time. If both employees attempt to modify the same record, Employee 1's changes and Employee 2's changes might be made to the database at the same time. We wouldn't want to have a situation in which a record in the database contained corrupted information.

Rule 2 prohibits an employee from accessing a record in the database if another employee is updating a record in the database. If this situation were not prevented, it would be possible for Employee 4 to read the contents of record 2543 while Employee 1 was altering that same record. When Employee 4's computer displayed record 2543, the record would contain some of the old information and some of the updated information—this is certainly unacceptable. Rule 3 is needed in order to solve the same problem. The difference in the wording of rules 2 and 3 prevents the situation regardless of who gains access to the database record first—an employee who is trying to write or an employee who is attempting to read.

The last rule, rule 4, exists for performance reasons. It makes sense that if no employees are attempting to modify records in the database, the content of the database is not changing and, therefore, any and all employees who are simply retrieving records from the database should be allowed to do so.

OK, there you have the gist of the problem. Now the question is, how do we solve it?

The Bucket (BUCKET.EXE) application, listed in Figure 9-5 beginning on page 379, demonstrates the solution by synchronizing the access of five threads to a small database. In order to accomplish this synchronization, Bucket uses three of the kernel synchronization objects discussed in this chapter: manual-reset events, semaphores, and mutexes. Although Bucket manages only five threads (two updating the database and three reading the database), the groundwork presented easily extends itself to a situation in which virtually any number of threads (readers and/or writers) can be synchronized. The source code files, resource files, and make file for the application are in the BUCKET.09 directory on the companion disc.

When you invoke Bucket, the following dialog box appears:

The database being managed is a bucket that can contain no more than 100 balls. Initially the bucket is empty. The Bucket Writers section in the upper portion of the dialog box represents the two threads that add, remove, or change the different colored balls in the bucket. To the right of the thread number is a time value specified in seconds. For Writer 1, this value is 1. This means that every second, Writer 1 attempts to gain access to the bucket and add another ball. The scroll bar at the right of the seconds value allows you to change this delay time, which can range from 0 through 60 seconds. Writer 2 operates in the same way except that it starts out with an initial delay time of 3 seconds.

The bottom portion of the dialog box represents the three reader threads. These threads work similarly to the writer threads. After every specified number of seconds (0 through 60), each of the three reader threads erases the contents of its list box, counts the different colored balls in the bucket, and updates the list box to display the results.

The important thing to remember here is that all the threads are being synchronized. If a writer currently has permission to add, remove, or change a ball in the bucket, neither the other writer nor any of the readers will be granted access to the bucket. On the other hand, if a reader has access to the bucket and is counting the balls, any of the other readers requesting access to do the same will gain access, but none of the writers will be allowed to change any of the balls in the bucket until all the readers are finished.

Now that you see how the program operates, let's turn our attention to the source code listed in Figure 9-5.

Important

A point that I have been trying to drive home throughout this entire chapter is that thread synchronization bugs are extremely difficult to locate and fix. As it turns out, I am far from immune to this problem myself (as several readers have so kindly pointed out to me). The Bucket sample that appears in the first edition of this book has bugs in it. I have (well, at least I'm pretty sure this time that I have) corrected the bugs in Bucket, and I have also improved the application's code and clarity significantly. If you used any code from my first edition's Bucket sample, you might want to examine this updated version and see whether you need to make any enhancements to your own code.

The SWMRG Compound Synchronization Object

When I started to fix Bucket for this edition of the book, I realized that the code that Bucket was using in the first edition for its thread synchronization was too complicated and error prone—a better method was definitely called for. Because the single-writer/multiple-reader scenario is a classic synchronization problem, I thought it best to create a generic, reusable object to solve it. This way, if any of you reading this need to solve this classic problem, you can just steal my code and incorporate it into your own application with few or no changes whatsoever. The result of my labor is something I like to call SWMRG (I pronounce it *swimerge*); it stands for single-writer/multiple-reader guard.

A SWMRG object is a data structure of my own creation. This SWMRG data structure and the functions that manipulate it can be found in the SWMRG.H and SWMRG.C files in the BUCKET.09 directory on the companion disc. A SWMRG object is a compound synchronization object designed specifically for handling the classic single-writer/ multiple-reader synchronization problem. I call it a compound synchronization object because it uses three kernel objects: a mutex, a semaphore, and a manual-reset event. I discuss how it uses these later. For now, I'll simply discuss how an application uses a SWMRG object.

Let me start off by saying that you use a SWMRG object in exactly the same way you would use a CRITICAL_SECTION object. First you must create an instance of a SWMRG object in your application. As with CRITICAL_SECTION objects, you usually create a SWMRG object as a global variable so that all threads in the process have access to it:

```
#include "SWMRG.h"
SWMRG g_SWMRG;     // The global SWMRG object
```

Also, the data members in a SWMRG object should be considered opaque to the application—only the functions supplied in SWMRG.C reference the members in the structure; the application should never need to touch these data members. This is also how CRITICAL_SECTION objects are used.

Before any thread in the process can synchronize itself using the SWMRG object, the SWMRG object must be initialized (usually in the application's *WinMain* function). A SWMRG object is initialized by calling the *SWMRGInitialize* function:

```
BOOL  SWMRGInitialize (PSWMRG pSWMRG, LPCTSTR lpszName);
```

As you can see, the first parameter must be the address of a SWMRG object and the second parameter allows you to specify a name for the object. Although the *SWMRGInitialize* function is similar to the *InitializeCriticalSection* function, there is one really big difference: I have designed the SWMRG object so that it can be accessed by threads running in different processes. In order to do this, however, you must pass a string name as the *lpszName* parameter. This technique is similar to creating a mutex object and specifying a name for it. If you don't want to share the SWMRG object across processes, you should pass NULL for the *lpszName* parameter. I'll talk more about using the SWMRG object across processes a little later in this chapter.

When the process is ending and you are sure that no writer or reader threads will attempt to access the SWMRG object, the SWMRG object should be destroyed by calling the *SWMRGDelete* function:

```
void SWMRGDelete (PSWMRG pSWMRG);
```

Now, in between the calls to *SWMRGInitialize* and *SWMRGDelete*, any writer or reader thread can use the SWMRG object for synchronization. The interface is very simple. When a writer thread needs access to the shared data resource, it must first call a function that is similar to the *EnterCriticalSection* function:

```
DWORD SWMRGWaitToWrite (PSWMRG pSWMRG, DWORD dwTimeout);
```

The writer thread passes the address of the SWMRG object as the first parameter and a time-out value for the second parameter. This is another area in which SWMRG objects vary from critical sections: with a SWMRG object, you can specify a time-out value while waiting. *SWMRG-WaitToWrite* will return either WAIT_OBJECT_0 or WAIT_TIMEOUT.

If the writer thread was granted exclusive access to the shared data resource because *SWMRGWaitToWrite* returned WAIT_OBJECT_0, it must call *SWMRGDoneWriting* when it no longer needs access to the data. Calling *SWMRGDoneWriting* allows other writer or reader threads the opportunity to access the shared resource:

```
void SWMRGDoneWriting (PSWMRG pSWMRG);
```

This function is similar to the *LeaveCriticalSection* function.

So far we have discussed only the writer thread side of using a SWMRG object. Now let's discuss how a reader thread uses the SWMRG object. When a reader thread wants to access the shared data resource, it calls *SWMRGWaitToRead*:

```
DWORD SWMRGWaitToRead (PSWMRG pSWMRG, DWORD dwTimeout);
```

This function is similar to the *SWMRGWaitToWrite* function in that it takes the same parameters and has the same return values. The difference is in what it does internally, which we'll discuss shortly.

When a reader thread is done accessing the shared data, it must call *SWMRGDoneReading* so that a writer thread has the opportunity to access the shared data resource:

```
void SWMRGDoneReading (PSWMRG pSWMRG);
```

Of course, a writer thread will be granted access only if no reader threads are currently accessing the resource.

It's time now to discuss how the SWMRG object is actually implemented. We'll begin by examining the data members of the SWMRG structure:

```
typedef struct SingleWriterMultiReaderGuard {
    // This mutex guards access to the other objects
    // managed by this data structure and also indicates
    // when there are no writer threads writing.
    HANDLE hMutexNoWriter;

    // This manual-reset event is signaled when
    // there are no reader threads reading.
    HANDLE hEventNoReaders;
```

(continued)

```
// This semaphore is used simply as a counter that is
// accessible between multiple processes. It is NOT
// used for thread synchronization.
// The count is the number of reader threads reading.
HANDLE hSemNumReaders;

} SWMRG, *PSWMRG;
```

This data structure consists of three handles to kernel synchronization objects. The first handle, *hMutexNoWriter*, is used by the SWMRG functions to indicate whether a writer thread has access to the shared data resource. Remember that a writer thread having access to the resource locks out all other writer threads as well as all reader threads. So a mutex object seems an excellent choice because only one thread at a time can own a mutex object. When the mutex is signaled, we know that no writer thread is currently accessing the data.

The second handle, *hEventNoReaders*, indicates whether any reader threads are currently accessing the data. If no reader threads are accessing the data, this manual-reset event object is signaled.

The third handle, *hSemNumReaders*, indicates the number of reader threads that are currently accessing the shared resource. The SWMRG functions do not use this semaphore for synchronization purposes— they use it as a counter. The SWMRG object must maintain a counter that indicates the number of reader threads that are simultaneously accessing the data. This way, when the last reader thread calls *SWMRGDoneReading*, the counter goes to 0 and the *hEventNoReaders* event can be signaled by calling the *SetEvent* function.

When I was developing SWMRG, I originally had a long variable declared in the SWMRG structure instead of this handle to a semaphore. I used this variable to count the number of reader threads accessing the resource. But then, as I continued to develop the SWMRG code, I got to the point where I wanted to make it work for threads in other processes. This meant that the counter variable needed to be accessible in each process's address space. So I thought about creating a memory-mapped file and mapping a view of this file into each process's address space when *SWMRGInitialize* is called. The thing I hated about this method was that a memory-mapped file can be no smaller than a page and all I needed was a 4-byte value. For a system with a page size of 4096 bytes, this meant a 102,400 percent overhead; on a system with a page size of 8192 (such as the DEC Alpha), the overhead would be 202,400 percent!

After racking my brain for a while, I realized that a semaphore kernel object maintains a counter, is accessible across processes, and uses much less than 4096 bytes of memory. So I create a semaphore and use this as my counter. Whenever I want to decrement the counter, I call *WaitForSingleObject*, passing the handle to the semaphore; and whenever I want to increment the counter, I call *ReleaseSemaphore*. The problem with using semaphores as counters is that you can't query the current value of the semaphore. The only thing you can do is check to see whether the semaphore has a count of 0 by calling *WaitForSingleObject* with a time out value of 0. If *WaitForSingleObject* returns WAIT_TIME-OUT, the semaphore's count is 0; and if WAIT_OBJECT_0 is returned, the semaphore's count is greater than 0. This is all that we can know about the semaphore, and fortunately, this is all that the SWMRG object functions need to know. More on this later.

I've placed a lot of comments in the SWMRG.C file to explain each of the functions, but I'll also discuss them briefly here in the text.

The *SWMRGInitialize* function is used to initialize the SWMRG object. Basically, it creates the mutex, event, and semaphore objects. In order for threads in different processes to share the SWMRG object, each process must allocate its very own instance of a SWMRG object. Then a thread in each process must pass the address of its SWMRG object as well as a name for the object when calling *SWMRGInitialize*. *SWMRGInitialize* uses this name when creating the mutex, event, and semaphore. For example, if you call *SWMRGInitialize*, passing *"Jeff"* for the *lpszName* parameter, the mutex object is created with the name *SWMRGMutexNoWriterJeff*, the event object is created with the name *SWMRGEventNoReadersJeff*, and the semaphore object is created with the name *SWMRGSemNumReadersJeff*. The static *ConstructObjName* function is a small helper function that *SWMRGInitialize* calls in order to append the *lpszName* parameter to the kernel object name's prefix.

When a thread in another process calls *SWMRGInitialize* and passes the same name for the *lpszName* parameter, the calls to create the various kernel objects will see that kernel objects with the same names already exist and will return handles to the existing objects rather than create new objects. The threads in the different processes will be synchronized.

The *SWMRGDelete* function is by far the simplest of the functions. It calls *CloseHandle* three times, once for each kernel object.

When a writer thread is ready to modify the shared data resource, it must first request permission to do so by calling the *SWMRGWaitToWrite* function. This function calls the Win32 *WaitForMultipleObjects* function, telling it to wait for both the *hMutexNoWriter* mutex and the *hEventNo-Readers* event. If *WaitForMultipleObjects* returns WAIT_OBJECT_0, the thread knows that there are no other writer threads and no reader threads using the shared resource. If the function returns WAIT_TIME-OUT, the writer thread knows that it is not safe to modify the shared resource because there is another writer thread or at least one reader thread currently accessing the data.

When a writer thread has completed modifying the shared resource, it must call the *SWMRGDoneWriting* function. This function releases the *hMutexNoWriter* semaphore so that any other writer or reader threads will see that there are no writer threads accessing the data.

When a reader thread is ready to read the shared data resource, it must first request permission to do so by calling the *SWMRGWaitToRead* function. This function calls *WaitForSingleObject*, passing the *hMutexNo-Writer* mutex handle. This is because a reader thread can always read the resource if there is no writer thread currently accessing the resource. If the call to *WaitForSingleObject* times out while waiting for the mutex, *SWMRGWaitToRead* returns WAIT_TIMEOUT.

However, if the call to *WaitForSingleObject* successfully obtains ownership of the mutex, the semaphore that maintains the count of reader threads must be incremented. This is done by simply calling *Release-Semaphore*, passing it the *hSemNumReaders* handle and a value of 1 for the *cReleaseCount* parameter. The *ReleaseSemaphore* function returns the previous count of the semaphore in a DWORD whose address is passed as the last parameter. *SWMRGWaitToRead* examines this value, and, if there were no reader threads accessing the shared resource prior to calling *ReleaseSemaphore*, *SWMRGWaitToRead* resets the *hEventNoReaders* manual-reset event. Resetting this event object indicates that there are some reader threads accessing the shared data. If this reader thread is not the first reader thread to access the data, the *hEventNoReaders* event will already be in the nonsignaled state so there is no reason to call *ResetEvent* again.

Just before *SWMRGWaitToRead* returns, it must call *ReleaseMutex*, passing the *hMutexNoWriter* handle. This is necessary because when *SWMRGWaitToRead* successfully waits for this mutex, the mutex becomes nonsignaled as a side effect. This indicates, of course, that there is a writer thread accessing the data. We must correct this side effect by calling *ReleaseMutex* so that the other threads know that a writer thread is not actually accessing the shared data.

The last function to discuss is *SWMRGDoneReading*. A reader thread must call this function when it has completed accessing the shared data. *SWMRGDoneReading* first calls *WaitForSingleObject*, passing the *hMutex-NoWriter* handle, because the thread that is calling *SWMRGDoneReading* must have exclusive access to the *hEventNoReaders* and *hSemNumReaders* objects. This thread needs to alter the states of these objects, and other writer and reader threads must not be able to examine the states of these objects until the thread that has finished reading has completely updated them. Because the *SWMRGWaitToWrite*, *SWMRGDoneWriting*, *SWMRG-WaitToRead*, and *SWMRGDoneReading* functions all must successfully wait on the *hMutexNoWriter* mutex before continuing, a reader thread calling *SWMRGDoneReading* can block these other threads until it has updated the event and semaphore objects.

After *SWMRGDoneReading* has successfully waited for the *hMutex-NoWriter* object, it must decrement the number of reader threads by calling *WaitForSingleObject*, passing the *hSemNumReaders* handle. Remember that successfully waiting for a semaphore object means that the system automatically decrements the count of the semaphore by 1. Now that the semaphore has been decremented, *SWMRGDoneReading* must check to see whether the reader thread is the last reader thread.

Determining whether this thread is the last reader thread is not as straightforward as I would have hoped. It would be easy if Win32 offered a function that returned the current count associated with a semaphore, but Win32 does not offer such a function. So the only thing I can do is call *WaitForSingleObject*, passing the *hSemNumReaders* handle and a time-out value of 0. This tells the system to return WAIT_OBJECT_0 if the semaphore's count is greater than 0, or WAIT_TIMEOUT if the semaphore's count is 0. If WAIT_TIMEOUT is returned, I know that this reader thread is the last one and I set the *fLastReader* variable to TRUE. *SWMRGDoneReading* must also change the *hEventNoReaders* event to the signaled state by calling *SetEvent*.

If this thread is *not* the last reader thread, I have done a very bad thing: by successfully waiting on the *hSemNumReaders* semaphore, I have decremented its count one more value than I should have. I must compensate for this by incrementing the count back to its original value. I do this by calling *ReleaseSemaphore*. When I was first developing the SWMRG code, I forgot to do this, causing a very bad synchronization problem that eventually suspended all of my reader and writer threads. Fortunately, hung threads are an indication of a bug, and I was able to catch this bug and correct it in the code you see in Figure 9-5.

Finally, just before *SWMRGDoneReading* returns, it must release the *hMutexNoWriter* mutex by calling *ReleaseMutex*. As with the *SWMRGWait-ToRead* function, this is necessary so that any other writer and reader threads can now wake up and continue their business.

The Bucket Sample Source Code

When you invoke Bucket, the first thing it does is initialize a SWMRG synchronization object. Because the Bucket sample application is the only application that needs access to the mutex, event, and semaphore objects, NULL is passed to *SWMRGInitialize*'s *lpszName* parameter. After the SWMRG object has been initialized, Bucket calls *DialogBox* in order to display its user interface.

Displaying the dialog box causes the system to send a WM_INIT-DIALOG message. In the processing of the *Dlg_OnInitDialog* function, the scroll bars are initialized and the two writer and three reader threads are created. The handles to these five threads are saved in a global array because they'll be needed to cleanly terminate the process. All these threads work in exactly the same way. Each thread performs a small amount of initialization and then enters a *while* loop that terminates only when the global *g_lTerminate* variable is set to 1. (When the application starts, this variable is initialized to 0; we'll come back to this variable shortly.)

Inside the *while* loop, each thread first calls the Win32 *Sleep* function, passing it a value that is determined by the thread's associated scroll bar value:

```
Sleep(1000 * GetDlgItemInt(g_hwndDlg, nNumID, NULL, FALSE));
```

This call to *Sleep* simulates the writer or reader thread doing other work that does not require access to the shared data resource. When a writer thread awakens, it calls the *SWMRGWaitToWrite* function; when a reader thread awakens, it calls the *SWMRGWaitToRead* function. When a writer thread's call to *SWMRGWaitToWrite* returns, the writer thread knows that no other writer thread or reader thread has access to the data. The writer thread then calls the *Bucket_AlterContents* function to change the contents of the bucket.

When a reader thread's call to *SWMRGWaitToRead* returns, it knows that no writer threads are accessing the bucket, but other reader threads might be accessing it. The reader thread calls the *Bucket_DumpToLB* function, which examines the contents of the bucket (without altering the contents) and places the results in the thread's respective list box.

When a writer or reader thread has completed its access to the bucket, it calls *SWMRGDoneWriting* or *SWMRGDoneReading*, depending on the type of thread. This lets another writer or reader thread access the bucket. Then the *while* loop iterates back to the top.

Now we get to the point of discussing how the writer and reader threads know when to terminate. When the user closes the dialog box, the process's primary thread, which is responsible for managing the application's user interface, returns from the call to *DialogBox* in the program's *WinMain* function and executes the following line of code:

```
InterlockedIncrement((PLONG) &g_lTerminate);
```

This call increments the global *g_lTerminate* variable from 0 to 1. Eventually all the writer and reader threads will see that this variable has changed, indicating that they should terminate. The *InterlockedIncrement* function atomically changes the value of the long variable whose address is passed to it. This means that any threads attempting to examine the value of the *g_lTerminate* values will be momentarily suspended until the *InterlockedIncrement* function has completely updated the long variable's value. (The *InterlockedIncrement* function is discussed in more detail in the last section of this chapter.)

Because the *g_lTerminate* variable has been incremented, the writer and reader threads will eventually stop running. They might not stop for quite some time, however—if they are busy performing work their *while* loops might not iterate for a while. In order to clean up nicely, the primary thread must wait for all the threads to terminate. It does this by calling *WaitForMultipleObjects*, passing the handles to the five threads. Remember that these handles were saved in a global array when the *Dlg_OnInitDialog* function was called. When all the threads have terminated, *WaitForMultipleObjects* returns and the primary thread calls *Close-Handle*, passing each of the writer and reader thread handles.

Finally the primary thread calls *SWMRGDelete* so that the *hMutex-NoWriter*, *hEventNoReaders*, and *hSemNumReaders* objects have their usage counts decremented, thereby freeing these objects.

When I was testing Bucket's process and thread termination, I used the PERFMON.EXE application that ships with Windows NT to be sure that everything was working correctly. After starting BUCKET.EXE, I started PERFMON.EXE, selected the Add To Chart option from the Edit menu, and got the dialog box shown on the next page.

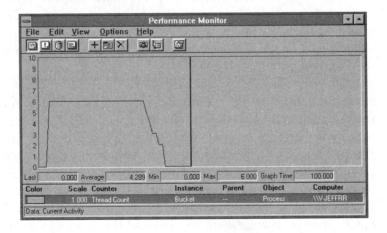

In the dialog box above, I set the Object field to Process, the Instance field to Bucket, and the Counter field to Thread Count. Then I clicked on the Add button. This caused PerfMon to monitor the number of threads that were running in the Bucket process. The chart produced appears below:

You can see from the chart that the Bucket application went from zero threads to six threads almost immediately. But then, around the time when the vertical bar was under the toolbar button that looks like a camera, I closed the dialog box. Bucket's primary thread immediately incremented the *g_lTerminate* variable to 1, and it looks as if three threads saw this change right away and terminated. Then, after a little delay, the fourth thread iterated back to the top of its *while* loop, saw the change, and terminated. A little later the fifth thread saw the changed variable and terminated. When the fifth thread terminated, the primary thread awakened immediately and also terminated. This is why the chart shows such a steep drop from two threads to zero threads.

The PERFMON.EXE application is an incredibly useful program that many developers ignore. This is an extremely minor example of what it can do. I am always finding new uses for PerfMon and encourage you to spend time experimenting with it to find out how it can give you additional perspectives on your own applications.

Bucket.ico

BUCKET.C

```
/******************************************************************
Module name: Bucket.C
Notices: Copyright (c) 1995 Jeffrey Richter
******************************************************************/


#include "..\AdvWin32.H"      /* See Appendix B for details. */
#include <windows.h>
#include <windowsx.h>

#pragma warning(disable: 4001)        /* Single-line comment */

#include <tchar.h>
#include <stdio.h>                // For sprintf
#include <stdlib.h>               // For rand
#include <process.h>             // For _beginthreadex
#include "Resource.H"

#include "SWMRG.H"


//////////////////////////////////////////////////////////////////


// Single-writer/multiple-reader guard synchronization object
SWMRG g_SWMRG;

// Array of thread handles needed for process termination
HANDLE g_hThreads[5];

// Flag indicating when the threads should terminate
// The flag is volatile because it is changed asynchronously.
long volatile g_lTerminate = 0;

// Window handle of dialog box
HWND g_hwndDlg = NULL;
```

Figure 9-5.

The Bucket application.

(continued)

Figure 9-5. *continued*

```
///////////////////////////////////////////////////////////
////// Data and routines for manipulating the bucket ///////
///////////////////////////////////////////////////////////

// Enumerated list of valid ball colors
typedef enum {
   BC_FIRSTBALLCLR,
   // BC_NULL indicates an empty space in the bucket.
   BC_NULL = BC_FIRSTBALLCLR,
   BC_BLACK,
   BC_RED,
   BC_GREEN,
   BC_BLUE,
   BC_WHITE,
   BC_YELLOW,
   BC_ORANGE,
   BC_CYAN,
   BC_GRAY,
   BC_LASTBALLCLR = BC_GRAY
} BALLCOLOR;


// String list of valid ball colors
const TCHAR *szBallColors[] = {
   NULL,
   __TEXT("Black"),
   __TEXT("Red"),
   __TEXT("Green"),
   __TEXT("Blue"),
   __TEXT("White"),
   __TEXT("Yellow"),
   __TEXT("Orange"),
   __TEXT("Cyan"),
   __TEXT("Gray")
};


// Maximum number of balls in the bucket
#define MAX_BALLS    100


// Initially the bucket is empty.
// The bucket is volatile because its contents
// change asynchronously.
BALLCOLOR volatile g_Bucket[MAX_BALLS] = { BC_NULL };
```

(continued)

Figure 9-5. *continued*

```
////////////////////////////////////////////////////////////////


void Bucket_AlterContents (void) {

   // Add/remove a randomly colored ball to or from the bucket.
   g_Bucket[rand() % MAX_BALLS] = (BALLCOLOR) (rand() % 10);
}



////////////////////////////////////////////////////////////////


void Bucket_DumpToLB (HWND hwndLB) {

   int nBallNum;
   int nBallColor[BC_LASTBALLCLR - BC_FIRSTBALLCLR + 1] =
      { 0 };

   BALLCOLOR BallColor;
   TCHAR szBuf[50];

   // Calculate how many balls of each color are in the bucket.
   for (nBallNum = 0; nBallNum < MAX_BALLS; nBallNum++) {
      // Get the color of the nBallNum'th ball.
      BallColor = g_Bucket[nBallNum];

      // Increment the total for balls of this color.
      nBallColor[BallColor]++;
   }



   // Empty the list box.
   ListBox_ResetContent(hwndLB);

   // Build the contents of the list box.
   BallColor = BC_FIRSTBALLCLR;
   for (; BallColor <= BC_LASTBALLCLR; BallColor++) {

      if (szBallColors[BallColor] != NULL) {
         _stprintf(szBuf, __TEXT("%s: %*s%2d"),
            szBallColors[BallColor],
            7 - lstrlen(szBallColors[BallColor]), __TEXT(" "),
            nBallColor[BallColor]);
```

(continued)

Figure 9-5. *continued*

```
        } else {
            _stprintf(szBuf, __TEXT("Total:    %2d"),
                MAX_BALLS - nBallColor[BallColor]);
        }

        ListBox_AddString(hwndLB, szBuf);
    }
}


///////////////////////////////////////////////////////////////


DWORD WINAPI Writer (LPVOID lpvParam) {
    int nWriterNum = (int) lpvParam, nNumID;

    switch (nWriterNum) {
        case 1:
            nNumID = IDC_WRITE1NUM;
            break;

        case 2:
            nNumID = IDC_WRITE2NUM;
            break;

        default:
            nNumID = 0;              // We should never get here.
            break;
    }


    // Continue looping until the process has been terminated.
    while (!g_lTerminate) {

        // Go to sleep for the user-defined amount of time.
        Sleep(1000 *
            GetDlgItemInt(g_hwndDlg, nNumID, NULL, FALSE));

        // Wait until safe to write: no writers and no readers.
        SWMRGWaitToWrite(&g_SWMRG, INFINITE);

        // Write to the shared data (the bucket).
        Bucket_AlterContents();
```

(continued)

Figure 9-5. *continued*

```
        // Inform the other writers/readers that we are done.
        SWMRGDoneWriting(&g_SWMRG);
    }

    return(0);
}



//////////////////////////////////////////////////////////////////


DWORD WINAPI Reader (LPVOID lpvParam) {
    int nReaderNum = (int) lpvParam, nNumID = 0;
    HWND hwndLB = NULL;

    // Get the window handle of the reader's display list box.
    // Get the ID of the reader's number static control.
    switch (nReaderNum) {
        case 1:
            nNumID = IDC_READ1NUM;
            hwndLB  = GetDlgItem(g_hwndDlg, IDC_READ1LIST);
            break;

        case 2:
            nNumID = IDC_READ2NUM;
            hwndLB  = GetDlgItem(g_hwndDlg, IDC_READ2LIST);
            break;

        case 3:
            nNumID = IDC_READ3NUM;
            hwndLB  = GetDlgItem(g_hwndDlg, IDC_READ3LIST);
            break;

        default:
            nNumID = 0;                 // We should never get here.
            hwndLB  = NULL;
            break;
    }


    // Continue looping until the process has been terminated.
    while (!g_lTerminate) {
```

(continued)

Figure 9-5. *continued*

```
        // Go to sleep for the user-defined amount of time.
        Sleep(1000 *
            GetDlgItemInt(g_hwndDlg, nNumID, NULL, FALSE));

        // Wait until safe to read: no writers.
        SWMRGWaitToRead(&g_SWMRG, INFINITE);

        // Read from the shared data (the bucket).
        Bucket_DumpToLB(hwndLB);

        // Inform the other writers/readers that we are done.
        SWMRGDoneReading(&g_SWMRG);
    }
    return(0);
}


///////////////////////////////////////////////////////////////


BOOL Dlg_OnInitDialog (HWND hwnd, HWND hwndFocus,
    LPARAM lParam) {

    DWORD dwThreadID;
    int x;

    // Save the handle of the dialog box in a global so that
    // the threads can easily gain access to it. This must
    // be done before creating the threads.
    g_hwndDlg = hwnd;

    // Associate an icon with the dialog box.
    SetClassLong(hwnd, GCL_HICON, (LONG)
        LoadIcon((HINSTANCE) GetWindowLong(hwnd, GWL_HINSTANCE),
        __TEXT("Bucket")));


    // Initialize the scroll bar values for the bucket writers.
    ScrollBar_SetRange(GetDlgItem(hwnd, IDC_WRITE1SCRL),
        0, 60, FALSE);
    ScrollBar_SetPos(GetDlgItem(hwnd, IDC_WRITE1SCRL), 1, TRUE);
    SetDlgItemInt(hwnd, IDC_WRITE1NUM, 1, FALSE);
```

(continued)

Figure 9-5. *continued*

```
    ScrollBar_SetRange(GetDlgItem(hwnd, IDC_WRITE2SCRL),
        0, 60, FALSE);
    ScrollBar_SetPos(GetDlgItem(hwnd, IDC_WRITE2SCRL), 3, TRUE);
    SetDlgItemInt(hwnd, IDC_WRITE2NUM, 3, FALSE);


    // Initialize the scroll bar values for the bucket readers.
    ScrollBar_SetRange(GetDlgItem(hwnd, IDC_READ1SCRL),
        0, 60, FALSE);
    ScrollBar_SetPos(GetDlgItem(hwnd, IDC_READ1SCRL), 2, TRUE);
    SetDlgItemInt(hwnd, IDC_READ1NUM, 2, FALSE);

    ScrollBar_SetRange(GetDlgItem(hwnd, IDC_READ2SCRL),
        0, 60, FALSE);
    ScrollBar_SetPos(GetDlgItem(hwnd, IDC_READ2SCRL), 4, TRUE);
    SetDlgItemInt(hwnd, IDC_READ2NUM, 4, FALSE);

    ScrollBar_SetRange(GetDlgItem(hwnd, IDC_READ3SCRL),
        0, 60, FALSE);
    ScrollBar_SetPos(GetDlgItem(hwnd, IDC_READ3SCRL), 7, TRUE);
    SetDlgItemInt(hwnd, IDC_READ3NUM, 7, FALSE);

    // Create the two writer and three reader threads.
    // Note: these threads MUST be created AFTER all other
    // synchronization objects.
    for (x = 0; x <= 1; x++) {
        g_hThreads[x] = BEGINTHREADEX(NULL, 0, Writer,
            (LPVOID) (x + 1), 0, &dwThreadID);
    }

    for (x = 2; x <= 4; x++) {
        g_hThreads[x] = BEGINTHREADEX(NULL, 0, Reader,
            (LPVOID) (x - 1), 0, &dwThreadID);
    }

    return(TRUE);
}


///////////////////////////////////////////////////////////////


void Dlg_OnHScroll (HWND hwnd, HWND hwndCtl,
    UINT code, int pos) {
```

(continued)

Figure 9-5. *continued*

```
    int posCrnt, posMin, posMax;

    posCrnt = ScrollBar_GetPos(hwndCtl);
    ScrollBar_GetRange(hwndCtl, &posMin, &posMax);

    switch (code) {
        case SB_LINELEFT:
            posCrnt--;
            break;

        case SB_LINERIGHT:
            posCrnt++;
            break;

        case SB_PAGELEFT:
            posCrnt -= 10;
            break;

        case SB_PAGERIGHT:
            posCrnt += 10;
            break;

        case SB_THUMBTRACK:
            posCrnt = pos;
            break;

        case SB_LEFT:
            posCrnt = 0;
            break;

        case SB_RIGHT:
            posCrnt = posMax;
            break;
    }

    if (posCrnt < 0)
        posCrnt = 0;

    if (posCrnt > posMax)
        posCrnt = posMax;

    ScrollBar_SetPos(hwndCtl, posCrnt, TRUE);

    SetDlgItemInt(hwnd, GetDlgCtrlID(hwndCtl) - 1,
        posCrnt, FALSE);
}
```

(continued)

Figure 9-5. *continued*

```
/////////////////////////////////////////////////////////////////

void Dlg_OnVScroll (HWND hwnd, HWND hwndCtl,
   UINT code, int pos) {

   int posCrnt, posMin, posMax;

   posCrnt = ScrollBar_GetPos(hwndCtl);
   ScrollBar_GetRange(hwndCtl, &posMin, &posMax);

   switch (code) {
      case SB_LINEUP:
         posCrnt--;
         break;

      case SB_LINEDOWN:
         posCrnt++;
         break;

      case SB_PAGEUP:
         posCrnt -= 10;
         break;

      case SB_PAGEDOWN:
         posCrnt += 10;
         break;

      case SB_THUMBTRACK:
         posCrnt = pos;
         break;

      case SB_TOP:
         posCrnt = 0;
         break;

      case SB_BOTTOM:
         posCrnt = posMax;
         break;
   }

   if (posCrnt < 0)
      posCrnt = 0;
```

(continued)

Figure 9-5. *continued*

```
    if (posCrnt > posMax)
        posCrnt = posMax;

    ScrollBar_SetPos(hwndCtl, posCrnt, TRUE);

    SetDlgItemInt(hwnd, GetDlgCtrlID(hwndCtl) - 1,
        posCrnt, FALSE);
}


//////////////////////////////////////////////////////////////


void Dlg_OnCommand (HWND hwnd, int id,
    HWND hwndCtl, UINT codeNotify) {

    switch (id) {
        case IDCANCEL:
            EndDialog(hwnd, id);
            break;
    }
}




//////////////////////////////////////////////////////////////


BOOL CALLBACK Dlg_Proc (HWND hDlg, UINT uMsg,
    WPARAM wParam, LPARAM lParam) {

    BOOL fProcessed = TRUE;

    switch (uMsg) {
        HANDLE_MSG(hDlg, WM_INITDIALOG, Dlg_OnInitDialog);
        HANDLE_MSG(hDlg, WM_COMMAND, Dlg_OnCommand);
        HANDLE_MSG(hDlg, WM_HSCROLL, Dlg_OnHScroll);
        HANDLE_MSG(hDlg, WM_VSCROLL, Dlg_OnVScroll);

        default:
            fProcessed = FALSE;
            break;
    }

    return(fProcessed);
}
```

(continued)

Figure 9-5. *continued*

```
/////////////////////////////////////////////////////////////


int WINAPI WinMain (HINSTANCE hinstExe,
    HINSTANCE hinstPrev, LPSTR lpszCmdLine, int nCmdShow) {

    int x;

    // Initialize the single-writer/multiple-reader
    // guard synchronization object. This must be done
    // before any thread attempts to use it.
    SWMRGInitialize(&g_SWMRG, NULL);


    // Display the process's user interface.
    DialogBox(hinstExe, MAKEINTRESOURCE(IDD_BUCKET),
        NULL, Dlg_Proc);

    // When the user shuts down the process, clean up.
    // 1. Inform the threads that the process is terminating.
    InterlockedIncrement((PLONG) &g_lTerminate);

    // 2. Wait for all of the threads to terminate. This
    // might take a long time because some threads might be
    // sleeping and therefore not checking the g_lTerminate
    // variable.
    WaitForMultipleObjects(ARRAY_SIZE(g_hThreads), g_hThreads,
        TRUE, INFINITE);

    // 3. Close all of our handles to the threads.
    for (x = 0; x < ARRAY_SIZE(g_hThreads); x++)
        CloseHandle(g_hThreads[x]);


    // 4. Delete the single-writer/multiple-reader guard
    // synchronization object. This must be done when it
    // is known that no threads will attempt to use it.
    SWMRGDelete(&g_SWMRG);

    return(0);
}


//////////////////////// End Of File ////////////////////////
```

(continued)

Figure 9-5. *continued*

SWMRG.C

```
/****************************************************************
Module name: SWMRG.C
Notices: Copyright (c) 1995 Jeffrey Richter
****************************************************************/


#include "..\AdvWin32.H"      /* See Appendix B for details. */
#include <windows.h>

#pragma warning(disable: 4001)       /* Single-line comment */

#include <string.h>
#include <tchar.h>

#include "SWMRG.H"                  // The header file


///////////////////////////////////////////////////////////////


static LPCTSTR ConstructObjName (
   LPCTSTR lpszPrefix, LPCTSTR lpszSuffix,
   LPTSTR lpszFullName, size_t cbFullName, PBOOL fOk) {
   *fOk = TRUE;   // Assume success.

   if (lpszSuffix == NULL)
      return(NULL);

   if ((_tcslen(lpszPrefix) + _tcslen(lpszSuffix)) >=
      cbFullName) {
      // If the strings will overflow the buffer,
      // indicate an error.
      *fOk = FALSE;
      return(NULL);
   }

   _tcscpy(lpszFullName, lpszPrefix);
   _tcscat(lpszFullName, lpszSuffix);
   return(lpszFullName);
}
```

(continued)

Figure 9-5. *continued*

```
//////////////////////////////////////////////////////////////


BOOL SWMRGInitialize (PSWMRG pSWMRG, LPCTSTR lpszName) {
   TCHAR szFullObjName[100];
   LPCTSTR lpszObjName;
   BOOL fOk;

   // Initialize all data members to NULL so that we can
   // accurately check whether an error has occurred.
   pSWMRG->hMutexNoWriter = NULL;
   pSWMRG->hEventNoReaders = NULL;
   pSWMRG->hSemNumReaders = NULL;


   // This mutex guards access to the other objects
   // managed by this data structure and also indicates
   // whether any writer threads are writing.
   // Initially no thread owns the mutex.
   lpszObjName = ConstructObjName(
      __TEXT("SWMRGMutexNoWriter"), lpszName,
      szFullObjName, ARRAY_SIZE(szFullObjName), &fOk);
   if (fOk)
      pSWMRG->hMutexNoWriter =
         CreateMutex(NULL, FALSE, lpszObjName);

   // Create the manual-reset event that is signaled when
   // no reader threads are reading.
   // Initially no reader threads are reading.
   lpszObjName = ConstructObjName(
      __TEXT("SWMRGEventNoReaders"), lpszName,
      szFullObjName, ARRAY_SIZE(szFullObjName), &fOk);
   if (fOk)
      pSWMRG->hEventNoReaders =
         CreateEvent(NULL, TRUE, TRUE, lpszObjName);

   // Initialize the variable that indicates the number of
   // reader threads that are reading.
   // Initially no reader threads are reading.
   lpszObjName = ConstructObjName(
      __TEXT("SWMRGSemNumReaders"), lpszName,
      szFullObjName, ARRAY_SIZE(szFullObjName), &fOk);
   if (fOk)
      pSWMRG->hSemNumReaders =
         CreateSemaphore(NULL, 0, 0x7FFFFFFF, lpszObjName);
```

(continued)

Figure 9-5. *continued*

```
    if ((NULL == pSWMRG->hMutexNoWriter)   ||
        (NULL == pSWMRG->hEventNoReaders)  ||
        (NULL == pSWMRG->hSemNumReaders)) {
      // If a synchronization object could not be created,
      // destroy any created objects and return failure.
      SWMRGDelete(pSWMRG);
      fOk = FALSE;
    } else {
      fOk = TRUE;
    }

    // Return TRUE upon success, FALSE upon failure.
    return(fOk);
}


///////////////////////////////////////////////////////////////


void SWMRGDelete (PSWMRG pSWMRG) {

    // Destroy any synchronization objects that were
    // successfully created.
    if (NULL != pSWMRG->hMutexNoWriter)
      CloseHandle(pSWMRG->hMutexNoWriter);

    if (NULL != pSWMRG->hEventNoReaders)
      CloseHandle(pSWMRG->hEventNoReaders);

    if (NULL != pSWMRG->hSemNumReaders)
      CloseHandle(pSWMRG->hSemNumReaders);
}


///////////////////////////////////////////////////////////////


DWORD SWMRGWaitToWrite (PSWMRG pSWMRG, DWORD dwTimeout) {
    DWORD dw;
    HANDLE aHandles[2];

    // We can write if the following are true:
    // 1. The mutex guard is available and
    //    no other threads are writing.
```

(continued)

Figure 9-5. *continued*

```
    // 2. No threads are reading.
    aHandles[0] = pSWMRG->hMutexNoWriter;
    aHandles[1] = pSWMRG->hEventNoReaders;
    dw = WaitForMultipleObjects(2, aHandles, TRUE, dwTimeout);

    if (dw != WAIT_TIMEOUT) {
       // This thread can write to the shared data.

       // Because a writer thread is writing, the mutex should
       // not be released. This stops other writers and readers.
    }

    return(dw);
}


//////////////////////////////////////////////////////////////////


void SWMRGDoneWriting (PSWMRG pSWMRG) {
    // Presumably, a writer thread calling this function has
    // successfully called WaitToWrite. This means that we
    // do not have to wait on any synchronization objects
    // here because the writer already owns the mutex.

    // Allow other writer/reader threads to use
    // the SWMRG synchronization object.
    ReleaseMutex(pSWMRG->hMutexNoWriter);
}


//////////////////////////////////////////////////////////////////


DWORD SWMRGWaitToRead (PSWMRG pSWMRG, DWORD dwTimeout) {
    DWORD dw;
    LONG lPreviousCount;

    // We can read if the mutex guard is available
    // and no threads are writing.
    dw = WaitForSingleObject(pSWMRG->hMutexNoWriter, dwTimeout);

    if (dw != WAIT_TIMEOUT) {
       // This thread can read from the shared data.
```

(continued)

Figure 9-5. *continued*

```
      // Increment the number of reader threads.
      ReleaseSemaphore(pSWMRG->hSemNumReaders, 1,
         &lPreviousCount);
      if (lPreviousCount == 0) {
         // If this is the first reader thread,
         // set the event to reflect this.
         ResetEvent(pSWMRG->hEventNoReaders);
      }

      // Allow other writer/reader threads to use
      // the SWMRG synchronization object.
      ReleaseMutex(pSWMRG->hMutexNoWriter);
   }

   return(dw);
}


//////////////////////////////////////////////////////////////


void SWMRGDoneReading (PSWMRG pSWMRG) {
   BOOL fLastReader;

   HANDLE aHandles[2];

   // We can stop reading if the mutex guard is available,
   // but when we stop reading we must also decrement the
   // number of reader threads.
   aHandles[0] = pSWMRG->hMutexNoWriter;
   aHandles[1] = pSWMRG->hSemNumReaders;
   WaitForMultipleObjects(2, aHandles, TRUE, INFINITE);

   fLastReader =
      (WaitForSingleObject(pSWMRG->hSemNumReaders, 0)
         == WAIT_TIMEOUT);

   if (fLastReader) {
      // If this is the last reader thread,
      // set the event to reflect this.
      SetEvent(pSWMRG->hEventNoReaders);
   } else {
```

(continued)

Figure 9-5. *continued*

```
        // If this is NOT the last reader thread, we successfully
        // waited on the semaphore. We must release the semaphore
        // so that the count accurately reflects the number
        // of reader threads.
        ReleaseSemaphore(pSWMRG->hSemNumReaders, 1, NULL);
    }


    // Allow other writer/reader threads to use
    // the SWMRG synchronization object.
    ReleaseMutex(pSWMRG->hMutexNoWriter);
}


/////////////////////////// End Of File ///////////////////////////
```

SWMRG.H

```
/*****************************************************************
Module name: SWMRG.H
Notices: Copyright (c) 1995 Jeffrey Richter
*****************************************************************/


// The single-writer/multiple-reader guard
// compound synchronization object
typedef struct SingleWriterMultiReaderGuard {
    // This mutex guards access to the other objects
    // managed by this data structure and also indicates
    // whether any writer threads are writing.
    HANDLE hMutexNoWriter;

    // This manual-reset event is signaled when
    // no reader threads are reading.
    HANDLE hEventNoReaders;

    // This semaphore is used simply as a counter that is
    // accessible between multiple processes. It is NOT
    // used for thread synchronization.
    // The count is the number of reader threads reading.
    HANDLE hSemNumReaders;

} SWMRG, *PSWMRG;
```

(continued)

Figure 9-5. *continued*

```
////////////////////////////////////////////////////////////

// Initializes a SWMRG structure. This structure must be
// initialized before any writer or reader threads attempt
// to wait on it.
// The structure must be allocated by the application, and
// the structure's address is passed as the first parameter.
// The lpszName parameter is the name of the object. Pass
// NULL if you do not want to share the object.
BOOL  SWMRGInitialize (PSWMRG pSWMRG, LPCTSTR lpszName);


// Deletes the system resources associated with a SWMRG
// structure. The structure must be deleted only when
// no writer or reader threads in the calling process
// will wait on it.
void  SWMRGDelete (PSWMRG pSWMRG);


// A writer thread calls this function to know when
// it can successfully write to the shared data.
DWORD SWMRGWaitToWrite (PSWMRG pSWMRG, DWORD dwTimeout);


// A writer thread calls this function to let other threads
// know that it no longer needs to write to the shared data.
void  SWMRGDoneWriting (PSWMRG pSWMRG);


// A reader thread calls this function to know when
// it can successfully read the shared data.
DWORD SWMRGWaitToRead  (PSWMRG pSWMRG, DWORD dwTimeout);


// A reader thread calls this function to let other threads
// know that it no longer needs to read the shared data.
void  SWMRGDoneReading (PSWMRG pSWMRG);


///////////////////////// End Of File /////////////////////////
```

(continued)

Figure 9-5. *continued*

```
BUCKET.RC
//Microsoft Visual C++ generated resource script.
//
#include "Resource.h"

#define APSTUDIO_READONLY_SYMBOLS
/////////////////////////////////////////////////////////////////
//
// Generated from the TEXTINCLUDE 2 resource.
//
#include "afxres.h"


/////////////////////////////////////////////////////////////////
#undef APSTUDIO_READONLY_SYMBOLS


/////////////////////////////////////////////////////////////////
//
// Icon
//

Bucket                  ICON    DISCARDABLE    "Bucket.Ico"


/////////////////////////////////////////////////////////////////
//
// Dialog
//

IDD_BUCKET DIALOG DISCARDABLE  12, 48, 216, 168
STYLE WS_MINIMIZEBOX ¦ WS_POPUP ¦ WS_VISIBLE ¦ WS_CAPTION
      ¦ WS_SYSMENU
CAPTION "Bucket Synchronization"
FONT 8, "Courier"
BEGIN
    GROUPBOX        "Bucket &Writers",IDC_STATIC,4,0,108,48
    RTEXT           "1:",IDC_STATIC,8,16,12,8,SS_NOPREFIX
    RTEXT           "100",IDC_WRITE1NUM,20,16,16,8,SS_NOPREFIX
    SCROLLBAR       IDC_WRITE1SCRL,40,16,68,10
    RTEXT           "2:",IDC_STATIC,8,32,12,8,SS_NOPREFIX
    RTEXT           "100",IDC_WRITE2NUM,20,32,16,8,SS_NOPREFIX
    SCROLLBAR       IDC_WRITE2SCRL,40,32,68,10
    GROUPBOX        "Bucket &Readers",IDC_STATIC,4,56,208,108
    RTEXT           "1:",IDC_STATIC,20,68,12,8,SS_NOPREFIX
    RTEXT           "100",IDC_READ1NUM,36,68,16,8,SS_NOPREFIX
```

(continued)

Figure 9-5. *continued*

```
        SCROLLBAR       IDC_READ1SCRL,8,80,10,80,SBS_VERT
        LISTBOX         IDC_READ1LIST,20,80,48,80,
                        LBS_NOINTEGRALHEIGHT | WS_VSCROLL
                        | WS_TABSTOP
        RTEXT           "2:",IDC_STATIC,88,68,12,8,SS_NOPREFIX
        RTEXT           "100",IDC_READ2NUM,104,68,16,8,SS_NOPREFIX
        SCROLLBAR       IDC_READ2SCRL,76,80,10,80,SBS_VERT
        LISTBOX         IDC_READ2LIST,88,80,48,80,
                        LBS_NOINTEGRALHEIGHT |  WS_VSCROLL
                        | WS_TABSTOP
        RTEXT           "3:",IDC_STATIC,156,68,12,8,SS_NOPREFIX
        RTEXT           "100",IDC_READ3NUM,172,68,16,8,SS_NOPREFIX
        SCROLLBAR       IDC_READ3SCRL,144,80,10,80,SBS_VERT
        LISTBOX         IDC_READ3LIST,156,80,48,80,
                        LBS_NOINTEGRALHEIGHT | WS_VSCROLL
                        | WS_TABSTOP
END


#ifdef APSTUDIO_INVOKED
/////////////////////////////////////////////////////////////////
//
// TEXTINCLUDE
//

1 TEXTINCLUDE DISCARDABLE
BEGIN
    "Resource.h\0"
END

2 TEXTINCLUDE DISCARDABLE
BEGIN
    "#include ""afxres.h""\r\n"
    "\0"
END

3 TEXTINCLUDE DISCARDABLE
BEGIN
    "\r\n"
    "\0"
END


/////////////////////////////////////////////////////////////////
#endif     // APSTUDIO_INVOKED
```

(continued)

Figure 9-5. *continued*

```
#ifndef APSTUDIO_INVOKED
/////////////////////////////////////////////////////////////////
//
// Generated from the TEXTINCLUDE 3 resource.
//


/////////////////////////////////////////////////////////////////
#endif    // not APSTUDIO_INVOKED
```

Auto-Reset Events

Auto-reset events behave more like mutexes and semaphores than manual-reset events do. When a thread calls *SetEvent* to signal an event, the event stays signaled until another thread that is waiting for the event is awakened. Just before the waiting thread resumes, the system automatically resets the event to the nonsignaled state. Using an auto-reset event in this way has the effect of allowing only one thread waiting for the event to resume execution. Any other threads waiting for the event are left suspended, still waiting. You have no control over which of the suspended threads will resume execution—the operating system makes that decision. This statement is true not only of events but of all synchronization objects. If multiple waits are satisfied, the highest-priority thread will run.

You can manipulate an auto-reset event by using the same functions that manipulate a manual-reset event: *SetEvent*, *ResetEvent*, and *PulseEvent*. Usually, you don't use the *ResetEvent* function, however, because the system automatically resets an auto-reset event before *WaitForSingleObject* and *WaitForMultipleObjects* return.

The *PulseEvent* function performs the same operations for manual-reset events as it does for auto-reset events—that is, *PulseEvent* signals the event, releases a thread waiting for the event, and resets the event. However, there is one small difference between calling *PulseEvent* for an auto-reset event and calling it for a manual-reset event: Pulsing an auto-reset event releases only a single thread that is waiting for the event, even if several threads are waiting. By contrast, pulsing a manual-reset event releases all the threads waiting for the event.

The Document Statistics Sample Application

The DocStats (DOCSTATS.EXE) application, listed in Figure 9-6 beginning on page 403, demonstrates the use of auto-reset events. The source code files, resource files, and make file for the application are in the DOCSTATS.09 directory on the companion disc.

To run DocStats, enter the following line from a command shell:

```
DOCSTATS PathName
```

PathName indicates any ANSI text file available on your system.

DocStats analyzes the specified file and generates a message box that indicates the number of characters, words, and lines in the file. What makes DocStats exciting is the way it accomplishes this heroic task.

First DocStats creates three threads, one for each of the items (characters, words, and lines) to be counted. These threads are suspended until a global buffer contains data for them to process. Next DocStats opens the specified file and loads the first 1024 bytes of the file into the global data buffer. Now that the data is ready to be processed, DocStats notifies the three suspended threads that they can resume execution to process the global data.

While the three threads are processing the file data, the primary thread suspends itself so that it won't immediately loop around and read the next 1024 bytes from the data file. The primary thread waits until all three counting threads have completed processing the data before it reads the next chunk of data from the file. If the primary thread doesn't wait and reads the next chunk of data, that data overwrites the previous chunk of data in the global buffer while the three secondary threads are still processing it—a big no-no. When the primary thread has read the last chunk of the file's data, it closes the file, retrieves the results calculated by the three secondary threads, and displays the results.

The most interesting aspect of DocStats is how it synchronizes the execution of the primary thread with the three secondary threads. Initially, when the primary thread starts executing, it creates six auto-reset events—two for each secondary thread. One of these events notifies a single secondary thread that the primary thread has read the data from the file and that this data can now be processed. The handles to these events are stored in the *g_hEventsDataReady* array. When these events are created, they are initially set to nonsignaled, which indicates that the data buffer is not ready for processing.

The second of the two events indicates that the secondary thread has processed the file's data contained in the global buffer and that it's suspending itself, waiting for the primary thread to indicate that the next chunk of data has been read and is ready to be processed. The handles to these events are stored in the *g_hEventsProcIdle* array. When these events are created, they are initially set to signaled, which indicates that the secondary threads are idle.

Next the primary thread creates the three secondary threads. None of these threads are created in the suspended state—all are allowed to begin executing. The handles to these three threads are stored in the *hThreads* array. All three threads operate in the same way. After they begin executing, they immediately enter a loop that iterates with each chunk of file data read by the primary thread. However, before any of the secondary threads can start processing the global buffer, they must wait until the buffer has been initialized. So the first action in this loop is a call to *WaitForSingleObject*, passing the handle of an event contained in the *g_hEventsDataReady* array.

The primary thread then opens the file and waits for all three of the secondary threads to indicate that they are not processing the data in the global buffer. For the first iteration, all the event handles in the *g_hEventsProcIdle* array are signaled, so the primary thread won't need to wait at all. The primary thread reads the first 1024 bytes into the global buffer and, after reading the data, signals the three waiting threads that the data is ready by calling *SetEvent* three times, once for each event in the *g_hEventsDataReady* array.

When these events become signaled, the secondary threads wake up and begin processing the file's data. Because these are auto-reset events, the events are automatically set back to the nonsignaled state, indicating that the data is *not* ready for processing. The result is that the secondary threads have indicated that the data is not ready for processing—but they have already resumed execution and are no longer checking the events. The threads continue to run, thinking that the data is ready—and it is.

When I was first designing this application, I tried to get by with using only one event to signal that the data was ready. After all, there was only one block of data, and it seemed to me that one event should be able to indicate to all of the secondary threads that the block of data was ready. But I wasn't able to solve this problem using only a single event.

When I tried using a single event, one of the secondary threads would see that the data was ready, and because an auto-reset event was used, the event would be reset to the nonsignaled state. This would happen before the other two secondary threads saw that the event had been signaled. As a result, the other two secondary threads would never get a chance to process the data. By using three different events to represent the "data-ready" event, each thread can look for its own event without affecting the other threads.

After each of the three secondary threads has scanned the whole buffer, each calls *SetEvent* on its respective event contained in the *g_hEventsProcIdle* array. This call signals back to the primary thread that the secondary thread is finished accessing the buffer. Remember, the primary thread calls *WaitForMultipleObjects* at the top of its loop. This means that it will wait until all three of the secondary threads have completed processing the buffer and set their respective events to signaled before it reads the next chunk of the file's data.

When the primary thread's call to *WaitForMultipleObjects* returns, the three *g_hEventsProcIdle* events are automatically reset to their nonsignaled state, indicating that the secondary threads are not idle and are processing data. In reality, they are still waiting for the data-ready events to be signaled.

Let's consider what would happen if the *g_hEventsProcIdle* events were not automatically reset to nonsignaled. And imagine that we're running the program on a single-CPU system and that threads are allowed to execute for a full hour before being preempted.

In this case, the primary thread could read the file's data, set the three data-ready events to signaled, and loop back around to the top of its loop. This time, it would be waiting for the three *g_hEventsProcIdle* events to be signaled, and if they weren't automatically reset to nonsignaled, the wait would end and the primary thread would read the next chunk of data into the buffer all before the secondary threads had a chance to process the contents of the previous chunk—a bug in the program!

I'm sure you see the problem here. I know that having the CPU dedicated to a single thread for a full hour before preempting it is a bit excessive, but extreme thinking is a good practice when creating multithreaded applications. Writing and designing multithreaded applications isn't easy. A number of possible gotchas can occur. I've found it tremendously helpful to imagine that the computer system I'm using to implement my application actually preempts threads once an hour. It's always easier to consider the potential problem up front rather than let the system discover it for you.

As it turns out, it took me quite a few tries before I got DocStats to execute correctly. Even a machine that preempts threads every 20 milliseconds is enough for the application to fail.

Now back to DocStats. After the primary thread has finished reading the file's data, the secondary threads must return the results of their calculations. They do this by executing a return statement at the end of their thread functions, using the result as the function's return value. Once again, the primary thread calls *WaitForMultipleObjects*, suspending itself until all three secondary threads have terminated. The suspending is done by waiting for the thread handles contained in the *hThreads* array rather than waiting for any events.

After all three of the secondary threads have terminated, the primary thread calls *GetExitCodeThread* to get each thread's return value. The primary thread then calls *CloseHandle* for all six events and all three threads so that the system resources are freed. Finally, DocStats constructs a string using the three threads' exit codes and displays the results in a message box.

DocStats.ico

DOCSTATS.C

```
/*****************************************************************
Module name: DocStats.C
Notices: Copyright (c) 1995 Jeffrey Richter
*****************************************************************/


#include "..\AdvWin32.H"        /* See Appendix B for details. */
#include <windows.h>
#include <windowsx.h>


#pragma warning(disable: 4001)          /* Single-line comment */


#include <tchar.h>
#include <stdio.h>                 // For sprintf
#include <string.h>
#include <process.h>               // For _beginthreadex
#include "Resource.H"
```

Figure 9-6.
The DocStats application.

(continued)

Figure 9-6. *continued*

```
//////////////////////////////////////////////////////////////


typedef enum {
   STAT_FIRST = 0,
   STAT_LETTERS = STAT_FIRST,
   STAT_WORDS,
   STAT_LINES,
   STAT_LAST = STAT_LINES
} STATTYPE;

HANDLE g_hEventsDataReady[STAT_LAST - STAT_FIRST + 1];
HANDLE g_hEventsProcIdle[STAT_LAST - STAT_FIRST + 1];

BYTE g_bFileBuf[1024];
DWORD g_dwNumBytesInBuf;

DWORD WINAPI LetterStats (LPVOID lpvParam);
DWORD WINAPI WordStats (LPVOID lpvParam);
DWORD WINAPI LineStats (LPVOID lpvParam);


//////////////////////////////////////////////////////////////


int WINAPI WinMain (HINSTANCE hinstExe,
   HINSTANCE hinstPrev, LPSTR lpszCmdLine, int nCmdShow) {

   HANDLE hThreads[STAT_LAST - STAT_FIRST + 1];
   HANDLE hFile;
   DWORD dwNumLetters = 0, dwNumWords = 0, dwNumLines = 0;
   DWORD dwThreadID;
   TCHAR szBuf[150];
   LPTSTR lpszCmdLineT;


   // Get the name of the file.
   // We must use GetCommandLine here instead of WinMain's
   // lpszCmdLine parameter because lpszCmdLine is always an
   // ANSI string, never a Unicode string. GetCommandLine
   // returns ANSI or Unicode depending on how we
   // have compiled.
   lpszCmdLineT = _tcschr(GetCommandLine(), __TEXT(' '));

   if (lpszCmdLineT != NULL) {
```

(continued)

Figure 9-6. *continued*

```
        // We found a space after the executable's filename.
        // Now let's skip over any white space to get to the
        // first argument.
        while (*lpszCmdLineT == __TEXT(' '))
            lpszCmdLineT++;
    }

    if ((lpszCmdLineT == NULL) || (*lpszCmdLineT == 0)) {
        // If a space was not found, or if there are no arguments
        // after the executable's filename, display an
        // error message.

        MessageBox(NULL,
            __TEXT("You must enter a filename on ")
            __TEXT("the command line."),
            __TEXT("DocStats"), MB_OK);
        return(0);
    }


    // Open the file for reading.
    hFile = CreateFile(lpszCmdLineT, GENERIC_READ, 0,
        NULL, OPEN_EXISTING, FILE_ATTRIBUTE_NORMAL, NULL);
    if (hFile == INVALID_HANDLE_VALUE) {
        // File open failed.
        MessageBox(NULL, __TEXT("File could not be opened."),
            __TEXT("DocStats"), MB_OK);
        return(0);
    }

    // Signaled when not processing buffer
    g_hEventsDataReady[STAT_LETTERS] =
        CreateEvent(NULL, FALSE, FALSE, NULL);
    g_hEventsProcIdle[STAT_LETTERS] =
        CreateEvent(NULL, FALSE, TRUE, NULL);

    g_hEventsDataReady[STAT_WORDS] =
        CreateEvent(NULL, FALSE, FALSE, NULL);
    g_hEventsProcIdle[STAT_WORDS] =
        CreateEvent(NULL, FALSE, TRUE, NULL);

    g_hEventsDataReady[STAT_LINES] =
        CreateEvent(NULL, FALSE, FALSE, NULL);
    g_hEventsProcIdle[STAT_LINES] =
        CreateEvent(NULL, FALSE, TRUE, NULL);
```

(continued)

Figure 9-6. *continued*

```
// Create all the threads. Threads MUST be
// created AFTER the event objects.
hThreads[STAT_LETTERS] = BEGINTHREADEX(NULL, 0,
   LetterStats, NULL, 0, &dwThreadID);
hThreads[STAT_WORDS]   = BEGINTHREADEX(NULL, 0,
   WordStats, NULL, 0, &dwThreadID);
hThreads[STAT_LINES]   = BEGINTHREADEX(NULL, 0,
   LineStats, NULL, 0, &dwThreadID);


do {
   // Wait for the worker threads to be idle.
   WaitForMultipleObjects(STAT_LAST - STAT_FIRST + 1,
      g_hEventsProcIdle, TRUE, INFINITE);

   // Read part of the file into the global memory buffer.
   ReadFile(hFile, g_bFileBuf, ARRAY_SIZE(g_bFileBuf),
      &g_dwNumBytesInBuf, NULL);

   // Signal the works that the data is ready.
   SetEvent(g_hEventsDataReady[STAT_LETTERS]);
   SetEvent(g_hEventsDataReady[STAT_WORDS]);
   SetEvent(g_hEventsDataReady[STAT_LINES]);

} while (g_dwNumBytesInBuf != 0);


// All the statistics for the file have been accumulated;
// time to clean up.
CloseHandle(hFile);

// Wait for all the threads to return.
WaitForMultipleObjects(STAT_LAST - STAT_FIRST + 1, hThreads,
   TRUE, INFINITE);

GetExitCodeThread(hThreads[STAT_LETTERS], &dwNumLetters);
CloseHandle(hThreads[STAT_LETTERS]);
CloseHandle(g_hEventsDataReady[STAT_LETTERS]);
CloseHandle(g_hEventsProcIdle[STAT_LETTERS]);

GetExitCodeThread(hThreads[STAT_WORDS], &dwNumWords);
CloseHandle(hThreads[STAT_WORDS]);
CloseHandle(g_hEventsDataReady[STAT_WORDS]);
CloseHandle(g_hEventsProcIdle[STAT_WORDS]);
```

(continued)

Figure 9-6. *continued*

```
      GetExitCodeThread(hThreads[STAT_LINES], &dwNumLines);
      CloseHandle(hThreads[STAT_LINES]);
      CloseHandle(g_hEventsDataReady[STAT_LINES]);
      CloseHandle(g_hEventsProcIdle[STAT_LINES]);

      _stprintf(szBuf,
         __TEXT("Num letters = %d, Num words = %d, ")
         __TEXT("Num lines = %d"),
         dwNumLetters, dwNumWords, dwNumLines);

      MessageBox(NULL, szBuf, __TEXT("DocStats"), MB_OK);
      return(0);
}


//////////////////////////////////////////////////////////////////

DWORD WINAPI LetterStats (LPVOID lpvParam) {
   DWORD dwNumLetters = 0, dwByteIndex;
   BYTE bByte;

   do {
      // Wait for the data to be ready
      WaitForSingleObject(g_hEventsDataReady[STAT_LETTERS],
         INFINITE);

      dwByteIndex = 0;
      for (; dwByteIndex < g_dwNumBytesInBuf; dwByteIndex++) {

         bByte = g_bFileBuf[dwByteIndex];

         // This program works only on ANSI files. Regardless
         // of whether we compile DocStats for ANSI or for
         // Unicode, we must always call the ANSI version of
         // IsCharAlpha.
         if (IsCharAlphaA(bByte))
            dwNumLetters++;
      }

      // Data processed; signal that we are done.
      SetEvent(g_hEventsProcIdle[STAT_LETTERS]);
   } while (g_dwNumBytesInBuf > 0);

   return(dwNumLetters);
}
```

(continued)

Figure 9-6. *continued*

```
///////////////////////////////////////////////////////////////


DWORD WINAPI WordStats (LPVOID lpvParam) {
   DWORD dwNumWords = 0, dwByteIndex;
   BYTE bByte;
   BOOL fInWord = FALSE, fIsWordSep;

   do {
      // Wait for the data to be ready.
      WaitForSingleObject(g_hEventsDataReady[STAT_WORDS],
         INFINITE);

      dwByteIndex = 0;
      for (; dwByteIndex < g_dwNumBytesInBuf; dwByteIndex++) {

         bByte = g_bFileBuf[dwByteIndex];

         // This program works only on ANSI files. Regardless
         // of whether we compile DocStats for ANSI or for
         // Unicode, we must always call the ANSI version
         // of strchr.
         fIsWordSep = (strchr(" \t\n\r", bByte) != NULL);

         if (!fInWord && !fIsWordSep) {
            dwNumWords++;
            fInWord = TRUE;
         } else {
            if (fInWord && fIsWordSep) {
               fInWord = FALSE;
            }
         }
      }

      // Data processed; signal that we are done.
      SetEvent(g_hEventsProcIdle[STAT_WORDS]);
   } while (g_dwNumBytesInBuf > 0);

   return(dwNumWords);
}


///////////////////////////////////////////////////////////////


DWORD WINAPI LineStats (LPVOID lpvParam) {
```

(continued)

Figure 9-6. *continued*

```
    DWORD dwNumLines = 0, dwByteIndex;
    BYTE bByte;

    do {
        // Wait for the data to be ready.
        WaitForSingleObject(g_hEventsDataReady[STAT_LINES],
            INFINITE);

        dwByteIndex = 0;
        for (; dwByteIndex < g_dwNumBytesInBuf; dwByteIndex++) {

            bByte = g_bFileBuf[dwByteIndex];

            // This program works only on ANSI files. Regardless
            // of whether we compile DocStats for ANSI or for
            // Unicode, we must always compare the byte to an
            // ANSI version of '\n'.
            if ('\n' == bByte)
                dwNumLines++;
        }

        // Data processed; signal that we are done.
        SetEvent(g_hEventsProcIdle[STAT_LINES]);

    } while (g_dwNumBytesInBuf > 0);

    return(dwNumLines);
}


//////////////////////// End Of File ////////////////////////
```

DOCSTATS.RC
```
//Microsoft Visual C++ generated resource script.
//
#include "Resource.h"

#define APSTUDIO_READONLY_SYMBOLS
/////////////////////////////////////////////////////////////////
//
// Generated from the TEXTINCLUDE 2 resource.
//
#include "afxres.h"
```

(continued)

Figure 9-6. *continued*

```
/////////////////////////////////////////////////////////////
#undef APSTUDIO_READONLY_SYMBOLS


/////////////////////////////////////////////////////////////
//
// Icon
//

DocStats                ICON    DISCARDABLE    "DocStats.Ico"

#ifdef APSTUDIO_INVOKED
/////////////////////////////////////////////////////////////
//
// TEXTINCLUDE
//

1 TEXTINCLUDE DISCARDABLE
BEGIN
    "Resource.h\0"
END

2 TEXTINCLUDE DISCARDABLE
BEGIN
    "#include ""afxres.h""\r\n"
    "\0"
END

3 TEXTINCLUDE DISCARDABLE
BEGIN
    "\r\n"
    "\0"
END


/////////////////////////////////////////////////////////////
#endif   // APSTUDIO_INVOKED


#ifndef APSTUDIO_INVOKED
/////////////////////////////////////////////////////////////
//
// Generated from the TEXTINCLUDE 3 resource.
//


/////////////////////////////////////////////////////////////
#endif    // not APSTUDIO_INVOKED
```

Thread Suspension

WaitForSingleObject and *WaitForMultipleObjects* are the functions that a thread most commonly calls to suspend itself until certain criteria are met. However, there are a few other functions that a thread can call to suspend itself. The following sections discuss these functions briefly.

Sleep

The simplest of these functions is *Sleep*:

```
VOID Sleep(DWORD cMilliseconds);
```

This function causes the thread to suspend itself until *cMilliseconds* have elapsed. Note that *Sleep* allows a thread to voluntarily give up the remainder of its time slice. Even a call to *Sleep* passing a value of 0 causes the CPU to stop executing the current thread and assign itself to the next waiting thread. The CritSecs program discussed earlier uses this technique.

Asynchronous File I/O

Asynchronous file I/O allows a thread to start a file-read or file-write operation without having to wait for the read or write operation to complete. For example, if an application needs to load a large file into memory, the application could tell the system to load the file into memory. Then, as the system loads the file, the application can be busy performing other tasks—creating windows, initializing internal data structures, and so on. When the initialization is complete, the application can suspend itself, waiting for the system to notify it that the file has been read.

File objects are synchronizable kernel objects, which means that you can call *WaitForSingleObject*, passing the handle of a file. While the system is performing the asynchronous I/O, the file object is in the non-signaled state. As soon as the file operation is complete, the system changes the state of the file object to signaled so that the thread knows that the file operation has completed. At this point, the thread continues execution.

Asynchronous file I/O is discussed in more detail in Chapter 13.

WaitForInputIdle

A thread can also suspend itself by calling *WaitForInputIdle*:

```
DWORD WaitForInputIdle(HANDLE hProcess, DWORD dwTimeout);
```

This function waits until the process identified by *hProcess* has no input pending in the thread that created the application's first window. This function is useful for a parent process. The parent process spawns a child process to do some work. When the parent process's thread calls *CreateProcess*, the parent's thread continues to execute while the child process is initializing. It might be that the parent's thread needs to get the handle of a window created by the child. The only way for the parent's thread to know when the child process has been fully initialized is for the parent's thread to wait until the child is no longer processing any input. So after the call to *CreateProcess*, the parent's thread would place a call to *WaitForInputIdle*.

You might also use *WaitForInputIdle* when you need to force keystrokes into an application. Let's say that you post the following messages to the main window of an application:

WM_KEYDOWN	with a virtual key of VK_MENU
WM_KEYDOWN	with a virtual key of VK_F
WM_KEYUP	with a virtual key of VK_F
WM_KEYUP	with a virtual key of VK_MENU
WM_KEYDOWN	with a virtual key of VK_O
WM_KEYUP	with a virtual key of VK_O

This sequence has the effect of sending Alt+F, O to an application, which, for most English-language applications, will select the application's File Open menu command. Selecting this command displays a dialog box; however, before the dialog box can appear, Windows must load the dialog box template from the file and cycle through all the controls in the template, calling *CreateWindow* for each one. This can take some time. So the application that posted the WM_KEY* messages can now call *WaitForInputIdle*, which causes the application to wait until the dialog box has been completely created and is ready for user input. The application can now force additional keys into the dialog box and its controls so that it can continue doing whatever it needs to do.

This particular problem was faced by many developers writing for 16-bit Windows. Applications wanted to post messages to a window but didn't know exactly when the window was created and ready. The *WaitForInputIdle* function solves this problem.

MsgWaitForMultipleObjects

A thread can call the *MsgWaitForMultipleObjects* function to cause the thread to wait for its own messages:

```
DWORD MsgWaitForMultipleObjects(DWORD dwCount, LPHANDLE lpHandles,
    BOOL bWaitAll, DWORD dwMilliseconds, DWORD dwWakeMask);
```

The *MsgWaitForMultipleObjects* function is similar to the *WaitForMultipleObjects* function, with the addition of the *dwWakeMask* parameter. This parameter can be used by an application to determine whether it should awaken to process certain types of messages. For example, if a thread wants to suspend itself until a keyboard or mouse message is in the queue, the application can make the following call:

```
MsgWaitForMultipleObjects(0, NULL, TRUE, INFINITE,
    QS_KEY | QS_MOUSE);
```

This statement says that we're not passing any handles of synchronization objects, as indicated by passing 0 and NULL for the *dwCount* and *lpHandles* parameters. We're telling the function to wait for all objects to be signaled. But because we're specifying only one object to wait on, the *fWaitAll* parameter could have easily been FALSE without altering the effect of this call. We are also telling the system that we want to wait however long it takes until either a keyboard message or a mouse message is available in the thread's input queue.

The legal domain of possible values that can be specified in the last parameter is the same as the values that can be passed to the *GetQueueStatus* function, which is discussed in Chapter 10. The *MsgWaitForMultipleObjects* function can be useful if your program is waiting for a particular object to become signaled and you want to allow the user to interrupt the wait. If your program is waiting for the object to become signaled and the user presses a key, the thread is awakened and the *MsgWaitForMultipleObjects* function returns. Normally, when the *WaitForMultipleObjects* function returns, it returns the index of the object that became signaled to satisfy the call (WAIT_OBJECT_0 to WAIT_OBJECT_0+*dwCount*−1). Adding the *dwWakeMask* parameter is like adding another handle to the call. If *MsgWaitForMultipleObjects* is satisfied because of the wake mask, the return value will be WAIT_OBJECT_0+*dwCount*. The FileChng application in Chapter 13 demonstrates how to use this function.

WaitForDebugEvent

The Win32-based operating systems offer excellent debugging support. When a debugger starts executing, it attaches itself to a debugee. The debugger simply sits idle waiting for the operating system to notify it of debug events related to the debugee. A debugger waits for these events by calling:

```
BOOL WaitForDebugEvent(LPDEBUG_EVENT lpde, DWORD dwTimeout);
```

When a debugger calls *WaitForDebugEvent*, the debugger's thread is suspended. The system will notify the debugger that a debug event has occurred by allowing the call to *WaitForDebugEvent* to return. The structure pointed to by the *lpde* parameter is filled by the system before it awakens the thread. This structure contains information regarding the debug event that has just occurred.

The Interlocked Family of Functions

The last three functions we'll discuss are *InterlockedIncrement*, *Interlocked-Decrement*, and *InterlockedExchange*:

```
LONG InterlockedIncrement(LPLONG lplValue);

LONG InterlockedDecrement(LPLONG lplValue);

LONG InterlockedExchange(LPLONG lplTarget, LONG lValue);
```

The sole purpose of these functions is to change the value of a long variable. These functions guarantee that the thread changing the long variable has exclusive access to this variable—no other thread will be able to change this variable at the same time. This is true even if the two threads are being executed simultaneously by two different CPUs in the same machine.

It is important to note that all the threads should attempt to modify the shared long variable by calling these functions; no thread should ever attempt to modify the shared variable by using simple C statements:

```
// The long variable shared by many threads
LONG lValue;
  :

// Incorrect way to increment the long
lValue++;
  :
```

```
// Correct way to increment the long
InterlockedIncrement(&lValue);
```

Normally, the way to protect the long variable from being corrupted would be to use a form of synchronization, such as mutexes. But because the manipulation of a long variable is so common and useful, Microsoft added these three functions to the Win32 API.

The calls to *InterlockedIncrement* and *InterlockedDecrement* add 1 to and subtract 1 from the long variable whose address you pass as the *lplValue* parameter to the functions. These functions *do not* return the new value of the long variable. Instead, they return a value that compares the new value of the long to 0. If the result of incrementing or decrementing the long variable causes the long variable to be 0, the functions return 0. If the value of the long becomes less than 0, the functions return a value that is less than 0. And you can probably guess that if the long variable becomes greater than 0, the functions return a value that is greater than 0. The return value is almost never the actual value of the long variable. I use both of these functions in the MULTINST.C and MODUSE.C source files, which are described in Chapter 11.

The third function, *InterlockedExchange*, is used to completely replace the current value of the long whose address is passed in the *lplTarget* parameter with a long value that is passed in the *lValue* parameter. Again, this function protects the long variable from any other thread that is attempting to change the variable at the same time.

Another point about using these functions: no *Interlocked* function is available for one thread to read the value of a long while another thread is attempting to change the long because the function isn't necessary. If one thread calls *InterlockedIncrement* while another thread reads the contents of the long, the value read from the long will always be valid. The thread might get the value of the long before *InterlockedIncrement* changes the variable, or the thread might get the value after *Interlocked-Increment* changes the value. The thread has no idea which value it gets, but it is guaranteed to get a valid value and not a value that is partially incremented.

WINDOW MESSAGES AND ASYNCHRONOUS INPUT

Microsoft had some pretty big goals in mind when it started designing the Win32 environment: virtual memory management, preemptive multitasking, and security, to name just a few. The idea behind many of these goals was to create a robust environment in which one application could not adversely affect other applications. This is an area where the 16-bit Windows environment is significantly lacking.

Unfortunately, in order to offer these improvements Microsoft was forced to change many things that 16-bit Windows programmers have become accustomed to. For example, the Win32 system processes a user's keyboard and mouse input in a completely different manner than the 16-bit Windows environment. For many applications, these changes to the environment will require that pieces of the application be redesigned rather than simply ported to Win32. These changes are the focus of this chapter.

Multitasking

I think multitasking is the single most important new feature that separates 16-bit Windows from Win32. Although 16-bit Windows can run multiple applications simultaneously, it runs the applications non-preemptively. That is, one application must tell the operating system that it's finished processing before the scheduler can assign another application execution time, which creates problems for both users and application developers.

For users, it means that control of the system is lost for an arbitrary time period decided by the application (not the user). If an application

417

takes a long time to execute a particular task, such as formatting a floppy disk, the user can't switch away from that task and work with a word processor while the formatting continues in the background. This situation is unfortunate because users want to make the most of their time.

Developers for 16-bit Windows recognize this and try to implement their applications so that they execute tasks in spurts. For example, a formatting program might format a single track on a floppy disk and then return control to 16-bit Windows. Once 16-bit Windows has control, it can respond to other tasks for the user. When the user is idle, 16-bit Windows returns control to the format program so that another track can be formatted.

Well, this method of sharing time between tasks works, but it makes implementing a program significantly more difficult. One way the formatting program can accomplish its tasks is to set a timer for itself using the *SetTimer* function. The program is then notified with WM_TIMER messages when it's time to execute another part of the process. This type of implementation involves the following problems:

- 16-bit Windows offers a limited number of timers for application use. What should the program do if a timer is not available— not allow the user to format a disk until another application using a timer is terminated?

- The program must keep track of its progress. The formatting program must save, either in global variables or in a dynamically allocated block of memory, information such as the letter of the drive it is formatting, the track that has just been formatted, and so forth.

- The program code can't include a function that formats a disk; instead, it must include a function that formats a single track of a disk. This means that the functions in the program must be broken up in a way that is not natural for a programmer to implement. You don't usually design an algorithm thinking that the processor needs to be able to jump into the middle of it. You can imagine how difficult implementation would be if your algorithm required a series of nested loops to perform its operations and the processor needed to jump into the innermost loop.

- WM_TIMER messages occur at regular intervals. So if an application sets a timer to go off every second, WM_TIMER messages are received 60 times every minute. This is true whether a user is running the application on a 25-MHz 386 or a 90-MHz Pentium. If a user has a faster machine, the program should take advantage of that.

Another favorite method 16-bit Windows developers use to help their applications behave more courteously toward other applications involves the *PeekMessage* function. When an application calls *PeekMessage*, the application tells 16-bit Windows, "I have more work to process, but I'm willing to postpone doing it if another application needs to do something."

This method makes the code easier to implement because the implementer can design the algorithms assuming that the computer won't jump into the middle of a process. This method also doesn't require any timers and doesn't have any special system resource requirements. The method does have two problems, however: the implementer must sprinkle *PeekMessage* loops throughout the code, and the application must be written to handle all kinds of asynchronous events. For example, a spreadsheet might be recalculating cell values when another application attempts to initiate a DDE conversation with it. It is incredibly difficult to test your application to verify that it performs correctly in all possible scenarios.

As it turns out, even when developers use these methods to help their applications behave in a friendlier way, their programs still don't multitask smoothly. Sometimes a user might click on another application's window, and a full second or more might go by before 16-bit Windows changes to the active application. More important, though, if an application bug causes the application never to call *PeekMessage* or return control to 16-bit Windows, the entire 16-bit Windows system effectively hangs. At this point, the user can't switch to another application, can't save on disk any work that was in progress, and, more often than not, is forced to reboot the computer. This is totally unacceptable!

The Win32 environment solves these problems (and more that I haven't even mentioned) with preemptive multitasking. By adding a preemptive multitasking capability to Windows NT and Windows 95, Microsoft has done much more than allow multiple applications to run simultaneously. The environment is much more robust because a single application can't control all the system resources.

Preemptive Time Scheduling

In 16-bit Windows, there is only one thread of execution. That is, the microprocessor travels in a linear path from functions in one application to functions in another application, frequently dipping into the operating system's code. Whenever the user moves from executing one application, or task, to another, the operating system code performs a task switch. A task switch simply means that the operating system saves the state of the CPU's registers before deactivating the current task and restores the registers for the newly activated task. Notice that I said the operating system is responsible for performing the task switch. Because the system has only one thread of execution, if any code enters an infinite loop the thread can never access the operating system code that performs the task switch, and the system hangs.

In addition, 16-bit Windows uses the concepts of modules and tasks. A module identifies an executable file that is loaded into memory. Every time an instance of the executable file is invoked, 16-bit Windows calls this instance a task. With few exceptions, resources (that is, memory blocks or windows) created (allocated) when the task is executing become owned by the particular task. Some resources, such as icons and cursors, are actually owned by the module, which allows these resources to be shared by all of the module's tasks.

Win32 still uses the term module to identify an executable file loaded into memory. However, Win32 takes the concept of a task and breaks it down into two new concepts—*processes* and *threads*.

As discussed in Chapter 2, a process refers to an instance of a running program. For example, if a single instance of Notepad and two instances of Calc are running, three processes are running in the system. And, as discussed in Chapter 3, a thread describes a path of execution within a process. When an executable file is invoked, the operating system creates both a process and a thread. For example, when the user invokes a Win32 application, the system locates the program's EXE file, creates a process and a thread for the new instance, and tells the CPU to start executing the thread beginning with the C run-time startup code, which in turn calls your *WinMain* function. When the thread terminates (returns from *WinMain*), the system destroys the thread and the process.

Every process has at least one thread; the system schedules CPU time among threads of a process, not among processes themselves. After a thread begins executing, it can create additional threads within the process. These threads execute until they are destroyed or until they terminate on their own. The number of threads that can be created is limited only by system resources.

While a thread is executing, the system can steal the CPU away from the thread and give the CPU to another thread. But the CPU cannot be interrupted while it is executing a single instruction (a CPU instruction, not a line of source code). The operating system's ability to interrupt a thread at (almost) any time and assign the CPU to a waiting thread is called *preemptive multitasking*.

The life span of a process is directly tied to the threads it owns. Threads within a process have lives of their own too. New threads are created, existing threads are paused and restarted, and other threads are terminated. When all the threads in a process terminate, the system terminates the process, frees any resources owned by the process, and removes the process from memory.

Most objects allocated by a thread are owned by the process that also owns the thread. For example, a block of memory allocated by a thread is owned by the process, not by the thread. All of the global and static variables in an application are also owned by the process. And all GDI objects (pens, brushes, bitmaps) are owned by the process. Most User objects (windows, menus, accelerator tables) are owned by the thread that created them or loaded them into memory. Only three User objects—icons, cursors, and window classes—are owned by a process instead of by a thread.

An understanding of ownership is important so that you know what can be shared. If a process has seven threads operating within it and one thread makes a call to allocate a block of memory, the block of memory can then be accessed from any of the seven threads. This access can cause several problems if all the threads attempt to read and write from the same block simultaneously. Synchronizing several threads is discussed further in Chapter 9.

Ownership is also important because the Win32 system is much better than 16-bit Windows about cleaning up after a thread or a process terminates. If a thread terminates and neglects to destroy a window that it created, the system ensures that the window is destroyed, not sitting around somewhere soaking up precious memory and system resources. For example, if a thread creates or loads a cursor into memory and then the thread is terminated, the cursor is not destroyed. This is because the cursor is owned by the process and not by the thread. When the process terminates, the system ensures that the cursor is destroyed. In 16-bit Windows, a task has the equivalent of one and only one thread. As a result, the concept of ownership is less complicated.

Thread Queues and Message Processing

Much of the work performed by Win32 applications is initiated by window messages. In the 16-bit Windows environment, there's a single thread of execution. If your application sends a message to a window created by another task, your task stops running and the code to process the message starts running. After the message is processed, the system returns to your task's code so that it can continue executing. In a multithreaded environment, things are quite different.

In Win32, the code in a window procedure must be executed by the thread that created the window, which might not be the same thread that sent the message. In order to let other threads process messages, some sort of cooperation must occur in which the calling thread notifies the receiving thread that it needs it to perform an action. Then the calling thread suspends itself until the receiving thread has completed the request. In this section, we'll take a look at the various methods threads can use to send and post window messages.

Win32 Message Queue Architecture

As I have already said, one of the main goals of Win32 is to offer a robust environment for all the applications running. In order to meet this goal, each thread must run in an environment in which it believes that it is the only thread running. More specifically, each thread must have message queues that are totally unaffected by other threads. In addition, each thread must have a simulated environment that allows the thread to maintain its own notion of keyboard focus, window activation, mouse capture, and so on.

Whenever a thread is created, the system also creates a THREAD-INFO structure and associates this data structure with the thread. This THREADINFO structure contains a set of member variables that are used to make the thread think that it is running in its very own environment. The THREADINFO structure is an internal (undocumented) data structure that identifies the thread's message queue, virtualized input queue, and wake flags, as well as a number of variables that are used for the thread's local input state. Figure 10-1 illustrates how THREADINFO structures are associated with three threads.

The remainder of this chapter is dedicated to discussing the THREADINFO structure's data members.

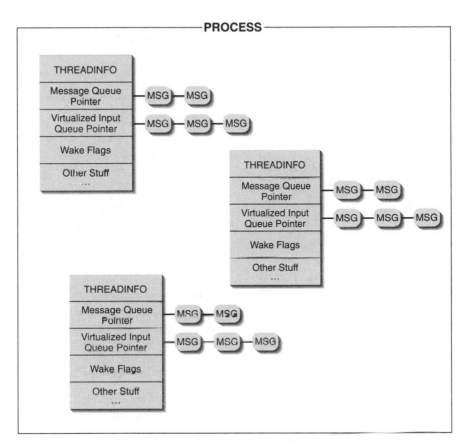

Figure 10-1.
Three threads with their respective THREADINFO structures.

Posting Messages to a Thread's Message Queue

In Win32, every thread has its very own message queue. If a single process creates 10 threads, there will be 10 message queues. Messages are placed in a message queue by calling the *PostMessage* function:

```
BOOL PostMessage(HWND hWnd, UINT Msg, WPARAM wParam,
    LPARAM lParam);
```

When a thread calls this function, the system determines which thread created the window identified by the *hWnd* parameter and posts the specified message to the appropriate thread's message queue. *PostMessage* returns immediately after posting the message—the calling thread has no idea whether the posted message was processed by the specified window's window procedure. In fact, it is possible that the specified window will never receive the posted message. This could happen if the thread that created the specified window were to somehow terminate before processing all of the messages in its queue.

In 16-bit Windows, each task has its own message queue so that every application doesn't have to process the messages destined for other applications. By default, this message queue is large enough to hold up to eight messages. An application is able to increase or decrease the queue size by calling the *SetMessageQueue* function. This function exists in the Win32 API but is unnecessary because messages are stored in a linked list and there is no limit to the number of messages that can be placed in the list. In Win32, each thread's message queue is maintained as a doubly linked list. As messages are posted to the queue, MSG structures are linked onto the end of the linked list. When a message is pulled off the message queue, the system returns the first message in the linked list. The THREADINFO structure contains the pointer to the first message in the linked list rather than the actual message queue.

PostMessage's return value indicates whether there was enough room in the queue to post the specified message. For 16-bit Windows, *PostMessage* returns FALSE if the queue is full. For Win32, it is nearly impossible for *PostMessage* to ever return FALSE.

A message can also be placed in a thread's message queue by calling *PostThreadMessage*:

```
BOOL PostThreadMessage(DWORD idThread, UINT Msg, WPARAM wParam,
    LPARAM lParam);
```

The desired thread is identified by the first parameter, *idThread*. When this message is placed in the queue, the *hWnd* member in the MSG structure will be set to NULL. This function is usually called when an application performs some special processing in its main message loop. The main message loop for the thread is written so that, after *GetMessage* or *PeekMessage* retrieves a message, the code checks for an *hWnd* of NULL and can examine the *msg* member of the MSG structure to perform the special processing. If the thread determines that this message is not destined for a window, *DispatchMessage* is not called, and the message loop iterates to retrieve the next message. (The PMRest application presented in Chapter 16 demonstrates the use of the *PostThreadMessage* function.)

Like the *PostMessage* function, this function returns immediately after posting the message to the thread's queue. The calling thread has no idea when or if the message gets processed.

The *PostThreadMessage* function replaces the 16-bit Windows function *PostAppMessage.*

Sending Messages to a Window

Window messages can be sent directly to a window procedure by using the *SendMessage* function:

```
LRESULT SendMessage(HWND hWnd, UINT Msg, WPARAM wParam,
   LPARAM lParam);
```

The window procedure will process the message and, only after the message has been processed, *SendMessage* will return to the caller. Because of its synchronous nature, *SendMessage* is used more frequently than either *PostMessage* or *PostThreadMessage* in Windows programming. The calling thread knows that the window message has been completely processed before the next line of code executes.

If the thread calling *SendMessage* is sending a message to a window created by the same thread, *SendMessage* is very simple: it just calls the specified window's window procedure as a subroutine. When the window procedure is finished processing the message, it returns a 32-bit value back to *SendMessage*. *SendMessage* returns this 32-bit value to the calling thread.

If a thread is sending a message to a window created by another thread, the internal workings of *SendMessage* are far more complicated.[1] Win32 requires that a window's message be processed by the thread that created the window. So if you call *SendMessage* to send a message to a window created by another process, and therefore to another thread, your thread cannot possibly process the window message because your thread is not running in the other process's address space and therefore does not have access to the window procedure's code and data. In fact, your thread is suspended while the other thread is processing the message. So in order to send a window message to a window created by another thread, the system must perform the actions discussed on the next page.

---

1. This is true even if the two threads are in the same process.

First, the sent message is appended to the receiving thread's message queue, which has the effect of setting the QS_SENDMESSAGE flag (discussed later) for that thread. Second, if the receiving thread is already executing code and isn't waiting for messages (on a call to *GetMessage*, *PeekMessage*, or *WaitMessage*), the sent message can't be processed—the system won't interrupt the thread in order to process the message immediately. When the receiving thread is waiting for messages, the system first checks to see whether the QS_SENDMESSAGE wake flag is set, and if it is, the system scans the list of messages in the message queue to find the first sent message. It is possible that several sent messages could pile up in this queue. For example, several threads could each send a message to a single window at the same time. When this happens, the system simply appends these messages to the receiving thread's message queue.

When the receiving thread is waiting for messages, the system simply locates the first sent message in the queue and calls the appropriate window procedure to process the message. If there are no more sent messages in the message queue, the QS_SENDMESSAGE wake flag is turned off. While the receiving thread is processing the message, the thread that called *SendMessage* is sitting idle. After the message is processed, the window procedure's return value is returned and the thread that called *SendMessage* is resumed so that it can continue execution.

While a thread is waiting for *SendMessage* to return, it basically sits idle. It is allowed to perform one task, however: if another thread in the system sends a message to a window created by a thread that is waiting for *SendMessage* to return, the system will process the sent message immediately. The system doesn't have to wait for the thread to call *GetMessage*, *PeekMessage*, or *WaitMessage* in this case.

Because the Win32 subsystem uses this method to handle the sending of interthread messages, it's possible that your thread could hang. For example, let's say that the thread processing the sent message has a bug and enters an infinite loop. What happens to the thread that called *SendMessage*? Will it ever be resumed? Does this mean that a bug in one application has the ability to hang another application? The answer is yes!

Four functions allow you to write code defensively to protect yourself from this situation.

The first function is *SendMessageTimeout*:

```
LRESULT SendMessageTimeout(HWND hwnd, UINT uMsg, WPARAM wParam,
    LPARAM lParam, UINT fuFlags, UINT uTimeout, LPDWORD lpdwResult);
```

It allows you to specify the maximum amount of time you are willing to wait for another thread to respond to your message. The first four parameters are the same parameters that you pass to *SendMessage*. For the *fuFlags* parameter you can pass SMTO_NORMAL, SMTO_ABORT-IFHUNG, or SMTO_BLOCK, or a combination of SMTO_ABORTIF-HUNG and SMTO_BLOCK.

The SMTO_ABORTIFHUNG flag tells *SendMessageTimeout* to check whether the receiving thread is in a hung state,[2] and if so, to return immediately. The SMTO_BLOCK flag causes the calling thread not to process any other sent messages until *SendMessageTimeout* returns. The SMTO_NORMAL flag is defined as 0 in WINUSER.H; this is the flag to use if you don't specify either of the other two.

Earlier in this section I said that a thread can be interrupted while waiting for a sent message to return so that it can process another sent message. Using the SMTO_BLOCK flag stops the system from allowing this interruption. You should use this flag only if your thread could not process a sent message while waiting for its sent message to be processed. Using SMTO_BLOCK could create a deadlock situation until the timeout expires—for example, if you send a message to another thread and that thread needs to send a message to your thread. In this case, neither thread can continue processing, and both threads effectively hang.

The *uTimeout* parameter specifies the number of milliseconds you are willing to wait for a result. If the function is successful, TRUE is returned and the result of the message is copied into the buffer whose address you specify in the *lpdwResult* parameter.

By the way, if you call *SendMessageTimeout* to send a message to a window created by the calling thread, the system simply calls the window procedure and places the return value in *lpdwResult*. Because all processing must take place with one thread, the code following the call to *SendMessageTimeout* cannot start executing until after the message has been processed.

The second function that can help in sending interthread messages is:

```
BOOL SendMessageCallback(HWND hwnd, UINT uMsg, WPARAM wParam,
    LPARAM lParam, SENDASYNCPROC lpResultCallBack, DWORD dwData);
```

---

2. The operating system considers a thread to be hung if the thread stops processing messages for more than 5 seconds.

Again, the first four parameters are the same as those used by the *Send-Message* function. When a thread calls *SendMessageCallback*, the function sends the message off to the receiving thread and immediately returns so that your thread can continue processing. When the receiving thread has finished processing the message, the system notifies your thread by calling a function that you write using the following prototype:

```
VOID CALLBACK ResultCallBack(HWND hwnd, UINT uMsg, DWORD dwData,
    LRESULT lResult);
```

You must pass the address to this function as the *lpResultCallBack* parameter of *SendMessageCallback*. When this function is called, it is passed the handle of the window that finished processing the message and the message value in the first two parameters. The third parameter, *dwData*, will always be the value that you passed in the *dwData* parameter to *SendMessageCallback*. The system simply takes whatever you specify here and passes it directly to your *ResultCallBack* function. The last parameter passed to your *ResultCallBack* function is the result from the window procedure that processed the message.

Your thread is not really notified of the result from the processed message as soon as the receiving window procedure returns. Instead, the system keeps a queue of returned messages; it can call your *ResultCallBack* function only while your thread is calling *GetMessage*, *PeekMessage*, *WaitMessage*, or one of the *SendMessage*∗ functions.

The *SendMessageCallback* function has another use. Win32 offers a method by which you can broadcast a message to all the existing overlapped windows in the system by calling *SendMessage* and passing HWND_BROADCAST (defined as –1) as the *hwnd* parameter. Use this method only to broadcast a message whose return value you aren't interested in because the function can return only a single LRESULT. But by using the *SendMessageCallback* function, you can broadcast a message to every overlapped window and see the result of each. Your *ResultCallBack* function will be called with the result of every window processing the message.

If you call *SendMessageCallback* to send a message to a window created by the calling thread, the system immediately calls the window procedure, and then, after the message is processed, the system calls the *ResultCallBack* function. After the *ResultCallBack* function returns, execution begins at the line following the call to *SendMessageCallback*.

The third new function that can help in sending interthread messages is:

```
BOOL SendNotifyMessage(HWND hwnd, UINT Msg, WPARAM wParam,
    LPARAM lParam);
```

SendNotifyMessage places a message in the receiving thread's queue and returns to the calling thread immediately. This should sound familiar because this is exactly what the *PostMessage* function does. However, *SendNotifyMessage* differs from *PostMessage* in two ways.

First, if *SendNotifyMessage* sends a message to a window created by another thread, the sent message has higher priority than posted messages placed in the receiving thread's queue. In other words, messages that the *SendNotifyMessage* function places in a queue are always retrieved before messages that the *PostMessage* function posts to a queue.

Second, when you are sending a message to a window created by the calling thread, *SendNotifyMessage* works exactly like the *SendMessage* function: *SendNotifyMessage* doesn't return until the message has been processed.

As it turns out, most messages sent to a window are used for notification purposes. That is, the message is sent because the window needs to be aware that a state change has occurred so that it can perform some processing before you carry on with your work. For example, WM_ACTIVATE, WM_DESTROY, WM_ENABLE, WM_SIZE, WM_SETFOCUS, and WM_MOVE, just to name a few, are all notifications that are sent to a window by the system instead of being posted. However, these messages are notifications to the window; the system doesn't have to stop running so that the window procedure can process these messages. In contrast, when the system sends a WM_CREATE message to a window, the system must wait until the window has finished processing the message. If the return value is –1, the window is not created.

The fourth new function that can help in sending interthread messages is:

```
BOOL ReplyMessage(LRESULT lResult);
```

This function is different from the three previously discussed functions. Whereas the three *Send** functions are used by the thread sending a message to protect itself from hanging, *ReplyMessage* is called by the thread receiving the window message. When a thread calls *ReplyMessage*, it is telling the system that it has completed enough work to know the result of the message and that the sending thread can have this result and continue executing.

The thread calling *ReplyMessage* specifies the result of processing the message in the *lResult* parameter. After *ReplyMessage* is called, the thread that sent the message resumes, and the thread processing the message continues to process the message. Neither thread is suspended, and both can continue executing normally. When the thread processing the message returns from its window procedure, any value that it returns is simply ignored.

The problem with *ReplyMessage* is that it has to be called from within the window procedure that is receiving the message and not by the thread that called one of the *Send** functions. So you are better off writing defensive code by replacing your calls to *SendMessage* with one of the three new *Send** functions instead of relying on the implementer of a window procedure to make calls to *ReplyMessage*.

Waking a Thread

When a thread calls *GetMessage* or *WaitMessage* and there are no messages for the thread or windows created by the thread, the system can suspend the thread so that it is not scheduled any CPU time. However, when a message is posted or sent to the thread, the system sets a wake flag indicating that the thread should now be scheduled CPU time in order to process the message. Under normal circumstances, the user is not typing or moving the mouse and there are no messages being sent to any of the windows. This means that most of the threads in the system are not being scheduled any CPU time.

When a thread is running, it can query the status of its queues by calling the *GetQueueStatus* function, shown below:

```
DWORD GetQueueStatus(UINT fuFlags);
```

The *fuFlags* parameter is a flag or a series of flags ORed together that allows you to test for specific wake bits. The table below shows the possible flag values and their meanings:

Flag	Message in the Queue
QS_KEY	WM_KEYUP, WM_KEYDOWN, WM_SYSKEYUP, or WM_SYSKEYDOWN
QS_MOUSE	Same as QS_MOUSEMOVE ¦ QS_MOUSEBUTTON
QS_MOUSEMOVE	WM_MOUSEMOVE
QS_MOUSEBUTTON	WM_?BUTTON*[1]
QS_PAINT	WM_PAINT

1. Where ? is L, M, or R, and * is DOWN, UP, or DBLCLK.

(continued)

continued

Flag	Message in the Queue
QS_POSTMESSAGE	Posted message (other than from a hardware input event)
QS_SENDMESSAGE	Message sent by another thread
QS_TIMER	WM_TIMER
QS_HOTKEY	WM_HOTKEY
QS_INPUT	Same as QS_MOUSE ¦ QS_KEY
QS_ALLEVENTS	Same as QS_INPUT ¦ QS_POSTMESSAGE ¦ QS_TIMER ¦ QS_PAINT ¦ QS_HOTKEY[2]
QS_ALLINPUT	Same as QS_ALLEVENTS ¦ QS_SENDMESSAGE

2. The QS_SENDMESSAGE flag is not ORed into the QS_ALLEVENTS flag because it's reserved for internal use by the system.

When you call the *GetQueueStatus* function, the *fuFlags* parameter tells *GetQueueStatus* the types of messages to check for in the queues. The fewer the number of QS_* identifiers you OR together, the faster the call executes. Then, when *GetQueueStatus* returns, the types of messages currently in the thread's queues can be found in the high-word of the return value. This returned set of flags will always be a subset of what you asked for. For example, if you make the following call:

```
BOOL fPaintMsgWaiting = HIWORD(GetQueueStatus(QS_TIMER)) & QS_PAINT;
```

the value of *fPaintMsgWaiting* will always be FALSE whether or not a WM_PAINT message is waiting in the queue, because QS_PAINT was not specified as a flag in the parameter passed to *GetQueueStatus*.

The low-word of *GetQueueStatus*'s return value indicates the types of messages that have been added to the queue and that haven't been processed since the last call to *GetQueueStatus*, *GetMessage*, or *PeekMessage*.

Not all the wake flags are treated equally. For the QS_MOUSE-MOVE flag, as long as an unprocessed WM_MOUSEMOVE message exists in the queue, the flag is turned on. When *GetMessage* or *PeekMessage* (with PM_REMOVE) pulls the last WM_MOUSEMOVE message from the queue, the flag is turned off until a new WM_MOUSEMOVE message is placed in the input queue. The QS_KEY, QS_MOUSEBUTTON, and QS_HOTKEY flags work in the same way for their respective messages.

The QS_PAINT flag is handled differently. If a window created by the thread has an invalid region, the QS_PAINT flag is turned on. When the area occupied by all windows created by this thread becomes validated (usually by a call to *ValidateRect*, *ValidateRegion*, or *BeginPaint*), the QS-_PAINT flag is turned off. This flag is turned off only when all windows created by the thread are validated. Calling *GetMessage* or *PeekMessage* has no effect on this wake flag.

The QS_POSTMESSAGE flag is set whenever at least one message is in the thread's message queue. This doesn't include hardware event messages that are in the thread's virtualized input queue. When all the messages in the thread's message queue have been processed and the queue is empty, this flag is reset.

The QS_TIMER flag is set whenever a timer (created by the thread) goes off. After the WM_TIMER event is returned by *GetMessage* or *PeekMessage*, the QS_TIMER flag is reset until the timer goes off again.

The QS_SENDMESSAGE flag indicates that another thread has sent a message to a window that was created by your thread. This flag is used by the system internally to identify and process messages being sent from one thread to another. It's not used for messages that a thread sends to itself. Although you can use the QS_SENDMESSAGE flag, it's very rare that you'd need to. I've never seen an application use this flag.

There is another queue status flag that is not documented—QS_QUIT. When a thread calls *PostQuitMessage*, the QS_QUIT flag is turned on. The system does not actually append a WM_QUIT message to the thread's message queue. The *GetQueueStatus* function does not return the state of this flag.

When a thread calls *GetMessage* or *PeekMessage*, the system must examine the state of the thread's queues and determine which message should be processed. Figure 10-2 and the following list illustrate the steps that the system performs when determining which message the thread should process next.

1. If the QS_SENDMESSAGE flag is turned on, the system sends the message to the proper window procedure. Both the *GetMessage* and *PeekMessage* functions handle this processing internally and do not return to the thread after the window procedure has processed the message; instead, these functions sit and wait for another message to process.

2. If there are messages in the thread's message queue, *GetMessage* and *PeekMessage* fill the MSG structure passed to these functions and then the functions return. The thread's message loop usually calls *DispatchMessage* at this point to have the message processed by the appropriate window procedure.

(continued)

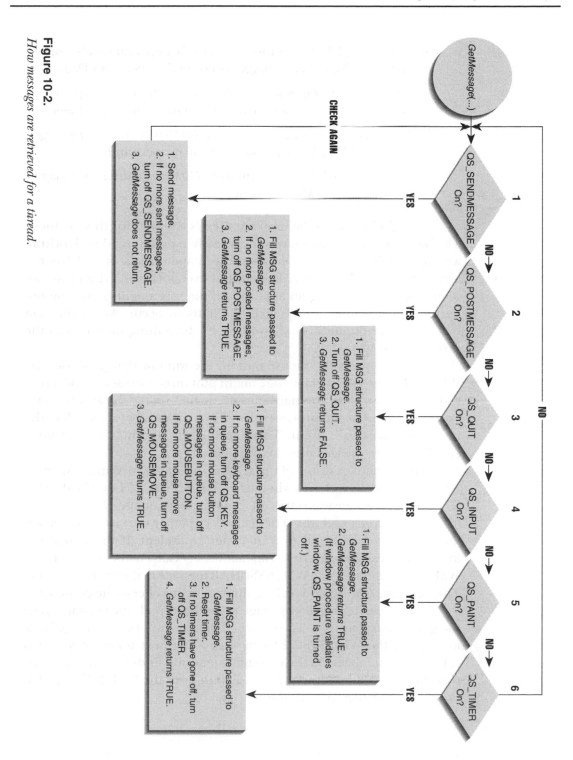

Figure 10-2.
How messages are retrieved for a thread.

3. If the QS_QUIT flag is turned on, *GetMessage* and *PeekMessage* return a WM_QUIT message and reset the QS_QUIT flag.

4. If there are messages in the thread's virtualized input queue, *GetMessage* and *PeekMessage* return the hardware input message.

5. If the QS_PAINT flag is turned on, *GetMessage* and *PeekMessage* return a WM_PAINT message for the proper window.

6. If the QS_TIMER flag is turned on, *GetMessage* and *PeekMessage* return a WM_TIMER message.

It might be hard to believe, but there's a reason for this madness. The big assumption that Microsoft made when designing this algorithm was that applications should be user-driven and that the user drives the applications by creating hardware input events (keyboard and mouse operations). While using an application, the user might press a mouse button, which causes a sequence of events to occur. An application makes each of the individual events occur by posting messages to the thread's message queue.

So if you press the mouse button, the window that processes the WM_LBUTTONDOWN message might post three messages to different windows. Because it's the hardware event that sparks these three software events, the system processes the software events before sending the user's next hardware event. This explains why the message queue is checked before the virtualized input queue.

An excellent example of this is a call to *TranslateMessage*. The *TranslateMessage* function checks whether a WM_KEYDOWN or a WM_SYS-KEYDOWN message was retrieved from the input queue. If one of these messages was retrieved, the system checks whether the virtual key information can be converted to a character equivalent. If the virtual key information can be converted, *TranslateMessage* calls *PostMessage* to place a WM_CHAR message or a WM_SYSCHAR message in the message queue. The next time *GetMessage* is called, the system first checks the contents of the message queue and, if a message exists there, pulls the message from the queue and returns it. The returned message will be the WM_CHAR message or the WM_SYSCHAR message. The next time *GetMessage* is called, the system checks the message queue and finds it empty. The system then checks the input queue, where it finds the WM_(SYS)KEYUP message. *GetMessage* returns this message.

Because the system works this way, the following sequence of hardware events,

```
WM_KEYDOWN
WM_KEYUP
```

generates the following sequence of messages to your window procedure (assuming that the virtual key information can be converted to a character equivalent):

```
WM_KEYDOWN
WM_CHAR
WM_KEYUP
```

Now let's get back to discussing how the system decides what messages to return from *GetMessage* and *PeekMessage*. After the system checks the message queue and before it checks the virtualized input queue, it checks the QS_QUIT flag. Remember that the QS_QUIT flag is set when the thread calls *PostQuitMessage*. Calling *PostQuitMessage* is similar to calling *PostMessage*, which places the message at the end of the message queue and causes the message to be processed before the input queue is checked. So why does *PostQuitMessage* set a flag instead of placing a WM_QUIT message in the message queue? There are two reasons.

First, in 16-bit Windows a queue can hold up to only eight messages. If the queue is full and the application attempts to post a WM_QUIT message to the queue, the WM_QUIT message gets lost and the application never terminates. Because the WM_QUIT message is handled as a special flag, the message never gets lost. Of course, in Win32 this reason is no longer valid because Win32 queues are linked lists that grow dynamically. The second reason for handling the QS_QUIT flag this way is to let the application finish processing all the other posted messages before the system terminates the application. So if you have the following code fragment:

```
case WM_CLOSE:
   PostQuitMessage(0);
   PostMessage(hwnd, WM_USER, 0, 0);
   :
   :
```

the WM_USER message will be retrieved from the queue before a WM_QUIT message, even though the WM_USER message is posted to the queue after *PostQuitMessage* is called.

Now we come to the last two messages: WM_PAINT and WM_TIMER. A WM_PAINT message has low priority because painting the screen is a slow process. If a WM_PAINT message were sent every time a window became invalid, the system would be too slow to use. By placing WM_PAINT messages after keyboard input, the system runs much faster. For example, you can select a menu item that invokes a dialog box, choose an item from the box, and press Enter all before the dialog box even appears on the screen. If you type fast enough, your keystroke messages will always be pulled from the queue before any WM_PAINT messages. When you press Enter to accept the dialog box options, the dialog box window is destroyed and the system resets the QS_PAINT flag.

The last message, WM_TIMER, has an even lower priority than a WM_PAINT message. To understand why, think about the Clock application that ships with the system. Clock updates its display every time it receives a WM_TIMER message. Imagine that WM_TIMER messages are returned before WM_PAINT messages and that Clock sets a timer of such short duration that it just goes off continuously, never allowing a WM_PAINT message to be returned from *GetMessage*. In this case, Clock would never paint itself—it would just keep updating its internal time but would never get a WM_PAINT message.

Important

Remember that the *GetMessage* and *PeekMessage* functions check only the wake flags and message queues of the calling thread. This means that threads can never retrieve messages from a queue that's attached to another thread, including messages for threads that are part of the same process.

Sending Data with Messages

I have already explained that Win32 does not allow two applications to share a memory block by passing the handle of the memory block from one process to another. I have also said that you cannot share the block by passing the address to the data's location from one process to another. Both of these methods for sharing data work in 16-bit Windows but fail under Win32 for the same reason: each process has its own address space.

If you want to share memory between applications, I recommend using memory-mapped files as explained in Chapter 7. However, let's look at a situation in which one process prepares a block of data for sharing with other applications. After the data is prepared, the creating process needs to signal the other applications that the data is ready. The creating process can accomplish this in several ways. One way is to use event objects as discussed in Chapter 9. Another way is to send a window message to a window in the other process. In this section, we'll examine how the system transfers data between processes using window messages.

Some window messages specify the address of a block of memory in their *lParam* parameter. For example, the WM_SETTEXT message uses the *lParam* parameter as a pointer to a zero-terminated string that identifies the new text for the window. Consider the following call:

```
SendMessage(FindWindow(NULL, "Calculator"), WM_SETTEXT,
   0, (LPARAM) "A Test Caption");
```

This call seems harmless enough—it determines the window handle of the Calculator application's window and attempts to change its caption to *A Test Caption*. But let's take a closer look at what happens here.

The string of the new title is contained in your process's address space. So the address of this string in your process space will be passed as the *lParam* parameter. When the window procedure for Calculator's window receives this message, it looks at the *lParam* parameter and attempts to manipulate what it thinks is a zero-terminated string in order to make it the new title.

But the address in *lParam* points to a string in your process's address space—not in Calculator's address space. This is a big problem because a memory access violation is sure to occur. But if you execute the line above, you'll see that it works successfully. How can this be?

The answer is that the system looks specifically for the WM_SET-TEXT message and handles it differently from the way it handles most other messages. When you call *SendMessage*, the code in the function checks whether you are trying to send a WM_SETTEXT message. If you are, it packs the zero-terminated string from your address space into a block of memory that it is going to share with the other process. Then it sends the message to the thread in the other process. When the receiving thread is ready to process the WM_SETTEXT message, it determines the location, in its own address space, of the shared block of memory that contains a copy of the new window text. The *lParam* parameter is initialized to point to this address, and the WM_SETTEXT message is dispatched to the appropriate window procedure. Boy, doesn't this seem like a lot of work?

Fortunately, most messages don't require this type of processing, which takes place only when an application sends interprocess messages. Special processing like this has to be performed for any message whose *wParam* or *lParam* parameters represent a pointer to a data structure.

Let's look at another case that requires special handling by the system—the WM_GETTEXT message. Suppose your application contains the following code:

```
char szBuf[200];
SendMessage(FindWindow(NULL, "Calculator"), WM_GETTEXT,
    sizeof(szBuf), (LPARAM) szBuf);
```

The WM_GETTEXT message requests that Calculator's window procedure fill the buffer pointed to by *szBuf* with the title of its window. When you send this message to a window in another process, the system must actually send two messages. First the system sends a WM_GETTEXT-LENGTH message to the window. The window procedure responds by returning the number of characters required to hold the window's title. The system can use this count to allocate a block of memory that will end up being shared between the two processes.

Once the memory block has been allocated, the system can send the WM_GETTEXT message to fill the memory block. Then the system switches back to the process that called *SendMessage* in the first place, copies the data from the shared memory block into the buffer pointed to by *szBuf*, and returns from the call to *SendMessage*.

Well, all this is fine and good if you are sending messages that the system is aware of, but what if you create your own (WM_USER + x) message that you want to send from one process to a window in another? The system will not know that you want it to allocate a shared block of memory and to update pointers when sending. If you want to do this, you can use the new WM_COPYDATA message:

```
COPYDATASTRUCT cds;
SendMessage(hwndReceiver, WM_COPYDATA,
    (WPARAM) hwndSender, (LPARAM) &cds);
```

COPYDATASTRUCT is a structure defined in WINUSER.H, and it looks like this:

```
typedef struct tagCOPYDATASTRUCT {
    DWORD dwData;
    DWORD cbData;
    PVOID lpData;
} COPYDATASTRUCT;
```

When you're ready to send some data to a window in another process, you must first initialize the COPYDATASTRUCT structure. The *dwData* member is reserved for your own use. You can place any 32-bit value in it. For example, you might have occasion to send different types or categories of data to the other process. You can use this value to indicate the content of the data you are sending.

The *cbData* member specifies the number of bytes that you want to transfer to the other process, and the *lpData* member points to the first byte of the data. The address pointed to by *lpData* is, of course, in the sender's address space.

When *SendMessage* sees that you are sending a WM_COPYDATA message, it allocates a block of memory *cbData* bytes in size and copies the data from your address space to this block. It then sends the message to the destination window. When the receiving window procedure processes this message, the *lParam* parameter points to a COPYDATA-STRUCT that exists in the address space of the receiving process. The *lpData* member of this structure points to the copied block of memory, and the address has been changed to reflect where the memory exists in the receiving process's address space.

There are three important things to note about the WM_COPY-DATA message. First, always send this message; never post it. You can't post a WM_COPYDATA message because the system must free the copied memory after the receiving window procedure has processed the message. If you post the message, the system doesn't know when the WM_COPYDATA message is processed and therefore can't free the copied block of memory.

The second item of note is that it takes some time for the system to make a copy of the data in the other process's address space. This means that you shouldn't have another thread that modifies the contents of the memory block running in the sending application until the call to *SendMessage* returns.

The third thing to be aware of is that the WM_COPYDATA message works for sending data from a Win32 process to a 16-bit Windows application and vice versa. This is probably the best way to communicate across the 16-bit to 32-bit boundary.

The CopyData Sample Application

The CopyData application (COPYDATA.EXE), listed in Figure 10-3 beginning on page 441, demonstrates how to use the WM_COPYDATA message to send a block of data from one application to another. The source code files, resource files, and make file for the application are in the COPYDATA.10 directory on the companion disc. You'll need to have at least two copies of CopyData running to see it work. Each time you start a copy of CopyData, it presents a dialog box that looks like this:

To see data copied from one application to another, first change the text in the Data1 and Data2 edit controls. Then click on one of the two Send Data* To Other Windows buttons, and the program sends the data to all the running instances of CopyData. Each instance updates the contents of its own edit box to reflect the new data.

The list below describes how CopyData works. When a user clicks on one of the two buttons, CopyData performs the following:

1. Initializes the *dwData* member of COPYDATASTRUCT with 0 if the user clicked on the Send Data1 To Other Windows button or 1 if the user clicked on the Send Data2 To Other Windows button.

2. Retrieves the length of the text string (in characters) from the appropriate edit box and adds 1 for a zero-terminating character. This value is converted from a number of characters to a number of bytes by multiplying by sizeof(TCHAR), and the result is then placed in the *cbData* member of COPYDATA-STRUCT.

3. Calls *HeapAlloc* to allocate a block of memory large enough to hold the length of the string in the edit box plus its zero-terminating character. The address of this block is stored in the *lpData* member of COPYDATASTRUCT.

4. Copies the text from the edit box into this memory block.

At this point, everything is ready to be sent to the other windows. To determine which windows to send the WM_COPYDATA message to, CopyData performs the following:

1. Gets the handle of the first window that is a sibling to the instance of CopyData the user is running.

2. Gets the text of CopyData's title bar.

3. Cycles through all the sibling windows, comparing each window's title bar to CopyData's title bar. If the titles match, the WM_COPYDATA message is sent to the sibling window. Because I didn't do any special checks in this loop, the instance of CopyData that is calling *SendMessage* will send itself a WM_COPYDATA message. This demonstrates that WM_COPYDATA messages can be sent and received from the same thread.

4. After all the windows have been checked, CopyData calls *Heap-Free* to free the memory block that it was using to hold the edit box text.

And that's all there is to sending data from one application to another using messages.

CopyData.ico

```
COPYDATA.C
/*********************************************************
Module name: CopyData.C
Notices: Copyright (c) 1995 Jeffrey Richter
*********************************************************/


#include "..\AdvWin32.H"      /* See Appendix B for details. */
#include <windows.h>
#include <windowsx.h>

#pragma warning(disable: 4001)        /* Single-line comment */

#include <tchar.h>
#include "Resource.H"


///////////////////////////////////////////////////////////////////////


// Microsoft does not include message cracker macros for
// the WM_COPYDATA message in WINDOWSX.H.
// I have written them here....

/* BOOL Cls_OnCopyData(HWND hwnd, HWND hwndFrom,
   PCOPYDATASTRUCT cds) */
```

Figure 10-3.
The CopyData application.

(continued)

441

Figure 10-3. *continued*

```
#define HANDLE_WM_COPYDATA(hwnd, wParam, lParam, fn) \
   ((fn)((hwnd), (HWND)(wParam), \
   (PCOPYDATASTRUCT)lParam), 0L)

#define FORWARD_WM_COPYDATA(hwnd, hwndFrom, cds, fn) \
   (BOOL)(UINT)(DWORD)(fn)((hwnd), WM_COPYDATA, \
   (WPARAM)(hwndFrom), (LPARAM)(cds))


///////////////////////////////////////////////////////////////

BOOL Dlg_OnCopyData(HWND hwnd, HWND hwndFrom,
   PCOPYDATASTRUCT cds) {

   Edit_SetText(
      GetDlgItem(hwnd, cds->dwData ? IDC_DATA2 : IDC_DATA1),
      cds->lpData);
   return(TRUE);
}


///////////////////////////////////////////////////////////////

BOOL Dlg_OnInitDialog (HWND hwnd, HWND hwndFocus,
   LPARAM lParam) {

   // Associate an icon with the dialog box.
   SetClassLong(hwnd, GCL_HICON, (LONG)
      LoadIcon((HINSTANCE) GetWindowLong(hwnd, GWL_HINSTANCE),
      __TEXT("CopyData")));

   // Initialize the edit control with some test data.
   Edit_SetText(GetDlgItem(hwnd, IDC_DATA1),
      __TEXT("Some test data"));
   Edit_SetText(GetDlgItem(hwnd, IDC_DATA2),
      __TEXT("Some more test data"));

   return(TRUE);
}


///////////////////////////////////////////////////////////////

void Dlg_OnCommand (HWND hwnd, int id, HWND hwndCtl,
   UINT codeNotify) {
```

(continued)

Figure 10-3. *continued*

```
HWND hwndEdit, hwndSibling;
COPYDATASTRUCT cds;
TCHAR szCaption[100], szCaptionSibling[100];

switch (id) {
   case IDC_COPYDATA1:
   case IDC_COPYDATA2:
      if (codeNotify != BN_CLICKED)
         break;

      hwndEdit = GetDlgItem(hwnd,
         (id == IDC_COPYDATA1) ? IDC_DATA1 : IDC_DATA2);

      // Prepare the contents of the COPYDATASTRUCT.
      // 0 = ID_DATA1, 1 = ID_DATA2
      cds.dwData = (DWORD) ((id == IDC_COPYDATA1) ? 0 : 1);

      // Get the length of the data block
      // that we are sending.
      cds.cbData = (Edit_GetTextLength(hwndEdit) + 1) *
         sizeof(TCHAR);

      // Allocate a block of memory to hold the string.
      cds.lpData = HeapAlloc(GetProcessHeap(),
         HEAP_ZERO_MEMORY, cds.cbData);

      // Put the edit control's string in the data block.
      Edit_GetText(hwndEdit, cds.lpData, cds.cbData);

      // Find the first overlapped window in the list.
      hwndSibling = GetFirstSibling(hwnd);

      // Get the caption of our window.
      GetWindowText(hwnd, szCaption,
         ARRAY_SIZE(szCaption));

      while (IsWindow(hwndSibling)) {
         // Get the caption of the potential
         // window to send the data to.
         GetWindowText(hwndSibling, szCaptionSibling,
            ARRAY_SIZE(szCaptionSibling));

         if (_tcscmp(szCaption, szCaptionSibling) == 0) {
            // If the window's caption is the same as ours,
            // send the data. This may mean that we are
```

(continued)

Figure 10-3. *continued*

```
                    // sending the message to ourselves. This is OK;
                    // it demonstrates that WM_COPYDATA can be
                    // used to send data to ourselves.
                    FORWARD_WM_COPYDATA(hwndSibling, hwnd,
                        &cds, SendMessage);
                }

                // Get the handle of the next overlapped window.
                hwndSibling = GetNextSibling(hwndSibling);
            }

            // Free the data buffer.
            HeapFree(GetProcessHeap(), 0, cds.lpData);
            break;

        case IDCANCEL:
            EndDialog(hwnd, id);
            break;
    }
}


///////////////////////////////////////////////////////////////

BOOL CALLBACK Dlg_Proc (HWND hDlg, UINT uMsg,
    WPARAM wParam, LPARAM lParam) {

    BOOL fProcessed = TRUE;

    switch (uMsg) {
        HANDLE_MSG(hDlg, WM_INITDIALOG, Dlg_OnInitDialog);
        HANDLE_MSG(hDlg, WM_COMMAND, Dlg_OnCommand);
        HANDLE_MSG(hDlg, WM_COPYDATA, Dlg_OnCopyData);

        default:
            fProcessed = FALSE;
            break;
    }
    return(fProcessed);
}


///////////////////////////////////////////////////////////////

int WINAPI WinMain (HINSTANCE hinstExe,
    HINSTANCE hinstPrev, LPSTR lpszCmdLine, int nCmdShow) {
```

(continued)

Figure 10-3. *continued*

```
    DialogBox(hinstExe, MAKEINTRESOURCE(IDD_COPYDATA),
        NULL, Dlg_Proc);

    return(0);
}


/////////////////////// End Of File ///////////////////////
```

COPYDATA.RC

```
//Microsoft Visual C++ generated resource script.
//
#include "Resource.h"

#define APSTUDIO_READONLY_SYMBOLS
/////////////////////////////////////////////////////////////////
//
// Generated from the TEXTINCLUDE 2 resource.
//
#include "afxres.h"


/////////////////////////////////////////////////////////////////
#undef APSTUDIO_READONLY_SYMBOLS


/////////////////////////////////////////////////////////////////
//
// Dialog
//

IDD_COPYDATA DIALOG DISCARDABLE  38, 36, 220, 42
STYLE WS_MINIMIZEBOX | WS_POPUP | WS_VISIBLE | WS_CAPTION
    | WS_SYSMENU
CAPTION "WM_COPYDATA Message Share Application"
FONT 8, "System"
BEGIN
    LTEXT           "Data&1:",IDC_STATIC,4,4,24,12
    EDITTEXT        IDC_DATA1,28,4,76,12
    PUSHBUTTON      "&Send Data1 to other windows",
                    IDC_COPYDATA1,112,4,104,14,WS_GROUP
    LTEXT           "Data&2:",IDC_STATIC,4,24,24,12
    EDITTEXT        IDC_DATA2,28,24,76,12
    PUSHBUTTON      "Send &Data2 to other windows",
                    IDC_COPYDATA2,112,24,104,
                    14,WS_GROUP
END
```

(continued)

Figure 10-3. *continued*

```
/////////////////////////////////////////////////////////////
//
// Icon
//

CopyData                ICON    DISCARDABLE     "CopyData.Ico"

#ifdef APSTUDIO_INVOKED
/////////////////////////////////////////////////////////////
//
// TEXTINCLUDE
//

1 TEXTINCLUDE DISCARDABLE
BEGIN
    "Resource.h\0"
END

2 TEXTINCLUDE DISCARDABLE
BEGIN
    "#include ""afxres.h""\r\n"
    "\0"
END

3 TEXTINCLUDE DISCARDABLE
BEGIN
    "\r\n"
    "\0"
END

/////////////////////////////////////////////////////////////
#endif    // APSTUDIO_INVOKED


#ifndef APSTUDIO_INVOKED
/////////////////////////////////////////////////////////////
//
// Generated from the TEXTINCLUDE 3 resource.
//


/////////////////////////////////////////////////////////////
#endif    // not APSTUDIO_INVOKED
```

Deserialized Input

Serialized input (used by 16-bit Windows) is when the system processes the user's input (keyboard and mouse events) in the order in which the input was entered by the user. The events are removed from the system queue as various applications request them. For example, let's say that the user types *ABC*, Alt+Tab, *XYZ* at the keyboard. This means that seven keyboard hardware events are added to the system queue.[3] The application with keyboard focus retrieves the *ABC* messages from the system queue and displays the characters in its client area. Let's say a bug in the program causes it to enter an infinite loop whenever it receives the letter *C*. At this point, the whole system is hung. Alt+Tab and *XYZ* will never be read from the system queue. In fact, if the user attempts to activate another application using the mouse, the mouse event will be appended to the system queue after the last keystroke event. And as you might expect, this mouse event will never be retrieved from the system queue either. The user has no recourse now but to reboot the computer.

Microsoft did try to improve this situation. Support was added to 16-bit Windows so that a user can press Ctrl+Alt+Del if an application is no longer responding to the system. When the system detects this input, it locates the currently active application and attempts to remove it from memory. My experience with this feature has been that 16-bit Windows usually cannot recover from the hung application gracefully and I still need to reboot.

The solution to this serialized input problem is *deserialized input*. With deserialized input, one hardware event isn't necessarily processed before another event. I know what you're thinking: "Does this mean that if you type *ABC* at the keyboard the thread will receive *CAB*?" No, of course not. However, it does mean that if you type *ABC*, Alt+Tab, *XYZ*, the thread that becomes active after Alt+Tab might process *XYZ* before the first thread finishes processing *ABC*.

In Win32, input is applied on a thread-level basis instead of on the systemwide basis employed by 16-bit Windows. A thread receives hardware events in the order in which the user enters them, which is how the system deserializes the hardware input.

---

3. Actually, more than seven events are appended to the system queue. For example, each keystroke generates a WM_KEYDOWN and a WM_KEYUP event. I am calling it seven events just to simplify the discussion.

How Input Is Deserialized

When the system starts running, the system creates a special thread for itself called the *raw input thread* (RIT). When the user presses and releases a key, presses and releases a mouse button, or moves the mouse, the device driver for the hardware device appends a hardware event to the RIT's queue. This causes the RIT to wake up; examine the event at the head of its queue; translate the event into the appropriate WM-_KEY*, WM_?BUTTON*, or WM_MOUSEMOVE message; and post the message to the appropriate thread's virtualized input queue.

As shown in Figure 10-1 on page 423, each thread has its very own message queue and virtualized input queue. Every time a thread creates a window, the system places all messages posted for this window in the creating thread's queue.

Assume the following scenario: a process creates two threads, Thread A and Thread B. Thread A then creates a window—Win A—and Thread B creates two windows—Win B and Win C. Figure 10-4 illustrates this scenario. If a thread in the system posts a message to Win A, this message is placed in Thread A's message queue. Any messages posted for either Win B or Win C are placed in Thread B's message queue.

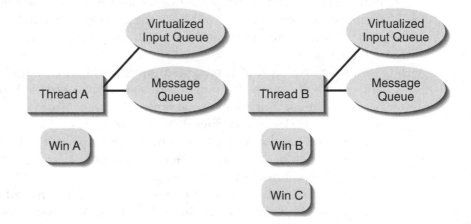

Figure 10-4.
Messages for Win A go in Thread A's queues; messages for Win B and Win C go in Thread B's queues.

When the RIT processes a hardware event, it must determine which virtualized input queue should receive the event. For a mouse event, the RIT first determines which window is under the mouse cursor and then places the mouse event (WM_?BUTTON* or WM_MOUSEMOVE) in the virtualized input queue associated with the thread that created the window. For a keystroke event, the RIT determines which thread is the foreground thread—that is, the thread with which the user is currently working. The appropriate keyboard message is placed in the virtualized input queue associated with this foreground thread.

In order for the system to switch threads, regardless of whether a thread is processing input, the RIT must examine each hardware input event before posting the event to a thread's virtualized input queue. For example, the RIT checks for the following key combinations and performs the corresponding action:

Key Combination	Windows 95	Windows NT
Alt+Tab	Activates another window connecting its thread to the RIT	Activates another window connecting its thread to the RIT
Alt+Esc	Activates another window connecting its thread to the RIT	Activates another window connecting its thread to the RIT
Ctrl+Esc	Pops open the Taskbar's Start menu	Displays the system's Task Manager
Ctrl+Alt+Del	Displays the system's Close Program dialog box	Displays the Windows NT Security dialog box

Sharing Thread Virtualized Input Queues

You can force two or more threads to share the same virtualized input queue and local input state variables (discussed later) by using the *AttachThreadInput* function:

```
BOOL AttachThreadInput(DWORD idAttach, DWORD idAttachTo,
  BOOL fAttach);
```

This function tells the system to let two threads share the same virtualized input queue, as illustrated in Figure 10-5 on the next page. The first parameter, *idAttach*, is the ID of the thread containing the virtualized input queue you no longer want. The second parameter, *idAttachTo*, is the ID of the thread containing the virtualized input queue you want the threads to share. The last parameter, *fAttach*, is TRUE if you want the sharing to occur or FALSE if you want to separate the two threads' virtualized input queues again. You can tell several threads to share the same virtualized input queue by making successive calls to the *Attach-ThreadInput* function.

Returning to the earlier example, let's say that Thread B calls *Attach-ThreadInput*, passing Thread B's ID as the first parameter, Thread A's ID as the second parameter, and TRUE as the last parameter:

```
AttachThreadInput(idThreadB, idThreadA, TRUE);
```

Now every hardware input event destined for either Win B or Win C will be appended to Thread A's virtualized input queue. Thread B's virtualized input queue will no longer receive input events unless the two queues are detached by calling *AttachThreadInput* a second time, passing FALSE as the *fAttach* parameter.

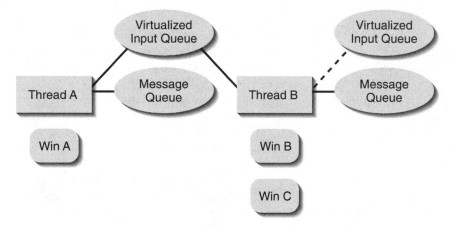

Figure 10-5.
*Hardware messages for Win A, Win B, and Win C go in Thread A's
virtualized input queue.*

When you attach two threads to the same virtualized input queue, each thread still maintains its own message queue. Every time you attach another thread to the same virtualized input queue, you are making the system behave more and more like 16-bit Windows. After all, in 16-bit Windows all the tasks are attached to a single input queue—the system queue. In fact, when you run 16-bit Windows applications under Windows 95 or Windows NT, the system makes sure that all the 16-bit Windows applications share a single input queue for backward compatibility because 16-bit Windows applications expect this behavior.

If you make all threads share a single queue, you severely curtail the robustness of the Win32 system. If one application receives a keystroke and hangs, another application can't receive any input. So think twice or three times before using the *AttachThreadInput* function.

> Windows NT 3.5 allows 16-bit Windows applications to run in separate address spaces. All the 16-bit applications in a single address space have their input queues attached to one another. However, if two 16-bit applications are running in different address spaces, the system does not attach their input queues. This makes Windows NT run 16-bit Windows applications more robustly than 16-bit Windows did. If a 16-bit Windows application hangs, all other 16-bit Windows applications in the same address space also hang. However, 16-bit Windows applications running in separate address spaces are not affected.
>
> This feature does not exist in Windows NT 3.1 or Windows 95.

The system implicitly attaches the virtualized input queues of several threads if an application installs a journal record hook or a journal playback hook. When the hook is uninstalled, the system automatically restores all the threads so that they are using the same input queues they were using before the hook was installed.

When an application installs a journal record hook, it tells the system that it wants to be notified of all hardware events entered by the user. The application usually saves or records this information. In another session, the application installs a journal playback hook, which causes the system to ignore the user's input and to expect the application that installed the hook to play back the events it recorded earlier.

Playing back the recorded events simulates the user repeating his or her hardware input. The Recorder application that Microsoft ships with 16-bit Windows allows users to record events for later playback by installing journal record and journal playback hooks. You'll notice that Recorder is not shipped with Windows 95 or Windows NT—this is because Recorder compromises the robustness of the system.

There is one other instance in which the system implicitly calls *AttachThreadInput* on your behalf. Let's say you have an application that creates two threads. The first thread creates a dialog box. After the dialog box has been created, the second thread calls *CreateWindow*, using the WS_CHILD style, and passes the handle of the dialog box to be the child's parent. The system implicitly calls *AttachThreadInput* with the child window's thread to tell the child's thread that it should use the same input queue that the dialog box thread is using. This action forces input to be synchronized among all the child windows in the dialog box. As you'll see later in this chapter, it's possible for windows created by different threads to look as if they all have the input focus simultaneously, which can confuse an end user. When you attach the input queues, only one window will appear to have the focus.

Local Input State

Back when programmers were developing applications for MS-DOS, it could always be presumed that the running application would be the only active application. As a result, applications frequently assumed that the whole display was theirs for the writing, the memory theirs for the allocating, the disk space theirs for the accessing, the keystrokes theirs for the taking, the CPU theirs for the computing—you get the idea.

Well, 16-bit Windows came around and programmers had to learn to cooperate with one another. Many programs, all running simultaneously, had to share the limited system resources. An application had to restrict its output to a small rectangular region on the display; allocate memory only when needed (as well as try to make it discardable); relinquish control of itself to other applications on certain keystrokes; and purposely put itself to sleep so that other applications could get a little CPU time. If an application was not as friendly as it should be, a user had no recourse but to terminate the piggish application or run it alone, which obviously defeated the idea of a multitasking environment.

Under Win32, much of this is still true. Developers still design their applications to use a small rectangular region on the display for output, allocate memory only when needed, and so on. The big difference is that Win32 makes applications behave courteously. The system forces limits on the amount of memory that an application can hog. It monitors the keyboard and allows the user to switch to another application whether the currently active application wants to allow this or not. It preempts a running application and gives time to another application regardless of how hungry for processing time the current application is.[4]

Who are the winners now that the system has so much control over the applications we write? Both the users and the developers. Because

---

4. You can set your process's priority class high; however, doing so might starve processes at a lower priority, making the lower-priority processes unresponsive. But even if you set a process's priority class high, the system still gives the user the ability to terminate the process.

the system does all this no matter what we as programmers might do to stop it, we can relax a little and stop worrying about crowding out other applications. A big part of making this work is the concept of the *local input state.*

Each thread has its very own input state, which is managed inside a thread's THREADINFO structure (discussed earlier). This input state consists of the thread's virtualized input queue as well as a set of variables. These variables keep track of the following input state management information:

Keyboard input and window focus information, such as

- Which window has keyboard focus

- Which window is active

- Which keys that are pressed on the keyboard are stored in the synchronous key state array

- The state of the caret

Mouse cursor management information, such as

- Which window has mouse capture

- The shape of the mouse cursor

- The visibility of the mouse cursor

Because each thread gets its very own set of input state variables, each thread has a different notion of focus window, mouse capture window, and so on. From a thread's perspective, either one of its windows has keyboard focus or no window in the system has keyboard focus, either one of its windows has mouse capture or no window has mouse capture, and so on. As you might expect, this separatism has several ramifications, which we'll discuss in this chapter.

Keyboard Input and Focus

Win32 and 16-bit Windows handle keyboard input in very different ways. When I was first getting started with Win32, I tried to understand how the system handles keyboard input by drawing on my knowledge of 16-bit Windows. As it turned out, my knowledge of how 16-bit Windows handles keyboard input made it *more* difficult to understand both how Win32 handles keyboard input and how it changes the input focus between windows.

In Win32, the RIT directs the user's keyboard input to a thread's virtualized input queue—not to a window. The RIT places the keyboard events into the thread's virtualized input queue without referring to a particular window. When the thread calls *GetMessage*, the keyboard event is removed from the queue and assigned to the window (created by the thread) that currently has input focus. Figure 10-6 illustrates this process.

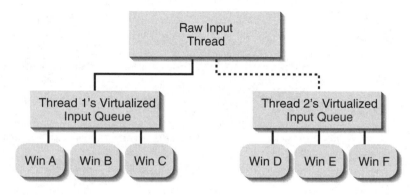

Figure 10-6.
The RIT directs the user's keyboard input to one thread's virtualized input queue at a time.

To instruct a different window to accept keyboard input, you need to specify to which thread's virtualized input queue the RIT should direct keyboard input *and* tell the thread's input state variables which window will have keyboard focus. Calling *SetFocus* alone does not accomplish both tasks. If Thread 1 is currently receiving input from the RIT, a call to *SetFocus*, passing the handle of Win A, Win B, or Win C, causes the focus to change. The window losing focus removes its focus rectangle or hides its caret, and the window gaining focus draws a focus rectangle or shows its caret.

However, let's say that Thread 1 is still receiving input from the RIT, and it calls *SetFocus*, passing the handle of Win E. In this case, the system prevents the call to *SetFocus* from doing anything because the window for which you are trying to set focus is not using the virtualized input queue that is currently "connected" to the RIT. After Thread 1 executes this call, there is no change in focus, and the appearance of the screen doesn't change.

In another situation, Thread 1 might be connected to the RIT and Thread 2 might call *SetFocus*, passing the handle of Win E. In this case, Thread 2's local input state variables are updated to reflect that Win E is the window to receive keyboard input the next time the RIT directs keystrokes to Thread 2. The call doesn't cause the RIT to direct input to Thread 2's virtualized input queue.

Because Win E now has focus for Thread 2, it receives a WM_SET-FOCUS message. If Win E is a pushbutton, it draws a focus rectangle for itself, so two windows with focus rectangles might appear on the screen. I found this very disconcerting at first—and now that I've seen it happen a few more times, I still find it disconcerting. You should be careful when you call *SetFocus* so that this situation doesn't occur.

By the way, if you give focus to a window that displays a caret when it receives a WM_SETFOCUS message, you can produce several windows on the screen that display carets simultaneously. This can be a bit disconcerting to a user.

When focus is transferred from one window to another using conventional methods (such as clicking on a window with the mouse), the window losing focus receives a WM_KILLFOCUS message. If the window receiving focus belongs to a thread other than the thread associated with the window losing focus, the local input state variables of the thread that created the window losing focus are updated to reflect that no window has focus. Calling *GetFocus* at this time returns NULL, which makes the thread think that no window currently has the focus. This can be problematic when you're porting a 16-bit Windows application to Win32 because most 16-bit Windows applications never expect *GetFocus* to return NULL.

The *SetActiveWindow* function activates a top-level window in the system:

```
HWND SetActiveWindow(HWND hwnd);
```

In 16-bit Windows, an application typically calls this function to bring another application to the foreground. In Win32, this function behaves just like the *SetFocus* function. That is, if a thread calls *SetActiveWindow*, passing the handle of a window owned by a different thread, the system does nothing. But if the window was created by the same thread making the call, the system changes the active window.

The complement of *SetActiveWindow* is the *GetActiveWindow* function:

```
HWND GetActiveWindow(VOID);
```

This function works just like the *GetFocus* function except that it returns the handle of the active window indicated by the calling thread's local input state variables. So if the active window is owned by another thread, *GetActiveWindow* returns NULL.

These functions behave differently under Win32 than they do under 16-bit Windows for a reason: Microsoft is taking control away from applications and giving it back to the users. The assumption is that users find it disconcerting when windows pop up in the foreground under program control.

For example, a user might start a lengthy process in Application A and switch to Application B. When Application A is finished, it may activate its main window. You certainly wouldn't want Application A's main window to pop up on top of Application B's window while the user is still working with Application B. This could catch the user by surprise. Also, the user might not immediately notice that Application A's window had popped up on top of Application B's window, and the user might enter text into Application A by mistake. This could have disastrous effects.

However, sometimes an application really needs to bring a window to the foreground. The following functions not only change the window focus for a thread but also instruct the RIT to direct keystrokes to a different thread. One of these functions, the *SetForegroundWindow* function, is new for Win32:

```
BOOL SetForegroundWindow(HWND hwnd);
```

This function brings the window identified by the *hwnd* parameter to the foreground. The system also activates the window and gives it the focus. This function sets the foreground window regardless of which thread created the window. The complementary function is *GetForegroundWindow*:

```
HWND GetForegroundWindow(VOID);
```

This function returns the handle of the window that is currently in the foreground.

Other functions that can alter a window's z-order, activation status, and focus status include *BringWindowToTop* and *SetWindowPos*. The *BringWindowToTop* function, shown below, exists in both 16-bit Windows and Win32:

```
BOOL BringWindowToTop(HWND hwnd);
```

As long as the thread calling *BringWindowToTop* is in the foreground when you call this function, Win32 activates the window you specify regardless of which thread created the window. Win32 both redirects the RIT to the thread that created the window and sets the focus window for the thread's local input state variables. If the thread calling *BringWindowToTop* is not the foreground thread, the window order doesn't change.

The *SetWindowPos* function, shown below, brings a window to the foreground or the background by passing HWND_TOP or HWND_BOTTOM as the second parameter:

```
BOOL SetWindowPos(HWND hwnd, HWND hwndInsertAfter,
   int x, int y, int cx, int cy, UINT fuFlags);
```

Actually, *BringWindowToTop* is implemented internally as a call to *SetWindowPos* passing HWND_TOP as the second parameter.

Another aspect of keyboard management and the local input state is that of the synchronous key state array. Every thread's local input state variables include a synchronous key state array, but all threads share a single asynchronous key state array. These arrays reflect the state of all keys on a keyboard at any given time. The *GetAsyncKeyState* function determines whether the user is currently pressing a key on the keyboard:

```
SHORT GetAsyncKeyState(int nVirtKey);
```

The *nVirtKey* parameter identifies the virtual key code of the key to check. The high-bit of the result indicates whether the key is currently pressed (1) or not (0). I have often used this function during the processing of a single message to check whether the user has released the primary mouse button. I pass the virtual key value VK_LBUTTON and wait for the high bit of the return value to be 0. This function has changed slightly for Win32. In Win32, *GetAsyncKeyState* always returns 0 (not pressed) if the thread calling the function did not create the window that currently has the input focus.

The *GetKeyState* function, shown below, differs from the *GetAsyncKeyState* function because it returns the keyboard state at the time the most recent keyboard message was removed from the thread's queue:

```
SHORT GetKeyState(int nVirtKey);
```

This function is not affected by which window has input focus and can be called at any time. For a more detailed discussion of these two key state arrays and these functions, refer to my article about keystroke processing, "Simulating Keyboard Input Between Programs Requires a (Key)Stroke of Genius," in the December 1992 issue of *Microsoft Systems Journal*.

Mouse Cursor Management

Mouse cursor management is another component of the local input state. Because the mouse, like the keyboard, must be shared among all the different threads, Win32 must not allow a single thread to monopolize the mouse cursor by altering its shape or confining it to a small area of the screen. In this section, we'll take a look at how the mouse cursor is managed by the system.

One aspect of mouse cursor management is the cursor's hide/show capability. Let's say that a 16-bit Windows application calls *ShowCursor-(FALSE)*, causing the mouse cursor to be hidden, and the application never calls *ShowCursor(TRUE)*. The user wouldn't be able to see the mouse when using a different application.

Win32 wouldn't allow this to happen. The system hides the cursor whenever the mouse is positioned over a window created by the thread that called *ShowCursor(FALSE)* and shows it whenever the cursor is positioned over a window not created by this thread.

Another aspect of mouse cursor management is the ability to clip the cursor to a rectangular region of the screen. In 16-bit Windows, it is possible for an application to clip the mouse cursor by calling the *Clip-Cursor* function:

```
BOOL ClipCursor(CONST RECT *lprc);
```

This function causes the mouse to be constrained within the screen coordinates specified in the rectangle pointed to by the *lprc* parameter. Again, we have the problem in which one application should not be able to limit the movement of the mouse cursor on the screen. But Win32 must also allow an application to clip a mouse cursor's motion to a specified rectangle. So the system allows the application to set the clipping rectangle and confines the mouse to that region of the screen. Then, if an asynchronous activation event occurs (when the user clicks on another application's window, when a call to *SetForegroundWindow* is made, or when Ctrl+Esc is pressed), the system stops clipping the cursor's movement, allowing the cursor to move freely across the entire screen.

Now we move to the issue of mouse capture. When a window "captures" the mouse (by calling *SetCapture*), it requests that all mouse messages be directed from the RIT to the thread's virtualized input queue and that all mouse messages from the virtualized input queue be directed to the window that set capture. This capturing of mouse messages continues until the application later calls *ReleaseCapture*.

Under 16-bit Windows, if an application calls *SetCapture* but never calls *ReleaseCapture*, mouse messages can never be directed to any other window in the system. Again, we have a situation that Win32 cannot allow, but solving this problem is a bit tricky. When an application calls *SetCapture*, the RIT is directed to place all mouse messages in the thread's virtualized input queue. *SetCapture* also sets the local input state variables for the thread that called *SetCapture*.

As soon as the user releases all mouse buttons, the RIT no longer directs mouse messages solely to the thread's virtualized input queue. Instead, the RIT directs mouse messages to the input queue associated with the window that is directly beneath the mouse cursor. This is normal behavior when the mouse is not captured.

However, the thread that originally called *SetCapture* still thinks that mouse capture is in effect. This means that whenever the mouse is positioned over any window created by the thread that has capture set, the mouse messages will be directed to the capture window for that thread. In other words, when the user releases all mouse buttons, mouse capture is no longer performed on a systemwide level—it is now performed on a thread-local level.

In addition, if the user attempts to activate a window created by another thread, the system automatically sends mouse button down and mouse button up messages to the thread that set capture. Then the system updates the thread's local input state variables to indicate that the thread no longer has mouse capture. It is clear from this implementation that Microsoft expects mouse clicking-and-dragging to be the most common reason for using mouse capture. If you are using mouse capture with techniques other than click-and-drag, you will definitely have to experiment to see how things may have changed from 16-bit Windows to Win32.

The final local input state variable pertaining to the mouse is its cursor shape. Whenever a thread calls *SetCursor* to change the shape of the mouse cursor, the local input state variables are updated to reflect the mouse cursor shape. In other words, the local input state variables always remember the most recent shape of the mouse cursor set by the thread.

Let's say that the user moves the mouse over your window, your window receives a WM_SETCURSOR message, and you call *SetCursor* to change the mouse cursor to an hourglass. After the call to *SetCursor*, you have code that enters into a lengthy process. (An infinite loop is a good example of a lengthy process.) Now the user moves the mouse cursor out of your window and over the window belonging to another application. In 16-bit Windows, the mouse cursor doesn't change, but in Windows 95 and Windows NT the mouse cursor can be changed by the other window procedure.

Local input state variables are not required in order for a thread to change the mouse cursor's shape when another thread executes a lengthy procedure. But now let's move the mouse cursor back into your window that is still executing its lengthy procedure. The system wants to send WM_SETCURSOR messages to the window, but the window is unable to retrieve them because it is still looping. So the system looks at the most recently set mouse cursor shape (contained in the thread's local input state variables) and automatically sets the mouse cursor back to this shape (the hourglass, in this example). This gives the user visual feedback that the process is still working and that the user must wait.

The Local Input State Laboratory Sample Application

The LISLab application (LISLAB.EXE), listed in Figure 10-7 beginning on page 467, is a laboratory that allows you to experiment with how local input states work. The source code files, resource files, and make file for the application are in the LISLAB.10 directory on the companion disc. Before invoking the application, you will want to run the Program Manager application. If you are running Windows NT, the Program Manager will already be running. If you are running Windows 95, however, you must invoke the Program Manager manually by doing the following: select the Start button, choose Run, and then type *PROGMAN* and click on the OK button.

After the Program Manager is running, you can start LISLab and see the following dialog box appear:

In the upper left corner is the Windows group box. The five entries in this box are updated once a second—that is, once every second the dialog box receives a WM_TIMER message, and in response, it calls the following functions: *GetFocus, GetActiveWindow, GetForegroundWindow, Get-Capture,* and *GetClipCursor.* The first four of these functions return window handles. From these window handles, I can determine the window's class and caption and display this information. Remember that these window handles are being retrieved from my own thread's local input state variables.

If I activate another application (such as the Program Manager), the Focus and Active entries change to (No Window) and the Foreground entry changes to [Progman] Program Manager. Notice that by activating the Program Manager you make LISLab think that no window has focus and that no window is active.

Next you can experiment with changing the window focus. First select SetFocus from the Function combo box at the upper right corner of the Local Input State Lab dialog box. Then enter the delay time (in seconds) that you want LISLab to wait before calling *SetFocus.* For this experiment, you'll probably want to specify a delay of 0 seconds. I'll explain shortly how the Delay field is used.

Next select a window that you want to pass in the call to *SetFocus.* You select a window using the Program Manager Windows And Self list box on the left side of the Local Input State Lab dialog box. For this experiment, select [Progman] Program Manager in the list box. Now you are ready to call *SetFocus.* Simply click on the Delay button, and watch what happens to the Windows group box—nothing. The system doesn't perform a focus change.

If you really want *SetFocus* to change focus to the Program Manager, you can click on the Attach To ProgMan button. Clicking on this button causes LISLab to call:

```
AttachThreadInput(GetWindowThreadProcessId(g_hwndPM, NULL),
   GetCurrentThreadId(), TRUE);
```

This call tells LISLab's thread to use the same virtualized input queue as that of the Program Manager. In addition, LISLab's thread will also share the same local input state variables used by the Program Manager.

If after clicking on the Attach To ProgMan button you click on the Program Manager window, LISLab's dialog box looks like the figure shown on the following page.

Notice that now, because the input queues are attached, LISLab can follow window focus changes made in the Program Manager. The dialog box on the next page shows that the Main group currently has the focus. If we continue to manipulate group windows in the Program Manager, LISLab will continue to update its display and show us which Program Manager window has focus, which window is active, and so on.

Now we can move back to LISLab, click on the Delay button, and have *SetFocus* attempt to give the Program Manager focus. This time the call to *SetFocus* succeeds because the input queues are attached.

You can continue to experiment by placing calls to *SetActiveWindow*, *SetForegroundWindow*, *BringWindowToTop*, and *SetWindowPos* by selecting the desired function from the Function combo box. Try calling these functions both when the input queues are attached and when they are detached, and notice the differences.

Now I'll explain why I include the delay option. The delay option causes LISLab to call the specified function after the number of seconds indicated. An example will help illustrate why you need it. First make sure that LISLab is detached from the Program Manager by clicking on the Detach From ProgMan button. Then select -> This Dialog Box <- from the Program Manager Windows And Self list box. Next select SetFocus from the Function combo box, and enter a delay of 10 seconds. Finally, click on the Delay button, and then quickly click on the Program Manager window to make it active. You must make the Program Manager active before the 10 seconds elapse.

While LISLab is waiting for the 10 seconds to elapse, it displays the word Pending to the right of the seconds value. After the 10 seconds, Pending is replaced by Executed, and the result of calling the function is displayed. If you watch carefully, LISLab will give focus to the Function combo box and show that the combo box now has the focus. But the Program Manager will still be receiving your keystrokes. LISLab's thread thinks that the combo box has the focus, and the Program Manager's thread thinks that one of its windows has the focus. However, the RIT remains "connected" to the Program Manager's thread.

One final point about windows and the focus: both the *SetFocus* and *SetActiveWindow* functions return the handle to the window that originally had the focus or was active. The information for this window is displayed in the PrevWnd field in the LISLab dialog box. Also, just before LISLab calls *SetForegroundWindow*, it calls *GetForegroundWindow* to get the handle of the window that was originally in the foreground. This information is also displayed in the PrevWnd field.

It's time to move on to experiments involving the mouse cursor. Whenever you move the mouse over LISLab's dialog box (but not over any of its child windows), the mouse is displayed as a vertical arrow. As mouse messages are sent to the dialog box, they are also added to the Mouse Messages Received list box. In this way, you know when the dialog box is receiving mouse messages. If you move the mouse outside the dialog box or over one of its child windows, you'll see that messages are no longer added to the list box.

Now move the mouse to the right of the dialog box over the text Click Right Mouse Button To Set Capture, and click and hold the right mouse button. When you do this, LISLab calls *SetCapture* and passes the handle of LISLab's dialog box. Notice that LISLab reflects that it has capture by updating the Windows group box at the top.

Without releasing the right mouse button, move the mouse over LISLab's child windows and watch the mouse messages being added to the list box. Notice that if you move the mouse outside of LISLab's dialog box, LISLab continues to be notified of mouse messages. The mouse cursor retains its vertical arrow shape no matter where you move the mouse on the screen. This is exactly how mouse capture works in 16-bit Windows.

But now we're ready to see where the system behaves differently. Release the right mouse button, and watch what happens. The capture window reflected at the top of LISLab continues to show that LISLab thinks it still has mouse capture. However, if you move the mouse outside of LISLab's dialog box, the cursor no longer remains a vertical arrow and mouse messages stop going to the Mouse Messages Received list box. If you move the mouse over any of LISLab's child windows, you'll see that capture is still in effect because all the windows are using the same set of local input state variables. This is very different from the way 16-bit Windows works.

When you're done experimenting with mouse capture, you can turn it off using one of two techniques:

- Double-click the right mouse button anywhere in the Local Input State Lab dialog box to have LISLab place a call to *ReleaseCapture*.

- Click on a window created by a thread other than LISLab's thread. When you do this, the system automatically sends mouse button up and mouse button down messages to LISLab's dialog box.

Regardless of which method you choose, watch how the Capture field in the Windows group box changes to reflect that no window has mouse capture.

There are only two more mouse-related experiments: one experiment involves clipping the mouse cursor's movement to a rectangle, and one experiment involves cursor visibility. When you click on the Set To(0,0)-(200,200) button, LISLab executes the following code:

```
RECT rc;
  :
  :
SetRect(&rc, 0, 0, 200, 200);
ClipCursor(&rc);
```

This causes the mouse cursor to be confined in the upper left corner of the screen. If you use Alt+Tab to select another application's window, you'll notice that the clipping rectangle stays in effect. The system automatically stops clipping the mouse and allows it to traverse the entire screen when you perform any of the following operations:

Windows 95	Click on another application's title bar and move the window.
Windows NT	Click on another application's title bar. (You don't have to move the window.)
Windows NT	Invoke and dismiss the Task Manager.

You can also click on the Remove button in the Local Input State Lab dialog box (assuming that the button is in the clipping rectangle) to remove the clipping rectangle.

Clicking on the Hide Cursor or Show Cursor button causes LISLab to execute the following code:

```
ShowCursor(FALSE);
```

or

```
ShowCursor(TRUE);
```

When you hide the mouse cursor, it doesn't appear when you move the mouse over LISLab's dialog box. But the moment you move the mouse outside this dialog box, the cursor appears again. Use the Show Cursor button to counteract the effect of the Hide Cursor button. Note that the effects of hiding the cursor are cumulative. That is, if you click on the Hide Cursor button five times, you must click on the Show Cursor button five times to make the cursor visible.

The last experiment involves using the Infinite Loop button. When you click on this button, LISLab executes the following code:

```
SetCursor(LoadCursor(NULL, IDC_NO));
for (;;)
    ;
```

The first line changes the mouse cursor to a slashed circle, and the second line executes an infinite loop. After you click on the Infinite Loop button, LISLab stops responding to any input whatsoever. If you move the mouse over LISLab's dialog box, the cursor remains as the slashed circle. However, if you move the mouse outside the dialog box, the cursor changes to reflect the cursor of the window over which it is located. You can use the mouse to manipulate these other windows.

If you move the mouse back over LISLab's dialog box, the system sees that LISLab is not responding and automatically changes the cursor back to its most recent shape—the slashed circle. In 16-bit Windows, an application executing an infinite loop hangs not only the application but the whole system. As you can see, on a Win32-based operating system an infinite loop is just a minor inconvenience to the user.

Notice that if you move a window over the hung Local Input State Lab dialog box and then move it away, the system sends LISLab a WM_PAINT message. But the system also realizes that the thread is not responding. The system helps out here by repainting the window for the unresponsive application. Of course, the system cannot repaint the window correctly because it doesn't know what the application is supposed to be doing, so the system simply erases the window's background and redraws the frame.

Now the problem is that we have a window on the screen that isn't responding to anything we do. How do we get rid of it? On Windows 95, we must first press Ctrl+Alt+Del to display the Close Program window shown below:

And on Windows NT, we must first press Ctrl+Esc to display the Task List window shown below:

Then we simply select the application we want to terminate—Local Input State Lab, in this case—and click on the End Task button. The system will attempt to terminate LISLab in a nice way but will notice that the application isn't responding. This causes the system to display the following dialog box:

Local Input State Lab

This Windows application cannot respond to the End Task request. It may be busy, waiting for a response from you, or it may have stopped executing.

o Press Cancel to cancel and return to Windows NT.

o Press End Task to close this application immediately. You will lose any unsaved information in this application.

o Press Wait to give the application 5 seconds to finish what it is doing and then try to close the application again.

[Wait] [End Task] [Cancel]

Choosing End Task causes the system to forcibly remove LISLab from the system. The Wait button (available only if you are running under Windows NT) delays the action; choose it if you think that an application will respond to input again within 5 seconds. We know that LISLab won't respond because its infinite loop will never end. The Cancel button tells the system that you changed your mind and no longer want to terminate the application. Choose End Task to remove LISLab from the system.

The whole point of these experiments is to demonstrate the system's robustness. It's almost impossible for one application to place the operating system in a state that would render the other applications unusable. Also, note that both Windows 95 and Windows NT automatically free all resources that were allocated by threads in the terminated process—there are no memory leaks!

LISLab.ico

LISLAB.C
```
/**********************************************************
Module name: LISLab.C
Notices: Copyright (c) 1995 Jeffrey Richter
**********************************************************/


#include "..\AdvWin32.h"      /* See Appendix B for details. */
#include <windows.h>
#include <windowsx.h>

#pragma warning(disable: 4001)        /* Single-line comment */
```

Figure 10-7.   *(continued)*
The LISLab application.

467

Figure 10-7. *continued*

```
#include <tchar.h>
#include <string.h>
#include <stdio.h>                          // For sprintf
#include "Resource.H"


///////////////////////////////////////////////////////////////////


#define TIMER_DELAY (1 * 1000) // 1 second * 1000 milliseconds

UINT  g_uTimerId = 1;
int   g_nEventId = 0;
DWORD g_dwEventTime = 0;
HWND  g_hwndSubject = NULL;
HWND  g_hwndPM = NULL;


///////////////////////////////////////////////////////////////////


void CalcWndText (HWND hwnd, LPTSTR szBuf, int nLen) {
   TCHAR szClass[50], szCaption[50], szBufT[150];

   if (hwnd == (HWND) NULL) {
      _tcscpy(szBuf, __TEXT("(no window)"));
      return;
   }


   if (!IsWindow(hwnd)) {
      _tcscpy(szBuf, __TEXT("(invalid window)"));
      return;
   }


   GetClassName(hwnd, szClass, ARRAY_SIZE(szClass));
   GetWindowText(hwnd, szCaption, ARRAY_SIZE(szCaption));

   _stprintf(szBufT, __TEXT("[%s] %s"), (LPTSTR) szClass,
      (*szCaption == 0) ? (LPTSTR) __TEXT("(no caption)")
      : (LPTSTR) szCaption);
   _tcsncpy(szBuf, szBufT, nLen - 1);
   szBuf[nLen - 1] = 0; // Force zero-terminated string
}
```

(continued)

Figure 10-7. *continued*

```
/////////////////////////////////////////////////////////////////

// To minimize stack use, one instance of WALKWINDOWTREEDATA
// is created as a local variable in WalkWindowTree() and a
// pointer to it is passed to WalkWindowTreeRecurse.

// Data used by WalkWindowTreeRecurse
typedef struct {
    HWND  hwndLB;          // Handle to the output list box
    HWND  hwndParent;      // Handle to the parent
    int   nLevel;          // Nesting depth
    int   nIndex;          // List box item index
    TCHAR szBuf[100];      // Output buffer
    int   iBuf;            // Index into szBuf
} WALKWINDOWTREEDATA, *LPWALKWINDOWTREEDATA;


void WalkWindowTreeRecurse (LPWALKWINDOWTREEDATA pWWT) {

    const int nIndexAmount = 2;
    HWND hwndChild;


    pWWT->nLevel++;

    if (!IsWindow(pWWT->hwndParent))
        return;

    for (pWWT->iBuf = 0;
        pWWT->iBuf < pWWT->nLevel * nIndexAmount; pWWT->iBuf++)
        pWWT->szBuf[pWWT->iBuf] = __TEXT(' ');

    CalcWndText(pWWT->hwndParent, &pWWT->szBuf[pWWT->iBuf],
        ARRAY_SIZE(pWWT->szBuf) - pWWT->iBuf);
    pWWT->nIndex = ListBox_AddString(pWWT->hwndLB, pWWT->szBuf);
    ListBox_SetItemData(pWWT->hwndLB, pWWT->nIndex,
        pWWT->hwndParent);

    hwndChild = GetFirstChild(pWWT->hwndParent);
    while (hwndChild != NULL) {
        pWWT->hwndParent = hwndChild;
        WalkWindowTreeRecurse(pWWT);
        hwndChild = GetNextSibling(hwndChild);
    }
```

(continued)

Figure 10-7. *continued*

```
    pWWT->nLevel--;
}


///////////////////////////////////////////////////////////////////


void WalkWindowTree (HWND hwndLB, HWND hwndParent) {

    WALKWINDOWTREEDATA WWT;

    WWT.hwndLB = hwndLB;
    WWT.hwndParent = hwndParent;
    WWT.nLevel = -1;

    WalkWindowTreeRecurse(&WWT);
}


///////////////////////////////////////////////////////////////////


BOOL Dlg_OnInitDialog (HWND hwnd, HWND hwndFocus,
    LPARAM lParam) {

    HWND hwndT;

    // Associate an icon with the dialog box.
    SetClassLong(hwnd, GCL_HICON, (LONG)
        LoadIcon((HINSTANCE) GetWindowLong(hwnd, GWL_HINSTANCE),
        __TEXT("LISLab")));

    g_uTimerId = SetTimer(hwnd, g_uTimerId, TIMER_DELAY, NULL);

    hwndT = GetDlgItem(hwnd, IDC_WNDFUNC);
    ComboBox_AddString(hwndT, __TEXT("SetFocus"));
    ComboBox_AddString(hwndT, __TEXT("SetActiveWindow"));
    ComboBox_AddString(hwndT, __TEXT("SetForegroundWnd"));
    ComboBox_AddString(hwndT, __TEXT("BringWindowToTop"));
    ComboBox_AddString(hwndT, __TEXT("SetWindowPos-TOP"));
    ComboBox_AddString(hwndT, __TEXT("SetWindowPos-BTM"));
    ComboBox_SetCurSel(hwndT, 0);


    // Fill the PMWnds list box with our window and the
    // windows of the Program Manager.
```

(continued)

Figure 10-7. *continued*

```
    // First our own dialog box
    hwndT = GetDlgItem(hwnd, IDC_PMWNDS);
    ListBox_AddString(hwndT,
        __TEXT("---> This dialog box <---"));

    ListBox_SetItemData(hwndT, 0, hwnd);
    ListBox_SetCurSel(hwndT, 0);

    // Now the windows of the Program Manager
    g_hwndPM = FindWindow(__TEXT("PROGMAN"), NULL);
    WalkWindowTree(hwndT, g_hwndPM);

    return(TRUE);
}


///////////////////////////////////////////////////////////////


void Dlg_OnDestroy (HWND hwnd) {
    if (g_uTimerId != 0)
        KillTimer(hwnd, g_uTimerId);
}


///////////////////////////////////////////////////////////////


void Dlg_OnCommand (HWND hwnd, int id, HWND hwndCtl,
    UINT codeNotify) {

    HWND hwndT;
    RECT rc;

    switch (id) {

        case IDCANCEL:
            EndDialog(hwnd, 0);
            break;

        case IDC_FUNCSTART:
            g_dwEventTime = GetTickCount() + 1000 *
                GetDlgItemInt(hwnd, IDC_DELAY, NULL, FALSE);
            hwndT = GetDlgItem(hwnd, IDC_PMWNDS);
```

(continued)

Figure 10-7. *continued*

```
            g_hwndSubject = (HWND)
               ListBox_GetItemData(hwndT,
                  ListBox_GetCurSel(hwndT));
            g_nEventId =
               ComboBox_GetCurSel(GetDlgItem(hwnd, IDC_WNDFUNC));
            SetWindowText(GetDlgItem(hwnd, IDC_EVENTPENDING),
               __TEXT("Pending"));
            break;

         case IDC_THREADATTACH:
            AttachThreadInput(
               GetWindowThreadProcessId(g_hwndPM, NULL),
               GetCurrentThreadId(), TRUE);
            break;

         case IDC_THREADDETACH:
            AttachThreadInput(
               GetWindowThreadProcessId(g_hwndPM, NULL),
               GetCurrentThreadId(), FALSE);
            break;

         case IDC_SETCLIPRECT:
            SetRect(&rc, 0, 0, 200, 200);
            ClipCursor(&rc);
            break;

         case IDC_REMOVECLIPRECT:
            ClipCursor(NULL);
            break;

         case IDC_HIDECURSOR:
            ShowCursor(FALSE);
            break;

         case IDC_SHOWCURSOR:
            ShowCursor(TRUE);
            break;

         case IDC_INFINITELOOP:
            SetCursor(LoadCursor(NULL, IDC_NO));
            for (;;)
               ;
            break;
      }
   }
```

(continued)

Figure 10-7. *continued*

```
//////////////////////////////////////////////////////////


BOOL Dlg_OnSetCursor (HWND hwnd, HWND hwndCursor,
   UINT codeHitTest, UINT msg) {

   SetCursor(LoadCursor(NULL, IDC_UPARROW));
   return(TRUE);
}


//////////////////////////////////////////////////////////


void AddStr (HWND hwndLB, LPCTSTR szBuf) {
   int nIndex;

   do {
      nIndex = ListBox_AddString(hwndLB, szBuf);
      if (nIndex == LB_ERR)
         ListBox_DeleteString(hwndLB, 0);
   } while (nIndex == LB_ERR);

   ListBox_SetCurSel(hwndLB, nIndex);
}


//////////////////////////////////////////////////////////


int Dlg_OnRButtonDown (HWND hwnd, BOOL fDoubleClick,
   int x, int y, UINT keyFlags) {

   TCHAR szBuf[100];
   _stprintf(szBuf,
      __TEXT("Capture=%-3s, Msg=RButtonDown, ")
      __TEXT("DblClk=%-3s, x=%5d, y=%5d"),
      (GetCapture() == NULL) ? __TEXT("No") : __TEXT("Yes"),
      fDoubleClick ? __TEXT("Yes") : __TEXT("No"), x, y);

   AddStr(GetDlgItem(hwnd, IDC_MOUSEMSGS), szBuf);
   if (!fDoubleClick) {
      SetCapture(hwnd);
   } else {
```

(continued)

Figure 10-7. *continued*

```
        ReleaseCapture();
    }
    return(0);
}


//////////////////////////////////////////////////////////////////


int Dlg_OnRButtonUp (HWND hwnd, int x, int y, UINT keyFlags) {
    TCHAR szBuf[100];
    _stprintf(szBuf,
        __TEXT("Capture=%-3s, Msg=RButtonUp,   x=%5d, y=%5d"),
        (GetCapture() == NULL)
            ? __TEXT("No") : __TEXT("Yes"), x, y);

    AddStr(GetDlgItem(hwnd, IDC_MOUSEMSGS), szBuf);
    return(0);
}


//////////////////////////////////////////////////////////////////


int Dlg_OnLButtonDown (HWND hwnd, BOOL fDoubleClick,
    int x, int y, UINT keyFlags) {

    TCHAR szBuf[100];
    _stprintf(szBuf,
        __TEXT("Capture=%-3s, Msg=LButtonDown, ")
        __TEXT("DblClk=%-3s, x=%5d, y=%5d"),
        (GetCapture() == NULL) ? __TEXT("No") : __TEXT("Yes"),
        fDoubleClick ? __TEXT("Yes") : __TEXT("No"), x, y);

    AddStr(GetDlgItem(hwnd, IDC_MOUSEMSGS), szBuf);
    return(0);
}


//////////////////////////////////////////////////////////////////


void Dlg_OnLButtonUp (HWND hwnd, int x, int y,
    UINT keyFlags) {
    TCHAR szBuf[100];
```

(continued)

Figure 10-7. *continued*

```
    _stprintf(szBuf,
        __TEXT("Capture=%-3s, Msg=LButtonUp,   x=%5d, y=%5d"),
        (GetCapture() == NULL)
            ? __TEXT("No") : __TEXT("Yes"), x, y);

    AddStr(GetDlgItem(hwnd, IDC_MOUSEMSGS), szBuf);
}


///////////////////////////////////////////////////////////////


void Dlg_OnMouseMove (HWND hwnd, int x, int y,
    UINT keyFlags) {

    TCHAR szBuf[100];

    _stprintf(szBuf,
        __TEXT("Capture=%-3s, Msg=MouseMove,  x=%5d, y=%5d"),
            (GetCapture() == NULL)
            ? __TEXT("No") : __TEXT("Yes"), x, y);

    AddStr(GetDlgItem(hwnd, IDC_MOUSEMSGS), szBuf);
}


///////////////////////////////////////////////////////////////


void Dlg_OnTimer (HWND hwnd, UINT id) {
    TCHAR szBuf[100];
    RECT rc;
    HWND hwndT;

    CalcWndText(GetFocus(), szBuf, ARRAY_SIZE(szBuf));
    SetWindowText(GetDlgItem(hwnd, IDC_WNDFOCUS), szBuf);

    CalcWndText(GetCapture(), szBuf, ARRAY_SIZE(szBuf));
    SetWindowText(GetDlgItem(hwnd, IDC_WNDCAPTURE), szBuf);

    CalcWndText(GetActiveWindow(), szBuf, ARRAY_SIZE(szBuf));
    SetWindowText(GetDlgItem(hwnd, IDC_WNDACTIVE), szBuf);

    CalcWndText(GetForegroundWindow(), szBuf,
        ARRAY_SIZE(szBuf));
```

(continued)

Figure 10-7. *continued*

```
SetWindowText(GetDlgItem(hwnd, IDC_WNDFOREGROUND), szBuf);

GetClipCursor(&rc);
_stprintf(szBuf,
   __TEXT("left=%d, top=%d, right=%d, bottom=%d"),
   rc.left, rc.top, rc.right, rc.bottom);
SetWindowText(GetDlgItem(hwnd, IDC_CLIPCURSOR), szBuf);


if ((g_dwEventTime == 0) ||
   (GetTickCount() < g_dwEventTime))
   return;

switch (g_nEventId) {
   case 0:  // SetFocus
      g_hwndSubject = SetFocus(g_hwndSubject);
      break;

   case 1:  // SetActiveWindow
      g_hwndSubject = SetActiveWindow(g_hwndSubject);
      break;

   case 2:  // SetForegroundWindow
      hwndT = GetForegroundWindow();
      SetForegroundWindow(g_hwndSubject);
      g_hwndSubject = hwndT;
      break;

   case 3:  // BringWindowToTop
      BringWindowToTop(g_hwndSubject);
      break;

   case 4:  // SetWindowPos w/HWND_TOP
      SetWindowPos(g_hwndSubject, HWND_TOP, 0, 0, 0, 0,
         SWP_NOMOVE | SWP_NOSIZE);
      g_hwndSubject = (HWND) 1;
      break;

   case 5:  // SetWindowPos w/ HWND_BOTTOM
      SetWindowPos(g_hwndSubject, HWND_BOTTOM, 0, 0, 0, 0,
         SWP_NOMOVE | SWP_NOSIZE);
      g_hwndSubject = (HWND) 1;
      break;
}
```

(continued)

Figure 10-7. *continued*

```
    if (g_hwndSubject == (HWND) 1) {
        SetWindowText(GetDlgItem(hwnd, IDC_PREVWND),
            __TEXT("Can't tell."));
    } else {
        CalcWndText(g_hwndSubject, szBuf, ARRAY_SIZE(szBuf));
        SetWindowText(GetDlgItem(hwnd, IDC_PREVWND), szBuf);
    }

    g_hwndSubject = NULL; g_nEventId = 0; g_dwEventTime = 0;
    SetWindowText(GetDlgItem(hwnd, IDC_EVENTPENDING),
        __TEXT("Executed"));
}


///////////////////////////////////////////////////////////////

BOOL CALLBACK Dlg_Proc (HWND hDlg, UINT uMsg,
    WPARAM wParam, LPARAM lParam) {

    BOOL fProcessed = TRUE;

    switch (uMsg) {
        HANDLE_MSG(hDlg, WM_INITDIALOG,      Dlg_OnInitDialog);
        HANDLE_MSG(hDlg, WM_DESTROY,         Dlg_OnDestroy);
        HANDLE_MSG(hDlg, WM_COMMAND,         Dlg_OnCommand);

        HANDLE_MSG(hDlg, WM_MOUSEMOVE,       Dlg_OnMouseMove);

        HANDLE_MSG(hDlg, WM_LBUTTONDOWN,     Dlg_OnLButtonDown);
        HANDLE_MSG(hDlg, WM_LBUTTONDBLCLK,   Dlg_OnLButtonDown);
        HANDLE_MSG(hDlg, WM_LBUTTONUP,       Dlg_OnLButtonUp);

        HANDLE_MSG(hDlg, WM_RBUTTONDOWN,     Dlg_OnRButtonDown);
        HANDLE_MSG(hDlg, WM_RBUTTONDBLCLK,   Dlg_OnRButtonDown);
        HANDLE_MSG(hDlg, WM_RBUTTONUP,       Dlg_OnRButtonUp);

        HANDLE_MSG(hDlg, WM_SETCURSOR,       Dlg_OnSetCursor);
        HANDLE_MSG(hDlg, WM_TIMER,           Dlg_OnTimer);

        default:
            fProcessed = FALSE;
            break;
    }
    return(fProcessed);
}
```

(continued)

Figure 10-7. *continued*

```
//////////////////////////////////////////////////////////////


int WINAPI WinMain (HINSTANCE hinstExe,
   HINSTANCE hinstPrev, LPSTR lpszCmdLine, int nCmdShow) {

   DialogBox(hinstExe, MAKEINTRESOURCE(IDD_LISLAB),
      NULL, Dlg_Proc);

   return(0);
}


/////////////////////// End Of File //////////////////////////
```

LISLAB.RC

```
//Microsoft Visual C++ generated resource script.
//
#include "Resource.h"

#define APSTUDIO_READONLY_SYMBOLS
//////////////////////////////////////////////////////////////
//
// Generated from the TEXTINCLUDE 2 resource.
//
#include "afxres.h"


//////////////////////////////////////////////////////////////
#undef APSTUDIO_READONLY_SYMBOLS


//////////////////////////////////////////////////////////////
//
// Icon
//

LISLab                    ICON    DISCARDABLE    "LISLab.Ico"

//////////////////////////////////////////////////////////////
//
// Dialog
//

IDD_LISLAB DIALOG DISCARDABLE  12, 38, 284, 204
```

(continued)

Figure 10-7. *continued*

```
STYLE WS_MINIMIZEBOX ¦ WS_POPUP ¦ WS_VISIBLE ¦ WS_CAPTION
      ¦ WS_SYSMENU
CAPTION "Local Input State Lab"
FONT 8, "MS Sans Serif"
BEGIN
        GROUPBOX            "Windows",IDC_STATIC,4,0,192,56
        LTEXT               "Focus:",IDC_STATIC,8,12,23,8
        LTEXT               "Focus window info",IDC_WNDFOCUS,
                            52,12,140,8
        LTEXT               "Active:",IDC_STATIC,8,20,24,8
        LTEXT               "Active window info",IDC_WNDACTIVE,
                            52,20,140,8
        LTEXT               "Foreground:",IDC_STATIC,8,28,40,8
        LTEXT               "Foreground window info",
                            IDC_WNDFOREGROUND,52,28,140,8
        LTEXT               "Capture:",IDC_STATIC,8,36,29,8
        LTEXT               "Capture window info",IDC_WNDCAPTURE,
                            52,36,140,8
        LTEXT               "Clip Cursor:",IDC_STATIC,8,44,39,8
        LTEXT               "Cursor clipping info",IDC_CLIPCURSOR,
                            52,44,140,8
        LTEXT               "Function:",IDC_STATIC,200,4,32,8
        COMBOBOX            IDC_WNDFUNC,200,14,82,54,
                            CBS_DROPDOWNLIST ¦ WS_VSCROLL
                            ¦ WS_TABSTOP
        PUSHBUTTON          "Dela&y:",IDC_FUNCSTART,200,30,26,14
        EDITTEXT            IDC_DELAY,228,30,24,12,ES_AUTOHSCROLL
        LTEXT               "Executed",IDC_EVENTPENDING,252,30,32,10
        LTEXT               "PrevWnd:",IDC_STATIC,200,46,34,8
        LTEXT               "Previous window info",IDC_PREVWND,
                            208,54,76,18
        LTEXT               "&Program Manager windows and Self:",
                            IDC_STATIC,4,60,119,8
        LISTBOX             IDC_PMWNDS,4,72,192,42,WS_VSCROLL
                            ¦ WS_TABSTOP
        PUSHBUTTON          "&Attach to ProgMan",IDC_THREADATTACH,
                            200,84,80,12
        PUSHBUTTON          "&Detach from ProgMan",IDC_THREADDETACH,
                            200,100,80,12
        LTEXT               "&Mouse messages received:",IDC_STATIC,
                            4,116,89,8
        LISTBOX             IDC_MOUSEMSGS,4,128,192,42,WS_VSCROLL
                            ¦ WS_TABSTOP
        LTEXT               "Click right mouse button to set capture.\
\n\nDouble-click right mouse button to release capture.",
                            IDC_STATIC,200,128,80,42
```

(continued)

Figure 10-7. *continued*

```
    LTEXT              "Clipping rect:",IDC_STATIC,4,172,44,8
    PUSHBUTTON         "&Set to(0, 0)-(200, 200)",IDC_SETCLIPRECT,
                       52,172,88,12
    PUSHBUTTON         "&Remove",IDC_REMOVECLIPRECT,144,172,52,12
    PUSHBUTTON         "Hide cursor",IDC_HIDECURSOR,4,188,52,12
    PUSHBUTTON         "Show cursor",IDC_SHOWCURSOR,60,188,52,12
    PUSHBUTTON         "&Infinite loop",IDC_INFINITELOOP,
                       200,188,80,12,WS_GROUP | NOT WS_TABSTOP
END


#ifdef APSTUDIO_INVOKED
/////////////////////////////////////////////////////////////////////////
//
// TEXTINCLUDE
//

1 TEXTINCLUDE DISCARDABLE
BEGIN
    "Resource.h\0"
END

2 TEXTINCLUDE DISCARDABLE
BEGIN
    "#include ""afxres.h""\r\n"
    "\0"
END

3 TEXTINCLUDE DISCARDABLE
BEGIN
    "\r\n"
    "\0"
END


/////////////////////////////////////////////////////////////////////////
#endif    // APSTUDIO_INVOKED


#ifndef APSTUDIO_INVOKED
/////////////////////////////////////////////////////////////////////////
//
// Generated from the TEXTINCLUDE 3 resource.
//


/////////////////////////////////////////////////////////////////////////
#endif    // not APSTUDIO_INVOKED
```

DYNAMIC-LINK LIBRARIES

Dynamic-link libraries (DLLs) have been the cornerstone of Windows since the very first version of the operating system. All the functions in the Win32 API are contained in DLLs. The three most important DLLs are KERNEL32.DLL, which consists of functions for managing memory, processes, and threads; USER32.DLL, which consists of functions for performing user-interface tasks such as window creation and message sending; and GDI32.DLL, which consists of functions for drawing graphical images and displaying text.

Windows also comes with several other DLLs that contain functions for performing more specialized tasks. For example, ADVAPI32.DLL contains functions for object security, registry manipulation, and event logging; COMDLG32.DLL contains the common dialogs (such as File Open and File Save); and LZ32.DLL supports file decompression.

In this chapter, I discuss how you can create Win32 DLLs for your own applications. In addition, the end of the chapter describes some advanced techniques that require the use of DLLs; you'll find other advanced techniques in Chapter 16.

Creating a Dynamic-Link Library

It is often easier to create a dynamic-link library than it is to create an application. This is because a dynamic-link library usually consists of a set of autonomous functions that any application can use. There is usually no support code for processing message loops or creating windows within DLLs. A dynamic-link library is simply a set of source code modules, with each module containing a set of functions. These functions are written with the expectation that an application (EXE file) or another DLL will call them. After all the source code files have been compiled, they are then linked by the linker just as an application's EXE file would be.

However, for a DLL you must specify the /DLL switch to the linker. This switch causes the linker to emit slightly different information into the resulting DLL file image so that the operating system loader recognizes the file image as a dynamic-link library rather than an application.

In order for an application (or another DLL) to call functions contained within a DLL, the DLL's file image must first be mapped into the calling process's address space. This can be accomplished using one of two methods: implicit load-time linking or explicit run-time linking. These methods will be discussed shortly.

Once a DLL's file image is mapped into the calling process's address space, the DLL's functions are available to all the threads running within the process. In fact, the DLL loses almost all of its identity as a DLL: to all the threads in the process, the DLL's code and data simply look like additional code and data that just happen to be in the process's address space. Whenever a thread calls any DLL function, the DLL function looks at the thread's stack to retrieve its passed parameters and also uses the thread's stack for any local variables that the DLL function might need. In addition, any objects created by code in the DLL's functions are owned by the calling thread or process—a DLL never owns anything in Win32.

For example, if *VirtualAlloc* is called by a function in a DLL, the region of address space is reserved from the address space of the calling thread's process. If the DLL is later unmapped from the process's address space, the address space region remains reserved because the system does not keep track of the fact that a function in the DLL reserved the region. The reserved region is owned by the process and will be freed only if a thread somehow calls the *VirtualFree* function or if the process terminates.

As you already know, the global and static variables of an EXE file are not shared between multiple, running instances of the same EXE. Windows 95 ensures this by allocating storage for the EXE's global and static variables when the EXE is mapped into the process's address space; Windows NT ensures this by using the copy-on-write mechanism discussed in Chapter 4. Global and static variables in a DLL are handled in exactly the same way. When one process maps a DLL image file into its address space, the system creates instances of the global and static data variables as well. Later in this chapter, I discuss a technique that allows a DLL to share its global and static variables across multiple mappings of the DLL. However, this technique is not the default in Win32—you must perform some additional actions in order to get this behavior.

16 ·ᐧ· 32

DLLs are managed quite differently in 16-bit Windows than in Win32. In 16-bit Windows, loading a DLL means that, in a sense, the DLL becomes part of the operating system. After the DLL is loaded, any and all applications currently running immediately have access to the DLL and the functions that the DLL contains. In the Win32 environment, a DLL *must* be mapped into the process's address space before an application can successfully call functions in the DLL.

The 16-bit Windows environment and the Win32 environment handle a DLL's global and static data quite differently as well. In 16-bit Windows, each DLL has its own data segment. This data segment houses all the static and global variables needed by the DLL as well as the DLL's own private local heap. When a DLL function allocates memory using *LocalAlloc*, the memory that satisfies this request is taken from the DLL's data segment. This segment, like all segments, is limited to 64 KB.

This design allows applications to easily share data among multiple processes because the DLL's local heap is available to the DLL regardless of which process called the function contained in the DLL. Here is an example of how a DLL can be used for sharing data between two applications:

```
HLOCAL g_hData = NULL;

void SetData (LPVOID lpvData, int nSize) {
   LPVOID lpv;
   g_hData = LocalAlloc(LMEM_MOVEABLE, nSize);
   lpv = LocalLock(g_hData);
   memcpy(lpv, lpvData, nSize);
   LocalUnlock(g_hData);
}

void GetData (LPVOID lpvData, int nSize) {
   LPVOID lpv = LocalLock(g_hData);
   memcpy(lpvData, lpv, nSize);
   LocalUnlock(g_hData);
}
```

When *SetData* is called, it allocates a block of memory out of the DLL's data segment, copies the data pointed to by the *lpvData* parameter into the block, and saves the handle to the block in a global variable, *g_hData*. A totally different application can now call *GetData*. *GetData* uses the global variable identifying the local memory handle, locks the block, copies the data into the buffer identified by the *lpvData* parameter, and returns. This is an easy way to share data between two processes in 16-bit Windows.

(continued)

16 -•- 32

continued

Of course, this method doesn't work at all in Win32 for two reasons. First, DLLs in Win32 don't receive their own local heaps. Second, a Win32 DLL's global and static variables are not shared among multiple mappings of the DLL—the system creates an instance of the global *g_hData* variable for each process, and each instance will not have the same value when the DLL is mapped into multiple processes' address spaces.

Mapping a DLL into a Process's Address Space

As I mentioned earlier, in order for a thread to call a function in a DLL, the DLL's file image must be mapped into the address space of the calling thread's process. There are two ways that this can be accomplished: implicitly linking to functions in the DLL and explicitly loading the DLL.

Implicit Linking

Implicit linking is the most common method for mapping a DLL's file image into a process's address space. When you link an application, you must specify a set of LIB files to the linker. Each LIB file contains the list of functions that a DLL file is allowing an application (or another DLL) to call. When the linker sees that the application is calling a function that is referenced in a DLL's LIB file, the linker embeds information into the resultant EXE file image that indicates the name of the DLL containing the functions that the EXE requires. When the operating system loads an EXE file, the system examines the contents of the EXE file image to see which DLLs must be loaded in order for the application to run. The system then attempts to map the required DLL file images into the process's address space. When searching for the DLL, the system looks for the file image in the following locations:

1. The directory containing the EXE image file

2. The process's current directory

3. The Windows system directory

4. The Windows directory

5. The directories listed in the PATH environment variable

If the DLL file cannot be found, the operating system displays a message box that looks something like the one on the facing page and immediately terminates the entire process.

When using this method, any DLL file images mapped into the process's address space are not unmapped until the process is terminated.

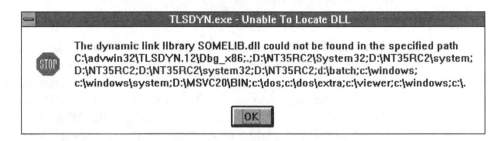

Explicit Linking

A DLL's file image can be explicitly mapped into a process's address space when one of the process's threads calls either the *LoadLibrary* or the *LoadLibraryEx* function:

```
HINSTANCE LoadLibrary(LPCTSTR lpszLibFile);

HINSTANCE LoadLibraryEx(LPCTSTR lpszLibFile, HANDLE hFile,
    DWORD dwFlags);
```

Both of these functions locate a file image on the user's system (using the same search algorithm discussed in the previous section) and attempt to map the DLL's file image into the calling process's address space. The HINSTANCE value returned from both of these functions identifies the virtual memory address where the file image was mapped. If the DLL could not be mapped into the process's address space, the functions return NULL.

Under 16-bit Windows, *LoadLibrary* indicates that an error has occurred by returning a handle value less than 32. The value returned indicates the reason for the failure. In Win32, NULL is always returned if an error occurs. To determine the reason for the error, the thread must call *GetLastError.*

You'll notice that the *LoadLibraryEx* function has two additional parameters: *hFile* and *dwFlags*. The *hFile* parameter is reserved for future use and must be NULL for now.

For the *dwFlags* parameter, you must specify either 0 or any combination of the following three flags: DONT_RESOLVE_DLL_REFERENCES, LOAD_LIBRARY_AS_DATAFILE, and LOAD_WITH_ALTERED_ SEARCH_PATH. These flags are discussed briefly below:

DONT_RESOLVE_DLL_REFERENCES Specifying this flag tells the system to map the DLL into the calling process's address space. Normally, when a DLL is mapped into a process's address space the system calls a special function in the DLL, usually named *DllMain* (discussed later in this chapter), that is used to initialize the DLL. Specifying the DONT_RESOLVE_DLL_REFERENCES flag causes the system to simply map the file image without calling the *DllMain* function.

In addition, a DLL might import functions contained in another DLL. When the system maps a DLL into a process's address space, the system also checks to see whether any additional DLLs are required by the DLL and automatically loads these DLLs as well. When the DONT-_RESOLVE_DLL_REFERENCES flag is specified, the system does not automatically load any of these additional DLLs into the process's address space.

LOAD_LIBRARY_AS_DATAFILE This flag is very similar to the DONT-_RESOLVE_DLL_REFERENCES flag. That is, the system simply maps the DLL into the process's address space as though it were a data file. No additional time is spent by the system in preparation to execute any code in the file. For example, when a DLL is mapped into a process's address space, the system examines some information in the DLL in order to determine which page protection attributes should be assigned to different sections of the file. When you don't specify the LOAD_LIBRARY-_AS_DATAFILE flag, the system sets the page protection attributes the same way it would if it were expecting to execute code in the file.

You might want to use this flag for several reasons. First, if you have a DLL that contains only resources and no functions, you might want to specify this flag. This way, the DLL's file image gets mapped into the process's address space and you can then use the HINSTANCE value returned from *LoadLibraryEx* in calls to functions that load resources. You might also use the LOAD_LIBRARY_AS_DATAFILE flag if you want to use resources that are contained inside an EXE file. Normally, loading an EXE file starts a new process, but you can also use the *LoadLibraryEx* function to map an EXE file's image into a process's address space. Again, once you have the mapped EXE's HINSTANCE value, you can access resources contained within it. Because an EXE file does not have the *DllMain* function, you'll have to specify the LOAD_LIBRARY_AS-_DATAFILE flag when calling *LoadLibraryEx* to load an EXE file.

LOAD_WITH_ALTERED_SEARCH_PATH   Specifying this flag changes the search algorithm used by *LoadLibraryEx* in order to locate the specified DLL file. Normally, *LoadLibraryEx* searches for files in the order shown at the bottom of page 484. However, if the LOAD_WITH_AL-TERED_SEARCH_PATH flag is specified, *LoadLibraryEx* searches for the file using the following algorithm:

1. The directory specified in the *lpszLibFile* parameter

2. The process's current directory

3. The Windows system directory

4. The Windows directory

5. The directories listed in the PATH environment variable

When explicitly loading a DLL, you may explicitly unmap the file image from the process's address space at any time by calling the *Free-Library* function:

```
BOOL FreeLibrary(HINSTANCE hinstDll);
```

When calling *FreeLibrary*, you must pass the HINSTANCE value that identifies the DLL that you want to free. This value was returned by an earlier call to *LoadLibrary* or *LoadLibraryEx*.

In reality, the *LoadLibrary* and *LoadLibraryEx* functions increment a usage count associated with the specified library, and the *FreeLibrary* function decrements the library's usage count. For example, the first time you call *LoadLibrary* to load a DLL, the system maps the DLL's file image into the calling process's address space and associates a usage count of 1 with the DLL. If a thread in the same process later calls *LoadLibrary* to load the same DLL file image, the system does not map the DLL file image into the process's address space a second time. Instead, the system simply increments the usage count associated with the DLL. In order for the DLL file image to be unmapped from the process's address space, threads in the process must call *FreeLibrary* twice—the first call to *FreeLibrary* simply decrements the DLL's usage count to 1, and the second call to *FreeLibrary* decrements the DLL's usage count to 0. When the system sees that a DLL's usage count has reached 0, the system automatically unmaps the DLL's file image from the process's address space. After the DLL's file image is unmapped, any thread that attempts to call a function in the DLL will raise an access violation because the code at the specified address is no longer mapped into the process's address space.

Notice that the system maintains a DLL's usage count on a per-process basis. That is, if a thread in Process A makes the following call:

```
HINSTANCE hinstDll = LoadLibrary("MyLib.DLL");
```

and then a thread in Process B makes the exact same call, MYLIB.DLL is mapped into both processes' address spaces—the DLL's usage count in Process A and the DLL's usage count in Process B are both 1. If a thread in Process B later calls:

```
FreeLibrary(hinstDll);
```

the DLL's usage count with respect to Process B becomes 0, and the DLL is unmapped from Process B's address space. However, the mapping of the DLL in Process A's address space is unaffected, and the DLL's usage count with respect to Process A remains 1.

A thread can call the *GetModuleHandle* function:

```
HINSTANCE GetModuleHandle(LPCTSTR lpszModuleName);
```

to determine whether a DLL is mapped into its process's address space. For example, the following code loads MYLIB.DLL only if it is not already mapped into the process's address space:

```
HINSTANCE hinstDll;
hinstDll = GetModuleHandle("MyLib");    // DLL extension assumed
if (hinstDll == NULL) {
   hinstDll = LoadLibrary("MyLib");     // DLL extension assumed
}
```

You can also determine the full pathname of a DLL (or an EXE) if all you have is the DLL's HINSTANCE value by using the *GetModuleFileName* function:

```
DWORD GetModuleFileName(HINSTANCE hinstModule,
   LPTSTR lpszPath, DWORD cchPath);
```

The first parameter is the DLL's (or EXE's) HINSTANCE. The second parameter, *lpszPath*, is the address of the buffer where the function will put the file image's full pathname. The third and last parameter, *cchPath*, specifies the size of the buffer in characters.

The 16-bit Windows API has a *GetModuleUsage* function:

```
int GetModuleUsage(HINSTANCE hinstDll);
```

When you pass this function the HINSTANCE value of a loaded DLL, the system returns the usage count of the DLL. The usage count tells you how many times *FreeLibrary* would have to be called before the DLL would actually be unloaded. Remember that in 16-bit Windows, DLLs become part of the operating system and are available to all running tasks. Because DLLs in Win32 become part of the calling process's address space rather than part of the operating system itself, *GetModuleUsage* is no longer supported in the Win32 API.

Personally, I think Microsoft should have kept *GetModuleUsage* in the Win32 API because it's useful to know the usage count of a DLL with respect to the calling process. The operating system keeps track of this information internally already—it would have been easy for Microsoft to modify *GetModuleUsage* so that it simply returned this information.

There is another Win32 function that you can use to decrement a DLL's usage count:

```
VOID FreeLibraryAndExitThread(HINSTANCE hinstDll,
   DWORD dwExitCode);
```

This function is implemented in KERNEL32.DLL as follows:

```
VOID FreeLibraryAndExitThread(HINSTANCE hinstDll,
   DWORD dwExitCode) {
   FreeLibrary(hinstDll);
   ExitThread(dwExitCode);
}
```

At first glance this doesn't look like such a big deal, and you might ask yourself why Microsoft went to the trouble to create the *FreeLibraryAndExitThread* function. The reason has to do with the following scenario: Suppose you are writing a DLL that, when it is first mapped into a process's address space, creates a thread. When the thread is finished performing its work, the thread can unmap the DLL from the process's address space. In order for the thread to unmap the DLL, the thread must call *FreeLibrary* and then immediately call *ExitThread*.

But if the thread calls *FreeLibrary* and *ExitThread* individually, a very serious problem occurs. The problem, of course, is that the call to *FreeLibrary* unmaps the DLL from the process's address space immediately. By the time the call to *FreeLibrary* returns, the code that contains the call to *ExitThread* is no longer available and the thread will attempt to execute nothing. This will cause an access violation to be raised, and the entire process will be terminated!

However, if the thread calls *FreeLibraryAndExitThread*, this function calls *FreeLibrary*, causing the DLL to be immediately unmapped. The next instruction executed is in KERNEL32.DLL, not in the DLL that has just been unmapped. This means that the thread can continue executing and can call *ExitThread*. *ExitThread* will cause the thread to terminate and will not return.

Granted, you will probably not have much need for the *FreeLibrary-AndExitThread* function. I have had a need for it only once myself, and I was performing a very specialized task. Also, at the time I was writing my code for Windows NT 3.1, which did not offer this function. So I was very glad to see that Microsoft had added it to Windows NT 3.5 and Windows 95.

The DLL's Entry/Exit Function

A Win32 DLL can, optionally, have a single entry/exit function. The system calls this DLL entry/exit function at various times that I will discuss later. These calls are informational and are usually used by a DLL to perform any per-process or per-thread initialization and cleanup. If your DLL doesn't require these notifications, you do not have to implement this function in your DLL source code. For example, if you create a DLL that contains only resources, you do not need to implement this function. If you do have this entry/exit function, it must look like this:

```
BOOL WINAPI DllMain (HINSTANCE hinstDll, DWORD fdwReason,
   LPVOID lpvReserved) {

   switch (fdwReason) {
      case DLL_PROCESS_ATTACH:
         // The DLL is being mapped into
         // the process's address space.
         break;

      case DLL_THREAD_ATTACH:
         // A thread is being created.
         break;

      case DLL_THREAD_DETACH:
         // A thread is exiting cleanly.
         break;
```

```
    case DLL_PROCESS_DETACH:
        // The DLL is being unmapped from
        // the process's address space.
        break;
    }
    return(TRUE);
}
```

When producing DLLs for 16-bit Windows, you always need to link a small assembly language module into your DLL. This module performs some low-level initialization and calls your *LibMain* function, passing parameters that the system has passed to the assembly language module in CPU registers. Fortunately, Microsoft includes the source code for this module on the SDK disks. The assembled OBJ file is also included on the SDK disks, which is helpful to those of us who don't own a macro assembler.

As mentioned earlier, Win32 is designed as a portable API capable of running on different hardware platforms using different CPUs. To accomplish this, Microsoft needed to remove the necessity for any assembly language modules. This means that to create a DLL, you need only to write your code and link it as if it were an application. Most of your DLLs should port directly to Win32 with very little modification. The two areas that will require modification are the *LibMain* and *Windows Exit Procedure (WEP)* functions.

In 16-bit Windows, the system calls the library's *LibMain* function whenever the library is loaded into the system and calls the library's *WEP* function whenever the library is being removed from the system. Conceptually, the *WEP* function was a nice addition to 16-bit Windows (it didn't exist prior to version 3.0), but there were many problems with the way that Windows made use of the function. In low-memory situations, the *WEP* function could actually be called before the *LibMain* function, and it might be called using the Kernel's very small stack. This meant that using local variables in the *WEP* function might cause the entire system to crash. You'll be happy to know that all these problems have been solved in Win32.

The *DllMain* function replaces the *LibMain* and *WEP* functions used in 16-bit Windows DLLs.

The operating system calls this entry/exit function at various times. Whenever the function is called, the *hinstDll* parameter contains the instance handle of the DLL. Like the *hinstExe* parameter to *WinMain*, this value identifies the virtual memory address of where the DLL's file image was mapped in the process's address space. Usually, you'll save this parameter in a global variable so that you can use it in calls that load resources, such as *DialogBox* and *LoadString*. The last parameter, *lpvReserved*, is reserved and is usually passed to you as NULL.

The *fdwReason* parameter indicates why the system is calling the function. This parameter can be one of four possible values: DLL_PROCESS_ATTACH, DLL_PROCESS_DETACH, DLL_THREAD_ATTACH, or DLL_THREAD_DETACH. These values and their meanings are discussed in the following sections.

DLL_PROCESS_ATTACH

When a DLL is first mapped into a process's address space, the system calls the DLL's *DllMain* function, passing it a value of DLL_PROCESS_ATTACH for the *fdwReason* parameter. This happens only when the DLL's file image is first mapped. If a thread later calls *LoadLibrary* or *LoadLibraryEx* for a DLL that is already mapped into the process's address space, the operating system simply increments the DLL's usage count; it does *not* call the DLL's *DllMain* function again with a value of DLL_PROCESS_ATTACH.

When processing DLL_PROCESS_ATTACH, a DLL should perform any process-relative initialization required by functions contained within the DLL. For example, the DLL might contain functions that need to use their own heap (created in the process's address space). The DLL's *DllMain* function could create this heap by calling *HeapCreate* during its processing of the DLL_PROCESS_ATTACH notification. The handle to the created heap could be saved in a global variable that the DLL functions have access to.

When *DllMain* is processing a DLL_PROCESS_ATTACH notification, *DllMain*'s return value indicates whether the DLL's initialization was successful. If, for example, the call to *HeapCreate* was successful, you should return TRUE from *DllMain*. If the heap could not be created, return FALSE. For any of the other *fdwReason* values—DLL_PROCESS_DETACH, DLL_THREAD_ATTACH, and DLL_THREAD_DETACH—the system ignores the return value from *DllMain*.

Of course, there must be some thread in the system that is responsible for executing the code in the *DllMain* function. When a new process is created, the system allocates the process's address space and then maps the EXE file image and all of the required DLL file images into the process's address space. Then the system creates the process's primary thread and uses this thread to call each of the DLL's *DllMain* functions with a value of DLL_PROCESS_ATTACH. After all of the mapped DLLs have responded to this notification, the system causes the process's primary thread to begin executing the EXE's C run-time startup code, followed by the EXE's *WinMain* function. If any of the DLL's *DllMain* functions return FALSE, indicating unsuccessful initialization, the system terminates the entire process, removing all the file images from its address space and displaying a message box to the user stating that the process could not be started.

Now let's look at what happens when a DLL is loaded explicitly. When a thread in a process calls *LoadLibrary* or *LoadLibraryEx*, the system locates the specified DLL and maps the DLL into the process's address space. Then the system calls the DLL's *DllMain* function with a value of DLL_PROCESS_ATTACH, using the thread that placed the call to *LoadLibrary* or *LoadLibraryEx*. After the DLL's *DllMain* function has processed the notification, the system allows the call to *LoadLibrary* or *LoadLibraryEx* to return, and the thread continues processing as normal. If the *DllMain* function returned FALSE, indicating that the initialization was unsuccessful, the system automatically unmaps the DLL's file image from the process's address space and NULL is returned from the call to *LoadLibrary* or *LoadLibraryEx*.

In 16-bit Windows, a DLL's *LibMain* function is called only once, when the DLL is loaded. If other applications are loaded and require the same DLL, 16-bit Windows doesn't call the DLL's *LibMain* function again. In contrast, a Win32 DLL's *DllMain* function is called with a value of DLL_PROCESS_ATTACH every time the DLL is mapped into another process's address space. If 10 applications require LIBXYZ.DLL, LIBXYZ's *DllMain* is called 10 times with a value of DLL_PROCESS_ATTACH.

DLL_PROCESS_DETACH

When a DLL is unmapped from a process's address space, the system calls the DLL's *DllMain* function, passing it an *fdwReason* value of DLL-_PROCESS_DETACH. A DLL should perform any process-relative cleanup when processing this value. For example, a DLL might call *HeapDestroy* to destroy a heap that it created during the DLL_PROCESS-_ATTACH notification.

Important

If a DLL's *DllMain* function is called with an *fdwReason* value of DLL-_PROCESS_ATTACH and *DllMain* returns FALSE, indicating unsuccessful initialization, the system will still call the DLL's *DllMain* function with a value of DLL_PROCESS_DETACH. For this reason, you must make sure that you don't try to clean up anything that wasn't successfully initialized.

For example, examine the *DllMain* function below to see whether you can determine where a possible memory access violation might occur:

```
BOOL WINAPI DllMain(HINSTANCE hinstDll, DWORD fdwReason,
   LPVOID lpvReserved) {

   static PVOID pvData = NULL;
   BOOL fOk = TRUE;   // Assume success.

   switch (fdwReason) {
     case DLL_PROCESS_ATTACH:
        pData = HeapAlloc(GetProcessHeap(), 0, 1000);
        if (pData == NULL)
           fOk = FALSE;
        break;

     case DLL_PROCESS_DETACH:
        HeapFree(GetProcessHeap(), 0, pData);
        break;
   }

   return(fOk);   // Used only for DLL_PROCESS_ATTACH
}
```

The code looks harmless enough. When the DLL is attached to the process's address space, a small memory block is allocated. If the block could not be allocated, *DllMain* returns FALSE, indicating that the DLL was unable to initialize properly. When the DLL is unmapped from the

(continued)

Important

continued

process's address space, the allocated memory block is freed. Here's the problem: In the fragment on the previous page, you'll see that if a library's *DllMain* returns FALSE when processing its DLL_PROCESS-_ATTACH notification, the system calls *DllMain* again with a value of DLL_PROCESS_DETACH. This means that *HeapFree* will be called to free a memory block, even though that memory block was never allocated successfully. To correct the problem, you must rewrite the DLL_PROCESS_DETACH case as follows:

```
case DLL_PROCESS_DETACH:
   if (pvData != NULL)
      HeapFree(GetProcessHeap(), 0, pvData);
   break;
```

If the DLL is being unmapped because the process is terminating, the thread that calls *ExitProcess* is responsible for executing the *DllMain* function's code. Under normal circumstances, this is the application's primary thread. When your *WinMain* function returns to the C run-time library's startup code, the startup code explicitly calls the *ExitProcess* function to terminate the process.

If the DLL is being unmapped because a thread in the process called *FreeLibrary*, the *DllMain* function code is executed by the thread that called *FreeLibrary*. The call to *FreeLibrary* will not return until after the *DllMain* function has finished executing.

Important

If a process terminates because some thread in the system calls *Terminate-Process*, the system does *not* call the DLL's *DllMain* function with a value of DLL_PROCESS_DETACH. This means that any DLLs mapped into the process's address space will not have the chance to perform any cleanup before the process terminates. This could result in the loss of data. The *TerminateProcess* function should be used only as a last resort!

Figure 11-1 on the following page shows the steps that are performed when a thread calls *LoadLibrary*.

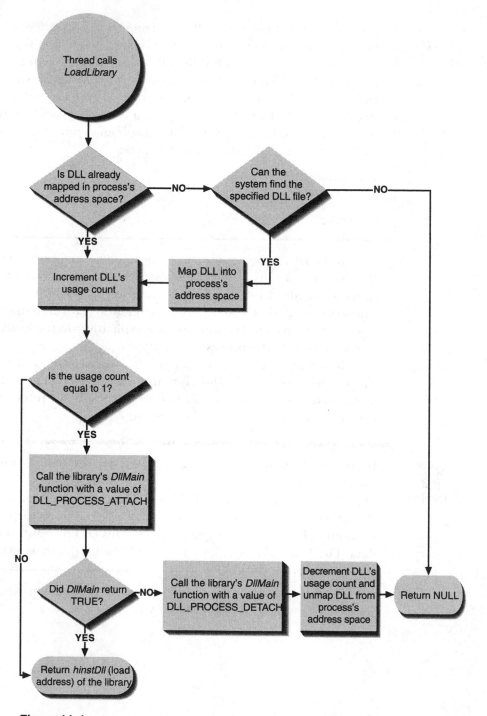

Figure 11-1.
The steps performed by the system when a thread calls LoadLibrary.

Figure 11-2 shows the steps that are performed when a thread calls *FreeLibrary*.

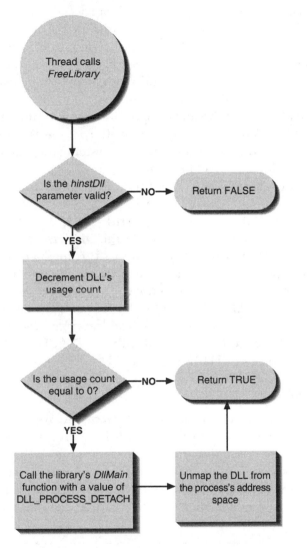

Figure 11-2.
The steps performed by the system when a thread calls FreeLibrary.

DLL_THREAD_ATTACH

When a thread is created in a process, the system examines all of the DLL file images currently mapped into the process's address space and calls each of these DLL's *DllMain* functions with a value of DLL_THREAD-_ATTACH. This notification tells all the DLLs to perform any per-thread initialization. For example, the DLL version of the C run-time library allocates a block of data so that a multithreaded application can safely use functions contained in the C run-time library.

The newly created thread is responsible for executing the code in all of the DLL's *DllMain* functions. Only after all the DLLs have had a chance to process this notification will the system allow the new thread to begin executing its thread function.

If a process already has several threads running in it when a new DLL is mapped into its address space, the system does *not* call the DLL's *DllMain* function with a value of DLL_THREAD_ATTACH for any of the already existing threads. The system calls the DLL's *DllMain* with a value of DLL_THREAD_ATTACH only if the DLL is mapped into the process's address space at the time that a new thread is created.

Also note that the system does not call any *DllMain* functions with a value of DLL_THREAD_ATTACH for the process's primary thread. Any DLLs that are mapped into the process's address space when the process is first invoked receive the DLL_PROCESS_ATTACH notification but do not receive the DLL_THREAD_ATTACH notification.

DLL_THREAD_DETACH

When a thread terminates by calling *ExitThread*,[1] the system examines all the DLL file images currently mapped into the process's address space and calls each DLL's *DllMain* function with a value of DLL_THREAD-_DETACH. This notification tells all the DLLs to perform any per-thread cleanup. For example, the DLL version of the C run-time library frees the data block that it uses to manage multithreaded applications.

---

1. If you allow your thread function to return instead of calling *ExitThread*, the system calls the *ExitThread* function automatically.

Important

If a thread terminates because a thread in the system calls *Terminate-Thread*, the system does *not* call all of the DLL's *DllMain* functions with a value of DLL_THREAD_DETACH. This means that any DLLs mapped into the process's address space will not have the chance to perform any cleanup before the thread terminates. This may result in the loss of data. Like *TerminateProcess*, *TerminateThread* should be used only as a last resort!

If any threads are still running when the DLL is detached, *DllMain* is not called with DLL_THREAD_DETACH for any of the threads. You might want to check for this in your DLL_PROCESS_DETACH processing so that you can perform any necessary cleanup.

Because of the rules stated above, it is possible to have the following situation occur: A thread in a process calls *LoadLibrary* to load a DLL, causing the system to call the DLL's *DllMain* function with a value of DLL_PROCESS_ATTACH. Next the thread that loaded the DLL exits, causing the DLL's *DllMain* function to be called again, this time with a value of DLL_THREAD_DETACH. Notice that the DLL is being notified that the thread is detaching but that it never received a DLL_THREAD-_ATTACH notifying the library that the thread had attached. For this reason, you must be extremely careful when performing any thread-relative cleanup. Fortunately, most programs are written so that the thread that calls *LoadLibrary* is the same thread that calls *FreeLibrary*.

How the System Serializes Calls to *DllMain*

The system serializes calls to a DLL's *DllMain* function. To understand what I mean, consider the following scenario. A process has two threads, Thread A and Thread B. The process also has a DLL, SOMEDLL.DLL, mapped into its address space. Both threads are about to call the *CreateThread* function in order to create two more threads: Thread C and Thread D.

When Thread A calls *CreateThread* to create Thread C, the system calls SOMEDLL's *DllMain* function with a value of DLL_THREAD_AT-TACH. While Thread C is executing the code in the *DllMain* function, Thread B calls *CreateThread* in order to create Thread D. The system needs to call the *DllMain* function again with a value of DLL_THREAD-_ATTACH, this time having Thread D execute the code. However, calls to *DllMain* are serialized by the system, and the system will suspend Thread D until Thread C has completely processed the code in *DllMain* and returned.

After Thread C has finished processing the *DllMain* function, it can begin executing its thread function. Now the system wakes up Thread D and allows it to process the code in *DllMain*. When it returns, Thread D will begin processing its thread function.

Normally, you don't even think about this *DllMain* serialization. The reason I am making a big deal out of it is that I worked with someone who had a bug in his code caused by *DllMain* serialization. His code looked something like this:

```
BOOL WINAPI DllMain (HINSTANCE hinstDll, DWORD fdwReason,
   LPVOID lpvReserved) {

   HANDLE hThread;
   DWORD dwThreadId;

   switch (fdwReason) {
   case DLL_PROCESS_ATTACH:
      // The DLL is being mapped into the
      // process's address space.

      // Create a thread to do some stuff.
      hThread = CreateThread(NULL, 0, SomeFunction, NULL,
         0, &dwThreadId);

      // Suspend our thread until the new thread terminates.
      WaitForSingleObject(hThread, INFINITE);

      // We no longer need access to the new thread.
      CloseHandle(hThread);
      break;

   case DLL_THREAD_ATTACH:
      // A thread is being created.
      break;

   case DLL_THREAD_DETACH:
      // A thread is exiting cleanly.
      break;

   case DLL_PROCESS_DETACH:
      // The DLL is being unmapped from the
      // process's address space.
      break;
   }
   return(TRUE);
}
```

It took us several hours to discover the problem with the code on the previous page. Can you see it? When *DllMain* receives a DLL_PROCESS_ATTACH notification, a new thread is created. The system needs to call this *DllMain* function again with a value of DLL_THREAD_ATTACH. However, the new thread is suspended because the thread that caused the DLL_PROCESS_ATTACH notification to be sent to *Dll-Main* has not finished processing yet. The problem is the call to *WaitForSingleObject*. This function suspends the currently executing thread until the new thread terminates. However, the new thread will never get a chance to run, let alone terminate, because it is suspended waiting for the current thread to exit the *DllMain* function. What we have here is a deadlock situation—both threads are forever suspended!

When I first started thinking about ways to solve this problem, I discovered the *DisableThreadLibraryCalls* function:

```
BOOL DisableThreadLibraryCalls(HINSTANCE hinstDll);
```

This function was introduced with Windows NT 3.5 and exists in Windows 95 as well.

When you call *DisableThreadLibraryCalls*, you are telling the system that you do not want DLL_THREAD_ATTACH and DLL_THREAD_DETACH notifications sent to the specified DLL's *DllMain* function. It seemed reasonable to me that, if we told the system not to send DLL notifications to the DLL, the deadlock situation would not occur. However, when I tested my solution (below), I soon discovered that the problem was not solved.

```
BOOL WINAPI DllMain (HINSTANCE hinstDll, DWORD fdwReason,
   LPVOID lpvReserved) {

   HANDLE hThread;
      DWORD dwThreadId;

   switch (fdwReason) {
   case DLL_PROCESS_ATTACH:
      // The DLL is being mapped into the process's address space.

      // Prevent the system from calling DllMain
      // when threads are created or destroyed.
      DisableThreadLibraryCalls(hinstDll);

      // Create a thread to do some stuff.
      hThread = CreateThread(NULL, 0, SomeFunction, NULL,
         0, &dwThreadId);
```

(continued)

501

```
        // Suspend our thread until the new thread terminates.
        WaitForSingleObject(hThread, INFINITE);

        // We no longer need access to the new thread.
        CloseHandle(hThread);
        break;

    case DLL_THREAD_ATTACH:
        // A thread is being created.
        break;

    case DLL_THREAD_DETACH:
        // A thread is exiting cleanly.
        break;

    case DLL_PROCESS_DETACH:
        // The DLL is being unmapped from the process's address
        // space.
        break;
    }
    return(TRUE);
}
```

Upon further research I discovered why. When a process is created, the system also creates a mutex object. Each process has its own mutex object—the mutex object is not shared by multiple processes. The purpose of this mutex object is to synchronize all of a process's threads when the threads call the *DllMain* functions of the DLLs mapped into the process's address space.

When the *CreateThread* function is called, the system first creates the thread kernel object and the thread's stack. Then the system internally calls the *WaitForSingleObject* function, passing the handle of the process's mutex object. Once the new thread has ownership of the mutex, the system makes the new thread call each of the DLL's *DllMain* functions with a value of DLL_THREAD_ATTACH. Only after all of the DLL's *DllMain* functions have been called does the system call *ReleaseMutex* to relinquish ownership of the process's mutex object. Because the system works this way, adding the call to *DisableThreadLibraryCalls* does prevent the threads from deadlocking. The only way I could think of to prevent the threads from being suspended was to redesign this part of the source code so that *WaitForSingleObject* is not called inside any DLL's *DllMain* function.

DllMain and the C Run-Time Library

In the discussion of the *DllMain* function on the previous page, I have been assuming that you are using Microsoft's Visual C++ compiler to build your dynamic-link library. When you write a DLL, it is likely that you will need some startup assistance from the C run-time library. For example, say that you are building a DLL that contains a global variable and that this global variable is an instance of a C++ class. Before the DLL can safely use the global variable, the variable must have its constructor called—this is a job for the C run-time library's DLL startup code.

When you link your DLL, the linker embeds the address of the DLL's entry/exit function in the resulting DLL file image. You specify the address of this function using the linker's /ENTRY switch. By default, when you use Microsoft's linker and specify the /DLL switch, the linker assumes that the entry function is called *_DllMainCRTStartup*. This function is contained inside the C run-time's static-link library and is embedded in your DLL file image when you link your DLL.

Now, when your DLL file image is mapped into a process's address space, the system actually calls this *_DllMainCRTStartup* function instead of your *DllMain* function. The *_DllMainCRTStartup* function initializes the C run-time library and ensures that any global or static C++ objects are constructed when *_DllMainCRTStartup* receives the DLL_PROCESS-_ATTACH notification. After any C run-time initialization has been performed, the *_DllMainCRTStartup* function calls your *DllMain* function.

When the DLL receives a DLL_PROCESS_DETACH notification, the system again calls the *_DllMainCRTStartup* function. This time, the function calls your *DllMain* function, and when *DllMain* returns, *_DllMainCRTStartup* calls any destructors for any global or static C++ objects in the DLL. The *_DllMainCRTStartup* function is also responsible for doing any additional C run-time–related initialization and cleanup when DLL_THREAD_ATTACH and DLL_THREAD_DETACH notifications are sent to the DLL.

I mentioned earlier in this chapter that you do not have to implement a *DllMain* function in your DLL's source code. If you don't have your own *DllMain* function, the C run-time library has its own implementation of a *DllMain* function that looks like this:

```
BOOL WINAPI DllMain(HINSTANCE hinstDll, DWORD fdwReason,
   LPVOID lpReserved) {

   return(TRUE);
}
```

When the linker links your DLL, it will link the C run-time's implementation of the *DllMain* function if the linker cannot find a *DllMain* function in your DLL's OBJ files.

Exporting Functions and Variables from a DLL

When you create a DLL, you are creating a set of functions that you want an EXE or other DLLs to be able to call. When a DLL function is made available to an EXE or another DLL file, the function is said to be *exported*. Win32 makes it possible to export global data variables as well as functions. In this section, we look at the steps you need to perform in order to export a DLL's functions and global variables.

The code below (taken from a DLL's source file) shows how to export a function called *Add* and a global integer variable called *g_nUsageCount* from a DLL:

```
__declspec(dllexport) int Add (int nLeft, int nRight) {
   return(nLeft + nRight);
}

__declspec(dllexport) int g_nUsageCount = 0;
```

For the most part, nothing in this code should be new to you except for the *__declspec(dllexport)*. Microsoft's C/C++ compiler recognizes this as a new keyword. When the compiler compiles the *Add* function and the *g_nUsageCount* variable, the compiler embeds some additional information in the resulting OBJ file. This information is intended to be parsed and processed by the linker when all of the OBJ files for the DLL are linked.

When the DLL is linked, the linker detects this embedded information about the exported function and variable. The linker then automatically produces a LIB file that contains the list of symbols exported by the DLL. This LIB file will, of course, be required to link any EXE that calls the exported functions in the DLL. In addition to creating the LIB file, the linker also embeds a table of exported symbols in the resulting DLL file. Each entry in this table consists of the exported function's or variable's name and the address at which the function or variable is located within the DLL's file image. The linker ensures that the list is sorted alphabetically by symbol name.

You can run the DumpBin utility that comes with Visual C++ to see what the export table looks like. The sample output on the opposite page shows a fragment of the Windows 95 KERNEL32.DLL's export table:

```
DUMPBIN -EXPORTS KERNEL32.DLL

Microsoft (R) COFF Binary File Dumper Version 2.50
Copyright (C) Microsoft Corp 1992-94. All rights reserved.


Dump of file kernel32.dll

File Type: DLL

        Section contains the following Exports for KERNEL32.dll

              0 characteristics
       2EAC6946 time date stamp Mon Oct 24 19:11:18 1994
           0.0 version
             1 base
           320 # functions
           320 # names

        ordinal hint    name

              1    0    AddAtomA  (000334b2)
              2    1    AddAtomW  (000108a9)
              3    2    AddConsoleAliasA  (0001094b)
              4    3    AddConsoleAliasW  (0001094b)
              5    4    AllocConsole  (0001707e)
              6    5    AllocLSCallback  (0002250a)
              7    6    AllocMappedBuffer  (00031b4f)
              8    7    AllocSLCallback  (0002253d)
              9    8    BackupRead  (00010930)
              A    9    BackupSeek  (0001091e)
              B    A    BackupWrite  (00010930)
              C    B    Beep  (000108c4)
              D    C    BeginUpdateResourceA  (000108c4)
              E    D    BeginUpdateResourceW  (000108c4)
              F    E    BuildCommDCBA  (00033f45)
             10    F    BuildCommDCBAndTimeoutsA  (00033f70)
             11   10    BuildCommDCBAndTimeoutsW  (000108df)
             12   11    BuildCommDCBW  (000108c4)
             13   12    CallNamedPipeA  (00033dae)
             14   13    CallNamedPipeW  (00010930)
                          :
                          :
            316  315    lstrcmpiA  (00032c80)
            317  316    lstrcmpiW  (000108c4)
            318  317    lstrcpy  (00032cba)
            319  318    lstrcpyA  (00032cba)
```

(continued)

```
31A   319    lstrcpyW   (000108c4)
31B   31A    lstrcpyn   (00032cf4)
31C   31B    lstrcpynA  (00032cf4)
31D   31C    lstrcpynW  (000108df)
31E   31D    lstrlen    (00032d6b)
31F   31E    lstrlenA   (00032d6b)
320   31F    lstrlenW   (000108a9)
```

Summary

```
 4000  .data
 6000  .edata
12000  .rsrc
41000  .text
 3000  LOCKCODE
 3000  LOCKDATA
 2000  _FREQASM
 2000  _INIT
```

As you can see, the symbols are in alphabetical order, and the number in parentheses identifies the symbol's address in the DLL file image. The hint column simply indicates the entry number in the list; the first entry is 0. The value in the ordinal column is always 1 greater than the value in the hint column.

Important

Many developers are used to exporting DLL functions by assigning functions an ordinal value. This is especially true if you are coming from a 16-bit Windows background. However, Microsoft does not publish ordinal values for the Win32 system DLLs. When your EXE or DLL links to any Win32 function, Microsoft wants you to link using the symbol's name. If you decide to link by ordinal, you run the risk that your application will not run on other Win32 platforms.

In fact, this has happened to me. I published a sample application in the *Microsoft Systems Journal* that used ordinal numbers. My application ran fine on Windows NT 3.1, but when Windows NT 3.5 came out, my application did not run correctly. In order to fix the problem, I had to replace the ordinal numbers with function names. Now the application runs on both Windows NT 3.1 and Windows NT 3.5.

I asked Microsoft why they are getting away from ordinals and got this response: "We [Microsoft] feel that the PE format provides the benefit of ordinals (fast lookup) with the flexibility of import by name. We can add APIs at any time. Ordinals are very hard to manage in a large project with multiple implementations."

(continued)

Important

continued

You can use ordinals for any DLLs that you create and have your EXE files link to these DLLs by ordinal. Microsoft guarantees that this method will continue to work even in future versions of the operating system. However, I personally am avoiding the use of ordinals in my own work and will link by name only from now on.

16-·-32

In order to produce a 16-bit Windows EXE or DLL file, the 16-bit linker requires the use of a module definitions (DEF) file. This DEF file has been the source of many problems for Windows programmers, and Microsoft is working to make DEF files a thing of the past as far as Win32 EXEs and DLLs are concerned. For the most part, Microsoft has replaced DEF files with new linker switches.

As of this writing, there are only two situations in which you require a DEF file to produce a Win32 EXE or DLL: when you want to use function forwarders and when you want to import a function with a name other than its exported name. Both of these uses of DEF files are extremely obscure and should not be an issue for 99.999 percent of all EXEs and DLLs written.

Importing Functions and Variables from a DLL

When you want your EXE to call functions or access variables contained within a DLL, you must tell the compiler that the functions or variables that you want to access are contained inside a DLL. For example, the code fragment below shows how to import the *Add* function and the *g_nUsage-Count* variable exported by the DLL discussed on page 504:

```
__declspec(dllimport) int Add (int nLeft, int nRight);

__declspec(dllimport) int g_nUsageCount;
```

Like *__declspec(dllexport)*, *__declspec(dllimport)* is a new keyword recognized by Microsoft's C/C++ compiler. This keyword informs the compiler that the *Add* function and the *g_nUsageCount* variable are contained in a DLL that the EXE will have access to when it loads. This causes the compiler to generate special code when accessing these imported symbols.

The compiler also embeds special information in the resulting OBJ file. This information is used in linking the EXE file. It tells the linker which functions it needs to look for in the various LIB files in order to successfully link the EXE file image. When the linker is attempting to link the EXE, it looks for the imported functions and variables. As the linker discovers which LIB file contains the imported symbols, the linker adds entries to an import table. Each entry contains the name of the DLL file that contains the symbol, and also contains the name of the symbol itself. When the linker finally writes the EXE file image to the hard drive, the image contains this import table.

You can run the DumpBin utility that comes with Visual C++ to see what the import table looks like. The sample output below shows the Windows 95 CALC.EXE's import table:

```
DUMPBIN -IMPORTS CALC.EXE

Microsoft (R) COFF Binary File Dumper Version 2.50
Copyright (C) Microsoft Corp 1992-94. All rights reserved.


Dump of file calc.exe

File Type: EXECUTABLE IMAGE

        Section contains the following Imports

            SHELL32.dll
            2EAC769C time date stamp Mon Oct 24 20:08:12 1994
                7E982F73    32    ShellAboutA

            KERNEL32.dll
            2EAC6964 time date stamp Mon Oct 24 19:11:48 1994
                BFFA1F51   184    GlobalUnlock
                BFF936B8   16C    GlobalAlloc
                BFFA1EA7   17D    GlobalReAlloc
                BFFA1EC9   17E    GlobalSize
                BFF936EB   16E    GlobalCompact
                BFFA1F73   175    GlobalFree
                BFFA1F0D   17A    GlobalLock
                BFFA2D6B   321    lstrlenA
                BFFA2D31   312    lstrcatA
                BFFA35DE   2F4    WriteProfileStringA
                BFFA3186   115    GetModuleHandleA
                BFFA3248   13F    GetStartupInfoA
                BFF9F4FC    F8    GetEnvironmentStrings
                BFF9F4EE    C8    GetCommandLineA
```

```
BFF96741    29E    Sleep
BFFA2C46    315    lstrcmpA
BFFA3581    13A    GetProfileStringA
BFF8C136    2B8    UnhandledExceptionFilter
BFFA3167    113    GetModuleFileNameA
BFFAAB12    BE     GetACP
BFFAAB18    11F    GetOEMCP
BFFAAB1E    C1     GetCPInfo
BFF8E3D4    141    GetStdHandle
BFF8E4DF    104    GetFileType
BFF94904    2C4    VirtualFree
BFF9476E    2C3    VirtualAlloc
BFFA21EE    21F    RaiseException
BFFAAC19    1FB    MultiByteToWideChar
BFFAB259    2DD    WideCharToMultiByte
BFFA1E78    12D    GetProcAddress
BFF9FCFD    10B    GetLastError
BFF936B8    1D8    LocalAlloc
BFFA1FFC    1DF    LocalReAlloc
BFFA2CBA    31B    lstrcpyA
BFFA354F    136    GetProfileIntA
BFF8A63D    15B    GetTickCount
BFF937D4    1DC    LocalFree
BFF8A150    161    GetVersion
BFF9F25B    7B     ExitProcess
BFF8BE06    23B    RtlUnwind

USER32.dll
2EAC7672 time date stamp Mon Oct 24 20:07:30 1994
BFF610F6    223    WinHelpA
BFF62386    D6     GetDC
BFF6446D    122    GetWindowRect
BFF62D77    45     CreateDialogParamA
BFF616A8    30     CheckRadioButton
BFF64950    165    LoadStringA
BFF63B36    192    RegisterClassA
BFF642DF    112    GetSysColorBrush
BFF64DB4    157    LoadCursorA
BFF64D9E    15B    LoadIconA
BFF61639    1C5    SetDlgItemTextA
BFF64416    DB     GetDlgItem
BFF62042    B6     FillRect
BFF64798    1DA    SetRect
BFF62B9E    2E     CheckMenuItem
BFF61A54    110    GetSubMenu
BFF62302    F1     GetMenu
```

(continued)

```
BFF6147E    1EB    SetWindowPos
BFF616C9    16B    MapDialogRect
BFF6203C    138    InvalidateRect
BFF6236E    1C8    SetFocus
BFF64597    14A    IsIconic
BFF642BE    111    GetSysColor
BFF623E4     7F    DestroyMenu
BFF61B41    208    TrackPopupMenuEx
BFF61251    161    LoadMenuA
BFF61E22    19F    ReleaseCapture
BFF62376    1B6    SetCapture
BFF64450     DA    GetDlgCtrlID
BFF62BA6     A4    EnableMenuItem
BFF6470D    144    IsClipboardFormatAvailable
BFF61F5C    1A0    ReleaseDC
BFF64527    1A7    ScreenToClient
BFF623B8     80    DestroyWindow
BFF623A8    18D    PostQuitMessage
BFF64F9B     77    DefWindowProcA
BFF623EC    172    MessageBeep
BFF61720    123    GetWindowTextA
BFF619F7     98    DrawFrameControl
BFF644AD     CC    GetClientRect
BFF62EF9    1F4    ShowCursor
BFF62B62    1BE    SetCursor
BFF61798     A9    EndPaint
BFF619FD     95    DrawEdge
BFF61747      9    BeginPaint
BFF62B50     36    CloseClipboard
BFF63F9B     29    CharUpperA
BFF61165     CE    GetClipboardData
BFF62F01    184    OpenClipboard
BFF61510    1EC    SetWindowTextA
BFF61F70     A6    EnableWindow
BFF61689     2D    CheckDlgButton
BFF61F64    1F7    ShowWindow
BFF623D4    217    UpdateWindow
BFF611A1     4F    CreateWindowExA
BFF64BD0    1AD    SendMessageA
BFF61255    153    LoadAcceleratorsA
BFF64AD7     FD    GetMessageA
BFF64B96    146    IsDialogMessageA
BFF64B3C    20A    TranslateAcceleratorA
BFF64B03    20D    TranslateMessage
BFF63DDB     85    DispatchMessageA
BFF63902    173    MessageBoxA
```

```
GDI32.dll
2EAC7672 time date stamp Mon Oct 24 20:07:30 1994
    BFF344AD   C2   GetStockObject
    BFF3133F   94   GetDeviceCaps
    BFF310E1   D3   GetTextMetricsA
    BFF34C28  135   SetTextColor
    BFF34C2F  114   SeFtBkColor
    BFF3219E  145   TextOutA
    BFF31B26   CF   GetTextExtentPointA
    BFF324A9  115   SetBkMode
    BFF3214F  10E   SelectObject
    BFF32461   4G   DeleteObject

Summary

1000 .bss
2000 .data
1000 .idata
1000 .rdata
2000 .reloc
2000 .rsrc
A000 .text
```

When an EXE file is invoked, the operating system loader examines the EXE's import table and attempts to locate and map any required DLLs into the process's address space. The loader then obtains the addresses of the symbols referenced by the EXE file and saves these addresses in a table. Naturally, this can take some processing time—but it is done only when the process is first invoked. Whenever the application references one of these symbols, the code generated by the compiler pulls the symbol's address from the table and completes the link. The number to the left of the imported symbol is called a *hint* and is used by the loader to speed up the process of resolving the symbol's address. The number to the left of the hint is the address of the function if the executable file has been bound.[2]

When you want to import a symbol, you do not have to use the *__declspec(dllimport)* keyword. Instead, you can simply use the standard C *extern* keyword. However, the compiler is able to produce slightly more efficient code if it knows ahead of time that the symbol you are referencing is going to be imported from a DLL's LIB file. So I highly recommend that you use the *__declspec(dllimport)* keyword for imported function and data symbols.

---

2. A DLL is bound using the BIND utility; this utility does not ship with Visual C++ but is included in the Win32 SDK.

A thread can obtain the address of a DLL's exported function or variable by calling the *GetProcAddress* function:

```
FARPROC GetProcAddress(HINSTANCE hinstDll, LPCSTR lpszProc);
```

The *hinstDll* parameter specifies the handle to the DLL. The return value from *LoadLibrary* or *LoadLibraryEx* identifies this handle value. The *lpsz-Proc* parameter can take one of two forms. First, it can be the address to a zero-terminated string containing the name of the function whose address we want:

```
lpfn = GetProcAddress(hinstDll, "SubclassProgManFrame");
```

Notice that the *lpszProc* parameter is prototyped as an LPCSTR, as opposed to an LPCTSTR. This means that the *GetProcAddress* function will accept only ANSI strings—you cannot pass a Unicode string to this function. This is because the function and variable symbols are always stored as ANSI strings in the DLL's export table.

The second form the *lpszProc* parameter can take indicates the ordinal number of the function whose address we want:

```
lpfn = GetProcAddress(hinstDll, MAKEINTRESOURCE(2));
```

This usage assumes that we know that the *SubclassProgManFrame* function was assigned the ordinal value of 2 by the creator of the DLL.[3]

Either method provides the address to the *SubclassProgManFrame* function contained inside the DLL. If the function cannot be found, *GetProcAddress* returns NULL. There are some subtle disadvantages in using either method. The first method works more slowly than the second because the system must perform string comparisons and searches on the function name string passed in. In the second method, if you pass an ordinal number that hasn't been assigned to any of the exported functions, *GetProcAddress* might return a non-NULL value. (This is true for 16-bit Windows as well.) This return value will trick your application into thinking that you have a valid address when in fact you don't. Attempting to call this address will almost certainly cause the thread to raise an access violation. Early in my Windows programming career, I didn't fully understand this behavior and was burned by it several times—watch out. (This behavior is yet another reason to avoid ordinals in favor of symbol names.)

---

3. See the important note on page 506 pertaining to the use of ordinal values.

A DLL's Header File

Usually, when you create a DLL you also create a header file. This header file has the prototypes for all the functions and variables that the DLL is exporting. When you compile your EXE's source code files, you will include this header file. Often you will want to include this header file when you compile the DLL's source code files as well. In order to create a single header file that you can include for both the EXE's and the DLL's source code files, you should create the header file as follows:

```
#if !defined(_MYLIB_)
#define MYLIBAPI __declspec(dllimport)
#else
#define MYLIBAPI __declspec(dllexport)
#endif

MYLIBAPI int Add (int nLeft, int nRight);
MYLIBAPI int g_nUsageCount;
```

Then, at the top of your DLL's source code files, include the above header file as follows:

```
#define _MYLIB_
#include "MYLIB.H"
    :
    :
```

When you create the header as I've just described, MYLIBAPI expands to __*declspec(dllexport)*, which matches the explicit usage of __*declspec(dllexport)* in the DLL's source code. This usage forces the *Add* function and the *g_nUsageCount* variable to be exported. The compiler would complain if the header file prototyped these symbols as imported while the source code defined the same symbols as exported. Because MYLIBAPI expands to __*declspec(dllexport)* when compiling the DLL's code, the compiler does not complain and the code compiles cleanly.

For the EXE's source code files, include the MYLIB.H header file without defining *_MYLIB_* first. This will cause MYLIBAPI to expand to __*declspec(dllimport)*, and the compiler will know that you are expecting these symbols to be imported. If you examine the Windows header files, such as WINUSER.H, you'll see that Microsoft uses the same technique that I've just explained here.

Sharing Data Across Mappings of an EXE or a DLL

As you know by now, the system creates instances of any global or static variables contained in an EXE or a DLL file image for multiple mappings of the file image. In other words, if an EXE has a global variable and you invoke two or more instances of the application, each process gets its very own copy of the global variable—the multiple instances of the EXE do not share a single copy of the global variable. Normally, this is exactly what we want. However, there are some occasions when it is useful and convenient for multiple mappings of an EXE to share a single instance of a variable.

For example, Win32 offers no easy way to determine whether the user is running multiple instances of an application. But if you could get all the instances to share a single global variable, this global variable could reflect the number of instances running. When the user invoked an instance of the application, the new instance's thread could simply check the value of the global variable (which had been updated by another instance), and if the count were greater than 1, the second instance could notify the user that only one instance of the application is allowed to run and the second instance would terminate.

This section discusses a technique that allows you to share variables among all instances of an EXE or a DLL. But before we get heavily into the details, you'll need a little background information.

The Sections of an EXE or a DLL

Every EXE or DLL file image is composed of a collection of sections. By convention, each standard section name begins with a period. For example, when you compile your program, the compiler places all the code in a section called .text. The compiler also places all the uninitialized data in a .bss section and all the initialized data in a .data section.

Each standard section has a combination of the following attributes associated with it:

Attribute	Meaning
READ	The bytes in the section can be read from.
WRITE	The bytes in the section can be written to.
SHARED	The bytes in the section are shared across multiple instances.
EXECUTE	The bytes in the section can be executed.

By running the DumpBin utility, you can see the list of sections in an executable or a DLL. The following listing shows the result of running the DumpBin utility on both the PMREST.EXE and PMRSTSUB.DLL files, the sample programs presented in Chapter 16:

```
DUMPBIN -SUMMARY PMREST.EXE
Microsoft (R) COFF Binary File Dumper Version 2.50
Copyright (C) Microsoft Corp 1992-94. All rights reserved.


Dump of file pmrest.exe

File Type: EXECUTABLE IMAGE

        Summary

            1000 .bss
            1000 .data
            1000 .idata
            1000 .rdata
            1000 .reloc
            1000 .rsrc
            1000 .text

DUMPBIN -SUMMARY PMRSTSUB.DLL
Microsoft (R) COFF Binary File Dumper Version 2.50
Copyright (C) Microsoft Corp 1992-94. All rights reserved.


Dump of file pmrstsub.dll

File Type: DLL

        Summary

            1000 .bss
            1000 .data
            1000 .edata
            1000 .idata
            1000 .rdata
            1000 .reloc
            1000 .rsrc
            1000 .text
            1000 Shared
```

In addition to the summary list of sections above, you can get a more detailed list of each section by specifying the -HEADERS switch to DumpBin.

The table below shows the names of some of the more common sections and what each contains:

Section Name	Contains
.text	Application's or DLL's code
.bss	Uninitialized data
.rdata	Read-only run-time data
.rsrc	Resources
.edata	Exported names table
.data	Initialized data
.xdata	Exception handling table
.idata	Imported names table
.CRT	Read-only C run-time data
.reloc	Fixup table information
.debug	Debugging information
.tls	Thread-local storage

Notice how the PMRSTSUB.DLL has an additional section—called Shared—that does not exist in the application's file. I created this section myself. You can easily create sections when compiling an application or a DLL by using the following directive when you compile:

```
#pragma data_seg("segname")
```

So for example, the PMRSTSUB.C file contains these lines:

```
#pragma data_seg("Shared")

DWORD g_dwThreadIdPMRestore = 0;
HWND  g_hwndPM = NULL;

#pragma data_seg()
```

When the compiler compiles this code, it creates a new section—Shared—and places all the *initialized* data variables that it sees after the pragma in this new section. In the example above, the two variables—*g_dwThreadIdPMRestore* and *g_hwndPM*—are both placed in the Shared section. Following the two variables, the *#pragma dataseg()* line tells the compiler to stop putting variables in the Shared section and to start putting them back in the default data section. It is extremely important to note that the compiler will store only initialized variables in the new section. The compiler always places uninitialized variables in the .bss section. For example, if I had removed the initializations from the previous code fragment as follows, the compiler would have ended up putting all these variables in the .bss section and none of them in the Shared section:

```
#pragma data_seg("Shared")

DWORD  g_dwThreadIdPMRestore;
HWND   g_hwndPM;

#pragma data_seg()
```

Probably the most common reason to put variables in their own section is to share them among multiple mappings of an application or a DLL. By default, each mapping of an application or a DLL gets its very own set of variables. However, you can group into their own section any variables that you want to share among all mappings of an application or a DLL. When you group variables, the system doesn't create new instances of the variables for every mapping of the application or DLL.

Just telling the compiler to place certain variables in their own section is not enough to share those variables. You must also tell the linker that the variables in a particular section are to be shared. You can do this by using the -SECTION switch on the linker's command line:

```
-SECTION:name, attributes
```

Following the colon, place the name of the section for which you want to alter attributes.

For PMRSTSUB.DLL, we want to change the attributes of the Shared section. You must specify the attributes of the section following the comma. Use an *R* for READ, a *W* for WRITE, an *S* for SHARED, and an *E* for EXECUTE. So to make the Shared section readable, writable, and shared, the switch must look like this:

```
-SECTION:Shared,RWS
```

If you want to change the attributes of more than one section, you must specify the -SECTION switch multiple times—once for each section for which you want to change attributes.[4]

---

4. The PMRSTSUB.C file uses the following line to embed this linker directive in the OBJ file:

```
#pragma comment(lib, "msvcrt " "-section:Shared,rws")
```

By embedding this directive in the source code file, you don't have to remember to change any linker switches in the project's settings.

Although it is possible to create shared sections, sharing sections is greatly discouraged for two reasons. First, sharing memory in this way violates B-level security policy. Second, sharing variables means that an error in one application can affect the operation of another application because there is no way to protect a block of data from being randomly written to by an application.

Pretend that you have written two applications, each requiring the user to enter a password. However, you decide to add a feature to your applications that makes things a little easier on the user: if the user is already running one of the applications when the second is started, the second application examines the contents of shared memory in order to get the password. This way, the user doesn't need to enter the password a second time if one of the programs is already being used.

This sounds innocent enough. After all, no other applications but your own load the DLL and know where to find the password contained within the shared section. However, hackers lurk about, and if they want to get your password, all they need to do is write a small program of their own to load your company's DLL and monitor the shared memory blocks. When the user enters a password, the hacker's program can learn the user's password.

An industrious program such as the hacker's might also try to repeatedly guess at passwords and write them to the shared memory. Once the program guesses the correct password, it can send all kinds of commands to one of the two applications.

Perhaps this problem could be solved if there were a way to grant access to only certain applications for loading a particular DLL. But currently this is not the case—any program can call *LoadLibrary* to explicitly load a DLL.

The ModUse Sample Application

Earlier in this chapter, I said that Win32 does not support the *GetModuleUsage* function offered by 16-bit Windows. However, by using shared memory, you can implement the *GetModuleUsage* function yourself. The MODUSE.EXE and MODULE.DLL files demonstrate how to do this. Figure 11-3 shows MODULE.DLL, which we'll look at first. The source code files, resource files, and make file for the application are in the MODUSE.11 directory on the companion disc.

MODULE.C

```
/*********************************************************
Module name: Module.C
Notices: Copyright (c) 1995 Jeffrey Richter
*********************************************************/


#include "..\AdvWin32.H"      /* See Appendix B for details. */
#include <windows.h>

#pragma warning(disable: 4001)       /* Single-line comment */

#define _MODULELIB_
#include "Module.H"


///////////////////////////////////////////////////////////


// Instruct the compiler to put the g_lModuleUsage data
// variable in its own data section, called Shared. We
// then instruct the linker that we want the data in this
// section to be shared by all instances of this application.
#pragma data_seg("Shared")

LONG g_lModuleUsage = 0;

#pragma data_seg()


///////////////////////////////////////////////////////////


// Instruct the linker to make the Shared section
// readable, writable, and shared.
#pragma comment(lib, "msvcrt " "-section:Shared,rws")


///////////////////////////////////////////////////////////


// 'g_uMsgModCountChange' could be shared, but I chose not to.
UINT g_uMsgModCntChange = 0;
```

Figure 11-3.   *(continued)*

The Module dynamic-link library.

Figure 11-3. *continued*

```
/////////////////////////////////////////////////////////////

BOOL WINAPI DllMain (HINSTANCE hinstDll, DWORD fdwReason,
   LPVOID lpvReserved) {

   switch (fdwReason) {

   case DLL_PROCESS_ATTACH:
      // DLL is attaching to the address
      // space of the current process.

      // Increment this module's usage count when it is
      // attached to a process.
      InterlockedIncrement((PLONG) &g_lModuleUsage);

      // Reserve a systemwide window message for ourselves.
      // This message is used to notify all of the top-level
      // windows that this module's usage count has changed.
      g_uMsgModCntChange =
         RegisterWindowMessage(__TEXT("MsgModUsgCntChange"));

      // Notify all of the top-level windows that this
      // module's usage count has changed.
      PostMessage(HWND_BROADCAST, g_uMsgModCntChange, 0, 0);
      break;

   case DLL_THREAD_ATTACH:
      // A new thread is being created in the current process.
      break;

   case DLL_THREAD_DETACH:
      // A thread is exiting cleanly.
      break;

   case DLL_PROCESS_DETACH:
      // The calling process is detaching
      // the DLL from its address space.

      // Decrement this module's usage count when it
      // gets detached from a process.
      InterlockedDecrement((PLONG) &g_lModuleUsage);
```

(continued)

Figure 11-3. *continued*

```
        // Notify all of the top-level windows that this
        // module's usage count has changed.
        PostMessage(HWND_BROADCAST, g_uMsgModCntChange, 0, 0);

        break;
    }

    return(TRUE);
}


//////////////////////////////////////////////////////////////////


MODULEAPI LONG GetModuleUsage (void) {
    return(g_lModuleUsage);
}

//////////////////////// End Of File ////////////////////////
```

MODULE.H
```
/*********************************************************
Module name: Module.H
Notices: Copyright (c) 1995 Jeffrey Richter
*********************************************************/


#if !defined(_MODULELIB_)
#define MODULEAPI __declspec(dllimport)
#else
#define MODULEAPI __declspec(dllexport)
#endif


// Function to return the module's usage count.
MODULEAPI LONG GetModuleUsage (void);


//////////////////////// End Of File ////////////////////////
```

(continued)

Figure 11-3. *continued*

MODULE.RC

```
//Microsoft Visual C++ generated resource script.
//
#include "Module.rh"

#define APSTUDIO_READONLY_SYMBOLS
/////////////////////////////////////////////////////////////////////////////
//
// Generated from the TEXTINCLUDE 2 resource.
//
#include "afxres.h"


/////////////////////////////////////////////////////////////////////////////
#undef APSTUDIO_READONLY_SYMBOLS


#ifdef APSTUDIO_INVOKED
/////////////////////////////////////////////////////////////////////////////
//
// TEXTINCLUDE
//

1 TEXTINCLUDE DISCARDABLE
BEGIN
    "Module.rh\0"
END

2 TEXTINCLUDE DISCARDABLE
BEGIN
    "#include ""afxres.h""\r\n"
    "\0"
END

3 TEXTINCLUDE DISCARDABLE
BEGIN
    "\r\n"
    "\0"
END


/////////////////////////////////////////////////////////////////////////////
#endif    // APSTUDIO_INVOKED
```

(continued)

Figure 11-3. *continued*

```
#ifndef APSTUDIO_INVOKED
/////////////////////////////////////////////////////////////////////
//
// Generated from the TEXTINCLUDE 3 resource.
//


/////////////////////////////////////////////////////////////////////
#endif    // not APSTUDIO_INVOKED
```

The most important thing to note in MODULE.C is that I have created a global variable, *g_lModuleUsage*, in its very own section and have specified that this section be shared by specifying the -SECTION switch to the linker. I have also initialized *g_lModuleUsage* to be –1. Now, whenever MODULE.DLL is mapped into a process's address space, *DllMain* is called with a value of DLL_PROCESS_ATTACH. The DLL processes this call by calling:

```
InterlockedIncrement(&g_lModuleUsage);
```

This call increments the *g_lModuleUsage* variable. You might wonder why I increment this long by calling *InterlockedIncrement* instead of just using:

```
g_lModuleUsage++;
```

I admit that the difference between the two statements is subtle, and that most of the time you wouldn't even notice a difference and everything would work just fine. However, if I use only the C postfix increment operator, there is a potential problem. If two processes call *LoadLibrary* to load MODULE.DLL into memory at the same time, the value of *g_lModuleUsage* can become corrupted. Actually, this would probably never happen on a single-CPU machine because the CPU can preempt a thread only in between machine instructions. But on a multiprocessor machine, several CPUs can access the same memory location simultaneously. By using *InterlockedIncrement*, the system guarantees that no more than one CPU can access the 4 bytes of memory at any one time.

The next step in maintaining MODULE.DLL's usage count is to decrement the usage count whenever *DllMain* is called with a value of DLL_PROCESS_DETACH. When this happens, *g_lUsageCount* is decremented by making a call to *InterlockedDecrement*. See Chapter 9 for more information on the *InterlockedIncrement* and *InterlockedDecrement* functions.

The only other function in this DLL is *GetModuleUsage*:

```
LONG GetModuleUsage(void);
```

This function accepts no parameters and simply returns the value in the *g_lUsageCount* variable. An application can now call this function to determine the number of processes that have mapped MODULE.DLL into their own address spaces.

To make this demonstration a little more exciting, I also created the ModUse (MODUSE.EXE) sample application, listed in Figure 11-4. This is a very simple program that displays a dialog box. After the dialog box is displayed, its dialog box procedure simply sits around and waits for the registered window message[5] "MsgModCntChange". This message is registered by MODULE.DLL when its *DllMain* function is called with a value of DLL_PROCESS_ATTACH. This same message is registered by MODUSE.EXE first when its *WinMain* function is called. The value for the message is saved in the global *g_uMsgModCntChange* variable.

Whenever the DLL is attached or detached from a process, it calls

```
PostMessage(HWND_BROADCAST, g_uMsgCntChange, 0, 0);
```

This causes the value of the registered window message to be broadcast to all the overlapped windows in the system. The only windows that will recognize this systemwide window message are the dialog boxes created by any active instances of the ModUse application. MODUSE.C's dialog box procedure contains an explicit check for this registered window message:

```
if (uMsg == g_uMsgModCntChange) {
    SetDlgItemInt(hDlg, IDC_MODCNT, GetModuleUsage(), FALSE);
}
```

When this message is received, the DLL's *GetModuleUsage* function is called to get the current module usage. This value is then placed in a static window control that is a child of the dialog box.

When you run the ModUse program, the MODULE.DLL file is implicitly mapped into the process's address space. The attachment of this DLL to the process causes the registered message to be posted to all the overlapped windows in the system. The windows will ignore this message except for the dialog box displayed by ModUse. When the dialog box receives the message, it calls the *GetModuleUsage* function in the DLL to

---

5. For more information about using registered window messages, see the *RegisterWindow-Message* function in the *Microsoft Win32 Programmer's Reference*.

obtain MODULE.DLL's usage count, which is 1. This value is then placed in the dialog box:

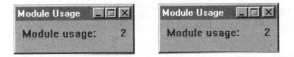

If you run a second instance of ModUse, the same sequence of events will occur. This time, MODULE.DLL's usage count is 2, and two dialog boxes that can process the registered window message are displayed. Both dialog box procedures call *GetModuleUsage*, see that the count is 2, and then update their static controls appropriately:

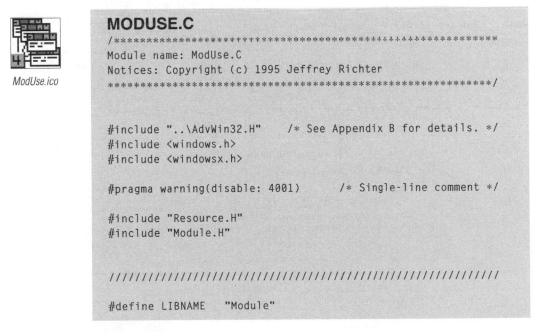

This technique for sharing data in a section across multiple file mappings is not limited to DLLs alone—applications (EXEs) can also use it. For an application, the data is shared among all running instances of the application.

ModUse.ico

```
MODUSE.C
/************************************************************
Module name: ModUse.C
Notices: Copyright (c) 1995 Jeffrey Richter
************************************************************/


#include "..\AdvWin32.H"      /* See Appendix B for details. */
#include <windows.h>
#include <windowsx.h>

#pragma warning(disable: 4001)        /* Single-line comment */

#include "Resource.H"
#include "Module.H"


//////////////////////////////////////////////////////////////

#define LIBNAME    "Module"
```

Figure 11-4.   *(continued)*
The ModUse application.

Figure 11-4. *continued*

```
#if defined(_X86_)
   #if defined(_DEBUG)
      #pragma comment(lib, "Dbg_x86\\" LIBNAME)
   #else
      #pragma comment(lib, "Rel_x86\\" LIBNAME)
   #endif
#elif defined(_MIPS_)
   #if defined(_DEBUG)
      #pragma comment(lib, "Dbg_MIPS\\" LIBNAME)
   #else
      #pragma comment(lib, "Rel_MIPS\\" LIBNAME)
   #endif
#elif defined(_ALPHA_)
   #if defined(_DEBUG)
      #pragma comment(lib, "Dbg_Alph\\" LIBNAME)
   #else
      #pragma comment(lib, "Rel_Alph\\" LIBNAME)
   #endif
#else
   #error Modification required for this CPU platform.
#endif


///////////////////////////////////////////////////////////////


UINT g_uMsgModCntChange = 0;


///////////////////////////////////////////////////////////////


BOOL Dlg_OnInitDialog (HWND hwnd, HWND hwndFocus,
   LPARAM lParam) {

   // Associate an icon with the dialog box.
   SetClassLong(hwnd, GCL_HICON, (LONG)
      LoadIcon((HINSTANCE) GetWindowLong(hwnd, GWL_HINSTANCE),
         __TEXT("ModUse")));

   // Force the static control to be initialized correctly.
   PostMessage(hwnd, g_uMsgModCntChange, 0, 0);
   return(TRUE);
}

///////////////////////////////////////////////////////////////
```

(continued)

Figure 11-4. *continued*

```
void Dlg_OnCommand (HWND hwnd, int id, HWND hwndCtl,
   UINT codeNotify) {

   switch (id) {
      case IDCANCEL:
         EndDialog(hwnd, id);
         break;
   }
}


//////////////////////////////////////////////////////////////


BOOL CALLBACK Dlg_Proc (HWND hDlg, UINT uMsg,
   WPARAM wParam, LPARAM lParam) {

   BOOL fProcessed = TRUE;

   if (uMsg == g_uMsgModCntChange) {
      SetDlgItemInt(hDlg, IDC_USAGECOUNT,
         GetModuleUsage(), FALSE);
   }

   switch (uMsg) {
      HANDLE_MSG(hDlg, WM_INITDIALOG, Dlg_OnInitDialog);
      HANDLE_MSG(hDlg, WM_COMMAND, Dlg_OnCommand);

      default:
         fProcessed = FALSE;
         break;
   }
   return(fProcessed);
}


//////////////////////////////////////////////////////////////


int WINAPI WinMain (HINSTANCE hinstExe,
   HINSTANCE hinstPrev, LPSTR lpszCmdLine, int nCmdShow) {

   // Get the numeric value of the systemwide window message
   // used by the module to notify all top-level windows when
```

(continued)

Figure 11-4. *continued*

```
    // the module's usage count has changed.
    g_uMsgModCntChange =
        RegisterWindowMessage(__TEXT("MsgModUsgCntChange"));

    DialogBox(hinstExe, MAKEINTRESOURCE(IDD_MODUSE),
        NULL, Dlg_Proc);

    return(0);
}



/////////////////////// End Of File ///////////////////////
```

MODUSE.RC

```
//Microsoft Visual C++ generated resource script.
//
#include "Resource.h"

#define APSTUDIO_READONLY_SYMBOLS
/////////////////////////////////////////////////////////////
//
// Generated from the TEXTINCLUDE 2 resource.
//
#include "afxres.h"


/////////////////////////////////////////////////////////////
#undef APSTUDIO_READONLY_SYMBOLS


#ifdef APSTUDIO_INVOKED
/////////////////////////////////////////////////////////////
//
// TEXTINCLUDE
//

1 TEXTINCLUDE DISCARDABLE
BEGIN
    "Resource.h\0"
END

2 TEXTINCLUDE DISCARDABLE
BEGIN
    "#include ""afxres.h""\r\n"
    "\0"
END
```

(continued)

Figure 11-4. *continued*

```
3 TEXTINCLUDE DISCARDABLE
BEGIN
    "\r\n"
    "\0"
END


//////////////////////////////////////////////////////////////
#endif    // APSTUDIO_INVOKED


//////////////////////////////////////////////////////////////
//
// Dialog
//

IDD_MODUSE DIALOG DISCARDABLE  0, 0, 76, 20
STYLE WS_MINIMIZEBOX | WS_POPUP | WS_VISIBLE | WS_CAPTION
      | WS_SYSMENU
CAPTION "Module Usage"
FONT 8, "System"
BEGIN
    LTEXT          "Module usage:",IDC_STATIC,4,4,49,
                   0,SS_NOPREFIX
    RTEXT          "#",IDC_USAGECOUNT,56,4,16,12,SS_NOPREFIX
END


//////////////////////////////////////////////////////////////
//
// Icon
//

ModUse                 ICON    DISCARDABLE    "ModUse.Ico"

#ifndef APSTUDIO_INVOKED
//////////////////////////////////////////////////////////////
//
// Generated from the TEXTINCLUDE 3 resource.
//


//////////////////////////////////////////////////////////////
#endif    // not APSTUDIO_INVOKED
```

The MultInst Sample Application

In 16-bit Windows, many programmers used the value of *hinstPrev*, which 16-bit Windows passed to *WinMain* to determine whether an instance of an application was already running. Applications that allowed only one instance of themselves to run at a time would check the value of *hinstPrev*, and, if its value wasn't NULL, they would terminate. Under Win32, the value of *hinstPrev* passed to *WinMain* is always NULL. Because of this, an application cannot easily determine whether another instance of itself is running.

One way for an application to know how many instances of itself are running is to use the shared data section technique just discussed. The MultInst (MULTINST.EXE) sample application, listed in Figure 11-5, demonstrates how to allow only one instance of an application to run. The source code files, resource files, and make file for the application are in the MULTINST.11 directory on the companion disc.

MultInst.ico

```
MULTINST.C
/********************************************************************
Module name: MultInst.C
Notices: Copyright (c) 1995 Jeffrey Richter
********************************************************************/


#include "..\AdvWin32.H"    /* See Appendix B for details. */
#include <windows.h>

#pragma warning(disable: 4001)      /* Single-line comment */


#include "Resource.H"


////////////////////////////////////////////////////////////////////


// We instruct the compiler to put the g_lUsageCount data
// variable in its own data section, called Shared. We
// then instruct the linker that we want the data in this
// section to be shared by all instances of this application.
#pragma data_seg("Shared")

LONG g_lUsageCount = -1;

#pragma data_seg()
```

Figure 11-5.
The MultInst application.

(continued)

Figure 11-5. *continued*

```
///////////////////////////////////////////////////////////////


// Instruct the linker to make the Shared section
// readable, writable, and shared.
#pragma comment(lib, "msvcrt " "-section:Shared,rws")



///////////////////////////////////////////////////////////////


int WINAPI WinMain (HINSTANCE hinstExe,
    HINSTANCE hinstPrev, LPSTR lpszCmdLine, int nCmdShow) {

    // An instance is running; increment the counter.
    BOOL fFirstInstance =
        (InterlockedIncrement(&g_lUsageCount) == 0);

    // If more than one instance is running, tell
    // the user and terminate the program.
    if (!fFirstInstance) {
        MessageBox(NULL,
            __TEXT("Application is already running - ")
            __TEXT("Terminating this instance."),
            __TEXT("Multiple Instance"),
              MB_OK | MB_ICONINFORMATION);
    } else {

        // We are the only instance running;
        // wait for the user to terminate us.
        MessageBox(NULL,
            __TEXT("Running first instance of application.\n")
            __TEXT("Select OK to terminate."),
            __TEXT("Multiple Instance"),
              MB_OK | MB_ICONINFORMATION);
    }

    // We are no longer running; decrement the usage counter.
    InterlockedDecrement(&g_lUsageCount);

    return(0);
}



///////////////////////// End Of File /////////////////////////
```

(continued)

Figure 11-5. *continued*

```
MULTINST.RC
//Microsoft Visual C++ generated resource script.
//
#include "Resource.h"

#define APSTUDIO_READONLY_SYMBOLS
/////////////////////////////////////////////////////////////////////
//
// Generated from the TEXTINCLUDE 2 resource.
//
#include "afxres.h"


/////////////////////////////////////////////////////////////////////
#undef APSTUDIO_READONLY_SYMBOLS


#ifdef APSTUDIO_INVOKED
/////////////////////////////////////////////////////////////////////
//
// TEXTINCLUDE
//

1 TEXTINCLUDE DISCARDABLE
BEGIN
    "Resource.h\0"
END

2 TEXTINCLUDE DISCARDABLE
BEGIN
    "#include ""afxres.h""\r\n"
    "\0"
END

3 TEXTINCLUDE DISCARDABLE
BEGIN
    "\r\n"
    "\0"
END


/////////////////////////////////////////////////////////////////////
#endif    // APSTUDIO_INVOKED
```

(continued)

Figure 11-5. *continued*

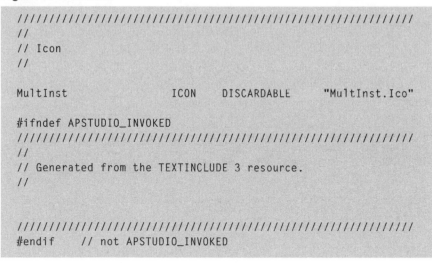

```
//////////////////////////////////////////////////////////////
//
// Icon
//

MultInst                ICON    DISCARDABLE    "MultInst.Ico"

#ifndef APSTUDIO_INVOKED
//////////////////////////////////////////////////////////////
//
// Generated from the TEXTINCLUDE 3 resource.
//


//////////////////////////////////////////////////////////////
#endif    // not APSTUDIO_INVOKED
```

THREAD-LOCAL STORAGE

Sometimes it's convenient to associate data with an instance of an object. For example, window extra bytes associate data with a specific window by using the *SetWindowWord* and *SetWindowLong* functions. Thread-local storage (TLS) allows you to associate data with a specific thread of execution. For example, you might want to associate the creation time of a thread with a thread. Then, when the thread terminates, you can determine the lifetime of the thread.

The C run-time library uses TLS. Because the library was designed years before multithreaded applications, most functions in the library are intended for use with single threaded applications. The *strtok* function is an excellent example. The first time an application calls *strtok*, the function passes the address to a string and saves the address of the string in its own static variable. Then, when you make future calls to *strtok*, passing NULL, the function refers to the saved string address.

In a multithreaded environment, it's possible that one thread can call *strtok*, and then, before it can make another call, another thread can also call *strtok*. In this case, the second thread causes *strtok* to overwrite its static variable with a new address, which happens unbeknownst to the first thread. And the first thread's future calls to *strtok* use the second thread's string, which can lead to all kinds of difficult-to-find-and-fix bugs.

To fix this problem, the C run-time uses TLS, which means each thread is assigned its very own string pointer that is reserved for use by the *strtok* function. Other C run-time functions that require the same treatment include *asctime* and *gmtime*.

TLS can be a lifesaver if your application relies heavily on global or static variables. Fortunately, software developers tend to minimize the use of such variables and rely much more on automatic (stack-based) variables and data passing via function parameters. This is good because stack-based variables are always associated with a particular thread.

It is both fortunate and unfortunate that the standard C library has existed for so many years. It has been implemented and reimplemented by various compiler vendors; no C compiler would be worth buying if it didn't include the standard C library. Programmers have used it for years and will continue to do so, which means that the prototype and behavior of functions such as *strtok* must remain exactly as the standard C library describes them. If the C run-time library were to be redesigned today, it would be designed for environments that support multithreaded applications, and extreme measures would be taken to avoid the use of global and static variables.

In my own software projects, I avoid global variables as much as possible. If your application uses global and static variables, I strongly suggest that you examine each variable and investigate the possibilities for changing it to a stack-based variable. This effort can save you an enormous amount of time if you decide to add additional threads to your application, and even single-threaded applications can benefit.

Although the two TLS techniques discussed in this chapter can be used in both applications and DLLs, you will more frequently find them useful when creating DLLs because DLLs often don't know the structure of the application to which they are linked. If you're writing an application (vs. a DLL), you typically know how many threads will be created and how those threads will be used. The application developer can then create makeshift methods or, better yet, use stack-based methods (local variables) for associating data with each created thread.

A DLL implementer typically doesn't know how the application to which it is linked creates and uses threads. TLS was created with the intent of helping the DLL developer. However, the information discussed in this chapter can be used just as easily by an application developer.

Dynamic Thread-Local Storage

An application takes advantage of dynamic thread-local storage by calling a set of four functions. Although these functions can be used by an application or a DLL, they are most often used by DLLs.

Figure 12-1 shows the internal data structures that Windows 95 and Windows NT use for managing TLS.

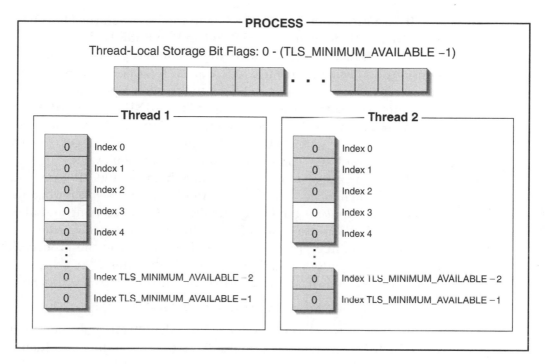

Figure 12-1.
Internal data structures that manage thread-local storage.

The figure shows a single set of in-use flags for each process running in the system. Each flag is either FREE or INUSE, indicating whether the TLS slot is in use. Microsoft guarantees that at least TLS_MINIMUM_AVAILABLE bit flags will be available on all Win32 platforms. By the way, TLS_MINIMUM_AVAILABLE is defined as 64 in WINNT.H. On some platforms, the system might actually expand this flag array to accommodate the needs of the application or the DLL.

To use dynamic TLS, a call must first be made to *TlsAlloc*:

```
DWORD TlsAlloc(VOID);
```

This function instructs the system to scan the bit flags in the process and locate a FREE flag. The system then changes the flag from FREE to INUSE, and *TlsAlloc* returns the index of the flag in the bit array. A DLL (or an application) usually saves the index in a global variable.[1]

---

1. This is one of those times when a global variable is actually the better choice because the value is used on a per-process basis rather than a per-thread basis.

If *TlsAlloc* cannot find a FREE flag in the list, it returns TLS_OUT-_OF_INDEXES (defined as 0xFFFFFFFF in WINBASE.H).

The first time *TlsAlloc* is called, the system recognizes that the first flag is FREE and changes the flag to INUSE, and *TlsAlloc* returns 0. That's 99 percent of what *TlsAlloc* does. I'll get to the other 1 percent later.

When a thread is created, an array of TLS_MINIMUM_AVAILABLE 32-bit values (LPVOIDs) is allocated, initialized to 0, and associated with the thread by the system. As Figure 12-1 shows, each thread gets its own array, and each LPVOID in the array can store any 32-bit value.

Before you can store information in a thread's LPVOID array, you must know which index in the array is available for use—this is what the earlier call to *TlsAlloc* is for. Conceptually, *TlsAlloc* is reserving an index for you. If *TlsAlloc* returns index 3, it is effectively saying that index 3 is reserved for you in every thread currently executing in the process as well as in any threads that might be created in the future.

To place a value in a thread's array, you call the *TlsSetValue* function:

```
BOOL TlsSetValue(DWORD dwTlsIndex, LPVOID lpvTlsValue);
```

This function puts an LPVOID value or any other 32-bit value, identified by the *lpvTlsValue* parameter, into the thread's array at the index identified by the *dwTlsIndex* parameter. The value of *lpvTlsValue* is associated with the thread making the call to *TlsSetValue*. If the call is successful, TRUE is returned.

A thread changes its own array when it calls *TlsSetValue*. But a thread cannot set a thread-local storage value for another thread. Personally, I wish there were another *Tls* function that allowed one thread to store data in another thread's array, but no such function exists. Currently the only way to pass initialization data from one thread to another is to pass a single 32-bit value to *CreateThread* or *_beginthreadex*. *CreateThread* or *_beginthreadex* then passes this value to the thread function as its only parameter.

When calling *TlsSetValue*, be extremely careful that you always pass an index returned from an earlier call to *TlsAlloc*. Microsoft designed these functions to be as fast as possible and, in so doing, gave up error checking. If you pass an index that was never allocated by a call to *TlsAlloc*, the system stores the 32-bit value in the thread's array anyway—no error check is performed.

To retrieve a value from a thread's array, you call *TlsGetValue*:

```
LPVOID TlsGetValue(DWORD dwTlsIndex);
```

This function returns the value that was associated with the TLS slot at index *dwTlsIndex*. Like *TlsSetValue*, *TlsGetValue* looks only at the array that belongs to the calling thread. And again like *TlsSetValue*, *TlsGetValue* performs no test to check the validity of the passed index.

When you come to a point in your process where you no longer need to reserve a TLS slot among all threads, you should call *TlsFree*:

```
BOOL TlsFree(DWORD dwTlsIndex);
```

This function simply tells the system that this slot no longer needs to be reserved. The INUSE flag managed by the process's bit flags array is set to FREE again and might be allocated in the future if a thread later calls *TlsAlloc*. *TlsFree* returns TRUE if the function is successful. Attempting to free a slot that was not allocated results in an error.

Using Dynamic Thread-Local Storage

Usually, if a DLL uses TLS, it calls *TlsAlloc* when its *DllMain* function is called with DLL_PROCESS_ATTACH, and it calls *TlsFree* when *DllMain* is called with DLL_PROCESS_DETACH. The calls to *TlsSetValue* and *Tls-GetValue* are most likely made during calls to functions contained within the DLL.

One method for adding TLS to an application is to add it when you need it. For example, you might have a function in a DLL that works similarly to *strtok*. The first time your function is called, the thread passes a pointer to a 40-byte structure. You need to save this structure so that future calls can reference it. So you might code your function like this:

```
DWORD g_dwTlsIndex;      // Assume that this is initialized
                         // with the result of a call to TlsAlloc.
    :
    :

void MyFunction (LPSOMESTRUCT lpSomeStruct) {
    if (lpSomeStruct != NULL) {
        // The caller is priming this function.

        // See if we already allocated space to save the data.
        if (TlsGetValue(g_dwTlsIndex) == NULL) {
            // Space was never allocated. This is the first
            // time this function has ever been called by this thread.
```

(continued)

```
        TlsSetValue(g_dwTlsIndex,
            HeapAlloc(GetProcessHeap(), 0,
                sizeof(*lpSomeStruct)));
    }

    // Memory already exists for the data; save the newly
    // passed values.
    memcpy(TlsGetValue(g_dwTlsIndex), lpSomeStruct,
        sizeof(*lpSomeStruct));

} else {

    // The caller already primed the function. Now it
    // wants to do something with the saved data.

    // Get the address of the saved data.
    lpSomeStruct = (LPSOMESTRUCT) TlsGetValue(g_dwTlsIndex);

    // The saved data is pointed to by lpSomeStruct; use it.
    .
    .
    .
}
```

If the application's thread never calls *MyFunction*, a memory block is never allocated for the thread.

It might seem that 64 (at least) TLS locations are more than you will ever need. However, keep in mind that an application can dynamically link to several DLLs. One DLL can allocate 10 TLS indexes, a second DLL can allocate 5 indexes, and so on. So it is always best to reduce the number of TLS indexes you need. The best way to do this is to use the same method that *MyFunction* uses above. Sure, I can save all 40 bytes across 10 TLS indexes, but doing so is not only wasteful, it makes working with the data difficult. Instead, allocate a memory block for the data and simply save the pointer in a single TLS index just as *MyFunction* does.

When I discussed the *TlsAlloc* function earlier, I described only 99 percent of what it did. To help you understand the remaining 1 percent, look at this code fragment:

```
DWORD dwTlsIndex;
LPVOID lpvSomeValue;
.
.
.
dwTlsIndex = TlsAlloc();
TlsSetValue(dwTlsIndex, (LPVOID) 12345);
TlsFree(dwTlsIndex);
```

```
// Assume that the dwTlsIndex value returned from
// this call to TlsAlloc is identical to the index
// returned by the earlier call to TlsAlloc.
dwTlsIndex = TlsAlloc();

lpvSomeValue = TlsGetValue(dwTlsIndex);
```

What do you think *lpvSomeValue* contains after the code above executes? 12345? The answer is 0. *TlsAlloc*, before returning, cycles through every thread existing in the process and places a 0 in each thread's array at the newly allocated index. This is very fortunate.

It's possible that an application will call *LoadLibrary* to load a DLL. And the DLL might call *TlsAlloc* to allocate an index. Then the thread might call *FreeLibrary* to remove the DLL. The DLL should free its index with a call to *TlsFree*, but who knows which values the DLL code placed in any of the thread's arrays? Next a thread calls *LoadLibrary* to load a different DLL into memory. This DLL also calls *TlsAlloc* when it starts and gets the same index used by the previous DLL. If *TlsAlloc* didn't set the returned index for all threads in the process, a thread might see an old value and the code might not execute correctly.

For example, this new DLL might want to check whether memory for a thread has ever been allocated by calling *TlsGetValue,* as in the code fragment shown above. If *TlsAlloc* doesn't clear out the array entry for every thread, the old data from the first DLL is still available. If a thread calls *MyFunction*, *MyFunction* thinks that a memory block has already been allocated and calls *memcpy* to copy the new data into what *MyFunction* thinks is a memory block. This could have disastrous results. Fortunately, *TlsAlloc* initializes the array elements so that the disaster can never happen.

The Dynamic Thread-Local Storage Sample Application

The TLSDyn (TLSDYN.EXE) application, listed in Figure 12-2 beginning on page 544, demonstrates how to take advantage of dynamic TLS. The program implicitly links to a dynamic-link library called SOMELIB.DLL, listed in Figure 12-3 beginning on page 550. This dynamic-link library allocates a single TLS index when it receives its DLL_PROCESS_ATTACH notification and frees this TLS index when it receives a DLL_PROCESS-_DETACH notification. The source code files, resource files, and make files for TLSDyn and SOMELIB.DLL are in the TLSDYN.12 directory on the companion disc.

SOMELIB.DLL contains a function called *LoadResString*. When this function is called, it first checks whether the calling thread previously called *LoadResString*. *LoadResString* determines this by calling *TlsGetValue* and checking whether the return value is NULL. A NULL value indicates a first-time call to *LoadResString*. In this case, *LoadResString* allocates a block of memory from the process's heap and stores the address of the block in the calling thread's TLS slot.

Whether or not this is the first time this thread is calling *Load-ResString*, we have an address to a block of memory in the heap allocated for this thread. *LoadResString* now calls *LoadString* to load a string from the DLL's string table into this block of memory. This string is now associated with the calling thread.

Finally, *LoadResString* increments an internal counter (stored in the static variable *nStringId*) and returns the address of the loaded string resource. Every time a thread calls *LoadResString*, a different string is retrieved from the DLL's string table.

Now let's look at how the TLSDyn application works. When you invoke it, the following message box appears:

String Before Dialog Box

String #0

OK

When *WinMain* begins executing, it makes a call to the *LoadRes-String* function, which in turn loads String #0 from the DLL's string table and associates the string with the process's primary thread. The primary thread then makes a call to *MessageBox* in order to show you that it was successful.

After you click on the OK button, the primary thread creates a dialog box and five threads. Each of these threads makes its own initial call to *LoadResString* so that each will have its own associated string. Then each thread iterates through a loop four times. With each iteration, each thread creates a string containing the thread number and its associated string. The string is then added to the list box. After all five threads have completed their loops, a dialog box appears as shown on the facing page.

The order of the strings might be different on your machine. Simply note that the *LoadResString* function assigns every thread its own string. Also note that if no thread in the program ever makes a call to

```
Dynamic Thread Local Storage          _ □ ×
Execution log:
Thread #1: String #1                    ▲
Thread #5: String #2
Thread #4: String #3
Thread #3: String #4
Thread #2: String #5
Thread #1: String #1
Thread #2: String #5
Thread #1: String #1
Thread #3: String #4
Thread #1: String #1
Thread #4: String #3
Thread #2: String #5
Thread #5: String #2
Thread #3: String #4
Thread #2: String #5
Thread #4: String #3
Thread #3: String #4
Thread #5: String #2
Thread #4: String #3
Thread #5: String #2                    ▼
```

LoadResString, memory isn't allocated from the heap for this thread. We could allocate the memory in the *DllMain* function whenever the program received either a DLL_PROCESS_ATTACH or a DLL_PROCESS-_DETACH notification, but that would mean allocating memory from the heap for all threads created by the process, even if they never called *LoadResString*. The method used by SOMELIB.DLL is more efficient.

After the program runs, you can terminate it, which causes another message box to appear:

```
String After Dialog Box    ×
 String #6

      ┌─────────┐
      │   OK    │
      └─────────┘
```

This message box appears as a result of *WinMain* making another call to *LoadResString*. *LoadResString* associates a new string with the primary thread, overwriting the original string, String #0.

Notice how the *DllMain* function in SOMELIB.C cleans up after itself when it receives either a DLL_THREAD_DETACH or a DLL-_PROCESS_DETACH. In both cases, the DLL checks whether memory from the heap was allocated for the thread and, if so, frees that memory block. Although the memory would be freed automatically when TLSDyn terminated, it's best to clean up yourself. Always check that memory is in fact allocated before attempting to free it (just as *DllMain* does). Also, notice how *TLSFree* is called when *DllMain* is notified that the library is being detached from the process.

Now suppose that an application is already running when one of its threads calls *LoadLibrary* to attach to SOMELIB.DLL. SOMELIB's *DllMain* allocates a TLS index that is guaranteed to be unique for all existing threads and all new threads for this process. Let's say that some threads call *LoadResString*, which results in memory allocation, and a thread calls *FreeLibrary* to detach SOMELIB.DLL. *DllMain* receives a DLL_PROCESS_DETACH message and frees any memory block associated with the calling thread. But what about other threads in the process that might have called *LoadResString*? The memory allocated by these threads will never be freed—we have a pretty bad memory leak here.

Unfortunately, this problem has no good solutions. Your DLL needs to track its allocations in an array, and when it receives a DLL_PROCESS_DETACH notification, it needs to traverse through all the pointers in the array and call *HeapFree* for each one.

TLSDyn.ico

TLSDYN.C

```
/**************************************************************
Module name: TLSDyn.C
Notices: Copyright (c) 1995 Jeffrey Richter
**************************************************************/


#include "..\AdvWin32.H"      /* See Appendix B for details. */
#include <windows.h>
#include <windowsx.h>


#pragma warning(disable: 4001)      /* Single-line comment */

#include <tchar.h>
#include <stdio.h>       // For sprintf
#include <process.h>     // For _beginthreadex
#include "SomeLib.H"

#include "Resource.H"
```

Figure 12-2.   *(continued)*
The TLSDyn application.

Figure 12-2. *continued*

```
///////////////////////////////////////////////////////////


#define LIBNAME   "SomeLib"

#if defined(_X86_)
   #if defined(_DEBUG)
      #pragma comment(lib, "Dbg_x86\\" LIBNAME)
   #else
      #pragma comment(lib, "Rel_x86\\" LIBNAME)
   #endif
#elif defined(_MIPS_)
   #if defined(_DEBUG)
      #pragma comment(lib, "Dbg_MIPS\\" LIBNAME)
   #else
      #pragma comment(lib, "Rel_MIPS\\" LIBNAME)
   #endif
#elif defined(_ALPHA_)
   #if defined(_DEBUG)
      #pragma comment(lib, "Dbg_Alph\\" LIBNAME)
   #else
      #pragma comment(lib, "Rel_Alph\\" LIBNAME)
   #endif
#else
   #error Modification required for this CPU platform.
#endif


///////////////////////////////////////////////////////////


HWND g_hwndLog = NULL;


///////////////////////////////////////////////////////////


DWORD WINAPI ThreadFunc (LPVOID lpvThreadParm) {
   int nThreadNum = (int) lpvThreadParm;
   int nNumCycles = 4;
   TCHAR szBuf[100];
   LPCTSTR szString = LoadResString();
```

(continued)

Figure 12-2. *continued*

```
    while (nNumCycles--) {
        _stprintf(szBuf, __TEXT("Thread #%d: %s"),
            nThreadNum, szString);

        ListBox_AddString(g_hwndLog, szBuf);

        Sleep(nThreadNum * 50);
    }
    return(0);
}


///////////////////////////////////////////////////////////////


BOOL Dlg_OnInitDialog (HWND hwnd, HWND hwndFocus,
    LPARAM lParam) {

    int nThreadNum;

    // Associate an icon with the dialog box.
    SetClassLong(hwnd, GCL_HICON, (LONG)
        LoadIcon((HINSTANCE) GetWindowLong(hwnd, GWL_HINSTANCE),
        __TEXT("TLSDyn")));

    g_hwndLog = GetDlgItem(hwnd, IDC_LOG);


    for (nThreadNum = 1; nThreadNum <= 5; nThreadNum++) {
        HANDLE hThread;
        DWORD dwIDThread;

        hThread = BEGINTHREADEX(NULL, 0, ThreadFunc,
            (LPVOID) nThreadNum, 0, &dwIDThread);

        CloseHandle(hThread);
    }

    return(TRUE);
}
```

(continued)

Figure 12-2. *continued*

```
///////////////////////////////////////////////////////////


void Dlg_OnCommand (HWND hwnd, int id, HWND hwndCtl,
   UINT codeNotify) {

   switch (id) {
      case IDCANCEL:
         EndDialog(hwnd, id);
         break;
   }
}


///////////////////////////////////////////////////////////


BOOL CALLBACK Dlg_Proc (HWND hDlg, UINT uMsg,
   WPARAM wParam, LPARAM lParam) {

   BOOL fProcessed = TRUE;

   switch (uMsg) {
      HANDLE_MSG(hDlg, WM_INITDIALOG, Dlg_OnInitDialog);
      HANDLE_MSG(hDlg, WM_COMMAND, Dlg_OnCommand);

      default:
         fProcessed = FALSE;
         break;
   }
   return(fProcessed);
}


///////////////////////////////////////////////////////////


int WINAPI WinMain (HINSTANCE hinstExe,
   HINSTANCE hinstPrev, LPSTR lpszCmdLine, int nCmdShow) {

   MessageBox(NULL, LoadResString(),
      __TEXT("String Before Dialog Box"), MB_OK);
```

(continued)

547

Figure 12-2. *continued*

```
    DialogBox(hinstExe, MAKEINTRESOURCE(IDD_TLSDYN),
        NULL, Dlg_Proc);

    MessageBox(NULL, LoadResString(),
        __TEXT("String After Dialog Box"), MB_OK);

    return(0);
}



///////////////////////// End Of File /////////////////////////
```

TLSDYN.RC
```
//Microsoft Visual C++ generated resource script.
//
#include "Resource.h"

#define APSTUDIO_READONLY_SYMBOLS
/////////////////////////////////////////////////////////////////
//
// Generated from the TEXTINCLUDE 2 resource.
//
#include "afxres.h"


/////////////////////////////////////////////////////////////////
#undef APSTUDIO_READONLY_SYMBOLS


#ifdef APSTUDIO_INVOKED
/////////////////////////////////////////////////////////////////
//
// TEXTINCLUDE
//

1 TEXTINCLUDE DISCARDABLE
BEGIN
    "Resource.h\0"
END

2 TEXTINCLUDE DISCARDABLE
BEGIN
    "#include ""afxres.h""\r\n"
    "\0"
END
```

(continued)

Figure 12-2. *continued*

```
3 TEXTINCLUDE DISCARDABLE
BEGIN
    "\r\n"
    "\0"
END


/////////////////////////////////////////////////////////////////
#endif    // APSTUDIO_INVOKED


/////////////////////////////////////////////////////////////////
//
// Icon
//

TLSDyn                ICON    DISCARDABLE    "TLSDyn.Ico"


/////////////////////////////////////////////////////////////////
//
// Dialog
//

IDD_TLSDYN DIALOG DISCARDABLE  25, 21, 147, 180
STYLE WS_MINIMIZEBOX | WS_VISIBLE | WS_CAPTION | WS_SYSMENU
CAPTION "Dynamic Thread Local Storage"
FONT 8, "System"
BEGIN
    LTEXT           "Execution &log:",IDC_STATIC,4,4,47,8
    LISTBOX         IDC_LOG,4,16,140,160,NOT LBS_NOTIFY
                    | LBS_NOINTEGRALHEIGHT | WS_VSCROLL
END


#ifndef APSTUDIO_INVOKED
/////////////////////////////////////////////////////////////////
//
// Generated from the TEXTINCLUDE 3 resource.
//


/////////////////////////////////////////////////////////////////
#endif    // not APSTUDIO_INVOKED
```

SOMELIB.C

```
/*************************************************************
Module name: SomeLib.C
Notices: Copyright (c) 1995 Jeffrey Richter
*************************************************************/


#include "..\AdvWin32.H"      /* See Appendix B for details. */
#include <windows.h>

#pragma warning(disable: 4001)        /* Single-line comment */

#include "SomeLib.RH"


#define _SOMELIBLIB_
#include "SomeLib.H"


///////////////////////////////////////////////////////////////


DWORD g_dwTlsIndex = TLS_OUT_OF_INDEXES;

// Per mapping instance data for this DLL
HINSTANCE g_hinstDll = NULL;


///////////////////////////////////////////////////////////////


BOOL WINAPI DllMain (HINSTANCE hinstDll, DWORD fdwReason,
   LPVOID lpvReserved) {

   LPTSTR lpszStr;

   switch (fdwReason) {

      case DLL_PROCESS_ATTACH:
         // DLL is attaching to the address space
         // of the current process.
         g_hinstDll = hinstDll;

         // Allocate a thread-local storage index.
         g_dwTlsIndex = TlsAlloc();
```

Figure 12-3.
The SomeLib.DLL file.

(continued)

Figure 12-3. *continued*

```
        if (g_dwTlsIndex == TLS_OUT_OF_INDEXES) {
            // The TLS index couldn't be allocated--have the
            // DLL return that initialization was
            // NOT successful.
            return(FALSE);
        }

        break;

    case DLL_THREAD_ATTACH:
        // A new thread is being created in the process.
        break;

    case DLL_THREAD_DETACH:
        // A thread is exiting cleanly.

        // Ensure that the TLS index was
        // allocated successfully.
        if (g_dwTlsIndex != TLS_OUT_OF_INDEXES) {

            // Get the pointer to the allocated memory.
            lpszStr = TlsGetValue(g_dwTlsIndex);

            // Test whether memory was ever allocated
            // for this thread.
            if (lpszStr != NULL) {
                HeapFree(GetProcessHeap(), 0, lpszStr);
            }
        }
        break;

    case DLL_PROCESS_DETACH:
        // The calling process is detaching the DLL
        // from its address space.

        // Ensure that the TLS index was
        // allocated successfully.
        if (g_dwTlsIndex != TLS_OUT_OF_INDEXES) {

            // Get the pointer to the allocated memory.
            lpszStr = TlsGetValue(g_dwTlsIndex);

            // Test whether memory was ever allocated
            // for this thread.
```

(continued)

Figure 12-3. *continued*

```
            if (lpszStr != NULL) {
                HeapFree(GetProcessHeap(), 0, lpszStr);
            }

            // Free the TLS index.
            TlsFree(g_dwTlsIndex);
        }
        break;
    }
    return(TRUE);
}


//////////////////////////////////////////////////////////////////


#define RESSTR_SIZE     (1000 * sizeof(TCHAR))

SOMELIBAPI LPCTSTR LoadResString (void) {
    static int nStringId = 0;

    LPTSTR lpszStr = TlsGetValue(g_dwTlsIndex);

    if (lpszStr == NULL) {
        lpszStr = HeapAlloc(GetProcessHeap(), 0, RESSTR_SIZE);
        TlsSetValue(g_dwTlsIndex, lpszStr);
    }

    LoadString(g_hinstDll, IDS_STRINGFIRST + nStringId,
        lpszStr, RESSTR_SIZE);

    nStringId = (nStringId + 1) % IDS_STRINGNUM;

    return(lpszStr);
}


///////////////////////// End Of File /////////////////////////
```

SOMELIB.H

```
/*************************************************************
Module name: SomeLib.H
Notices: Copyright (c) 1995 Jeffrey Richter
*************************************************************/
```

(continued)

Figure 12-3. *continued*

```
#if !defined(_SOMELIBLIB_)
#define SOMELIBAPI __declspec(dllimport)
#else
#define SOMELIBAPI __declspec(dllexport)
#endif


// IDs for use by the string table resource
#define IDS_STRINGLAST    (IDS_STRINGFIRST + 9)
#define IDS_STRINGNUM     (IDS_STRINGLAST - \
                           IDS_STRINGFIRST + 1)


// Function to return the address of a string in memory
SOMELIBAPI LPCTSTR LoadResString (void);


/////////////////////////// End Of File ///////////////////////////
```

```
SOMELIB.RC
//Microsoft Visual C++ generated resource script.
//
#include "SomeLib.rh"

#define APSTUDIO_READONLY_SYMBOLS
/////////////////////////////////////////////////////////////////////
//
// Generated from the TEXTINCLUDE 2 resource.
//
#include "afxres.h"


/////////////////////////////////////////////////////////////////////
#undef APSTUDIO_READONLY_SYMBOLS


#ifdef APSTUDIO_INVOKED
/////////////////////////////////////////////////////////////////////
//
// TEXTINCLUDE
//

1 TEXTINCLUDE DISCARDABLE
```

(continued)

Figure 12-3. *continued*

```
BEGIN
    "SomeLib.rh\0"
END

2 TEXTINCLUDE DISCARDABLE
BEGIN
    "#include ""afxres.h""\r\n"
    "\0"
END

3 TEXTINCLUDE DISCARDABLE
BEGIN
    "\r\n"
    "\0"
END


/////////////////////////////////////////////////////////////////
#endif    // APSTUDIO_INVOKED


/////////////////////////////////////////////////////////////////
//
// String Table
//

STRINGTABLE DISCARDABLE
BEGIN
    1008                    "String #8"
    1009                    "String #9"
END

STRINGTABLE DISCARDABLE
BEGIN
    IDS_STRINGFIRST         "String #0"
    1001                    "String #1"
    1002                    "String #2"
    1003                    "String #3"
    1004                    "String #4"
    1005                    "String #5"
    1006                    "String #6"
    1007                    "String #7"
END


#ifndef APSTUDIO_INVOKED
```

(continued)

Figure 12-3. *continued*

```
///////////////////////////////////////////////////////////
//
// Generated from the TEXTINCLUDE 3 resource.
//


///////////////////////////////////////////////////////////
#endif    // not APSTUDIO_INVOKED
```

Static Thread-Local Storage

Static thread-local storage uses the same concept as dynamic TLS—it associates data with a thread. However, static TLS is much easier to use in your code because you don't need to call any functions to take advantage of it.

Let's say that you want to associate a start time with every thread created by your application. All you need to do is declare the start-time variable as follows:

```
__declspec(thread) DWORD gt_dwStartTime = 0;
```

The *__declspec(thread)* prefix in the line above is a new modifier that Microsoft added to the Visual C++ compiler. It tells the compiler that the corresponding variable should be placed in its own section inside the EXE or DLL file. The variable following *__declspec(thread)* must be declared as either a global variable or a static variable inside (or outside) a function. You can't declare a local variable to be of type *__declspec(thread)*. This shouldn't be a problem because local variables are always associated with a specific thread anyway. I use the *gt_* prefix for global TLS variables and *st_* for static TLS variables.

When the compiler compiles your program, it puts all the TLS variables into their own section named, unsurprisingly enough, .tls. The linker combines all the .tls sections together from all the object modules to produce one big .tls section in the resulting EXE or DLL file.

To actually make static TLS work, the operating system needs to get involved. When your application is loaded into memory, the system looks for the .tls section in your EXE file and dynamically allocates a block of memory large enough to hold all the static TLS variables. Every time the code in your application refers to one of these variables, the reference resolves to a memory location contained in the allocated block of memory. As a result, the compiler must generate additional code in order to reference the static TLS variables, which makes your application both larger in size and slower to execute. On an $x86$ CPU, three additional machine instructions are generated for every reference to a static TLS variable.

If another thread is created in your process, the system traps it and automatically allocates another block of memory to contain the new thread's static TLS variables. The new thread has access only to its own static TLS variables and isn't able to access the TLS variables belonging to any other thread.

That's basically how static TLS works. Now let's add DLLs to the story. It's likely that your application will use static TLS variables and that you will link to a DLL that also wants to use static TLS variables. When the system loads your application, it first determines the size of your application's .tls section and adds the value to the size of any .tls sections contained in any DLLs to which your application links. When threads are created in your process, the system automatically allocates a block of memory large enough to hold all the TLS variables required by your application and all the implicitly linked DLLs. This is pretty cool.

But let's look at what happens when your application calls *Load-Library* to link to a DLL that also contains static TLS variables. The system needs to look at all the threads that already exist in the process and enlarge their TLS memory blocks to accommodate the additional memory requirements of the new DLL. Also, if *FreeLibrary* is called to free a DLL containing static TLS variables, the memory block associated with each thread in the process should be compacted.

Alas, this is too much for the operating system to manage. The system allows libraries containing static TLS variables to be explicitly loaded at run time; however, the TLS data isn't properly initialized, and any attempt to access it may result in an access violation. This is the only disadvantage of using static TLS; this problem doesn't occur when using dynamic TLS. Libraries that use dynamic TLS can be loaded at run time and freed at run time with no problems at all.

The Static Thread-Local Storage Sample Application

The TLSStat (TLSSTAT.EXE) application, listed in Figure 12-4 beginning on page 559, demonstrates the use of static TLS. The source code files, resource files, and make file for the application are in the TLSSTAT.12 directory on the companion disc. When you first invoke TLSStat, the following dialog box appears:

This dialog box allows you to dynamically create new threads and monitor their execution.

The following line is included near the top of TLSSTAT.C:

```
__declspec(thread) DWORD gt_dwStartTime = 0;
```

This line declares a static TLS variable called *gt_dwStartTime*. The system creates a new instance of this variable every time a new thread is created in the process. Whenever any thread refers to *gt_dwStartTime*, that thread is always referring to its own copy of this variable.

Clicking on the Create Thread button dynamically creates a new thread by allocating a data structure from the heap and filling the members of the structure with information that needs to be passed to the newly created thread. This information includes the thread number, the number of cycles that the thread should execute, and the duration of each cycle. The pointer to this data structure is then passed to *_beginthreadex*, which passes the pointer to the thread function. The thread function is responsible for freeing this memory block when it no longer needs it.[2]

---

2. While I was writing this section of code, I thought it would be useful to have a new Win32 function that offered some way for one thread to alter the thread-local storage variables used by another thread. If this function existed, I probably could have avoided using the heap altogether by simply assigning values to the new thread.

When each new thread begins, it records the system time in the *gt_dwStartTime* variable and starts executing a loop. As each iteration of the loop begins, the thread displays the total amount of time that the thread has been in existence in the Thread Execution Log list box.

You should notice that in this example I could have done away with the *gt_dwStartTime* variable by creating a local (stack-based) variable called *dwStartTime* and placing it inside *ThreadFunc*. In fact, this would have been a better way to write the application because it would have avoided the additional size and speed overhead incurred when using static TLS. However, if I had done this, the demonstration program would no longer have demonstrated static TLS.

The real point I'm trying to make is that an application "understands" the nature of the program, whereas a DLL most likely doesn't. This is why TLS was really designed for DLLs, although it can be used in applications.

Before creating a thread, you can set the number of iterations in the loop and the duration of each iteration by adjusting the contents of the Num Of Cycles and Cycle Time (Secs) edit boxes. Because a new thread can take several seconds to execute, you can create additional threads before the first thread finishes executing by adjusting the Num Of Cycles and Cycle Time (Secs) edit boxes and clicking on the Create Thread button again. The screen shot below was taken while three threads were executing simultaneously:

The three threads were created using the following settings:

Thread Number	Num Of Cycles	Cycle Time (Secs)
1	10	3
2	5	2
3	3	1

Every time a new thread is created, the Thread Number value is incremented. You can reset the application by clicking on the Clear button, which causes the Thread Number value to reset to 1 and the contents of the list box to be cleared.

One last thing to note. When you terminate TLSStat, it displays the following message box:

TLS Static

Total time running application=115841

OK

The box displays the total amount of time that the application (or primary thread) has been executing by referencing its own *gt_dwStartTime* TLS variable.

TLSStat.ico

TLSSTAT.C

```
/*************************************************************
Module name: TLSStat.C
Notices: Copyright (c) 1995 Jeffrey Richter
*************************************************************/


#include "..\AdvWin32.H"    /* See Appendix B for details. */
#include <windows.h>
#include <windowsx.h>

#pragma warning(disable: 4001)      /* Single-line comment */

#include <tchar.h>
#include <stdlib.h>                 // For rand
```

Figure 12-4.
The TLSStat application.

(continued)

Figure 12-4. *continued*

```
#include <stdio.h>              // For sprintf
#include <process.h>            // For _beginthreadex
#include "Resource.H"


////////////////////////////////////////////////////////////////


// Structure used to pass data from one thread to another
typedef struct {
    int nThreadNum;        // The number used for recordkeeping
    int nNumCycles;        // Number of iterations in the loop
    DWORD dwCycleTime;     // Time spent in each loop iteration
} THREADDATA, *LPTHREADDATA;

// Global handle to list box window used for
// logging execution
HWND g_hwndLogLB = NULL;


// Our global static TLS variable
// to hold each thread's start time
// The system will automatically allocate one of these
// for every thread created in this process.
__declspec(thread) DWORD gt_dwStartTime = 0;



////////////////////////////////////////////////////////////////


DWORD WINAPI ThreadFunc (LPVOID lpvThreadParm) {
    // The parameter passed to us is a pointer to a THREADDATA
    // structure. Let's save it in a local variable.
    LPTHREADDATA lpThreadData = (LPTHREADDATA) lpvThreadParm;

    TCHAR szBuf[100];

    // Store the thread's start time in its very
    // own static TLS variable.
    gt_dwStartTime = GetTickCount();

    // Write a log entry stating that we're starting.
    _stprintf(szBuf, __TEXT("Thread started: %d"),
        lpThreadData->nThreadNum);
    ListBox_AddString(g_hwndLogLB, szBuf);
    ListBox_SetCurSel(g_hwndLogLB, 0);
```

(continued)

Figure 12-4. *continued*

```
    // Start doing some work....
    while (lpThreadData->nNumCycles--) {
        // Write to the log how many cycles this thread
        // has left before it dies and how long this thread
        // has been running.
        _stprintf(szBuf,
            __TEXT("Thread %d, Cycles left=%d, time running=%d"),
            lpThreadData->nThreadNum, lpThreadData->nNumCycles,
            GetTickCount() - gt_dwStartTime);

        ListBox_AddString(g_hwndLogLB, szBuf);

        // Sleep for awhile and let other threads run.
        Sleep(lpThreadData->dwCycleTime);
    }

    // This thread is done executing; write a log entry
    // that says so and displays the total execution time
    // of the thread.
    _stprintf(szBuf, __TEXT("Thread ended: %d, total time=%d"),
        lpThreadData->nThreadNum,
        GetTickCount() - gt_dwStartTime);
    ListBox_AddString(g_hwndLogLB, szBuf);

    // The thread is responsible for deleting the THREADDATA
    // structure that was allocated by the primary thread.
    HeapFree(GetProcessHeap(), 0, lpvThreadParm);

    return(0);
}


///////////////////////////////////////////////////////////////////


BOOL Dlg_OnInitDialog (HWND hwnd, HWND hwndFocus,
    LPARAM lParam) {

    // Associate an icon with the dialog box.
    SetClassLong(hwnd, GCL_HICON, (LONG)
        LoadIcon((HINSTANCE) GetWindowLong(hwnd, GWL_HINSTANCE),
        __TEXT("TLSStat")));

    // Default the thread number to 1.
    SetDlgItemInt(hwnd, IDC_THREADNUM, 1, FALSE);
```

(continued)

Figure 12-4. *continued*

```
    // Default the number of cycles to 10.
    SetDlgItemInt(hwnd, IDC_NUMCYCLES, 10, FALSE);

    // Default the maximum cycle time to 3 seconds.
    SetDlgItemInt(hwnd, IDC_CYCLETIME, 3, FALSE);

    // Save the handle of the dialog box in a global
    // variable so that it can be accessed easily from
    // the thread function.
    g_hwndLogLB = GetDlgItem(hwnd, IDC_LOG);

    // Let's start with the Create Thread
    // button having focus.
    SetFocus(GetDlgItem(hwnd, IDOK));

    // I set focus, so the Dialog Manager shouldn't.
    return(FALSE);
}


///////////////////////////////////////////////////////////////


void Dlg_OnCommand (HWND hwnd, int id, HWND hwndCtl,
    UINT codeNotify) {

    DWORD        dwIDThread;
    HANDLE       hThread;
    LPTHREADDATA lpThreadData;

    switch (id) {

        case IDC_CLEAR:
            // Reset the application.
            SetDlgItemInt(hwnd, IDC_THREADNUM, 1, FALSE);
            ListBox_ResetContent(g_hwndLogLB);
            break;

        case IDOK:
            // Allocate a block of memory that can be used to
            // give data from this thread to the new thread we
            // are about to create.
            lpThreadData = (LPTHREADDATA)
                HeapAlloc(GetProcessHeap(), 0,
                    sizeof(THREADDATA));
```

(continued)

Figure 12-4. *continued*

```
      if (lpThreadData == NULL) {
         // Memory could not be allocated; display message
         // box and break.
         MessageBox(hwnd,
            __TEXT("Error creating ThreadData"),
            __TEXT("TLS Static"), MB_OK);
         break;
      }

      // Fill the memory block with the data from
      // the dialog box.
      lpThreadData->nThreadNum =
         GetDlgItemInt(hwnd, IDC_THREADNUM, NULL, FALSE);
      lpThreadData->nNumCycles =
         GetDlgItemInt(hwnd, IDC_NUMCYCLES, NULL, FALSE);

      // Multiply the cycle time by 1000
      // to convert to seconds.
      lpThreadData->dwCycleTime = (DWORD)
         (1000 * GetDlgItemInt(hwnd,
            IDC_CYCLETIME, NULL, FALSE));

      // Increment the thread number for the next thread.
      SetDlgItemInt(hwnd, IDC_THREADNUM,
         lpThreadData->nThreadNum + 1, FALSE);

      // Create the new thread and pass it the address of
      // our allocated memory block containing the
      // attributes that the thread should use. The
      // thread is responsible for freeing the memory
      // block when it no longer needs it.
      hThread = BEGINTHREADEX(NULL, 0, ThreadFunc,
            (LPVOID) lpThreadData, 0, &dwIDThread);

      if (hThread != NULL) {
         // If the thread was created successfully, close
         // the handle because this thread never needs
         // to refer to the new thread again.
         CloseHandle(hThread);

      } else {
```

(continued)

Figure 12-4. *continued*

```
             // The thread could not be created;
             // display message box and break.
             MessageBox(hwnd,
                __TEXT("Error creating the new thread"),
                __TEXT("TLS Static"), MB_OK);
             HeapFree(GetProcessHeap(), 0,
                (LPVOID) lpThreadData);
          }
          break;

       case IDCANCEL:
          EndDialog(hwnd, id);
          break;
    }
}


//////////////////////////////////////////////////////////////

BOOL CALLBACK Dlg_Proc (HWND hDlg, UINT uMsg,
    WPARAM wParam, LPARAM lParam) {

   BOOL fProcessed = TRUE;

   switch (uMsg) {
      HANDLE_MSG(hDlg, WM_INITDIALOG, Dlg_OnInitDialog);
      HANDLE_MSG(hDlg, WM_COMMAND, Dlg_OnCommand);

      default:
         fProcessed = FALSE;
         break;
   }
   return(fProcessed);
}


//////////////////////////////////////////////////////////////

int WINAPI WinMain (HINSTANCE hinstExe,
    HINSTANCE hinstPrev, LPSTR lpszCmdLine, int nCmdShow) {

   TCHAR szBuf[100];
```

(continued)

Figure 12-4. *continued*

```
    // The primary thread also gets its own TLS copy
    // of the gt_dwStartTime variable. Let's initialize it to
    // the time when the application started executing.
    gt_dwStartTime = GetTickCount();

    DialogBox(hinstExe, MAKEINTRESOURCE(IDD_TLSSTAT),
        NULL, Dlg_Proc);

    // The user has terminated the dialog box; let's show
    // how long the whole application has been running.
    _stprintf(szBuf,
        __TEXT("Total time running application=%d."),
        GetTickCount() - gt_dwStartTime);
    MessageBox(NULL, szBuf, __TEXT("TLS Static"), MB_OK);

    return(0);
}


/////////////////////////// End Of File ///////////////////////////
```

```
TLSSTAT.RC
//Microsoft Visual C++ generated resource script.
//
#include "Resource.h"

#define APSTUDIO_READONLY_SYMBOLS
/////////////////////////////////////////////////////////////////////
//
// Generated from the TEXTINCLUDE 2 resource.
//
#include "afxres.h"


/////////////////////////////////////////////////////////////////////
#undef APSTUDIO_READONLY_SYMBOLS


#ifdef APSTUDIO_INVOKED
/////////////////////////////////////////////////////////////////////
//
// TEXTINCLUDE
//
```

(continued)

Figure 12-4. *continued*

```
1 TEXTINCLUDE DISCARDABLE
BEGIN
    "Resource.h\0"
END

2 TEXTINCLUDE DISCARDABLE
BEGIN
    "#include ""afxres.h""\r\n"
    "\0"
END

3 TEXTINCLUDE DISCARDABLE
BEGIN
    "\r\n"
    "\0"
END


/////////////////////////////////////////////////////////////////
#endif    // APSTUDIO_INVOKED


/////////////////////////////////////////////////////////////////
//
// Dialog
//

IDD_TLSSTAT DIALOG DISCARDABLE  18, 18, 180, 215
STYLE WS_MINIMIZEBOX ¦ WS_VISIBLE ¦ WS_CAPTION ¦ WS_SYSMENU
CAPTION "Static Thread Local Storage"
FONT 8, "Helv"
BEGIN
    LTEXT           "Thread number:",IDC_STATIC,4,4,52,8
    RTEXT           "1",IDC_THREADNUM,60,4,13,8
    PUSHBUTTON      "Clea&r",IDC_CLEAR,104,4,56,14
    LTEXT           "&Num of cycles:",IDC_STATIC,4,20,50,8
    EDITTEXT        IDC_NUMCYCLES,68,20,28,13
    LTEXT           "&Cycle time (secs):",IDC_STATIC,
                    4,36,59,8
    EDITTEXT        IDC_CYCLETIME,68,36,28,13
    DEFPUSHBUTTON   "Create &thread",IDOK,104,36,
                    56,14,WS_GROUP
    LTEXT           "Thread execution &log:",IDC_STATIC,
                    4,56,72,8
    LISTBOX         IDC_LOG,4,68,172,144,NOT LBS_NOTIFY
                    ¦ WS_VSCROLL ¦
                    WS_GROUP ¦ WS_TABSTOP
END
```

(continued)

Figure 12-4. *continued*

```
///////////////////////////////////////////////////////////////
//
// Icon
//

TLSStat                    ICON     DISCARDABLE     "TLSStat.Ico"

#ifndef APSTUDIO_INVOKED
///////////////////////////////////////////////////////////////
//
// Generated from the TEXTINCLUDE 3 resource.
//


///////////////////////////////////////////////////////////////
#endif    // not APSTUDIO_INVOKED
```

CHAPTER THIRTEEN

FILE SYSTEMS AND FILE I/O

One important aspect of any operating system is the way in which it manages files. In good old MS-DOS, managing files is about all the operating system did, especially when 16-bit Windows was running on top of it. 16-bit Windows pretty much took care of everything except the manipulation of files on hard disks and floppy disks, which it left up to MS-DOS. (As time went on, though, 16-bit Windows took on more of even this responsibility by adding direct 32-bit access support and going right to the disk controller to manipulate the system's paging file.)

Now both Windows 95 and Windows NT have greatly enhanced 32-bit file support for managing the user's files and drives. In fact, both of these operating systems sport an installable file system that is capable of supporting multiple file systems—all of them simultaneously.

The File Allocation Table (FAT) file system is the familiar file system currently used by all versions of MS-DOS. Windows 95 has extended the MS-DOS file system by adding support for long filenames. Microsoft expects this feature to be extremely compelling to end users and hopes that application developers will update their software to handle long filenames appropriately. Windows NT 3.5 also supports long filenames on FAT partitions in order to be compatible with Windows 95. Windows NT 3.1, however, doesn't offer this support.

Although Windows NT supports two additional disk drive file systems, the High Performance File System (HPFS) and the NT File System (NTFS), the FAT file system will probably be the most common file system used. For users who need to boot flexibly between MS-DOS, Windows 95, and Windows NT, the FAT file system will certainly be the file system of choice because all the user's files will be accessible to all the operating systems. Note too that the FAT file system is the only file system that can be used on floppy disks.

HPFS, originally designed for use with the OS/2 operating system, was created to overcome many of the limitations of the FAT file system. However, it didn't deal with data corruption problems very well at all. In the event of a system crash, it was possible that some important file-related information wouldn't be written back to the disk. The next time OS/2 was booted, a CHKDSK that could take several hours to reconstruct the important file-related data would have to be performed. Windows NT supports the HPFS file system for backward compatibility with the files of users who are upgrading from OS/2 to Windows NT and don't want to reformat their hard disks just yet.

NTFS is, as its name implies, brand-new for Windows NT. It's the next-generation file system after HPFS; the problems associated with HPFS have been fixed in NTFS, and NTFS has several new features as well. The most important of the new features is a file system recovery scheme that allows for quick restoration of disk-based data after a system failure.

Other features of NTFS include the ability to manipulate extremely large storage media and to have filenames of up to 255 characters in length (just like the new FAT file system in Windows 95 and Windows NT 3.5). Several security features, such as execute-only files (which make it far more difficult for a virus to attach itself to an application), have been added. NTFS stores all filenames and directory names by means of the international Unicode. This means among other things that files will retain their names when they're copied to systems that use different languages. For POSIX compatibility, NTFS supports file system features such as hard links, case-sensitive filenames, and the ability to retain information regarding when a file was last opened.

NTFS was designed to be extended. Features that will be supported include transaction-based operations to support fault tolerant applications, user-controlled version numbers for files, multiple data streams per file, flexible options for file naming and file attributes, and support for the popular file servers. For security-minded installations, NTFS will certainly become the standard, and it should eventually replace the FAT file system standard.

The CD-ROM File System (CDFS) is used specifically for a CD-ROM drive, once considered a high-ticket peripheral for a personal computer. Today a CD-ROM drive is becoming more a necessity than a luxury. More and more software is becoming available on CD-ROM, and Windows 95 and Windows NT themselves are available on CD-ROM. In the future more software programs will use CD-ROMs as their distribution medium because CD-ROMs offer several advantages:

- CD-ROMs are less expensive to mass-produce when compared to the sheer number of floppy disks involved in so much of software distribution. This should lower the cost of retail software products.

- Because the average end user doesn't have CD-ROM duplication equipment, it's much harder for end users to pirate copies of software distributed on CD-ROM. People who want to use the software will have to buy it. This should also help lower the cost of retail software products.

- CD-ROMs are more reliable than floppies because CD-ROMs aren't magnetic and therefore, unlike floppies, aren't subject to magnetic disturbances.

- Data can be accessed directly from a CD-ROM without having to be installed on your hard drive. This can save enormous amounts of precious hard disk space.

- Applications are much easier to install from a CD-ROM because you don't have to baby-sit the computer, switching floppies on demand.

Microsoft's having built CD-ROM support directly into Windows 95 and Windows NT will certainly help to promote the use and wide acceptance of CD-ROMs in the marketplace.

The best aspect of all these file systems is that they provide simultaneous operating system support. If you are using Windows NT, you can easily have one partition on your hard disk formatted for HPFS and another formatted for NTFS. Then you can easily copy files from either of these partitions to a floppy disk formatted for the FAT file system.

Win32's Filename Conventions

So that Win32 can support several different file systems, all the file systems must observe some ground rules. The most important rule is that each file system must organize files into a hierarchical directory tree just as the FAT file system does. Directory names and filenames in the pathname must be separated by the backslash (\) character. In addition to the rules for constructing pathnames, there are rules for constructing directory names and filenames.

■ All pathnames must be zero-terminated.

■ Directory names and filenames must not contain the backslash separator character (\), a character whose ASCII value is in the range 0 through 31, or any character explicitly disallowed by any of the file systems.

■ Directory names and filenames can be created in mixed case, but users must anticipate that searches for directories and files will always be performed by means of case-insensitive comparisons. If a file called ReadMe.Txt already exists and you try to name another file README.TXT, the naming of the second file will fail.

■ When used to specify a directory name, the period (.) identifies the current directory. For example, the pathname .\README.TXT indicates that the file is in the current directory.

■ When used to specify a directory name, two periods (..) identify the parent directory of the current directory. For example, the pathname ..\README.TXT indicates that the file is in the current directory's parent directory.

■ When used as part of a directory name or filename, a period (.) separates individual components of the name. For example, in the file README.TXT, the period separates the file's name (in the smaller sense) from the file's extension.

■ Directory names and filenames must not contain some special characters; these include the less than sign (<), the greater than sign (>), the colon (:), the double quotation marks ("), and the pipe (¦).

All file systems supported by Win32 must follow these ground rules. The differences among the file systems have to do with how each file system interprets the ground rules and with the additional features or information a file system adds that distinguishes it from others. For example, the NTFS file system allows directories and files to be secured, whereas the FAT and HPFS file systems do not.

System and Volume Operations

Let's look at the file system at the highest level first and work our way down to the nitty-gritty stuff. At the highest level, your application might need to know what logical drives exist in the user's environment. The most primitive call you can make to determine this is:

```
DWORD GetLogicalDrives(void);
```

This function simply returns a 32-bit value in which each bit represents whether a logical drive exists. For example, if the system has a drive A, bit 0 will be set, and if the system has a drive Z, bit 25 will be set.

You can determine whether a particular drive letter was assigned to a logical drive on the system by executing this function:

```
BOOL DoesDriveExist (TCHAR cDriveLetter) {
   cDriveLetter = (TCHAR) CharUpper(cDriveLetter);
   return(GetLogicalDrives() & (1 << (cDriveLetter - __TEXT('A'))));
}
```

The result from *GetLogicalDrives* can also be used to count the number of logical drives in the system:

```
UINT GetNumDrivesInSys (void) {
   DWORD dw = GetLogicalDrives();
   UINT uDrivesInSys = 0;

   // Repeat until there are no more drives.
   while (dw != 0) {

      if (dw & 1) {
         // If low-bit is set, drive exists.
         uDrivesInSys++;
      }

      // Shift all the drive information down 1 bit.
      dw >>= 1;
   }

   // Return number of logical drives.
   return(uDrivesInSys);
}
```

The *GetLogicalDrives* function is very fast but doesn't return a lot of useful information. The *GetLogicalDriveStrings* function doesn't require all the bit manipulations and returns more complete information:

```
DWORD GetLogicalDriveStrings(DWORD cchBuffer, LPTSTR lpszBuffer);
```

This function fills the buffer pointed to by *lpszBuffer* with the root directory information associated with every logical drive on the system. The *cchBuffer* parameter tells the function the maximum size of the buffer. The function returns the number of characters required to hold all the data. When calling this function, you should always compare the return value with the value passed in the *cchBuffer* parameter. If the return value is smaller, the buffer was large enough to hold all of the data. If the return value is larger, there was more data than could fit into the buffer.

The best way to use this function is to call it once, passing in 0 as the *cchBuffer* parameter. Then use the return value to dynamically allocate a block of memory of the size returned by the call to *GetLogicalDriveStrings*. Then call the function again, this time passing in the address of the newly allocated buffer:

```
DWORD dw = GetLogicalDriveStrings(0, NULL);
LPTSTR lpDriveStrings = HeapAlloc(GetProcessHeap(), 0, dw *
    sizeof(TCHAR));
GetLogicalDriveStrings(dw, lpDriveStrings);
```

The contents of the returned buffer have the same format as an environment string buffer: that is, items separated by a zero character with an extra, terminating zero character at the end. For example, on my machine the buffer comes back looking like this:

```
A:\<null>
B:\<null>
C:\<null>
D:\<null>
E:\<null>
F:\<null>
G:\<null>
<null>
```

Under Windows 95, the *GetLogicalDriveStrings* function has no useful implementation and simply returns 0; calling *GetLastError* returns ERROR_CALL_NOT_IMPLEMENTED.

Now that you have the root directories for every logical drive on the system, you might want to determine exactly what type of drive each is located on. You can use *GetDriveType*:

```
UINT GetDriveType(LPTSTR lpszRootPathName);
```

The *GetDriveType* function returns the type of drive identified by the *lpszRootPathName* parameter. Here are the possible return values:

Identifier	Meaning
0	Drive type can't be determined.
1	Root directory doesn't exist.
DRIVE_REMOVEABLE	Disk can be removed from the drive. This value is returned for floppy drives.
DRIVE_FIXED	Disk can't be removed from the drive. This value is returned for hard drives.
DRIVE_REMOTE	Drive is a remote drive. This value is returned for network drives.
DRIVE_CDROM	Drive is a CD-ROM drive.
DRIVE_RAMDISK	Drive is a RAM disk.

You might be familiar with the 16-bit Windows version of the *GetDriveType* function:

```
UINT GetDriveType(int nDriveNumber);
```

You'll want to take note of some differences in the Win32 version. First, Win32's version of this function takes a pointer to a zero-terminated string as its parameter, whereas the 16-bit Windows version accepts an integer identifying the drive to be tested (A = 0, B = 1, and so on).

Using an integer instead of a string has always been a problem for 16-bit Windows programmers. Using MS-DOS's JOIN command, you can logically connect a drive to another drive as a subdirectory of the second drive's root directory. For example, if you execute:

```
JOIN A: C:\DRIVE-A
```

MS-DOS creates a new logical directory called DRIVE-A as a subdirectory of drive C's root directory. If you were to issue the following command:

```
DIR C:\DRIVE-A
```

the contents of the floppy disk in drive A would be displayed. Using the 16-bit Windows *GetDriveType* function, you can pass only a drive letter to the function. In this case, we would have to pass the value 2 (for drive C) and *GetDriveType* would return DRIVE_FIXED. Using the Win32 version of *GetDriveType*, you can pass C:\DRIVE-A as the parameter. In this case, the Win32 version will return DRIVE_REMOVEABLE, which is the correct value.

As it turns out, Microsoft made so many improvements to the file systems in Windows 95 and Windows NT that the JOIN command is no longer necessary and is not supported. In MS-DOS, the SUBST command is the complement of the JOIN command. Whereas the JOIN command attaches the root directory of a drive as a subdirectory to another drive, the SUBST command creates a new drive letter for a subdirectory on another drive. The SUBST command is not as useful under Windows 95 and Windows NT as it was under MS-DOS, and Microsoft discouraged its use for 16-bit Windows, but unlike JOIN, SUBST is still supported in Win32, and there are no problems with using it.

Another big limitation of the 16-bit Windows version of *GetDriveType* is that it doesn't always return as much information as you'd like. If you query the type of a CD-ROM drive, DRIVE_REMOVEABLE is returned, and if you query the type of a RAM disk, DRIVE_FIXED is returned. Frequently, applications that really need to make use of this information are required to make additional tests to determine whether a drive is really a CD-ROM or a RAM disk.

Getting Volume-Specific Information

When developing a Win32 application, you should always keep in mind that the user might be using any combination of the present four file systems (FAT, HPFS, NTFS, and CDFS) and that new file systems will emerge in the future.[1] Any new file systems will need to follow the ground rules, and with a little extra work you can write an application so that it runs correctly regardless of which file system or systems the user is using. If your application needs some specific information about a particular file system, it can call *GetVolumeInformation*:

```
BOOL GetVolumeInformation(LPTSTR lpRootPathName,
    LPTSTR lpVolumeNameBuffer, DWORD nVolumeNameSize,
    LPDWORD lpVolumeSerialNumber, LPDWORD lpMaximumComponentLength,
    LPDWORD lpFileSystemFlags, LPTSTR lpFileSystemNameBuffer,
    DWORD nFileSystemNameSize);
```

---

1. Even as you read this, Microsoft is hard at work on a new file system called OFS (Object File System), which will help realize Bill Gates's vision of "Information at Your Fingertips."

The *GetVolumeInformation* function returns file system–specific information associated with the directory path specified in the *lpRootPath-Name* parameter. Most of the remaining parameters are pointers to buffers or DWORDs that the function will fill.

GetVolumeInformation returns the name of the volume in *lpVolume-NameBuffer*. For the FAT file system, this is the label of the floppy disk drive or the hard drive. The *nVolumeNameSize* parameter indicates the maximum size of the buffer in characters. The DWORD pointed to by the *lpVolumeSerialNumber* parameter gets filled with the serial number of the volume. If you are not interested in this information, NULL can be passed as the *lpVolumeSerialNumber* parameter.

The serial number is most useful when another disk has been inserted in the drive. Starting with MS-DOS 4.0, the FORMAT command puts serial number information on a disk. This way, even if two disks have the same volume label, each has its own unique serial number. If the user removes one disk and inserts the other, the volume labels could be the same but the serial numbers would be different. An application can check to determine whether the user has swapped disks.

The DWORD pointed to by the *lpMaximumComponentLength* parameter gets filled with the maximum number of characters supported for directory names and filenames. For the FAT, HPFS, NTFS, and CDFS file systems, the value is 255. Many applications hard-code lengths in their source code for pathname and filename buffers. This is a big no-no! For many applications, everything might seem OK at first, as the application manipulates files and paths with short filenames; but when the application manipulates files with long filenames, you'll get stack overwrites, invalid memory accesses, and other assorted problems.

When you are developing an application, create some lo-o-ong filenames and some hu-u-uge pathnames, and bury some of your application's data files deep down in the bowels of the directory hierarchy to see how your application performs. It's much better for you to catch file system problems during development rather than after you ship.

Another easy-to-forget consideration is Unicode. If you are using Unicode in your application, your buffers need to be twice as big. Only the FAT and the NTFS file systems store filenames as Unicode strings, and the system knows whether your application manipulates Unicode filenames. When you request paths and filenames, the system will perform any and all conversions for you, but you must ensure that your buffers will be big enough to hold the results of these conversions.

The DWORD pointed to by the *lpFileSystemFlags* parameter is filled with flags about the file system. Here are the possible values:

Flag Identifier	Meaning
FS_CASE_IS_PRESERVED	The case of a filename is preserved when the name is put on disk.
FS_CASE_SENSITIVE	The file system supports case-sensitive filename lookup.
FS_UNICODE_STORED_ON_DISK	The file system supports Unicode in filenames as they appear on disk.
FS_PERSISTENT_ACLS	The file system preserves and enforces access control lists (NTFS only).

The *lpFileSystemNameBuffer* parameter points to a buffer that *Get-VolumeInformation* will fill with the name of the file system (FAT, HPFS, NTFS, or CDFS). The last parameter, *nFileSystemNameSize*, is the maximum size of the *lpFileSystemNameBuffer* buffer in characters.

Most of the information returned by *GetVolumeInformation* is determined when the user's disk is formatted, and it can't be changed unless the user's disk is reformatted. The one piece of information that you can change without reformatting is the disk's volume label. You can change it by calling:

```
BOOL SetVolumeLabel(LPTSTR lpRootPathName, LPTSTR lpVolumeName);
```

The first parameter of *SetVolumeLabel* is the root directory of the file system whose volume label you want to change. If you specify NULL here, the system changes the volume label for the process's current disk. The *lpVolumeName* parameter indicates the new name you want the volume to have. Specifying NULL here causes *SetVolumeLabel* to remove any volume label from the disk.

Another function you can call to get disk volume information is the *GetDiskFreeSpace* function:

```
BOOL GetDiskFreeSpace(LPTSTR lpszRootPathName,
   LPDWORD lpSectorsPerCluster, LPDWORD lpBytesPerSector,
   LPDWORD lpFreeClusters, LPDWORD lpClusters);
```

The *GetDiskFreeSpace* function returns space availability statistics about the volume identified by the *lpszRootPathName* parameter. All the bytes available on floppy disks and hard drives are packaged together into sectors, usually with 512 bytes per sector. Sectors are then grouped together to form clusters. In the FAT file system, the number of sectors per cluster can vary dramatically, as this table indicates:

Disk Type	Sectors per Cluster
360-KB floppy disk	2
1.2-MB floppy disk	4
200-MB hard disk	8
400-MB hard disk	32

When parts of a disk are allocated to a file, the minimum amount of memory that can be allocated to a file is a single cluster. For example, a 10-byte file would occupy 2 sectors, or 1 KB (2 × 512 bytes), on a 360-KB floppy; but the same file would occupy 8 sectors, or 4 KB (8 × 512 bytes), on a 200-MB hard disk.

Let's say that we have two 1-KB files on a floppy disk and try to copy both files to a 200-MB hard drive that has only 4 KB of free space. The first file will be copied successfully, but there will be insufficient disk space on the hard drive for the second file. We've tried to copy 2 KB of data into a 4-KB space and failed. On very large media, this cluster overhead can become a serious problem.

While I was writing the first edition of this book, I upgraded my 250-MB hard drive to a 1-GB hard drive. I also decided to partition the new drive into two 512-MB partitions. Each partition used 32 sectors per cluster. This meant that a 1-byte file required a minimum of 16 KB. After I'd finished installing about 200 MB of file data, the amount of wasted space was about 100 MB. That 100 MB of wasted space was almost half my original hard drive's total capacity. I was impressed by the extent of the clustering overhead. I quickly repartitioned my new hard drive into several partitions, each about 250 MB because clusters for a 250-MB drive contain only 8 sectors each.

From the values returned by the *GetDiskFreeSpace* function, you can calculate the total disk space, the amount of free disk space, and the amount of used disk space:

```
DWORD dwSectorsPerCluster, dwBytesPerSector;
DWORD dwFreeClusters, dwClusters;
```

(continued)

```
DWORD dwTotalDiskSpace, dwFreeDiskSpace, dwUsedDiskSpace;

GetDiskFreeSpace("C:\\", &dwSectorsPerCluster,
    &dwBytesPerSector, &dwFreeClusters, &dwClusters);

dwTotalDiskSpace =
    dwSectorsPerCluster * dwBytesPerSector * dwClusters;

dwFreeDiskSpace =
    dwSectorsPerCluster * dwBytesPerSector * dwFreeClusters;

dwUsedDiskSpace =
    dwSectorsPerCluster * dwBytesPerSector *
      (dwClusters - dwFreeClusters);
    .
    .
    .
```

One other function you can use to manipulate a disk's volume is the *DeviceIoControl* function:

```
BOOL DeviceIoControl(HANDLE hDevice, DWORD dwIoControlCode,
    LPVOID lpvInBuffer, DWORD cbInBuffer,
    LPVOID lpvOutBuffer, DWORD cbOutBuffer,
    LPDWORD lpcbBytesReturned, LPOVERLAPPED lpOverlapped);
```

The *DeviceIoControl* function is used to send commands to or request information directly from a disk's device driver. The *hDevice* parameter specifies a handle to a disk device. This handle is obtained by placing a call to the *CreateFile* function. If you want to get a device handle to a floppy drive or to a single partition on a hard drive, call *CreateFile* as shown here.

```
hDevice = CreateFile("\\\\.\\X:",
    0, FILE_SHARE_WRITE, NULL, OPEN_EXISTING, 0, NULL);
```

The *X* in the first parameter represents the drive letter for the device. To obtain a device handle to drive C, for example, make this call:

```
hDevice = CreateFile("\\\\.\\C:",
    0, FILE_SHARE_WRITE, NULL, OPEN_EXISTING, 0, NULL);
```

You can get a device handle to a physical hard disk by calling *CreateFile* like this:

```
hDevice = CreateFile("\\\\.\\PhysicalDriveN",
    0, FILE_SHARE_WRITE, NULL, OPEN_EXISTING, 0, NULL);
```

The *N* in the first parameter represents a hard drive on the user's system. The first hard drive on the system would be drive 0. You can get the device handle to a physical disk only if you have administrative privileges; otherwise, the call will fail.

Once you have a valid device handle, you can pass the handle as the first parameter of the *DeviceIoControl* function. The second parameter of *DeviceIoControl* specifies the command you want to send to the device. Here is a list of the possible values:

Command Identifier	Meaning
FSCTL_DISMOUNT_VOLUME	Dismounts a volume
FSCTL_LOCK_VOLUME	Locks a volume
FSCTL_UNLOCK_VOLUME	Unlocks a volume
IOCTL_DISK_CHECK_VERIFY	Checks for a change in a removable media device
IOCTL_DISK_EJECT_MEDIA	Ejects medium from a SCSI device
IOCTL_DISK_FORMAT_TRACKS	Formats a contiguous set of disk tracks
IOCTL_DISK_GET_DRIVE_GEOMETRY	Obtains information on the physical disk's geometry
IOCTL_DISK_GET_DRIVE_LAYOUT	Provides information about each partition on a disk
IOCTL_DISK_GET_MEDIA_TYPES	Obtains information about media support
IOCTL_DISK_GET_PARTITION_INFO	Obtains disk partition information
IOCTL_DISK_LOAD_MEDIA	Loads medium into a device
IOCTL_DISK_MEDIA_REMOVAL	Enables or disables the media eject mechanism
IOCTL_DISK_PERFORMANCE	Provides disk performance information
IOCTL_DISK_REASSIGN_BLOCKS	Maps disk blocks to the spare-block pool
IOCTL_DISK_SET_DRIVE_LAYOUT	Partitions a disk
IOCTL_DISK_SET_PARTITION_INFO	Sets the disk partition type
IOCTL_DISK_VERIFY	Performs a logical format of a disk extent
IOCTL_SERIAL_LSRMST_INSERT	Enables or disables the placement of line and modem status data into the data stream

The meanings of the remaining *DeviceIoControl* parameters depend on the operation you passed in the *dwIoControlCode* parameter. For example, if you want to format tracks, you must allocate and initialize a FORMAT_PARAMETERS structure:

```
typedef struct _FORMAT_PARAMETERS {
   MEDIA_TYPE MediaType;
   DWORD StartCylinderNumber;
   DWORD EndCylinderNumber;
   DWORD StartHeadNumber;
   DWORD EndHeadNumber;
} FORMAT_PARAMETERS;
```

and pass the address to this structure in *DeviceIoControl*'s *lpvInBuffer* parameter. You must also pass the length of this structure, in bytes, in the *cbInBuffer* parameter. When you're formatting tracks, the *DeviceIoControl* function doesn't return any special information to you—only the news that the function succeeded (TRUE) or failed (FALSE).

If you are requesting a disk's geometry information, you must allocate a DISK_GEOMETRY structure:

```
typedef struct _DISK_GEOMETRY {
   MEDIA_TYPE  MediaType;
   LARGE_INTEGER  Cylinders;
   DWORD   TracksPerCylinder;
   DWORD   SectorsPerTrack;
   DWORD   BytesPerSector;
} DISK_GEOMETRY;
```

and pass the address and the length of this structure (in bytes) as the *lpvOutBuffer* and *cbOutBuffer* parameters, respectively. You'll also want to pass the address of a DWORD variable as the *lpcbBytesReturned* parameter. Just before *DeviceIoControl* returns, it fills this structure with the disk device's geometry and fills the DWORD pointed to by *lpcbBytesReturned* with the number of bytes copied into the buffer.

Because requesting a disk's geometry doesn't require that you pass any information into *DeviceIoControl*, you can pass NULL and 0 as the *lpvInBuffer* and *cbInBuffer* parameters. Similarly, because formatting tracks doesn't cause *DeviceIoControl* to return information, you can pass NULL and 0 for the *lpvOutBuffer* and *cbOutBuffer* parameters.

For some operations, such as disk formatting, *DeviceIoControl* can format the disk asynchronously. If *DeviceIoControl* is to perform an operation asynchronously, the device must be opened by a specification of the

FILE_FLAG_OVERLAPPED flag when *CreateFile* is called, and you must pass in the address of an OVERLAPPED structure as the *lpOverlapped* parameter of *DeviceIoControl*. The *hEvent* member of this structure must also contain the handle of a manual-reset event. The other members of the OVERLAPPED structure are ignored by the *DeviceIoControl* function.

If *DeviceIoControl* completes the operation before returning, *DeviceIoControl* returns TRUE. If the operation hasn't been completed by the time *DeviceIoControl* returns, FALSE is returned. When the operation is complete, the manual-reset event gets signaled. You should call *GetOverlappedResult* (discussed later, in the asynchronous file I/O section of this chapter) when the thread needs to sleep until the operation has been completed.

When you have finished calling *DeviceIoControl*, you must close the device handle by calling *CloseHandle*. More information on using the *DeviceIoControl* function can be found in the *Microsoft Win32 Programmer's Reference*.

The Disk Information Viewer Sample Application

The DiskInfo (DISKINFO.EXE) application, listed in Figure 13-1 beginning on page 586, demonstrates the use of most of the functions we've just surveyed. The source code files, resource files, and make file for the application are in the DISKINFO.13 directory on the companion disc. When you execute DiskInfo, the Disk Volume Information Viewer dialog box appears. On the next two pages, this dialog box shows the results when I select various logical drives on my computer.

The combo box at the top of the dialog box shows all the logical drives connected to the system. This information is obtained by a call to *GetLogicalDriveStrings*. When you select a logical drive, the remaining fields in the dialog box change to show information about the newly selected drive. The Drive Type field is updated by a call to *GetDriveType*, the fields in the Volume Information group box are updated by a call to *GetVolumeInformation*, and the fields in the Disk Free Space group box are updated by a call to *GetDiskFreeSpace*.

When DISKINFO.EXE is run on Windows 95, it cannot obtain the logical drive string information because the *GetLogicalDriveStrings* function is not implemented. So DiskInfo constructs the set of drive strings by using the drive information returned from a call to *GetLogicalDrives* instead.

Disk Volume Information Viewer

Logical drive strings: a:\

Drive type: Removable

Volume information

Volume name: RAISTLIN
Serial number: 3961702622
Component length: 255
Flags: FS_CASE_IS_PRESERVED

FS_UNICODE_STORED_ON_DISK

File System: FAT

Disk free space

Sectors/Cluster: 1
Bytes/Sector: 512
Free clusters: 2826
Clusters: 2847

Disk Volume Information Viewer

Logical drive strings: c:\

Drive type: Fixed

Volume information

Volume name: RINCEWIND
Serial number: 170596557
Component length: 255
Flags: FS_CASE_IS_PRESERVED

FS_UNICODE_STORED_ON_DISK

File System: FAT

Disk free space

Sectors/Cluster: 16
Bytes/Sector: 512
Free clusters: 6350
Clusters: 41427

Disk Volume Information Viewer

Logical <u>d</u>rive strings: [d:\]

Drive type: CD-ROM

Volume information

Volume name: NEC
Serial number: 1629624025
Component length: 255
Flags: FS_CASE_IS_PRESERVED

File System: CDFS

Disk free space

Sectors/Cluster: 16
Bytes/Sector: 2048
Free clusters: 0
Clusters: 16745

Disk Volume Information Viewer

Logical <u>d</u>rive strings: [x:\]

Drive type: Remote

Volume information

Volume name: arwen_d
Serial number: 0
Component length: 255
Flags: FS_CASE_IS_PRESERVED
                    FS_CASE_SENSITIVE
                    FS_UNICODE_STORED_ON_DISK
                    FS_PERSISTENT_ACLS
File System: NTFS

Disk free space

Sectors/Cluster: 32
Bytes/Sector: 512
Free clusters: 13824
Clusters: 63999

DiskInfo.ico

DISKINFO.C

```
/**************************************************************
Module name: DiskInfo.C
Notices: Copyright (c) 1995 Jeffrey Richter
**************************************************************/


#include "..\AdvWin32.H"     /* See Appendix B for details. */
#include <windows.h>
#include <windowsx.h>

#pragma warning(disable: 4001)       /* Single-line comment */

#include <tchar.h>
#include <stdio.h>                  // For sprintf
#include <string.h>                 // For strchr
#include "Resource.H"


///////////////////////////////////////////////////////////////


void Dlg_FillDriveInfo (HWND hwnd, LPTSTR lpszRootPathName) {
   // Variables for processing the drive type information
   int nDriveType;
   LPCTSTR p;

   // Variables for processing the volume information
   TCHAR szBuf[200];
   TCHAR lpVolumeNameBuffer[200];
   DWORD dwVolumeSerialNumber, dwMaximumComponentLength;
   DWORD dwFileSystemFlags;
   TCHAR lpFileSystemNameBuffer[50];

   // Variables for processing the disk space information
   DWORD dwSectorsPerCluster, dwBytesPerSector;
   DWORD dwFreeClusters, dwClusters;


   // Get the drive type information.
   nDriveType = GetDriveType(lpszRootPathName);
   switch (nDriveType) {
      case 0:
         p = __TEXT("Cannot be determined.");
         break;
```

Figure 13-1.
The DiskInfo application.

(continued)

Figure 13-1. *continued*

```
        case 1:
            p = __TEXT("Path does not exist.");
            break;

        case DRIVE_REMOVABLE:
            p = __TEXT("Removable");
            break;

        case DRIVE_FIXED:
            p = __TEXT("Fixed");
            break;

        case DRIVE_REMOTE:
            p = __TEXT("Remote");
            break;

        case DRIVE_CDROM:
            p = __TEXT("CD-ROM");
            break;

        case DRIVE_RAMDISK:
            p = __TEXT("RAM disk");
            break;

        default:
            p = __TEXT("Unknown");
            break;
    }

    SetWindowText(GetDlgItem(hwnd, IDC_DRIVETYPE), p);



    // Get the volume information.
    if (GetVolumeInformation(lpszRootPathName,
        lpVolumeNameBuffer,
        ARRAY_SIZE(lpVolumeNameBuffer), &dwVolumeSerialNumber,
        &dwMaximumComponentLength, &dwFileSystemFlags,
        lpFileSystemNameBuffer,
        ARRAY_SIZE(lpFileSystemNameBuffer))) {

        _stprintf(szBuf, __TEXT("%s\n%u\n%u\n"),
            lpVolumeNameBuffer, dwVolumeSerialNumber,
            dwMaximumComponentLength);
```

(continued)

Figure 13-1. *continued*

```
    if (dwFileSystemFlags & FS_CASE_IS_PRESERVED)
        _tcscat(szBuf, __TEXT("FS_CASE_IS_PRESERVED"));
    _tcscat(szBuf, __TEXT("\n"));

    if (dwFileSystemFlags & FS_CASE_SENSITIVE)
        _tcscat(szBuf, __TEXT("FS_CASE_SENSITIVE"));
    _tcscat(szBuf, __TEXT("\n"));

    if (dwFileSystemFlags & FS_UNICODE_STORED_ON_DISK)
        _tcscat(szBuf, __TEXT("FS_UNICODE_STORED_ON_DISK"));
    _tcscat(szBuf, __TEXT("\n"));

    if (dwFileSystemFlags & FS_PERSISTENT_ACLS)
        _tcscat(szBuf, __TEXT("FS_PERSISTENT_ACLS"));
    _tcscat(szBuf, __TEXT("\n"));

    _tcscat(szBuf, lpFileSystemNameBuffer);
  } else {
    _tcscpy(szBuf, __TEXT("NO VOLUME INFO"));
  }
  SetWindowText(GetDlgItem(hwnd, IDC_VOLINFO), szBuf);


  // Get the disk space information.
  if (GetDiskFreeSpace(lpszRootPathName,
    &dwSectorsPerCluster, &dwBytesPerSector,
    &dwFreeClusters, &dwClusters)) {

    _stprintf(szBuf, __TEXT("%u\n%u\n%u\n%u"),
        dwSectorsPerCluster, dwBytesPerSector,
        dwFreeClusters, dwClusters);
  } else {
    _tcscpy(szBuf, __TEXT("NO\nDISK\nSPACE\nINFO"));
  }
  SetWindowText(GetDlgItem(hwnd, IDC_DISKINFO), szBuf);
}



///////////////////////////////////////////////////////////////


BOOL Dlg_OnInitDialog (HWND hwnd, HWND hwndFocus,
   LPARAM lParam) {
```

(continued)

Figure 13-1. *continued*

```
DWORD  dwNumBytesForDriveStrings;
HANDLE hHeap;
LPTSTR lp;
TCHAR  szLogDrive[100];
HWND   hwndCtl = GetDlgItem(hwnd, IDC_LOGDRIVES);
int    nNumDrives = 0, nDriveNum;

// Associate an icon with the dialog box.
SetClassLong(hwnd, GCL_HICON, (LONG)
   LoadIcon((HINSTANCE) GetWindowLong(hwnd, GWL_HINSTANCE),
   __TEXT("DiskInfo")));

// Get the number of bytes needed to hold all
// the logical drive strings.
dwNumBytesForDriveStrings =
   GetLogicalDriveStrings(0, NULL) * sizeof(TCHAR);

if (dwNumBytesForDriveStrings != 0) {
   // The GetLogicalDriveStrings function is
   // supported on this platform.

   // Allocate memory from the heap for the drive
   // string names.
   hHeap = GetProcessHeap();
   lp = (LPTSTR) HeapAlloc(hHeap, HEAP_ZERO_MEMORY,
      dwNumBytesForDriveStrings);

   // Get the drive string names in our buffer.
   GetLogicalDriveStrings(HeapSize(hHeap, 0, lp), lp);

   // Parse the memory block, and fill the combo box.
   while (*lp != 0) {
      ComboBox_AddString(hwndCtl, lp);
      nNumDrives++;
      lp = _tcschr(lp, 0) + 1;   // Point to next string.
   }

   HeapFree(hHeap, 0, lp);
} else {
   // The GetLogicalDriveStrings function is NOT
   // supported on this platform--Windows 95.
   DWORD dwDriveMask = GetLogicalDrives();
   for (nDriveNum = 0; dwDriveMask != 0; ) {
```

(continued)

Figure 13-1. *continued*

```
        wsprintf(szLogDrive, __TEXT("%c:\\"),
           (TCHAR) (__TEXT('A') + nDriveNum));
           ComboBox_AddString(hwndCtl, szLogDrive);

        nDriveNum++;             // Increment the drive number.
        dwDriveMask >>= 1;   // Check next bit.
     }
  }

  // Initialize the volume information for the first fixed
  // drive so that we don't try to read volume
  // information from a drive that doesn't contain a
  // diskette.
  for (nDriveNum = 0; nDriveNum < nNumDrives; nDriveNum++) {
     ComboBox_GetLBText(hwndCtl, nDriveNum, szLogDrive);
     if (GetDriveType(szLogDrive) == DRIVE_FIXED)
        break;
  }

  if (nDriveNum == nNumDrives) {
     // There are no fixed drives--just use the
     // first drive.
     ComboBox_GetLBText(hwndCtl, nDriveNum = 0, szLogDrive);
  }

  // Select the first fixed drive, or select the first
  // drive if no fixed drives exist.
  ComboBox_SetCurSel(hwndCtl, nDriveNum);

  Dlg_FillDriveInfo(hwnd, szLogDrive);

  return(TRUE);
}


////////////////////////////////////////////////////////////////


void Dlg_OnCommand (HWND hwnd, int id, HWND hwndCtl,
  UINT codeNotify) {

  TCHAR szLogDrive[100];

  switch (id) {
    case IDC_LOGDRIVES:
       if (codeNotify != CBN_SELCHANGE)
          break;
```

(continued)

Figure 13-1. *continued*

```
        ComboBox_GetText(hwndCtl, szLogDrive,
            ARRAY_SIZE(szLogDrive));
        Dlg_FillDriveInfo(hwnd, szLogDrive);
        break;

    case IDCANCEL:
        EndDialog(hwnd, id);
        break;
    }
}


///////////////////////////////////////////////////////////////


BOOL CALLBACK Dlg_Proc (HWND hDlg, UINT uMsg,
    WPARAM wParam, LPARAM lParam) {

    BOOL fProcessed = TRUE;

    switch (uMsg) {
        HANDLE_MSG(hDlg, WM_INITDIALOG, Dlg_OnInitDialog);
        HANDLE_MSG(hDlg, WM_COMMAND, Dlg_OnCommand);

        default:
            fProcessed = FALSE;
            break;
    }
    return(fProcessed);
}


///////////////////////////////////////////////////////////////


int WINAPI WinMain (HINSTANCE hinstExe,
    HINSTANCE hinstPrev, LPSTR lpszCmdLine, int nCmdShow) {

    DialogBox(hinstExe, MAKEINTRESOURCE(IDD_DISKINFO),
        NULL, Dlg_Proc);

    return(0);
}


////////////////////////// End Of File //////////////////////////
```

(continued)

Figure 13-1. *continued*

```
DISKINFO.RC
//Microsoft Visual C++ generated resource script.
//
#include "Resource.h"

#define APSTUDIO_READONLY_SYMBOLS
/////////////////////////////////////////////////////////////////
//
// Generated from the TEXTINCLUDE 2 resource.
//
#include "afxres.h"


/////////////////////////////////////////////////////////////////
#undef APSTUDIO_READONLY_SYMBOLS


#ifdef APSTUDIO_INVOKED
/////////////////////////////////////////////////////////////////
//
// TEXTINCLUDE
//

1 TEXTINCLUDE DISCARDABLE
BEGIN
    "Resource.h\0"
END

2 TEXTINCLUDE DISCARDABLE
BEGIN
    "#include ""afxres.h""\r\n"
    "\0"
END

3 TEXTINCLUDE DISCARDABLE
BEGIN
    "\r\n"
    "\0"
END


/////////////////////////////////////////////////////////////////
#endif    // APSTUDIO_INVOKED
```

(continued)

Figure 13-1. *continued*

```
//////////////////////////////////////////////////////////////
//
// Dialog
//

IDD_DISKINFO DIALOG DISCARDABLE  15, 24, 198, 176
STYLE DS_NOIDLEMSG ¦ WS_MINIMIZEBOX ¦ WS_POPUP ¦ WS_VISIBLE
    ¦ WS_CAPTION ¦ WS_SYSMENU
CAPTION "Disk Volume Information Viewer"
FONT 8, "System"
BEGIN
    LTEXT           "Logical &drive strings:",IDC_STATIC,
                    4,4,70,8
    COMBOBOX        IDC_LOGDRIVES,78,4,80,76,CBS_DROPDOWNLIST
                    ¦ WS_GROUP ¦ WS_TABSTOP
    LTEXT           "Drive type:",IDC_STATIC,4,20,37,8
    LTEXT           "Text",IDC_DRIVETYPE,48,20,96,8
    GROUPBOX        "&Volume information",IDC_STATIC,4,32,
                    192,84,WS_GROUP ¦ WS_TABSTOP
    LTEXT           "Volume name:\nSerial number:\n\
Component length:\nFlags:\n\n\n\nFile System:",
                    IDC_STATIC,8,44,64,64
    LTEXT           "Label\n12345678\n10\nFS_CASE_IS_PRESERVED\
\nFS_CASE_SENSITIVE\nFS_UNICODE_STORED_ON_DISK\
\nFS_PERSISTENT_ACLS\nNTFS",
                    IDC_VOLINFO,77,44,116,68,SS_NOPREFIX
    GROUPBOX        "Disk free &space",IDC_STATIC,4,120,
                    108,48,WS_GROUP ¦ WS_TABSTOP
    LTEXT           "Sectors/Cluster:\nBytes/Sector:\
\nFree clusters:\nClusters:",
                    IDC_STATIC,8,132,52,32
    RTEXT           "8\n512\n300\n400",IDC_DISKINFO,64,132,
                    44,32,SS_NOPREFIX
END


//////////////////////////////////////////////////////////////
//
// Icon
//

DISKINFO                ICON    DISCARDABLE     "DiskInfo.Ico"

#ifndef APSTUDIO_INVOKED
```

(continued)

Figure 13-1. *continued*

```
///////////////////////////////////////////////////////////////////
//
// Generated from the TEXTINCLUDE 3 resource.
//


///////////////////////////////////////////////////////////////////
#endif    // not APSTUDIO_INVOKED
```

Directory Operations

Every process has a directory associated with it called the current directory. By default, file operations are performed inside the process's current directory. When a process is first created, it inherits the current directory used by its parent process.

Getting the Current Directory

A process determines its current directory by calling:

```
DWORD GetCurrentDirectory(DWORD cchCurDir, LPTSTR lpszCurDir);
```

The *GetCurrentDirectory* function fills the buffer pointed to by *lpszCurDir* with the process's current path. The *cchCurDir* parameter indicates the maximum size of the buffer in characters. If the function fails, 0 is returned; otherwise, the function returns the number of characters copied to the buffer, not including the terminating zero. If the buffer isn't large enough to hold the current path, the return value indicates the number of characters required to hold the path. To ensure that *GetCurrentDirectory* succeeds, you need to write code similar to this:

```
TCHAR szCurDir[MAX_PATH];

DWORD dwResult = GetCurrentDirectory(
   sizeof(szCurDir) / sizeof(TCHAR), szCurDir);

if (dwResult == 0) {
   // Total function failure
} else {
   if (dwResult < (sizeof(szCurDir) / sizeof(TCHAR))) {
      // Buffer was big enough for the full path
   } else {
      // Buffer was too small
   }
}
```

Notice the use of MAX_PATH in this routine. The MAX_PATH value is defined in WINDEF.H as 260. For MS-DOS development, some C compilers define a macro called _MAX_PATH as only 80. The big difference in this value is attributable to the long filenames now supported by Windows 95 and Windows NT. It's difficult to stress enough the significance of long filename support. I've seen too many programs that create buffers for filenames along these lines:

```
char szFileName[13];    // "Filename" + '.' + "ext" + zero byte
```

These buffers will be far too small to hold long filenames. It's likely that a function in the application will overwrite a buffer because the application will make the assumption that filenames will never be more than 13 characters long.

One way to handle the longer filenames is to make your buffers much larger. Using MAX_PATH as we've just seen is an example of this approach. Unfortunately, the Win32 header files don't define a macro called MAX_FILE, but you could define MAX_FILE as 260 as well.

This approach would work for today's long filenames, but a new file system in the future might allow filenames as long as 512 characters. So the best way to allocate buffers for file system components is dynamically, by first calling *GetVolumeInformation* and checking the value returned in the buffer pointed to by the *lpMaximumComponentLength* parameter.

Changing the Current Directory

A process can change its current directory by calling:

```
BOOL SetCurrentDirectory(LPTSTR lpszCurDir);
```

Changing the current directory alters the current directory of only the process making the call; the change of directory doesn't affect any other running processes. However, if the process making the call spawns a new process after changing its current directory, the new process will inherit the current directory of the parent, which will now be the directory that was specified in the last call to *SetCurrentDirectory*.

Getting the System Directory

In addition to getting its own current directory, an application can determine the system directory by calling:

```
UINT GetSystemDirectory(LPTSTR lpszSysPath, UINT cchSysPath);
```

The *GetSystemDirectory* function fills the buffer pointed to by *lpszSys-Path* with the system directory name. Usually, this directory will be something like this:

```
C:\WINDOWS\SYSTEM     (Windows 95)
C:\WINNT\SYSTEM32     (Windows NT)
```

The return values for *GetSystemDirectory* should be interpreted just as they were for the *GetCurrentDirectory* function. Applications typically don't use the system directory for anything. In fact, on shared versions of Windows, the system directory is protected so that files can't be created in the directory; nor can files already in the system directory be modified. A benefit of this protection is that viruses won't be able to attach themselves to any of the files contained in the system directory.

Getting the Windows Directory

If a process wants to create or write to a file that is to be shared by multiple processes, the process can use the Windows directory. The path of the Windows directory can be obtained by calling:

```
UINT GetWindowsDirectory(LPTSTR lpszWinPath, UINT cchWinPath);
```

The *GetWindowsDirectory* function fills the buffer pointed to by *lpszWinPath* with the Windows directory. Usually, this directory will be something like this:

```
C:\WINDOWS     (Windows 95)
C:\WINNT       (Windows NT)
```

When running a shared version of Windows, the system creates a Windows directory private to each user. This is the only directory guaranteed to be private for an individual user. If a user wants to keep certain files hidden from all other users, the files must be created either in the Windows directory or in a subdirectory of the Windows directory.

Creating and Removing Directories

Finally, there are two additional functions for manipulating directories:

```
BOOL CreateDirectory(LPTSTR lpszPath, LPSECURITY_ATTRIBUTES lpsa);
```

and

```
BOOL RemoveDirectory(LPTSTR lpszDir);
```

As their names imply, these functions allow a process to create and remove a directory, respectively. When creating a directory, a process can specify a SECURITY_ATTRIBUTES structure in order to assign special privileges to the directory. For example, an application could create the directory so that another user couldn't go into or remove the directory.

Both these functions return TRUE when they're successful and FALSE when they fail. *RemoveDirectory* will fail if the directory contains files or other subdirectories or if the process doesn't have delete access for removing the directory.

Copying, Deleting, Moving, and Renaming Files

Both 16-bit Windows and MS-DOS have always lacked a function for copying files from one place to another. Applications have typically implemented this important functionality by opening a source file for reading and creating a destination file for writing. Then, using a buffer, the application would read part of the source file into memory and write the buffer back out to the destination file. After the source file had been read and written, the application would close both files. And the time stamp of the destination file would reflect the time of the copy—not the time of the source file's last update. This problem would usually have to be fixed by the addition of a few more function calls.

Copying a File

With Win32, we finally have an operating system call available to us for copying files:

```
BOOL CopyFile(LPTSTR lpszExistingFile, LPTSTR lpszNewFile,
    BOOL fFailIfExists);
```

CopyFile is a simple function that copies the file identified by the *lpszExistingFile* parameter to a new file whose pathname is specified by the *lpszNewFile* parameter. The last parameter, *fFailIfExists*, specifies whether you want the function to fail if a file already exists that matches the name pointed to by the *lpszNewFile* parameter. If a file with the same name does exist and *fFailIfExists* is TRUE, the function fails; otherwise, the function destroys the existing file and creates the new file. *CopyFile* returns TRUE if it is successful. Only closed files or files that are open with read-access only can be copied. The function fails if any process has the existing file open with write-access.

Deleting a File

Deleting a file by means of the *DeleteFile* function is even easier than copying a file:

```
BOOL DeleteFile(LPTSTR lpszFileName);
```

This function deletes the file identified by the *lpszFileName* parameter and returns TRUE if successful. The function fails if the specified file doesn't exist or if the file is open. If any process has the file open, the file can't be deleted.

Under Windows 95, the *DeleteFile* function will actually delete an open file, whereas Windows NT guards against this possibility. Deleting an open file, of course, means that the file may lose data. It is up to you to ensure that files are closed prior to deleting them with *DeleteFile*.

Moving a File

Two functions allow you to move a file from one directory to another directory:

```
BOOL MoveFile(LPTSTR lpszExisting, LPTSTR lpszNew);
```

and

```
BOOL MoveFileEx(LPTSTR lpszExisting, LPTSTR lpszNew,
   DWORD fdwFlags);
```

Both functions move the existing file, which is identified by the *lpszExisting* parameter, to the new location identified by the *lpszNew* parameter. The *lpszNew* parameter must include the name of the file. For example, this instruction won't move the CLOCK.EXE file from the WINNT directory on drive C to the root directory of drive C:

```
MoveFile("C:\\WINNT\\CLOCK.EXE", "C:\\");
```

This instruction will:

```
MoveFile("C:\\WINNT\\CLOCK.EXE", "C:\\CLOCK.EXE");
```

Moving a file is not always identical to copying the file to another location and then deleting the original file. If you are moving a file from one directory to another directory on the same drive, *MoveFile* and

MoveFileEx don't move any of the data in the file at all. Both functions simply remove the file's entry in the first directory and add a new entry to the second directory the file is supposedly copied to. Simply adjusting the directory entries "copies" a file significantly faster because no data is moved around. Less disk space is needed during the move too. When a file is moved from one drive to another, the system must actually create a duplicate file before it deletes the original. At the moment after the copy and before the deletion of the original, there are two whole copies of the file in existence. If the file is huge, this can take up a serious amount of disk space.

If the system had to copy and delete a file it was moving from one directory to another on the same drive, the function might fail because of insufficient disk space. If the file were 1 MB long and only 512 KB of disk space were available, the system wouldn't be able to copy the file before deleting the original. But since only directory entries are altered, no additional disk space is required and the move is much more likely to succeed.

If the move does succeed, both *MoveFile* and *MoveFileEx* return TRUE. The move can fail if insufficient disk space is available for interdrive moves or if a filename matching the name specified in *lpszNew* already exists.

You wouldn't be able to guess it from their names, but both *MoveFile* and *MoveFileEx* can also be used to change the name of a subdirectory. For example, to change the name of the subdirectory UTILITY to TOOLS, use this statement:

```
MoveFile("C:\\UTILITY", "C:\\TOOLS");
```

It would certainly be useful if *MoveFile* and *MoveFileEx* could move an entire subdirectory tree elsewhere in the drive's directory hierarchy, but these functions are not capable of this sweeping kind of operation. To move a subdirectory tree to another location on the same drive, you would have to use the *FindFirstFile*, *FindNextFile*, and *FindClose* functions discussed later in this chapter to walk down the directory hierarchy three different times. The first time you'd need to call *CreateDirectory* to create a similar directory structure in the new location. The second time you'd need to call *MoveFile* to move each individual file in the directory structure. The last time you'd need to call *RemoveDirectory* to remove the old directory hierarchy.

The Differences Between *MoveFile* and *MoveFileEx*

By offering one more parameter, *fdwFlags*, *MoveFileEx* gives you more control over moving a file or renaming a subdirectory than the *MoveFile* function does.

Under Windows 95, the *MoveFileEx* function has no useful implementation and simply returns FALSE; calling *GetLastError* returns ERROR-_CALL_NOT_IMPLEMENTED.

MoveFileEx comes into its own when moving a file fails because a filename matching the name specified in *lpszNew* already exists. To destroy the existing file and give the moved file the same name anyway, you can specify the MOVEFILE_REPLACE_EXISTING flag when you call *MoveFileEx*. This flag has no effect when you're renaming a subdirectory.

By default, *MoveFileEx* will not move a file from one drive to another drive. If you want to allow this behavior, you must specify the MOVE-FILE_COPY_ALLOWED flag. On Windows NT, the *MoveFile* function calls the *MoveFileEx* function internally, specifying the MOVEFILE-_COPY_ALLOWED flag, so you don't have to worry about this if you use the *MoveFile* function instead of the *MoveFileEx* function. Like the MOVE-FILE_REPLACE_EXISTING flag, this flag has no effect when you're renaming a subdirectory.

The last flag, MOVEFILE_DELAY_UNTIL_REBOOT, provokes some interesting behavior. If this flag is specified, the system doesn't move the file or rename the directory at the time the call is placed. Instead, it keeps a list in the registry of all the files that have been moved with this flag specified. Then, the next time the operating system is booted, the system examines the registry and moves or renames all the files in the list. The files are moved or renamed just after the drives are checked and before any paging files are created.

The MOVEFILE_DELAY_UNTIL_REBOOT flag is customarily used by installation programs. Let's say that you recently received a new device driver for your video card. When you try to install the new driver, the system can't delete or overwrite the old video driver because the file is still in use by the system. In this case, the Setup program will copy the new driver into another directory, leaving the original driver file. Setup will then issue a call to *MoveFileEx*, specifying the current path of the new file in the *lpszExisting* parameter and the location where the file should

be in the *lpszNew* parameter. Setup will also pass the MOVEFILE_DELAY-
_UNTIL_REBOOT flag to *MoveFileEx*. The system will add the new path
to its list in the registry and simply return to Setup. When the system is
rebooted, it will replace the old video driver with the new driver before
the system is fully started. Once the system is up, the new device driver
will be used instead of the old one.

One other way in which *MoveFileEx* differs from *MoveFile* is that it
provides a novel way of deleting a file. You can delete a file with
MoveFileEx by passing NULL as the *lpszNew* parameter. In a sense, you
are telling the system you want to move the existing file (*lpszExisting*) to
nowhere, which has the effect of deleting the file.

Renaming a File

There is no *RenameFile* function. Renaming a file is accomplished by calling *MoveFile* or *MoveFileEx*. To rename a file, all you do is move the file
from its directory to the same directory. To rename CLOCK.EXE to
WATCH.EXE, for example, you'd use this statement:

```
MoveFile("C:\\WINNT\\CLOCK.EXE", "C:\\WINNT\\WATCH.EXE");
```

Because we are not moving the file from one drive to another drive or
from one directory to another directory, the system simply removes
WINNT's directory entry for CLOCK.EXE and adds a new directory
entry for WATCH.EXE—the file is effectively renamed.

The Setup program could have copied the new video device driver
file to the system directory, giving it a different name. Then the Setup
program would issue a call to *MoveFileEx*, still specifying the MOVE-
FILE_DELAY_UNTIL_REBOOT flag. This time, since the file would
already be in the correct directory, rebooting the system would have the
effect of renaming the file instead of actually copying it.

I'd like to see Microsoft enhance these file functions by adding
wildcard support. Wouldn't it be nice to be able to issue a command like
this one:

```
DeleteFile("*.BAK");
```

and have the system delete all of the BAK files in the current directory?
Currently, if you want to do a mass deletion you must create a list of all the
BAK files in the current directory first and then call *DeleteFile* for each file.
To create a list of the BAK files, you would use *FindFirstFile*, *FindNextFile*,
and *FindClose*—functions we'll discuss in detail later in this chapter.

Creating, Opening, and Closing Files

In 16-bit Windows, files are created and opened by means of the *OpenFile*, *_lcreat*, and *_lopen* functions. For backward compatibility, these functions were carried over into Win32, but they're considered obsolete, and you should avoid using them. For Win32 applications, files should be created or opened by means of the much more powerful *CreateFile* function:

```
HANDLE CreateFile(LPCTSTR lpszName, DWORD fdwAccess,
    DWORD fdwShareMode, LPSECURITY_ATTRIBUTES lpsa,
    DWORD fdwCreate, DWORD fdwAttrsAndFlags, HANDLE hTemplateFile);
```

When you call this function, the *lpszName* parameter identifies the name of the file you want to create or open. The *fdwAccess* parameter specifies how you want to access the data in the file. You can specify GENERIC_READ if you are going to read from the file, GENERIC_WRITE if you are going to write to the file, or GENERIC_READ | GENERIC-_WRITE if you are going to both read from and write to the file.

The *fdwShareMode* parameter specifies file sharing privileges. In Windows 95 and Windows NT more so than in 16-bit Windows, it's likely that a single file can and will be accessed by several computers at the same time (in a networking environment) or by several processes at the same time (in a multithreaded environment). The potential for file sharing means that you must give some thought to whether you should and how you will restrict other computers or processes from accessing the data in the file. The *fdwShareMode* flag can be set to 0, FILE_SHARE-_READ, and FILE_SHARE_WRITE. Specifying 0 means that, after you open the file, the file cannot be opened again until you've closed it.

Probably the most common flag to use here is FILE_SHARE-_READ. This flag tells the system that the same file may be opened again as long as the opener intends only to read from the file. Any attempts to open the file for writing will fail as long as you have the file open. The last flag, FILE_SHARE_WRITE, is rarely used. It tells the system that the same file may be opened again as long as the opener intends only to write to the file. If you specify FILE_SHARE_READ | FILE_SHARE-_WRITE, you tell the system that the file may be opened by others, allowing them to both read from and write to the file at will.

Of course, a strange situation can come up. Let's say that a process has opened a file for reading and has specified the FILE_SHARE_READ flag. Now another process comes along and tries to open the file, passing

0 for the *fdwShareMode* parameter. This means that the second process wants to open the file but doesn't want to allow anybody else to open the file for reading or writing. But another process already has the file open for reading. In such a case, the system won't allow the second open to succeed since it can't guarantee that the first process will stop accessing the file while the second process has the file open.

The fourth parameter of *CreateFile* is *lpsa*. As always, this parameter points to a SECURITY_ATTRIBUTES structure that allows you to specify security information with the file's associated kernel object. The parameter can be NULL if you don't want any special security for the file object.

The *fdwCreate* parameter specifies flags that allow you to fine-tune the behavior of *CreateFile*. You must specify only one of these flags:

Identifier	Meaning
CREATE_NEW	Tells *CreateFile* to create a new file and to fail if a file with the same name already exists.
CREATE_ALWAYS	Tells *CreateFile* to create a file regardless of whether a file with the same name already exists. If the file already exists, *CreateFile* overwrites the existing file.
OPEN_EXISTING	Tells *CreateFile* to open an existing file and to fail if the file doesn't already exist.
OPEN_ALWAYS	Tells *CreateFile* to open a file if it exists and to create the file if it doesn't exist.
TRUNCATE_EXISTING	Tells *CreateFile* to open an existing file and truncate its size to 0 bytes and to fail if the file doesn't already exist. The GENERIC_WRITE flag must be used with this flag.

CreateFile's *fdwAttrsAndFlags* parameter has two purposes: it assigns special attributes to the file if the file is being created, and it alters the method that the system uses to read from and write to a file. If *CreateFile* is opening an existing file, the attribute information in *fdwAttrsAndFlags* is ignored but the flag information is used.

Let's look at the file attributes listed on the next page first, and then we'll look at the file flags. Most of the attributes will already be familiar to you because they originated with the MS-DOS FAT file system.

Identifier	Meaning
FILE_ATTRIBUTE_ARCHIVE	The file is an archive file. Applications use this flag to mark files for backup or removal. When *CreateFile* creates a new file, this flag is automatically set.
FILE_ATTRIBUTE_HIDDEN	The file is hidden. It won't be included in an ordinary directory listing.
FILE_ATTRIBUTE_NORMAL	The file has no other attributes set. This attribute is valid only if it's used alone.
FILE_ATTRIBUTE_READONLY	The file is read-only. Applications can read the file but can't write to it or delete it.
FILE_ATTRIBUTE_SYSTEM	The file is part of the operating system or is used exclusively by the operating system.

In addition to those familiar attributes, Win32 offers one more file attribute: FILE_ATTRIBUTE_TEMPORARY. Use FILE_ATTRIBUTE_TEMPORARY if you are creating a temporary file. When *CreateFile* creates a file with the temporary attribute, it tries to keep the file's data in memory instead of on the disk. This makes accessing the file's contents much faster. If you keep writing to the file and the system can no longer keep the data in RAM, the operating system will be forced to start writing the data to the hard disk. You can improve the system's performance by combining the FILE_ATTRIBUTE_TEMPORARY flag with the FILE_FLAG_DELETE_ON_CLOSE flag (discussed on the next page). Normally, the system purges a file's cache when the file is closed. However, if the system sees that the file is to be deleted when it is closed, the system doesn't need to purge its cache.

Now let's turn our attention to the file flags. Most of these flags are signals that tell the system how you intend to use a file. The system can then optimize its caching algorithms to help your application work more efficiently with the file.

Let's start with the case in which you don't want the system to help you at all with file buffering. If you don't want the system to perform any buffering on a file, use the FILE_FLAG_NO_BUFFERING flag. This flag tells the device driver that you are supplying the disk buffers used for file I/O and that the system should perform no read-ahead or disk caching of the file at all. Because the device driver is using your buffers, you must read from and write to the file on sector boundaries, and the buffer addresses must be aligned on disk sector boundaries in memory. You can use the *GetDiskFreeSpace* function to determine the sector size the file system is using.

The next two flags, FILE_FLAG_RANDOM_ACCESS and FILE-_FLAG_SEQUENTIAL_SCAN, are used to tell the system whether you intend to access a file randomly or sequentially. Setting one or the other of these flags is simply a hint to the system so that it can optimize its caching. You can access the file any way you want to after using one of these flags, but access may not be as fast as possible if you access the file differently from the way you told the system you would.

When you've set the FILE_FLAG_SEQUENTIAL_SCAN flag, the system expects the file to be accessed from the beginning through to the end. If you perform any direct seeks on the file, you are violating the system's expectation and it won't be able to use the optimum caching it has set for sequential access.

The last cache-related flag is FILE_FLAG_WRITE_THROUGH. The FILE_FLAG_WRITE_THROUGH flag disables intermediate caching of file-write operations in order to reduce the potential for data loss. When you specify this flag, the system writes all file modifications directly to the disk. However, the system still maintains an internal cache of the file's data, and file-read operations use the cached data (if available) instead of reading data directly from the disk. When this flag is used to open a file on a network server, the Win32 file-write functions do not return to the calling thread until the data is actually written to the server's disk drive.

That's it for the buffer-related flags. The remaining *CreateFile fdwAttrsAndFlags* flags don't seem to fall into any one category.

Use the FILE_FLAG_DELETE_ON_CLOSE flag to have the system delete the file after the file is closed. This flag is most frequently used with the FILE_ATTRIBUTE_TEMPORARY attribute. When these two flags are used together, your application can create a temporary file, write to it, read from it, and close it. When the file is closed, the system automatically deletes the file—what a convenience! If your process closes its handle to the file and the same file is opened by somebody else, the system won't immediately close the file. The system will wait until all open handles to the file are closed before deleting it.

Use the FILE_FLAG_BACKUP_SEMANTICS flag in backup and restore software. Before opening or creating any files, the system normally performs security checks to be sure that the process trying to open or create a file has the requisite access privileges. However, backup and restore software is special in that it can override certain file security checks. When you specify the FILE_FLAG_BACKUP_SEMANTICS flag, the system checks to be sure that a process has the access rights and, if it does, allows the file to be opened for backup or restore purposes only.

Use the FILE_FLAG_POSIX_SEMANTICS flag to tell the system to use POSIX rules for accessing a file. File systems used by POSIX allow case-sensitive filenames. This means that the files named JEFFREY.DOC, Jeffrey.Doc, and jeffrey.doc are all different files. MS-DOS, 16-bit Windows, Win32, and OS/2 were designed to expect that filenames would be case-insensitive. Use the FILE_FLAG_POSIX_SEMANTICS flag with extreme caution. If you use this flag when you create a file, that file might not be accessible to MS-DOS, 16-bit Windows, Win32, or OS/2 applications.

The last flag, FILE_FLAG_OVERLAPPED, tells the system that you want to access a file asynchronously. In MS-DOS and 16-bit Windows, files must be accessed synchronously; that is, when you make a call to read from a file, your program is suspended, waiting for the information to be read. Once the information has been read, your program regains control and continues executing.

File I/O is slow when compared with most other operations. If a user wants to save a document and print it, the user must wait for the file to be saved before starting to print the document. Wouldn't it be nice if, when the user told the application to save the document, the application told the system to write the data without the application's having to wait until the file-write operation was complete? The system could use another thread to write the file data while the application's main thread continued to respond to requests, such as a request to print, from the user.

The Win32 API allows you to perform asynchronous file I/O. You can tell the system to write or read the file in the background while you continue processing. When the system has finished the background process, it will notify you. If you can't continue processing until all the data has been read or written, you can suspend your thread until the file I/O is complete. This method of working with files is discussed in detail later in this chapter.

Under Windows 95, the asynchronous file I/O functions have no useful implementation and simply return FALSE; calling *GetLastError* returns ERROR_CALL_NOT_IMPLEMENTED.

CreateFile's last parameter, *hTemplateFile*, either identifies the handle of an open file or is NULL. If *hTemplateFile* identifies a file handle, *CreateFile* ignores the *fdwAttrsAndFlags* parameter completely and uses the attributes and flags associated with the file identified by *hTemplateFile*. The file identified by *hTemplateFile* must have been opened with the GENERIC_READ flag for this to work. If *CreateFile* is opening an existing file (as opposed to creating a new file), the *hTemplateFile* parameter is ignored.

If *CreateFile* succeeds in creating or opening a file, the handle of the file is returned. If *CreateFile* fails, INVALID_HANDLE_VALUE is returned.

Important

Most Win32 functions that return a handle return NULL if the function fails. However, *CreateFile* returns INVALID_HANDLE_VALUE (defined as 0xFFFFFFFF) instead. I have often seen code like this:

```
HANDLE hFile = CreateFile(...);
if (hFile == NULL) {
   // File not created
} else {
   // File created OK
}
.
.
.
```

The code is incorrect. Here's the correct way to check for an invalid file handle:

```
HANDLE hFile = CreateFile(...);
if (hFile == INVALID_HANDLE_VALUE) {
   // File not created
} else {
   // File created OK
}
.
.
.
```

Now you know all the possibilities available to you for creating and opening a file. The next two sections discuss how to read from and write to an open file synchronously and asynchronously. For now, just imagine that we've finished using the file. We tell the system that we no longer need to access the file by closing it using the ever-popular:

```
BOOL CloseHandle(HANDLE hObject);
```

where *hObject* identifies the handle of the file that was returned by the earlier call to *CreateFile*.

Reading and Writing Files Synchronously

This section discusses the Win32 functions for reading and writing files. These functions and methods are based on procedures that should be familiar to anyone who has ever performed file I/O on any operating system. Win32 offers these familiar functions, but I recommend that anyone interested in doing 32-bit file I/O consider using Win32's memory-mapped files. Memory-mapped files offer more convenient file access. More information about memory-mapped files and how to use them appears in Chapter 7.

Without a doubt, the easiest and most commonly used method for reading from and writing to files uses the following two functions:

```
BOOL ReadFile(HANDLE hFile, LPVOID lpBuffer,
    DWORD nNumberOfBytesToRead, LPDWORD lpNumberOfBytesRead,
    LPOVERLAPPED lpOverlapped);
```

and

```
BOOL WriteFile(HANDLE hFile, CONST VOID *lpBuffer,
    DWORD nNumberOfBytesToWrite, LPDWORD lpNumberOfBytesWritten,
    LPOVERLAPPED lpOverlapped);
```

The *ReadFile* and *WriteFile* functions are similar to the 16-bit Windows *_lread* and *_lwrite* functions, which are included in the Win32 API for backward compatibility only. The *hFile* parameter identifies the handle of the file you want to access. The *lpBuffer* parameter points to the buffer to which the file's data should be read or to the buffer containing the data that should be written out to the file. The *nNumberOfBytesToRead* and *nNumberOfBytesToWrite* parameters tell *ReadFile* and *WriteFile* how many bytes to read from the file and how many bytes to write to the file, respectively.

The 16-bit Windows functions _lread and _lwrite return the number of bytes actually read from or written to the file. For *ReadFile* and *WriteFile*, you need to pass the address of a DWORD, *lpNumberOfBytesRead* or *lpNumberOfBytesWritten*, that the functions will fill with this information.

Use the last parameter, *lpOverlapped*, if you want to read from or write to the file asynchronously. If you're doing synchronous file I/O, simply pass NULL for the *lpOverlapped* parameter. We'll look into this parameter in more detail in the section on asynchronous file I/O.

Windows 95 does not support any form of asynchronous file I/O except on serial devices. Therefore, you must pass NULL to *ReadFile* and *WriteFile*'s *lpOverlapped* parameter unless the *hFile* parameter identifies a serial device.

Both *ReadFile* and *WriteFile* return TRUE if successful. By the way, *ReadFile* can be called only for files that were created or opened with the GENERIC_READ flag. Likewise, *WriteFile* can be called only if the file was created or opened with the GENERIC_WRITE flag.

When *CreateFile* returns a handle to a file, the system associates a file pointer with the handle. Initially, this file pointer is set to 0; so if you call *ReadFile* immediately after a call to *CreateFile* you will start reading from offset 0 in the file. If you read 100 bytes into memory, the system updates the pointer associated with the file handle so that the next call to *ReadFile* starts reading at the 101st byte in the file. Remember that a file pointer is associated with a file handle and not with file operations or the file kernel object itself. For example, look at this code:

```
HFILE hFile = CreateFile(...);
ReadFile(hFile, lpBuffer, 100, &dwBytesRead, NULL);
WriteFile(hFile, lpBuffer, 100, &dwBytesWritten, NULL);
```

In the code fragment above, the first 100 bytes from the file are read into the buffer and these same 100 bytes are written to the file. The bytes are written from offset 100 in the file to offset 199. If there is another file operation after the call to *WriteFile*, it will start at offset 200 in the file.

It's also possible to open the same file two or more times. Every time the file is opened, a new file handle is returned. Because a file pointer is associated with each file handle, file manipulations using one file handle don't affect the pointer associated with other file handles, even if all handles refer to the same file. Look at the code below:

```
HFILE hFile1 = CreateFile("MYFILE.DAT", ...);
HFILE hFile2 = CreateFile("MYFILE.DAT", ...);
ReadFile(hFile1 lpBuffer, 100, &dwBytesRead, NULL);
WriteFile(hFile2, lpBuffer, 100, &dwBytesWritten, NULL);
```

In this code, the first 100 bytes from MYFILE.DAT are read into a buffer. After this read, the pointer associated with *hFile1* points to the 101st byte in the file. Now the code writes 100 bytes back to the same file. In this case, the pointer associated with *hFile2* is still initialized to 0, causing the first 100 bytes in MYFILE.DAT to be overwritten with the same data that was originally read from the file. The net result is that there is no change to the contents of the file. But after the calls to *ReadFile* and *WriteFile* have been completed, both handles' file pointers point to the 101st byte in the file.

Positioning a File Pointer

If you need to access a file randomly, you will need to alter the file pointer associated with the file's handle. You do this by calling *SetFilePointer*:

```
DWORD SetFilePointer(HANDLE hFile, LONG lDistanceToMove,
   PLONG lpDistanceToMoveHigh, DWORD dwMoveMethod);
```

The *hFile* parameter identifies the file handle the pointer is associated with. The *lDistanceToMove* parameter tells the system by how many bytes you want to move the pointer. The number you specify is added to the current value of the file's pointer, so a negative number has the effect of stepping backward in the file. For most files, being able to move the pointer forward or backward by a 32-bit value is good enough. But for those really big files, you might need a 64-bit value.

This is exactly what the *lpDistanceToMoveHigh* parameter is for. If you are moving the pointer within plus or minus 2 GB of its current position, pass NULL in the *lpDistanceToMoveHigh* parameter. If you want to move the pointer somewhere within 18 billion GB of its current position, you need to pass the high 32-bit part of this value in the *lpDistance-ToMoveHigh* parameter. Actually, you can't pass the high 32-bit part of the value directly; you must store the value in a variable and pass the address of this variable as the parameter.

The reason for this indirection is that *SetFilePointer* returns the previous location of the file pointer. If all you are interested in is the low 32 bits of this pointer, the function returns that value directly. If you are also interested in the high 32 bits of the pointer, the *SetFilePointer* function fills the variable pointed to by *lpDistanceToMoveHigh* before it returns.

The last parameter, *dwMoveMethod*, tells *SetFilePointer* how to interpret the two parameters *lDistanceToMove* and *lpDistanceToMoveHigh*. Here are the three possible values you can pass via *dwMoveMethod* to specify the starting point for the move:

Identifier	Meaning
FILE_BEGIN	The file's pointer becomes the unsigned value specified by the two *DistanceToMove* parameters.
FILE_CURRENT	The file's pointer is added to the signed value specified by the two *DistanceToMove* parameters.
FILE_END	The file's pointer becomes the number of bytes in the file added to the signed value specified by the two *DistanceToMove* parameters. The *DistanceToMove* parameters should identify a negative number in this case.

If *SetFilePointer* fails to alter the file's pointer, it returns 0xFFFFFFFF and the contents of the *lpDistanceToMoveHigh* buffer will contain NULL. Since it is possible for a large file to be positioned successfully to location 0xFFFFFFFF, it is better to verify that *SetFilePointer* is successful by calling *GetLastError* and checking to see whether it returns NO_ERROR.

Setting the End of a File

Usually, the system takes care of setting the end of a file when the file is closed. However, you might sometimes want to make a file smaller or larger. On those occasions, call:

```
BOOL SetEndOfFile(HANDLE hFile);
```

This *SetEndOfFile* function changes the length of a file so that the value indicated by the file pointer becomes the length of the file. For example, if you wanted to force a file to be 1024 bytes long, you'd use *SetEndOfFile* this way:

```
HFILE hFile = CreateFile(...);
SetFilePointer(hFile, 1024, NULL, FILE_BEGIN);
SetEndOfFile(hFile);
CloseHandle(hFile);
```

If you use the Explorer or the File Manager to examine the directory containing this file, you'll see that the file is exactly 1024 bytes long.

Forcing Cached Data to Be Written to Disk

You'll remember from our look at the *CreateFile* function that there were quite a few flags you could pass to alter the way in which the system cached file data. Win32 also offers a function you can use to force all unwritten file data to be flushed to disk:

```
BOOL FlushFileBuffers(HANDLE hFile);
```

The *FlushFileBuffers* function forces all the buffered data that is associated with a file identified by the *hFile* parameter to be flushed to disk. The file must have been created or opened with the GENERIC_WRITE flag. If the function is successful, TRUE is returned. Usually, you won't need to call this function. The system will guarantee that all of the buffered data will be flushed to disk when the file is closed.

Locking and Unlocking Regions of a File

The FILE_SHARE_READ and FILE_SHARE_WRITE flags let you tell the system whether and how a file can be opened by others. But think of a company that has a large customer database that contains 1 million records. Such a database is probably opened by almost everyone in the company. If everybody is performing searches only, that's fine—the file can always be opened with just the FILE_SHARE_READ flag specified.

But what if a group in the company needs to enter additional names and addresses in the customer database? These employees will need to open the database for writing. And somehow write access will need to be coordinated so that when one employee is appending a record to the database, another employee won't be able to append a record at the same time. If both employees were able to write to the database simultaneously, the integrity of the database would be compromised. File locking is a solution to this problem.

File locking is similar to using the FILE_SHARE_* flags, but the FILE_SHARE_* flags affect an entire file, whereas file locking affects small sections of a file. For example, if a customer moves to a new address, you'll need to update the customer's record. Before you write out the new information, you'll want to be sure that no one else can access the customer's data record while you're updating it. You'll want to lock that part of the database by calling:

```
BOOL LockFile(HANDLE hFile, DWORD dwFileOffsetLow,
    DWORD dwFileOffsetHigh, DWORD cbLockLow, DWORD cbLockHigh);
```

The first parameter, *hFile*, identifies the handle to the file you want to lock a subsection of. The next two parameters, *dwFileOffsetLow* and *dwFile-OffsetHigh*, specify the 64-bit offset into the file where you want to begin the file lock. The last two parameters, *cbLockLow* and *cbLockHigh*, specify the number of bytes you want to lock. If you were going to update the 100th customer in the database, you would use *LockFile* this way:

```
LockFile(hFile, sizeof(CUSTOMER_RECORD) * (100 - 1), 0,
    sizeof(CUSTOMER_RECORD), 0);
```

If *LockFile* is successful, TRUE is returned. While a region of a file is locked, all other processes that try to read from or write to the locked region will fail. This is why it's crucial to check the number of bytes read or written when *ReadFile* and *WriteFile* return—in case some other process has already locked regions of the file. You must design your program to handle such a case gracefully, perhaps by allowing the user to close other applications and try to read or write the data again.

It's perfectly legal to lock a region that falls beyond the current end of the file. You'd want to do that when you were adding customer records to the end of the file. You'd lock the region of the file just beyond the end of the file and write the new customer record to this region.

Note that you can't lock a region that includes an already locked region. The second call to *LockFile* below, for example, will fail:

```
LockFile(hFile, sizeof(CUSTOMER_RECORD) * (100 - 1), 0,
    sizeof(CUSTOMER_RECORD), 0);

LockFile(hFile, sizeof(CUSTOMER_RECORD) * (100 - 2), 0,
    2 * sizeof(CUSTOMER_RECORD), 0);
```

In the first call to *LockFile*, we locked the 100th customer record. In the second call, we're trying to lock the 99th through 100th customer records. Since the 100th record has already been locked, this second call fails.

Naturally, when you have finished with a locked region of a file, you'll need to unlock it:

```
BOOL UnlockFile(HANDLE hFile, DWORD dwFileOffsetLow,
    DWORD dwFileOffsetHigh, DWORD cbUnlockLow, DWORD cbUnlockHigh);
```

The *UnlockFile* parameters correspond to the *LockFile* parameters, and the return value is the same. When you unlock a region, you must unlock it in the same way that it was locked. For example, the calls on the following page won't work together correctly.

```
LockFile(hFile, sizeof(CUSTOMER_RECORD) * (100 - 1), 0,
    sizeof(CUSTOMER_RECORD), 0);

LockFile(hFile, sizeof(CUSTOMER_RECORD) * (100 - 2), 0,
    sizeof(CUSTOMER_RECORD), 0);

UnlockFile(hFile, sizeof(CUSTOMER_RECORD) * (100 - 2), 0,
    2 * sizeof(CUSTOMER_RECORD), 0);
```

The first two calls to *LockFile* lock the 100th and 99th records of the database, respectively. Then the call to *UnlockFile* tries to unlock both records with one call. This call to *UnlockFile* will fail. If two separate calls are made to *LockFile*, two separate and similar calls must be made to *UnlockFile*.

Important

Remember to unlock all locked regions of a file before you close the file or terminate the process.

There are two other functions you can call to lock and unlock a region of a file:

```
BOOL LockFileEx(HANDLE hFile, DWORD dwFlags, DWORD dwReserved,
    DWORD nNumberOfBytesToLockLow, DWORD nNumberOfBytesToLockHigh,
    LPOVERLAPPED lpOverlapped);
```

and

```
BOOL UnlockFileEx(HANDLE hFile, DWORD dwReserved,
    DWORD nNumberOfBytesToUnlockLow,
    DWORD nNumberOfBytesToUnlockHigh,
    LPOVERLAPPED lpOverlapped);
```

The *LockFileEx* and *UnlockFileEx* functions offer a superset of the *LockFile* and *UnlockFile* file capabilities.

Under Windows 95, the *LockFileEx* and *UnlockFileEx* functions have no useful implementations and simply return FALSE; calling *GetLastError* returns ERROR_CALL_NOT_IMPLEMENTED.

LockFileEx adds two capabilities to *LockFile*. You can use *LockFileEx* to lock a region of a file so that no other process can write to the locked region, as with *LockFile*, but with *LockFileEx* you can allow other processes to continue reading from the locked region. By default, the *LockFileEx* function requests such a shared lock; you can request an exclusive lock by ORing with the LOCKFILE_EXCLUSIVE_LOCK flag in the *dwFlags* parameter. (*LockFile* uses the LOCKFILE_EXCLUSIVE_LOCK flag when it calls *LockFileEx*.)

The other capability *LockFileEx* adds to *LockFile* is that you can tell *LockFileEx* to wait until a lock is granted if a thread in your process asks to lock a region of a file that is already locked by another process. In such a case, the *LockFile* function would return immediately, indicating that the call had failed. If your thread couldn't continue processing unless it could lock the region of the file, you would have to call *LockFile* repeatedly until it was able to lock the region and return TRUE. To simplify your program, you can call *LockFileEx*, which by default won't return until it has been able to lock the region of the file you've asked it to. If you want the function to return immediately, regardless of whether it can lock the region, OR the LOCKFILE_FAIL_IMMEDIATELY flag into the *dwFlags* parameter.

Most of the other *LockFileEx* parameters—*hFile*, *nNumberOfBytesToLockLow*, and *nNumberOfBytesToLockHigh*—are self-explanatory. The *dwReserved* parameter is reserved for Microsoft's future use, so it should always be 0. The last parameter, *lpOverlapped*, must point to an OVERLAPPED structure:

```
typedef struct _OVERLAPPED {
    DWORD   Internal;
    DWORD   InternalHigh;
    DWORD   Offset;
    DWORD   OffsetHigh;
    HANDLE hEvent;
} OVERLAPPED;
typedef OVERLAPPED *LPOVERLAPPED;
```

The only members of the OVERLAPPED structure that *LockFileEx* uses are the *Offset* and *OffsetHigh* members; *LockFileEx* ignores all the other members. Before calling *LockFileEx*, you must initialize the *Offset* and *OffsetHigh* members so that they indicate the starting byte of the region of the file you want to lock.

When you're ready to unlock the locked region of the file, you can call either *UnlockFile* or *UnlockFileEx*. The *UnlockFileEx* function will someday offer enhancements of *UnlockFile*. It currently offers no capabilities in addition to those offered by *UnlockFile*.

Reading and Writing Files Asynchronously

Compared to most other operations carried out by a computer, file I/O is one of the slowest. The CPU is much faster at performing arithmetic operations and even painting the screen than it is at reading data from or writing data to a file. And depending on the type of medium involved—CD-ROM, hard disk, or floppy disk—file I/O can take an excruciatingly long time. Under MS-DOS and 16-bit Windows, the time it took an application to read data from or write data out to a file was precious time wasted during which the user couldn't continue working with the application.

By taking advantage of Win32's multithreaded architecture, you can perform asynchronous file I/O. That is, you can tell the system to read from or write to the disk file while the rest of the code in your application continues to execute in parallel. Suppose you were developing a simple database application. When the user opened a database, you'd have to have your application read the contents of the database into memory as well as into an index file. After the user selected the OK button in the File Open dialog box, your application would display an hourglass cursor while the database file was opened and read. After reading the database records into memory, the application would have to open the index file and read the index as well. While all this work went on, the hourglass cursor would be displayed and the user wouldn't be able to start manipulating the records in the database until all the files had been read.

By taking advantage of asynchronous file I/O, you can cut this file opening time down substantially. If the user will run the database application on a machine with several CPUs, one CPU could be assigned responsibility for opening and reading the database records and another CPU could be assigned responsibility for opening and reading the index file. Since each of these tasks would be assigned to its very own CPU, the two tasks could execute at the same time. This would reduce the time it would take to open the database, and the user would be able to start manipulating records much sooner.

Of course, the file containing the index for the database would probably be much smaller than the file containing the records themselves. The index file would probably be loaded into memory before the database records were loaded. The application couldn't allow the user access until both files had been completely read into memory, though. So that the application would know when both files had been completely read, you'd have to use some form of thread synchronization.

As I said earlier, Windows 95 does not perform any file I/O asynchronously. When calling the *ReadFile* and *WriteFile* functions, you must pass NULL for the *lpOverlapped* structure unless you are manipulating serial devices. If you are not using serial devices and are targeting only Windows 95 and not Windows NT, you might want to skip ahead to the section "Manipulating File Attributes" beginning on page 642.

To access a data file asynchronously, you must first create or open the file by calling *CreateFile*, specifying the FILE_FLAG_OVERLAPPED flag in the *fdwAttrsAndFlags* parameter. This flag notifies the system that you intend to access the file asynchronously.

Once the file is open, you can read from and write to it by using the *ReadFile* and *WriteFile* functions we've already seen in the discussion of synchronous file I/O:

```
BOOL ReadFile(HANDLE hFile, LPVOID lpBuffer,
   DWORD nNumberOfBytesToRead, LPDWORD lpNumberOfBytesRead,
   LPOVERLAPPED lpOverlapped);
```

and

```
BOOL WriteFile(HANDLE hFile, CONST VOID *lpBuffer,
   DWORD nNumberOfBytesToWrite, LPDWORD lpNumberOfBytesWritten,
   LPOVERLAPPED lpOverlapped);
```

However, when you use the *ReadFile* and *WriteFile* functions to perform asynchronous file I/O, you must pass the address to an initialized OVERLAPPED structure as the *lpOverlapped* parameter. Win32 uses the word *overlapped* in this context to indicate that the time spent performing the file operation overlaps the time your thread spends doing other things. Here's the form of an OVERLAPPED structure again:

```
typedef struct _OVERLAPPED {
   DWORD    Internal;
   DWORD    InternalHigh;
   DWORD    Offset;
   DWORD    OffsetHigh;
   HANDLE   hEvent;
} OVERLAPPED;
typedef OVERLAPPED *LPOVERLAPPED;
```

When you call either *ReadFile* or *WriteFile*, you must allocate an OVERLAPPED structure (usually on your function's stack as a local variable) and initialize the *Offset, OffsetHigh,* and *hEvent* members of the structure. The *Offset* and *OffsetHigh* members indicate the byte position within the file at which you want the file operation to begin. For example, if you want to read 100 bytes from the file starting at byte position 345, write:

```
// Open file for asynchronous file I/O.
HANDLE hFile = CreateFile(..., FILE_FLAG_OVERLAPPED, ...);

// Create a buffer to hold the data.
BYTE bBuffer[100];

// Boolean value to indicate whether read started successfully
BOOL fReadStarted;

// DWORD used for the number of bytes read
DWORD dwNumBytesRead;

// Initialize an OVERLAPPED structure to tell
// the system where to start reading the data.
OVERLAPPED Overlapped;
Overlapped.Offset = 345;
Overlapped.OffsetHigh = 0;

Overlapped.hEvent = NULL;    // Explained later

// Start reading the data asynchronously.
fReadStarted = ReadFile(hFile, bBuffer, sizeof(bBuffer),
    &dwNumBytesRead, &Overlapped);

// Code below ReadFile executes while the system
// reads the file's data into the buffer.
  :
  :
```

Note several things as you perform asynchronous file I/O. In synchronous file I/O, each file handle has a file pointer associated with it. When another request to read from or write to the file is made, the system knows to start accessing the file at the location identified by the file pointer. After the operation is complete, the system updates the file pointer automatically so that the next operation can pick up where the last operation left off.

Things work quite differently in asynchronous file I/O. Imagine what would happen if you didn't have to use an OVERLAPPED structure. If your code placed a call to *ReadFile* immediately followed by another call to *ReadFile* (for the same file handle), the system wouldn't know where to start reading the file for the second call to *ReadFile*. You probably wouldn't want to start reading the file at the same location used by the first call to *ReadFile*. You might want to start the second read at the byte in the file following the last byte read by the first call to *ReadFile*. To avoid confusion, Microsoft designed *ReadFile* and *WriteFile* so that for every asynchronous I/O operation the starting byte in the file must be specified in the OVERLAPPED structure.

The next thing to notice is that in the code on the previous page the call to *ReadFile* has NULL passed in the *lpNumberofBytesRead* parameter. Since you are performing asynchronous file I/O, it's likely that the call to *ReadFile* will actually return before all the data has been read into the buffer. Because all the data won't have been read from the file when *ReadFile* returns, *ReadFile* can't possibly fill the buffer pointed to by the *lpNumberOfBytesRead* parameter with a meaningful value. However, you'll notice that I still must pass a valid address to *ReadFile*, or an access violation is raised. This concept extends to asynchronous file writes. When you call *WriteFile* to initiate an asynchronous file write, you must pass a valid address for the *lpNumberOfBytesWritten* parameter.

The last thing to notice is the return value from *ReadFile*. For synchronous file I/O, *ReadFile* returns regardless of whether the data was read successfully. For asynchronous file I/O, *ReadFile* returns before all the data has been read and can therefore return only a value that indicates whether the data has begun to be read. Similarly, for asynchronous file I/O, *WriteFile*'s return value indicates only whether the write operation has begun. *ReadFile* and *WriteFile* both return FALSE if an error occurred in the call. For example, both functions return FALSE if the *hFile* parameter is an invalid file handle.

Once the asynchronous file operation has begun, your thread can continue initializing or do any other processing it sees fit to do. Eventually, you will need to synchronize your thread with the file I/O operation. In other words, you'll hit a point in your thread's code at which the thread can't continue to execute unless the data from the file is fully loaded into the buffer.

Win32 considers a file handle to be a synchronization object—that is, it can be in either a signaled or a nonsignaled state. When you call *ReadFile* or *WriteFile*, one of the first things these functions do is reset the file handle to its nonsignaled state. Then, when all the data has been read from or written to the file, the system sets the file handle to the signaled state. By calling the *WaitForSingleObject* or *WaitForMultipleObjects* function, your thread can determine when the asynchronous file operation has completed—that is, when the file handle has been set to the signaled state. Here is an extension of the code we've been looking at:

```
// Open file for asynchronous file I/O.
HANDLE hFile = CreateFile(..., FILE_FLAG_OVERLAPPED, ...);

// Create a buffer to hold the data.
BYTE bBuffer[100];

// Boolean value to indicate whether read started successfully
BOOL fReadStarted;

// DWORD used for the number of bytes read
DWORD dwNumBytesRead;

// Initialize an OVERLAPPED structure to tell
// the system where to start reading the data.
OVERLAPPED Overlapped;
Overlapped.Offset = 345;
Overlapped.OffsetHigh = 0;

Overlapped.hEvent = NULL;    // Explained later

// Start reading the data asynchronously.
fReadStarted = ReadFile(hFile, bBuffer, sizeof(bBuffer),
    &dwNumBytesRead, &Overlapped);

// Code below ReadFile executes while the system
// reads the file's data into the buffer.
    :
    :

// The thread can't continue until we know that all
// the requested data has been read into our buffer.
WaitForSingleObject(hFile, INFINITE);

// Initialization complete and file data read;
// the thread can continue.
    :
    :
```

Something important is missing from this code. We should be checking to be sure that the file operation has completed successfully before we allow the thread to continue running. We can get the result of an asynchronous file operation by calling:

```
BOOL GetOverlappedResult(HANDLE hFile, LPOVERLAPPED lpOverlapped,
    LPDWORD lpcbTransfer, BOOL fWait);
```

When we call the *GetOverlappedResult* function, the *hFile* and *lpOverlapped* parameters must indicate the same file handle and OVERLAPPED structure that were used in the call to *ReadFile* or *WriteFile*. The *lpcbTransfer* parameter points to a DWORD that will be filled with the number of bytes that were successfully transferred to or from the buffer during the write or read operation. If you aren't interested in this information, you must still pass a valid address here to avoid an access violation.

The last parameter, *fWait*, is a Boolean value that tells *GetOverlappedResult* whether it should wait until the overlapped file operation is complete before returning. If *fWait* is FALSE, *GetOverlappedResult* doesn't wait and returns immediately to the application. An application can call *GetOverlappedResult*, passing TRUE for the *fWait* parameter, to suspend the thread while an operation continues execution, instead of calling *WaitForSingleObject* as in the code we just looked at.

GetOverlappedResult returns TRUE if the function is successful. If you pass FALSE for the *fWait* parameter and the file operation has not yet been completed, *GetOverlappedResult* will return FALSE. You can determine whether the call failed or whether the file operation is still proceeding by following the call to *GetOverlappedResult* with a call to *GetLastError*. If *GetLastError* returns ERROR_IO_INCOMPLETE, the call was good but the file operation is still in progress.

Under Windows 95, the *GetOverlappedResult* function works only on serial devices or on files opened by using the *DeviceIoControl* function.

Note that you can't reuse the OVERLAPPED structure in your application until the file operation has been completed. The example shown below is totally incorrect:

```
void Func1 (void) {

    // Open file for asynchronous file I/O.
    HANDLE hFile = CreateFile(..., FILE_FLAG_OVERLAPPED, ...);

    // Create a buffer to hold the data.
    BYTE bBuffer[100];

    Func2(hFile, bBuffer, sizeof(bBuffer));
    :
    :

}
```

(continued)

```
void Func2 (HANDLE hFile, LPVOID bBuffer, DWORD dwBufSize) {

    DWORD dwNumBytesRead;

    // Initialize an OVERLAPPED structure to tell
    // the system where to start reading the data.
    OVERLAPPED Overlapped;
    memset(&Overlapped, 0, sizeof(Overlapped));

    // Start reading the data asynchronously.
    fReadStarted = ReadFile(hFile, bBuffer,
        dwBufSize, &dwNumBytesRead, &Overlapped);
}
```

This code fragment is incorrect because the locally defined OVERLAPPED structure in *Func2* will go out of scope when *Func2* returns. The system remembers the address of the OVERLAPPED structure when you call *ReadFile* or *WriteFile*. When the file operation is complete, the system needs to reference the *Internal, InternalHigh,* and *hEvent* members of the structure. If the structure goes out of scope, the system will manipulate whatever garbage happens to be on the stack—and this could introduce difficult-to-find bugs into your application!

The *Internal* and *InternalHigh* members of the OVERLAPPED structure, which the system must update when the file operation is complete, were reserved for internal use during very early betas of Windows NT. As time went on, it became clear to Microsoft that the information contained in these members would be useful to all of us. They left the names of the members *Internal* and *InternalHigh* so that any code already relying on these names wouldn't have to be changed. If the file operation is completed because of an error, the *Internal* member contains a system-dependent status. The *InternalHigh* member is updated with the number of bytes that have been transferred. This is the same value that is put into the buffer pointed to by the *lpcbTransfer* parameter of *GetOverlappedResult*.

There is one more thing to watch out for when you try to perform asynchronous file I/O. Suppose you were trying to carry out multiple asynchronous operations on the same file at the same time. Say that you wanted to read a sequence of bytes from the beginning of the file and simultaneously write another sequence of bytes to the end of the file. In this situation, you can't synchronize your thread by waiting for the file handle to become signaled.

The handle becomes signaled as soon as either of the file operations completes, so if you call *WaitForSingleObject*, passing it the file handle, you will be unsure when *WaitForSingleObject* returns, and whether it returned because the read operation was completed or because the write operation was completed. Clearly, there needs to be a better way to perform asynchronous file I/O so that we don't run into this predicament—fortunately, there is.

The last member of the OVERLAPPED structure, *hEvent*, identifies an event synchronization kernel object you must create by calling *CreateEvent*. When the system completes an asynchronous file I/O operation, it checks to see whether the *hEvent* member of the OVERLAPPED structure is NULL. If *hEvent* is not NULL, the system signals the event by calling *SetEvent* using *hEvent* as the event handle. The system also sets the file handle to the signaled state just as it did before. However, if you are using events to determine when a file operation has been completed, you shouldn't wait for the file handle object to become signaled—wait for the event instead.

Performing Multiple Asynchronous File I/O Operations Simultaneously

If you want to perform multiple asynchronous file I/O operations simultaneously, you should create an event for each of the operations, initialize the *hEvent* member in each of the file operations' OVERLAPPED structure, and then call *ReadFile* or *WriteFile*. When you reach the point in your code at which you need to synchronize with the completion of the file operation, simply call *WaitForSingleObject*. But instead of passing the file's handle, pass the handle to the event that you stored in the OVERLAPPED structure. With this scheme, you can easily and reliably perform multiple asynchronous file I/O operations simultaneously using the same file handle.

You can use the *GetOverlappedResult* function to synchronize your application with its impending file I/O. If you pass TRUE in as the *fWait* parameter for *GetOverlappedResult*, the function internally calls *WaitForSingleObject* and passes the *hEvent* member of the OVERLAPPED structure.

The potential problem here is that, if you are using an auto-reset event instead of a manual-reset event to signal the end of a file operation, you might permanently suspend your thread. If you use an auto-reset event and call *WaitForSingleObject* from your own code to wait for the file operation to be completed, the event will be reset automatically to the nonsignaled state when *WaitForSingleObject* returns. If you then call *GetOverlappedResult* to determine the number of bytes that were successfully transferred and pass TRUE for *fWait*, you will cause *GetOverlappedResult*

623

to make its own call to *WaitForSingleObject*. When *GetOverlappedResult* does this, the call to *WaitForSingleObject* will never return because the file operation already completed will have caused the event to become signaled. The event won't be signaled again. *GetOverlappedResult* will never return to your thread's code, and the thread will be hung!

Alertable Asynchronous File I/O

Win32 offers another set of file I/O functions that allow you to perform asynchronous file I/O:

```
BOOL ReadFileEx(HANDLE hFile, LPVOID lpBuffer,
    DWORD nNumberOfBytesToRead, LPOVERLAPPED lpOverlapped,
    LPOVERLAPPED_COMPLETION_ROUTINE lpCompletionRoutine);
```

and

```
BOOL WriteFileEx(HANDLE hFile, CONST VOID *lpBuffer,
    DWORD nNumberOfBytesToWrite, LPOVERLAPPED lpOverlapped,
    LPOVERLAPPED_COMPLETION_ROUTINE lpCompletionRoutine);
```

Under Windows 95, the *ReadFileEx* and *WriteFileEx* functions have no useful implementation and simply return FALSE; calling *GetLastError* returns ERROR_CALL_NOT_IMPLEMENTED.

The *ReadFileEx* and *WriteFileEx* functions allow you to start a file I/O operation just as the asynchronous functions *ReadFile* and *WriteFile* do. The difference is that, with the *ReadFileEx* and *WriteFileEx* alertable functions, you must also pass the address to a callback function, called a *completion routine*. This routine must have the following prototype:

```
VOID FileIOCompletionRoutine(DWORD fdwError, DWORD cbTransferred,
    LPOVERLAPPED lpo);
```

I'll get back to this completion routine function shortly. First let's look at how the system handles the asynchronous file I/O operation.

When you call *ReadFileEx* or *WriteFileEx*, the system queues your file request into a system buffer. The system periodically (and asynchronously) examines the buffer of queued requests and performs the specified operations. As the file operations are completed, the system creates a list of the completed events and associates this list with the thread that originally called *ReadFileEx* or *WriteFileEx*. For example, the following code queues three different asynchronous file operations:

```
hFile = CreateFile(...);

// Perform first ReadFileEx.
ReadFileEx(hFile, ...);

// Perform first WriteFileEx.
WriteFileEx(hFile, ...);

// Perform second ReadFileEx.
ReadFileEx(hFile, ...);

SomeFunc();
```

If the call to *SomeFunc* takes some time to execute, the system will complete the three file operations before *SomeFunc* returns. While the thread is executing the *SomeFunc* function, the system is creating a list of file I/O completion records for the thread. The list might look something like this:

```
1st WriteFileEx completed
2nd ReadFileEx completed
1st ReadFileEx completed
```

This list of events is maintained in internal data structures—you have no access to the list. You'll also notice from the list that the system can execute your queued file operations in any order and that file operations you invoke last may be completed first and vice versa.

The completed file operations are just queued—the system doesn't call the *FileIOCompletionRoutine* function as soon as each file operation is completed. If you want to suspend your thread and allow the system to call the *FileIOCompletionRoutine* function for each of the file operations as it's completed, you must call one of three alertable functions:

```
DWORD SleepEx(DWORD dwTimeout, BOOL fAlertable);
```

or

```
DWORD WaitForSingleObjectEx(HANDLE hObject, DWORD dwTimeout,
   BOOL fAlertable);
```

or

```
DWORD WaitForMultipleObjectsEx(DWORD cObjects,
   LPHANDLE lphObjects, BOOL fWaitAll. DWORD dwTimeout,
   BOOL fAlertable);
```

All three extended functions work exactly as their nonalertable counterparts (*Sleep*, *WaitForSingleObject*, and *WaitForMultipleObjects*) do, except that the alertable functions have that additional parameter, *fAlertable*. If you pass FALSE for the *fAlertable* value, you are saying that the function is not alertable, which makes the function operate just as the nonalertable versions described in Chapter 9, the thread synchronization chapter. In fact, the *Sleep*, *WaitForSingleObject*, and *WaitForMultipleObjects* functions are implemented internally as calls to the alertable versions of the functions, with FALSE passed for the *fAlertable* parameter.

If you pass TRUE for *fAlertable*, the system puts your thread to sleep while it waits for file I/O operations to be completed. While your thread is asleep, the system checks the list of completed file I/O operations. If the system finds a completed I/O operation, it wakes up your thread and calls the *FileIOCompletionRoutine* function. When the *FileIOCompletionRoutine* function returns, the system removes the entry from the list and checks again to see whether there are any more. If there are, the system again wakes your thread and calls the *FileIOCompletionRoutine* function.

Important

The thread that calls an extended wait function must be the same thread that called the file I/O function.

When the list of completed file operations is empty, the system wakes up your thread again and returns from the call to *SleepEx*, *WaitForSingleObjectEx*, or *WaitForMultipleObjectsEx*. The return value from any of these three functions will be WAIT_IO_COMPLETION if the function returned because the *FileIOCompletionRoutine* was executed one or more times.

If you call one of the extended wait functions and there are no completed file operations to be processed, the functions work just as though you had called them and passed FALSE for the *fAlertable* parameter. If, while the system waits, a single file operation or several file operations are completed, your thread wakes, the system calls *FileIOCompletionRoutine* using your thread for all the finished operations, and then these functions return WAIT_IO_COMPLETION.

These alertable functions in their extended form are most useful in a client/server situation. You might have a server application that guards a database of information. You might also have a client application that periodically needs to request data from the server application. The server and client applications would communicate with each other using named pipes.

The server application would start by calling *ReadFileEx* and then pass to the server the handle to a named pipe instead of the handle to a file. When a client application sent information to the server through the named pipe, the asynchronous call would read the client's request and call the *FileIOCompletionRoutine* function. The *FileIOCompletionRoutine* function would interpret the client's request and locate the requested information in the database. The server would do this by initiating its own call to *ReadFileEx*. When the database information had been read, another *FileIOCompletionRoutine* call would be executed and the retrieved data would be transferred back through the named pipe to the client application.

The Alertable I/O Sample Application

The AlertIO (ALERTIO.EXE) application, listed in Figure 13-2 beginning on page 630, demonstrates the use of alertable file I/O. The source code files, resource files, and make file for the application are in the ALERTIO.13 directory on the companion disc. The program simply copies a file the user specifies to a new file called ALERTIO.CPY. When the user executes AlertIO, the Alertable I/O File Copy dialog box appears:

The user clicks on the Browse button to select the file to be copied. To best see the effects of using the alertable I/O functions, it's a good idea to select a large file (the Win32 API help file, API32.HLP, for instance). After you've selected a file to be copied, the Source File and File Size fields are updated.

When the user clicks on the Copy button, the program opens the source file, creates the destination file (saving both file handles in the global *g_hFileSrc* and *g_hFileDst* variables), and begins copying the file. After the file has been copied, the file handles are closed.

The file is copied by means of four internal buffers. Each buffer is a different size, as shown below:

Buffer Number	Size in Bytes
0	32768
1	16384
2	10922
3	8192

The entire file will be copied, piece by piece, using these buffers. First, four chunks of the file, one chunk per buffer, will be read. These file-read operations are initiated by calls to the *ReadFileEx* function. The address of the *InputCompletion* function is specified in the call to *ReadFileEx*, causing *InputCompletion* to be called automatically when the file-read operation for an individual buffer has been completed. Because the buffers are different sizes, the reads might not be finished in the order they were requested.

After the four initial reads have been initiated, the program enters a loop that executes until the destination file has been written or until a file copy error occurs.

```
while ((g_CopyStatus != csError) &&
       (g_CopyStatus != csDoneWriting)) {

   // Put this thread to sleep until it is awakened by
   // an alertable file I/O completion.
   SleepEx(INFINITE, TRUE);
}
```

Inside the loop, the thread calls *SleepEx*, the alertable version of the *Sleep* function. If the system is still performing the asynchronous file-read operations, the call to *SleepEx* causes the thread to be suspended. However, as soon as the asynchronous buffer reads have been completed, the thread is in an alertable state and executes the *InputCompletion* function once for each of the completed buffer reads.

The code inside the *InputCompletion* function first verifies that the part of the file has been read into the buffer successfully. Then it calls *WriteFileEx* so that the contents of the buffer are written to the destination file. The call to *WriteFileEx* writes the contents of the buffer to the same byte offset in the destination as the offset that was used when the source data was read from the source file. The call to *WriteFileEx* also specifies the address of the *OutputCompletion* function so that the system will automatically call the *OutputCompletion* function after all file-write operations have been completed and the thread is in an alertable state.

During the file copy, the Alertable I/O File Copy dialog box, shown below, indicates whether information is being read from the source file into a buffer or whether data is being written from a buffer to the destination file.

From left to right, each line shows a buffer number, whether the data is being read into or written out from the buffer, the location in the source or destination file at which the data is being read from or written to, and the number of bytes in the buffer that will be read or written.

Most of the time, the number of bytes written will be the number of bytes that were read. However, when the last part of the source file is read into a buffer, it often doesn't completely fill the buffer. Therefore, when the information in this buffer is written to the destination file, only the actual number of bytes that were read is written, not the size in bytes of the whole buffer. If the whole buffer were written, the destination file would end up larger than the source file.

AlertIO.ico

ALERTIO.C

```
/****************************************************************
Module name: AlertIO.C
Written by: Jim Harkins and Jeffrey Richter
Notices: Copyright (c) 1995 Jeffrey Richter
****************************************************************/


#include "..\AdvWin32.H"   /* See Appendix B for details. */
#include <windows.h>
#include <windowsx.h>

#pragma warning(disable: 4001)      /* Single-line comment */

#include <tchar.h>
#include <stdio.h>
#include <stdlib.h>
#include "Resource.H"


///////////////////////////////////////////////////////////////


#define BUFFSIZE (32 * 1024)
#define BUFFNUM  4

#define DSTFILENAME      __TEXT("AlertIO.CPY")

// Status of the copy
// Note:  This is an ordered list (i.e., < and > operators are
// used on this type).

typedef enum {
   csCopying,
   csDoneReading,
   csDoneWriting,
   csError,
} COPYSTATUS;


HWND g_hwndLB = NULL;

// Data used by copy
HANDLE g_hFileSrc, g_hFileDst;
```

Figure 13-2.   *(continued)*
The AlertIO application.

Figure 13-2. *continued*

```
// hEvent contains the buffer number
OVERLAPPED g_Overlapped[BUFFNUM];

// Pointer to file copy buffers
BYTE g_bBuffers[BUFFSIZE * BUFFNUM];

// Offset in source file where next read begins
DWORD  g_dwNextReadOffset = 0;

// Status of the file copy
COPYSTATUS g_CopyStatus = csCopying;

DWORD g_dwLastError = NO_ERROR;

int g_nReadsInProgress     = 0;
int g_nMaxReadsInProgress  = 0;
int g_nCompletedReads      = 0;
int g_nWritesInProgress    = 0;
int g_nMaxWritesInProgress = 0;
int g_nCompletedWrites     = 0;


VOID WINAPI InputCompletion (DWORD fdwError,
    DWORD cbTransferred, LPOVERLAPPED lpo);

VOID WINAPI OutputCompletion (DWORD fdwError,
    DWORD cbTransferred, LPOVERLAPPED lpo);


//////////////////////////////////////////////////////////////////

// This function constructs a string using the format string
// passed and the variable number of arguments and adds the
// string to the list box identified by the global
// g_hwndLB variable.
void AddStr (LPCTSTR szFmt, ...) {
   TCHAR szBuf[150];
   int nIndex;
   va_list va_params;

   // Make va_params point to the first argument after szFmt.
   va_start(va_params, szFmt);
```

(continued)

Figure 13-2. *continued*

```
    // Build the string to be displayed.
    _vstprintf(szBuf, szFmt, va_params);

    do {
        // Add the string to the end of the list box.
        nIndex = ListBox_AddString(g_hwndLB, szBuf);

        // If the list box is full, delete the first item in it.
        if (nIndex == LB_ERR)
            ListBox_DeleteString(g_hwndLB, 0);

    } while (nIndex == LB_ERR);

    // Select the newly added item.
    ListBox_SetCurSel(g_hwndLB, nIndex);

    // Indicate that we're done referencing
    // the variable arguments.
    va_end(va_params);
}


///////////////////////////////////////////////////////////////////


void ReadNext (LPOVERLAPPED lpOverlapped) {
    BOOL  fReadOk;
    DWORD dwLastError;
    int nBufSize = BUFFSIZE / ((int) lpOverlapped->hEvent + 1);

    if (csCopying != g_CopyStatus) {
        // Either an error has occurred or we have read past
        // the end of the file. In either case,
        // let's not start to read a new block from the file.
        return;
    }

    // The file is still being copied.

    // Figure out where to start
    // reading the next portion of the file.
    lpOverlapped->Offset = g_dwNextReadOffset;
    lpOverlapped->OffsetHigh = 0;
```

(continued)

Figure 13-2. *continued*

```
    // Set the global file offset variable so that it knows
    // where it should begin reading the next time.
    g_dwNextReadOffset += nBufSize;


    AddStr(__TEXT("%d: Read, Offset=%d, Len=%d."),
        (int) lpOverlapped->hEvent, lpOverlapped->Offset,
        nBufSize);


    // Initiate the alertable read from the
    // file into the appropriate buffer.
    fReadOk = ReadFileEx(g_hFileSrc,
        g_bBuffers + (int) lpOverlapped->hEvent * BUFFSIZE,
        nBufSize, lpOverlapped, InputCompletion);


    if (fReadOk) {
        // The read is successful; update the counters.
        g_nReadsInProgress++;
        g_nMaxReadsInProgress =
            max(g_nMaxReadsInProgress, g_nReadsInProgress);
    } else {
        // The read is unsuccessful.
        // Get the reason for the failure.
        dwLastError = GetLastError();


        if (ERROR_HANDLE_EOF == dwLastError) {
            // Read failed because of an attempt to read past the
            // end of the file; set global status indicator.
            g_CopyStatus = csDoneReading;
            AddStr(__TEXT("%d: Read past end-of-file."),
                (int) lpOverlapped->hEvent);
        } else {
            // Read failed because of another error;
            // set global status indicator and global error.
            g_CopyStatus = csError;
            g_dwLastError = dwLastError;


            AddStr(__TEXT("%d: Read caused an error (%d)."),
                (int) lpOverlapped->hEvent, g_dwLastError);
        }
    }
}
```

(continued)

Figure 13-2. *continued*

```
///////////////////////////////////////////////////////////////


VOID WINAPI InputCompletion (DWORD fdwError,
    DWORD cbTransferred, LPOVERLAPPED lpOverlapped) {

    BOOL fWriteOk;

    // Signal that a read has been completed.
    g_nReadsInProgress--;

    switch (fdwError) {
        case 0:
            // The read has been completed successfully.
            g_nCompletedReads++;

            AddStr(__TEXT("%d: Write, Offset=%d, Len=%d."),
                (int) lpOverlapped->hEvent, lpOverlapped->Offset,
                cbTransferred);

            // Write this buffer to the destination file.
            // The OVERLAPPED structure contains the offset
            // the buffer was read from. This is the same offset
            // the buffer should be written to.
            fWriteOk = WriteFileEx(g_hFileDst,
                g_bBuffers + (int) lpOverlapped->hEvent * BUFFSIZE,
                cbTransferred, lpOverlapped, OutputCompletion);

            if (fWriteOk) {
                // The write is successful; update the counters.
                g_nWritesInProgress++;
                g_nMaxWritesInProgress = max(
                    g_nMaxWritesInProgress, g_nWritesInProgress);
            } else {
                // The write is unsuccessful.
                // Get the reason for the failure, and set global
                // status indicator and global error.
                g_CopyStatus = csError;
                g_dwLastError = GetLastError();

                AddStr(__TEXT("%d: Write caused an error (%d)."),
                    (int) lpOverlapped->hEvent, g_dwLastError);
            }
            break;
```

(continued)

Figure 13-2. *continued*

```
        case ERROR_HANDLE_EOF:
            // Read past the end of the file.
            // Update the global status indicator.
            g_CopyStatus = csDoneReading;
            AddStr(__TEXT("%d: Done reading source file."),
                (int) lpOverlapped->hEvent);
            break;
    }
}


///////////////////////////////////////////////////////////////////////


VOID WINAPI OutputCompletion (DWORD fdwError,
    DWORD cbTransferred, LPOVERLAPPED lpOverlapped) {

    // Signal that a write has been completed.
    g_nWritesInProgress--;

    if (fdwError == 0) {
        // The write has been completed successfully.
        g_nCompletedWrites++;

        // Start reading the next chunk of the file if we're not
        // done reading the file yet.
        if (csCopying == g_CopyStatus) {
            ReadNext(lpOverlapped);
        }

        // Test to see whether this was the last write, and if
        // so, update the global status indicator so that the
        // main copy loop will know the file has been copied.
        if ((g_CopyStatus == csDoneReading) &&
            (g_nWritesInProgress == 0)) {
            g_CopyStatus = csDoneWriting;
            AddStr(__TEXT("%d: Done writing destination file."),
                (int) lpOverlapped->hEvent);
        }
    }
}
```

(continued)

Figure 13-2. *continued*

```
///////////////////////////////////////////////////////////////

BOOL FileCopy (LPCTSTR pszFileSrc, LPCTSTR pszFileDst) {
  int nBuffer;

  // Open the existing source file for input.
  g_hFileSrc = CreateFile(pszFileSrc, GENERIC_READ,
    FILE_SHARE_READ, NULL, OPEN_EXISTING,
    FILE_ATTRIBUTE_NORMAL | FILE_FLAG_OVERLAPPED |
    FILE_FLAG_SEQUENTIAL_SCAN, NULL);

  if (g_hFileSrc == INVALID_HANDLE_VALUE) {
    g_dwLastError = GetLastError();
    return(FALSE);
  }

  // Create the new destination file for output.
  g_hFileDst = CreateFile(pszFileDst, GENERIC_WRITE,
    0, NULL, CREATE_ALWAYS,
    FILE_ATTRIBUTE_NORMAL | FILE_FLAG_OVERLAPPED |
    FILE_FLAG_SEQUENTIAL_SCAN, NULL);

  if (g_hFileDst == INVALID_HANDLE_VALUE) {
    CloseHandle(g_hFileSrc);
    g_dwLastError = GetLastError();
    return(FALSE);
  }

  // Get ready to start copying the file.
  g_CopyStatus = csCopying;
  g_dwNextReadOffset      = 0;
  g_nReadsInProgress      = 0;
  g_nMaxReadsInProgress   = 0;
  g_nCompletedReads       = 0;
  g_nWritesInProgress     = 0;
  g_nMaxWritesInProgress  = 0;
  g_nCompletedWrites      = 0;

  // Start the copy engine by allowing the buffers to begin
  // reading data from the file.
  for (nBuffer = 0; nBuffer < BUFFNUM; nBuffer++) {
    g_Overlapped[nBuffer].hEvent = (HANDLE) nBuffer;
    ReadNext(&g_Overlapped[nBuffer]);
  }
```

(continued)

Figure 13-2. *continued*

```
      // Loop until an error has occurred or until the
      // destination file has been written.
      while ((g_CopyStatus != csError) &&
            (g_CopyStatus != csDoneWriting)) {

         // Put this thread to sleep until it's awakened by
         // an alertable file I/O completion.
         SleepEx(INFINITE, TRUE);
      }


      CloseHandle(g_hFileDst);
      CloseHandle(g_hFileSrc);

      if (g_CopyStatus == csError) {
         SetLastError(g_dwLastError);
         AddStr(__TEXT("File copy error %d."), g_dwLastError);
      } else {
         AddStr(__TEXT("File copied successfully."));
      }

      // Put some statistical information in the list box.
      AddStr(__TEXT("Max reads in progress=%d."),
         g_nMaxReadsInProgress);
      AddStr(__TEXT("Completed reads=%d."), g_nCompletedReads);
      AddStr(__TEXT("Max writes in progress=%d."),
         g_nMaxWritesInProgress);
      AddStr(__TEXT("Completed writes=%d."), g_nCompletedWrites);

      return(g_CopyStatus != csError);
   }



   ///////////////////////////////////////////////////////////////


   BOOL Dlg_OnInitDialog (HWND hwnd, HWND hwndFocus,
      LPARAM lParam) {

      // Save the handle of the dialog's list box in a global
      // so that the threads can easily gain access to it.
      g_hwndLB = GetDlgItem(hwnd, IDC_LOG);


      // Associate an icon with the dialog box.
      SetClassLong(hwnd, GCL_HICON, (LONG)
```

(continued)

Figure 13-2. *continued*

```
      LoadIcon((HINSTANCE) GetWindowLong(hwnd, GWL_HINSTANCE),
      __TEXT("AlertIO")));


   // Disable the Copy button because no file
   // has been selected yet.
   EnableWindow(GetDlgItem(hwnd, IDOK), FALSE);

   return(TRUE);
}



///////////////////////////////////////////////////////////////////


void Dlg_OnCommand (HWND hwnd, int id,
   HWND hwndCtl, UINT codeNotify) {

   TCHAR szPathname[_MAX_DIR];
   BOOL fOk;
   OPENFILENAME ofn;

   switch (id) {
      case IDOK:
         // Copy the source file to the destination file.
         ListBox_ResetContent(g_hwndLB);
         Static_GetText(GetDlgItem(hwnd, IDC_SRCFILE),
            szPathname, sizeof(szPathname));
         SetCursor(LoadCursor(NULL, IDC_WAIT));
         FileCopy(szPathname, DSTFILENAME);
         break;

      case IDC_BROWSE:
         memset(&ofn, 0, sizeof(ofn));
         ofn.lStructSize = sizeof(ofn);
         ofn.hwndOwner = hwnd;
         ofn.lpstrFilter = __TEXT("*.*\0");

         _tcscpy(szPathname, __TEXT("*.*"));
         ofn.lpstrFile = szPathname;

         ofn.nMaxFile = sizeof(szPathname);
         ofn.Flags = OFN_FILEMUSTEXIST;
         fOk = GetOpenFileName(&ofn);
```

(continued)

Figure 13-2. *continued*

```
        if (fOk) {
            HANDLE hFile;
            Static_SetText(GetDlgItem(hwnd, IDC_SRCFILE),
                szPathname);
            hFile = CreateFile(szPathname, GENERIC_READ,
                0, NULL, OPEN_EXISTING, 0, NULL);

            SetDlgItemInt(hwnd, IDC_SRCFILESIZE,
                GetFileSize(hFile, NULL), FALSE);
            CloseHandle(hFile);
        }

        // Enable the Copy button if the user selected
        // a valid pathname.
        GetWindowText(GetDlgItem(hwnd, IDC_SRCFILE),
            szPathname, sizeof(szPathname));
        EnableWindow(GetDlgItem(hwnd, IDOK),
            szPathname[0] != __TEXT('('));

        if (fOk) {
            // If the user pressed the OK button in the file
            // dialog box, change focus to the Copy button.
            FORWARD_WM_NEXTDLGCTL(hwnd, GetDlgItem(hwnd, IDOK),
                TRUE, SendMessage);
        }
        break;

    case IDCANCEL:
        EndDialog(hwnd, id);
        break;
    }
}


////////////////////////////////////////////////////////////////


BOOL CALLBACK Dlg_Proc (HWND hDlg, UINT uMsg,
    WPARAM wParam, LPARAM lParam) {

    BOOL fProcessed = TRUE;

    switch (uMsg) {
        HANDLE_MSG(hDlg, WM_INITDIALOG, Dlg_OnInitDialog);
        HANDLE_MSG(hDlg, WM_COMMAND, Dlg_OnCommand);
```

(continued)

Figure 13-2. *continued*

```
    default:
        fProcessed = FALSE;
        break;
    }

    return(fProcessed);
}


///////////////////////////////////////////////////////////////


int WINAPI WinMain (HINSTANCE hinstExe,
    HINSTANCE hinstPrev, LPSTR lpszCmdLine, int nCmdShow) {

    DialogBox(hinstExe, MAKEINTRESOURCE(IDD_ALERTIO),
        NULL, Dlg_Proc);

    return(0);
}


/////////////////////////// End Of File ///////////////////////////
```

ALERTIO.RC

```
//Microsoft Visual C++ generated resource script.
//
#include "Resource.h"

#define APSTUDIO_READONLY_SYMBOLS
///////////////////////////////////////////////////////////////
//
// Generated from the TEXTINCLUDE 2 resource.
//
#include "afxres.h"


///////////////////////////////////////////////////////////////
#undef APSTUDIO_READONLY_SYMBOLS


///////////////////////////////////////////////////////////////
//
// Icon
//

AlertIO                 ICON    DISCARDABLE     "AlertIO.Ico"
```

(continued)

Figure 13-2. *continued*

```
///////////////////////////////////////////////////////////////
//
// Dialog
//

IDD_ALERTIO DIALOG DISCARDABLE  18, 18, 158, 158
STYLE WS_MINIMIZEBOX | WS_POPUP | WS_CAPTION | WS_SYSMENU
CAPTION "Alertable I/O File Copy"
FONT 8, "System"
BEGIN
    PUSHBUTTON       "&Browse...",IDC_BROWSE,4,4,52,12
    LTEXT            "Source file:",IDC_STATIC,5,20,40,8
    LTEXT            "(use Browse to select a file)",
                     IDC_SRCFILE,46,20,108,8,SS_NOPREFIX
    LTEXT            "File size:",IDC_STATIC,68,8,36,8
    LTEXT            "0",IDC_SRCFILESIZE,104,8,36,8
    DEFPUSHBUTTON    "&Copy",IDOK,100,40,52,12
    LTEXT            "Execution &log:",IDC_STATIC,4,45,48,8
    LISTBOX          IDC_LOG,4,56,148,100,NOT LBS_NOTIFY |
                     LBS_NOINTEGRALHEIGHT | WS_VSCROLL
                     | WS_TABSTOP
END


#ifdef APSTUDIO_INVOKED
///////////////////////////////////////////////////////////////
//
// TEXTINCLUDE
//

1 TEXTINCLUDE DISCARDABLE
BEGIN
    "Resource.h\0"
END

2 TEXTINCLUDE DISCARDABLE
BEGIN
    "#include ""afxres.h""\r\n"
    "\0"
END

3 TEXTINCLUDE DISCARDABLE
BEGIN
    "\r\n"
    "\0"
END
```

(continued)

Figure 13-2. *continued*

```
///////////////////////////////////////////////////////////////
#endif     // APSTUDIO_INVOKED


#ifndef APSTUDIO_INVOKED
///////////////////////////////////////////////////////////////
//
// Generated from the TEXTINCLUDE 3 resource.
//


///////////////////////////////////////////////////////////////
#endif     // not APSTUDIO_INVOKED
```

Manipulating File Attributes

A set of attributes is associated with every file. Many of the file attributes are initialized when the file is created, some are altered when a file is accessed, and some can be altered specifically under program control. Often you might not have any interest in altering the values but just want to see what the current attributes are for a file. Most file attributes have to do with flag settings, file size, and file time stamps.

File Flags

A file's attributes are initially set when the file is created with the *Create-File* function. When *CreateFile* is called, the *fdwAttrsAndFlags* parameter specifies the attributes the file should have when it is created. To see what these attributes are later, an application can call:

```
DWORD GetFileAttributes(LPTSTR lpszFileName);
```

The *GetFileAttributes* function retrieves the attributes associated with the file identified by the *lpszFileName* parameter. When the function returns, you can AND the return value with any of the identifiers we saw in the discussion of *CreateFile*'s *fdwAttrsAndFlags* parameter earlier in this chapter:

> FILE_ATTRIBUTE_ARCHIVE
> FILE_ATTRIBUTE_DIRECTORY
> FILE_ATTRIBUTE_HIDDEN

```
FILE_ATTRIBUTE_NORMAL
FILE_ATTRIBUTE_READONLY
FILE_ATTRIBUTE_SYSTEM
```

Although it's not frequently done, you can alter any of these file attributes by calling *SetFileAttributes*:

```
BOOL SetFileAttributes(LPTSTR lpFileName, DWORD dwFileAttributes);
```

SetFileAttributes returns TRUE if it successfully alters the file's attributes. The code below, for example, turns off the archive flag for CALC.EXE:

```
DWORD dwFileAttributes = GetFileAttributes("CALC.EXE");
dwFileAttributes &= ~FILE_ATTRIBUTE_ARCHIVE;
SetFileAttributes("CALC.EXE", dwFileAttributes);
```

File Size

You might also want to query a file's size by calling *GetFileSize*:

```
DWORD GetFileSize(HANDLE hFile, LPDWORD lpdwFileSizeHigh);
```

You'll immediately notice that the *GetFileSize* function requires that the file be open and that the handle to the file be passed as the *hFile* parameter. *GetFileSize* returns the low 32-bit value representing the file's size directly. If you are interested in the high 32-bit part of the file's size, you need to pass an address to a DWORD that *GetFileSize* will fill with this information. A file's size can be altered only by writing to the file or by calling *SetEndOfFile*.

File Time Stamps

In MS-DOS, and more specifically in FAT file systems prior to Windows 95 and Windows NT 3.5, a file has only one time stamp associated with it—the stamp indicating the last time the file was written to. But in the new FAT file systems, as well as in HPFS and NTFS, a file can have three time stamps associated with it: the date and time the file was created, the date and time the file was last accessed, and the date and time the file was last written to. To retrieve the time stamp information for a file, call:

```
BOOL GetFileTime(HANDLE hFile, LPFILETIME lpftCreation,
    LPFILETIME lpftLastAccess, LPFILETIME lpftLastWrite);
```

For files stored on early FAT file systems, the creation time and the last access time will be 0. As with *GetFileSize*, the file must be opened before the call to *GetFileTime* is made so that we can pass its file handle as the *hFile* parameter. The next three parameters are all pointers to FILETIME structures:

```
typedef struct _FILETIME {
    DWORD dwLowDateTime;
    DWORD dwHighDateTime;
} FILETIME, *PFILETIME, *LPFILETIME;
```

If you aren't interested in when the file was created, you can pass NULL in as the *lpftCreation* parameter. The same is true for either of the other two time stamp parameters.

The 64-bit value composed of the *dwLowDateTime* and *dwHighDateTime* members in the FILETIME structure represents the number of 100-nanosecond intervals since January 1, 1601. I'll grant you that this isn't very useful, but the date does, after all, mark the start of a new quadricentury. Still not too impressed? I guess Microsoft didn't think you'd be too impressed either, so they wrote some additional functions to help you realize the usefulness of file times.

Perhaps all you need to do is check to see which of two files is older. That's easy:

```
LONG CompareFileTime(LPFILETIME lpft1, LPFILETIME lpft2);
```

CompareFileTime returns one of these long values:

Result of CompareFileTime	Meaning
−1	*lpft1* is less than (older than) *lpft2*
0	*lpft1* is same (age) as *lpft2*
+1	*lpft1* is greater than (younger than) *lpft2*

Using *CompareFileTime*, you can also check to see whether a file was written to the last time it was accessed:

```
lResult = CompareFileTime(&ftLastAccess, &ftLastWrite);
if (lResult == 0) {
    // Last access was a write
} else {
    // Last access was not a write
}
```

You might want to show the user one of the file's time stamps. In this case, you will need to convert FILETIME structures to SYSTEM-TIME structures or vice versa using:

```
BOOL FileTimeToSystemTime(LPFILETIME lpft, LPSYSTEMTIME lpst);
```

and

```
BOOL SystemTimeToFileTime(LPSYSTEMTIME lpst, LPFILETIME lpft);
```

These functions convert the time stamp easily between the FILE-TIME and SYSTEMTIME structures. A SYSTEMTIME structure looks like this:

```
typedef struct _SYSTEMTIME {
    WORD wYear;
    WORD wMonth;
    WORD wDayOfWeek;
    WORD wDay;
    WORD wHour;
    WORD wMinute;
    WORD wSecond;
    WORD wMilliseconds;
} SYSTEMTIME;
typedef SYSTEMTIME *PSYSTEMTIME, *LPSYSTEMTIME;
```

With this information, it's easy to construct a string that will be meaningful to an end user. Note that when you convert from SYSTEMTIME to FILETIME, the *wDayOfWeek* member in the SYSTEMTIME structure is ignored.

You can convert a file's time to local time and back again by using these functions:

```
BOOL FileTimeToLocalFileTime(LPFILETIME lpft,
    LPFILETIME lpftLocal);
```

and

```
BOOL LocalFileTimeToFileTime(LPFILETIME lpftLocal,
    LPFILETIME lpft);
```

Both these functions take two pointers to FILETIME structures. When you use these functions, be careful not to pass the same address as both parameters—the functions won't work correctly.

And if you're an MS-DOS and FAT diehard who doesn't want to port the existing file time stamp code in your applications over to the new way of doing things just yet, you can use these two functions to convert a FILETIME structure to the time format used by MS-DOS and vice versa:

```
BOOL FileTimeToDosDateTime(LPFILETIME lpft,
    LPWORD lpwDOSDate, LPWORD lpwDOSTime);
```

and

```
BOOL DosDateTimeToFileTime(WORD wDOSDate, WORD wDOSTime,
    LPFILETIME lpft);
```

The *FileTimeToDosDateTime* function takes the address of the FILE-TIME structure containing the file's time and converts it to two WORD values that MS-DOS uses—one WORD for the date and the other WORD for the time.

Important

Under Windows 95, the *FileTimeToDosDateTime* and *DosDateTimeToFileTime* functions allow dates up to 12/31/2099. Under Windows NT, these functions allow dates up to 12/31/2107.

After you have manipulated and converted the time values all you want, you can change the time associated with a file by calling *GetFileTime*'s complementary function:

```
BOOL SetFileTime(HANDLE hFile, LPFILETIME lpftCreation,
    LPFILETIME lpftLastAccess, LPFILETIME lpftLastWrite);
```

If you don't want to change the creation time stamp of the file, you can pass NULL in for the *lpftCreation* parameter.

The other way to get the attribute information associated with a file is to call the *GetFileInformationByHandle* function:

```
BOOL GetFileInformationByHandle(HANDLE hFile,
    LPBY_HANDLE_FILE_INFORMATION lpFileInformation);
```

This function requires the handle of an open file identified by the *hFile* parameter and the address of a BY_HANDLE_FILE_INFORMA-TION structure, which the function fills with information about the file:

```
typedef struct _BY_HANDLE_FILE_INFORMATION {
    DWORD dwFileAttributes;
    FILETIME ftCreationTime;
    FILETIME ftLastAccessTime;
    FILETIME ftLastWriteTime;
    DWORD dwVolumeSerialNumber;
    DWORD nFileSizeHigh;
    DWORD nFileSizeLow;
```

```
        DWORD nNumberOfLinks;
        DWORD nFileIndexHigh;
        DWORD nFileIndexLow;
} BY_HANDLE_FILE_INFORMATION,
    *PBY_HANDLE_FILE_INFORMATION, *LPBY_HANDLE_FILE_INFORMATION;
```

The *GetFileInformationByHandle* function gathers all of the attribute information available for the file. In addition to the file attributes contained in the *dwFileAttributes* member and the three time stamps contained in the *ftCreationTime, ftLastAccessTime,* and *ftLastWriteTime* members, the function gets the serial number of the disk volume on which the file resides in the *dwVolumeSerialNumber* member, and the file's size in the *nFileSizeHigh* and *nFileSizeLow* members. It finds the number of links (used by the POSIX subsystem in Windows NT) in the *nNumberOfLinks* member.

The system assigns every file, each time it's opened, a unique ID contained in the *nFileIndexHigh* and *nFileIndexLow* members. The ID might not be constant across openings of the file and will almost definitely be different if the file is opened during a different session. However, if one application opens a file and another application opens the same file, the ID will be the same. An application can use the ID in conjunction with the volume's serial number to determine whether two (or more) different file handles actually reference the same file.

Searching for Files

Almost all applications use files. Because an application can create many files and because applications are often designed to read files created by other applications (Microsoft Excel can read Lotus 1-2-3 files, for example), file searching has become a common task—so common, in fact, that Microsoft has created a set of common dialog boxes that help users search their drives for particular files. For some applications, though, the File Open and File Save As dialog boxes aren't enough. Some applications might need to search for files or allow access to files using methods not accommodated by the standard file dialog boxes.

One common operation is to convert a simple filename or a file with a relative path to its full pathname. In 16-bit Windows, a call to *OpenFile* using the OF_PARSE flag accomplishes the conversion. In Win32, the call is to:

```
DWORD GetFullPathName(LPCTSTR lpszFile, DWORD cchPath,
    LPTSTR lpszPath, LPTSTR *ppszFilePart);
```

The *GetFullPathName* function accepts a filename (and optional path information) in the *lpszFile* parameter. The function then uses the current drive and current directory information associated with the process, calculates the full pathname for the file, and fills the buffer pointed to by *lpszPath*. The *cchPath* parameter indicates the maximum size of the buffer for the drive and path in characters. In the *ppszFilePart* parameter, you must pass the address of an LPTSTR variable. *GetFullPathName* will fill the variable with the address within *lpszPath* at which the filename resides. Applications can use this information when they construct their caption text.

For example, if I am using Windows 95 Wordpad and open a file called HIMOM.TXT, Wordpad's caption becomes

```
HIMOM.TXT - Wordpad
```

This last parameter, *ppszFilePart,* is simply a convenience. You could get the address of the filename by calling:

```
szFilePart = strrchr(szPath, '\\') + 1;
```

GetFullPathName doesn't really search for a file on the system. It just converts a filename to its full pathname. In fact, *GetFullPathName* doesn't examine anything on the disk at all. If you want to actually scan the user's disks for a file, you can use:

```
DWORD SearchPath(LPCTSTR lpszPath, LPCTSTR lpszFile,
   LPCSTR lpszExtension, DWORD cchReturnBuffer,
   LPTSTR lpszReturnBuffer, LPTSTR *plpszFilePart);
```

The *SearchPath* function looks for a file in a list of directories you specify. You pass the list of paths to be scanned in the *lpszPath* parameter. If this parameter is NULL, the file is searched for in the paths in the following order:

1. The directory from which the application was loaded

2. The current directory

3. The Windows system directory

4. The Windows directory

5. The directories listed in the PATH environment variable

You specify the file you want to search for in the *lpszFile* parameter. If the *lpszFile* parameter includes an extension, you should pass NULL in for the *lpszExtension* parameter; otherwise, you can pass an extension in the *lpszExtension* parameter that must begin with a period. The extension is appended to the filename only if the filename doesn't have an extension already. The last three parameters have the same meanings as the last three parameters of the *GetFullPathName* function.

Another method of looking for files allows you to find a file by traversing the user's entire hard disk, looking at every directory and file in existence if you want. You tell the system what directory to start in and the filename to search for by calling *FindFirstFile*:

```
HANDLE FindFirstFile(LPTSTR lpszSearchFile,
   LPWIN32_FIND_DATA lpffd);
```

The *FindFirstFile* function tells the system you want to search for a file. The first parameter, *lpszSearchFile*, points to a zero-terminated string containing a filename. The filename can include wildcard characters (* and ?), and you can preface the filename with a starting path. The *lpffd* parameter is the address to a WIN32_FIND_DATA structure:

```
typedef struct _WIN32_FIND_DATA {
   DWORD dwFileAttributes;
   FILETIME ftCreationTime;
   FILETIME ftLastAccessTime;
   FILETIME ftLastWriteTime;
   DWORD nFileSizeHigh;
   DWORD nFileSizeLow;
   DWORD dwReserved0;
   DWORD dwReserved1;
   CHAR cFileName[ MAX_PATH ];
   CHAR cAlternateFileName[ 14 ];
} WIN32_FIND_DATA, *PWI32_FIND_DATA, *LPWIN32_FIND_DATA;
```

If *FindFirstFile* succeeds in locating a file matching the filespec in the specified directory, it fills in the members of the WIN32_FIND_DATA structure and returns a handle. If *FindFirstFile* fails to find a file that matches the filespec, it returns INVALID_HANDLE_VALUE, and the structure isn't changed.

Important

Like the *CreateFile* function, the *FindFirstFile* function returns INVALID-_HANDLE_VALUE when it fails rather than NULL.

The WIN32_FIND_DATA structure contains information about the matching file—its attributes, its time stamps, and its size. At the end of the structure are two names for the file. The *cFileName* member is the real name of the file. This is the member you should use most often. The *cAlternateFileName* is a synthesized name for the file.

Let's say you are using a program designed for 16-bit Windows. When you select the application's File Open dialog box, you see a list of the files in the current directory. If the current directory is on an NTFS file system and the names of the files in that directory average 50 characters, what gets displayed?

Under OS/2, a program that wasn't designed to recognize HPFS filenames couldn't see HPFS files at all. For Win32, Microsoft decided (correctly) that such files should be made accessible to the user. Well, since the 16-bit Windows application isn't prepared to work with long filenames, the system must convert the long filenames to fit an 8.3 system. This converted, or alternate, filename is what you'll find in the *cAlternateFileName* member of the WIN32_FIND_DATA structure.

For short filenames, of course, the contents of the *cFileName* and *cAlternateFileName* members will be identical, and for long filenames, the *cFileName* member will contain the real name and the *cAlternateFileName* member will contain the synthesized name. For example, the filename "Hello Mom and Dad" can have a truncated, or alternate, name "HELLOM~1."

Important

There is a *GetShortPathName* function:

```
DWORD GetShortPathName (LPCTSTR lpszLongPath, LPTSTR lpszShortPath,
   DWORD cchBuffer);
```

You pass the address to a buffer containing a file's long name in the *lpszLongPath* parameter, and the function fills the buffer pointed to by the *lpszShortPath* parameter with the file's corresponding short name. You must pass the size, in characters, of the *lpszShortPath* buffer in the *cchBuffer* parameter. The function returns the number of characters copied to the *lpszShortPath* buffer.

If *FindFirstFile* has successfully found a matching file, you can call *FindNextFile* to search for the next file matching the file specification originally passed to *FindFirstFile*:

```
BOOL FindNextFile(HANDLE hFindFile, LPWIN32_FIND_DATA lpffd);
```

The *hFindFile* parameter is the handle that was returned by the earlier call to *FindFirstFile*, and the *lpffd* parameter is, again, the address to a WIN32_FIND_DATA structure—not necessarily the same structure you used in the earlier call to *FindFirstFile*, although it can be if you'd like.

If *FindNextFile* is successful, it returns TRUE and fills the WIN32-_FIND_DATA structure. If the function can't find a match, it returns FALSE.

When you have finished finding files, you must close the handle returned by *FindFirstFile* by calling *FindClose*:

```
BOOL FindClose(HANDLE hFindFile);
```

Important

This is one of the very few times in Win32 that you don't call *CloseHandle* to close a handle. You must call *FindClose* instead so that some additional bookkeeping information maintained by the system will also be freed.

The *FindFirstFile* and *FindNextFile* functions just cycle through all the files (and subdirectories) within a single directory you've specified. If you want to walk up and down the entire directory hierarchy, you will need to write a recursive function.

The Directory Walker Sample Application

The DirWalk (DIRWALK.EXE) application, listed in Figure 13-3 beginning on page 654, demonstrates use of the *FindFirstFile*, *FindNextFile*, *FindClose*, *GetCurrentDirectory*, and *SetCurrentDirectory* functions to walk the entire directory tree of a disk volume. The source code files, resource files, and make file for the application are in the DIRWALK.13 directory on the companion disc. When the user executes DIRWALK.EXE, it starts at the root directory of the current drive, walks the whole tree, and displays a dialog box containing a list box that shows the entire drive's directory tree. On the next page, you'll see how the Directory Walker dialog box appears when DirWalk is run on my machine.

When the dialog box receives its WM_INITDIALOG message, it performs some simple initialization and calls the *DirWalk* function located in DIRWALK.C:

```
void DirWalk (HWND hwndTreeLB, LPCTSTR pszRootPath);
```

The *hwndTreeLB* parameter is the handle of the list box window that the function should fill, and the *pszRootPath* is the starting directory. The call to *DirWalk* passes "\\" in the *pszRootPath* parameter so that the directory walk starts at the root of the current drive. It would certainly be possible to specify a different directory here so that the tree would be walked from the specified directory downward.

When the *DirWalk* function is called, it performs some initialization before calling the *DirWalkRecurse* function. This recursive function will be called by itself over and over as different levels of the drive's directory tree are walked. Before the directory tree can be walked, *DirWalk* performs some initialization by saving the current directory in a temporary variable and then setting the current directory to the path specified in the *pszRootPath* parameter.

Then the thread is ready to start walking by calling *DirWalkRecurse*. This function first adds the current directory to the list box. Then it calls *FindFirstFile* to get the name of the first file in the current directory. If a file is found, its name is displayed and *FindNextFile* is called in order to get the next file in the directory.

After all the files have been displayed, *DirWalkRecurse* tests the *fRecurse* member of the DIRWALKDATA structure to see if it should recurse into subdirectories. In the DirWalk sample application, this member will always be TRUE. I added the *fRecurse* member because these functions are used in the FILECHNG.EXE application, presented later in this chapter.

When *DirWalkRecurse* needs to go into a subdirectory, it calls *FindFirstChildDir*. This little function, which appears in DIRWALK.C, is a simple wrapper around the *FindFirstFile* function. *FindFirstChildDir* filters out all the filenames in a directory and returns only subdirectory names. The helper function *FindNextChildDir* is just a wrapper around the *FindNextFile* function that also filters out filenames.

As each subdirectory is found, *DirWalkRecurse* moves into the new subdirectory and calls itself so that the new subtree can be walked. After the subtree is walked, *DirWalkRecurse* calls:

```
SetCurrentDirectory(__TEXT(".."));
```

so that the current directory is restored to what it was before making the recursive call to *DirWalkRecurse*.

Before any tree walking can start, the *DirWalk* function creates a local DIRWALKDATA structure, called *DW*, on the stack. This structure contains information used by *DirWalkRecurse*.

When I first wrote this program, I had all the members inside the DIRWALKDATA structure as local variables declared inside *DirWalkRecurse*. Then, each time *DirWalkRecurse* called itself, another set of these variables was created on the stack. As I soon discovered, this can eat up quite a bit of stack space if a directory tree goes down pretty deep, so I looked for a more efficient method of storing these variables.

The next method I tried was to create the DIRWALKDATA members as static variables. That way, I thought, there would be only one set of them and they wouldn't be allocated on the stack at all. This sounded pretty good to me except that it meant that the *DirWalk* and *DirWalkRecurse* functions were no longer multithread safe. If two threads wanted to walk the tree simultaneously, they would be sharing the same static local variables—with undesirable effects. This realization led me to modify the program again.

I made all of the variables static thread-local storage variables by putting *__declspec(thread)* in front of each one. This, I thought, would force a new set of the static variables for every thread created in the process. The only thing I didn't like about this approach was that a set of these variables would be created for every thread, even for those threads that never called *DirWalk* or *DirWalkRecurse*.

This problem could be fixed by using dynamic thread-local storage. This way, I reasoned, I'd be allocating only a TLS index, which isn't a memory allocation anyway. Then, when *DirWalk* was called, it would call *HeapAlloc* to allocate a DIRWALKDATA structure and store the address of this structure using *TlsSetValue*. This dynamic approach solved the problem of allocating additional memory for threads that never called *DirWalk*, and as a bonus, the memory containing the data structure would be around only while the *DirWalk* function was being called. Just before *DirWalk* returned, it would free the buffer.

After I got to this point, the best solution finally hit me: create a data structure on the stack for the thread, and provide just the pointer to the structure with each recursive call. This solution is what you see in the sample program's code. This method creates the variables on the stack, memory is allocated for them only when it is needed, and only a 4-byte pointer is passed on the stack with each recursive call. This seems to me to be the best compromise among all of the possibilities.

In spite of all this effort, it turns out that *DirWalk* and *DirWalkRecurse* are still not multithread safe. Can you guess why? Because of the calls to *SetCurrentDirectory*. You should think of the current directory as being stored in a global variable for a process. If you change the current directory in one thread, you are changing it for all threads in the process. To make *DirWalk* and *DirWalkRecurse* multithread safe, you would have to get rid of the calls to *SetCurrentDirectory*. You could get rid of the calls to *SetCurrentDirectory* by managing the walked path in a string variable and by calling *FindFirstDir* using a full path instead of using paths relative to the current directory. Since I also wanted to demonstrate the use of the *GetCurrentDirectory* and *SetCurrentDirectory* functions, I leave this last modification of the program as an exercise for you.

DirWalk.ico

DIRWALK.C

```
/******************************************************************
Module name: DirWalk.C
Written by: Jim Harkins and Jeffrey Richter
Notices: Copyright (c) 1995 Jeffrey Richter
******************************************************************/
```

Figure 13-3.
The DirWalk application.

(continued)

Figure 13-3. *continued*

```c
#include "..\AdvWin32.H"      /* See Appendix B for details. */
#include <windows.h>
#include <windowsx.h>

#pragma warning(disable: 4001)        /* Single-line comment */

#include <tchar.h>
#include <stdlib.h>
#include <stdio.h>               // For sprintf
#include <string.h>
#include "Resource.H"


///////////////////////////////////////////////////////////////


void DirWalk (HWND hwndTreeLB, LPCTSTR pszRootPath,
   BOOL fRecurse);


///////////////////////////////////////////////////////////////


BOOL Dlg_OnInitDialog (HWND hwnd, HWND hwndFocus,
   LPARAM lParam) {

   RECT rc;

   // Associate an icon with the dialog box.
   SetClassLong(hwnd, GCL_HICON, (LONG)
      LoadIcon((HINSTANCE) GetWindowLong(hwnd, GWL_HINSTANCE),
      __TEXT("DirWalk")));

   DirWalk(GetDlgItem(hwnd, IDC_TREE), __TEXT("\\"), TRUE);

   GetClientRect(hwnd, &rc);
   SetWindowPos(GetDlgItem(hwnd, IDC_TREE), NULL,
      0, 0, rc.right, rc.bottom, SWP_NOZORDER);

   return(TRUE);
}
```

(continued)

Figure 13-3. *continued*

```
///////////////////////////////////////////////////////////


void Dlg_OnSize (HWND hwnd, UINT state, int cx, int cy) {
    SetWindowPos(GetDlgItem(hwnd, IDC_TREE), NULL, 0, 0,
        cx, cy, SWP_NOZORDER);
}



///////////////////////////////////////////////////////////


void Dlg_OnCommand (HWND hwnd, int id, HWND hwndCtl,
    UINT codeNotify) {

    switch (id) {
        case IDCANCEL:
            EndDialog(hwnd, id);
            break;

        case IDOK:
            // Call the recursive routine to walk the tree.
            DirWalk(GetDlgItem(hwnd, IDC_TREE), __TEXT("\\"),
                TRUE);
            break;
    }
}



///////////////////////////////////////////////////////////


BOOL IsChildDir (WIN32_FIND_DATA *lpFindData) {

    return(
        (lpFindData->dwFileAttributes &
            FILE_ATTRIBUTE_DIRECTORY) &&
        (lpFindData->cFileName[0] != __TEXT('.')));
}
```

(continued)

Figure 13-3. *continued*

```
///////////////////////////////////////////////////////////////


BOOL FindNextChildDir (HANDLE hFindFile,
   WIN32_FIND_DATA *lpFindData) {

   BOOL fFound = FALSE;

   do {
      fFound = FindNextFile(hFindFile, lpFindData);
   } while (fFound && !IsChildDir(lpFindData));

   return(fFound);
}



///////////////////////////////////////////////////////////////


HANDLE FindFirstChildDir (LPTSTR szPath,
   WIN32_FIND_DATA *lpFindData) {

   BOOL fFound;
   HANDLE hFindFile = FindFirstFile(szPath, lpFindData);

   if (hFindFile != INVALID_HANDLE_VALUE) {
      fFound = IsChildDir(lpFindData);

      if (!fFound)
         fFound = FindNextChildDir(hFindFile, lpFindData);

      if (!fFound) {
         FindClose(hFindFile);
         hFindFile = INVALID_HANDLE_VALUE;
      }
   }
   return(hFindFile);
}
```

(continued)

Figure 13-3. *continued*

```
////////////////////////////////////////////////////////////////


// To minimize stack use, one instance of the DIRWALKDATA
// structure is created as a local variable in DirWalk,
// and a pointer to it is passed to DirWalkRecurse.

// Data used by DirWalkRecurse
typedef struct {
   HWND   hwndTreeLB;    // Handle to the output list box
   int    nDepth;        // Nesting depth
   BOOL   fRecurse;      // Set to TRUE to list subdirectories.
   TCHAR  szBuf[1000];   // Output formatting buffer
   int    nIndent;       // Indentation character count
   BOOL   fOk;           // Loop control flag
   BOOL   fIsDir;        // Loop control flag
   WIN32_FIND_DATA FindData; // File information
} DIRWALKDATA, *LPDIRWALKDATA;



////////////////////////////////////////////////////////////////


// Walk the directory structure and fill a list box with
// filenames. If pDW->fRecurse is set, list any child
// directories by recursively calling DirWalkRecurse.
void DirWalkRecurse (LPDIRWALKDATA pDW) {
   HANDLE hFind;

   pDW->nDepth++;

   pDW->nIndent = 3 * pDW->nDepth;
   _stprintf(pDW->szBuf, __TEXT("%*s"), pDW->nIndent,
      __TEXT(""));

   GetCurrentDirectory(ARRAY_SIZE(pDW->szBuf) - pDW->nIndent,
      &pDW->szBuf[pDW->nIndent]);
   ListBox_AddString(pDW->hwndTreeLB, pDW->szBuf);

   hFind = FindFirstFile(__TEXT("*.*"), &pDW->FindData);
   pDW->fOk = (hFind != INVALID_HANDLE_VALUE);
```

(continued)

Figure 13-3. *continued*

```
    while (pDW->fOk) {
        pDW->fIsDir = pDW->FindData.dwFileAttributes &
            FILE_ATTRIBUTE_DIRECTORY;
        if (!pDW->fIsDir ||
            (!pDW->fRecurse && IsChildDir(&pDW->FindData))) {

            _stprintf(pDW->szBuf,
                pDW->fIsDir ? __TEXT("%*s[%s]") : __TEXT("%*s%s"),
                pDW->nIndent, __TEXT(""),
                pDW->FindData.cFileName);

            ListBox_AddString(pDW->hwndTreeLB, pDW->szBuf);
        }
        pDW->fOk = FindNextFile(hFind, &pDW->FindData);
    }
    if (hFind != INVALID_HANDLE_VALUE)
        FindClose(hFind);

    if (pDW->fRecurse) {
        // Get the first child directory.
        hFind = FindFirstChildDir(
            __TEXT("*.*"), &pDW->FindData);
        pDW->fOk = (hFind != INVALID_HANDLE_VALUE);
        while (pDW->fOk) {
            // Change into the child directory.
            if (SetCurrentDirectory(pDW->FindData.cFileName)) {

                // Perform the recursive walk into the child
                // directory. Remember that some members of pDW
                // will be overwritten by this call.
                DirWalkRecurse(pDW);

                // Change back to the child's parent directory.
                SetCurrentDirectory(__TEXT(".."));
            }

            pDW->fOk = FindNextChildDir(hFind, &pDW->FindData);
        }

        if (hFind != INVALID_HANDLE_VALUE)
            FindClose(hFind);
    }
    pDW->nDepth--;
}
```

(continued)

Figure 13-3. *continued*

```
///////////////////////////////////////////////////////////////


// Walk the directory structure and fill a list box with
// filenames. This function sets up a call to
// DirWalkRecurse, which does the real work.

void DirWalk (
    HWND hwndTreeLB,          // List box to fill
    LPCTSTR pszRootPath,      // Starting point of the tree walk
    BOOL fRecurse) {          // Expand subdirectories.

    TCHAR szCurrDir[_MAX_DIR];
    DIRWALKDATA DW;

    // Clear out the list box.
    ListBox_ResetContent(hwndTreeLB);

    // Save the current directory so that it can
    // be restored later.
    GetCurrentDirectory(ARRAY_SIZE(szCurrDir), szCurrDir);

    // Set the current directory to where we want
    // to start walking.
    SetCurrentDirectory(pszRootPath);

    // nDepth is used to control indenting. The value -1 will
    // cause the first level to display flush left.
    DW.nDepth = -1;

    DW.hwndTreeLB = hwndTreeLB;
    DW.fRecurse = fRecurse;

    // Call the recursive function to walk the subdirectories.
    DirWalkRecurse(&DW);

    // Restore the current directory to what it was
    // before the function was called.
    SetCurrentDirectory(szCurrDir);
}
```

(continued)

Figure 13-3. *continued*

```
//////////////////////////////////////////////////////////////

BOOL CALLBACK Dlg_Proc (HWND hDlg, UINT uMsg,
   WPARAM wParam, LPARAM lParam) {

   BOOL fProcessed = TRUE;

   switch (uMsg) {
      HANDLE_MSG(hDlg, WM_INITDIALOG,  Dlg_OnInitDialog);
      HANDLE_MSG(hDlg, WM_SIZE,        Dlg_OnSize);
      HANDLE_MSG(hDlg, WM_COMMAND,     Dlg_OnCommand);

      default:
         fProcessed = FALSE;
         break;
   }
   return(fProcessed);
}


//////////////////////////////////////////////////////////////


int WINAPI WinMain (HINSTANCE hinstExe,
   HINSTANCE hinstPrev, LPSTR lpszCmdLine, int nCmdShow) {

   DialogBox(hinstExe, MAKEINTRESOURCE(IDD_DIRWALK),
      NULL, Dlg_Proc);

   return(0);
}


///////////////////////// End Of File /////////////////////////
```

DIRWALK.RC
```
//Microsoft Visual C++ generated resource script.
//
#include "Resource.h"

#define APSTUDIO_READONLY_SYMBOLS
```

(continued)

Figure 13-3. *continued*

```
///////////////////////////////////////////////////////////////
//
// Generated from the TEXTINCLUDE 2 resource.
//
#include "afxres.h"


///////////////////////////////////////////////////////////////
#undef APSTUDIO_READONLY_SYMBOLS



///////////////////////////////////////////////////////////////
//
// Icon
//


DirWalk                 ICON    DISCARDABLE     "DirWalk.Ico"


///////////////////////////////////////////////////////////////
//
// Dialog
//


IDD_DIRWALK DIALOG DISCARDABLE  10, 18, 250, 250
STYLE WS_MINIMIZEBOX | WS_MAXIMIZEBOX | WS_POPUP | WS_VISIBLE
    | WS_CAPTION | WS_SYSMENU | WS_THICKFRAME
CAPTION "Directory Walker"
FONT 8, "System"
BEGIN
    LISTBOX         IDC_TREE,0,0,0,0,NOT LBS_NOTIFY
                    | LBS_NOINTEGRALHEIGHT | NOT WS_BORDER
                    | WS_VSCROLL | WS_HSCROLL | WS_GROUP
                    | WS_TABSTOP
END



#ifdef APSTUDIO_INVOKED
///////////////////////////////////////////////////////////////
//
// TEXTINCLUDE
//


1 TEXTINCLUDE DISCARDABLE
BEGIN
    "Resource.h\0"
END
```

(continued)

Figure 13-3. *continued*

```
2 TEXTINCLUDE DISCARDABLE
BEGIN
    "#include ""afxres.h""\r\n"
    "\0"
END

3 TEXTINCLUDE DISCARDABLE
BEGIN
    "\r\n"
    "\0"
END

/////////////////////////////////////////////////////////////////////////
#endif    // APSTUDIO_INVOKED


#ifndef APSTUDIO_INVOKED
/////////////////////////////////////////////////////////////////////////
//
// Generated from the TEXTINCLUDE 3 resource.
//


/////////////////////////////////////////////////////////////////////////
#endif    // not APSTUDIO_INVOKED
```

File System Change Notifications

There are so many applications that would like to be notified when something in the file system has been altered. You probably haven't noticed it, but the Windows 95 File Open common dialog box updates its window automatically to reflect any changes made to the file system. To see this in action, perform the following experiment. Select the File Open menu option in any application that displays the File Open common dialog box. Now, from the command prompt, copy a file from a floppy disk to the directory that is currently viewed in the dialog box. After the file is copied, the dialog box will automatically update its contents to show that the new file is now present in the viewed directory.

This has been a feature long wished for in 16-bit Windows—and actually, 16-bit Windows does have a function, *FileCDR*, that an application can call in order to be notified of changes in the file system. There are two problems with *FileCDR*, though: it's an undocumented function, and it allows only one application at a time to get file system notifications. If another application calls the *FileCDR* function, the first application will stop getting notifications.

So many people requested that applications be notified dynamically of file system changes that Microsoft built direct support for this capability into Windows 95 and Windows NT. Here is how it works. First your application must tell the system that it's interested in being notified of file system changes by calling *FindFirstChangeNotification*:

```
HANDLE FindFirstChangeNotification(LPTSTR lpszPath,
    BOOL fWatchSubTree, DWORD fdwFilter);
```

The *lpszPath* parameter specifies the root of the directory tree that you want to monitor. You can specify the root directory of a drive or any subdirectory. If you specify a subdirectory, you won't be notified of events occurring in directories above the specified subdirectory. If you want to monitor directory trees on different drives, you must make multiple calls to *FindFirstChangeNotification*—one for each drive that you want to monitor.

The second parameter *fWatchSubTree*, tells the system whether you want to watch events that occur in directories beneath the *lpszPath* directory. If you pass FALSE, you will be notified only of events that occur in the single directory you've specified.

In the *fdwFilter* parameter, you tell the system what type of file changes you're interested in. You can combine the *fdwFilter* flags by ORing them. Here's the list of valid flags and their meanings:

Flag	Meaning
FILE_NOTIFY_CHANGE_FILE_NAME	A file has been created, renamed, or deleted.
FILE_NOTIFY_CHANGE_DIR_NAME	A directory has been created, renamed, or deleted.
FILE_NOTIFY_CHANGE_ATTRIBUTES	A file's attribute has changed.
FILE_NOTIFY_CHANGE_SIZE	A file's size has changed.
FILE_NOTIFY_CHANGE_LAST_WRITE	A file's last write time has changed.
FILE_NOTIFY_CHANGE_SECURITY	A security descriptor for a directory or file has been changed.

Note that the system frequently buffers file changes. A file's size doesn't change, for example, until buffered information is flushed to the disk. You will be notified of the change in the file size only when the system flushes the data to disk, not when an application actually changes the data.

If *FindFirstChangeNotification* is successful, it returns a handle your thread can use with the various synchronization functions such as *WaitForSingleObject* and *WaitForMultipleObjects*. If you pass an invalid parameter, such as a nonexistent path, INVALID_HANDLE_VALUE is returned.

Important

Like the *CreateFile* and *FindFirstFile* functions, the *FindFirstChangeNotification* function returns INVALID_HANDLE_VALUE when it fails rather than NULL.

Personally, I think it would have made more sense to name the *FindFirstChangeNotification* function something like *CreateFileChangeNotification* because the function doesn't really find a file change at all; it simply creates a file change notification object and returns its handle.

Once you have the notification object's handle, you can use it in calls to the *WaitForSingleObject* and *WaitForMultipleObjects* functions. Whenever a change occurs in the file system that meets the criteria you specified in the call to *FindFirstChangeNotification*, the object will become signaled. You can think of a file change notification object as a manual-reset event with some additional logic built into it—when a change occurs in the file system, the event is signaled. When your call to *WaitForSingleObject* or *WaitForMultipleObjects* returns, you know that you need to walk the drive's directory tree (starting from *lpszPath*) so that you can refresh the directory and file information in your application.

Note that the system accumulates many file changes and notifies you of them all at once. For example, if the user entered this command on the command line:

```
deltree .    (Windows 95)
rmdir . /s   (Windows NT)
```

to erase all of the files in the current directory and all its subdirectories, the command shell's thread might delete several files before the system signaled the file change notification object, allowing your thread to resume execution. The handle won't be signaled separately for every single file change. This greatly improves performance.

When the file change notification object is signaled, your thread wakes up and you can perform whatever operations you want to. When you have finished, you must call *FindNextChangeNotification*:

```
BOOL FindNextChangeNotification(HANDLE hChange);
```

The *FindNextChangeNotification* function resets the file change notification object to its nonsignaled state, similar to calling *ResetEvent*. However, this is where file change notification objects differ from manual-reset events. While your thread was walking the drive's directory tree, the command shell's thread might have preempted your thread and been able to continue deleting more files and directories. The call to *FindNextChangeNotification* checks to see whether this has happened, and if more file change events have occurred since the object became signaled, the object is not reset to the nonsignaled state and remains signaled.

That way, if your thread waits for the object again, the wait will be satisfied immediately and you will again walk the drive's directory tree. You should always wait for a file change notification object after every call to *FindNextChangeNotification*. Without this wait, your thread might miss a file change event.

As usual, when you no longer want file change notifications, you must close the object. You close the file change notification object by calling:

```
BOOL FindCloseChangeNotification(HANDLE hChange);
```

Important

> This is one of the very few times in Win32 that you don't call *CloseHandle* to close a handle. You must call *FindCloseChangeNotification* instead so that the system deletes any record of file changes that have been made since the file change notification object was last signaled.

The File Change Sample Application

The FileChng (FILECHNG.EXE) application, listed in Figure 13-4 beginning on page 669, uses the three change notification functions to monitor changes made to a drive's directory tree. The source code files, resource files, and make file for the application are in the FILECHNG.13 directory on the companion disc. When the user executes FileChng, the File Change Notifications dialog box appears:

Before the program starts monitoring file changes, you must tell it what you are interested in monitoring by setting some or all of the parameters in the Filters group box. When you click on the Start button, the program retrieves all of the parameters from the dialog box controls and calls *FindFirstChangeNotification* so that the system will start to notify the program of any file system changes. The program also resets the Notification Count value to 0 and performs an initial directory tree walk starting at the path you've specified, filling the list box with a list of the directories and files in the tree.

The program then sits idle waiting for the system to signal the file change notification object. When a change occurs in the file system that matches your filter criteria, the system signals the notification object, causing FileChng's thread to wake up, increment the Notification Count value, and rewalk the directory tree. After each walk, the thread calls *FindNextChangeNotification* and waits for the object again. You can stop monitoring changes to the file system by clicking on the Stop button or by changing some of the notification criteria values.

The program code is pretty self-explanatory, but I do want to draw your attention to the *WinMain* function, which I've structured differently from *WinMain* in the other sample programs in this book. I wanted to write the FileChng program so that it had only a single thread of execution. To do this, I needed a method whereby my thread could suspend itself until either a window message entered the thread's queues or the file change notification object became signaled. I racked my brain for a while and then remembered the *MsgWaitForMultipleObjects* function.

This function was just what the doctor ordered. It's just like *WaitFor-MultipleObjects* except that it also checks for window messages. Using *MsgWaitForMultipleObjects* meant that I couldn't create a modal dialog box for this program, though, because modal dialog boxes call *GetMessage* for their message processing and there would be no way for me to wait for the file change notification object. Since I had to get more involved with the message loop for the program, I had to use *CreateDialog* instead of *DialogBox* in order to create a modeless dialog box. Then I had to code the message loop myself.

Here's a little more detail on what the program does. First it calls *CreateDialog* to create a modeless dialog box that will be the user interface for the program. Next the thread starts executing the message loop, which repeatedly checks the *fQuit* variable to find out when it should terminate. The *fQuit* variable is initialized to FALSE when the program starts and is set to TRUE when a WM_QUIT message is pulled from the thread's queue.

Once in the message loop, the thread checks whether the handle to the file change notification object is valid and stores the result in the *fWait4FileChanges* variable. The handle won't be valid if the user hasn't clicked on the Start button yet. Then the program makes this call:

```
dwResult = MsgWaitForMultipleObjects(
   (fWait4FileChanges) ? 1 : 0,
   &s_hChange, FALSE, INFINITE, QS_ALLEVENTS);
```

If there is a valid handle to a file change notification object, the call to *MsgWaitForMultipleObjects* tells the system to wait either for this object to become signaled or for a message to enter one of the thread's message queues. If the handle is invalid, the thread will just wait until a message is available.

When the system awakens the thread, the thread checks to see what the reason is. If it has been awakened because of a file change, the Notification Count value is incremented, the directory tree is rewalked, and *FindNextChangeNotification* is called. The thread then loops around to the top of the message loop and makes another call to *MsgWaitFor-MultipleObjects*.

If the thread has been awakened because of a window message, the message must now be retrieved from the queue by a call to *PeekMessage* specifying the PM_REMOVE flag. Next *IsDialogMessage* is called, passing the retrieved message. This call allows the user to navigate through the controls in the modeless dialog box using the keyboard. If the message isn't a navigational keyboard message, the thread checks to see whether it is a WM_QUIT message. If it is, the *fQuit* variable is set to TRUE, causing the message loop to terminate before it begins its next iteration.

If the message isn't a navigational keyboard message and is also not a WM_QUIT message, *TranslateMessage* is called, followed by *DispatchMessage*, just as they would be called in any normal message loop.

You'll notice that I call *PeekMessage* in a loop here—I do this in order to give the user interface a higher priority than the processing for file change notifications.

FileChng.ico

FILECHNG.C

```
/**************************************************************
Module name: FileChng.C
Written by: Jim Harkins and Jeffrey Richter
Notices: Copyright (c) 1995 Jeffrey Richter
**************************************************************/


#include "..\AdvWin32.H"        /* See Appendix B for details. */
#include <windows.h>
#include <windowsx.h>


#pragma warning(disable: 4001)        /* Single-line comment */


#include <tchar.h>
#include <stdio.h>
#include <stdlib.h>
#include <string.h>
#include "Resource.H"



///////////////////////////////////////////////////////////////


void DirWalk (HWND hwndTreeLB, LPCTSTR pszRootPath,
   BOOL fRecurse);

HANDLE g_hChange = INVALID_HANDLE_VALUE;
int    g_nCount = 0;
```

Figure 13-4.   *(continued)*
The FileChng application.

Figure 13-4. *continued*

```
//////////////////////////////////////////////////////////////


void Dlg_ErrorBox (LPCTSTR pszSource) {
   TCHAR szBuf[100];    // Output formatting buffer.

   _stprintf(szBuf, __TEXT("%s reported error %lu"),
     pszSource, GetLastError());

   MessageBox(NULL, szBuf, __TEXT("File Change"), MB_OK);
}


//////////////////////////////////////////////////////////////


DWORD Dlg_GetFilter (HWND hwnd) {
   DWORD fdwFilter = 0;

   if (IsDlgButtonChecked(hwnd, IDC_FILENAME))
     fdwFilter |= FILE_NOTIFY_CHANGE_FILE_NAME;

   if (IsDlgButtonChecked(hwnd, IDC_DIRNAME))
     fdwFilter |= FILE_NOTIFY_CHANGE_DIR_NAME;

   if (IsDlgButtonChecked(hwnd, IDC_ATTRIBS))
     fdwFilter |= FILE_NOTIFY_CHANGE_ATTRIBUTES;

   if (IsDlgButtonChecked(hwnd, IDC_SIZEFLTR))
     fdwFilter |= FILE_NOTIFY_CHANGE_SIZE;

   if (IsDlgButtonChecked(hwnd, IDC_LASTWRITE))
     fdwFilter |= FILE_NOTIFY_CHANGE_LAST_WRITE;

   if (IsDlgButtonChecked(hwnd, IDC_SECURITY))
     fdwFilter |= FILE_NOTIFY_CHANGE_SECURITY;

   return(fdwFilter);
}

//////////////////////////////////////////////////////////////


// Validate the dialog box controls and configure a
// valid call to FindFirstChangeNotification:
// at least one filter flag must be set, and
```

(continued)

Figure 13-4. *continued*

```
// the path must be valid.
BOOL Dlg_Validate (HWND hwnd) {
   BOOL  fValid = FALSE;
   TCHAR szPath[_MAX_DIR];

   // Test to see whether at least one flag is set.
   if (0 != Dlg_GetFilter(hwnd)) {

      // Verify that the path exists.
      GetDlgItemText(hwnd, IDC_PATH, szPath,
         ARRAY_SIZE(szPath));
      fValid = SetCurrentDirectory(szPath);
   }
   return(fValid);
}


///////////////////////////////////////////////////////////////


// Stop close change notification.
void Dlg_CloseChange (HWND hwnd) {
   BOOL fDisableFocus =
      (GetFocus() == GetDlgItem(hwnd, IDC_STOP));

   EnableWindow(GetDlgItem(hwnd, IDC_STOP), FALSE);

   if (Dlg_Validate(hwnd)) {
      EnableWindow(GetDlgItem(hwnd, IDC_START), TRUE);
      if (fDisableFocus) {
         SetFocus(GetDlgItem(hwnd, IDC_START));
      }
   } else {
      fDisableFocus = fDisableFocus ||
         (GetFocus() == GetDlgItem(hwnd, IDC_START));

      EnableWindow(GetDlgItem(hwnd, IDC_START), FALSE);
      if (fDisableFocus) {
         SetFocus(GetDlgItem(hwnd, IDC_INCSUBDIRS));
      }
   }

   if (INVALID_HANDLE_VALUE != g_hChange) {
      if (!FindCloseChangeNotification(g_hChange)) {
         Dlg_ErrorBox(__TEXT("FindCloseChangeNotification"));
      }
```

(continued)

Figure 13-4. *continued*

```
      g_hChange = INVALID_HANDLE_VALUE;
   }
}


/////////////////////////////////////////////////////////////


// Start close change notification.
void Dlg_OpenChange (HWND hwnd) {
   TCHAR szPath[_MAX_DIR];
   BOOL fDisableFocus =
      (GetFocus() == GetDlgItem(hwnd, IDC_START));

   Dlg_CloseChange(hwnd);

   g_nCount = 0;
   SetDlgItemInt(hwnd, IDC_NCOUNT, g_nCount, FALSE);

   GetDlgItemText(hwnd, IDC_PATH, szPath, ARRAY_SIZE(szPath));

   g_hChange = FindFirstChangeNotification(szPath,
      IsDlgButtonChecked(hwnd, IDC_INCSUBDIRS),
      Dlg_GetFilter(hwnd));

   if (INVALID_HANDLE_VALUE == g_hChange) {
      Dlg_ErrorBox(__TEXT("FindFirstChangeNotification"));
      g_hChange = INVALID_HANDLE_VALUE;
   } else {
      EnableWindow(GetDlgItem(hwnd, IDC_START), FALSE);
      EnableWindow(GetDlgItem(hwnd, IDC_STOP), TRUE);

      if (fDisableFocus) {
         SetFocus(GetDlgItem(hwnd, IDC_STOP));
      }

      DirWalk(GetDlgItem(hwnd, IDC_TREE), szPath,
         IsDlgButtonChecked(hwnd, IDC_INCSUBDIRS));
   }
}


/////////////////////////////////////////////////////////////


BOOL Dlg_OnInitDialog (HWND hwnd, HWND hwndFocus,
   LPARAM lParam) {
   TCHAR szPath[_MAX_DIR];
```

(continued)

Figure 13-4. *continued*

```
    // Associate an icon with the dialog box.
    SetClassLong(hwnd, GCL_HICON, (LONG)
        LoadIcon((HINSTANCE) GetWindowLong(hwnd, GWL_HINSTANCE),
        __TEXT("FileChng")));

    // Path defaults to the current path
    GetCurrentDirectory(ARRAY_SIZE(szPath), szPath);
    SetDlgItemText(hwnd, IDC_PATH, szPath);

    Dlg_CloseChange(hwnd);

    return(TRUE);
}


///////////////////////////////////////////////////////////////////


void Dlg_OnCommand (HWND hwnd, int id, HWND hwndCtl,
    UINT codeNotify) {

    switch (id) {
        case IDC_PATH:
            // If change notification is started and
            // the user updates the path,
            // stop notifications.
            if (EN_CHANGE == codeNotify) {
                Dlg_CloseChange(hwnd);
            }
            break;

        case IDC_INCSUBDIRS:
        case IDC_FILENAME:
        case IDC_DIRNAME:
        case IDC_ATTRIBS:
        case IDC_SIZEFLTR:
        case IDC_LASTWRITE:
        case IDC_SECURITY:
        case IDC_STOP:
            Dlg_CloseChange(hwnd);
            break;

        case IDC_START:
            Dlg_OpenChange(hwnd);
            break;
```

(continued)

Figure 13-4. *continued*

```
      case IDCANCEL:
         Dlg_CloseChange(hwnd);
         PostQuitMessage(0);
         break;
   }
}


///////////////////////////////////////////////////////////////


BOOL CALLBACK Dlg_Proc (HWND hDlg, UINT uMsg, WPARAM wParam,
   LPARAM lParam) {

   BOOL fProcessed = TRUE;

   switch (uMsg) {
      HANDLE_MSG(hDlg, WM_INITDIALOG, Dlg_OnInitDialog);
      HANDLE_MSG(hDlg, WM_COMMAND, Dlg_OnCommand);

      default:
         fProcessed = FALSE;
         break;
   }
   return(fProcessed);
}


///////////////////////////////////////////////////////////////


int WINAPI WinMain (HINSTANCE hinstExe,
   HINSTANCE hinstPrev, LPSTR lpszCmdLine, int nCmdShow) {

   HWND  hwnd;
   MSG   msg;
   DWORD dwResult;
   BOOL  fQuit = FALSE, fWait4FileChanges;
   TCHAR szPath[_MAX_DIR];

   // Create a modeless dialog box instead of a modal
   // dialog box because we need to have more control over
   // the message loop processing.
   hwnd = CreateDialog(hinstExe,
      MAKEINTRESOURCE(IDD_FILECHNG), NULL, Dlg_Proc);
```

(continued)

Figure 13-4. *continued*

```
// Continue to loop until a WM_QUIT
// message comes out of the queue.
while (!fQuit) {

    // Do we have a valid file change notification handle?
    fWait4FileChanges = (INVALID_HANDLE_VALUE != g_hChange);

    // If we do, wait until a file change occurs OR until
    // a message shows up in our queue.
    dwResult = MsgWaitForMultipleObjects(
        (fWait4FileChanges) ? 1 : 0,
        &g_hChange, FALSE, INFINITE, QS_ALLEVENTS);


    if (fWait4FileChanges && (WAIT_OBJECT_0 == dwResult)) {
        // We awoke because of a file change notification.
        // Let's update the list box.

        // Increment the counter indicating the number
        // of notifications we have received.
        SetDlgItemInt(hwnd, IDC_NCOUNT, ++g_nCount, FALSE);

        // Get the root path and fill the list box with the
        // list of files in the path and the root
        // directory's subdirectories if the Include
        // Subdirectories check box is checked.
        GetDlgItemText(hwnd, IDC_PATH, szPath,
            ARRAY_SIZE(szPath));
        DirWalk(GetDlgItem(hwnd, IDC_TREE), szPath,
            IsDlgButtonChecked(hwnd, IDC_INCSUBDIRS));

        // Tell the system that we processed the
        // notification.
        FindNextChangeNotification(g_hChange);
    } else {

        // We awoke because there is at least one message in
        // the queue. Let's dispatch all the queued messages.
        while (PeekMessage(&msg, NULL, 0, 0, PM_REMOVE)) {

            // Call IsDialogMessage so that the keyboard can
            // be used to control focus in the dialog box.
            if (!IsDialogMessage(hwnd, &msg)) {
                if (msg.message == WM_QUIT) {
                    // If we have a WM_QUIT message,
```

(continued)

Figure 13-4. *continued*

```
                        // set the flag so that the
                        // loop terminates.
                        fQuit = TRUE;
                    } else {
                        // Not a WM_QUIT message. Translate it
                        // and dispatch it.
                        TranslateMessage(&msg);
                        DispatchMessage(&msg);
                    }
                } // if (!IsDialogMessage())
            } // while messages are still in the queue
        } // if file change notification OR message
    } // while (!fQuit)

    // The application is terminating. Destroy the modeless
    // dialog box.
    DestroyWindow(hwnd);

    return(0);
}


////////////////////////////////////////////////////////////


// The following functions are taken directly from DirWalk.C.


////////////////////////////////////////////////////////////


BOOL IsChildDir (WIN32_FIND_DATA *lpFindData) {

    return(
        (lpFindData->dwFileAttributes &
            FILE_ATTRIBUTE_DIRECTORY) &&
        (lpFindData->cFileName[0] != __TEXT('.')));
}


////////////////////////////////////////////////////////////


BOOL FindNextChildDir (HANDLE hFindFile,
    WIN32_FIND_DATA *lpFindData) {
```

(continued)

Figure 13-4. *continued*

```
   BOOL fFound = FALSE;

   do {
      fFound = FindNextFile(hFindFile, lpFindData);
   } while (fFound && !IsChildDir(lpFindData));

   return(fFound);
}


/////////////////////////////////////////////////////////////////


HANDLE FindFirstChildDir (LPTSTR szPath,
   WIN32_FIND_DATA *lpFindData) {

   BOOL fFound;
   HANDLE hFindFile = FindFirstFile(szPath, lpFindData);

   if (hFindFile != INVALID_HANDLE_VALUE) {
      fFound = IsChildDir(lpFindData);

      if (!fFound)
         fFound = FindNextChildDir(hFindFile, lpFindData);

      if (!fFound) {
         FindClose(hFindFile);
         hFindFile = INVALID_HANDLE_VALUE;
      }
   }
   return(hFindFile);
}


/////////////////////////////////////////////////////////////////


// To minimize stack use, one instance of the DIRWALKDATA
// structure is created as a local variable in DirWalk,
// and a pointer to it is passed to DirWalkRecurse.

// Data used by DirWalkRecurse
typedef struct {
   HWND   hwndTreeLB;   // Handle to the output list box
   int    nDepth;       // Nesting depth
   BOOL   fRecurse;     // Set to TRUE to list subdirectories.
```

(continued)

Figure 13-4. *continued*

```
   TCHAR   szBuf[500];    // Output formatting buffer
   int     nIndent;       // Indentation character count
   BOOL    fOk;           // Loop control flag
   BOOL    fIsDir;        // Loop control flag
   WIN32_FIND_DATA FindData; // File information
} DIRWALKDATA, *LPDIRWALKDATA;


///////////////////////////////////////////////////////////////


// Walk the directory structure, and fill a list box with
// filenames. If pDW->fRecurse is set, list any child
// directories by recursively calling DirWalkRecurse.
void DirWalkRecurse (LPDIRWALKDATA pDW) {
   HANDLE hFind;

   pDW->nDepth++;

   pDW->nIndent = 3 * pDW->nDepth;
   _stprintf(pDW->szBuf, __TEXT("%*s"), pDW->nIndent,
      __TEXT(""));

   GetCurrentDirectory(ARRAY_SIZE(pDW->szBuf) - pDW->nIndent,
      &pDW->szBuf[pDW->nIndent]);
   ListBox_AddString(pDW->hwndTreeLB, pDW->szBuf);

   hFind = FindFirstFile(__TEXT("*.*"), &pDW->FindData);
   pDW->fOk = (hFind != INVALID_HANDLE_VALUE);
   while (pDW->fOk) {
      pDW->fIsDir = pDW->FindData.dwFileAttributes &
         FILE_ATTRIBUTE_DIRECTORY;
      if (!pDW->fIsDir ||
         (!pDW->fRecurse && IsChildDir(&pDW->FindData))) {
         _stprintf(pDW->szBuf,
            pDW->fIsDir ? __TEXT("%*s[%s]") : __TEXT("%*s%s"),
            pDW->nIndent, __TEXT(""),
            pDW->FindData.cFileName);

         ListBox_AddString(pDW->hwndTreeLB, pDW->szBuf);
      }
      pDW->fOk = FindNextFile(hFind, &pDW->FindData);
   }

   if (hFind != INVALID_HANDLE_VALUE)
      FindClose(hFind);
```

(continued)

Figure 13-4. *continued*

```
    if (pDW->fRecurse) {
        // Get the first child directory.
        hFind = FindFirstChildDir(
            __TEXT("*.*"), &pDW->FindData);
        pDW->fOk = (hFind != INVALID_HANDLE_VALUE);
        while (pDW->fOk) {
            // Change into the child directory.
            if (SetCurrentDirectory(pDW->FindData.cFileName)) {

                // Perform the recursive walk into the child
                // directory. Remember that some members of pDW
                // will be overwritten by this call.

                DirWalkRecurse(pDW);

                // Change back to the child's parent directory.
                SetCurrentDirectory(__TEXT(".."));
            }

            pDW->fOk = FindNextChildDir(hFind, &pDW->FindData);
        }

        if (hFind != INVALID_HANDLE_VALUE)
            FindClose(hFind);
    }

    pDW->nDepth--;
}


//////////////////////////////////////////////////////////////////


// Walk the directory structure, and fill a list box with
// filenames. This function sets up a call to
// DirWalkRecurse, which does the real work.

void DirWalk (HWND hwndTreeLB, LPCTSTR pszRootPath,
    BOOL fRecurse) {

    TCHAR szCurrDir[_MAX_DIR];
    DIRWALKDATA DW;

    // Clear out the list box.
    ListBox_ResetContent(hwndTreeLB);
```

(continued)

Figure 13-4. *continued*

```
    // Save the current directory so that it can be
    // restored later.
    GetCurrentDirectory(ARRAY_SIZE(szCurrDir), szCurrDir);

    // Set the current directory to where we want to
    // start walking.
    SetCurrentDirectory(pszRootPath);

    // nDepth is used to control indenting. The value -1 will
    // cause the first level to display flush left.
    DW.nDepth = -1;

    DW.hwndTreeLB = hwndTreeLB;
    DW.fRecurse = fRecurse;

    // Call the recursive function to walk the subdirectories.
    DirWalkRecurse(&DW);

    // Restore the current directory to what it was before the
    // function was called.
    SetCurrentDirectory(szCurrDir);
}


/////////////////////// End Of File ///////////////////////
```

```
FILECHNG.RC
//Microsoft Visual C++ generated resource script.
//
#include "Resource.h"

#define APSTUDIO_READONLY_SYMBOLS
/////////////////////////////////////////////////////////////
//
// Generated from the TEXTINCLUDE 2 resource.
//
#include "afxres.h"


/////////////////////////////////////////////////////////////
#undef APSTUDIO_READONLY_SYMBOLS
```

(continued)

Figure 13-4. *continued*

```
//////////////////////////////////////////////////////////////
//
// Icon
//

FileChng                 ICON    DISCARDABLE    "FileChng.Ico"

//////////////////////////////////////////////////////////////
//
// Dialog
//

IDD_FILECHNG DIALOG DISCARDABLE  6, 18, 195, 237
STYLE WS_MINIMIZEBOX ! WS_VISIBLE ! WS_CAPTION ! WS_SYSMENU
CAPTION "File Change Notifications"
FONT 8, "Helv"
BEGIN
    LTEXT           "&Path:",IDC_STATIC,4,4,19,8
    EDITTEXT        IDC_PATH,24,4,166,12,ES_AUTOHSCROLL
    CONTROL         "&Include subdirectories",IDC_INCSUBDIRS,
                    "Button",BS_AUTOCHECKBOX ! WS_TABSTOP,
                    4,64,83,10
    LTEXT           "Notification count:",IDC_STATIC,
                    104,84,62,9,SS_NOPREFIX
    LTEXT           "0",IDC_NCOUNT,168,84,24,8,SS_NOPREFIX
    GROUPBOX        "Filters",IDC_STATIC,4,20,188,40
    CONTROL         "File &name",IDC_FILENAME,"Button",
                    BS_AUTOCHECKBOX ! WS_TABSTOP,8,32,42,10
    CONTROL         "&Dir name",IDC_DIRNAME,"Button",
                    BS_AUTOCHECKBOX ! WS_TABSTOP,8,44,40,10
    CONTROL         "&Attributes",IDC_ATTRIBS,"Button",
                    BS_AUTOCHECKBOX ! WS_TABSTOP,64,32,42,10
    CONTROL         "Si&ze",IDC_SIZEFLTR,"Button",
                    BS_AUTOCHECKBOX ! WS_TABSTOP,64,44,25,10
    CONTROL         "&Last write time",IDC_LASTWRITE,
                    "Button",BS_AUTOCHECKBOX ! WS_TABSTOP,
                    120,32,58,10
    CONTROL         "Securit&y",IDC_SECURITY,"Button",
                    BS_AUTOCHECKBOX ! WS_TABSTOP,
                    120,44,38,10
    DEFPUSHBUTTON   "&Start",IDC_START,124,64,32,14
    PUSHBUTTON      "S&top",IDC_STOP,160,64,32,14
    LTEXT           "&File list:",IDC_STATIC,4,84,27,8
```

(continued)

Figure 13-4. *continued*

```
        LISTBOX            IDC_TREE,4,96,188,136,NOT LBS_NOTIFY
                           | LBS_NOINTEGRALHEIGHT | WS_VSCROLL
                           | WS_HSCROLL | WS_TABSTOP
END


#ifdef APSTUDIO_INVOKED
/////////////////////////////////////////////////////////////////
//
// TEXTINCLUDE
//

1 TEXTINCLUDE DISCARDABLE
BEGIN
    "Resource.h\0"
END

2 TEXTINCLUDE DISCARDABLE
BEGIN
    "#include ""afxres.h""\r\n"
    "\0"
END

3 TEXTINCLUDE DISCARDABLE
BEGIN
    "\r\n"
    "\0"
END

/////////////////////////////////////////////////////////////////
#endif    // APSTUDIO_INVOKED


#ifndef APSTUDIO_INVOKED
/////////////////////////////////////////////////////////////////
//
// Generated from the TEXTINCLUDE 3 resource.
//


/////////////////////////////////////////////////////////////////
#endif    // not APSTUDIO_INVOKED
```

STRUCTURED EXCEPTION HANDLING

Close your eyes for a moment and imagine writing your application as though your code could never fail. That's right—there's always enough memory, no one ever passes you an invalid pointer, and files you count on always exist. Wouldn't it be a pleasure to write your code if you could make these assumptions? Your code would be so much easier to write, to read, and to understand. No more fussing with *if* statements here and *gotos* there—in each function, you'd just write your code top to bottom.

If this kind of straightforward programming environment seems like a dream to you, you'll love structured exception handling (SEH). The virtue of structured exception handling is that as you write your code, you can focus on getting your task done. If something goes wrong at run time, the system catches it and notifies you of the problem.

With SEH you can't totally ignore the possibility of an error in your code, but SEH does allow you to separate the main job from the error handling chores. This division makes it easy to concentrate on the problem at hand and focus on the possible errors later.

One of Microsoft's main motivations for adding structured exception handling to Win32 was to ease the development of Windows 95 and Windows NT and make the operating systems more robust. The developers of the Windows NT operating system and its various subsystems used SEH to make the system more robust. And we can use SEH to make our own applications more robust.

The burden of making SEH work falls more on the compiler than on the operating system. Your compiler must generate special code when exception blocks are entered into and exited from. The compiler must produce tables of support data structures to handle SEH and also must supply callback functions that the operating system can call so that exception blocks can be traversed. The compiler is also responsible for preparing stack frames and other internal information that is used and referenced by the operating system. Adding SEH support to a compiler is not an easy task, and you shouldn't be surprised if your favorite compiler vendor delays shipment of its Win32-capable compiler because of SEH implementation problems.

Nor should it surprise you that different compiler vendors implement structured exception handling in different ways. Fortunately, we can ignore compiler implementation details and just use the compiler's SEH capabilities.

Differences among compiler implementations of SEH could make it difficult to discuss in specific ways with specific code examples how you can take advantage of SEH. However, most compiler vendors follow Microsoft's suggested syntax. The syntax and keywords I use in my examples may differ from those of another company's compiler, but the main SEH concepts are the same. I'll use the Microsoft Visual C++ 2.0 compiler's syntax throughout this chapter.

Important

Don't confuse structured exception handling with C++ exception handling. C++ exception handling is a different form of exception handling, one that makes use of the new C++ keywords *catch* and *throw*. Microsoft has added C++ exception handling in Visual C++ version 2.0. Microsoft's implementation of C++ exception handling is implemented by taking advantage of the structured exception handling capabilities already present in the compiler and Windows operating systems.

Structured exception handling really consists of two main capabilities: termination handling and exception handling. We'll turn our attention to termination handlers first.

Termination Handlers

A termination handler guarantees that a block of code (the termination handler) will be called and executed regardless of how another section of code (the guarded body) is exited. The syntax (using the Microsoft Visual C++ 2.0 compiler) for a termination handler is as follows:

```
__try {
   // Guarded body
   .
   .
   .
}
__finally {
   // Termination handler
   .
   .
   .
}
```

The new __*try* and __*finally* keywords delineate the two sections of the termination handler. In the code fragment above, the operating system and the compiler work together to guarantee that the __*finally* block code in the termination handler will be executed no matter how the guarded body is exited. Regardless of whether you put a *return*, a *goto*, or even a call to *longjump* in the guarded body, the termination handler will be called. Here's the flow of code execution:

```
// 1. Code before the try block executes

__try {
   // 2. Code inside the try block executes
}
__finally {
   // 3. Code inside the finally block executes
}

// 4. Code after the finally block executes
```

Understanding Termination Handlers by Example

Because the compiler and the operating system are intimately involved with the execution of your code when you use SEH, I believe that the best way to demonstrate how SEH works is by examining source code samples and discussing the order in which the statements execute in each example.

Therefore, the next few sections show different source code fragments, and the text associated with each fragment explains how the compiler and operating system alter the execution order of your code.

Funcenstein1

To appreciate the ramifications of using termination handlers, let's examine a more concrete coding example on the next page.

```
DWORD Funcenstein1 (void) {
   DWORD dwTemp;

   // 1. Do any processing here.
   .
   .
   .
   __try {
      // 2. Request permission to access
      //    protected data, and then use it.
      WaitForSingleObject(g_hSem, INFINITE);

      g_dwProtectedData = 5;
      dwTemp = g_dwProtectedData;
   }
   __finally {
      // 3. Allow others to use protected data.
      ReleaseSemaphore(g_hSem, 1, NULL);
   }

   // 4. Continue processing.
   return(dwTemp);
}
```

In *Funcenstein1*, using the *try-finally* blocks really isn't doing very much for you. The code will wait for a semaphore, alter the contents of the protected data, save the new value in the local variable *dwTemp*, release the semaphore, and return the new value to the caller.

Funcenstein2

Now let's modify the function a little and see what happens:

```
DWORD Funcenstein2 (void) {
   DWORD dwTemp;

   // 1. Do any processing here.
   .
   .
   .
   __try {
      // 2. Request permission to access
      //    protected data, and then use it.
      WaitForSingleObject(g_hSem, INFINITE);

      g_dwProtectedData = 5;
      dwTemp = g_dwProtectedData;

      // Return the new value.
```

```
        return(dwTemp);
    }
    __finally {
        // 3. Allow others to use protected data.
        ReleaseSemaphore(g_hSem, 1, NULL);
    }

    // Continue processing--this code
    // will never execute in this version.
    dwTemp = 9;
    return(dwTemp);
}
```

In *Funcenstein2*, a *return* statement has been added to the end of the *try* block. This *return* statement tells the compiler that you want to exit the function and return the contents of the *dwTemp* variable, which now contains the value 5. However, if this *return* statement had been executed, the semaphore would not have been released by the thread—and no other thread would ever be able to gain control of the semaphore. As you can imagine, this kind of sequence can become a really big problem because threads waiting for the semaphore might never be able to resume execution.

However, by using the termination handler, you have avoided the premature execution of the *return* statement. When the *return* statement tries to exit the *try* block, the compiler makes sure that the code in the *finally* block executes first. The code inside the *finally* block is guaranteed to execute before the *return* statement in the *try* block is allowed to exit. In *Funcenstein2*, putting the call to *ReleaseSemaphore* into a termination handler block ensures that the semaphore will always be released—there is no chance for a thread to accidentally retain ownership of the semaphore, which would mean that all other threads waiting for the semaphore would never be scheduled CPU time.

After the code in the *finally* block executes, the function does, in fact, return. Any code appearing below the *finally* block doesn't execute because the function returns in the *try* block. Therefore, this function returns the value 5 and not the value 9.

You might be asking yourself how the compiler guarantees that the *finally* block executes before the *try* block can be exited. When the compiler examines your source code, it sees that you have coded a *return* statement inside a *try* block. Having seen this, the compiler generates code to save the return value (5 in our example) in a temporary variable created by the compiler. The compiler then generates code to execute the instructions contained inside the *finally* block; this is called a *local unwind.* More specifically, a local unwind occurs when the system executes the contents of a *finally* block because of the premature exit of code in a *try* block. After the instructions inside the *finally* block execute, the value in the compiler's temporary variable is retrieved and returned from the function.

As you can see, the compiler must generate additional code and the system must perform additional work to pull this whole thing off. On different CPUs, the steps necessary to make termination handling work vary. The MIPS and Alpha processors, for example, must execute several hundred or even several thousand instructions in order to capture the *try* block's premature return and call the *finally* block. You should avoid writing code that causes premature exits from the *try* block of a termination handler because the performance of your application could be adversely impacted. Later in this chapter, I'll discuss the __leave keyword, which can help you avoid writing code that forces local unwinds.

Exception handling is designed to capture exceptions (in our example, the premature *return*)—the exceptions to the rule that you expect to happen infrequently. If a situation is the norm, it's much more efficient to check for the situation explicitly rather than to rely on the structured exception handling capabilities of the operating system and your compiler to trap common occurrences.

Note that when the flow of control naturally leaves the *try* block and enters the *finally* block (as shown in *Funcenstein1*), the overhead of entering the *finally* block is minimal. On the *x86* CPUs using the Microsoft compiler, a single machine instruction is executed as execution leaves the *try* block to enter the *finally* block—I doubt that you will even notice this overhead at all in your application. When the compiler has to generate additional code and the system has to perform additional work, as in *Funcenstein2*, the overhead is much more noticeable.

Funcenstein3

Now let's modify the function again and take a look at what happens:

```
DWORD Funcenstein3 (void) {
   DWORD dwTemp;

   // 1. Do any processing here.
   :

   __try {
```

```
   // 2. Request permission to access
   //    protected data, and then use it.
   WaitForSingleObject(g_hSem, INFINITE);

   g_dwProtectedData = 5;
   dwTemp = g_dwProtectedData;

   // Try to jump over the finally block.
   goto ReturnValue;
   }

   __finally {
   // 3. Allow others to use protected data.
   ReleaseSemaphore(g_hSem, 1, NULL);
   }

   dwTemp = 9;
   // 4. Continue processing.
   ReturnValue:
   return(dwTemp);
}
```

In *Funcenstein3*, when the compiler sees the *goto* statement in the *try* block, it generates a local unwind to execute the contents of the *finally* block first. However, this time, after the code in the *finally* block executes, the code after the ReturnValue label is executed because no return occurs in either the *try* or the *finally* block. This code causes the function to return a 5. Again, because you have interrupted the natural flow of control from the *try* block into the *finally* block, you may incur a high performance penalty depending on the CPU your application is running on.

Funcfurter1

Now let's look at another scenario in which termination handling really proves its value. Look at this function:

```
DWORD Funcfurter1 (void) {
   DWORD dwTemp;

   // 1. Do any processing here.
   .
   .
   .
   __try {
   // 2. Request permission to access
   //    protected data, and then use it.
   WaitForSingleObject(g_hSem, INFINITE);
```

(continued)

```
        dwTemp = Funcinator(g_dwProtectedData);
    }
    __finally {
        // 3. Allow others to use protected data.
        ReleaseSemaphore(g_hSem, 1, NULL);
    }

    // 4. Continue processing.
    return(dwTemp);
}
```

Now imagine that the *Funcinator* function called in the *try* block contains a bug that causes an invalid memory access. In a 16-bit Windows application, this would present the user with the ever-popular Application Error dialog box. When the user dismissed the error dialog box, the application would be terminated. If the code were running in a Win32 application with no *try-finally* block, and the application were terminated because *Funcinator* generated an invalid memory access, the semaphore would still be owned and would never be released—any threads in other processes that were waiting for this semaphore would never be scheduled CPU time. But placing the call to *ReleaseSemaphore* in a *finally* block guarantees that the semaphore gets released even if some other function causes a memory access violation.

If termination handlers are powerful enough to capture an application terminating because of an invalid memory access, we should have no trouble believing that they will also capture *setjump/longjump* combinations and, of course, simple statements such as *break* and *continue*.

Pop Quiz Time: *FuncaDoodleDoo*

Now for a test. Can you guess what the function below returns?

```
DWORD FuncaDoodleDoo (void) {
    DWORD dwTemp = 0;

    while (dwTemp < 10) {

        __try {
            if (dwTemp == 2)
                continue;

            if (dwTemp == 3)
                break;
        }
```

```
    __finally {
       dwTemp++;
    }

    dwTemp++;
  }

  dwTemp += 10;
  return(dwTemp);
}
```

Let's analyze what the function does step by step. First *dwTemp* is set to 0. The code in the *try* block executes, but neither of the *if* statements evaluates to TRUE. Execution moves naturally to the code in the *finally* block, which increments *dwTemp* to 1. Then the instruction after the *finally* block increments *dwTemp* again, making it 2.

When the loop iterates, *dwTemp* is 2 and the *continue* statement in the *try* block will execute. Without a termination handler to force execution of the *finally* block before exit from the *try* block, execution would immediately jump back up to the *while* loop, *dwTemp* would not be changed, and we would have started an infinite loop. With a termination handler, the system notes that the *continue* statement causes the flow of control to exit the *try* block prematurely and moves execution to the *finally* block. In the *finally* block, *dwTemp* is incremented to 3. However, the code after the *finally* block doesn't execute because the flow of control moves back to *continue* and thus to the top of the loop.

Now we are processing the loop's third iteration. This time, the first *if* statement evaluates to FALSE, but the second *if* statement evaluates to TRUE. The system again catches our attempt to break out of the *try* block and executes the code in the *finally* block first. Now *dwTemp* is incremented to 4. Because a *break* statement was executed, control resumes after the loop. Thus, the code after the *finally* block and still inside the loop doesn't execute. The code below the loop adds 10 to *dwTemp* for a grand total of 14—the result of calling this function. It should go without saying that you should never actually write code like *FuncaDoodleDoo*. I placed the *continue* and *break* statements in the middle of the code only to demonstrate the operation of the termination handler.

Although a termination handler will catch most situations in which the *try* block would otherwise be exited prematurely, it can't cause the code in a *finally* block to be executed if the thread or process is terminated. A call to *ExitThread* or *ExitProcess* will immediately terminate the thread or process without executing any of the code in a *finally* block. Also, if your thread or process should die because some application called *TerminateThread* or *TerminateProcess*, the code in a *finally* block again won't execute. Some C run-time functions, such as *abort*, which in turn call *ExitProcess*, again preclude the execution of *finally* blocks. You can't do anything to prevent another application from terminating one of your threads or processes, but you can prevent your own premature calls to *ExitThread* and *ExitProcess*.

Funcenstein4

Let's take a look at one more termination handling scenario.

```
DWORD Funcenstein4 (void) {
    DWORD dwTemp;
    // 1. Do any processing here.
        :
        :
    __try {
        // 2. Request permission to access
        //      protected data, and then use it.
        WaitForSingleObject(g_hSem, INFINITE);

        g_dwProtectedData = 5;
        dwTemp = g_dwProtectedData;

        // Return the new value.
        return(dwTemp);
    }
    __finally {
        // 3. Allow others to use protected data.
        ReleaseSemaphore(g_hSem, 1, NULL);
        return(103);
    }

    // Continue processing--this code will never execute.
    dwTemp = 9;
    return(dwTemp);
}
```

In *Funcenstein4*, the *try* block will execute and try to return the value of *dwTemp* (5) back to *Funcenstein4*'s caller. As we noted in the discussion of *Funcenstein2*, trying to return prematurely from a *try* block causes the generation of code that puts the return value into a temporary variable created by the compiler. Then the code inside the *finally* block is executed. Notice that in this variation on *Funcenstein2* I have added a *return* statement to the *finally* block. Will *Funcenstein4* return 5 to the caller, or 103? The answer is that 103 will be returned because the *return* statement in the *finally* block causes the value 103 to be stored in the same temporary variable in which the value 5 has been stored, overwriting the 5. When the *finally* block completes execution, the value now in the temporary variable (103) is returned from *Funcenstein4* to its caller.

We've seen termination handlers do an effective job of rescuing execution from a premature exit of the *try* block, and we've also seen termination handlers produce an unwanted result because they prevented a premature exit of the *try* block. A good rule of thumb is to avoid any statements that would cause a premature exit of the *try* block part of a termination handler. In fact, it is always best to remove all *return*s, *continue*s, *break*s, *goto*s, and so on from inside both the *try* and the *finally* blocks of a termination handler and to put these statements outside the handler. Such a practice will cause the compiler to generate both a smaller amount of code because it won't have to catch premature exits from the *try* block and faster code because it will have fewer instructions to execute in order to perform the local unwind. In addition, your code will be much easier to read and maintain.

Funcarama1

We have pretty much covered the basic syntax and semantics of termination handlers. Now let's look at how a termination handler could be used to simplify a more complicated programming problem. Let's look at a function that doesn't take advantage of termination handlers at all.

```
BOOL Funcarama1 (void) {
    HANDLE hFile = INVALID_HANDLE_VALUE;
    LPVOID lpBuf = NULL;
    DWORD dwNumBytesRead;
    BOOL fOk;

    hFile = CreateFile("SOMEDATA.DAT", GENERIC_READ,
        FILE_SHARE_READ, NULL, OPEN_EXISTING,
        0, NULL);
    if (hFile == INVALID_HANDLE_VALUE) {
        return(FALSE);
    }

    lpBuf = VirtualAlloc(NULL, 1024, MEM_COMMIT,
        PAGE_READWRITE);
    if (lpBuf == NULL) {
        CloseHandle(hFile);
```

(continued)

693

```
      return(FALSE);
   }

   fOk = ReadFile(hFile, lpBuf, 1024,
      &dwNumBytesRead, NULL);
   if (!fOk || (dwNumBytesRead == 0)) {
      VirtualFree(lpBuf, MEM_RELEASE | MEM_DECOMMIT);
      CloseHandle(hFile);
      return(FALSE);
   }

   // Do some calculation on the data.
      :
      :

   // Clean up all the resources.
   VirtualFree(lpBuf, MEM_RELEASE | MEM_DECOMMIT);
   CloseHandle(hFile);
   return(TRUE);
}
```

All the error checking in *Funcarama1* makes the function difficult to read, which also makes the function difficult to understand, maintain, and modify.

Funcarama2

Of course, it's possible to rewrite *Funcarama1* so that it is a little cleaner and easier to understand:

```
BOOL Funcarama2 (void) {
   HANDLE hFile = INVALID_HANDLE_VALUE;
   LPVOID lpBuf = NULL;
   DWORD dwNumBytesRead;
   BOOL fOk, fSuccess = FALSE;

   hFile = CreateFile("SOMEDATA.DAT", GENERIC_READ,
      FILE_SHARE_READ, NULL, OPEN_EXISTING,
      0, NULL);

   if (hFile != INVALID_HANDLE_VALUE) {

      lpBuf = VirtualAlloc(NULL, 1024, MEM_COMMIT,
         PAGE_READWRITE);

      if (lpBuf != NULL) {

         fOk = ReadFile(hFile, lpBuf, 1024,
            &dwNumBytesRead, NULL);
```

```
        if (fOk && (dwNumBytesRead != 0)) {
           // Do some calculation on the data.
           :
           :
           fSuccess = TRUE;
        }

     }

     VirtualFree(lpBuf, MEM_RELEASE | MEM_DECOMMIT);

  }

  CloseHandle(hFile);
  return(fSuccess);
}
```

Funcarama2 is easier to understand, but it is still difficult to modify and maintain. Also, the indentation level gets to be pretty extreme as more conditional statements are added; with such a rewrite you soon end up writing code on the far right of your screen and wrapping statements after every five characters!

Funcarama3

Let's rewrite the first version, *Funcarama1*, to take advantage of an SEH termination handler:

```
DWORD Funcarama3 (void) {
  HANDLE hFile = INVALID_HANDLE_VALUE;
  LPVOID lpBuf = NULL;

  __try {
     DWORD dwNumBytesRead;
     BOOL fOk;

     hFile = CreateFile("SOMEDATA.DAT", GENERIC_READ,
        FILE_SHARE_READ, NULL, OPEN_EXISTING,
        0, NULL);
     if (hFile == INVALID_HANDLE_VALUE) {
        return(FALSE);
     }

     lpBuf = VirtualAlloc(NULL, 1024, MEM_COMMIT,
        PAGE_READWRITE);
     if (lpBuf == NULL) {
        return(FALSE);
     }
```

(continued)

```
    fOk = ReadFile(hFile, lpBuf, 1024,
        &dwNumBytesRead, NULL);
    if (!fOk || (dwNumBytesRead != 1024)) {
        return(FALSE);
    }

    // Do some calculation on the data.
    :
    :

}

__finally {
    // Clean up all the resources.
    if (lpBuf != NULL)
        VirtualFree(lpBuf, MEM_RELEASE | MEM_DECOMMIT);
    if (hFile != INVALID_HANDLE_VALUE)
        CloseHandle(hFile);
}
// Continue processing.
return(TRUE);
}
```

The real virtue of the *Funcarama3* version is that all of the function's clean-up code is localized in one place and one place only: the *finally* block. If we ever need to add some additional code to this function, we can simply add a single clean-up line in the *finally* block—we won't have to go back to every possible location of failure and add our clean-up line to each failure location.

Funcarama4: The Final Frontier

The real problem with the *Funcarama3* version is the overhead. As we noted after the discussion of *Funcenstein4*, we really should avoid putting *return* statements into *try* blocks as much as possible.

To help make such avoidance easier, Microsoft added another keyword, __*leave*, to its C++ compiler. Here is the *Funcarama4* version, which takes advantage of the new __*leave* keyword:

```
DWORD Funcarama4 (void) {
    HANDLE hFile = INVALID_HANDLE_VALUE;
    LPVOID lpBuf = NULL;

    // Assume that the function will not execute successfully.
    BOOL fFunctionOk = FALSE;
```

```
__try {
   DWORD dwNumBytesRead;
   BOOL fOk;

   hFile = CreateFile("SOMEDATA.DAT", GENERIC_READ,
      FILE_SHARE_READ, NULL, OPEN_EXISTING,
      0, NULL);
   if (hFile == INVALID_HANDLE_VALUE) {
      __leave;
   }

   lpBuf = VirtualAlloc(NULL, 1024, MEM_COMMIT,
      PAGE_READWRITE);

   if (lpBuf == NULL) {
      __leave;
   }

   fOk = ReadFile(hFile, lpBuf, 1024,
      &dwNumBytesRead, NULL);
   if (!fOk || (dwNumBytesRead == 0)) {
      __leave;
   }

   // Do some calculation on the data.
      :
      :
   // Indicate that the entire function executed successfully.
   fFunctionOk = TRUE;
}
__finally {
   // Clean up all the resources.
   if (lpBuf != NULL)
      VirtualFree(lpBuf, MEM_RELEASE | MEM_DECOMMIT);
   if (hFile != INVALID_HANDLE_VALUE)
      CloseHandle(hFile);
}
// Continue processing.
return(fFunctionOk);
}
```

The use of the __*leave* keyword in the *try* block causes a jump to the end of the *try* block. You can think of it as jumping to the *try* block's closing brace. Because the flow of control will exit *naturally* from the *try* block and enter the *finally* block, no overhead is incurred. However, it was necessary to introduce a new Boolean variable, *fFunctionOk*, to indicate the success or failure of the function—a relatively small price to pay.

When designing your functions to take advantage of termination handlers in this way, remember to initialize all of your resource handles to invalid values before entering your *try* block. Then, in the *finally* block, you can check to see which resources have been allocated successfully so that you'll know which ones to free. Another popular method for tracking which resources will need to be freed is to set a flag when a resource allocation is successful. Then the code in the *finally* block can examine the state of the flag to determine whether the resource needs freeing.

Notes About the *finally* Block

So far we have explicitly identified two scenarios that force the *finally* block to be executed:

- Normal flow of control from the *try* block into the *finally* block

- Local unwind: premature exit from the *try* block (*goto*, *longjump*, *continue*, *break*, *return*, and so on) forcing control to the *finally* block

A third scenario, a *global unwind,* occurred without explicit identification as such in the *Funcfurter1* function we saw earlier on pages 689 and 690. Inside the *try* block of this function was a call to the *Funcinator* function. If the *Funcinator* function caused a memory access violation, a global unwind caused *Funcfurter1*'s *finally* block to execute. We'll look at global unwinding in greater detail when we get to the exception filters and exception handlers section of this chapter.

Code in a *finally* block always starts executing as a result of one of these three situations. To determine which of the three possibilities caused the *finally* block to execute, you can call the intrinsic function[1] *AbnormalTermination*:

```
BOOL AbnormalTermination(VOID);
```

---

1. An intrinsic function is a special function recognized by the compiler. The compiler generates the code for the function in-line rather than generating code to call the function. For example, *memcpy* is an intrinsic function (if the /Oi compiler switch is specified). When the compiler sees a call to *memcpy*, it puts the *memcpy* code directly into the function that called *memcpy* instead of generating a call to the *memcpy* function. This usually has the effect of making your code run faster at the expense of code size.

The intrinsic *AbnormalTermination* function is different from the intrinsic *memcpy* function in that it exists only in an intrinsic form. No C run-time library contains the *Abnormal-Termination* function.

This intrinsic function can be called only from inside a *finally* block and returns a Boolean value indicating whether the *try* block associated with the *finally* block was exited prematurely. In other words, if the flow of control leaves the *try* block and naturally enters the *finally* block, *AbnormalTermination* will return FALSE. If the flow of control exits the *try* block abnormally—usually because a local unwind has been caused by a *goto, return, break,* or *continue* statement or because a global unwind has been caused by a memory access violation—a call to *AbnormalTermination* will return TRUE. If *AbnormalTermination* returns TRUE, it is not possible to distinguish whether a local unwind or a global unwind caused the *finally* block to execute. It is impossible to determine whether a *finally* block is executing because of a global or a local unwind.

Funcfurter2

Here is *Funcfurter2*, which demonstrates use of the *AbnormalTermination* intrinsic function:

```
DWORD Funcfurter2 (void) {
   DWORD dwTemp;

   // 1. Do any processing here.
   .
   .
   .

   __try {
      // 2. Request permission to access
      //    protected data, and then use it.
      WaitForSingleObject(g_hSem, INFINITE);

      dwTemp = Funcinator(g_dwProtectedData);
   }
   __finally {
      // 3. Allow others to use protected data.
      ReleaseSemaphore(g_hSem, 1, NULL);

      if (!AbnormalTermination()) {
         // No errors occurred in the try block, and
         // control flowed naturally from try into finally.
         .
         .
         .
      } else {

         // Something caused an exception, and
         // because there is no code in the try block
         // that would cause a premature exit, we must
```

(continued)

```
        // be executing in the finally block
        // because of a global unwind.

        // If there were a goto in the try block,
        // we wouldn't know how we got here.
        ⋮


      }
    }

  // 4. Continue processing.
  return(dwTemp);
}
```

Now that you know how to write termination handlers, you'll see that termination handlers can be even more useful and important when we look at exception filters and exception handlers later in the chapter. Before we move on, let's review the reasons for using termination handlers. Termination handlers:

- Simplify error processing because all cleanup is in one location and is guaranteed to execute

- Improve program readability

- Make code easier to maintain

- Have minimal speed and size overhead if used appropriately

The SEH Termination Sample Application

The SEHTerm (SEHTERM.EXE) application, listed in Figure 14-1 beginning on page 704, demonstrates the use of termination handlers by simulating the execution of a function that counts the number of words in a file. The source code files, resource files, and make file for the application are in the SEHTERM.14 directory on the companion disc. Here are the steps that the program's *Dlg_CountWordsInFile* function performs:

1. Opens the file.

2. Gets the size of the file.

3. Allocates a memory block using the result of step 2.

4. Reads the contents of the file into the allocated memory block.

5. Calculates the number of words in the file in the memory block.

After the calculation, the function cleans up everything it has done and returns the number of words counted:

6. Frees the memory block.

7. Closes the file.

8. Returns the number of words in the file. If an error occurred, returns −1.

During the initialization for this function, any of steps 1 through 4 could fail. If this happens, the function needs to clean up any allocations it's already made before returning −1 to the caller. Termination handlers ensure that everything is cleaned up properly.

When you first invoke SEHTerm, this dialog box appears:

In the Results Of Execution group box at the top of the dialog box, you get to specify which of the four initialization operations will succeed and which will fail. Remember, this program only simulates the work to be done; it doesn't actually open a file, read the file's contents, or count the number of words in the file. In a sense, you get to play operating system here—you can tell the simulation which operations you want to succeed and which operations you want to fail.

After you have set the four check boxes the way you want them, click on the Execute button. The simulation will now try to perform steps 1 through 4 in the list of steps that the *Dlg_CountWordsInFile* function performs. All four steps are performed from within a single *try* block. If any of the steps fails, a __*leave* statement in the *try* block is executed and processing moves immediately into the *finally* block, skipping the remainder of the code in the *try* block.

The code in the *finally* block examines the state of the initialization by checking the *hFile* and *lpvFileData* variables, and then it executes the appropriate clean-up routines. The Execution Log list box at the bottom of the SEH Termination Handler Test dialog box shows the result of each step of *Dlg_CountWordsInFile*'s execution.

In our first experiment, we'll allow all four operations to succeed. To simulate this success, we must be sure that all four check boxes are checked before we click on the Execute button. After the code executes, we can see the results in the Execution Log:

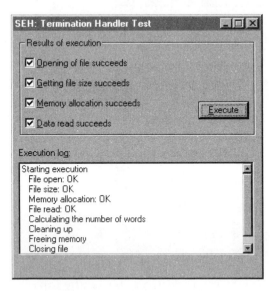

The Execution Log tells us that everything was successfully initialized, the number of words was calculated, and everything was cleaned up OK.

Now let's pretend that the memory allocation failed when the *Dlg-_CountWordsInFile* function attempted it. Here is the result:

The function opened the file, obtained its size, and tried to allocate a block of memory. When we forced this allocation to fail, execution jumped over the remainder of the *try* block code to an immediate execution of the *finally* block code. The code in the *finally* block can see that the file was opened successfully by checking the *hFile* variable. It calls *CloseHandle* to close the file.

The *finally* block code also checks the *lpvFileData* variable to see whether the memory allocation was successful. Since *lpvFileData* is NULL, the code doesn't try to free the memory block. That's why *Freeing memory* doesn't appear in the Execution Log this time.

The function will also return –1, indicating that an error has occurred. This causes the line *Error occurred in function* to appear in the Execution Log.

Let's do just one more experiment. You can try others on your own machine. On the next page is another simulation.

In this experiment, we force the opening of the file to fail and everything else to succeed. However, the code in the *try* block stops executing as soon as it can't open the file. In this case, the remainder of the initialization doesn't execute and the code in the *finally* block starts executing. The clean-up code sees that the file was never opened and that the memory block was never allocated and therefore does nothing.

You can experiment yourself by checking and unchecking the various options and clicking on the Execute button. Notice how the Execution Log changes with each test. As you experiment, it's a good idea to have the SEHTerm source code (which begins below) beside you to help you understand how termination handlers work.

SEHTerm.ico

SEHTERM.C

```
/**************************************************************
Module name: SEHTerm.C
Notices: Copyright (c) 1995 Jeffrey Richter
**************************************************************/


#include "..\AdvWin32.H"      /* See Appendix B for details. */
#include <windows.h>
#include <windowsx.h>
```

Figure 14-1.
The SEHTerm application.

(continued)

Figure 14-1. *continued*

```
#pragma warning(disable: 4001)         /* Single-line comment */

#include <tchar.h>
#include <stdio.h>
#include "Resource.H"


// The SIMULATION define should always be defined.
// It exists so that you can easily separate the simulation
// aspects of this program from the actual code that you would
// use to perform the various operations.
#define SIMULATION


///////////////////////////////////////////////////////////////

BOOL Dlg_OnInitDialog (HWND hwnd, HWND hwndFocus,
   LPARAM lParam) {

   // Associate an icon with the dialog box.
   SetClassLong(hwnd, GCL_HICON, (LONG)
      LoadIcon((HINSTANCE) GetWindowLong(hwnd, GWL_HINSTANCE),
      __TEXT("SEHTerm")));

   Button_SetCheck(GetDlgItem(hwnd, IDC_OPENSUCCEEDS), TRUE);
   Button_SetCheck(GetDlgItem(hwnd, IDC_SIZESUCCEEDS), TRUE);
   Button_SetCheck(GetDlgItem(hwnd, IDC_MEMSUCCEEDS),  TRUE);
   Button_SetCheck(GetDlgItem(hwnd, IDC_READSUCCEEDS), TRUE);
   return(TRUE);
}


///////////////////////////////////////////////////////////////

LONG Dlg_CountWordsInFile (HWND hwndLog,
   BOOL fOpenSucceeds, BOOL fFileSizeSucceeds,
   BOOL fMemSucceeds, BOOL fReadSucceeds) {

   HANDLE hFile = INVALID_HANDLE_VALUE;
   DWORD  dwFileSize = 0;
   LPVOID lpvFileData = NULL;
   BOOL   fFileReadOk = FALSE;
   LONG   lNumWords = -1;
   DWORD  dwLastError;
```

(continued)

Figure 14-1. *continued*

```
    __try {
        // Clear the Execution Log list box.
        ListBox_ResetContent(hwndLog);
        ListBox_AddString(hwndLog,
            __TEXT("Starting execution"));

        // Open the file.
#ifdef SIMULATION
        hFile = (fOpenSucceeds ?
            (HANDLE) !INVALID_HANDLE_VALUE :
            INVALID_HANDLE_VALUE);
#else
        hFile = CreateFile(...);
#endif
        if (hFile == INVALID_HANDLE_VALUE) {
            // The file could not be opened.
            ListBox_AddString(hwndLog,
                __TEXT("    File open: Fail"));
            __leave;
        } else {
            ListBox_AddString(hwndLog,
                __TEXT("    File open: OK"));
        }

        // Determine the size of the file.
#ifdef SIMULATION
        dwLastError = fFileSizeSucceeds ? NO_ERROR : !NO_ERROR;
#else
        dwFileSize = GetFileSize(hFile);
        dwLastError = GetLastError();
#endif

        if (dwLastError != NO_ERROR) {
            // The file size could not be obtained.
            ListBox_AddString(hwndLog,
                __TEXT("    File size: Fail"));
            __leave;
        } else {
            ListBox_AddString(hwndLog,
                __TEXT("    File size: OK"));
        }

        // Allocate a block of memory to store the entire file.
#ifdef SIMULATION
        lpvFileData = fMemSucceeds ? !NULL : NULL;
```

(continued)

Figure 14-1. *continued*

```
#else
        lpvFileData = HeapAlloc(GetProcessHeap(), 0, dwFileSize);
#endif
        if (lpvFileData == NULL) {
           // Allocation failed.
           ListBox_AddString(hwndLog,
               __TEXT("   Memory allocation: Fail"));
           __leave;
        } else {
           ListBox_AddString(hwndLog,
               __TEXT("   Memory allocation: OK"));
        }


        // Read the file into the buffer.
#ifdef SIMULATION
        fReadSucceeds = fReadSucceeds;
#else
        fReadSucceeds = ReadFile(hFile, lpvFileData, dwFileSize,
           NULL, NULL);
#endif
        if (!fReadSucceeds) {
           // The file's data could not be loaded into memory.
           ListBox_AddString(hwndLog,
               __TEXT("   File read: Fail"));
           __leave;
        } else {
           ListBox_AddString(hwndLog,
               __TEXT("   File read: OK"));
           fFileReadOk = TRUE;
        }

        // Calculate the number of words in the file.
        // The algorithm to calculate the number of words in the
        // file would go here. For simulation purposes, I'll
        // just set lNumWords to 37.
        ListBox_AddString(hwndLog,
           __TEXT("   Calculating the number of words"));
        lNumWords = 37;

     }  // try

     __finally {
        // Display a notification that we are cleaning up.
        ListBox_AddString(hwndLog, __TEXT("   Cleaning up"));
```

(continued)

Figure 14-1. *continued*

```
        // Guarantee that the memory is freed.
        if (lpvFileData != NULL) {
            ListBox_AddString(hwndLog,
                __TEXT("   Freeing memory"));
#ifndef SIMULATION
            HeapFree(GetProcessHeap(), 0, lpvFileData);
#endif
        }

        // Guarantee that the file is closed.
        if (hFile != INVALID_HANDLE_VALUE) {
            ListBox_AddString(hwndLog,
                __TEXT("   Closing file"));
#ifndef SIMULATION
            CloseHandle(hFile);
#endif
        }

    }  // finally

    return(lNumWords);
}


///////////////////////////////////////////////////////////


void Dlg_OnCommand (HWND hwnd, int id, HWND hwndCtl,
    UINT codeNotify) {

    TCHAR szBuf[100];
    LONG  lNumWords;

    switch (id) {
      case IDOK:
          lNumWords = Dlg_CountWordsInFile(
              GetDlgItem(hwnd, IDC_LOG),
              Button_GetCheck(GetDlgItem(hwnd,
                  IDC_OPENSUCCEEDS)),
              Button_GetCheck(GetDlgItem(hwnd,
                  IDC_SIZESUCCEEDS)),
              Button_GetCheck(GetDlgItem(hwnd, IDC_MEMSUCCEEDS)),
              Button_GetCheck(GetDlgItem(hwnd, IDC_READSUCCEEDS))
              );
```

(continued)

Figure 14-1. *continued*

```
        if (lNumWords == -1) {
           ListBox_AddString(GetDlgItem(hwnd, IDC_LOG),
              __TEXT("Error occurred in function."));
        } else {
             _stprintf(szBuf,
                __TEXT("Result: Words in file = %d"),
               lNumWords);
           ListBox_AddString(GetDlgItem(hwnd,
              IDC_LOG), szBuf);
        }

        break;

     case IDCANCEL:
        EndDialog(hwnd, id);
        break;
  }
}


///////////////////////////////////////////////////////////////////


BOOL CALLBACK DlgProc (HWND hDlg, UINT uMsg,
   WPARAM wParam, LPARAM lParam) {

   BOOL fProcessed = TRUE;

   switch (uMsg) {
      HANDLE_MSG(hDlg, WM_INITDIALOG, Dlg_OnInitDialog);
      HANDLE_MSG(hDlg, WM_COMMAND, Dlg_OnCommand);

      default:
         fProcessed = FALSE;
         break;
   }
   return(fProcessed);
}
```

(continued)

Figure 14-1. *continued*

```
////////////////////////////////////////////////////////////

int WINAPI WinMain (HINSTANCE hinstExe,
    HINSTANCE hinstPrev, LPSTR lpszCmdLine, int nCmdShow) {

    DialogBox(hinstExe, MAKEINTRESOURCE(IDD_SEHTERM),
        NULL, DlgProc);

    return(0);
}



///////////////////////// End Of File ////////////////////////
```

SEHTERM.RC

```
//Microsoft Visual C++ generated resource script.
//
#include "Resource.h"

#define APSTUDIO_READONLY_SYMBOLS
/////////////////////////////////////////////////////////////////
//
// Generated from the TEXTINCLUDE 2 resource.
//
#include "afxres.h"


/////////////////////////////////////////////////////////////////
#undef APSTUDIO_READONLY_SYMBOLS


#ifdef APSTUDIO_INVOKED
/////////////////////////////////////////////////////////////////
//
// TEXTINCLUDE
//

1 TEXTINCLUDE DISCARDABLE
BEGIN
    "Resource.h\0"
END
```

(continued)

Figure 14-1. *continued*

```
2 TEXTINCLUDE DISCARDABLE
BEGIN
    "#include ""afxres.h""\r\n"
    "\0"
END

3 TEXTINCLUDE DISCARDABLE
BEGIN
    "\r\n"
    "\0"
END

/////////////////////////////////////////////////////////////////////
#endif    // APSTUDIO_INVOKED


/////////////////////////////////////////////////////////////////////
//
// Dialog
//

IDD_SEHTERM DIALOG DISCARDABLE  18, 18, 214, 196
STYLE WS_MINIMIZEBOX ¦ WS_VISIBLE ¦ WS_CAPTION ¦ WS_SYSMENU
CAPTION "SEH: Termination Handler Test"
FONT 8, "Helv"
BEGIN
    GROUPBOX        "Results of execution",IDC_STATIC,5,5,
                    204,78,WS_GROUP
    CONTROL         "&Opening of file succeeds",
                    IDC_OPENSUCCEEDS,"Button",
                    BS_AUTOCHECKBOX ¦ WS_GROUP ¦ WS_TABSTOP,
                    10,20,92,10
    CONTROL         "&Getting file size succeeds",
                    IDC_SIZESUCCEEDS,"Button",
                    BS_AUTOCHECKBOX ¦ WS_GROUP ¦ WS_TABSTOP,
                    10,36,95,10
    CONTROL         "&Memory allocation succeeds",
                    IDC_MEMSUCCEEDS,"Button",
                    BS_AUTOCHECKBOX ¦ WS_GROUP ¦ WS_TABSTOP,
                    10,52,103,10
    CONTROL         "&Data read succeeds",IDC_READSUCCEEDS,
                    "Button", BS_AUTOCHECKBOX ¦ WS_GROUP
                    ¦ WS_TABSTOP,10,68,77,10
```

(continued)

711

Figure 14-1. *continued*

```
    PUSHBUTTON        "&Execute",IDOK,160,56,44,14,WS_GROUP
    LTEXT             "Execution lo&g:",IDC_STATIC,4,92,48,8
    LISTBOX           IDC_LOG,4,104,204,88,NOT LBS_NOTIFY
                      | WS_VSCROLL | WS_GROUP | WS_TABSTOP
END


/////////////////////////////////////////////////////////////////
//
// Icon
//


SEHTerm                   ICON    DISCARDABLE     "SEHTerm.Ico"

#ifndef APSTUDIO_INVOKED
/////////////////////////////////////////////////////////////////
//
// Generated from the TEXTINCLUDE 3 resource.
//


/////////////////////////////////////////////////////////////////
#endif    // not APSTUDIO_INVOKED
```

Exception Filters and Exception Handlers

An exception is an event you don't expect. In a well-written application, you don't expect attempts to access an invalid memory address or divide a value by 0. Nevertheless, such errors do occur. The CPU is responsible for catching invalid memory accesses and divides by 0, and it will raise an exception in response to these errors. When the CPU raises an exception, it's known as a *hardware exception*. We'll see later that the operating system and your applications can raise their own exceptions, known as *software exceptions.*

When a hardware or software exception is raised, the operating system offers your application the opportunity to see what type of exception was raised and allows the application to handle the exception itself. Here is the syntax for an exception handler:

```
__try {
  // Guarded body
  :
  :
}
```

```
__except (exception filter) {
   // Exception handler
   .
   .
   .
}
```

The new keyword is __except. Whenever you create a *try* block, it must be followed by either a *finally* block or an *except* block. A *try* block can't have both a *finally* block and an *except* block, and a *try* block can't have multiple *finally* or *except* blocks. However, it is possible to nest *try-finally* blocks inside *try-except* blocks and vice versa.

Understanding Exception Filters and Exception Handlers by Example

Unlike termination handlers, exception filters and exception handlers are executed directly by the operating system—the compiler has little to do with evaluating exception filters or executing exception handlers. The next six sections demonstrate the normal execution of *try-except* blocks, explain how and why the operating system evaluates exception filters, and show the circumstances under which the operating system executes the code inside of an exception handler.

Funcmeister1

Here's a more concrete coding example of a *try-except* block:

```
DWORD Funcmeister1 (void) {
   DWORD dwTemp;

   // 1. Do any processing here.
   .
   .

   __try {
      // 2. Perform some operation.
      dwTemp = 0;
   }
   __except (EXCEPTION_EXECUTE_HANDLER) {
      // Handle an exception; this never executes.
      .
      .
      .
   }

   // 3. Continue processing.
   return(dwTemp);
}
```

In the *Funcmeister1 try* block, we simply move a 0 into the *dwTemp* variable. This operation will never cause an exception to be raised, so the code inside the *except* block will never execute. Note this difference from *try-finally* behavior. After *dwTemp* is set to 0, the next instruction to execute is the *return* statement.

Although *return, goto, continue,* and *break* statements are strongly discouraged in the *try* block of a termination handler, no speed or code-size penalty is associated with using these statements inside the *try* block of an exception handler. Such a statement in the *try* block associated with an *except* block won't incur the overhead of a local unwind.

Funcmeister2

Let's modify the function and see what happens:

```
DWORD Funcmeister2 (void) {
   DWORD dwTemp = 0;

   // 1. Do any processing here.
   :
   :

   __try {
      // 2. Perform some operation(s).
      dwTemp = 5 / dwTemp;      // Generates an exception
      dwTemp += 10;             // Never executes
   }
   __except ( /* 3. Evaluate filter. */ EXCEPTION_EXECUTE_HANDLER) {
      // 4. Handle an exception.

      MessageBeep(0);
      :
      :

   }

   // 5. Continue processing.
   return(dwTemp);
}
```

In *Funcmeister2*, an instruction inside the *try* block calls for the attempt to divide 5 by 0. The CPU will catch this event and raise a hardware exception. When this exception is raised, the system will locate the beginning of the *except* block and evaluate the exception filter expression, an expression that must evaluate to one of the following three identifiers as defined in the Win32 EXCPT.H file:

Identifier	Defined As
EXCEPTION_EXECUTE_HANDLER	1
EXCEPTION_CONTINUE_SEARCH	0
EXCEPTION_CONTINUE_EXECUTION	−1

EXCEPTION_EXECUTE_HANDLER

In *Funcmeister2*, the exception filter expression evaluates to EXCEPTION_EXECUTE_HANDLER. This value basically says to the system: "I recognize the exception; that is, I had a feeling that this exception might occur sometime, and I've written some code to deal with it that I'd like to execute now." Execution immediately jumps to the code inside the *except* block (the exception handler code). After the code in the *except* block has executed, the system considers the exception to be handled and allows your application to continue executing.

This is pretty different from 16-bit Windows applications, where a divide by 0 causes a System Error box to appear that allows the user one option only: to close the application right then and there. In Win32 applications, you can trap the error, handle it in your own way, and allow your application to continue running without the user ever knowing that the error happened.

But where in the code does execution resume? With a little bit of thought, it's easy to imagine several possibilities.

The first possibility would be for execution to resume after the CPU instruction that generates the exception. In *Funcmeister2*, execution would resume with the instruction that adds 10 to *dwTemp*. This may seem like a reasonable thing to do, but in reality, most programs are written so that they cannot continue executing successfully if one of the earlier instructions fails to execute.

In *Funcmeister2*, the code can continue to execute normally; however, *Funcmeister2* is not the normal situation. Most likely, your code will be structured so that the CPU instructions following the instruction that generates the exception will expect a valid return value. For example, you might have a function that allocates memory, in which case a whole series of instructions will be executed to manipulate that memory. If the memory cannot be allocated, all the lines will fail, making the program generate exceptions repeatedly.

Here is another example of why execution cannot continue after the failed CPU instruction. Let's replace the C statement that generated the exception in *Funcmeister2* with the following line:

```
malloc(5 / dwTemp);
```

For the line above, the compiler generates CPU instructions to perform the division, pushes the result on the stack, and calls the *malloc* function. If the division fails, the code can't continue executing properly. The system has to push something on the stack; if it doesn't, the stack gets corrupted.

Fortunately, Microsoft has not made it possible for us to have the system resume execution on the instruction following the instruction that generates the exception. This decision saves us from potential problems like these.

The second possibility would be for execution to resume with the instruction that generated the exception. This is an interesting possibility. What if inside the *except* block you had this statement:

```
dwTemp = 2;
```

With this assignment in the *except* block, you could resume execution with the instruction that generated the exception. This time, you would be dividing 5 by 2, and execution would continue just fine without raising another exception. You can alter something and have the system retry the instruction that generated the exception. However, you should be aware that this technique can result in some subtle behaviors. We'll discuss this technique in the following section.

The third and last possibility would be for execution to pick up with the first instruction following the *except* block. This is actually what happens when the exception filter expression evaluates to EXCEPTION-_EXECUTE_HANDLER. After the code inside the *except* block finishes executing, control resumes at the first instruction after the *except* block.

EXCEPTION_CONTINUE_EXECUTION

Let's take a closer look at the exception filter to see how it evaluates to one of the three exception identifiers defined in EXCPT.H. In *Funcmeister2*, the EXCEPTION_EXECUTE_HANDLER identifier is hard-coded directly into the filter for simplicity's sake, but you can make the filter call a function that will determine which of the three identifiers should be returned. Let's look at another code example:

```
char g_szBuffer[100];

void FunclinRoosevelt1 (void) {
   int x = 0;
   char *lpBuffer = NULL;

   __try {
      *lpBuffer = 'J';
      x = 5 / x;
   }
   __except (OilFilter1(&lpBuffer)) {
      MessageBox(NULL, "An exception occurred", NULL, MB_OK);
   }
   MessageBox(NULL, "Function completed", NULL, MB_OK);
}

LONG OilFilter1 (char **lplpBuffer) {
   if (*lplpBuffer == NULL) {
      *lplpBuffer = g_szBuffer;
      return(EXCEPTION_CONTINUE_EXECUTION);
   }
   return(EXCEPTION_EXECUTE_HANDLER);
}
```

We first run into a problem when we try to put a '*J*' into the buffer
pointed to by *lpBuffer*. Unfortunately, we didn't initialize *lpBuffer* to point
to our global buffer *g_szBuffer*, and *lpBuffer* points to NULL instead. The
CPU will generate an exception and evaluate the exception filter in
the *except* block associated with the *try* block in which the exception occurred. In the *except* block, the *OilFilter1* function is passed the address of
the *lpBuffer* variable.

When *OilFilter1* gets control, it checks to see whether **lplpBuffer* is
NULL and, if it is, sets it to point to the global buffer *g_szBuffer*. The filter then returns EXCEPTION_CONTINUE_EXECUTION. When the
system sees that the filter evaluated to EXCEPTION_CONTINUE_EXE-
CUTION, it jumps back to the instruction that generated the exception
and tries to execute it again. This time, the instruction will succeed, and
'*J*' will be put into the first byte of the *g_szBuffer* buffer.

As the code continues to execute, we run up against the divide by 0
problem in the *try* block. Again the system evaluates the exception filter.
This time, *OilFilter1* sees that **lplpBuffer* is not NULL and returns EXCEP-
TION_EXECUTE_HANDLER, which tells the system to execute the
except block code. This causes a message box to appear displaying the
text *An exception occurred*.

As you can see, you can do an awful lot of work inside an exception filter. Of course, the filter must return one of the three exception identifiers, but the filter can also perform any other tasks you want it to.

Use EXCEPTION_CONTINUE_EXECUTION with Caution

As it turns out, trying to correct the situation shown in the function just discussed and having the system continue execution might or might not work—it depends on the target CPU for your application, on how your compiler generates instructions for C statements, and on your compiler options.

A compiler might generate two machine instructions to perform the statement:

```
*lpBuffer = 'J';
```

The first instruction would load the contents of *lpBuffer* into a register, and the second instruction would try to copy a *'J'* into the address to which the register points. It is this second instruction that would generate the exception. The exception filter would catch the exception, correct the value in *lpBuffer*, and tell the system to reexecute the second instruction. The problem is that the contents of the register wouldn't be changed to reflect the new value loaded into *lpBuffer*, and reexecuting the instruction would therefore generate another exception. We'd have an infinite loop!

Continuing execution might be fine if the compiler optimizes the code but might fail if the compiler doesn't optimize the code. This can be an incredibly difficult bug to fix, and you will have to examine the assembly language generated for your source code in order to determine what has gone wrong in your application. The moral of this story is to be very, very careful when returning EXCEPTION_CONTINUE_EXECUTION from an exception filter.

EXCEPTION_CONTINUE_SEARCH

The examples have been pretty tame so far. Let's shake things up a bit by adding a function call:

```
void FunclinRoosevelt2 (void) {
  char *lpBuffer = NULL;

  __try {
    FuncSinatra2(lpBuffer);
  }
  __except (OilFilter2(&lpBuffer)) {
```

```
      MessageBox(NULL, ...);
   }
}

void FuncSinatra2 (char *sz) {
   *sz = 0;
}

LONG OilFilter2 (char **lplpBuffer) {
   if (*lplpBuffer == NULL) {
      *lplpBuffer = g_szBuffer;
      return(EXCEPTION_CONTINUE_EXECUTION);
   }
   return(EXCEPTION_EXECUTE_HANDLER);
}
```

When *FunclinRoosevelt2* executes, it calls *FuncSinatra2*, passing it NULL. When *FuncSinatra2* executes, an exception is generated. Just as before, the system evaluates the exception filter associated with the most recently executing *try* block. In this example, the *try* block inside *FunclinRoosevelt2* is the most recently executing *try* block, so the system calls the *OilFilter2* function to evaluate the exception filter—even though the exception was generated inside the *FuncSinatra2* function.

Now let's shake things up a little more by adding another *try-except* block.

```
void FunclinRoosevelt3 (void) {

   char *lpBuffer = NULL;

   __try {
      FuncSinatra3(lpBuffer);
   }
   __except (OilFilter3(&lpBuffer)) {
      MessageBox(NULL, ...);
   }
}

void FuncSinatra3 (char *sz) {
   __try {
      *sz = 0;
   }
   __except (EXCEPTION_CONTINUE_SEARCH) {
      // This never executes.
         :
         :
   }
```

(continued)

```
}

LONG OilFilter3 (char **lplpBuffer) {
   if (*lplpBuffer == NULL) {
      *lplpBuffer = g_szBuffer;
      return(EXCEPTION_CONTINUE_EXECUTION);
   }
   return(EXCEPTION_EXECUTE_HANDLER);
}
```

Now, when *FuncSinatra3* tries to fill address NULL with 0, an exception is still generated but *FuncSinatra3*'s exception filter will get executed. *FuncSinatra3*'s exception filter is very simple and evaluates to EXCEPTION_CONTINUE_SEARCH. This identifier tells the system to walk up to the previous *try* block that's matched with an *except* block and call this previous *try* block's exception filter.

Because *FuncSinatra3*'s filter evaluates to EXCEPTION_CONTINUE_SEARCH, the system will walk up to the previous *try* block (in *FunclinRoosevelt3*) and evaluate its exception filter, *OilFilter3*. *OilFilter3* will see that *lpBuffer* is NULL, will set *lpBuffer* to point to the global buffer, and will then tell the system to resume execution on the instruction that generated the exception. This will allow the code inside *FuncSinatra3*'s *try* block to execute, but unfortunately, *FuncSinatra3*'s local *sz* variable will not have been changed, and resuming execution on the failed instruction will simply cause another exception to be generated. What we have here is another infinite loop!

You'll notice I said that the system walks up to the most recently executing *try* block that's matched with an *except* block and evaluates its filters. This means that any *try* blocks that are matched with *finally* blocks instead of *except* blocks are skipped by the system while it walks up the chain. The reason for this should be pretty obvious: *finally* blocks don't have exception filters and therefore give the system nothing to evaluate. If *FuncSinatra3* in the last example contained a *finally* block instead of its *except* block, the system would have started evaluating exception filters beginning with *FunclinRoosevelt3*'s *OilFilter3*.

Figure 14-2 shows a flowchart describing the actions taken by the system when an exception is generated.

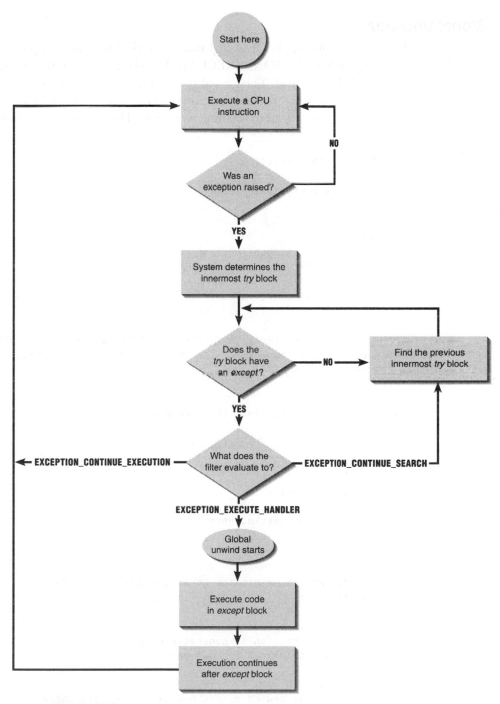

Figure 14-2.
How the system processes an exception.

Global Unwinds

Exception handling involves a global unwind. When an exception filter evaluates to EXCEPTION_EXECUTE_HANDLER, the system must perform a global unwind. The global unwind causes all of the outstanding *try-finally* blocks that started executing below the *try-except* block that is handling the exception to resume execution. These two functions are an example:

```
void FuncOStimpy1 (void) {

   // 1. Do any processing here.
   :
   :

   __try {
      // 2. Call another function.
      FuncORen1();

      // Code here never executes.
   }

   __except ( /* 6. Evaluate filter. */ EXCEPTION_EXECUTE_HANDLER) {
      // 8. After the unwind, the exception handler executes.
      MessageBox(NULL, ...);
   }

   // 9. Exception handled--continue execution.
   :
   :

}
void FuncORen1 (void) {
   DWORD dwTemp = 0;

   // 3. Do any processing here.
   :
   :

   __try {
      // 4. Request permission to access protected data.
      WaitForSingleObject(g_hSem, INFINITE);

      // 5. Modify the data.
      //    An exception is generated here.
      g_dwProtectedData = 5 / dwTemp;
   }
   __finally {
      // 7. Global unwind occurs because filter evaluated
      //    to EXCEPTION_EXECUTE_HANDLER.
```

```
      // Allow others to use protected data.
      ReleaseSemaphore(g_hSem, 1, NULL);
   }

   // Continue processing--never executes.
   .
   .
   .
}
```

FuncOStimpy1 and *FuncORen1* together illustrate the most confusing aspects of structured exception handling. The numbers at the beginnings of the comments show the order of execution, but let's hold hands and go through it together.

FuncOStimpy1 begins execution by entering its *try* block and calling *FuncORen1*. *FuncORen1* starts by entering its own *try* block and waits to obtain a semaphore. Once it has the semaphore, *FuncORen1* tries to alter the global data variable, *g_dwProtectedData*. However, the division by 0 causes an exception to be generated. The system grabs control now and searches for a *try* block matched with an *except* block. Since the *try* block in *FuncORen1* is matched by a *finally* block, the system searches upward for another *try* block. This time, it finds the *try* block in *FuncOStimpy1*, and it sees that *FuncOStimpy1*'s *try* block is matched by an *except* block.

The system now evaluates the exception filter that's associated with *FuncOStimpy1*'s *except* block and waits for the return value. When the system sees that the return value is EXCEPTION_EXECUTE_HANDLER, the system begins a global unwind in *FuncORen1*'s *finally* block. Note that the unwind takes place *before* the system begins execution of the code in *FuncOStimpy1*'s *except* block. For a global unwind, the system starts back at the bottom of all outstanding *try* blocks and searches this time for *try* blocks matched by *finally* blocks. The *finally* block that the system finds here is the one contained inside *FuncORen1*.

When the system executes the code in *FuncORen1*'s *finally* block, you can really see the power of structured exception handling. Because *FuncORen1*'s *finally* block is executed, the semaphore is released, allowing other threads to resume execution. If the call to *ReleaseSemaphore* were not contained inside the *finally* block, the semaphore would never be released.

After the code contained in the *finally* block has executed, the system continues to walk upward looking for outstanding *finally* blocks that need to be executed. In this example there are none. The system stops walking upward when it reaches the *try-except* block that decided to handle the exception. At this point, the global unwind is complete, and the system can execute the code contained inside the *except* block.

Figure 14-3 shows a flowchart that describes how the system performs a global unwind.

That's how structured exception handling works. SEH can be difficult to understand because the system really gets involved with the execution of your code. No longer does the code flow from top to bottom; the system gets involved and makes sections of code execute according to its notions of order. This order of execution is complex but predictable, and by following the flowcharts in Figure 14-2 and Figure 14-3, you should be able to use SEH with confidence.

Halting Global Unwinds

It's possible to stop the system from completing a global unwind by putting a *return* statement inside a *finally* block. Let's look at the code below:

```
void FuncMonkey (void) {
   __try {
      FuncFish();
   }
   __except (EXCEPTION_EXECUTE_HANDLER) {
      MessageBeep(0);
   }
   MessageBox(...);
}

void FuncFish (void) {
   FuncPheasant();
   MessageBox(...);
}

void FuncPheasant (void) {

   __try {
      strcpy(NULL, NULL);
   }

   __finally {
      return;
   }
}
```

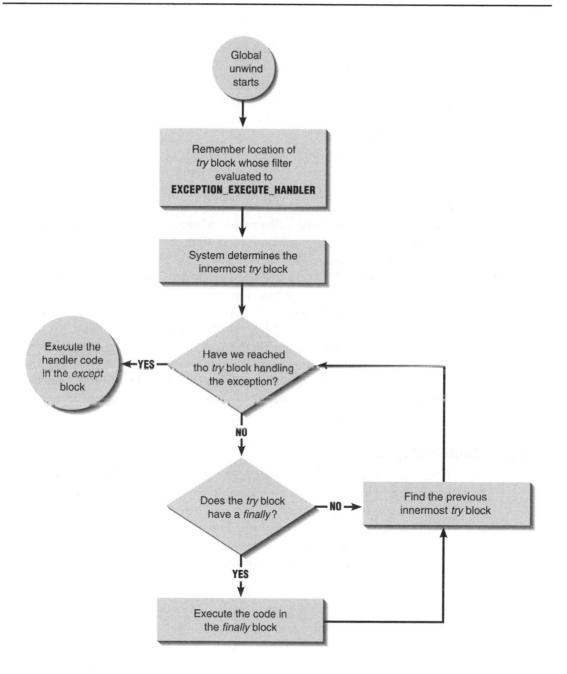

Figure 14-3.
How the system performs a global unwind.

When the *strcpy* function is called in *FuncPheasant*'s *try* block, a memory access violation exception will be generated. When this happens, the system will start scanning to see whether any exception filters exist that can handle the exception. The system will find that the exception filter in *FuncMonkey* wants to handle the exception, and the system will start a global unwind.

The global unwind starts by executing the code inside *Func-Pheasant*'s *finally* block. However, this block of code contains a *return* statement. The *return* statement causes the system to stop unwinding, and *FuncPheasant* will actually end up returning to *FuncFish*. *FuncFish* will continue executing and will display a message box on the screen. *FuncFish* will then return to *FuncMonkey*. The code in *FuncMonkey* continues executing by calling *MessageBox*.

Notice that the code inside *FuncMonkey*'s exception block never executes the call to *MessageBeep*. The *return* statement in *FuncPheasant*'s *finally* block causes the system to stop unwinding altogether, and execution continues as though nothing ever happened.

Microsoft has designed SEH to work this way on purpose. You might occasionally want to stop unwinding and allow execution to continue, and this method allows you to do this. Usually, though, this isn't the sort of thing you want to do. As a rule, be careful to avoid putting *return* statements inside *finally* blocks.

More About Exception Filters

Often an exception filter must analyze the situation before it can determine what value to return. For example, your handler might know what to do if a divide by 0 exception occurs, but it might not know how to handle a memory access exception. The exception filter has the responsibility for examining the situation and returning the appropriate value.

This code demonstrates a method for identifying the kind of exception that has occurred:

```
__try {
   x = 0;
   y = 4 / x;
}

__except ((GetExceptionCode() == EXCEPTION_INT_DIVIDE_BY_ZERO) ?
   EXCEPTION_EXECUTE_HANDLER : EXCEPTION_CONTINUE_SEARCH) {
   // Handle divide by zero exception.
}
```

The *GetExceptionCode* intrinsic function returns a value identifying the kind of exception that has occurred:

```
DWORD GetExceptionCode(VOID);
```

The following list of all predefined exceptions and their meanings is adapted from the Win32 documentation. The exception identifiers can be found in the Win32 WINBASE.H header file.

EXCEPTION_ACCESS_VIOLATION   The thread tried to read from or write to a virtual address for which it doesn't have the appropriate access.

EXCEPTION_ARRAY_BOUNDS_EXCEEDED   The thread tried to access an array element that is out of bounds, and the underlying hardware supports bounds checking.

EXCEPTION_BREAKPOINT   A breakpoint was encountered.

EXCEPTION_DATATYPE_MISALIGNMENT   The thread tried to read or write data that is misaligned on hardware that doesn't provide alignment. For example, 16-bit values must be aligned on 2-byte boundaries, 32-bit values on 4-byte boundaries, and so on.

EXCEPTION_FLT_DENORMAL_OPERAND   One of the operands in a floating-point operation is denormal. A denormal value is one that is too small to represent a standard floating-point value.

EXCEPTION_FLT_DIVIDE_BY_ZERO   The thread tried to divide a floating-point value by a floating-point divisor of 0.

EXCEPTION_FLT_INEXACT_RESULT   The result of a floating-point operation can't be represented exactly as a decimal fraction.

EXCEPTION_FLT_INVALID_OPERATION   Represents any floating-point exception not included in this list.

EXCEPTION_FLT_OVERFLOW   The exponent of a floating-point operation is greater than the magnitude allowed by the corresponding type.

EXCEPTION_FLT_STACK_CHECK   The stack overflowed or underflowed as the result of a floating-point operation.

EXCEPTION_FLT_UNDERFLOW   The exponent of a floating-point operation is less than the magnitude allowed by the type.

EXCEPTION_GUARD_PAGE   A thread attempted to access a page of memory that has the PAGE_GUARD protection attribute. The page is made accessible and an EXCEPTION_GUARD_PAGE exception is raised.

EXCEPTION_ILLEGAL_INSTRUCTION   A thread executed an invalid instruction. This exception is defined by the specific CPU architecture; executing an invalid instruction may cause a trap error on different CPUs.

EXCEPTION_IN_PAGE_ERROR   A page fault couldn't be satisfied because the file system or a device driver returned a read error.

EXCEPTION_INT_DIVIDE_BY_ZERO   The thread tried to divide an integer value by an integer divisor of 0.

EXCEPTION_INT_OVERFLOW   The result of an integer operation caused a carry out of the most significant bit of the result.

EXCEPTION_INVALID_DISPOSITION   An exception handler returned a value other than EXCEPTION_EXECUTE_HANDLER, EXCEPTION_CONTINUE_SEARCH, or EXCEPTION_CONTINUE-_EXECUTION.

EXCEPTION_NONCONTINUABLE_EXCEPTION   The thread tried to continue execution after a noncontinuable exception occurred.

EXCEPTION_PRIV_INSTRUCTION   The thread tried to execute an instruction whose operation is not allowed in the current machine mode.

EXCEPTION_SINGLE_STEP   A trace trap or other single-instruction mechanism signaled that one instruction has been executed.

EXCEPTION_STACK_OVERFLOW   The user stack is exhausted and cannot be expanded.

The *GetExceptionCode* intrinsic function can be called only in an exception filter (between the parentheses following *__except*) or inside an exception handler. The following code is legal:

```
__try {
   y = 0;
   x = 4 / y;
}
```

```
__except (
   ((GetExceptionCode() == EXCEPTION_ACCESS_VIOLATION) ||
    (GetExceptionCode() == EXCEPTION_INT_DIVIDE_BY_ZERO)) ?
   EXCEPTION_EXECUTE_HANDLER : EXCEPTION_CONTINUE_SEARCH) {

   switch (GetExceptionCode()) {
      case EXCEPTION_ACCESS_VIOLATION:
         // Handle the access violation.
            .
            .
            .
         break;

      case EXCEPTION_INT_DIVIDE_BY_ZERO:
         // Handle the integer divide by 0.
            .
            .
            .
         break;
   }
}
```

However, you cannot call *GetExceptionCode* from inside an exception filter function. To help you catch such errors, the compiler will produce a compilation error if you try to compile the following code:

```
__try {
   y = 0;
   x = 4 / y;
}

__except (CoffeeFilter()) {

   // Handle the exception.
      .
      .
      .
}

LONG CoffeeFilter (void) {
   // Compilation error: illegal call to GetExceptionCode.
   return((GetExceptionCode() == EXCEPTION_ACCESS_VIOLATION) ?
      EXCEPTION_EXECUTE_HANDLER : EXCEPTION_CONTINUE_SEARCH);
}
```

You can get this effect by rewriting the code this way:

```
__try {
   y = 0;
   x = 4 / y;
}
```

(continued)

```
__except (CoffeeFilter(GetExceptionCode())) {

   // Handle the exception.
      .
      .
      .
}

LONG CoffeeFilter (DWORD dwExceptionCode) {
   return((dwExceptionCode == EXCEPTION_ACCESS_VIOLATION) ?
      EXCEPTION_EXECUTE_HANDLER : EXCEPTION_CONTINUE_SEARCH);
}
```

Exception codes follow the rules for error codes in Win32 as defined inside the WINERROR.H file. Each DWORD is divided as shown in this table:

Bits:	31–30	29–28	27–16	15–0
Contents:	Severity	Flags	Facility code	Exception code
Meaning:	0 = Success	Bit 29	Programmer-defined	Programmer-defined
	1 = Informational	0 = Microsoft		
	2 = Warning	1 = Customer		
	3 = Error	Bit 28 is reserved (must be 0)		

The table below shows the meaning of all the system-defined exception codes:

Exception Code	Code	Severity
EXCEPTION_ACCESS_VIOLATION	0xC0000005	Error
EXCEPTION_ARRAY_BOUNDS_EXCEEDED	0xC000008C	Error
EXCEPTION_BREAKPOINT	0x80000003	Warning
EXCEPTION_DATATYPE_MISALIGNMENT	0x80000002	Warning
EXCEPTION_FLT_DENORMAL_OPERAND	0xC000008D	Error

(continued)

continued

Exception Code	Code	Severity
EXCEPTION_FLT_DIVIDE_BY_ZERO	0xC000008E	Error
EXCEPTION_FLT_INEXACT_RESULT	0xC000008F	Error
EXCEPTION_FLT_INVALID_OPERATION	0xC0000030	Error
EXCEPTION_FLT_OVERFLOW	0xC0000091	Error
EXCEPTION_FLT_STACK_CHECK	0xC0000032	Error
EXCEPTION_FLT_UNDERFLOW	0xC0000033	Error
EXCEPTION_GUARD_PAGE	0x80000001	Warning
EXCEPTION_ILLEGAL_INSTRUCTION	0xC000001D	Error
EXCEPTION_IN_PAGE_ERROR	0xC0000006	Error
EXCEPTION_INT_DIVIDE_BY_ZERO	0xC0000094	Error
EXCEPTION_INT_OVERFLOW	0xC0000035	Error
EXCEPTION_INVALID_DISPOSITION	0xC0000026	Error
EXCEPTION_NONCONTINUABLE_EXCEPTION	0xC0000025	Error
EXCEPTION_PRIV_INSTRUCTION	0xC0000096	Error
EXCEPTION_SINGLE_STEP	0x80000004	Warning
EXCEPTION_STACK_OVERFLOW	0xC00000FD	Error

GetExceptionInformation

When an exception occurs, the operating system pushes an EXCEP-
TION_RECORD structure, a CONTEXT structure, and an EXCEPTION-
_POINTERS structure on the stack of the thread that raised the
exception.

The EXCEPTION_RECORD structure contains CPU-independent
information about the raised exception, while the CONTEXT structure
contains CPU-dependent information about the raised exception. The
EXCEPTION_POINTERS structure has only two data members that are
pointers to the pushed EXCEPTION_RECORD and CONTEXT data
structures:

```
typedef struct _EXCEPTION_POINTERS {
   PEXCEPTION_RECORD ExceptionRecord;
   PCONTEXT ContextRecord;
} EXCEPTION_POINTERS;
```

In order to retrieve this information and use it in your own application, you will need to call the *GetExceptionInformation* function:

```
LPEXCEPTION_POINTERS GetExceptionInformation(VOID);
```

This intrinsic function returns a pointer to an EXCEPTION_POINTERS structure.

The most important thing to remember about the *GetException-Information* function is that it can be called only in an exception filter—never inside an exception handler and never inside an exception filter function because the CONTEXT, EXCEPTION_RECORD, and EXCEPTION_POINTERS data structures are valid only during the exception filter processing. Once control has been transferred to the exception handler, the data on the stack is destroyed, which is why the function can be called only during evaluation of the exception filter.

If you have a need to access the exception information from inside your exception handler block, you must save the EXCEPTION-_RECORD data structure and/or CONTEXT data structure pointed to by the EXCEPTION_POINTERS structure in one or more variables that you create. The code below demonstrates how to save both the EXCEPTION_RECORD and CONTEXT data structures:

```
void FuncSkunk (void) {
    // Declare variables that we can use to save the exception
    // record and the context if an exception should occur.
    EXCEPTION_RECORD SavedExceptRec;
    CONTEXT SavedContext;
    .
    .
    .
    __try {
        .
        .
        .
    }

    __except (
        SavedExceptRec =
            *(GetExceptionInformation())->ExceptionRecord,
        SavedContext =
            *(GetExceptionInformation())->ContextRecord,
        EXCEPTION_EXECUTE_HANDLER) {

        // We can use the SavedExceptRec and SavedContext
        // variables inside the handler code block.
```

```
    switch (SavedExceptRec.ExceptionCode) {
       .
       .
       .
    }
  }
  .
  .
  .
}
```

Notice the use of the C language's comma (,) operator in the exception filter. Many programmers aren't used to seeing this operator. It tells the compiler to execute the comma-separated expressions from left to right. When all of the expressions have been evaluated, the result of the last (or rightmost) expression is returned.

In *FuncSkunk*, the left expression will execute, which causes the EXCEPTION_RECORD structure on the stack to be stored in the *SavedExceptRec* local variable. The result of this expression is the value of *SavedExceptRec*. However, this result is discarded and the next expression to the right is evaluated. This second expression causes the CONTEXT structure on the stack to be stored in the *SavedContext* local variable. The result of the second expression is *SavedContext*, and again, this expression is discarded as the third expression is evaluated. This is a very simple expression that evaluates to EXCEPTION_EXECUTE-_HANDLER. The result of this rightmost expression is the result of the entire comma-separated expression.

Because the exception filter evaluated to EXCEPTION_EXE-CUTE_HANDLER, the code inside the *except* block executes. At this point, the *SavedExceptRec* and *SavedContext* variables have been initialized and can be used inside the *except* block. Note that it is important that the *SavedExceptRec* and *SavedContext* variables be declared outside the *try* block.

As you've probably guessed, the *ExceptionRecord* member of the EXCEPTION_POINTERS structure points to an EXCEPTION_RECORD structure:

```
typedef struct _EXCEPTION_RECORD {
   DWORD ExceptionCode;
   DWORD ExceptionFlags;
   struct _EXCEPTION_RECORD *ExceptionRecord;
   PVOID ExceptionAddress;
   DWORD NumberParameters;
   DWORD ExceptionInformation[EXCEPTION_MAXIMUM_PARAMETERS];
} EXCEPTION_RECORD;
```

The EXCEPTION_RECORD structure contains detailed, CPU-independent information about the exception that has most recently occurred:

- *ExceptionCode* contains the code of the exception. This is the same information that is returned from the *GetExceptionCode* intrinsic function.

- *ExceptionFlags* contains flags about the exception. Currently the only two values are 0 (which indicates a continuable exception) and EXCEPTION_NONCONTINUABLE (which indicates a noncontinuable exception). Any attempt to continue execution after a noncontinuable exception causes an EXCEPTION-_NONCONTINUABLE_EXCEPTION exception to be raised.

- *ExceptionRecord* points to an EXCEPTION_RECORD structure for another unhandled exception. While handling one exception, it is possible to raise another exception. For example, the code in your exception filter could attempt to divide a number by 0. Exception records can be chained to provide additional information when nested exceptions occur. A nested exception occurs if an exception is generated during the processing of an exception filter. If there are no unhandled exceptions, this member will contain NULL.

- *ExceptionAddress* specifies the address of the instruction in your code at which the exception occurred.

- *NumberParameters* specifies the number of parameters associated with the exception. This is the number of defined elements in the *ExceptionInformation* array.

- *ExceptionInformation* specifies an array of additional 32-bit arguments that describe the exception. For most exception codes, the array elements are undefined.

The last two members of the EXCEPTION_RECORD structure, *NumberParameters* and *ExceptionInformation*, offer the exception filter some additional information about the exception. Currently only one type of exception involves additional information: EXCEPTION-_ACCESS_VIOLATION. All other possible exceptions will have the *NumberParameters* member set to 0. When you look at the additional information about a generated exception, you can examine the *NumberParameters* member to see how many DWORDs of information are available.

For an EXCEPTION_ACCESS_VIOLATION exception, *Exception-Information[0]* contains a read-write flag that indicates the type of operation that caused the access violation. If this value is 0, the thread tried to read the inaccessible data. If this value is 1, the thread tried to write to an inaccessible address. *ExceptionInformation[1]* specifies the virtual address of the inaccessible data.

By using these members, you can produce exception filters that offer you a significant amount of information about your application. For example, you might write an exception filter like this one:

```
__try {
   :
   :
}
__except (ExpFltr(GetExceptionInformation()->ExceptionRecord)) {
   :
   :
}

LONG ExpFltr (LPEXCEPTION_RECORD lpER) {
   char szBuf[300], *p;
   DWORD dwExceptionCode = lpER->ExceptionCode;

   sprintf(szBuf, "Code = %x, Address = %x",
      dwExceptionCode, lpER->ExceptionAddress);

   // Find the end of the string.
   p = strchr(szBuf, 0);

   // I used a switch statement in case Microsoft adds
   // information for other exception codes in the future.
   switch (dwExceptionCode) {
      case EXCEPTION_ACCESS_VIOLATION:
         sprintf(p, "Attempt to %s data at address %x",
            lpER->ExceptionInformation[0] ? "read" : "write",
            lpER->ExceptionInformation[1]);
         break;

      default:
         break;
   }

   MessageBox(NULL, szBuf, "Exception",
      MB_OK | MB_ICONEXCLAMATION);

   return(EXCEPTION_CONTINUE_SEARCH);
}
```

The *ContextRecord* member of the EXCEPTION_POINTERS structure points to a CONTEXT structure. This structure is platform-dependent; that is, the contents of this structure will differ from one CPU platform to another. Here is the CONTEXT structure for an *x*86 CPU:

```
typedef struct _CONTEXT {

    // Flags describing contents of CONTEXT record
    DWORD ContextFlags;

    // Debug registers
    DWORD    Dr0;
    DWORD    Dr1;
    DWORD    Dr2;
    DWORD    Dr3;
    DWORD    Dr6;
    DWORD    Dr7;

    // Floating-point registers
    FLOATING_SAVE_AREA FloatSave;

    // Segment registers
    DWORD    SegGs;
    DWORD    SegFs;
    DWORD    SegEs;
    DWORD    SegDs;

    // Integer registers
    DWORD    Edi;
    DWORD    Esi;
    DWORD    Ebx;
    DWORD    Edx;
    DWORD    Ecx;
    DWORD    Eax;

    // Control registers
    DWORD    Ebp;
    DWORD    Eip;
    DWORD    SegCs;
    DWORD    EFlags;
    DWORD    Esp;
    DWORD    SegSs;

} CONTEXT;
```

Basically, this structure contains one member for each of the registers available on the CPU. When an exception is raised, you can find out even more information by examining the members of this structure. Unfortunately, realizing the benefit of such a possibility requires you to write platform-dependent code that recognizes the machine it's running on and uses the appropriate CONTEXT structure. The best way to handle this is to put #*ifdef*s into your code. The CONTEXT structures for the *x*86, MIPS, and Alpha CPUs are in the WINNT.H header file.

The SEH Exceptions Sample Application

The SEHExcpt (SEHEXCPT.EXE) sample application, listed in Figure 14-4 beginning on page 741, demonstrates the use of exception filters and handlers. The source code files, resource files, and make file for the application are in the SEHEXCPT.14 directory on the companion disc. When you invoke SEHExcpt, this dialog box appears:

When you click on the Execute button, the program calls *VirtualAlloc* to reserve a region of memory in the process's address space big enough to contain an array of 50 elements, each 4 KB in size. Notice that I said the region is reserved—not committed.

After reserving the region, the program tries to write to randomly selected elements in the array. You get to specify the number of accesses the program will try by entering a number in the Number Of Writes To Perform field.

For the first randomly selected element, an access violation exception will occur because memory has only been reserved, not committed. At this point, the exception filter, identified by the *ExpFilter* function in SEHEXCPT.C, gets called by the operating system.

This filter is responsible for calling *VirtualAlloc* again, but this time it passes MEM_COMMIT to *VirtualAlloc* in order to actually commit memory to the reserved region. But before the filter can do this, it must determine that the exception that it is filtering occurred because of an invalid memory access in the reserved region.

It's important that the program not accidentally absorb exceptions. When you implement an exception filter, be sure to perform whatever tests are necessary to ensure that you are actually handling the exception for which you designed the filter. If any other exception occurs that the filter can't handle, the filter must return EXCEPTION-_CONTINUE_SEARCH.

The *ExpFilter* function determines whether the occurring exception comes from an invalid array access by performing the following tests:

1. Is the exception code EXCEPTION_ACCESS_VIOLATION?

2. Had memory for the array been reserved when the exception occurred? An exception might have occurred before memory for the array was even reserved.

3. Is the address of the invalid memory access within the memory region reserved for the array?

If any of the three tests fails, the filter was not written to handle the occurring exception and the filter returns EXCEPTION_CONTINUE-_SEARCH. If all three tests succeed, the filter assumes that the invalid access was in the array and calls *CommitMemory*. *CommitMemory* determines whether the invalid memory access was an attempt to read from or to write to the array and creates a string to be displayed in the Execution Log list box. For this sample program, the memory access will always be an attempt to write to the memory. Finally, *CommitMemory* calls *VirtualAlloc* to commit memory to the region of the array memory occupied by the individual array element that was accessed.

When *CommitMemory* returns to the exception filter, the filter returns EXCEPTION_CONTINUE_EXECUTION. This causes the machine instruction that raised the exception to execute again. This time, the memory access will succeed because memory will have been committed.

Earlier in this chapter, I said that you must be careful when returning EXCEPTION_CONTINUE_EXECUTION from a filter. I said that there could be a problem if your compiler generates multiple machine instructions for a single C/C++ statement. In the case I've just discussed, there would *never* be a problem. This example is guaranteed to work on any CPU platform using any programming language or compiler because we are not trying to change any variables that the compiler might decide to load into registers.

OK, let's look at a sample run of the program:

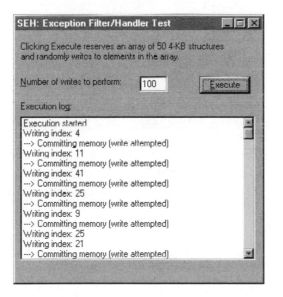

The log shows the results of performing 100 randomly selected write accesses to the array. At first the array had no memory committed to it, causing the exception filter to be invoked for array indexes 4, 11, 41, 25, and 9. But then index 25 was written to again. This time, no access violation occurred, and the exception filter didn't get called.

Now let's scroll to the bottom of the Execution Log:

```
SEH: Exception Filter/Handler Test

Clicking Execute reserves an array of 50 4-KB structures
and randomly writes to elements in the array.

Number of writes to perform:    100        Execute

Execution log:

Writing index: 31
Writing index: 8
Writing index: 44
Writing index: 39
---> Committing memory (write attempted)
Writing index: 26
Writing index: 23
Writing index: 37
Writing index: 38
Writing index: 18
Writing index: 32
Writing index: 29
Writing index: 41
Execution ended
```

At the end of the 100 accesses, very few exceptions occur because most of the array indexes have already been selected and memory for these indexes has been committed.

You'll notice that I put a *try-finally* block inside the *ExpFilter* function. I did this to demonstrate that it's perfectly legal and useful to use structured exception handling inside an exception filter. It's also possible to put *try-finally* or *try-except* blocks inside *finally* blocks or *except* blocks, and it's even possible to nest *try-finally* and *try-except* blocks inside one another. Nesting of exception handlers inside an exception filter will be demonstrated in the SEHSoft sample application, coming up a little later.

As with the SEHTerm program we looked at earlier, you can experiment with SEHExcpt yourself by changing the number of array accesses and seeing how this change affects the number of times that the exception filter is called.

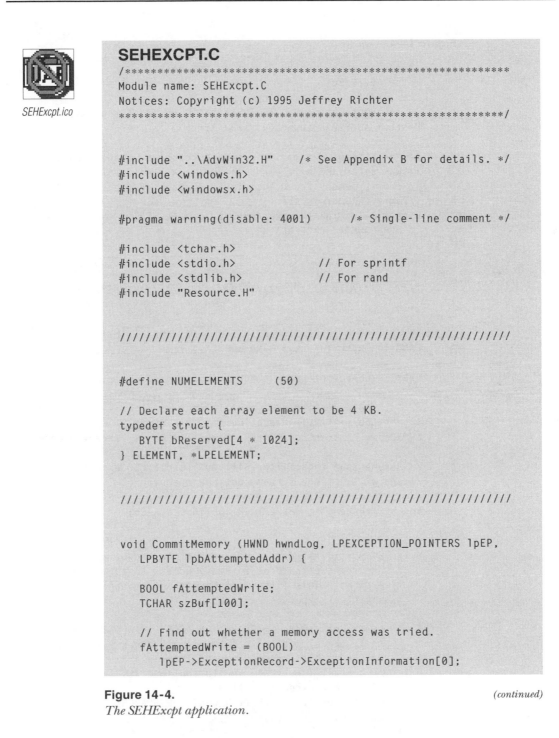

SEHExcpt.ico

SEHEXCPT.C

```
/*******************************************************************
Module name: SEHExcpt.C
Notices: Copyright (c) 1995 Jeffrey Richter
*******************************************************************/


#include "..\AdvWin32.H"     /* See Appendix B for details. */
#include <windows.h>
#include <windowsx.h>

#pragma warning(disable: 4001)        /* Single-line comment */

#include <tchar.h>
#include <stdio.h>                    // For sprintf
#include <stdlib.h>                   // For rand
#include "Resource.H"


///////////////////////////////////////////////////////////////


#define NUMELEMENTS       (50)

// Declare each array element to be 4 KB.
typedef struct {
   BYTE bReserved[4 * 1024];
} ELEMENT, *LPELEMENT;


///////////////////////////////////////////////////////////////


void CommitMemory (HWND hwndLog, LPEXCEPTION_POINTERS lpEP,
   LPBYTE lpbAttemptedAddr) {

   BOOL fAttemptedWrite;
   TCHAR szBuf[100];

   // Find out whether a memory access was tried.
   fAttemptedWrite = (BOOL)
      lpEP->ExceptionRecord->ExceptionInformation[0];
```

Figure 14-4.   *(continued)*
The SEHExcpt application.

Figure 14-4. *continued*

```
   // Add an entry to the Execution Log list box.
   _stprintf(szBuf,
      __TEXT("---> Committing memory (%s attempted)"),
      fAttemptedWrite ? __TEXT("write") : __TEXT("read"));
   ListBox_AddString(hwndLog, szBuf);

   // The attempted memory access did occur while the program
   // was accessing an element in our array. Let's try to
   // commit memory to an individual element of the reserved
   // array's address space.
   VirtualAlloc(lpbAttemptedAddr, sizeof(ELEMENT),
      MEM_COMMIT, PAGE_READWRITE);
}


///////////////////////////////////////////////////////////////


int ExpFilter (LPEXCEPTION_POINTERS lpEP, LPBYTE lpbArray,
   LONG lNumBytesInArray, HWND hwndLog) {

   LPBYTE lpbAttemptedAddr = NULL;

   // Get the exception code explaining
   // why the filter is executing.
   DWORD dwExceptionCode = lpEP->ExceptionRecord->ExceptionCode;

   // Assume that this filter will NOT handle the exception
   // and will let the system continue scanning
   // for other filters.
   int nFilterResult = EXCEPTION_CONTINUE_SEARCH;

   __try {
      // We must first determine whether the exception is
      // occurring because of a memory access to our array of
      // elements. This filter and handler do not process
      // any other types of exceptions.

      if (dwExceptionCode != EXCEPTION_ACCESS_VIOLATION) {
         // If the exception is not a memory access violation,
         // the exception doesn't come from an array element
         // access. The system should continue its search for
         // another exception filter.
         nFilterResult = EXCEPTION_CONTINUE_SEARCH;
         __leave;
      }
```

(continued)

Figure 14-4. *continued*

```
        if (lpbArray == NULL) {
            // The exception occurred either before the program
            // tried to reserve the address space, or the
            // array's address space was unsuccessfully reserved.
            nFilterResult = EXCEPTION_CONTINUE_SEARCH;
            __leave;
        }

        // Get the address of the attempted memory access.
        lpbAttemptedAddr = (LPBYTE)
            lpEP->ExceptionRecord->ExceptionInformation[1];

        if ((lpbAttemptedAddr < lpbArray) ||
            ((lpbArray + lNumBytesInArray) < lpbAttemptedAddr)) {

            // Address attempted is BELOW the beginning of the
            // array's reserved space or is ABOVE the end of the
            // array's reserved space. We'll let some other
            // filter handle this exception.
            nFilterResult = EXCEPTION_CONTINUE_SEARCH;
            __leave;
        }

        // This filter will handle the exception.

        CommitMemory(hwndLog, lpEP, lpbAttemptedAddr);

        // Memory is committed now. Let's restart the
        // instruction that caused the exception in the first
        // place. This time, the instruction will succeed
        // and not cause another exception.
        nFilterResult = EXCEPTION_CONTINUE_EXECUTION;
    }

    __finally {
    }

    // Now that memory is committed, we can continue execution
    // at the instruction that generated the exception in
    // the first place.
    return(nFilterResult);
}
```

(continued)

Figure 14-4. *continued*

```
//////////////////////////////////////////////////////////////


void Dlg_ReserveArrayAndAccessIt (HWND hwndLog,
   int nNumAccesses) {

   LPELEMENT lpArray = NULL;
   ELEMENT Element;
   TCHAR szBuf[100];
   int nElementNum;
   const LONG lNumBytesInArray = sizeof(ELEMENT) *
      NUMELEMENTS;

   // Clear the Execution Log list box.
   ListBox_ResetContent(hwndLog);
   ListBox_AddString(hwndLog, __TEXT("Execution started"));

   __try {
      // Reserve an address space large enough to
      // hold NUMELEMENTS number of ELEMENTs.
      lpArray = VirtualAlloc(NULL, lNumBytesInArray,
         MEM_RESERVE, PAGE_NOACCESS);

      while (nNumAccesses--) {
         // Get the index of a random element to access.
         nElementNum = rand() % NUMELEMENTS;

         // Try a write access.
         _stprintf(szBuf,
            __TEXT("Writing index: %d"), nElementNum);
         ListBox_AddString(hwndLog, szBuf);

         // The exception will occur on this line.
         lpArray[nElementNum] = Element;

      }  // while

      // We have finished the execution.
      ListBox_AddString(hwndLog, __TEXT("Execution ended"));

      // Decommit and free the array of ELEMENTs.
      VirtualFree(lpArray, 0, MEM_RELEASE);
   }  // __try
```

(continued)

Figure 14-4. *continued*

```
    __except (
        ExpFilter(GetExceptionInformation(), (LPBYTE) lpArray,
            lNumBytesInArray, hwndLog)) {

        // Because the filter never returns
        // EXCEPTION_EXECUTE_HANDLER, there is nothing
        // to do in the except block.

    }  // __except
}


//////////////////////////////////////////////////////////////////


BOOL Dlg_OnInitDialog (HWND hwnd, HWND hwndFocus,
    LPARAM lParam) {

    // Associate an icon with the dialog box.
    SetClassLong(hwnd, GCL_HICON, (LONG)
        LoadIcon((HINSTANCE) GetWindowLong(hwnd,
        GWL_HINSTANCE), __TEXT("SEHExcpt")));

    // Default the number of accesses to 100.
    SetDlgItemInt(hwnd, IDC_NUMACCESSES, 100, FALSE);
    return(TRUE);
}


//////////////////////////////////////////////////////////////////


void Dlg_OnCommand (HWND hwnd, int id,
    HWND hwndCtl, UINT codeNotify) {

    int  nNumAccesses;
    BOOL fTranslated;

    switch (id) {
        case IDOK:
            nNumAccesses = GetDlgItemInt(hwnd, IDC_NUMACCESSES,
                &fTranslated, FALSE);
```

(continued)

745

Figure 14-4. *continued*

```
        if (fTranslated) {
            Dlg_ReserveArrayAndAccessIt(
                GetDlgItem(hwnd, IDC_LOG), nNumAccesses);
        } else {
            MessageBox(hwnd,
                __TEXT("Invalid number of accesses."),
                __TEXT("SEHExcpt"), MB_OK);
        }
        break;

    case IDCANCEL:
        EndDialog(hwnd, id);
        break;
    }
}


///////////////////////////////////////////////////////////


BOOL CALLBACK Dlg_Proc (HWND hDlg, UINT uMsg,
    WPARAM wParam, LPARAM lParam) {

    BOOL fProcessed = TRUE;

    switch (uMsg) {
        HANDLE_MSG(hDlg, WM_INITDIALOG, Dlg_OnInitDialog);
        HANDLE_MSG(hDlg, WM_COMMAND, Dlg_OnCommand);

        default:
            fProcessed = FALSE;
            break;
    }
    return(fProcessed);
}


///////////////////////////////////////////////////////////
```

(continued)

Figure 14-4. *continued*

```
int WINAPI WinMain (HINSTANCE hinstExe,
   HINSTANCE hinstPrev, LPSTR lpszCmdLine, int nCmdShow) {
   DialogBox(hinstExe, MAKEINTRESOURCE(IDD_SEHEXCPT),
      NULL, Dlg_Proc);

   return(0);
}



///////////////////////// End Of File /////////////////////////
```

SEHEXCPT.RC

```
//Microsoft Visual C++ generated resource script.
//
#include "Resource.h"

#define APSTUDIO_READONLY_SYMBOLS
/////////////////////////////////////////////////////////////////////
//
// Generated from the TEXTINCLUDE 2 resource.
//
#include "afxres.h"


/////////////////////////////////////////////////////////////////////
#undef APSTUDIO_READONLY_SYMBOLS


#ifdef APSTUDIO_INVOKED
/////////////////////////////////////////////////////////////////////
//
// TEXTINCLUDE
//

1 TEXTINCLUDE DISCARDABLE
BEGIN
    "Resource.h\0"
END

2 TEXTINCLUDE DISCARDABLE
BEGIN
```

(continued)

Figure 14-4. *continued*

```
    "#include ""afxres.h""\r\n"
    "\0"
END

3 TEXTINCLUDE DISCARDABLE
BEGIN
    "\r\n"
    "\0"
END


/////////////////////////////////////////////////////////////////
#endif     // APSTUDIO_INVOKED


/////////////////////////////////////////////////////////////////
//
// Dialog
//

IDD_SEHEXCPT DIALOG DISCARDABLE  18, 18, 214, 200
STYLE WS_MINIMIZEBOX ¦ WS_VISIBLE ¦ WS_CAPTION ¦ WS_SYSMENU
CAPTION "SEH: Exception Filter/Handler Test"
FONT 8, "Helv"
BEGIN
    LTEXT           "Clicking Execute reserves an array of 50\
 4-KB structures and randomly writes to elements in the array.",
                    IDC_STATIC,4,8,188,24
    LTEXT           "&Number of writes to perform:",
                    IDC_STATIC,4,36,93,8
    EDITTEXT        IDC_NUMACCESSES,108,36,24,12
    PUSHBUTTON      "&Execute",IDD_SEHEXCPT,160,36,44,
                    14,WS_GROUP
    LTEXT           "Execution lo&g:",IDC_STATIC,4,56,48,8
    LISTBOX         IDC_LOG,4,68,204,128,NOT LBS_NOTIFY
                    ¦ WS_VSCROLL ¦
                    WS_GROUP ¦ WS_TABSTOP
END


/////////////////////////////////////////////////////////////////
//
// Icon
//

SEHEXCPT                ICON    DISCARDABLE     "SEHExcpt.Ico"

#ifndef APSTUDIO_INVOKED
```

(continued)

Figure 14-4. *continued*

```
////////////////////////////////////////////////////////////
//
// Generated from the TEXTINCLUDE 3 resource.
//


////////////////////////////////////////////////////////////
#endif     // not APSTUDIO_INVOKED
```

The SEH Sum Sample Application

The SEHSum (SEHSUM.EXE) sample application, listed in Figure 14-5 beginning on page 752, demonstrates how to use exception filters and exception handlers to recover gracefully from a stack overflow. The source code files, resource files, and make file for the application are in the SEHSUM.14 directory on the companion disc. You may want to review the section "A Thread's Stack" in Chapter 6 in order to fully understand how this application works.

The SEHSum application sums all of the numbers from 0 through x, where x is a number entered by the user. Of course, the simplest way to do this would be to create a function called *Sum* that simply performs the following calculation:

```
Sum = (x * (x + 1)) / 2;
```

For this sample, I have written the *Sum* function to be recursive.

When the program starts, it displays the dialog box shown below:

In this dialog box, you can enter a number in the edit control and then click on the Calculate button. This causes the program to create a new thread whose sole responsibility is to total all of the numbers between 0 and x. While the new thread is running, the program's primary thread tells the system not to schedule it any CPU time by calling *WaitForSingleObject*. When the new thread terminates, the system reschedules CPU time to the primary thread. The primary thread retrieves the

749

sum by getting the new thread's exit code through a call to *GetExitCode-Thread*. Finally—and this is extremely important—the primary thread closes its handle to the new thread so that the system can completely destroy the thread object and so that our application does not have a resource leak.

Now the primary thread examines the summation thread's exit code. If the exit code is UINT_MAX, it indicates that an error occurred—the summation thread overflowed the stack while totaling the numbers—and the primary thread will display a message box to this effect. If the exit code is not UINT_MAX, the summation thread completed successfully and the exit code is the summation. In this case, the primary thread will simply put the summation answer in the dialog box.

Now let's turn to the summation thread. The thread function for this thread is called *SumThreadFunc*. When this thread is created by the primary thread, it is passed the number of integers that it should total as its only parameter, *p*. The function then initializes the *uSum* variable to UINT_MAX, which means that the function is assuming that it will not complete successfully. Next *SumThreadFunc* sets up SEH so that it can catch any exception that might be raised while the thread executes. The recursive *Sum* function is then called in order to calculate the sum.

If the sum is calculated successfully, *SumThreadFunc* simply returns the value of the *uSum* variable; this is the thread's exit code. However, if an exception is raised while the *Sum* function is executing, the system will immediately evaluate the SEH filter expression. In other words, the system will call the *FilterFunc* function and pass it the code that identifies the raised exception. For a stack overflow exception, this code is EXCEPTION_STACK_OVERFLOW. If you want to see the program gracefully handle a stack overflow exception, tell the program to sum the first 44,000 numbers.

My *FilterFunc* function is very simple. It begins by assuming that it is not prepared to handle the type of exception that has been raised. When a filter does not know how to handle an exception, it should return EXCEPTION_CONTINUE_SEARCH. Then the filter should check to see whether the raised exception is EXCEPTION_STACK_OVERFLOW. If this is true, the filter should return EXCEPTION_EXECUTE_HANDLER. This indicates to the system that the filter was expecting this exception and that the code contained in the *except* block should execute. For this sample application, EXCEPTION_EXECUTE_HANDLER indicates that an error occurred while the thread was executing the *Sum* function and that the thread should simply exit returning UINT_MAX (the value in *uSumNum*) because I'm pretending that the *Sum* function was never called.

The last thing that I want to discuss is why I execute the *Sum* function in its own thread instead of just setting up an SEH block in the primary thread and calling the *Sum* function from within the *try* block. There are three reasons why I create this additional thread.

First, each time a thread is created, it gets its very own 1-MB stack region. If I called the *Sum* function from within the primary thread, some of the stack space would already be in use and the *Sum* function would not be able to use its full 1 MB of stack space. Granted, my sample is a very simple program and is probably not using all that much stack, but other programs will probably be more complicated. I can easily imagine a situation in which *Sum* might successfully total the integers from 0 through 1000; then, when *Sum* is called again later, the stack might be deeper, causing a stack overflow to occur when *Sum* is trying only to total the integers from 0 through 750. So to make the *Sum* function behave more consistently, I ensure that it has a full stack that has not been used by any other code.

The second reason for using a separate thread is that a thread is notified only once of a stack overflow exception. If I called the *Sum* function in the primary thread and a stack overflow occurred, the exception could be trapped and handled gracefully. However, at this point, all of the stack's reserved address space is committed with physical storage, and there are no more pages with the guard protection flag turned on. If the user performs another sum, the *Sum* function could overflow the stack and a stack overflow exception would not be raised. Instead, an access violation exception would be raised, and it would be too late to handle this situation gracefully.

The final reason for using a separate stack is so that the physical storage for the stack can be freed. Take this scenario as an example: The user asks the *Sum* function to calculate the sum of the integers from 0 through 30,000. This will require quite a bit of physical storage to be committed to the stack region. Then the user might do several summations in which the highest number is only 5000. In this case, there is a large amount of storage that is committed to the stack region but is no longer being used. This physical storage is allocated from the paging file. It's better to free this storage and give it back to the system and other processes. By having the *SumThreadFunc* thread terminate, the system automatically reclaims the physical storage that was committed to the stack's region.

SEHSum.ico

SEHSUM.C

```c
/****************************************************************
Module name: SEHSum.C
Notices: Copyright (c) 1995 Jeffrey Richter
****************************************************************/


#include "..\AdvWin32.H"      /* See Appendix B for details. */
#include <windows.h>
#include <windowsx.h>

#pragma warning(disable: 4001)        /* Single-line comment */

#include <limits.h>
#include <process.h>                  // For _beginthreadex
#include "Resource.H"


///////////////////////////////////////////////////////////////


// An example of calling Sum for uNum = 0 through 9
// uNum: 0 1 2 3  4  5  6  7  8  9 ...
// Sum:  0 1 3 6 10 15 21 28 36 45 ...
UINT Sum (UINT uNum) {

   if (uNum == 0)
      return(0);

   // Call Sum recursively.
   return(uNum + Sum(uNum - 1));
}


///////////////////////////////////////////////////////////////


long FilterFunc (DWORD dwExceptionCode) {

   // Assume that we do not know how to handle the exception;
   // tell the system to continue to search for an SEH
   // handler.
   long lRet = EXCEPTION_CONTINUE_SEARCH;
```

Figure 14-5.
The SEHSum application.

(continued)

Figure 14-5. *continued*

```
    if (dwExceptionCode == STATUS_STACK_OVERFLOW) {
       // If the exception raised is a stack overflow,
       // we do know how to handle it.
       lRet = EXCEPTION_EXECUTE_HANDLER;
    }

    return(lRet);
}


//////////////////////////////////////////////////////////////////


// The separate thread that is responsible for calculating the
// sum. I use a separate thread for the following reasons:
// 1. A separate thread gets its own 1 MB of stack space.
// 2. A thread can be notified of a stack overflow only once.
// 3. The stack's storage is freed when the thread exits.
DWORD WINAPI SumThreadFunc (PVOID p) {

    // The parameter, p, is really a UINT containing
    // the number of integers to sum.
    UINT uSumNum = (UINT) p;

    // uSum contains the summation of the numbers
    // from 0 through uSumNum. If the sum cannot be calculated,
    // a sum of UINT_MAX is returned.
    UINT uSum = UINT_MAX;

    __try {
       // To catch the stack overflow exception, we must
       // execute the Sum function while inside an SEH block.
       uSum = Sum(uSumNum);
    }
    __except (FilterFunc(GetExceptionCode())) {
       // If we get in here, it's because we have trapped
       // a stack overflow. We can now do whatever is
       // necessary to gracefully continue execution.
       // This sample application has nothing to do, so
       // no code is placed in this exception handler block.
    }
```

(continued)

Figure 14-5. *continued*

```
    // The thread's exit code is the sum of the first uSumNum
    // numbers, or UINT_MAX if a stack overflow occurred.
    return(uSum);
}


///////////////////////////////////////////////////////////////


BOOL Dlg_OnInitDialog (HWND hwnd, HWND hwndFocus,
    LPARAM lParam) {

    // Associate an icon with the dialog box.
    SetClassLong(hwnd, GCL_HICON, (LONG)
        LoadIcon((HINSTANCE) GetWindowLong(hwnd, GWL_HINSTANCE),
        __TEXT("Summation")));

    return(TRUE);
}


///////////////////////////////////////////////////////////////


void Dlg_OnCommand (HWND hwnd, int id,
    HWND hwndCtl, UINT codeNotify) {

    UINT uSumNum, uSum;
    BOOL fTranslated;
    DWORD dwThreadId;
    HANDLE hThread;

    switch (id) {
        case IDC_CALC:
            // Get the number of integers the user wants to sum.
            uSumNum = GetDlgItemInt(hwnd, IDC_SUMNUM,
                &fTranslated, FALSE);

            // Create a thread (with its own stack) that is
            // responsible for performing the summation.
            hThread = BEGINTHREADEX(NULL, 0, SumThreadFunc,
                (PVOID) uSumNum, 0, &dwThreadId);

            // The thread's exit code is the resulting summation.
```

(continued)

Figure 14-5. *continued*

```
        // We must first wait for the thread to terminate.
        WaitForSingleObject(hThread, INFINITE);

        // Now we can get the thread's exit code.
        GetExitCodeThread(hThread, (PDWORD) &uSum);

        // Finally, we close the handle to the thread so
        // that the system can destroy the thread object.
        CloseHandle(hThread);

        // Update the dialog box to show the result.
        if (uSum == UINT_MAX) {
            // If the thread's exit code is UINT_MAX, a stack
            // overflow occurred. Update the dialog box
            // and display a message box.
            SetDlgItemText(hwnd, IDC_ANSWER, __TEXT("Error"));
            MessageBox(GetFocus(),
                __TEXT("Summation could not be calculated"),
                NULL, MB_OK);
        } else {
            // The sum was calculated successfully;
            // update the dialog box.
            SetDlgItemInt(hwnd, IDC_ANSWER, uSum, FALSE);
        }

        break;

    case IDCANCEL:
        EndDialog(hwnd, id);
        break;
    }
}


//////////////////////////////////////////////////////////////////


BOOL CALLBACK Dlg_Proc (HWND hDlg, UINT uMsg,
    WPARAM wParam, LPARAM lParam) {

    BOOL fProcessed = TRUE;

    switch (uMsg) {
        HANDLE_MSG(hDlg, WM_INITDIALOG, Dlg_OnInitDialog);
        HANDLE_MSG(hDlg, WM_COMMAND, Dlg_OnCommand);
```

(continued)

Figure 14-5. *continued*

```
        default:
            fProcessed = FALSE;
            break;
    }

    return(fProcessed);
}



//////////////////////////////////////////////////////////////////////



int WINAPI WinMain (HINSTANCE hinstExe,
    HINSTANCE hinstPrev, LPSTR lpszCmdLine, int nCmdShow) {

    DialogBox(hinstExe, MAKEINTRESOURCE(IDD_SUMMATION),
        NULL, Dlg_Proc);

    return(0);
}



///////////////////////// End Of File /////////////////////////
```

SEHSUM.RC

```
//Microsoft App Studio generated resource script.
//
#include "Resource.h"

#define APSTUDIO_READONLY_SYMBOLS
//////////////////////////////////////////////////////////////////////
//
// Generated from the TEXTINCLUDE 2 resource.
//
#define APSTUDIO_HIDDEN_SYMBOLS
#include "windows.h"
#undef APSTUDIO_HIDDEN_SYMBOLS


//////////////////////////////////////////////////////////////////////
#undef APSTUDIO_READONLY_SYMBOLS
```

(continued)

Figure 14-5. *continued*

```
////////////////////////////////////////////////////////////////
//
// Icon
//

SUMMATION                     ICON    DISCARDABLE     "SEHSum.ICO"

////////////////////////////////////////////////////////////////
//
// Dialog
//

IDD_SUMMATION DIALOG DISCARDABLE  18, 18, 236, 40
STYLE WS_POPUP ¦ WS_CAPTION ¦ WS_SYSMENU
CAPTION "Summation"
FONT 8, "System"
BEGIN
    LTEXT           "Calculate the sum of the numbers from 0\
  through &x, where x is: ",
                    IDC_STATIC,4,4,188,12
    EDITTEXT        IDC_SUMNUM,192,4,40,13,ES_AUTOHSCROLL
    DEFPUSHBUTTON   "&Calculate",IDC_CALC,4,16,56,16
    LTEXT           "Answer:",IDC_STATIC,68,20,30,8
    LTEXT           "?",IDC_ANSWER,104,20,56,8
END

#ifdef APSTUDIO_INVOKED
////////////////////////////////////////////////////////////////
//
// TEXTINCLUDE
//

1 TEXTINCLUDE DISCARDABLE
BEGIN
    "Resource.h\0"
END

2 TEXTINCLUDE DISCARDABLE
BEGIN
    "#define APSTUDIO_HIDDEN_SYMBOLS\r\n"
    "#include ""windows.h""\r\n"
    "#undef APSTUDIO_HIDDEN_SYMBOLS\r\n"
    "#include ""sum.h""\r\n"
    "\0"
END
```

(continued)

Figure 14-5. *continued*

```
3 TEXTINCLUDE DISCARDABLE
BEGIN
    "\r\n"
    "\0"
END


/////////////////////////////////////////////////////////////////
#endif    // APSTUDIO_INVOKED


#ifndef APSTUDIO_INVOKED
/////////////////////////////////////////////////////////////////
//
// Generated from the TEXTINCLUDE 3 resource.
//


/////////////////////////////////////////////////////////////////
#endif    // not APSTUDIO_INVOKED
```

Software Exceptions

So far we have been looking at handling hardware exceptions in which the CPU catches an event and raises an exception. Often it's useful to raise software exceptions in which the operating system or your application raises its own exceptions. The *HeapAlloc* function provides a good occasion for software exception use. When you call the *HeapAlloc* function, you can specify the HEAP_GENERATE_EXCEPTIONS flag. Then, if *HeapAlloc* is unable to satisfy the memory request, *HeapAlloc* generates a STATUS_NO_MEMORY software exception.

If you want to take advantage of this exception, you can code your *try* block as though the memory allocation will always succeed and then, if the allocation fails, you can either handle the exception by using an *except* block or have your function clean up by matching the *try* block with a *finally* block.

Your application doesn't need to know whether it is processing a hardware exception or a software exception, and you implement your *try-finally* and *try-except* blocks identically. However, you can have portions of your code raise software exceptions themselves, just as *HeapAlloc* does. To raise a software exception in your code, call the *RaiseException* function:

```
VOID RaiseException(DWORD dwExceptionCode, DWORD dwExceptionFlags,
   DWORD cArguments, LPDWORD lpArguments);
```

The first parameter, *dwExceptionCode*, must be a value that identifies the raised exception. The *HeapAlloc* function passes STATUS_NO_MEM-ORY for this parameter. If you raise your own exception identifiers, you should follow the same format as the standard Win32 error codes as defined in the WINERROR.H file. You'll recall that each DWORD is divided as shown in this table:

Bits:	31–30	29–28	27–16	15–0
Contents:	Severity	Flags	Facility code	Exception code
Meaning:	0 = Success	Bit 29	Programmer-defined	Programmer-defined
	1 = Informational	0 = Microsoft		
	2 = Warning	1 = Customer		
	3 = Error	Bit 28 is reserved (must be 0)		

If you create your own exception code, fill out all four fields of the DWORD: bits 31 and 30 should contain the severity, bit 29 should be 1 (0 is reserved for Microsoft-created exceptions, such as *HeapAlloc*'s STATUS_NO_MEMORY), bit 28 should be 0, and bits 27 through 16 and bits 15 through 0 should be arbitrary values that you choose to iden-tify the section of your application that raised the exception.

RaiseException's second parameter, *dwExceptionFlags*, must be either 0 or EXCEPTION_NONCONTINUABLE. Specifying the EXCEPTION-_NONCONTINUABLE flag tells the system that the type of exception you are raising can't be continued. The EXCEPTION_NONCONTINU-ABLE flag is used internally in the operating system to signal fatal (nonrecoverable) errors.

When *HeapAlloc* raises the STATUS_NO_MEMORY exception, it uses the EXCEPTION_NONCONTINUABLE flag to tell the system that this exception cannot be continued and that it is illegal for an exception filter to evaluate to EXCEPTION_CONTINUE_EXECUTION. If this type of exception is raised and an exception filter does evaluate to

EXCEPTION_CONTINUE_EXECUTION, the system raises a new exception: EXCEPTION_NONCONTINUABLE_ EXCEPTION.

That's right—it is possible for an exception to be raised while the application is trying to process another exception. This of course makes sense. While we're at it, let's note that it's also possible for an invalid memory access to occur inside a *finally* block, an exception filter, or an exception handler. When this happens, the system stacks exceptions. Remember the *GetExceptionInformation* function? This function returns the address of an EXCEPTION_POINTERS structure. The *Exception-Record* member of the EXCEPTION_POINTERS structure points to an EXCEPTION_RECORD structure that contains another *ExceptionRecord* member. This member is a pointer to another EXCEPTION_RECORD, which contains information about the previously raised exception.

Usually the system is processing only one exception at a time and the *ExceptionRecord* member is NULL. However, if during the processing of one exception another exception is raised, the first EXCEPTION-_RECORD structure contains information about the most recently raised exception and the *ExceptionRecord* member of this first EXCEP-TION_RECORD structure points to the EXCEPTION_ RECORD structure for the previously raised exception. If additional exceptions have not been completely processed, you can continue to walk this linked list of EXCEPTION_RECORD structures to determine how to handle the exception.

RaiseException's third and fourth parameters, *cArguments* and *lpArguments*, are used to pass additional information about the generated exception. If you don't need additional arguments, you can pass NULL to *lpArguments*, in which case *RaiseException* ignores the *cArguments* parameter. If you do want to pass additional arguments, the *cArguments* parameter must indicate the number of elements in the DWORD array pointed to by the *lpArguments* parameter. This parameter cannot exceed EXCEPTION_MAXIMUM_PARAMETERS, which is defined in WINNT.H as 15.

During the processing of this exception, you can have an exception filter refer to the *NumberParameters* and *ExceptionInformation* members of the EXCEPTION_RECORD structure to examine the information in the *cArguments* and *lpArguments* parameters.

You might want to generate your own software exceptions in your application for any of several reasons. For example, you might want to send informational messages to the system's event log. Whenever a function in your application sensed some sort of problem, you could call *RaiseException* and have some exception handler further up the call tree look for certain exceptions and either add them to the event log or pop up a message box. You might also want to create software exceptions to signal internal fatal errors in your application. This would be much easier than trying to return error values all the way up the call tree.

The SEH Software Exceptions Sample Application

The SEHSoft (SEHSOFT.EXE) application, listed in Figure 14-6 beginning on page 764, demonstrates how to create and use your own software exceptions. The source code files, resource files, and make file for the application are in the SEHSOFT.14 directory on the companion disc. The program is based on the earlier SEHExcpt sample program. When you invoke SEHSoft, this dialog box appears:

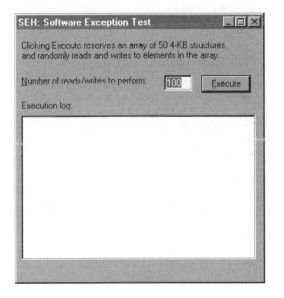

This box is similar to SEHExcpt's dialog box, but this program will try to read from as well as write to the array of elements.

In the *Dlg_ReserveArrayAndAccessIt* function, the access loop gets the index of a random element to access; it has been modified to then select another random number. This second number is used to determine whether the program should try to write the element to the array or read the element from the array.

You might be asking yourself what it means to read an element from the array if the array has never been initialized. You'd be quite correct to ask this. I have enhanced the program to automatically zero the contents of an array element when memory is committed because the program has tried to read an array element. I did this by raising a software exception.

Inside the *ExpFilter* function, instead of just calling *CommitMemory* as I did in SEHEXCPT.C, I put the call to *CommitMemory* into a *try* block. The filter expression for the *except* block associated with this *try* block checks whether the call to *CommitMemory* has generated an exception and whether that exception code is SE_ZERO_ELEM.

SE_ZERO_ELEM is a *#define* that identifies a software exception code I have created at the top of SEHSOFT.C:

```
// Useful macro for creating our own software exception codes
#define MAKESOFTWAREEXCEPTION(Severity, Facility, Exception) \
   ((DWORD) ( \
   /* Severity code */        (Severity << 30) ¦    \
   /* MS(0) or Cust(1) */     (1         << 29) ¦    \
   /* Reserved(0) */          (0         << 28) ¦    \
   /* Facility code */        (Facility  << 16) ¦    \
   /* Exception code */       (Exception <<  0)))

// Our very own software exception. This exception is raised
// when an element of the array needs to be initialized
// to all zeros.
#define SE_ZERO_ELEM    MAKESOFTWAREEXCEPTION(3, 0, 1)
```

The exception filter expression looks like this:

```
__except ((GetExceptionCode() == SE_ZERO_ELEM) ?
   (SavedExceptRec =
      *((GetExceptionInformation())->ExceptionRecord),
   EXCEPTION_EXECUTE_HANDLER) :
   EXCEPTION_CONTINUE_SEARCH) {
   :
   :
}
```

The exception handler is prepared to handle only SE_ZERO_ELEM exceptions. If *GetExceptionCode* returns any other exception, EXCEPTION_CONTINUE_SEARCH is returned. If the exception code is SE_ZERO_ELEM, EXCEPTION_EXECUTE_HANDLER should be returned so that the code inside the *except* block will be executed. But the code inside the *except* block will need access to the exception information, so a call to *GetExceptionInformation* is made before the return. EXCEPTION_EXECUTE_HANDLER and the information inside the EXCEPTION_RECORD structure are stored in the local *SavedExceptRec* variable.

Now that the code inside the *except* block is executing, it gets the address of the array element that needs to be zeroed by looking into the SavedExceptRec structure and calls *memset* to zero this one array element.

The only thing that I've left out is how the exception is generated. The code appears at the bottom of the *CommitMemory* function:

```
if (!fAttemptedWrite) {
    // The program is trying to read an array element
    // that has never been created. We'll raise our very own
    // software exception so that this array element will be
    // zeroed before it is accessed.
    RaiseException(SE_ZERO_ELEM, 0, 1, (LPDWORD) &lpAttemptedAddr);
}
```

If the attempted access is a read, the program calls *RaiseException*, passing it a SE_ZERO_ELEM software exception code and a 0 flag. We can also pass, using the third and fourth arguments, a maximum of EXCEPTION_MAXIMUM_PARAMETERS (15) parameters to the exception filter. In this example, I want to pass just one parameter to the filter: the address to the array element that needs to be zeroed. To do this, I send 1 as the third argument to *RaiseException* and the address to that parameter as the fourth argument.

Here is an example of what SEHSoft looks like when it's executed:

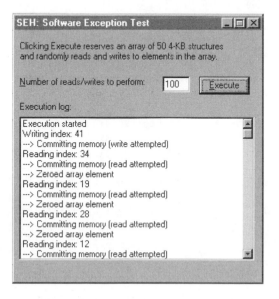

Every time the software exception is raised, the exception handler adds an entry to the Execution Log showing that it zeroed the array element.

SEHSoft.ico

SEHSOFT.C

```
/**************************************************************
Module name: SEHSoft.C
Notices: Copyright (c) 1995 Jeffrey Richter
**************************************************************/


#include "..\AdvWin32.H"    /* See Appendix B for details. */
#include <windows.h>
#include <windowsx.h>

#pragma warning(disable: 4001)       /* Single-line comment */

#include <tchar.h>
#include <stdio.h>               // For sprintf
#include <stdlib.h>              // For rand
#include "Resource.H"


//////////////////////////////////////////////////////////////


#define NUMELEMENTS       (50)

// Declare each array element to be 4 KB.
typedef struct {
   BYTE bReserved[4 * 1024];
} ELEMENT, *LPELEMENT;

// Useful macro for creating our own software exception codes
#define MAKESOFTWAREEXCEPTION(Severity, Facility, Exception) \
   ((DWORD) ( \
   /* Severity code */     (Severity  << 30) |       \
   /* MS(0) or Cust(1) */  (1         << 29) |       \
   /* Reserved(0) */       (0         << 28) |       \
   /* Facility code */     (Facility  << 16) |       \
   /* Exception code */    (Exception <<  0)))

// Our very own software exception. This exception is raised
// when an element of the array needs to be initialized
// to all zeros.
#define SE_ZERO_ELEM   MAKESOFTWAREEXCEPTION(3, 0, 1)
```

Figure 14-6. *(continued)*
The SEHSoft application.

Figure 14-6. *continued*

```
///////////////////////////////////////////////////////////


void CommitMemory(HWND hwndLog, LPEXCEPTION_POINTERS lpEP,
   LPBYTE lpbAttemptedAddr) {

   BOOL fAttemptedWrite;
   TCHAR szBuf[100];

   // Find out whether a memory read or write was tried.
   fAttemptedWrite = (BOOL)
      lpEP->ExceptionRecord->ExceptionInformation[0];

   // Add an entry to the Execution Log list box.
   _stprintf(szBuf,
      __TEXT("---> Committing memory (%s attempted)"),
      fAttemptedWrite ? __TEXT("write") : __TEXT("read"));
   ListBox_AddString(hwndLog, szBuf);

   // The attempted memory access did occur while the
   // program was accessing an element in our array.
   // Let's try to commit memory to an individual element
   // of the reserved array's address space.
   VirtualAlloc(lpbAttemptedAddr, sizeof(ELEMENT),
      MEM_COMMIT, PAGE_READWRITE);

   if (!fAttemptedWrite) {
      // The program is trying to read an array element
      // that has never been created. We'll raise our very
      // own software exception so that this array element
      // will be zeroed before it is accessed.
      RaiseException(SE_ZERO_ELEM, 0, 1,
         (LPDWORD) &lpbAttemptedAddr);
   }
}


///////////////////////////////////////////////////////////


int ExpFilter (LPEXCEPTION_POINTERS lpEP, LPBYTE lpbArray,
   LONG lNumBytesInArray, HWND hwndLog) {

   LPBYTE lpbAttemptedAddr = NULL;
```

(continued)

Figure 14-6. *continued*

```
// Get the exception code explaining
// why the filter is executing.
DWORD dwExceptionCode = lpEP->ExceptionRecord->ExceptionCode;

// Assume that this filter will NOT handle the exception
// and will let the system continue scanning
// for other filters.
int nFilterResult = EXCEPTION_CONTINUE_SEARCH;

__try {
   // Declare an EXCEPTION_RECORD structure that is local
   // to this __try frame. This variable is used in the
   // __except block below.
   EXCEPTION_RECORD SavedExceptRec;

   // We must first determine whether the exception is
   // occurring because of a memory access to our array of
   // elements. This filter and handler do not process
   // any other types of exceptions.

   if (dwExceptionCode != EXCEPTION_ACCESS_VIOLATION) {
      // If the exception is not a memory access violation,
      // the exception did not occur because of an array
      // element access. The system should continue its
      // search for another exception filter.
      nFilterResult = EXCEPTION_CONTINUE_SEARCH;
      __leave;
   }

   if (lpbArray == NULL) {
      // The exception occurred either before the program
      // tried to reserve the address space, or else the
      // array's address space was unsuccessfully reserved.
      nFilterResult = EXCEPTION_CONTINUE_SEARCH;
      __leave;
   }

   // Get the address of the attempted memory access.
   lpbAttemptedAddr = (LPBYTE)
      lpEP->ExceptionRecord->ExceptionInformation[1];

   if ((lpbAttemptedAddr < lpbArray) ||
      ((lpbArray + lNumBytesInArray) < lpbAttemptedAddr)) {
      // Address attempted is BELOW the beginning of the
      // array's reserved space or is ABOVE the end of the
```

(continued)

Figure 14-6. *continued*

```
            // array's reserved space. We'll let some other
            // filter handle this exception.
            nFilterResult = EXCEPTION_CONTINUE_SEARCH;
            __leave;
         }


         // *** The exception is to be handled by this filter.

         __try {
            // Call the function that commits memory to the
            // accessed array element. This function will raise
            // a software exception if read access was attempted.
            // In this case, we want to zero the contents of the
            // array element before the read continues.
            CommitMemory(hwndLog, lpEP, lpbAttemptedAddr);
         }

         // We want to handle the exception only if it is our
         // very own software exception telling us to zero the
         // contents of the array element. If this is the case, we
         // need to save the additional information given to us
         // with the SE_ZERO_ELEM exception code so that the
         // handler knows which array element to zero.
         __except ((GetExceptionCode() == SE_ZERO_ELEM) ?
            (SavedExceptRec =
               *((GetExceptionInformation())->ExceptionRecord),
            EXCEPTION_EXECUTE_HANDLER) :
            EXCEPTION_CONTINUE_SEARCH) {

            // Get the address of the array element to zero.
            LPELEMENT lpArrayElementToZero = (LPELEMENT)
               SavedExceptRec.ExceptionInformation[0];

            // Zero the array element before reading from it.
            memset((LPVOID) lpArrayElementToZero, 0,
               sizeof(ELEMENT));

            ListBox_AddString(hwndLog,
               __TEXT("---> Zeroed array element"));
         }

         // Memory is committed now; let's restart the
         // instruction that caused the exception in the first
         // place. This time, it will succeed and not cause
         // another exception.
```

(continued)

Figure 14-6. *continued*

```
      nFilterResult = EXCEPTION_CONTINUE_EXECUTION;
   }

   __finally {
   }

   // Now that memory is committed, we can continue execution
   // on the instruction that generated the exception in
   // the first place.
   return(nFilterResult);
}


///////////////////////////////////////////////////////////////

void Dlg_ReserveArrayAndAccessIt (HWND hwndLog,
   int nNumAccesses) {

   LPELEMENT lpArray = NULL;
   ELEMENT Element;
   TCHAR szBuf[100];
   int nElementNum = 0;
   const LONG lNumBytesInArray = sizeof(ELEMENT) *
      NUMELEMENTS;

   // Clear the Execution Log list box.
   ListBox_ResetContent(hwndLog);
   ListBox_AddString(hwndLog, __TEXT("Execution started"));

   __try {
      // Reserve an address space large enough to
      // hold NUMELEMENTS number of ELEMENTs.
      lpArray = VirtualAlloc(NULL, lNumBytesInArray,
         MEM_RESERVE, PAGE_NOACCESS);

      while (nNumAccesses--) {
         // Get the index of a random element to access.
         nElementNum = rand() % NUMELEMENTS;

         // Give us a 50 percent chance of reading and a
         // 50 percent chance of writing.
         if ((rand() % 2) == 0) {
            // Attempt a read access.
            _stprintf(szBuf, __TEXT("Reading index: %d"),
               nElementNum);
```

(continued)

Figure 14-6. *continued*

```
          ListBox_AddString(hwndLog, szBuf);

          // The exception will occur on this line.
          Element = lpArray[nElementNum];

      } else {

          // Attempt a write access.
          stprintf(szBuf, __TEXT("Writing index: %d"),
            nElementNum);
          ListBox_AddString(hwndLog, szBuf);

          // The exception will occur on this line.
          lpArray[nElementNum] = Element;
      }

   }  // while

   // We have finished the execution.
   ListBox_AddString(hwndLog, __TEXT("Execution ended"));

   // Decommit and free the array of ELEMENTs.
   VirtualFree(lpArray, 0, MEM_RELEASE);
   }  // __try

   __except (
      ExpFilter(GetExceptionInformation(), (LPBYTE) lpArray,
         lNumBytesInArray, hwndLog)) {

      // Because the filter never returns
      // EXCEPTION_EXECUTE_HANDLER, there is
      // nothing to do here.

   }  // __except
}


///////////////////////////////////////////////////////////////


BOOL Dlg_OnInitDialog (HWND hwnd, HWND hwndFocus,
   LPARAM lParam) {

   // Associate an icon with the dialog box.
```

(continued)

Figure 14-6. *continued*

```
    SetClassLong(hwnd, GCL_HICON, (LONG)
        LoadIcon((HINSTANCE) GetWindowLong(hwnd, GWL_HINSTANCE),
        __TEXT("SEHSoft")));

    // Default the number of accesses to 100.
    SetDlgItemInt(hwnd, IDC_NUMACCESSES, 100, FALSE);
    return(TRUE);
}


///////////////////////////////////////////////////////////////


void Dlg_OnCommand (HWND hwnd, int id,
    HWND hwndCtl, UINT codeNotify) {

    int  nNumAccesses;
    BOOL fTranslated;

    switch (id) {
      case IDOK:
        nNumAccesses = GetDlgItemInt(hwnd, IDC_NUMACCESSES,
            &fTranslated, FALSE);

        if (fTranslated) {
          Dlg_ReserveArrayAndAccessIt(
            GetDlgItem(hwnd, IDC_LOG), nNumAccesses);
        } else {
          MessageBox(hwnd,
            __TEXT("Invalid number of accesses."),
            __TEXT("SEHSoft"), MB_OK);
        }
        break;

      case IDCANCEL:
        EndDialog(hwnd, id);
        break;
    }
}


///////////////////////////////////////////////////////////////


BOOL CALLBACK Dlg_Proc (HWND hDlg, UINT uMsg,
    WPARAM wParam, LPARAM lParam) {
```

(continued)

Figure 14-6. *continued*

```
    BOOL fProcessed = TRUE;

    switch (uMsg) {
        HANDLE_MSG(hDlg, WM_INITDIALOG, Dlg_OnInitDialog);
        HANDLE_MSG(hDlg, WM_COMMAND, Dlg_OnCommand);

        default:
            fProcessed = FALSE;
            break;
    }
    return(fProcessed);
}


//////////////////////////////////////////////////////////////////


int WINAPI WinMain (HINSTANCE hinstExe,
    HINSTANCE hinstPrev, LPSTR lpszCmdline, int nCmdShow) {

    DialogBox(hinstExe, MAKEINTRESOURCE(IDD_SEHSOFT),
        NULL, Dlg_Proc);

    return(0);
}


//////////////////////// End Of File ////////////////////////
```

SEHSOFT.RC

```
//Microsoft Visual C++ generated resource script.
//
#include "Resource.h"

#define APSTUDIO_READONLY_SYMBOLS
//////////////////////////////////////////////////////////////////
//
// Generated from the TEXTINCLUDE 2 resource.
//
#include "afxres.h"


//////////////////////////////////////////////////////////////////
#undef APSTUDIO_READONLY_SYMBOLS
```

(continued)

Figure 14-6. *continued*

```
#ifdef APSTUDIO_INVOKED
///////////////////////////////////////////////////////////////
//
// TEXTINCLUDE
//

1 TEXTINCLUDE DISCARDABLE
BEGIN
    "Resource.h\0"
END

2 TEXTINCLUDE DISCARDABLE
BEGIN
    "#include ""afxres.h""\r\n"
    "\0"
END

3 TEXTINCLUDE DISCARDABLE
BEGIN
    "\r\n"
    "\0"
END


///////////////////////////////////////////////////////////////
#endif    // APSTUDIO_INVOKED


///////////////////////////////////////////////////////////////
//
// Dialog
//

IDD_SEHSOFT DIALOG DISCARDABLE  18, 18, 214, 200
STYLE WS_MINIMIZEBOX | WS_VISIBLE | WS_CAPTION | WS_SYSMENU
CAPTION "SEH: Software Exception Test"
FONT 8, "Helv"
BEGIN
    LTEXT           "Clicking Execute reserves an array of 50\
 4-KB structures and randomly reads and writes to elements\
 in the array.",
                    IDC_STATIC,4,8,188,24
    LTEXT           "&Number of reads/writes to perform:",
                    IDC_STATIC,4,36,
                    114,8
    EDITTEXT        IDC_NUMACCESSES,128,36,24,12
    PUSHBUTTON      "&Execute",IDOK,160,36,44,14,WS_GROUP
```

(continued)

Figure 14-6. *continued*

```
      LTEXT           "Execution lo&g:",IDC_STATIC,4,56,48,8
      LISTBOX         IDC_LOG,4,68,204,128,NOT LBS_NOTIFY
                      ¦ WS_VSCROLL ¦ WS_GROUP ¦ WS_TABSTOP
  END


  //////////////////////////////////////////////////////////////////
  //
  // Icon
  //

  SEHSOFT               ICON    DISCARDABLE     "SEHSoft.Ico"

  #ifndef APSTUDIO_INVOKED
  //////////////////////////////////////////////////////////////////
  //
  // Generated from the TEXTINCLUDE 3 resource.
  //


  //////////////////////////////////////////////////////////////////
  #endif    // not APSTUDIO_INVOKED
```

Unhandled Exceptions

All through this chapter, I've been pointing out that, when an exception is raised, the system tries to locate an exception filter that is willing to handle the exception. This is true, but it's actually not the first thing the system does when an exception occurs. When an exception is raised, the system first checks to see whether the process is attached to a debugger. If the process isn't attached to a debugger, the system then scans for exception filters.

If the process is being debugged, the system sends a debugging event to the debugger and fills out this EXCEPTION_DEBUG_INFO structure:

```
typedef struct _EXCEPTION_DEBUG_INFO {
   EXCEPTION_RECORD ExceptionRecord;
   DWORD dwFirstChance;
} EXCEPTION_DEBUG_INFO;
```

The EXCEPTION_DEBUG_INFO structure tells the debugger that an exception has occurred. The *ExceptionRecord* member contains the same information you would get by calling the *GetExceptionInformation* function. The debugger can use this information to determine how it wants to handle the exception. The *dwFirstChance* member will be set to nonzero. Typically, a debugger will be written to process breakpoint and single-step exceptions and can thus stop these exceptions from percolating up through your thread.

If a debugger is monitoring the process and handles the exception, the process is allowed to continue processing. The debugger can also decide to freeze the threads in the process and allow you to inspect the reason for the generated exception.

If the debugger doesn't handle the exception, the system scans your thread in search of an exception filter that returns either EXCEPTION_EXECUTE_HANDLER or EXCEPTION_CONTINUE-_EXECUTION. As soon as an exception filter returns one of these identifiers, execution continues as described for each identifier earlier in this chapter.

If the system reaches the top of the thread without locating an exception filter to handle the exception, the system notifies the debugger again. This time, the *dwFirstChance* member in the EXCEPTION-_DEBUG_INFO structure will be 0. The debugger can tell from this value that an unhandled exception occurred in one of the process's threads; the debugger will display a message box notifying you of this unhandled exception and will allow you to start debugging the process.

Unhandled Exceptions Without a Debugger Attached

But let's look at what happens if every exception filter returns EXCEPTION_CONTINUE_SEARCH when your process is not being debugged. In this case, the system traverses all the way to the top of the thread without finding an exception filter willing to handle the exception. When this happens, the system uses the SEH frame that was initialized in the system's *StartOfThread* function (see page 56 in Chapter 3) to call a built-in exception filter function called *UnhandledExceptionFilter*:

```
LONG UnhandledExceptionFilter(
    LPEXCEPTION_POINTERS lpexpExceptionInfo);
```

The first thing that this function does is check whether the process is being debugged; if so, *UnhandledExceptionFilter* returns EXCEPTION-_CONTINUE_SEARCH, which causes the debugger to be notified of the exception.

If the process is not being debugged, the function displays a message box notifying the user that an exception occurred in the process. This message box looks similar to the following on Windows 95:

On Windows NT, it looks like this:

In the Windows NT message box, the first paragraph of text indicates which exception occurred and the address of the instruction in the process's address space that generated the exception. It just so happens that a memory access violation caused this message box to appear, so the system can report the invalid memory address that was accessed and specify that the attempted access was for reading. The *UnhandledExceptionFilter* function gets this additional information by referencing the *ExceptionInformation* member of the EXCEPTION_RECORD structure generated for this exception.

Following the description of the exception, the message box indicates the user's two choices. The first is to click on the OK button, which

causes *UnhandledExceptionFilter* to return EXCEPTION_EXECUTE_HAN-
DLER. This causes the system to execute a built-in exception handler
that terminates the process by calling:

```
ExitProcess(GetExceptionCode());
```

The second choice, clicking on the Cancel button, is a developer's
dream come true. When you click on the Cancel button, *Unhandled-
ExceptionFilter* attempts to load a debugger and attach the debugger to
the process. With the debugger attached to the process, you can examine the state of variables, set breakpoints, restart the process, and do anything else you would normally do when you debug a process.

The real boon is that you can handle the failure of your application
when it occurs. Under most other operating systems, you must invoke
your application through the debugger in order to debug it. If an exception occurs in a process on one of these other operating systems, you
have to terminate the process, start a debugger, and invoke the application again using the debugger. The problem is that you would have to
try to reproduce the bug before you could fix it. And who knows what
the values of the different variables were when the problem originally
occurred? It's much harder to resolve a bug this way. The ability to
dynamically attach a debugger to a process as it's running is one of
Win32's best features.

UnhandledExceptionFilter invokes the debugger by looking into the
Registry. Specifically, the key contains the command line that *Unhandled-
ExceptionFilter* executes:

```
HKEY_LOCAL_MACHINE\SOFTWARE\Microsoft\
   Windows NT\CurrentVersion\AeDebug\Debugger
```

When you install Visual C++ 2.0, the value of this key is set to:

```
F:\MSVC\BIN\MSVC.EXE -p %ld -e %ld
```

This line tells the system which program to run (MSVC.EXE) and where
to find it (in F:\MSVC\BIN on my machine). *UnhandledExceptionFilter*
also passes two parameters on the command line to MSVC.EXE. The
first parameter is the ID of the process that is to be debugged. The second parameter identifies an inheritable manual-reset event that was created in the nonsignaled state by the *UnhandledExceptionFilter* function.
MSVC recognizes the *-p* and *-e* switches as identifying the process ID and
the event handle.

After the process ID and event handle are parsed into the string,
UnhandledExceptionFilter executes the debugger by calling *CreateProcess*

and waits for the manual-reset event to become signaled. The debugger can then attach itself to the process by calling *DebugActiveProcess* and passing it the ID of the process to be debugged:

```
BOOL DebugActiveProcess(DWORD idProcess);
```

When the debugger attaches to the process, the system sends debug events back to the debugger so that the debugger is aware of the process's state. For example, the system sends information about active threads in the process and about dynamic-link libraries mapped into the process's address space.

While the system is bringing the debugger up-to-date, all the threads in the debuggee are suspended, still waiting for the manual-reset event to become signaled. When the debugger is ready to let you debug the process, it calls the *SetEvent* function, passing the handle of the manual-reset event. The debugger can use the event's handle value directly because the event was created so that it could be inherited by any child processes of the debuggee. And because the *Unhandled ExceptionFilter* function in the process called *CreateProcess* to invoke the debugger, the debugger is a child of the process.

When the debuggee sees that the manual-reset event has become signaled, it wakes up, and *UnhandledExceptionFilter* returns EXCEP TION_CONTINUE_SEARCH. Returning EXCEPTION_CONTINUE-_SEARCH causes the unhandled exception to be filtered up again. This time, the process is being debugged, and the debugger will be notified of the exception.

Turning Off the Exception Message Box

There may be times when you don't want the exception message box to be displayed if an exception occurs. For example, you might not want the message box to appear in the shipping version of your product. If it did appear, it could easily lead an end user to accidentally start debugging your application. An end user needs only to click on the Cancel button in the message box to enter unfamiliar, scary territory—the debugger. There are several methods you can use to prevent this message box from appearing.

To prevent *UnhandledExceptionFilter* from displaying the exception message box, you can call the *SetErrorMode* function,

```
UINT SetErrorMode(UINT fuErrorMode);
```

passing it the SEM_NOGPFAULTERRORBOX identifier. Then, when *UnhandledExceptionFilter* is called to handle the exception, it simply terminates your application. The user is given no warning; the application just goes away.

Another method you can use to disable the message box is to place a *try-except* block around the entire contents of your *WinMain* function. Make sure that the exception filter always evaluates to EXCEPTION-_EXECUTE_HANDLER so that the exception is handled, preventing the system from calling the *UnhandledExceptionFilter* function. In *WinMain*'s exception handler, you can display a dialog box with some diagnostic information. The user can copy the information and report it to your customer service lines to help you track the sources of problems in your application. You should create the dialog box so that the user can only terminate the application and not invoke the debugger.

The problem with this method is that it catches only exceptions that occur in your process's primary thread. If any other threads are running, and an unhandled exception occurs in one of these threads, the system calls the built-in *UnhandledExceptionFilter* function. To fix this, you would need to include *try-except* blocks before all the thread functions in your code and in the *WinMain* function.

Because it is so easy to forget this when writing new code, Microsoft added another Win32 function, *SetUnhandledExceptionFilter*, to help you:

```
LPTOP_LEVEL_EXCEPTION_FILTER SetUnhandledExceptionFilter(
    LPTOP_LEVEL_EXCEPTION_FILTER lpTopLevelExceptionFilter);
```

After your process calls this function, an unhandled exception occurring in any of your process's threads causes your own exception filter to be called. You need to pass the address of this filter as the only parameter to *SetUnhandledExceptionFilter*. The prototype of this function looks like this:

```
LONG UnhandledExceptionFilter(
    LPEXCEPTION_POINTERS lpexpExceptionInfo);
```

You'll notice that this function is identical in form to the *Unhandled-ExceptionFilter* function. You can perform any processing you desire in your exception filter as long as you return one of the three EXCEP-TION_* identifiers. The following table shows what happens when each identifier is returned:

Identifier	What Happens
EXCEPTION_EXECUTE_HANDLER	The process simply terminates because the system doesn't perform any action in its exception handler block.
EXCEPTION_CONTINUE_EXECUTION	Execution continues at the instruction that raised the exception. You can modify the exception information referenced by the LPEXCEPTION_POINTERS parameter.
EXCEPTION_CONTINUE_SEARCH	The normal Win32 *UnhandledExceptionFilter* function is called.

To make the *UnhandledExceptionFilter* function the default filter again, you can simply call *SetUnhandledExceptionFilter* and pass it NULL. Also, whenever you set a new unhandled exception filter, *SetUnhandledExceptionFilter* returns the address of the previously installed exception filter. This address will be NULL if *UnhandledExceptionFilter* was the currently installed filter.

The last method for turning off *UnhandledExceptionFilter*'s message box is really designed for the software developer and not for the end user. Another subkey in the Registry affects the *UnhandledExceptionFilter* function:

```
HKEY_LOCAL_MACHINE\SOFTWARE\Microsoft\
   Windows NT\CurrentVersion\AeDebug\Auto
```

This Auto subkey can be set to either 0 or 1. If the Auto subkey is set to 1, *UnhandledExceptionFilter* does not display a message box showing the user the exception and immediately invokes the debugger. If the Auto subkey is set to 0, *UnhandledExceptionFilter* displays the exception message box first and operates as described in the previous section.

Calling *UnhandledExceptionFilter* Yourself

The *UnhandledExceptionFilter* function is a Win32 function that you can call directly from within your own code. Here is an example of how you can use it:

```
void Funcadelic (void) {
   __try {
      :
      :

   }
   __except (ExpFltr(GetExceptionInformation())) {
      :
      :

   }
}


LONG ExpFltr (LPEXCEPTION_POINTERS lpEP) {
   DWORD dwExceptionCode = lpEP->ExceptionRecord.ExceptionCode;

   if (dwExceptionCode == EXCEPTION_ACCESS_VIOLATION) {
      // Do some work here....
      return(EXCEPTION_CONTINUE_EXECUTION);
   }

   return(UnhandledExceptionFilter(lpEP));
}
```

In the *Funcadelic* function, an exception in the *try* block causes the *ExpFltr* function to be called. The *ExpFilter* function is passed the return value from *GetExceptionInformation*. Inside the exception filter, the exception code is determined and compared with EXCEPTION_ACCESS-_VIOLATION. If an access violation has occurred, the exception filter corrects the situation and returns EXCEPTION_CONTINUE_EXE-CUTION from the filter. The return value causes the system to continue execution at the instruction that originally caused the exception in the first place.

If any other exception has occurred, *ExpFltr* calls *Unhandled-ExceptionFilter*, passing it the address of the EXCEPTION_POINTERS structure. *UnhandledExceptionFilter* then displays a message box that allows you to terminate the process or to begin debugging the process. The return value from *UnhandledExceptionFilter* is returned from *ExpFltr*.

Windows NT–Specific: Unhandled Kernel-Mode Exceptions

So far in this chapter, we have looked at what happens when a user-mode thread generates an exception—but a kernel-mode thread might also generate an exception. Exceptions in kernel mode are handled exactly the same as exceptions in user mode. If a low-level virtual memory function generates an exception, the system checks whether any kernel-mode exception filters are prepared to handle the exception. If the system can't find an exception filter to handle the exception, the exception is unhandled. In the case of a kernel-mode exception, the unhandled exception is in the operating system and not in an application. Such an exception would be a serious bug in the operating system!

It isn't safe for the system to continue running if an unhandled exception occurs in kernel mode, so Windows NT doesn't call the *UnhandledExceptionFilter* function in such a case; instead, Windows NT switches the video mode back to text mode, displays some debugging information on the screen, and halts the system. You should jot down the debugging information and send it to Microsoft so that they can use it to correct the code in future versions of the operating system. You'll need to reboot your machine before you can do anything else; any unsaved work is lost.

UNICODE

With Microsoft Windows becoming more and more popular around the world, it is increasingly important that we, as developers, target the various international markets. Previously, it was common for U.S. versions of software to ship as much as six months prior to the shipping of international versions. But increasing international support in the operating system is making it easier to produce applications for international markets and therefore reducing the time lag between distribution of the U.S. and international versions of our software.

Windows has always offered support to help developers localize their applications. An application can get country-specific information from various functions and can examine Control Panel settings to determine the user's preferences. Windows even supports different fonts for our applications.

Character Sets

The real problem with localization has always been manipulating different character sets. For years, most of us have been coding text strings as a series of single-byte characters with a zero at the end. This is second nature to us. When we call *strlen*, it returns the number of characters in a zero-terminated array of single-byte characters.

The problem is that some languages and writing systems (kanji being the classic example) have so many symbols in their character sets that a single byte, which offers no more than 256 different symbols at best, is just not enough. So double-byte character sets (DBCSs) were created to support these languages and writing systems.

Single-Byte and Double-Byte Character Sets

In a double-byte character set, each character in a string consists of either 1 or 2 bytes. For Japanese kanji, if the first character is between 0x81 and 0x9F or between 0xE0 and 0xFC, you must look at the next byte to determine the full character in the string. Working with double-byte character sets is a programmer's nightmare because some characters are 1 byte wide and some are 2 bytes wide.

Simply placing a call to *strlen* doesn't really tell you how many characters are in the string—it tells you the number of bytes before you hit a terminating zero. The ANSI C run-time library has no functions that allow you to manipulate double-byte character sets. However, Visual C++ 2.0's run-time library does include a number of functions such as *_mbstrcat* that allow you to manipulate multibyte (that is, both single-byte and double-byte) character strings.

To help manipulate these DBCS strings, Win32 offers a set of helper functions, listed below:

Function	Description
LPTSTR CharNext(LPCTSTR lpszCurrentChar);	Returns the address of the next character in a string
LPTSTR CharPrev(LPCTSTR lpszStart, LPCTSTR lpszCurrentChar);	Returns the address of the previous character in a string
BOOL IsDBCSLeadByte(BYTE bTestChar);	Returns TRUE if the byte is the first byte of a DBCS character

The two functions *CharNext* and *CharPrev* allow you to traverse forward or backward through a DBCS string one character at a time. The third function, *IsDBCSLeadByte*, returns TRUE if the byte passed to it is the first byte of a 2-byte character.

Although these functions make manipulating DBCS strings a little easier, a better approach is definitely needed. Enter Unicode.

When Microsoft was porting the *AnsiNext* and *AnsiPrev* functions to the Win32 API, someone realized that the functions are really used by DBCS strings instead of ANSI strings and that the functions should undergo name change surgery. So the *AnsiNext* and *AnsiPrev* functions have been renamed and added to the Win32 API as *CharNext* and *CharPrev*: The Win32 header files define the following macros so that 16-bit Windows code ports easily to Win32:

```
#define AnsiNext CharNextA
#define AnsiPrev CharPrevA
```

Unicode: The Wide-Byte Character Set

Unicode is a standard founded by Apple and Xerox in 1988. In 1991, a consortium was created to develop and promote Unicode. The consortium consists of Adobe, Aldus, Apple, Borland, Digital, Go, IBM, Lotus, Metaphor, Microsoft, NeXT, Novell, the Research Libraries Group, Sun, Taligent, Unisys, WordPerfect, and Xerox. This group of companies is responsible for maintaining the Unicode standard. The full description of Unicode can be found in *The Unicode Standard: Worldwide Character Encoding, Version 1.0,* from Addison-Wesley.

Unicode offers a simple and consistent way of representing strings. All characters in a Unicode string are 16-bit values (2 bytes). There are no special bytes that indicate whether the next byte is part of the same character or is a new character. This means that you can traverse the characters in a string by simply incrementing or decrementing a pointer. Calls to functions such as *CharNext, CharPrev,* and *IsDBCSLeadByte* are no longer necessary.

Because Unicode represents each character with a 16-bit value, more than 65,000 characters are available, making it possible to encode all the characters that make up written languages throughout the world. This is a far cry from the 256 characters available with a single-byte character set.

Currently, Unicode code points[1] are defined for the Arabic, Chinese bopomofo, Cyrillic (Russian), Greek, Hebrew, Japanese kana, Korean hangul, and Latin (English) alphabets, as well as for others. A large number of punctuation marks, mathematical symbols, technical symbols, arrows, dingbats, diacritics, and other characters are also included

---

1. A code point is the position of a symbol in a character set.

in the character sets. When you add all these alphabets and symbols together, they total about 34,000 different code points, which leaves about half of the 65,000 total code points available for future expansion.

These 65,536 characters are divided into regions. The table below shows some of the regions and the characters that are assigned to them:

16-Bit Code	Characters
0000–007F	ASCII
0080–00FF	Latin1 characters
0100–017F	European Latin
0180–01FF	Extended Latin
0250–02AF	Standard phonetic
02B0–02FF	Modified letters
0300–036F	Generic diacritical marks
0370–03FF	Greek
0400–04FF	Cyrillic
0530–058F	Armenian
0590–05FF	Hebrew
0600–06FF	Arabic
0900–097F	Devanagari

Approximately 29,000 code points are currently unassigned but are reserved for future use. And approximately 6000 code points are reserved for your own personal use.

Why You Should Use Unicode

When developing an application, you should definitely consider taking advantage of Unicode. Even if you're not planning to localize your application today, developing with Unicode in mind will certainly simplify conversion in the future. In addition, Unicode:

- Enables easy data exchange between languages
- Allows you to distribute a single binary EXE or DLL file that supports all languages
- Improves the efficiency of your application (discussed in more detail later)

How to Write Unicode Source Code

Microsoft designed the Win32 API for Unicode so that it would have as little impact on your code as possible. In fact, it is possible to write a single source code file so that it can be compiled with or without using Unicode—you need only define two macros to make the change and then recompile.

Windows NT and Unicode

Windows NT is the first operating system to be built from the ground up using Unicode. All the core functions for creating windows, displaying text, performing string manipulations, and so forth expect Unicode strings. If you call any Win32 function and pass it an ANSI string, the system first converts the string to Unicode and then passes the Unicode string to the operating system. If you are expecting ANSI strings back from a function, the system converts the Unicode string to an ANSI string before returning to your application. All these conversions occur invisibly to you. Of course, there is a slight time overhead involved in order for the system to carry out all these string conversions.

For example, if you call *CreateWindowEx* and pass non-Unicode strings for the class name and window caption text, *CreateWindowEx* must allocate blocks of memory (in your process's default heap), convert the non-Unicode strings to Unicode strings and store the result in the allocated memory blocks, and make a function call to the Unicode version of *CreateWindowEx*.

For functions that fill buffers with strings, the system must convert from Unicode to non-Unicode equivalents before your application can process the string. Because the system must perform all these conversions, your application requires more memory and runs slower. You can make your application perform more efficiently by developing your application using Unicode from the start.

Windows 95 and Unicode

Windows 95 is not a completely new operating system. It has a 16-bit Windows heritage that was not designed to handle Unicode. Adding Unicode support would have been too large a task and was dropped from the product's feature list. For this reason, Windows 95, like its predecessors, does everything internally using ANSI strings.

It is still possible to write a Win32 application that processes Unicode characters and strings, but it is much harder to call the Win32 functions. For example, if you want to call *CreateWindowEx* and pass it ANSI strings, the call is very fast; no buffers need to be allocated from your process's default heap, and no string conversions need to be done. However, if you want to call *CreateWindowEx* and pass it Unicode strings, you must explicitly allocate buffers yourself and call Win32 functions to perform the conversion from Unicode to ANSI. You can then call *CreateWindowEx*, passing the ANSI strings. When *CreateWindowEx* returns, you can free the temporary buffers. This is far less convenient than using Unicode on Windows NT.

I will describe how you can perform these conversions under Windows 95 later in this chapter.

Unicode Support in the C Run-Time Library

To take advantage of Unicode character strings, some new data types have been defined. The standard C header file, STRING.H, has been modified to define a new data type named wchar_t, which is the data type of a Unicode character:

```
typedef unsigned short wchar_t;
```

For example, if you want to create a buffer to hold a Unicode string of up to 99 characters and a terminating zero character, you can use the following statement:

```
wchar_t szBuffer[100];
```

This statement creates an array of 100 16-bit values. Of course, the standard C run-time string functions, such as *strcpy*, *strchr*, and *strcat*, operate on ANSI strings only; they don't process Unicode strings correctly. So a new, complementary set of functions was created. Figure 15-1 shows the standard C ANSI string functions followed by their equivalent Unicode functions.

```
char * strcat(char *, const char *);
wchar_t * wcscat(wchar_t *, const wchar_t *);

char * strchr(const char *, int);
wchar_t * wcschr(const wchar_t *, wchar_t);
```

Figure 15-1. *(continued)*
Standard C ANSI string functions and their Unicode equivalents.

Figure 15-1. *continued*

```
int strcmp(const char *, const char *);
int wcscmp(const wchar_t *, const wchar_t *);

int _stricmp(const char *, const char *);
int _wcsicmp(const wchar_t *, const wchar_t *);

int strcoll(const char *, const char *);
int wcscoll(const wchar_t *, const wchar_t *);

int _stricoll(const char *, const char *);
int _wcsicoll(const wchar_t *, const wchar_t *);

char * strcpy(char *, const char *);
wchar_t * wcscpy(wchar_t *, const wchar_t *);

size_t strcspn(const char *, const char *);
size_t wcscspn(const wchar_t *, const wchar_t *);

char * _strdup(const char *);
wchar_t * _wcsdup(const wchar_t *);

size_t strlen(const char *);
size_t wcslen(const wchar_t *);

char * _strlwr(char *);
wchar_t * _wcslwr(wchar_t *);

char * strncat(char *, const char *, size_t);
wchar_t * wcsncat(wchar_t *, const wchar_t *, size_t);

int strncmp(const char *, const char *, size_t);
int wcsncmp(const wchar_t *, const wchar_t *, size_t);

int _strnicmp(const char *, const char *, size_t);
int _wcsnicmp(const wchar_t *, const wchar_t *, size_t);

char * strncpy(char *, const char *, size_t);
wchar_t * wcsncpy(wchar_t *, const wchar_t *, size_t);

char * _strnset(char *, int, size_t);
wchar_t * _wcsnset(wchar_t *, wchar_t, size_t);
```

(continued)

Figure 15-1. *continued*

```
char * strpbrk(const char *, const char *);
wchar_t * wcspbrk(const wchar_t *, const wchar_t *);

char * strrchr(const char *, int);
wchar_t * wcsrchr(const wchar_t *, wchar_t);

char * _strrev(char *);
wchar_t * _wcsrev(wchar_t *);

char * _strset(char *, int);
wchar_t * _wcsset(wchar_t *, wchar_t);

size_t strspn(const char *, const char *);
size_t wcsspn(const wchar_t *, const wchar_t *);

char * strstr(const char *, const char *);
wchar_t * wcsstr(const wchar_t *, const wchar_t *);

char * strtok(char *, const char *);
wchar_t * wcstok(wchar_t *, const wchar_t *);

char * _strupr(char *);
wchar_t * _wcsupr(wchar_t *);

size_t strxfrm (char *, const char *, size_t);
size_t wcsxfrm(wchar_t *, const wchar_t *, size_t);
```

Notice that all the new functions begin with *wcs*, which stands for *wide character set*. You simply replace the *str* prefix of any ANSI string function with the new *wcs* prefix in order to call the Unicode function.

Code that includes explicit calls to either the *str* functions or the *wcs* functions cannot be compiled easily for both ANSI and Unicode. Earlier in this chapter, I said it's possible to make a single source code file that can be compiled for both. To set up the dual capability, you include the new TCHAR.H file instead of including STRING.H.

TCHAR.H exists for the sole purpose of helping you create ANSI/Unicode generic source code files. It consists of a set of macros that you should use in your source code instead of making direct calls to either the *str* or the *wcs* function. If you define _UNICODE when you compile your source code, the macros reference the *wcs* set of functions. If you don't define _UNICODE, the macros reference the *str* set of functions. Figure 15-2 lists the macros in TCHAR.H and what they reference, depending on whether _UNICODE is defined:

TCHAR.H Macro	_UNICODE Defined	_UNICODE Not Defined
_tprintf	wprintf	printf
_ftprintf	fwprintf	fprintf
_stprintf	swprintf	sprintf
_sntprintf	_snwprintf	_snprintf
_vtprintf	vwprintf	vprintf
_vftprintf	vfwprintf	vfprintf
_vstprintf	vswprintf	vsprintf
_vvsntprintf	_vsnwprintf	_vsnprintf
_tscanf	wscanf	scanf
_ftscanf	fwscanf	fscanf
_stscanf	swscanf	sscanf
_fgettc	fgetwc	fgetc
_fgettchar	fgetwchar	fgetchar
_fgetts	fgetws	fgets
_fputtc	fputwc	fputc
_fputtchar	fputwchar	fputchar
_fputts	fputws	fputs
_gettc	getwc	getc
_getts	gctws	gets
_puttc	putwc	putc
_putts	putws	puts
_ungettc	ungetwc	ungetc
_tcstod	wcstod	strtod
_tcstol	wcstol	strtol
_tcstoul	wcstoul	strtoul
_tcscat	wcscat	strcat
_tcschr	wcschr	strchr
_tcscmp	wcscmp	strcmp
_tcscpy	wcscpy	strcpy
_tcscspn	wcspn	strcspn
_tcslen	wcslen	strlen
_tcsncat	wcsncat	strncat

Figure 15-2.
Macros in TCHAR.H and their references.

(continued)

Figure 15-2. *continued*

TCHAR.H Macro	_UNICODE Defined	_UNICODE Not Defined
_tcsncmp	wcsncmp	strncmp
_tcsncpy	wcsncpy	strncpy
_tcspbrk	wcspbrk	strpbrk
_tcsrchr	wcsrchr	strrchr
_tcsspn	wcsspn	strspn
_tcsstr	wcsstr	strstr
_tcstok	wcstok	strtok
_tcsdup	_wcsdup	strdup
_tcsicmp	_wcsicmp	stricmp
_tcsnicmp	_wcsnicmp	_strnicmp
_tcsnset	_wcsnset	_strnset
_tcsrev	_wcsrev	_strrev
_tcsset	_wcsset	_strset
_tcslwr	_wcslwr	_strlwr
_tcsupr	_wcsupr	_strupr
_tcsxfrm	wcsxfrm	strxfrm
_tcscoll	wcscoll	strcoll
_tcsicoll	_wcsicoll	_stricoll
_istalpha	iswalpha	isalpha
_istupper	iswupper	isupper
_istlower	iswlower	islower
_istdigit	iswdigit	isdigit
_istxdigit	iswxdigit	isxdigit
_istspace	iswspace	isspace
_istpunct	iswpunct	ispunct
_istalnum	iswalnum	isalnum
_istprint	iswprint	isprint
_istgraph	iswgraph	isgraph
_istcntrl	iswcntrl	iscntrl
_istascii	iswascii	isascii
_totupper	towupper	toupper
_totlower	towlower	tolower

By using the identifiers listed in the left column, you can write your source code so that it can be compiled using either Unicode or ANSI. This isn't quite the whole story, however. TCHAR.H includes some additional macros.

To define an array of string characters that is ANSI/Unicode generic, use the following new TCHAR data type. If _UNICODE is defined, TCHAR is declared as follows:

```
typedef wchar_t TCHAR;
```

If _UNICODE is not defined, TCHAR is declared as:

```
typedef char TCHAR;
```

Using this data type, you can allocate a string of characters as follows:

```
TCHAR szString[100];
```

You can also create pointers to strings:

```
TCHAR *szError = "Error";
```

However, there is a problem with the previous line. By default, Microsoft's C++ compiler compiles all strings as though they were ANSI strings, not Unicode strings. As a result, the compiler will compile this line correctly if _UNICODE is not defined but will generate an error if _UNICODE is defined. To generate a Unicode string instead of an ANSI string, you would have to rewrite the line as follows:

```
TCHAR *szError = L"Error";
```

An uppercase *L* before a literal string informs the compiler that the string should be compiled as a Unicode string. When the compiler places the string in the program's data section, it intersperses zero bytes between every character. The problem with this change is that now the program will compile successfully only if _UNICODE is defined. We need another macro that selectively adds the uppercase *L* before a literal string. This is the job of the _TEXT macro, also defined in TCHAR.H. If _UNICODE is defined, _TEXT is defined as:

```
#define _TEXT(x)    L ## x
```

and if _UNICODE is not defined, _TEXT is defined as:

```
#define _TEXT(x)    x
```

Using this macro, we can rewrite the line above so that it compiles correctly whether or not the _UNICODE macro is defined, as shown on the following page.

```
TCHAR *szError = _TEXT("Error");
```

The _TEXT macro can also be used for literal characters. For example, to check whether the first character of a string is an uppercase *J*, execute the following:

```
if (szError[0] == _TEXT('J')) {
    // First character is a 'J'
    .
    .
    .
} else {
    // First character is not a 'J'
    .
    .
    .
}
```

Unicode Data Types Defined by Win32

The Win32 header files define the data types listed below:

Data Type	Description
WCHAR	Unicode character
LPWSTR	Pointer to a Unicode string
LPCWSTR	Pointer to a constant Unicode string

These data types always refer to Unicode characters and strings. The Win32 header files also define the ANSI/Unicode generic data types LPTSTR and LPCTSTR. These data types point to either an ANSI string or a Unicode string, depending on whether the UNICODE macro is defined when you compile the module.

Notice that this time the UNICODE macro is not preceded by an underscore. The _UNICODE macro is used for the C run-time header files, and the UNICODE macro is used for the Win32 header files. You usually need to define both macros when compiling a source code module.

Unicode and ANSI Functions in Win32

Earlier I implied that there are two functions called *CreateWindowEx*: a *CreateWindowEx* that accepts Unicode strings and a second *CreateWindowEx* that accepts ANSI strings. This is true, but the two functions are actually prototyped as follows:

```
HWND WINAPI CreateWindowExW(DWORD dwExStyle, LPCWSTR lpClassName,
    LPCWSTR lpWindowName, DWORD dwStyle, int X, int Y,
    int nWidth, int nHeight, HWND hWndParent, HMENU hMenu,
    HINSTANCE hInstance, LPVOID lpParam);
```

and

```
HWND WINAPI CreateWindowExA(DWORD dwExStyle, LPCSTR lpClassName,
    LPCSTR lpWindowName, DWORD dwStyle, int X, int Y,
    int nWidth, int nHeight, HWND hWndParent, HMENU hMenu,
    HINSTANCE hInstance, LPVOID lpParam);
```

CreateWindowExW is the version that accepts Unicode strings. The uppercase *W* at the end of the function name stands for *wide*. Unicode characters are 16 bits each, so they are frequently referred to as wide characters. *CreateWindowExA* has an uppercase *A* at the end, which indicates that it accepts ANSI character strings.

But we usually just include a call to *CreateWindowEx* in our code and don't directly call either *CreateWindowExW* or *CreateWindowExA*. In WINUSER.II, *CreateWindowEx* is actually a macro defined as:

```
#ifdef UNICODE
#define CreateWindowEx   CreateWindowExW
#else
#define CreateWindowEx   CreateWindowExA
#endif // !UNICODE
```

Whether UNICODE is defined when you compile your source code module determines which version of *CreateWindowEx* is called. When you port a 16-bit Windows application to Win32, you probably won't define UNICODE when you compile. Any calls you make to *CreateWindowEx* evaluate to calls to *CreateWindowExA*—the ANSI version of *CreateWindowEx*. Because 16-bit Windows offers only an ANSI version of *CreateWindowEx*, your porting will go much easier.

Under Windows NT, Microsoft's source code for *CreateWindowExA* is simply a thunking, or translation, layer that allocates memory to convert ANSI strings to Unicode strings; the code then calls *CreateWindowExW*, passing the converted strings. When *CreateWindowExW* returns, *CreateWindowExA* frees its memory buffers and returns the window handle to you.

If you're creating dynamic-link libraries that other software developers will use, consider using this technique: Supply two entry points in the DLL—an ANSI version and a Unicode version. In the ANSI version, simply allocate memory, perform the necessary string conversions, and call the Unicode version of the function. (This process is demonstrated later in this chapter.)

Under Windows 95, Microsoft's source code for *CreateWindowExA* is the actual function that does the work. Windows 95 offers all the entry points to all the Win32 functions that accept a Unicode parameter, but these functions do not translate Unicode strings to ANSI strings—they just return failure. A call to *GetLastError* returns ERROR_CALL_NOT-_IMPLEMENTED. Only ANSI versions of these functions work properly. If your compiled code makes calls to any of the wide-character Win32 functions, your application will not run under Windows 95.

Certain functions in the Win32 API, such as *WinExec* and *OpenFile*, exist solely for backward compatibility with 16-bit Windows programs and should be avoided. You should replace any calls to *WinExec* and *OpenFile* with calls to the new *CreateProcess* and *CreateFile* functions. Internally, the old functions call the new functions anyway.

The big problem with the old functions is that they don't accept Unicode strings. When you call these functions, you must pass ANSI strings. All the new and nonobsolete functions, on the other hand, do have both ANSI and Unicode versions on Windows NT.

WinMain is a special, nonobsolete function that exists only in an ANSI version:

```
int WinMain(HINSTANCE hinstExe, HINSTANCE hinstPrev,
   LPSTR lpszCmdLine, int nCmdShow);
```

The string pointed to by the *lpszCmdLine* parameter is always an ANSI string, which is indicated by its type—LPSTR. If the type were LPTSTR, we might have guessed that the function existed in both ANSI and Unicode forms. But this function cannot exist in both forms because it's called by the C run-time library's startup code. Because you didn't compile the startup code yourself, Microsoft had to choose either ANSI or Unicode. For backward compatibility reasons, the string had to be ANSI.

This leads us to a new question: What do we do if we need to parse the command line as a Unicode string? The answer lies in the *Get-CommandLine* function. This function returns a pointer to the application's command line. As with most Win32 functions, it exists in both ANSI and Unicode versions. (The Unicode version is not fully implemented on Windows 95.)

```
#ifdef UNICODE
#define GetCommandLine   GetCommandLineW
#else
#define GetCommandLine   GetCommandLineA
#endif // !UNICODE
```

The difference between the buffer pointed to by the *lpszCmdLine* parameter and the buffer pointed to by *GetCommandLine* is that *lpszCmdLine*'s buffer doesn't contain the program's pathname, only the program's command-line arguments. The buffer returned by *GetCommandLine* includes the name of the executable program as well, which means that you'll need to skip this token in the buffer in order to retrieve the actual arguments.

Making Your Application ANSI- and Unicode-Aware

It's a good idea to start converting your application to make it Unicode-aware even if you don't plan to use Unicode right away. Here are the basic steps you should follow:

- Start thinking of text strings as arrays of characters, not as arrays of *char*s or arrays of bytes.

- Use generic data types (such as TCHAR and LPTSTR) for text characters and strings.

- Use explicit data types (such as BYTE and LPBYTE) for bytes, byte pointers, and data buffers.

- Use the _TEXT macro for literal characters and strings.

- Perform global replaces. (For example, replace LPSTR with LPTSTR.)

- Modify string arithmetic problems. (For example, convert *sizeof(szBuffer)* to *(sizeof(szBuffer) / sizeof(TCHAR))*.) This is the most difficult step to remember—I have forgotten to do this more times than I care to remember.

When I was developing the sample programs for the first edition of this book, I originally wrote them so that they compiled natively as ANSI only. Then, when I began to write this chapter, I knew that I wanted to encourage the use of Unicode and was going to create sample programs to demonstrate how easy it is to create programs that can be compiled in both Unicode and ANSI. I decided that the best course of action was to convert all the sample programs in the book so that they could be compiled in both Unicode and ANSI.

I converted all the programs in about four hours, which isn't bad, considering that I didn't have any prior conversion experience.

String Functions in Win32

The Win32 API also offers a set of functions for manipulating Unicode strings, as described below:

Function	Description
lstrcat	Concatenates one string onto the end of another
lstrcmp	Performs case-sensitive comparison of two strings
lstrcmpi	Performs case-insensitive comparison of two strings
lstrcpy	Copies one string to another location in memory
lstrlen	Returns the length of a string in characters

These functions are implemented as macros that call either the Unicode version of the function or the ANSI version of the function, depending on whether UNICODE is defined when the source module is compiled. For example, if UNICODE is not defined, *lstrcat* will expand to *lstrcatA*, and if UNICODE is defined, *lstrcat* will expand to *lstrcatW*.

Two Win32 string functions, *lstrcmp* and *lstrcmpi*, behave differently from their equivalent C run-time functions. The C run-time functions *strcmp*, *strcmpi*, *wcscmp*, and *wcscmpi* simply compare the values of the code points in the strings. That is, the functions ignore the meaning of the actual characters and simply check the numeric value of each character in the first string with the numeric value of the character in the second string. The Win32 functions *lstrcmp* and *lstrcmpi*, on the other hand, are implemented as calls to the new Win32 function *CompareString*:

```
int CompareString(LCID lcid, DWORD fdwStyle,
    LPCWSTR lpString1, int cch1, LPCTSTR lpString2, int cch2);
```

This function compares two Unicode strings. The first parameter to *CompareString* specifies a locale ID (LCID), a 32-bit value that identifies a particular language. *CompareString* uses this LCID to compare the two strings by checking the meaning of the characters as they apply to a particular language. This action is much more meaningful than the simple number comparison performed by the C run-time functions.

When any of the *lstrcmp* family of functions calls *CompareString*, the function passes the result of calling the Win32 *GetThreadLocale* function as the first parameter:

```
LCID GetThreadLocale(VOID);
```

Every time a thread is created, it is assigned a locale. This function returns the current locale setting for the thread.

The second parameter of *CompareString* identifies flags that modify the method used by the function to compare the two strings. The table below shows the possible flags:

Flag	Meaning
NORM_IGNORECASE	Ignore case differences
NORM_IGNOREKANATYPE	Do not differentiate between hiragana and katakana characters
NORM_IGNORENONSPACE	Ignore nonspacing characters
NORM_IGNORESYMBOLS	Ignore symbols
NORM_IGNOREWIDTH	Do not differentiate between a single-byte character and the same character as a double-byte character
SORT_STRINGSORT	Treat punctuation the same as symbols

When *lstrcmp* calls *CompareString*, it passes 0 for the *fdwStyle* parameter. But when *lstrcmpi* calls *CompareString*, it passes NORM_IGNORE-CASE. The remaining four parameters of *CompareString* specify the two strings and their respective lengths. If you pass –1 for the *cch1* parameter, the function assumes that the *lpString1* string is zero-terminated and calculates the length of the string. This also is true for the *cch2* parameter with respect to the *lpString2* string.

Other C run-time functions don't offer good support for manipulating Unicode strings. For example, the *tolower* and *toupper* functions don't properly convert characters with accent marks. To compensate for these deficiencies in the C run-time library, you'll need to call the Win32 functions described on the following page to convert the case of a Unicode string. These functions also work correctly for ANSI strings.

The first two functions,

```
LPTSTR CharLower(LPTSTR lpszString);
```

and

```
LPTSTR CharUpper(LPTSTR lpszString);
```

convert either a single character or an entire zero-terminated string. To convert an entire string, simply pass the address of the string. To convert a single character, you must pass the individual character as follows:

```
TCHAR cLowerCaseChar = CharLower((LPTSTR) szString[0]);
```

Casting the single character to an LPTSTR causes the high 16 bits of the pointer to be set to 0 and the low 16 bits to contain the character. When the function sees that the high 16 bits are 0, the function knows that you want to convert a single character rather than a whole string. The value returned will be a 32-bit value with the converted character in the low 16 bits.

The next two functions are similar to the previous two except that they convert the characters contained inside a buffer (which does not need to be zero-terminated):

```
DWORD CharLowerBuff(LPTSTR lpszString, DWORD cchString);
```

and

```
DWORD CharUpperBuff(LPTSTR lpszString, DWORD cchString);
```

Other C run-time functions, such as *isalpha*, *islower*, and *isupper*, return a value that indicates whether a given character is alphabetic, lowercase, or uppercase. The Win32 API offers functions that return this information as well, but the Win32 functions also consider the language indicated by the user in the Control Panel:

```
BOOL IsCharAlpha(TCHAR ch);

BOOL IsCharAlphaNumeric(TCHAR ch);

BOOL IsCharLower(TCHAR ch);

BOOL IsCharUpper(TCHAR ch);
```

The *printf* family of functions is the last group of C run-time functions we'll discuss. If you compile your source module with _UNICODE defined, the *printf* family of functions expects that all the character and string parameters represent Unicode characters and strings. However, if you compile without defining _UNICODE, the *printf* family expects that all the characters and strings passed to it are ANSI.

The Win32 function *wsprintf* is an enhanced version of the C runtime's *sprintf* function. It offers some additional field types that allow you to state explicitly whether a character or string is ANSI or Unicode. Using these extended field types, you can mix ANSI and Unicode characters and strings in a single call to *wsprintf*.

Resources

When the resource compiler compiles all your resources, the output file is a binary representation of the resources. String values in your resources (string tables, dialog box templates, menus, and so on) are always written as Unicode strings. Under both Windows 95 and Windows NT, the system performs internal conversions if your application doesn't define the UNICODE macro. For example, if UNICODE is not defined when you compile your source module, a call to *LoadString* will actually call the *LoadStringA* function. *LoadStringA* will then read the string from your resources and convert the string to ANSI. The ANSI representation of the string will be returned from the function to your application.

Text Files

To date, there have been very few Unicode text files. None of the text files that ship with any Microsoft operating system or product have been in Unicode. However, I expect that this trend may change in the future (albeit a long ways into the future). Certainly, the Windows NT Notepad application allows you to open both Unicode and ANSI files as well as to create them.

For many applications that open text files and process them, such as compilers, it would be convenient if, after opening a file, the application could determine whether the text file contained ANSI characters or Unicode characters. Windows NT 3.5 introduced the *IsTextUnicode* function, which can help make this distinction:

```
DWORD IsTextUnicode(CONST LPVOID lpvBuffer, int cb, LPINT lpResult);
```

The problem with text files is that there are no hard and fast rules as to their content. This makes it extremely difficult to determine whether the file contains ANSI or Unicode characters. *IsTextUnicode* uses a series of statistical and deterministic methods in order to guess at the content of the buffer. Since this is not an exact science, it is possible that *IsTextUnicode* will return an incorrect result.

The first parameter, *lpvBuffer*, identifies the address of a buffer that you want to test. The data is a void pointer because you don't know whether you have an array of ANSI characters or an array of Unicode characters.

The second parameter, *cb*, specifies the number of bytes that *lpv-Buffer* points to. Again, because you don't know what's in the buffer, *cb* is a count of bytes rather than a count of characters. Note that you do not have to specify the entire length of the buffer. Of course, the more bytes *IsTextUnicode* can test, the more accurate a response you're likely to get.

The third parameter, *lpResult*, is the address of an integer that you must initialize before calling *IsTextUnicode*. You initialize this integer to indicate which tests you want *IsTextUnicode* to perform. (See the *Microsoft Win32 Programmer's Reference* for details.) You can also pass NULL for this parameter, in which case *IsTextUnicode* will perform every test it can.

If *IsTextUnicode* thinks that the buffer contains Unicode text, TRUE is returned; otherwise, FALSE is returned. If specific tests were requested in the integer pointed to by the *lpResult* parameter, the function sets the bits in the integer before returning to reflect the results of each test.

Under Windows 95, the *IsTextUnicode* function has no useful implementation and simply returns FALSE; calling *GetLastError* returns ERROR-_CALL_NOT_IMPLEMENTED.

The FileRev sample application presented in Chapter 7 demonstrates the use of the *IsTextUnicode* function.

Translating Strings Between Unicode and ANSI

The Win32 function *MultiByteToWideChar* converts multibyte-character strings to wide-character strings:

```
int MultiByteToWideChar(UINT uCodePage, DWORD dwFlags,
   LPCSTR lpMultiByteStr, int cchMultiByte,
   LPWSTR lpWideCharStr, int cchWideChar);
```

The *uCodePage* parameter identifies a code page number that is associated with the multibyte string. The *dwFlags* parameter allows you to specify additional control that affects characters with diacritical marks, such as accents. Usually the flags aren't used, and 0 is passed in the *dwFlags* parameter. The *lpMultiByteStr* parameter specifies the string to be converted, and the *cchMultiByte* parameter indicates the length (in bytes) of the string. The function determines the length of the source string if you pass –1 for the *cchMultiByte* parameter.

The Unicode version of the string resulting from the conversion is written to the buffer located in memory at the address specified by the *lpWideCharStr* parameter. You must specify the maximum size of this buffer (in characters) in the *cchWideChar* parameter. If you call *MultiByteToWideChar*, passing 0 for the *cchWideChar* parameter, the function doesn't perform the conversion and instead returns the size of the buffer required for the conversion to succeed. Typically, you will convert a multibyte character string to its Unicode equivalent by performing the following steps:

1. Call *MultiByteToWideChar*, passing NULL for the *lpWideCharStr* parameter and 0 for the *cchWideChar* parameter.

2. Allocate a block of memory large enough to hold the converted Unicode string. This size is returned by the previous call to *MultiByteToWideChar*.

3. Call *MultiByteToWideChar* again, this time passing the address of the buffer as the *lpWideCharStr* parameter and the size returned by the first call to *MultiByteToWideChar* as the *cchWideChar* parameter.

4. Use the converted string.

5. Free the memory block occupying the Unicode string.

The Win32 function *WideCharToMultiByte* converts a wide-character string to its multibyte string equivalent, as shown below.

```
int WideCharToMultiByte(UINT uCodePage, DWORD dwFlags,
    LPCWSTR lpWideCharStr, int cchWideChar,
    LPSTR lpMultiByteStr, int cchMultiByte,
    LPCSTR lpDefaultChar, LPBOOL lpfUsedDefaultChar);
```

This function is very similar to the *MultiByteToWideChar* function. Again, the *uCodePage* parameter identifies the code page to be associated with the newly converted string. The *dwFlags* parameter allows you to specify additional control over the conversion. The flags affect characters with diacritical marks and characters that the system is unable to convert. Most often, you won't need this degree of control over the conversion, and you'll pass 0 for the *dwFlags* parameter.

The *lpWideCharStr* parameter specifies the address in memory of the string to be converted, and the *cchWideChar* parameter indicates the length (in characters) of this string. The function determines the length of the source string if you pass –1 for the *cchWideChar* parameter.

The multibyte version of the string resulting from the conversion is written to the buffer indicated by the *lpMultiByteStr* parameter. You must specify the maximum size of this buffer (in bytes) in the *cchMultiByte* parameter. Passing 0 as the *cchMultiByte* parameter of the *WideChar-ToMultiByte* function causes the function to return the size required by the destination buffer. You'll typically convert a wide-byte character string to a multibyte character string using a sequence of events similar to those discussed when converting a multibyte string to a wide-byte string.

You'll notice that the *WideCharToMultiByte* function accepts two parameters more than the *MultiByteToWideChar* function: *lpDefaultChar* and *lpfUsedDefaultChar*. These parameters are used by the *WideCharTo-MultiByte* function only if it comes across a wide character that doesn't have a representation in the code page identified by the *uCodePage* parameter. If the wide character cannot be converted, the function uses the character pointed to by the *lpDefaultChar* parameter. If this parameter is NULL, which is most common, the function uses a system default character. This default character is usually a question mark. This is dangerous for filenames because the question mark is a wildcard character.

The *lpfUsedDefaultChar* parameter points to a Boolean variable that the function sets to TRUE if at least one character in the wide-character string could not be converted to its multibyte equivalent. The function sets the variable to FALSE if all the characters convert successfully. You can test this variable after the function returns to check whether the wide-character string was converted successfully. Again, you usually pass NULL for this parameter.

For a more complete description of how to use these functions, please refer to the *Microsoft Win32 Programmer's Reference*.

You could use these two functions to easily create both Unicode and ANSI versions of functions. For example, you might have a dynamic-link library that contains a function that reverses all the characters in a string. You could write the Unicode version of the function as follows:

```
BOOL StringReverseW (LPWSTR lpWideCharStr) {

    // Get a pointer to the last character in the string.
    LPWSTR lpEndOfStr = lpWideCharStr + wcslen(lpWideCharStr) - 1;
    wchar_t cCharT;
```

```
    // Repeat until we reach the center character in the string.
    while (lpWideCharStr < lpEndOfStr) {
        // Save a character in a temporary variable.
        cCharT = *lpWideCharStr;

        // Put the last character in the first character.
        *lpWideCharStr = *lpEndOfStr;

        // Put the temporary character in the last character.
        *lpEndOfStr = cCharT;

        // Move in one character from the left.
        lpWideCharStr++;

        // Move in one character from the right.
        lpEndOfStr--;
    }

    // The string is reversed; return success.
    return(TRUE);
}
```

And you could write the ANSI version of the function so that it doesn't perform the actual work of reversing the string at all. Instead, you could write the ANSI version so that it converts the ANSI string to Unicode, passes the Unicode string to the *StringReverseW* function, and then converts the reversed string back to ANSI. The function would look like this:

```
BOOL StringReverseA (LPSTR lpMultiByteStr) {
    LPWSTR lpWideCharStr;
    int nLenOfWideCharStr;
    BOOL fOk = FALSE;

    // Calculate the number of characters needed to hold
    // the wide character version of the string.
    nLenOfWideCharStr = MultiByteToWideChar(CP_ACP, 0,
        lpMultiByteStr, -1, NULL, 0);

    // Allocate memory from the process's default heap to
    // accommodate the size of the wide-character string.
    // Don't forget that MultiByteToWideChar returns the
    // number of characters, not the number of bytes, so
    // you must multiply by the size of a wide character.
    lpWideCharStr = HeapAlloc(GetProcessHeap(), 0,
        nLenOfWideCharStr * sizeof(WCHAR));
```

(continued)

```
  if (lpWideCharStr == NULL)
    return(fOk);

  // Convert the multibyte string to a wide-character string.
  MultiByteToWideChar(CP_ACP, 0, lpMultiByteStr, -1,
    lpWideCharStr, nLenOfWideCharStr);

  // Call the wide-character version of this
  // function to do the actual work.
  fOk = StringReverseW(lpWideCharStr);

  if (fOk) {
    // Convert the wide-character string back
    // to a multibyte string.
    WideCharToMultiByte(CP_ACP, 0, lpWideCharStr, -1,
      lpMultiByteStr, strlen(lpMultiByteStr), NULL, NULL);
  }

  // Free the memory containing the wide-character string.
  HeapFree(GetProcessHeap(), 0, lpWideCharStr);

  return(fOk);
}
```

Finally, in the header file that you distribute with the dynamic-link library, you would prototype the two functions as follows:

```
BOOL StringReverseW (LPWSTR lpWideCharStr);
BOOL StringReverseA (LPSTR lpMultiByteStr);

#ifdef UNICODE
#define StringReverse   StringReverseW
#else
#define StringReverse   StringReverseA
#endif // !UNICODE
```

Windows NT: Window Classes and Procedures

When you register a new window class, you must tell the system the address of the window procedure responsible for processing messages for this class. For certain messages (such as WM_SETTEXT), the *lParam* parameter for the message is a pointer to a string. The system needs to know whether the window procedure requires that the string be in ANSI or Unicode before dispatching the message so that the message will be processed correctly.

You tell the system whether a window procedure expects ANSI strings or Unicode strings depending on which function you use to register the window class. If you construct the WNDCLASS structure and call *RegisterClassA*, the system thinks that the window procedure expects all strings and characters to be ANSI. Registering the window class with *RegisterClassW* causes the system to dispatch only Unicode strings and characters to the window procedure. Of course, the macro *RegisterClass* expands to either *RegisterClassA* or *RegisterClassW*, depending on whether UNICODE is defined when you compile the source module.

If you have a handle to a window, you can determine what type of characters and strings the window procedure expects by calling:

```
BOOL IsWindowUnicode(HWND hwnd);
```

If the window procedure for the specified window expects Unicode, the function returns TRUE; otherwise, FALSE is returned.

If you create an ANSI string and send a WM_SETTEXT message to a window whose window procedure expects Unicode strings, the system will automatically convert the string for you before sending the message. It is very rare that you'll ever need to call the *IsWindowUnicode* function.

The system will also perform automatic translations if you subclass a window procedure. Let's say that the window procedure for an edit control expects its characters and strings to be in Unicode. Then somewhere in your program you create an edit control and subclass the window's procedure by calling

```
LONG SetWindowLongA(HWND hwnd, int nIndex, LONG lNewLong);
```

or

```
LONG SetWindowLongW(HWND hwnd, int nIndex, LONG lNewLong);
```

and passing GWL_WNDPROC as the *nIndex* parameter and the address to your subclass procedure as the *lNewLong* parameter. But what happens if your subclass procedure expects ANSI characters and strings? This could potentially create a big problem. The system determines how to convert the strings and characters depending on which of the two functions above you use to perform the subclassing. If you call *SetWindowLongA*, you're telling the system that the new window procedure (your subclass procedure) is to receive ANSI characters and strings. In fact, if you were to call *IsWindowUnicode* after calling *SetWindowLongA*, you would see that it would return FALSE, indicating that the subclassed edit window procedure no longer expects Unicode characters and strings.

But now we have a new problem: how do we ensure that the original window procedure gets the correct type of characters and strings? The system needs to have two pieces of information to correctly convert the characters and strings. The first is the form that the characters and strings are currently in. We inform the system by calling either *Call-WindowProcA* or *CallWindowProcW*:

```
LRESULT CallWindowProcA(WNDPROC wndprcPrev, HWND hwnd,
    UINT uMsg, WPARAM wParam, LPARAM lParam);
```

or

```
LRESULT CallWindowProcW(WNDPROC wndprcPrev, HWND hwnd,
    UINT uMsg, WPARAM wParam, LPARAM lParam);
```

If the subclass procedure has ANSI strings that it wants to pass to the original window procedure, the subclass procedure must call *Call-WindowProcA*. If the subclass procedure has Unicode strings that it wants to pass to the original window procedure, the subclass procedure must call *CallWindowProcW*.

The second piece of information that the system needs is the type of characters and strings that the original window procedure expects. The system gets this information from the address of the original window procedure. When you call the *SetWindowLongA* or the *SetWindowLongW* function, the system checks to see whether you are subclassing a Unicode window procedure with an ANSI subclass procedure or vice versa. If you're not changing the type of strings expected, *SetWindowLong* simply returns the address of the original window procedure. If you're changing the type of characters and strings that the window procedure expects, *SetWindowLong* doesn't return the actual address of the original window procedure; instead, it returns a handle to an internal Win32 subsystem data structure.

This structure contains the actual address of the original window procedure and a value that indicates whether that procedure expects Unicode or ANSI strings. When you call *CallWindowProc*, the system checks whether you are passing a handle of one of the internal data structures or the actual address of a window procedure. If you're passing the address of a window procedure, the original window procedure is called and no character and string conversions need to be performed.

If, on the other hand, you're passing the handle of an internal data structure, the system converts the characters and strings to the appropriate type (Unicode or ANSI) and then calls the original window procedure.

BREAKING THROUGH PROCESS BOUNDARY WALLS

In the Win32 environment, each process gets its own 4-GB address space that can be accessed using 32-bit addresses ranging from 0x00000000 through 0xFFFFFFFF. When you use pointers to reference memory, the value of the pointer refers to a memory address in your own process's address space. It is not possible for your process to create a pointer that references memory belonging to another process. This way, if your process has a bug that overwrites memory at a random address, the bug can't affect the memory used by another process.

One of the biggest problems with the 16-bit Windows operating system is that all processes run in the same address space. If one process writes to memory, it is possible that the memory belongs to another process or, even worse, the operating system itself. With the individual address spaces used by Win32 it is very difficult for one process to affect another process.

Win32 processes running under Windows 95 actually share the 2-GB address space from 0x80000000 through 0xFFFFFFFF. Only memory-mapped files and system components are mapped into this region. For more information see Chapter 4 and Chapter 7.

Win32's separate address spaces are a great advantage for both developers and users. For developers, the Win32 environment is more likely to catch wild memory reads and writes. For users, the operating system is more robust because one application cannot bring down another process or the operating system. However, many 16-bit Windows-based programs take advantage of the fact that all programs share a single address space. These programs are now much more difficult for developers to port to Win32.

Here are some examples of situations that require breaking through process boundary walls to access another process's address space:

■ Subclassing a window created by another process

■ Debugging aids (for example, determining which DLLs another process is using)

■ Hooking other processes

In this chapter, I'll show you three mechanisms by which a Win32 process can break through the process boundary walls. All three are based on the concept of injecting a DLL into another process's address space.

Why Process Boundary Walls Need to Be Broken: An Example

Say that you want to subclass an instance of a window created by another process. You may recall that subclassing allows you to alter the behavior of a window. In 16-bit Windows, you simply call *SetWindowLong* to change the window procedure address in the window's memory block to point to a new (your own) *WndProc*. The entry for the *SetWindowLong* function in the Win32 documentation states that an application cannot subclass a window created by another process. This statement is not exactly true. The problem with subclassing another process's window really has to do with process address space boundaries. When you call *SetWindowLong* in both 16-bit Windows and Win32 to subclass a window,

```
SetWindowLong(hwnd, GWL_WNDPROC, MySubclassProc);
```

you are telling the system that all messages sent or posted to the window specified by *hwnd* should now be directed to *MySubclassProc* instead of the window's normal window procedure. In other words, whenever the system needs to dispatch a message to the specified window's *WndProc*, the system looks up its address and then makes a direct call to the *WndProc*. In this example, the system will see that the address of the *MySubclassProc* function is associated with the window and make a direct call to *MySubclassProc* instead.

The problem with subclassing a window created by another process in Win32 is that the subclass procedure is in another address space. Figure 16-1 shows a simplified view of how a window procedure receives messages. Process A is running and has created a window. The USER32 .DLL file is mapped into the address space of Process A. This mapping of USER32.DLL is responsible for receiving and dispatching all sent and posted messages destined for any window created by any thread running in Process A. When this mapping of USER32.DLL detects a message, it first determines the address of the window's *WndProc* and then calls it, passing the window handle, the message, and the *wParam* and *lParam* values. After the *WndProc* processes the message, USER32 loops back around and waits for another window message to be processed.

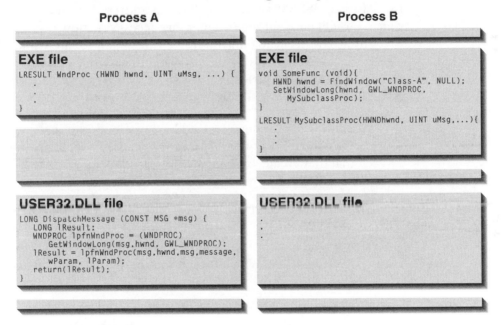

Figure 16-1.
A thread in Process B attempts to subclass a window created by a thread in Process A.

Now let's suppose that your process is Process B and you want to subclass a window created by a thread in Process A. Your code in Process B must first determine the handle to the window you want to subclass. This can be done easily in a variety of ways. The example shown in Figure 16-1 simply calls *FindWindow* to obtain the desired window. Next the thread in Process B calls *SetWindowLong* in an attempt to change the address of the window's *WndProc*. Notice that I wrote "attempt." In Win32, this call does nothing and simply returns NULL. The code in *SetWindowLong* checks to see whether one process is attempting to change the *WndProc* address for a window created by another process and simply ignores the call.

What if Win32's *SetWindowLong* function could change the window's *WndProc*? The system would associate the address of *MySubclassProc* with the specified window. Then when this window was sent a message, the USER32 code in Process A would retrieve the message, get the address of *MySubclassProc*, and attempt to call this address. But then there would be a big problem. *MySubclassProc* would be in Process B's address space, but Process A would be the active process. Obviously, if USER32 were to call this address, USER32 would be calling an address in Process A's address space, most likely resulting in a memory access violation.

To avoid this problem, you'd like the system to know that *MySubclassProc* is in Process B's address space and then have the system perform a context switch before calling the subclass procedure. There are several reasons why this additional functionality wasn't implemented:

- Subclassing windows created by threads in other processes is done fairly infrequently. Most applications subclass windows that they create, and the memory architecture of Win32 does not hinder this.

- Switching active processes is very expensive in terms of CPU time.

- A thread in Process B would have to execute the code in *MySubclassProc*. Which thread should the system try to use? An existing thread or a new thread?

- How could USER32 tell whether the address associated with the window was for a procedure in another process or in the same process?

Because there are no great solutions to these problems, Microsoft decided not to allow *SetWindowLong* to change the window procedure of a window created by another process.

But it is possible to subclass a window created by another process; you just have to go about it a different way. The problem isn't really a question of subclassing but more a question of process address space boundaries. If you could somehow get the code for your subclass procedure into Process A's address space, you could easily call *SetWindowLong* and pass Process A's address to *MySubclassProc*. I call this technique injecting a DLL into a process's address space. I know three ways to do this. Let's discuss each of these in turn, going from easiest to most difficult.

Injecting a DLL Using the Registry

If you have been using Windows 95 or Windows NT for any period of time, you should be familiar with the registry. If you're not, get familiar with it! The configuration for the entire system is maintained in the registry, and you can alter the behavior of the system by tweaking various settings. The entry that I'm going to discuss is in the following key:

```
HKEY_LOCAL_MACHINE\Software\Microsoft\Windows
 NT\CurrentVersion\Windows\AppInit_DLLs.
```

Windows 95 ignores this registry key. Therefore this technique cannot be used to inject a DLL under Windows 95.

The window below shows what the entries in this key look like when viewed from the Windows NT Registry Editor. The value for this key might contain a single DLL pathname or a set of DLL pathnames (separated by spaces). In the window, I have set the value to a single DLL pathname, C:\MYLIB.DLL.

Registry Editor - [HKEY_LOCAL_MACHINE on Local Machine]
Registry Edit Tree View Security Options Window Help

```
├─ Devices                          AppInit_DLLs : REG_SZ : C:\MyLib.DLL
├─ drivers.desc                     DeviceNotSelectedTimeout : REG_SZ : 15
├─ Drivers32                        Spooler : REG_SZ : yes
├─ Embedding                        swapdisk : REG_SZ :
├─ File Manager                     TransmissionRetryTimeout : REG_SZ : 45
├─ Font Drivers
├─ FontCache
├─ Fonts
├─ FontSubstitutes
├─ GRE_Initialize
├─ IniFileMapping
├─ MCI
├─ MCI Extensions
├─ MCI32
├─ Network
├─ NetworkCards
├─ Perflib
├─ Ports
├─ PrinterPorts
├─ ProfileList
├─ related.desc
├─ Userinstallable.drivers
├─ Windows
├─ Winlogon
└─ WOW
├─ OLE
├─ Program Groups
├─ Secure
└─ Windows 3.1 Migration Status
└─ SYSTEM
```

When you restart your machine and Windows NT initializes, the Win32 subsystem saves the value of this key. Then, whenever the USER32 .DLL library is mapped into a process, USER32 retrieves the saved value of this key from the Win32 subsystem and calls *LoadLibrary* for each of the DLLs specified in the string. As each library is loaded, the library's associated *DllMain* is called with an *fdwReason* value of DLL_PROCESS-_ATTACH so that each library can initialize itself. USER32 does not check whether each library has been successfully loaded or initialized.

Of all the methods for injecting a DLL, this is by far the easiest. All you need to do is add a value to an already existing registry key. But there are some disadvantages to this technique.

First, because the Win32 subsystem reads the value of this key during initialization, you must restart your computer after changing this value. Even logging off and logging back on won't work—you must restart. Of course, the opposite is also true; if you remove a DLL from this key's value, the system won't stop mapping the library until the computer is restarted.

Second, your DLL is mapped only into processes that also map USER32.DLL. While all GUI-based applications will map USER32, most console-based applications will not. So if you need to inject your DLL into a compiler or linker, this method will not work at all.

Third, your DLL is mapped into every GUI-based application. Most likely, you need only to inject your library into one or a few processes. The more processes your DLL is mapped into, the greater the chance of crashing the "container" processes. After all, your code is now being executed by threads running in these processes. If your code causes an infinite loop or accesses memory incorrectly, you are affecting the behavior and robustness of the processes in which your code is running. Therefore it is best to inject your library into as few processes as possible.

Finally, your DLL is mapped into every GUI-based application for its entire lifetime. This is similar to the previous problem. Since it is better to be mapped into just the processes that you need, it follows that it is best for the DLL to be mapped into those processes for the minimum amount of time. Suppose that when the user invokes your application, you want to subclass the Program Manager's main window. Your DLL doesn't have to be mapped into the Program Manager's address space until the user invokes your application. If the user later decides to terminate your application, you'll want to unsubclass the Program Manager's main window. In this case, your DLL no longer needs to be injected into the Program Manager's address space. It's best to keep your DLL injected only when necessary.

Injecting a DLL Using Windows Hooks

It is possible to inject a DLL into a process's address space using hooks. To get hooks to work in Win32 as they do in 16-bit Windows, Microsoft was forced to devise a mechanism that allows a DLL to be injected into the address space of another process. Let's look at an example.

Process A (a Spy++-like utility) installs a WH_GETMESSAGE hook to see messages processed by windows in the system. The hook is installed by calling *SetWindowsHookEx* as follows:

```
HHOOK hHook = SetWindowsHookEx(WH_GETMESSAGE, GetMsgProc,
    hinstDll, NULL);
```

The first parameter, WH_GETMESSAGE, indicates the type of hook to install. The second parameter, *GetMsgProc*, identifies the address (in your address space) of the function that the system should call whenever a window is about to process a message. The third parameter, *hinstDll*, identifies the DLL that contains the *GetMsgProc* function. In Win32, a DLL's *hinstDll* value actually identifies the 32-bit virtual memory address where the DLL is mapped into the process's address space. Finally, the last parameter, NULL, identifies the thread to hook. It is possible for one thread to call *SetWindowsHookEx* and to pass the ID of another thread in the system. By passing a value of NULL for this parameter, we are telling the system that we want to hook all threads in the system.

Now let's take a look at what happens:

1. A thread in Process B is about to dispatch a message to a window.

2. The system checks to see whether a WH_GETMESSAGE hook is installed on this thread.

3. The system checks to see whether the DLL containing the *GetMsgProc* function is mapped into Process B's address space.

4. If the DLL has not been mapped, the system forces the DLL to be mapped into Process B's address space and increments a lock count on the DLL's mapping in Process B.

5. The system looks at the DLL's *hinstDll* as it applies to Process B and checks to see whether the DLL's *hinstDll* is at the same location as it applies to Process A. If the *hinstDll*s are the same, the memory address of the *GetMsgProc* function is also the same in the two process address spaces. In this case, the system can simply call the *GetMsgProc* function in Process A's address space.

6. If the *hinstDll*s are different, the system must determine the virtual memory address of the *GetMsgProc* function in Process B's address space. This is determined with the following formula:

$$GetMsgProc\ B = hinstDll\ B + (GetMsgProc\ A - hinstDll\ A)$$

   By subtracting *hinstDll A* from *GetMsgProc A* you get the offset in bytes for the *GetMsgProc* function. Adding this offset to *hinstDll B* gives the location of the *GetMsgProc* function as it applies to the DLL's mapping in Process B's address space.

7. The system increments a lock count on the DLL's mapping in Process B.

8. The system calls the *GetMsgProc* function in Process B's address space.

9. When *GetMsgProc* returns, the system decrements a lock count on the DLL's mapping in Process B.

That's it. This is how hooks had to be implemented in the Win32 environment. You should note that when the system injects or maps the DLL containing the hook filter function the whole DLL is mapped—not just the hook filter function. This means that any and all functions contained in the DLL now exist and can be called from threads running in Process B's context.

So, to subclass a window created by a thread in another process, you can first set a WH_GETMESSAGE hook on the thread that created the window, and then, when the *GetMsgProc* function is called, call *SetWindowLong* to subclass the window. Of course, the subclass procedure must be in the same DLL as the *GetMsgProc* function.

Unlike the Registry method of injecting a DLL, this method allows you to unmap the DLL when it is no longer needed in the other process's address space by simply calling the following:

```
BOOL UnhookWindowsHookEx(HHOOK hhook);
```

When a thread calls the *UnhookWindowsHookEx* function, the system cycles through its internal list of processes into which it had to inject the DLL and decrements the DLL's lock count. When this lock count reaches 0, the DLL is automatically unmapped from the process's address space. You'll recall that just before the system calls the *GetMsgProc* function, the system increments the DLL's lock count. (See step 7 on the preceding page.) This prevents a memory access violation. Without incrementing this lock count, another thread running in the system could call *UnhookWindowsHookEx* while Process B's thread attempts to execute the code in the *GetMsgProc* function.

All this means that you can't subclass the window and immediately unhook the hook. The hook must stay in effect for the lifetime of the subclass.

The Program Manager Restore Sample Application

When I first got 16-bit Windows 3.0, I liked it right away. Even the new Program Manager shell was much better than the old MS-DOS Executive used with Windows 2.0. But there was one "feature" of the Program Manager I just didn't like: if the Program Manager was minimized and I closed my last running application, the Program Manager stayed minimized. At this point, there was nothing I could do except move the mouse all the way down to the bottom of my screen and double-click on the Program Manager so that I could execute another program.

Well, laziness being the mother of invention, I created (fanfare, please) PMRest. The source code files, resource files, and make file for the application are in the PMREST.16 directory on the companion disc. PMRest consists of a small executable program and a small DLL. The program (in conjunction with the DLL) subclasses the Program Manager. Whenever the Program Manager is running minimized and the user closes the last running application, the subclass procedure detects this and forces the Program Manager to automatically restore itself. This saves wear and tear on the mouse ball by not forcing the user to move the mouse over to the Program Manager to double-click on its icon.

When you run PMRest (PMREST.EXE), listed in Figure 16-2 beginning on page 821, it subclasses the Program Manager's main window. It calls the *SubclassProgManFrame* function contained in the PMRSTSUB .DLL, passing it the thread ID of PMRest's primary thread. You'll see why this is needed later.

If *SubclassProgManFrame* can subclass the Program Manager's main window successfully, *SubclassProgManFrame* returns TRUE. At this point, PMRest enters into a *GetMessage* loop:

```
while (GetMessage(&msg, NULL, 0, 0))
    ;
```

This loop simply causes PMRest to wait for a WM_QUIT message. PMRest doesn't create any windows itself, so there is no call to *Translate-Message* or *DispatchMessage*. When a WM_QUIT message is finally received, PMRest unhooks the hook that was set by the previous call to *Subclass-ProgManFrame* and terminates. Unhooking the hook causes the system to unmap PMRSTSUB.DLL from the Program Manager's address space.

So, as you can see, all the hard work is actually performed by the PMRSTSUB.DLL, listed in Figure 16-3 beginning on page 824. Let's take a look at what it does now.

SubclassProgManFrame first obtains the window handle of the Program Manager's main window by calling *FindWindow*:

```
g_hwndPM = FindWindow(__TEXT("PROGMAN"), NULL);
```

This window handle is then saved in a global variable, *g_hwndPM*. This variable is also shared between all views of this PMRSTSUB.DLL. If the Program Manager's window can't be found for some reason, *Subclass-ProgManFrame* returns FALSE to PMRest so that it can exit cleanly.

Now we're ready to subclass the Program Manager's window. PMRSTSUB.DLL does this by installing a WH_GETMESSAGE hook:

```
g_hHook = SetWindowsHookEx(WH_GETMESSAGE, GetMsgProc,
    g_hinstDll, GetWindowThreadProcessId(g_hwndPM, NULL));
```

The address of the hook filter function is identified by *GetMsgProc*, the handle of the module containing the function is identified by *g_hinstDll*, and the ID of the thread that we want to watch for events is the ID for the thread that created the Program Manager's main window. This thread ID is obtained by calling *GetWindowThreadProcessId*. *SetWindowsHookEx* returns the hook handle that identifies the installed hook. This handle is saved in the global *g_hHook* variable.

If the hook was installed successfully, we now force a benign window message to be posted to the Program Manager's main window:

```
PostMessage(g_hwndPM, WM_NULL, 0, 0);
```

When the thread that handles messages for the Program Manager calls *GetMessage* to retrieve the WM_NULL message, the system automatically maps PMRSTSUB.DLL into the address space of the Program Manager and calls the *GetMsgProc* filter function. The filter function checks that the message being processed is, in fact, a WM_NULL message that was destined for the Program Manager's main window. If not, *GetMsgProc* does nothing interesting and simply passes the hook notification on to the next installed WH_GETMESSAGE filter function.

If, on the other hand, a WM_NULL message is pulled from the thread's message queue and is destined for the Program Manager's main window, *GetMsgProc* calls the *SubclassWindow* macro (which is defined in WINDOWSX.H) to subclass the window. At this point, the PMRSTSUB .DLL is mapped into the Program Manager's address space, and the Program Manager's window is subclassed. From now on, any messages destined for the Program Manager's main window will be rerouted to our own subclass window procedure, *PMSubclass*.

We'll get to what the subclass procedure does in a minute. For now, let's get back to discussing PMRest's own thread. Assuming that the hook was installed successfully and that the WM_NULL message was posted to the Program Manager's main window, PMRSTSUB.DLL next adds two new top-level menu items to the Program Manager's menu bar:

```
hmenu = GetMenu(g_hwndPM);

AppendMenu(hmenu, MF_ENABLED | MF_STRING,
    IDM_PMRESTOREABOUT, "A&bout PM Restore...");
AppendMenu(hmenu, MF_ENABLED | MF_STRING,
    IDM_PMRESTOREREMOVE, "&Remove PM Restore");

DrawMenuBar(g_hwndPM);      // Update the new menu bar.
```

Finally, just before *SubclassProgManFrame* returns, it saves the ID of PMRest's primary thread into a global shared variable, *g_dwThreadId-PMRestore*.

Here's a summary of what has happened so far: the WH_GET-MESSAGE hook is still installed, any messages destined for the Program Manager's main window are being routed to the *PMSubclass* function, and the PMRest program is waiting for a WM_QUIT message at its *GetMessage* loop.

The *PMSubclass* function is designed to process only two different window messages—WM_ACTIVATEAPP and WM_COMMAND. For any other window message, *PMSubclass* simply calls *CallWindowProc* so that the message gets processed in its normal fashion.

If *PMSubclass* receives a WM_ACTIVATEAPP message, it calls the *PM_OnActivateApp* function to determine whether other windows belonging to other applications are running. If other applications are displaying windows, *PMSubclass* does nothing and passes the WM_AC-TIVATEAPP message on to the original window procedure. However, if *PM_OnActivateApp* determines that other processes aren't displaying windows, *PM_OnActivateApp* calls *ShowWindow*, forcing the Program Manager to be restored from its minimized state.

PMSubclass processes the WM_COMMAND message so that it can perform the necessary actions when one of the two new menu options has been selected by the user. When the user selects the About PM Restore option, the subclassing procedure displays PMRest's About dialog box. If the user selects the Remove PM Restore menu option, PMRSTSUB.DLL performs the following:

1. Restores the original window procedure of the Program Manager's main window.

2. Removes the two menu items that it added to the Program Manager's menu bar.

3. Posts a WM_QUIT message to PMRest's thread by calling *PostThreadMessage* and passing the ID of PMRest's thread. PMRest's thread ID was saved earlier in the global shared variable *g_dwThreadIdPMRestore*. This variable must be shared so that the Program Manager's mapping of PMRSTSUB.DLL can access this variable, which was initialized by PMREST.EXE's mapping of PMRSTSUB.DLL.

When I first wrote PMRest, I attempted to use a WH_CALLWND-PROC hook instead of a WH_GETMESSAGE hook and *sent* a WM-_NULL message instead of *posting* it. My method didn't work because, as it turns out, the system calls WH_CALLWNDPROC hook filter functions in the context of the process *sending* the message, not *receiving* the message. This meant that the hook filter function was called when PMRest called *SendMessage*, not when the Program Manager's window received the message. Because WH_CALLWNDPROC hooks work in this way, a view of the PMRSTSUB.DLL never got mapped into the Program Manager's address space.

PMRest.ico

PMREST.C

```c
/*******************************************************************
Module name: PMRest.C
Notices: Copyright (c) 1995 Jeffrey Richter
*******************************************************************/


#include "..\AdvWin32.H"     /* See Appendix B for details. */
#include <windows.h>

#pragma warning(disable: 4001)        /* Single-line comment */

#include <stdio.h>

#include "Resource.H"
#include "PMRstSub.H"


///////////////////////////////////////////////////////////////////


#define LIBNAME    "PMRstSub"

#if defined(_X86_)
   #if defined(_DEBUG)
      #pragma comment(lib, "Dbg_x86\\" LIBNAME)
   #else
      #pragma comment(lib, "Rel_x86\\" LIBNAME)
   #endif
#elif defined(_MIPS_)
   #if defined(_DEBUG)
      #pragma comment(lib, "Dbg_MIPS\\" LIBNAME)
   #else
      #pragma comment(lib, "Rel_MIPS\\" LIBNAME)
   #endif
#elif defined(_ALPHA_)
   #if defined(_DEBUG)
      #pragma comment(lib, "Dbg_Alph\\" LIBNAME)
   #else
      #pragma comment(lib, "Rel_Alph\\" LIBNAME)
   #endif
#else
   #error Modification required for this CPU platform.
#endif
```

Figure 16-2.
The PMRest application.

(continued)

Figure 16-2. *continued*

```
/////////////////////////////////////////////////////////////////


int WINAPI WinMain (HINSTANCE hinstExe,
   HINSTANCE hinstPrev, LPSTR lpszCmdLine, int nCmdShow) {

   MSG msg;

   // Find the Program Manager and modify its menu.
   if (!SubclassProgManFrame(GetCurrentThreadId()))
      return(1);

   // Begin message loop so that our application
   // doesn't terminate. If we did terminate, our subclass
   // function would be removed from memory. This means that
   // when the system tried to call the subclass function,
   // the system would jump to garbage and cause an access
   // violation.
   while (GetMessage(&msg, NULL, 0, 0))
      ;

   // Uninstall the WH_GETMESSAGE hook.
   // This causes the DLL to be unmapped
   // from the Program Manager.
   if (!UnhookWindowsHookEx(g_hHook)) {
      MessageBox(NULL, __TEXT("Error unhooking"),
         __TEXT("PM Restore"), MB_OK);
   }

   return(0);
}


//////////////////////// End Of File ////////////////////////
```

PMREST.RC
```
//Microsoft Visual C++ generated resource script.
//
#include "Resource.h"

#define APSTUDIO_READONLY_SYMBOLS
```

(continued)

Figure 16-2. *continued*

```
/////////////////////////////////////////////////////////////
//
// Generated from the TEXTINCLUDE 2 resource.
//
#include "afxres.h"


/////////////////////////////////////////////////////////////
#undef APSTUDIO_READONLY_SYMBOLS


#ifdef APSTUDIO_INVOKED
/////////////////////////////////////////////////////////////
//
// TEXTINCLUDE
//

1 TEXTINCLUDE DISCARDABLE
BEGIN
    "Resource.h\0"
END

2 TEXTINCLUDE DISCARDABLE
BEGIN
    "#include ""afxres.h""\r\n"
    "\0"
END

3 TEXTINCLUDE DISCARDABLE
BEGIN
    "\r\n"
    "\0"
END


/////////////////////////////////////////////////////////////
#endif    // APSTUDIO_INVOKED


/////////////////////////////////////////////////////////////
//
// Icon
//

PMRest                  ICON    DISCARDABLE     "PMRest.Ico"
```

(continued)

Figure 16-2. *continued*

```
#ifndef APSTUDIO_INVOKED
/////////////////////////////////////////////////////////////
//
// Generated from the TEXTINCLUDE 3 resource.
//


/////////////////////////////////////////////////////////////
#endif     // not APSTUDIO_INVOKED
```

PMRSTSUB.C

```
/*************************************************************
Module name: PMRstSub.C
Notices: Copyright (c) 1995 Jeffrey Richter
*************************************************************/


#include "..\AdvWin32.H"     /* See Appendix B for details. */
#include <windows.h>
#include <windowsx.h>

#pragma warning(disable: 4001)      /* Single-line comment */

#include "PMRstSub.RH"


#define _PMRSTSUBLIB_
#include "PMRstSub.H"



/////////////////////////////////////////////////////////////



// Forward references
LRESULT WINAPI GetMsgProc (int nCode, WPARAM wParam,
   LPARAM lParam);

LRESULT WINAPI PMSubclass (HWND hwnd, UINT uMsg,
   WPARAM wParam, LPARAM lParam);

BOOL WINAPI AnyAppsRunning (HWND hwnd, LPARAM lParam);
```

Figure 16-3.   *(continued)*
The PMRSTSUB.DLL file.

Figure 16-3. *continued*

```
///////////////////////////////////////////////////////////


// Instruct the compiler to put the g_dwThreadIdPMRestore and
// the g_hwndPM data variable in their own data section called
// Shared. We then instruct the linker that we want to
// share the data in this section with all instances of this
// application.
#pragma data_seg("Shared")

DWORD g_dwThreadIdPMRestore = 0;
HWND  g_hwndPM = NULL;

#pragma data_seg()


///////////////////////////////////////////////////////////


// Instruct the linker to make the Shared section
// readable, writable, and shared.
#pragma comment(lib, "msvcrt " "-section:Shared,rws")


///////////////////////////////////////////////////////////


// Nonshared variables
PMRSTSUBAPI HHOOK g_hHook = NULL;
WNDPROC   g_wpOrigPMProc = NULL;
HINSTANCE g_hinstDll = NULL;


///////////////////////////////////////////////////////////


BOOL WINAPI DllMain (HINSTANCE hinstDll, DWORD fdwReason,
  LPVOID lpvReserved) {

  switch (fdwReason) {

    case DLL_PROCESS_ATTACH:
      // DLL is attaching to the address space
      // of the current process.
```

(continued)

Figure 16-3. *continued*

```
        g_hinstDll = hinstDll;
        break;

    case DLL_THREAD_ATTACH:
        // A new thread is being created
        // in the current process.
        break;

    case DLL_THREAD_DETACH:
        // A thread is exiting cleanly.
        break;

    case DLL_PROCESS_DETACH:
        // The calling process is detaching the
        // DLL from its address space.
        break;
    }
    return(TRUE);
}


//////////////////////////////////////////////////////////////


// Menu IDs from Program Manager's menu
#define IDM_PMRESTOREABOUT      (4444)
#define IDM_PMRESTOREREMOVE     (4445)

PMRSTSUBAPI BOOL SubclassProgManFrame (DWORD
    dwThreadIdPMRestore) {

    HMENU hmenu;

    // Find the window handle of the Program Manager. Do not
    // specify a caption because the Program Manager's caption
    // changes depending on whether a group is maximized or not.
    g_hwndPM = FindWindow(__TEXT("PROGMAN"), NULL);

    if (!IsWindow(g_hwndPM)) {
        // If the Program Manager cannot be found,
        // we must terminate.
        MessageBox(NULL,
            __TEXT("Cannot find the Program Manager."),
            NULL, MB_OK);
        return(FALSE);
    }
```

(continued)

Figure 16-3. *continued*

```
    // First we must install a systemwide WH_GETMESSAGE hook.
    g_hHook = SetWindowsHookEx(WH_GETMESSAGE, GetMsgProc,
        g_hinstDll, GetWindowThreadProcessId(g_hwndPM, NULL));

    // The hook cannot be installed. (Maybe there is greater
    // security in this environment.)
    if (g_hHook == NULL)
        return(FALSE);

    // The hook was installed successfully; force a
    // benign message to the window so that the hook
    // function gets called.
    PostMessage(g_hwndPM, WM_NULL, 0, 0);


    // Get the menu handle to the Program Manager's Options menu.
    hmenu = GetMenu(g_hwndPM);

    AppendMenu(hmenu, MF_ENABLED | MF_STRING,
        IDM_PMRESTOREABOUT, __TEXT("A&bout PM Restore..."));
    AppendMenu(hmenu, MF_ENABLED | MF_STRING,
        IDM_PMRESTOREREMOVE, __TEXT("&Remove PM Restore"));

    DrawMenuBar(g_hwndPM);          // Update the new menu bar.

    // The window in the other process is subclassed.
    g_dwThreadIdPMRestore = dwThreadIdPMRestore;
    return(TRUE);
}


///////////////////////////////////////////////////////////////


LRESULT WINAPI GetMsgProc (int nCode, WPARAM wParam,
    LPARAM lParam) {

    static BOOL fPMSubclassed = FALSE;

    if (!fPMSubclassed && (nCode == HC_ACTION)  &&
        (wParam == PM_REMOVE) &&
        (((MSG *) lParam)->hwnd == g_hwndPM) &&
        (((MSG *) lParam)->message == WM_NULL)) {
```

(continued)

Figure 16-3. *continued*

```
      // If we have not yet subclassed the Program Manager
      // and it is retrieving a message
      // and the window handle identifies the Program Manager
      // and the message is a WM_NULL message

      // This DLL is now mapped into the Program Manager's
      // address space. Time to subclass the Program Manager.
      g_wpOrigPMProc = SubclassWindow(g_hwndPM, PMSubclass);

      // Remind ourselves that we have subclassed the
      // Program Manager so that we don't do it again if we
      // ever get another WM_NULL message.
      fPMSubclassed = TRUE;
   }

   return(CallNextHookEx(g_hHook, nCode, wParam, lParam));
}


///////////////////////////////////////////////////////////////


int PM_OnActivateApp (HWND hwnd, BOOL fActivate,
   DWORD dwThreadId) {

   BOOL fAnyWindowsUp;

   // The Program Manager is being either activated
   // or deactivated.
   if (!fActivate)
      return(0);      // PROGMAN being deactivated.

   if (!IsIconic(hwnd))
      return(0);      // PROGMAN isn't an icon.

   // Program Manager is being made active and is an icon.
   // Check whether any other applications are running.
   fAnyWindowsUp = (EnumWindows(AnyAppsRunning, 0) == 0);

   // If the enumeration was stopped prematurely, there must
   // be at least one other application running.
   if (fAnyWindowsUp)
      return(0);
```

(continued)

Figure 16-3. *continued*

```
    // No other apps running; restore PROGMAN to "open" state.
    ShowWindow(hwnd, SW_RESTORE);
    return(0);
}


///////////////////////////////////////////////////////////////////


// Function to process About box
BOOL WINAPI AboutProc (HWND hDlg, UINT uMsg,
    WPARAM wParam, LPARAM lParam) {

    BOOL fProcessed = TRUE;

    switch (uMsg) {
        case WM_INITDIALOG:
            break;

        case WM_COMMAND:
            switch (GET_WM_COMMAND_ID(wParam, lParam)) {
                case IDOK:
                case IDCANCEL:
                    if (GET_WM_COMMAND_CMD(wParam, lParam) ==
                        BN_CLICKED) {
                        EndDialog(hDlg,
                            GET_WM_COMMAND_ID(wParam, lParam));
                    }
                    break;

                default:
                    break;
            }
            break;

        default:
            fProcessed = FALSE;
            break;
    }
    return(fProcessed);
}
```

(continued)

Figure 16-3. *continued*

```
/////////////////////////////////////////////////////////////


void PM_OnCommand (HWND hwnd, int id, HWND hwndCtl,
   UINT codeNotify) {

   HMENU hmenu;

   switch (id) {

      case IDM_PMRESTOREABOUT:
         // The About PM Restore menu option
         // that we added was chosen.
         DialogBox(g_hinstDll, MAKEINTRESOURCE(IDD_ABOUT),
            hwnd, AboutProc);
         break;

      case IDM_PMRESTOREREMOVE:
         // Stop window subclassing by putting back the
         // address of the original window procedure.
         (void) SubclassWindow(hwnd, g_wpOrigPMProc);

         // Get the menu handle to the Program Manager's
         // Options menu.
         hmenu = GetMenu(hwnd);
         RemoveMenu(hmenu, IDM_PMRESTOREABOUT, MF_BYCOMMAND);
         RemoveMenu(hmenu, IDM_PMRESTOREREMOVE, MF_BYCOMMAND);
         DrawMenuBar(hwnd);       // Update the new menu bar.

         // Post WM_QUIT to our task to remove it from memory.
         PostThreadMessage(g_dwThreadIdPMRestore, WM_QUIT,
            0, 0);
         break;

      default: // Pass other WM_COMMANDs to original WndProc.
         break;
   }
}


/////////////////////////////////////////////////////////////
```

(continued)

Figure 16-3. *continued*

```
// Subclass function for the Program Manager. Any message for
// the Program Manager window comes here before reaching the
// original window function.
LRESULT WINAPI PMSubclass (HWND hwnd, UINT uMsg,
   WPARAM wParam, LPARAM lParam) {

   switch (uMsg) {
      case WM_ACTIVATEAPP:
         HANDLE_WM_ACTIVATEAPP(hwnd, wParam,
            lParam, PM_OnActivateApp);
         break;

      case WM_COMMAND:
         HANDLE_WM_COMMAND(hwnd, wParam, lParam,
            PM_OnCommand);
         break;

      default: // Pass other messages to original procedure.
         break;
   }

   // Call original window procedure and return the result to
   // whoever sent this message to the Program Manager.
   return(CallWindowProc(g_wpOrigPMProc, hwnd,
      uMsg, wParam, lParam));
}


//////////////////////////////////////////////////////////////////


// This callback function determines whether any
// windows exist that should stop us from restoring
// the Program Manager.
BOOL WINAPI AnyAppsRunning (HWND hwnd, LPARAM lParam) {

   // If the window is the Windows desktop,
   // continue enumeration.
   if (hwnd == GetDesktopWindow())
      return(1);

   // If the window is invisible (hidden),
   // continue enumeration.
   if (!IsWindowVisible(hwnd))
      return(1);
```

(continued)

Figure 16-3. *continued*

```
    // If the window was created by PROGMAN,
    // continue enumeration.
    if (GetWindowThreadProcessId(g_hwndPM, NULL) ==
        GetWindowThreadProcessId(hwnd, NULL))
        return(1);

    // For any other type of window, stop enumeration.
    return(0);
}



//////////////////////// End Of File ////////////////////////
```

PMRSTSUB.H

```
/***************************************************************
Module name: PMRstSub.H
Notices: Copyright (c) 1995 Jeffrey Richter
***************************************************************/


#if !defined(_PMRSTSUBLIB_)
#define PMRSTSUBAPI __declspec(dllimport)
#else
#define PMRSTSUBAPI __declspec(dllexport)
#endif


// External function and variable prototypes
PMRSTSUBAPI BOOL SubclassProgManFrame (DWORD ThreadIdPMRestore);

// The handle of the WH_GETMESSAGE hook
// This data member is shared between the DLL and the
// application.
PMRSTSUBAPI HHOOK g_hHook;



//////////////////////// End Of File ////////////////////////
```

(continued)

Figure 16-3. *continued*

PMRSTSUB.RC

```
//Microsoft Visual C++ generated resource script.
//
#include "PMRstSub.rh"

#define APSTUDIO_READONLY_SYMBOLS
/////////////////////////////////////////////////////////////////////
//
// Generated from the TEXTINCLUDE 2 resource.
//
#include "afxres.h"


/////////////////////////////////////////////////////////////////////
#undef APSTUDIO_READONLY_SYMBOLS


#ifdef APSTUDIO_INVOKED
/////////////////////////////////////////////////////////////////////
//
// TEXTINCLUDE
//

1 TEXTINCLUDE DISCARDABLE
BEGIN
    "PMRstSub.rh\0"
END

2 TEXTINCLUDE DISCARDABLE
BEGIN
    "#include ""afxres.h""\r\n"
    "\0"
END

3 TEXTINCLUDE DISCARDABLE
BEGIN
    "\r\n"
    "\0"
END


/////////////////////////////////////////////////////////////////////
#endif    // APSTUDIO_INVOKED
```

(continued)

Figure 16-3. *continued*

```
///////////////////////////////////////////////////////////////
//
// Dialog
//

IDD_ABOUT DIALOG DISCARDABLE  16, 20, 126, 59
STYLE WS_POPUP | WS_VISIBLE | WS_CAPTION | WS_SYSMENU
CAPTION "About Program Manager Restore"
FONT 8, "System"
BEGIN
    ICON            "PMRest",IDC_STATIC,4,16,18,20
    CTEXT           "Program Manager Restore\nCopyright (c)\
 1995 by:\nJeffrey Richter",
                    IDC_STATIC,22,8,100,28,NOT WS_GROUP
    DEFPUSHBUTTON   "&OK",IDOK,40,44,44,12
END


///////////////////////////////////////////////////////////////
//
// Icon
//

PMRest                  ICON    DISCARDABLE     "PMRest.Ico"

#ifndef APSTUDIO_INVOKED
///////////////////////////////////////////////////////////////
//
// Generated from the TEXTINCLUDE 3 resource.
//


///////////////////////////////////////////////////////////////
#endif    // not APSTUDIO_INVOKED
```

Injecting a DLL Using Remote Threads

This method of injecting a DLL was the most difficult to develop, but it offers the greatest amount of flexibility. It uses many of the new features in Win32: processes, threads, thread synchronization, structured exception handling, virtual memory management, and Unicode. (If you're unclear about any of these features, please refer to their respective chapters in this book.) To inject DLLs using this method, you need to create and execute threads in the target process's address space and access the physical storage committed to a thread's stack. But first you must understand how the system creates threads and how a thread uses its stack. You might want to refresh your memory on these details by referring to the section "The *CreateThread* Function" in Chapter 3 and the section "A Thread's Stack" in Chapter 6.

How a DLL Is Loaded

As we all know, the function *LoadLibrary* causes the system to load the specified library into the calling thread's process's address space:

```
HINSTANCE LoadLibrary(LPCTSTR lpszLibFile);
```

If you look up *LoadLibrary* in the WINBASE.H header file, you find the following:

```
HINSTANCE WINAPI LoadLibraryA(LPCSTR lpLibFileName);
HINSTANCE WINAPI LoadLibraryW(LPCWSTR lpLibFileName);
#ifdef UNICODE
#define LoadLibrary   LoadLibraryW
#else
#define LoadLibrary   LoadLibraryA
#endif // !UNICODE
```

There are actually two *LoadLibrary* functions: *LoadLibraryA* and *LoadLibraryW*. The only difference between them is the type of parameter that you pass to the function. If you have the library's filename stored as an ANSI string, you must call *LoadLibraryA* (the *A* stands for ANSI); if the filename is stored as a Unicode string, you must call *LoadLibraryW* (the *W* stands for wide characters). No single *LoadLibrary* function exists—only *LoadLibraryA* and *LoadLibraryW*. For most applications, the LoadLibrary macro expands to *LoadLibraryA*.

Win32 Functions That Affect Other Processes

By this point in the book you should have a pretty good understanding of threads and their stacks. But before I dive into further discussions about injecting a DLL into another process's address space, I want to briefly discuss the Win32 functions that allow one process to alter another. Very few functions allow one process to alter another process because it usually compromises the robustness of an application. Many of the functions that do allow a process to alter another process were created by Microsoft for use by debuggers. Most Win32-based applications should have very little or no need to call any of these functions. The two tables below show all of the Win32 functions that accept handles to processes and threads as parameters.

Win32 Process Function	Description
CreateProcess	Creates another process
FlushInstructionCache	Flushes another process's instruction cache
VirtualProtectEx	Changes access protection on another process's committed pages
VirtualQueryEx	Provides information about a range of pages in another process
GetProcessAffinityMask	Indicates the processors on which a process is allowed to run
GetProcessTimes	Obtains another process's timing information
GetProcessWorkingSetSize	Gets the minimum and maximum working set sizes for a specified process
SetProcessWorkingSetSize	Sets the minimum and maximum working set sizes for a specified process
TerminateProcess	Terminates another process
GetExitCodeProcess	Gets another process's exit code
CreateRemoteThread	Creates a thread in another process
ReadProcessMemory	Reads memory from another process's address space
WriteProcessMemory	Writes memory to another process's address space
GetPriorityClass	Gets another process's priority class
SetPriorityClass	Sets another process's priority class
WaitForInputIdle	Waits until another process has no input pending in its thread's input queue

Win32 Thread Function	Description
SetThreadAffinityMask	Sets the processors on which a thread is allowed to run
GetThreadPriority	Gets another thread's scheduling priority
SetThreadPriority	Sets another thread's scheduling priority

(continued)

Win32 Thread Function	Description
GetThreadTimes	Gets another thread's timing information
TerminateThread	Terminates another thread
GetExitCodeThread	Gets another thread's exit code
GetThreadSelectorEntry	Gets another thread's descriptor table entry (for *x86* systems only)
GetThreadContext	Gets a thread's CPU registers
SetThreadContext	Changes a thread's CPU registers
ResumeThread	Increments another thread's suspend count
SuspendThread	Decrements another thread's suspend count

Of all these functions, we need to use only seven in order to inject a DLL into another process's address space. Let's take a brief look at these seven functions.

CreateRemoteThread

CreateRemoteThread allows one process to create a thread that runs in the context of another process.

```
HANDLE CreateRemoteThread (HANDLE hProcess, LPSECURITY_ATTRIBUTES
    lpsa, DWORD cbStack, LPTHREAD_START_ROUTINE lpStartAddr,
    LPVOID lpvThreadParm, DWORD fdwCreate, LPDWORD lpIDThread);
```

CreateRemoteThread is identical to *CreateThread* except that it has one additional parameter, *hProcess*. The *hProcess* parameter identifies the process that is to own the newly created thread. The *lpStartAddr* parameter identifies the memory address of the thread function. This memory address is, of course, relative to the remote process—the thread function's code cannot be in your own process's address space.

In Windows NT, the more commonly used *CreateThread* function is implemented by calling *CreateRemoteThread*. *CreateThread* is implemented as follows:

```
HANDLE CreateThread (LPSECURITY_ATTRIBUTES lpsa, DWORD cbStack,
    LPTHREAD_START_ROUTINE lpStartAddr, LPVOID lpvThreadParm,
    DWORD fdwCreate, LPDWORD lpIDThread) {

    return(CreateRemoteThread(GetCurrentProcess(), lpsa, cbStack,
        lpStartAddr, lpvThreadParm, fdwCreate, lpIDThread));
}
```

Under Windows 95, the *CreateRemoteThread* function has no useful implementation and simply returns FALSE; calling *GetLastError* returns ERROR_CALL_NOT_IMPLEMENTED. (The *CreateThread* function contains the complete implementation of the code that creates a thread in the calling process.) Because *CreateRemoteThread* is not implemented, this technique cannot be used to inject a DLL under Windows 95.

GetThreadContext and *SetThreadContext*

The Win32 API contains just one data structure, called CONTEXT, that is CPU-specific. The code fragment below shows the CONTEXT structure for an *x*86 CPU. A CONTEXT structure is divided into five sections. CONTEXT_CONTROL contains the control registers of the CPU such as the instruction pointer, stack pointer, flags, and function return address. (Unlike the *x*86 processor, which pushes a function's return address on the stack when making a call, both MIPS and Alpha CPUs place a function's return address in a register when making a call.) CONTEXT_INTEGER identifies the CPU's integer registers; CONTEXT_FLOATING_POINT identifies the CPU's floating-point registers; CONTEXT_SEGMENTS identifies the CPU's segment registers (*x*86 only); and CONTEXT_DEBUG_REGISTERS identifies the CPU's debug registers (*x*86 only).

```
typedef struct _CONTEXT {

    //
    // The flags values within this flag control the contents of
    // a CONTEXT record.
    //
    // If the context record is used as an input parameter, then
    // for each portion of the context record controlled by a flag
    // whose value is set, it is assumed that that portion of the
    // context record contains valid context. If the context record
    // is being used to modify a thread's context, then only that
    // portion of the thread's context will be modified.
    //
    // If the context record is used as an IN OUT parameter to
    // capture the context of a thread, then only those portions
    // of the thread's context corresponding to set flags will be
    // returned.
    // The context record is never used as an OUT only parameter.
    //
```

```
        DWORD ContextFlags;

        //
        // This section is specified/returned if CONTEXT_DEBUG_REGISTERS
        // is set in ContextFlags. Note that CONTEXT_DEBUG_REGISTERS is
        // NOT included in CONTEXT_FULL.
        //

        DWORD   Dr0;
        DWORD   Dr1;
        DWORD   Dr2;
        DWORD   Dr3;
        DWORD   Dr6;
        DWORD   Dr7;

        //
        // This section is specified/returned if the
        // ContextFlags word contains the flag CONTEXT_FLOATING_POINT.
        //

        FLOATING_SAVE_AREA FloatSave;

        //
        // This section is specified/returned if the
        // ContextFlags word contains the flag CONTEXT_SEGMENTS.
        //

        DWORD   SegGs;
        DWORD   SegFs;
        DWORD   SegEs;
        DWORD   SegDs;

        //
        // This section is specified/returned if the
        // ContextFlags word contains the flag CONTEXT_INTEGER.
        //

        DWORD   Edi;
        DWORD   Esi;
        DWORD   Ebx;
        DWORD   Edx;
        DWORD   Ecx;
        DWORD   Eax;

        //
        // This section is specified/returned if the
        // ContextFlags word contains the flag CONTEXT_CONTROL.
        //
```

(continued)

```
        DWORD   Ebp;
        DWORD   Eip;
        DWORD   SegCs;              // MUST BE SANITIZED
        DWORD   EFlags;             // MUST BE SANITIZED
        DWORD   Esp;
        DWORD   SegSs;
```

`} CONTEXT;`

One member of a CONTEXT structure that does not correspond to any CPU registers is *ContextFlags*. This member exists in all CONTEXT structure definitions regardless of the CPU architecture. The *Context-Flags* member indicates to the *GetThreadContext* function which registers you are interested in retrieving. For example, if you wanted to get the control registers for a thread, you would write something like this:

```
// Create a CONTEXT structure.
CONTEXT Context;

// Tell the system that we are interested in only the
// control registers.
Context.ContextFlags = CONTEXT_CONTROL;

// Tell the system to get the registers associated with a thread.
GetThreadContext(hThread, &Context);

// The control register members in the CONTEXT structure
// reflect the thread's control registers. The other members
// are undefined.
```

Notice that you must first initialize the *ContextFlags* member in the CONTEXT structure prior to calling *GetThreadContext*. If you want to get a thread's control and integer registers, you should initialize *ContextFlags* as follows:

```
// Tell the system that we are interested
// in the control and integer registers.
Context.ContextFlags = CONTEXT_CONTROL | CONTEXT_INTEGER;
```

There is also an identifier that you can use to get all of the thread's important registers (that is, the ones Microsoft deems to be most commonly used):

```
// Tell the system we are interested
// in the important registers.
Context.ContextFlags = CONTEXT_FULL;
```

CONTEXT_FULL is defined in WINNT.H as shown in the table below:

CPU Type	Definition of CONTEXT_FULL
x86	CONTEXT_CONTROL ¦ CONTEXT_INTEGER ¦ CONTEXT_SEGMENTS
MIPS	CONTEXT_CONTROL ¦ CONTEXT_FLOATING_POINT ¦ CONTEXT_INTEGER
Alpha	CONTEXT_CONTROL ¦ CONTEXT_FLOATING_POINT ¦ CONTEXT_INTEGER

When *GetThreadContext* returns, you can easily examine any of the thread's register values, but remember this means writing code that is CPU-dependent. The table below lists the instruction pointer and stack pointer members of a CONTEXT structure according to the CPU type:

CPU Type	Instruction Pointer	Stack Pointer
x86	CONTEXT.Eip	CONTEXT.Esp
MIPS	CONTEXT.Fir	CONTEXT.IntSp
Alpha	CONTEXT.Fir	CONTEXT.IntSp

You'll notice that the MIPS and Alpha member names are the same for the instruction and stack pointers. The developers who ported Windows NT to the Alpha decided to use the same naming convention as the MIPS developers to make it easier for people writing CPU-dependent code for both the MIPS and the Alpha. If Windows NT is ported to other RISC architectures in the future, the member names may or may not be the same.

It's also possible for you to modify any of the members in the CONTEXT structure. Of course, changing any member in the CONTEXT structure does not change the registers associated with the thread. After you do change some of the members in the CONTEXT structure, you could call *SetThreadContext* to set the register values of the specified thread to reflect the values of CONTEXT's members.

```
BOOL SetThreadContext(HANDLE hThread, CONST CONTEXT *lpContext);
```

Before calling *SetThreadContext*, you must initialize the *ContextFlags* member of CONTEXT again, as shown below:

```
CONTEXT Context;

// Stop the thread from running.
SuspendThread(hThread);

// Get the thread's context registers.
Context.ContextFlags = CONTEXT_CONTROL;
GetThreadContext(hThread, &Context);

// Make the instruction pointer point to the address of your choice.
// Here I've arbitrarily set the address instruction pointer to
// 0x00010000.
#if defined(_ALPHA_)
Context.Fir = 0x00010000;
#elif defined(_MIPS_)
Context.Fir = 0x00010000;
#elif defined(_X86_)
Context.Eip = 0x00010000;
#else
#error Module contains CPU-specific code; modify and recompile.
#endif


// Set the thread's registers to reflect the changed values.
// It's not really necessary to reset the ControlFlags member
// because it was set earlier.
Context.ControlFlags = CONTEXT_CONTROL;
SetThreadContext(hThread, &Context);

// Resuming the thread will cause it to begin execution
// at address 0x00010000.
ResumeThread(hThread);
```

VirtualQueryEx and *VirtualProtectEx*

The *VirtualQueryEx* function returns information about a process's address space:

```
DWORD VirtualQueryEx(HANDLE hProcess, LPCVOID lpvAddress,
    PMEMORY_BASIC_INFORMATION pmbiBuffer, DWORD cbLength);
```

This function is very similar to the *VirtualQuery* function discussed in Chapter 6 except that *VirtualQueryEx* has one additional parameter, *hProcess*. This parameter allows you to select a process whose address space you wish to query.

The *VirtualProtectEx* function allows a thread in one process to alter the protection attributes on pages of physical storage that are used by another process:

```
BOOL VirtualProtectEx(HANDLE hProcess, LPVOID lpvAddress,
    DWORD cbSize, DWORD fdwNewProtect, LPDWORD pfdwOldProtect);
```

This function is very similar to the *VirtualProtect* function discussed in Chapter 6. Again, the only difference is that the *VirtualProtectEx* function has one additional parameter, *hProcess*.

ReadProcessMemory and *WriteProcessMemory*

The *ReadProcessMemory* and *WriteProcessMemory* functions allow a thread to copy data from its process's address space to another process's address space and vice versa.

```
BOOL ReadProcessMemory (HANDLE hProcess, LPVOID lpBaseAddress,
    LPVOID lpBuffer, DWORD cbRead, LPDWORD lpNumberOfBytesRead);

BOOL WriteProcessMemory (HANDLE hProcess, LPVOID lpBaseAddress,
    LPVOID lpBuffer, DWORD cbWrite, LPDWORD lpNumberOfBytesWritten);
```

The remote process is identified by the *hProcess* parameter. The *lpBaseAddress* parameter is the base address of memory in the remote process, *lpBuffer* is the base address of memory in the local process, *cbRead* and *cbWrite* are the requested number of bytes to transfer, and *lpNumberOfBytesRead* and *lpNumberOfBytesWritten* are filled on return with the number of bytes actually transferred.

Creating a Function to Inject a DLL into Any Process's Address Space

Now I'm ready (finally) to discuss the third method of injecting a DLL into another process. Up to this point, one problem has remained unsolved: a call to the *LoadLibrary* function causes the system to map the specified DLL into the address space of the process that owns the calling thread, when what you need to do is to force a thread in another process to call *LoadLibrary* for you.

Solving this problem was certainly a learning experience for me. I would say that my code went through a series of major revisions before I got to the final result, which you see in Figure 16-6 later in this chapter. I will not show the results of all the attempts, but I will try to explain how I was led to the final result, a function I named *InjectLib*.

Version 0: Why the Obvious Method Just Doesn't Work

On the surface, the simple solution to this problem seems to be the following:

```
HANDLE hProcessRemote;
DWORD dwThreadId;
HINSTANCE hinstKrnl = GetModuleHandle(__TEXT("Kernel32"));

CreateRemoteThread(hProcessRemote, NULL, 0,
   (LPTHREAD_START_ROUTINE)
     GetProcAddress(hinstKrnl, "LoadLibraryA"),
     "C:\\MYLIB.DLL", 0, &dwThreadId);
```

This call to *CreateRemoteThread* doesn't work the way you'd think, but let's first reexamine what I am trying to do here. I am trying to create a thread in the remote process. This thread should begin execution by calling *LoadLibraryA*. Fortunately, *LoadLibraryA* takes a single 32-bit parameter that is an address to an ANSI string identifying the DLL to be loaded. When *LoadLibraryA* is called to map a DLL into a process's address space, the DLL is mapped into the process that owns the thread that is calling *LoadLibraryA*. After *LoadLibraryA* loads the DLL, it should return to the *StartOfThread* function, and the thread then exits. Of course, MYLIB.DLL would forever be mapped into the remote process's address space because its lock count would never be decremented, but let's just take this problem one step at a time.

Can you see why the call above doesn't work? It's because the string "C:\\MYLIB.DLL" is in the calling process's address space. You are passing this string's address (in the local address space) to the remote thread. When *LoadLibraryA* is called by the remote thread, *LoadLibraryA* is going to think that the address identifies a string in its own address space and will try to process whatever's at that address. Most likely this will cause an access violation in the remote thread; the unhandled exception message box will be presented to the user, and the remote process will be terminated. That's right, the remote process will be terminated—not your process. You will have successfully crashed another process while yours continues to execute just fine!

What you really need to do now is somehow copy the string identifying the DLL into the address space of the remote process. So where do you copy this string to? This question will be answered as I progress.

You may be wondering why I bothered to get the address of *Load-LibraryA* by calling *GetProcAddress* instead of calling *CreateRemoteThread* like this:

```
CreateRemoteThread(hProcessRemote, NULL, 0, LoadLibraryA,
   "C:\\MYLIB.DLL", 0, &dwThreadId);
```

The reason is quite subtle. When you compile and link a Win32-based program, the resulting binary contains a jump table. This table consists of a series of thunks to called functions. So when your code calls a function such as *LoadLibraryA*, the linker actually generates a call to a thunk in your EXE's or your DLL's jump table. The jump table in turn makes a jump to the actual function. The linker does this to reduce the load time of your EXE or DLL and to save on memory.

If you used a direct reference to *LoadLibraryA* in the call to *CreateRemoteThread*, this would resolve to the address of the *LoadLibraryA* thunk in your jump table. Passing the address of the thunk as the starting address of the remote thread would cause the remote thread to begin executing who-knows-what. Again, the result most likely would be an access violation. To force a direct call to the *LoadLibraryA* function, bypassing the jump table, you need to get the exact location of *LoadLibraryA* by calling *GetProcAddress*.

The call to *CreateRemoteThread* assumes that KERNEL32.DLL is mapped to the same memory location in both the local and the remote processes' address spaces. Every application requires KERNEL32.DLL, and in my experience the system maps KERNEL32.DLL to the same address in every process. I can't think of a situation in which this isn't true. In fact, if you compile, link, and run the following program:

```
void __cdecl main (void) {
}
```

and then run PVIEW.EXE, you'll see that even this teeny-tiny program requires that NTDLL.DLL and KERNEL32.DLL be mapped into the process's address space.

Version 1: Hand-Coded Machine Language

The very first version of the *InjectLib* function that I actually implemented went like this. First I created a thread in the remote process by calling *CreateRemoteThread*:

```
hThread = CreateRemoteThread(hProcess, NULL, 1024, 0x00000000,
   NULL, CREATE_SUSPENDED, &dwThreadId);
```

This is a pretty bizarre way to create a thread because the address of the thread function is 0x00000000. This is sure to guarantee an access violation as soon as the thread starts running. However, note that I also specified the CREATE_SUSPENDED flag. This means that the thread will have an initial suspend count of 1 and will therefore not be scheduled any CPU time.

Next I had to locate the new thread's stack. I did this by calling *GetThreadContext* and examining the address contained in the stack pointer register.

From this address, I used *WriteProcessMemory* to copy the name of the DLL to the remote thread's stack. I then created a buffer in my own process's address space in which I placed hand-coded Intel *x*86 machine language to do the following:

```
mov     eax, <address of DLL pathname on stack>
push    eax             ; Push address of DLL's pathname
                        ; on the stack.
call    LoadLibraryA    ; Call LoadLibraryA function.
push    eax             ; Save the DLL's hinstDll
                        ; (returned in EAX) on the stack.
push    eax             ; Save the DLL's hinstDll again.
call    FreeLibrary     ; The DLL's hinstDll is on the stack
                        ; for this call.
call    ExitThread      ; Force the thread to terminate.
                        ; (DLL's hinstDll is the exit code.)
```

That's right, I looked up the machine language instructions for each of the assembly-language instructions above and filled this buffer with these instructions. Then I again called *WriteProcessMemory* to write this code to the remote thread's stack. I wrote this code just below the DLL's pathname.

Next I changed the remote thread's context structure so that the stack pointer pointed to the memory below the hand-coded machine language, and I changed the instruction pointer so that it pointed to the first byte of the hand-coded machine language. (See Figure 16-4.) I then called *SetThreadContext* to put the new values in the remote thread's registers.

Now I was all ready to go. All I had to do was call *ResumeThread*, and the remote thread would start executing my hand-coded machine language instructions, load the DLL, free the DLL, and exit the thread.

There are a number of points to discuss about this method. First, I needed to call *ExitThread* myself because I changed the instruction pointer. Remember that a thread's instruction pointer is initialized to point to

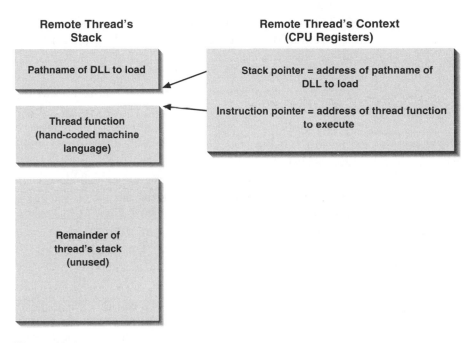

Remote Thread's Stack

Pathname of DLL to load

Thread function (hand-coded machine language)

Remainder of thread's stack (unused)

Remote Thread's Context (CPU Registers)

Stack pointer = address of pathname of DLL to load

Instruction pointer = address of thread function to execute

Figure 16-4.
The CPU registers of a remote thread pointing to the contents of another remote thread's stack.

the *StartOfThread* function. (See page 56 in Chapter 3 for a discussion of the *StartOfThread* function.) A side effect of my changing the instruction pointer was that the *StartOfThread* function would never execute. Normally, *StartOfThread* calls the thread function, but because I changed the instruction pointer register, *StartOfThread* did not call my thread function. Therefore, I couldn't put an Intel *x*86 RET instruction at the end of my code—the CPU would not know where to return. So, to make the remote thread terminate cleanly, I had to call *ExitThread* explicitly.

Second, if the library does not initialize properly, *LoadLibraryA* returns NULL to me. At this point, my code would push NULL on the stack and call *FreeLibrary*. This is probably not the best thing it could do. It would be better to compare the EAX register with zero, and call *FreeLibrary* only if EAX is nonzero. I didn't put this check in the code because I didn't want to figure out what the hand-coded machine language for these additional instructions would be. Instead, I thought that the *FreeLibrary* function would figure out that I was passing an invalid *hinstDll* value and would just return FALSE, indicating that the call was bad.

Third, skipping the execution of the *StartOfThread* function means that a default structured exception handling (SEH) frame is not set up properly for this thread. This is a problem only if the thread's code causes an exception to be raised. At first, you might not think that this is too bad a problem. After all, what could possibly go wrong with a call to *LoadLibraryA*, a call to *FreeLibrary*, and a call to *ExitThread*? Well, as you may remember from Chapter 11, this thread is also responsible for executing the library's *DllMain* function with an *fdwReason* value of DLL_PROCESS_ATTACH and an *fdwReason* value of DLL_PROCESS-_DETACH. If any of this code raises an unhandled exception, the system terminates the process on the spot without a message box or any notification to the end user whatsoever. Again, I could have written additional hand-coded machine language instructions to create an SEH frame, but this would have been *very* difficult. The implementation of SEH varies dramatically among given CPU architectures and is extremely complicated.

Finally, as you can see, the biggest problem with this whole approach is the hand-coded assembly language. As it is, I have already copped out on adding features or correcting potential problems because I didn't feel like figuring out the additional instructions. But I needed to redo all this work for each CPU platform. I did, in fact, go ahead and do this for the MIPS platform and was starting to do it for the Alpha when a friend suggested that there might be a way to write this code so that it was CPU-independent.

I have to admit that my friend and I were both skeptical at first, but we started tossing ideas around, and then we started typing up some of our ideas in Notepad. When it actually started to seem like there might be a way to do it, I started modifying my code (after making a backup of the original, of course). Several hours later (around 2:00 A.M.), we actually had something working on the Intel and MIPS platforms—which takes us to version 2.

Version 2: *AllocProcessMemory* and *CreateRemoteThread*

Eventually I wound up with a method that works something like this:

1. Allocate memory space in the remote process's address space.

2. Copy the code of a function from your process's address space to the remote process's address space. I will discuss this in detail later in this chapter.

3. Copy an INJLIBINFO data structure containing the DLL's pathname and other important data to the remote process's address space.

4. Call *CreateRemoteThread*, passing the remote address of the copied function as the *lpStartAddr* parameter and the remote address of the INJLIBINFO structure as the *lpvThreadParm* parameter.

5. Wait for the remote thread to exit.

6. Free the memory allocated in step 1.

Now let's look into each of these steps in more detail. Let's begin with how to allocate and free memory in another process's address space.

When I first started to look for a way to allocate memory in a remote process I looked feverishly for the two Win32 functions *VirtualAllocEx* and *VirtualFreeEx*. I knew that the Win32 API has a *VirtualQueryEx* function that allows a thread in one process to examine the state of memory owned by another process and a *VirtualProtectEx* function that allows a thread in one process to actually change the page protection of memory owned by another process. Given these two functions, I was sure that there must be *VirtualAllocEx* and *VirtualFreeEx* functions as well. But I was wrong! It seemed awfully strange to me that *VirtualAllocEx* and *VirtualFreeEx* functions didn't exist. There just had to be another way to allocate memory in another process's address space! Then I remembered that when I create a thread, the system allocates memory for the thread's stack—eureka! If I create a remote thread, the stack is allocated in the remote process's address space.

After I came to this realization, the implementation of functions to allocate and free memory in a remote process's address space was pretty straightforward. The result is shown in the PROCMEM.C file. (See Figure 16-5 beginning on page 854.) This file contains two functions, *Alloc-ProcessMemory* and *FreeProcessMemory*, which mimic the *ReadProcessMemory* and *WriteProcessMemory* functions.

Let's look at *AllocProcessMemory* first.

```
PVOID AllocProcessMemory (HANDLE hProcess, DWORD dwNumBytes);
```

As its name implies, this function allocates memory in another process's address space. The *hProcess* parameter identifies the process in whose address space memory should be allocated, and the *dwNumBytes* parameter indicates the number of bytes to allocate. The function returns the address where the memory was allocated in the remote process; if the memory could not be allocated, the function returns NULL.

Here is how the function works. First I call *CreateRemoteThread* as follows:

```
HINSTANCE hinstKrnl = GetModuleHandle(__TEXT("Kernel32"));
    :
    :

hThread = CreateRemoteThread(hProcess, NULL,
    dwNumBytes + sizeof(HANDLE),
    (LPTHREAD_START_ROUTINE)GetProcAddress(hinstKrnl, "ExitThread"),
    0, CREATE_SUSPENDED, &dwThreadId);
```

You know that creating a thread causes the system to allocate a stack for the thread. So for the third parameter to *CreateRemoteThread* I pass the number of bytes to commit for the thread's stack. This value is the number of bytes passed to *AllocProcessMemory* plus the size of a HANDLE. For reasons you'll see later, I need a place to save the thread handle; I chose to save it at the beginning of the allocated memory block.

I tell the system that the thread should start executing at the address where the *ExitThread* function resides. As soon as the thread starts executing, it immediately invokes *ExitThread*, passing it a parameter value of 0. This, of course, causes the thread to terminate immediately and the system to free the thread's stack. But I need the thread's stack to hang around for awhile, so I pass the CREATE_SUSPENDED flag to *CreateRemoteThread*. This flag tells the system not to let the thread execute—the CPU registers and the stack for the thread are initialized, but the thread is not scheduled any CPU time. After the system creates the remote thread, the thread's ID is placed in the *dwThreadId* variable and the handle to the thread is returned.

But why do I need to call *ExitThread* at all? It would be nice to create the remote thread as follows:

```
hThread = CreateRemoteThread(hProcess, NULL,
    dwNumBytes + sizeof(HANDLE),
    0x00000000, 0, CREATE_SUSPENDED, &dwThreadId);
```

This specifies that the remote thread should start executing at address 0x00000000, which would certainly cause a memory access violation if the thread resumed execution. However, I don't ever need to resume the thread. When the time comes to free the memory block, I could just make the following call:

```
TerminateThread(hThread, 0);
```

TerminateThread forces the system to terminate the thread. Unfortunately, under Windows NT *TerminateThread* does not cause the thread's stack to be freed. (See the discussion of the *TerminateThread* function on page 65 in Chapter 3.) *ExitThread*, however, does free a thread's stack. So, to ensure that the memory allocated in the remote process is freed, the remote thread calls *ExitThread* when it is resumed.

Now, after creating the remote thread, I need to determine where in the remote process's address space the stack is located. This is done as shown below:

```
CONTEXT Context;
    :
    :

Context.ContextFlags = CONTEXT_CONTROL;
GetThreadContext(hThread, &Context);

// Address of top of stack is in stack pointer register
```

GetThreadContext retrieves the CPU registers for the specified thread—in this case, the remote thread. The CONTEXT structure contains a stack pointer register that's initialized by the system when the thread is created and that contains the 32-bit memory address at the top of the stack. Actually, this address is 4 bytes above the top of the stack. When a function pushes something onto the stack, the CPU first decrements the stack pointer by 4 bytes and then puts the new data on the stack. You have to subtract 4 bytes (or the size of a 32-bit value) off the stack pointer address to get the address of the last 32-bit value on the stack.

The stack pointer's register name varies among CPUs, so I created a macro, STACKPTR, that abstracts the stack pointer's register name based on the CPU type. This is the only CPU-dependent portion of my code:

```
#if defined(_X86_)
#define STACKPTR(Context)   (Context.Esp)
#endif

#if defined(_MIPS_)
#define STACKPTR(Context)   (Context.IntSp)
#endif

#if defined(_ALPHA_)
#define STACKPTR(Context)   (Context.IntSp)
#endif
```

(continued)

```
#if !defined(STACKPTR)
#error Module contains CPU specific code; modify and recompile.
#endif
```

Notice that at the end I check to see if STACKPTR is defined. If not, I force the compilation to halt by taking advantage of the preprocessor's *#error* directive. If, in the future, this code is compiled for another CPU architecture, it'll have to be modified to abstract the new architecture's stack pointer register.

After I have the address of the top of the stack, I call *VirtualQueryEx*:

```
MEMORY_BASIC_INFORMATION mbi;
LPVOID pvMem;
    :
    :
VirtualQueryEx(hProcess, (PDWORD) STACKPTR(Context) - 1,
   &mbi, sizeof(mbi));
pvMem = (PVOID) mbi.BaseAddress;
```

As mentioned earlier, this function looks into the address space of another process and fills a MEMORY_BASIC_INFORMATION structure with data describing the nature of the memory. I am interested in the *BaseAddress* member of this structure. This member gives the memory address at the bottom of the stack's committed memory—this is the address of my allocated memory block.

At this point, I have the remote memory address to return to the caller. However, if I want to free the allocated memory later by calling *ResumeThread*, I must save the handle of the remote thread somewhere. I could have forced the caller to pass *AllocProcessMemory* the address of a HANDLE variable that I could fill before returning, but I didn't like this method for two reasons. One, the caller would need to know too much of my internal implementation of this function. Two, the caller would be responsible for maintaining this handle and passing the correct handle back to me when calling *FreeProcessMemory*.

Instead, I decided to save the thread's handle at the bottom of the newly allocated memory block in the remote process's address space. To do this, I write the thread's handle there by calling *WriteProcessMemory*.

```
fOk = WriteProcessMemory(hProcess, pvMem, &hThread,
   sizeof(hThread), &dwNumBytesXferred);
```

Next, I increment the pointer to the block by the size of a thread handle and return this address to the caller:

```
pvMem = (PVOID) ((PHANDLE) pvMem + 1);
return(pvMem);
```

Freeing the memory is much simpler. When the local thread wants to free the remote memory, it calls *FreeProcessMemory*:

```
BOOL FreeProcessMemory (HANDLE hProcess, PVOID pvMem);
```

and passes the remote process's handle and the memory address that was returned by the previous call to *AllocProcessMemory*. The first thing that *FreeProcessMemory* must do is get the handle to the remote thread. *AllocProcessMemory* stored this handle in the first 4 bytes of the allocated memory. So, to get it back, you must subtract the size of a thread handle from the memory address and call *ReadProcessMemory*:

```
pvMem = (PVOID) ((PHANDLE) pvMem - 1);
fOk = ReadProcessMemory(hProcess, pvMem, &hThread,
    sizeof(hThread), &dwNumBytesXferred);
```

Now all you have to do is allow the thread to begin executing. This is done by calling *ResumeThread*.

```
ResumeThread(hThread);
CloseHandle(hThread);
```

When the thread starts executing, it will immediately call *ExitThread*; the thread will stop running and the system will destroy the thread's stack. Also, the local thread must call *CloseHandle* so that you don't accidentally accumulate another thread handle in your process whenever a call to *AllocProcessMemory* is made.

The ProcMem Utility Functions

The *AllocProcessMemory* and *FreeProcessMemory* functions allocate and free memory in another process's address space. The code for these functions is contained in PROCMEM.C, listed in Figure 16-5 beginning on the next page. Any code that uses the functions should, of course, include the PROCMEM.H header file, also listed in Figure 16-5. These source code files are in the TINJLIB.16 directory on the companion disc.

PROCMEM.C

```
/***************************************************************
Module name: ProcMem.C
Notices: Copyright (c) 1995 Jeffrey Richter
***************************************************************/


#include "..\AdvWin32.H"      /* See Appendix B for details. */

#include <windows.h>
#pragma warning(disable: 4001)         /* Single-line comment */

#include "ProcMem.H"


///////////////////////////////////////////////////////////////


#if defined(_X86_)
#define STACKPTR(Context)  (Context.Esp)
#endif

#if defined(_MIPS_)
#define STACKPTR(Context)  (Context.IntSp)
#endif

#if defined(_ALPHA_)
#define STACKPTR(Context)  (Context.IntSp)
#endif

#if !defined(STACKPTR)
#error Module contains CPU-specific code; modify and recompile.
#endif


///////////////////////////////////////////////////////////////
```

Figure 16-5.   *(continued)*

The ProcMem utility functions.

Figure 16-5. *continued*

```
PVOID AllocProcessMemory (HANDLE hProcess, DWORD dwNumBytes) {
   CONTEXT Context;
   DWORD dwThreadId, dwNumBytesXferred, dwError;
   HANDLE hThread;
   HINSTANCE hinstKrnl = GetModuleHandle(__TEXT("Kernel32"));
   PVOID pvMem = NULL;
   MEMORY_BASIC_INFORMATION mbi;
   BOOL fOk = FALSE;      // Assume failure.

   __try {
      hThread = CreateRemoteThread(
         hProcess,
         NULL,              // Default security
         dwNumBytes + sizeof(HANDLE),
                            // Amount of memory to allocate in
                            // the remote process, plus 4 bytes
                            // for a thread handle.
         (LPTHREAD_START_ROUTINE)
            GetProcAddress(hinstKrnl, "ExitThread"),
                            // Address of function where thread
                            // should begin execution. We pass the
                            // address of ExitThread so that the
                            // stack will be destroyed.
         0,                 // Parameter passed to thread function.
                            // This will be passed to ExitThread.
         CREATE_SUSPENDED, // Flags. We must create the thread
                            // suspended so that the thread
                            // doesn't terminate before we use
                            // the allocated memory.
         &dwThreadId);      // The ID of the new thread

      if (hThread == NULL) {
         dwError = GetLastError();  // For debugging
         __leave;
      }

      Context.ContextFlags = CONTEXT_CONTROL;
      if (!GetThreadContext(hThread, &Context))
         __leave;
```

(continued)

Figure 16-5. *continued*

```
      // Determine the bottom address of the committed memory.
      if (sizeof(mbi) != VirtualQueryEx(hProcess,
         (PDWORD) STACKPTR(Context) - 1, &mbi, sizeof(mbi)))
         __leave;

      // Store the remote thread's handle in the bottommost
      // bytes of the allocated memory.
      pvMem = (PVOID) mbi.BaseAddress;

      fOk = WriteProcessMemory(hProcess, pvMem, &hThread,
         sizeof(hThread), &dwNumBytesXferred);

      if (!fOk)
         __leave;

      // Point past the thread's handle.
      pvMem = (PVOID) ((PHANDLE) pvMem + 1);
   }
   __finally {
      if (!fOk) {
         if (hThread) {
            ResumeThread(hThread);
            CloseHandle(hThread);
         }
         pvMem = NULL;
      }
   }

   return(pvMem);
}


///////////////////////////////////////////////////////////////////


BOOL FreeProcessMemory (HANDLE hProcess, PVOID pvMem) {
   BOOL fOk;
   HANDLE hThread;
   DWORD dwNumBytesXferred;


   // Get the handle of the remote thread from the block of
   // memory.
   pvMem = (PVOID) ((PHANDLE) pvMem - 1);
```

(continued)

Figure 16-5. *continued*

```
    fOk = ReadProcessMemory(hProcess, pvMem, &hThread,
        sizeof(hThread), &dwNumBytesXferred);

    if (fOk) {
        if (ResumeThread(hThread) == 0xffffffff) {
            // Resume failed, probably because the application
            // containing the handle overwrote the memory.
            fOk = FALSE;
        }
        CloseHandle(hThread);
    }

    return(fOk);
}


/////////////////////////// End Of File ///////////////////////////
```

PROCMEM.H
```
/****************************************************************
Module name: ProcMem.H
Notices: Written 1995 Jeffrey Richter
****************************************************************/


PVOID AllocProcessMemory (HANDLE hProcess, DWORD dwNumBytes);
BOOL  FreeProcessMemory (HANDLE hProcess, PVOID pvMem);


/////////////////////////// End Of File ///////////////////////////
```

The *InjectLib* Function

The *InjectLib* function, listed in Figure 16-6 beginning on page 864, shows how I injected a DLL into another process's address space. The source code files are in the TINJLIB.16 directory on the companion disc. First I'll discuss how I determine the amount of memory I need to allocate in the remote process's address space. After I allocate the memory, I "squirt" the *ThreadFunc* function and INJLIBINFO structure into this memory block and start the function executing.

When *ThreadFunc* runs in the remote process, it calls *LoadLibrary* to inject the function. The secret to creating a CPU-independent version of *ThreadFunc* is to write the function using a high-level language (C in this case) and let the compiler generate the machine-language code for the whole function. You can then copy the function from your address space to the remote process's address space and let the function execute. Regardless of the CPU type, the compiler will generate the proper machine language for this function.

When I was designing the *ThreadFunc* function, I had to keep in mind that in the local process's address space the function is located at one memory address, but that, when the function is copied to the remote process's address space, it almost definitely is not copied to the same address. This means that I had to design the function to contain no references to anything outside of itself! This is very difficult.

More specifically, the function could not contain any references to global or static variables because the references would be to exact memory locations, and the data variables would not exist in the remote process's address space. *ThreadFunc* also couldn't contain any direct references or calls to other functions. The compiler and linker optimize these calls to call thunks in the jump table, which would not be in the remote process.

The function also could not use more than a page's worth of local variables. Whenever the compiler sees that the amount of memory required by a single function's local variables is more than a page, the compiler generates a hidden call to the C run-time library's stack checking function. This call to the stack checking function is a direct reference to another function that would cause the remote thread to raise an exception when it was allowed to execute.

Even with all these prohibitions, you can still access the stack. So I put a pointer on the stack that points to an INJLIBINFO data structure containing all the information needed by *ThreadFunc*. The data structure contains three members:

```
typedef HINSTANCE (WINAPI *PROCLOADLIBRARY)(LPBYTE);
typedef BOOL (WINAPI *PROCFREELIBRARY)(HINSTANCE);

typedef struct {
    PROCLOADLIBRARY fnLoadLibrary;
    PROCFREELIBRARY fnFreeLibrary;
    BYTE pbLibFile[MAX_PATH * sizeof(WCHAR)];
} INJLIBINFO, *PINJLIBINFO;
```

The first member, *fnLoadLibrary*, holds the absolute address of either the *LoadLibraryA* or *LoadLibraryW* function, depending on whether the *pbLibFile* member contains an ANSI or a Unicode string. The second member, *fnFreeLibrary*, contains the absolute address of the *FreeLibrary* function. The last member, *pbLibFile*, contains either the ANSI or the Unicode version of the pathname for the DLL to be loaded.

When the remote thread executes *ThreadFunc*, *ThreadFunc* is passed the address to this data structure; the address was copied into the memory allocated by the earlier call to *AllocProcessMemory*. *ThreadFunc* simply calls one of the *LoadLibrary* functions:

```
HINSTANCE hinstDll;
hinstDll = pInjLibInfo->fnLoadLibrary(pInjLibInfo->pbLibFile);
```

Remember, this call will not return until the library's *DllMain* function has processed its DLL_PROCESS_ATTACH notification. When the call does return, the HINSTANCE of the DLL is saved in the local variable, *hinstDll*. Then, after the library has loaded and successfully initialized, *ThreadFunc* calls *FreeLibrary*:

```
if (hinstDll != NULL) {
   pInjLibInfo->fnFreeLibrary(hinstDll);
}
```

The call to *FreeLibrary* will not return until after the library's *DllMain* function has finished processing its DLL_PROCESS_DETACH notification.

Finally, *ThreadFunc* returns the HINSTANCE of the loaded DLL. (NULL is returned if the DLL failed to load successfully.) This return value becomes the exit code for this thread. As long as another thread in the system has a handle to this remote thread, the remote thread's thread kernel object remains in the system, and *GetExitCodeThread* can be called to retrieve the thread's exit code. This way, the thread running in the local process can determine whether the DLL loaded successfully.

You should notice two advantages of *ThreadFunc* over version 1's thread function. As mentioned earlier, the biggest advantage is that there is no hand-coded machine language at all. The second is that the remote *ThreadFunc* function is called by the *StartOfThread* function. This means that *ThreadFunc* can simply return when it is finished, rather than having to call *ExitThread*, and that the default structured exception handling frame is set up and ready to capture unhandled exceptions.

InjectLib, *InjectLibA*, *InjectLibW*, and *InjectLibWorA*

Now let's look at the function responsible for injecting the *ThreadFunc* function into the remote process's address space. Because I wanted to supply a complete library function, I created this function to have full ANSI and Unicode entry points. This means that there are two functions—one for ANSI (*InjectLibA*) and one for Unicode (*InjectLibW*)—as well as a macro, *InjectLib*, that expands to one of these two functions depending on whether UNICODE is defined during compilation.

```
BOOL InjectLibA (HANDLE hProcess, LPCSTR lpszLibFile);
BOOL InjectLibW (HANDLE hProcess, LPCWSTR lpszLibFile);


#ifdef UNICODE
#define InjectLib InjectLibW
#else
#define InjectLib InjectLibA
#endif // !UNICODE
```

The two function prototypes and the macro are defined in the INJLIB.H file. (See Figure 16-6.)

Both *InjectLibA* and *InjectLibW* are one-line stub functions that simply call the real workhorse function, *InjectLibWorA*. *InjectLibWorA* is a static function that cannot be called from any code outside the INJLIB.C file. (See Figure 16-6.) When the stub functions call *InjectLibWorA*, they pass the following:

- The handle of the process in which the library is to be injected.

- The address to the DLL's pathname. This may be either an ANSI string or a Unicode string.

- A Boolean value that indicates what type of string *lpszLibFile* is. TRUE indicates Unicode and FALSE indicates ANSI.

The value returned by *InjectLibWorA* indicates whether the DLL was successfully loaded in the remote process. *InjectLibA* and *InjectLibW* simply return *InjectLibWorA*'s return value back to their callers.

```
BOOL InjectLibA (HANDLE hProcess, LPCSTR lpszLibFile) {
    return(InjectLibWorA(hProcess, (LPBYTE) lpszLibFile, FALSE));
}

BOOL InjectLibW (HANDLE hProcess, LPCWSTR lpszLibFile) {
    return(InjectLibWorA(hProcess, (LPBYTE) lpszLibFile, TRUE));
}
```

So how does *InjectLibWorA* actually inject a DLL into another process's address space? The first step is to create and initialize an INJLIB-INFO data structure:

```
HINSTANCE hinstKrnl = GetModuleHandle(__TEXT("Kernel32"));

INJLIBINFO InjLibInfo;
:
:
InjLibInfo.fnLoadLibrary = (PROCLOADLIBRARY)
   GetProcAddress(hinstKrnl,
      (fUnicode ? "LoadLibraryW" : "LoadLibraryA"));
InjLibInfo.fnFreeLibrary = (PROCFREELIBRARY)
   GetProcAddress(hinstKrnl, "FreeLibrary");
InjLibInfo.pbLibFile[0] = 0;  // Initialized later
:
:
if (fUnicode)
   wcscpy((LPWSTR) InjLibInfo.pbLibFile, (LPCWSTR) pbLibFile);
else
   strcpy((LPSTR) InjLibInfo.pbLibFile, (LPCSTR) pbLibFile);
```

This structure is eventually copied into the memory allocated within the remote process. The structure is initialized by obtaining the absolute address of the *LoadLibraryA* or *LoadLibraryW* function as well as the *Free-Library* function. Then the DLL's pathname is copied from the *pbLibFile* parameter to the *pbLibFile* member of the INJLIBINFO structure.

The code assumes that both the local process and the remote process have KERNEL32.DLL mapped into their respective address spaces and that KERNEL32.DLL is mapped to the same address in both processes. As mentioned earlier, this is actually a very safe bet—I have never seen a situation where this failed to be the case.

Now I need to determine the size of the memory block to allocate in the remote process's address space. This memory block is going to hold a copy of *ThreadFunc* and a copy of INJLIBINFO. The size of *Thread-Func* is determined by taking its address in memory and subtracting the memory address of the function after it, *AfterThreadFunc*:

```
const int cbCodeSize = ((LPBYTE) (DWORD)
   AfterThreadFunc - (LPBYTE) (DWORD) ThreadFunc);
```

This assumes that the compiler and linker will place the *AfterThread-Func* function immediately after the *ThreadFunc* function in the resulting object code. For the Intel, MIPS, and Alpha compilers that ship with Visual C++, this is true. However, I've been told that an Alpha compiler (for operating systems other than Windows NT) compiles functions and places them backwards in the resulting object file. It's possible that other compilers for Windows NT might come up with a different result when subtracting *ThreadFunc* from *AfterThreadFunc*, which would break this code.

Even if a Windows NT–based compiler did reverse the functions, this problem would be easy to correct. You would simply need to add a function before *ThreadFunc* and call the new function *BeforeThreadFunc*. Then you could compare the address of *BeforeThreadFunc* with the address of *AfterThreadFunc* and subtract the memory address of *ThreadFunc* from the larger function. Of course, it's always possible that some future compiler will reorganize functions in a way I haven't anticipated, although I think this is unlikely.

So now you have the size of the *ThreadFunc* function, but you also need enough memory in the remote process to hold an INJLIBINFO structure:

```
const DWORD cbMemSize = cbCodeSize + sizeof(InjLibInfo) + 3;
```

You'll notice that I added *3* to the memory size above. This is because all structures must start on an even 32-bit boundary. The same is true for code. For example, if the *ThreadFunc* function required 65 bytes, and I put the INJLIBINFO structure immediately after the code, the structure would start at byte 65. As soon as the *ThreadFunc* function attempted to access the structure, the CPU would raise a datatype misalignment exception. For *x*86 architectures, this is not a problem because they automatically correct for misaligned data, but on RISC architectures, this is a really big problem. It wouldn't help to put the INJLIBINFO structure before *ThreadFunc*'s code. In calculating the size of the required memory block, I just assumed that in a worst case situation I'd need to leave at most a 3-byte gap after the code and before the structure.

The memory space is now allocated in the remote process using my *AllocProcessMemory* function.

```
pdwCodeRemote = (PDWORD) AllocProcessMemory(hProcess, cbMemSize);
```

When the system reserves stack space for a new thread, the system gives the memory pages of that space a protection of PAGE_READ-WRITE. This means that any attempt to read or write to the memory is OK, but if an attempt is made to execute code on these pages, the CPU raises an exception. This causes a small problem because I'm purposely putting code on the stack so that it can be executed. This problem is solved with a simple call to *VirtualProtectEx*:

```
fOk = VirtualProtectEx(hProcess, pdwCodeRemote, cbMemSize,
   PAGE_EXECUTE_READWRITE, &dwOldProtect);
```

This is the kind of problem that can go unnoticed for a long time. In fact, I figured it out only while writing this text—long after I had finished writing and testing the code on *x*86, MIPS, and Alpha platforms. How'd I manage that? While I was working on the code I must have tested it occasionally, and I should have immediately seen that the remote thread was raising exceptions, right? Well, Win32 supports these different page protections, but the CPU might not. In fact, the *x*86, MIPS, and Alpha CPUs all ignore the execute page protection. With these CPUs, if a page is readable, it's executable. I decided to add this call to *Virtual-ProtectEx* anyway for aesthetic reasons and because this code is more likely to work on future CPU architectures.

Now it's time to copy the *ThreadFunc* function and the INJLIBINFO structure over to the memory that was allocated in the remote process's address space:

```
fOk = WriteProcessMemory(hProcess, pdwCodeRemote,
   (LPVOID) (DWORD) ThreadFunc, cbCodeSize, &dwNumBytesXferred);

// Force the structure to begin on an even 32-bit boundary.
PINJLIBINFO pInjLibInfoRemote = (PINJLIBINFO)
   (pdwCodeRemote + ((cbCodeSize + 4) & ~3));

fOk = WriteProcessMemory(hProcess, pInjLibInfoRemote,
   &InjLibInfo, sizeof(InjLibInfo), &dwNumBytesXferred);
```

At this point, everything is initialized in the remote process. The next step is to create a remote thread that will execute the *ThreadFunc* function using the data in the INJLIBINFO structure. Since this thread will execute asynchronously with your local thread, you must put the local thread to sleep until you know that the remote thread has finished loading the DLL and exited:

```
HANDLE hThread = CreateRemoteThread(hProcess, NULL, 0,
   (LPTHREAD_START_ROUTINE) (DWORD) pdwCodeRemote,
   pInjLibInfoRemote, 0, &dwThreadId);

WaitForSingleObject(hThread, INFINITE);
```

After the remote thread has finished executing, you want to get the remote thread's exit code. This exit code is the HINSTANCE of the remotely loaded DLL. If the HINSTANCE is NULL, you know that the

DLL did not initialize successfully. *InjectLibWorA* returns FALSE if the HINSTANCE value is NULL, otherwise it returns TRUE. After you have the remote thread's exit code, you no longer need to maintain your handle to the remote thread and you can free the memory allocated in the remote process's address space:

```
GetExitCodeThread(hThread, (PDWORD) &hinstDllRemote);
CloseHandle(hThread);
FreeProcessMemory(hProcess, pdwCodeRemote);

return(hinstDllRemote != NULL);
```

```
INJLIB.C
/*************************************************************
Module name: InjLib.C
Notices: Copyright (c) 1995 Jeffrey Richter
*************************************************************/


#include "..\AdvWin32.H"      /* See Appendix B for details. */

#include <windows.h>
#pragma warning(disable: 4001)          /* Single-line comment */

#include "ProcMem.H"
#include "InjLib.H"



///////////////////////////////////////////////////////////////


typedef HINSTANCE (WINAPI *PROCLOADLIBRARY)(LPBYTE);
typedef BOOL (WINAPI *PROCFREELIBRARY)(HINSTANCE);

typedef struct {
   PROCLOADLIBRARY fnLoadLibrary;
   PROCFREELIBRARY fnFreeLibrary;
   BYTE pbLibFile[MAX_PATH * sizeof(WCHAR)];
} INJLIBINFO, *PINJLIBINFO;
```

Figure 16-6. *(continued)*
Implementation of the InjectLib *function.*

Figure 16-6. *continued*

```
////////////////////////////////////////////////////////////////

// Calls to the stack checking routine must be disabled.
#pragma check_stack (off)

static DWORD WINAPI ThreadFunc (PINJLIBINFO pInjLibInfo) {
   // There must be less than a page's worth of local
   // variables used in this function.
   HINSTANCE hinstDll;

   // Call LoadLibrary(A/W) to load the DLL.
   hinstDll = pInjLibInfo->
      fnLoadLibrary(pInjLibInfo->pbLibFile);

   // Calling LoadLibrary causes the system to map the DLL
   // into the remote process's address space and call
   // the DLL's DllMain with an fdwReason value of
   // DLL_PROCESS_ATTACH. The DLL can do whatever it wants to
   // during this processing. When DllMain returns, the system
   // returns the HINSTANCE of the DLL back from our call to
   // LoadLibrary. At this point, we call FreeLibrary,
   // passing the library's HINSTANCE in order to free it.

   // If the DLL could not be loaded, or if the library's
   // DllMain (DLL_PROCESS_ATTACH) returns FALSE, hinstDll
   // will come back as NULL.

   // If the library initialized successfully, free it.
   if (hinstDll != NULL) {
      // Calling FreeLibrary causes the system to call the
      // DLL's DllMain with a reason of DLL_PROCESS_DETACH.
      // The DLL can perform whatever cleanup is necessary.
      pInjLibInfo->fnFreeLibrary(hinstDll);
   }

   // The thread's exit code is the handle of the DLL.
   return((DWORD) hinstDll);
}
```

(continued)

Figure 16-6. *continued*

```
///////////////////////////////////////////////////////////////


// This function marks the memory address after ThreadFunc.
// ThreadFuncCodeSizeInBytes =
//     (PBYTE) AfterThreadFunc - (PBYTE) ThreadFunc.
static void AfterThreadFunc (void) {
}
#pragma check_stack


///////////////////////////////////////////////////////////////


static BOOL InjectLibWorA (HANDLE hProcess,
   const BYTE * const pbLibFile, BOOL fUnicode) {

   // Kernel32.DLL's HINSTANCE is used to get the
   // address of LoadLibraryA or LoadLibraryW and
   // FreeLibrary.
   HINSTANCE hinstKrnl = GetModuleHandle(__TEXT("Kernel32"));

   INJLIBINFO InjLibInfo;

   // The address to which code will be copied in the
   // remote process
   PDWORD pdwCodeRemote = NULL;

   // Calculate the number of bytes in the ThreadFunc
   // function.
   const int cbCodeSize = ((LPBYTE) (DWORD)
      AfterThreadFunc - (LPBYTE) (DWORD) ThreadFunc);

   // The address to which INJLIBINFO will be copied in
   // the remote process
   PINJLIBINFO pInjLibInfoRemote = NULL;

   // The number of bytes written to the remote process
   DWORD dwNumBytesXferred = 0;
```

(continued)

Figure 16-6. *continued*

```
// The handle and ID of the thread executing the
// remote copy of ThreadFunc
DWORD dwThreadId = 0;
const DWORD cbMemSize =
   cbCodeSize + sizeof(InjLibInfo) + 3;
HANDLE hThread = NULL;
HINSTANCE hinstDllRemote = NULL;

BOOL fOk = FALSE;
DWORD dwOldProtect;

// Initialize the INJLIBINFO structure here, and
// then copy it to memory in the remote process.
InjLibInfo.fnLoadLibrary = (PROCLOADLIBRARY)
   GetProcAddress(hinstKrnl,
      (fUnicode ? "LoadLibraryW" : "LoadLibraryA"));
InjLibInfo.fnFreeLibrary = (PROCFREELIBRARY)
   GetProcAddress(hinstKrnl, "FreeLibrary");
InjLibInfo.pbLibFile[0] = 0;   // Initialized later

__try {
   // Finish initializing the INJLIBINFO structure
   // by copying the desired DLL's pathname.
   if (fUnicode)
      wcscpy((LPWSTR) InjLibInfo.pbLibFile,
         (LPCWSTR) pbLibFile);
   else
      strcpy((LPSTR) InjLibInfo.pbLibFile,
         (LPCSTR) pbLibFile);

   // Allocate enough memory in the remote process's
   // address space to hold our ThreadFunc function
   // and an INJLIBINFO structure.
   pdwCodeRemote = (PDWORD)
      AllocProcessMemory(hProcess, cbMemSize);

   if (pdwCodeRemote == NULL)
      __leave;

   // Change the page protection of the allocated memory
   // to executable, read, and write.
   fOk = VirtualProtectEx(hProcess, pdwCodeRemote,
      cbMemSize, PAGE_EXECUTE_READWRITE, &dwOldProtect);
   if (!fOk)
      __leave;
```

(continued)

Figure 16-6. *continued*

```
    // Write a copy of ThreadFunc to the remote process.
    fOk = WriteProcessMemory(hProcess, pdwCodeRemote,
        (LPVOID) (DWORD) ThreadFunc, cbCodeSize,
        &dwNumBytesXferred);
    if (!fOk)
        __leave;


    // Write a copy of INJLIBINFO to the remote process.
    // (The structure MUST start on an even 32-bit boundary.)
    pInjLibInfoRemote = (PINJLIBINFO)
        (pdwCodeRemote + ((cbCodeSize + 3) & ~3));

    // Put INJLIBINFO in remote thread's memory block.
    fOk = WriteProcessMemory(hProcess, pInjLibInfoRemote,
        &InjLibInfo, sizeof(InjLibInfo), &dwNumBytesXferred);
    if (!fOk)
        __leave;


    hThread = CreateRemoteThread(hProcess, NULL, 0,
        (LPTHREAD_START_ROUTINE) (DWORD) pdwCodeRemote,
        pInjLibInfoRemote, 0, &dwThreadId);
    if (hThread == NULL)
        __leave;

    WaitForSingleObject(hThread, INFINITE);
} // __try
__finally {
    if (hThread != NULL) {
        GetExitCodeThread(hThread, (PDWORD) &hinstDllRemote);
        CloseHandle(hThread);
    }

    // Let the remote thread start executing the remote
    // ThreadFunc function using our modified stack, which
    // now contains an initialized INJLIBINFO structure.
    FreeProcessMemory(hProcess, pdwCodeRemote);
} //__finally

// Return TRUE if the DLL loaded successfully.
return(hinstDllRemote != NULL);
}
```

(continued)

Figure 16-6. *continued*

```
//////////////////////////////////////////////////////////////


BOOL WINAPI InjectLibA (HANDLE hProcess, LPCSTR lpszLibFile) {

   return(InjectLibWorA(hProcess, (LPBYTE) lpszLibFile,
      FALSE));
}


//////////////////////////////////////////////////////////////


BOOL WINAPI InjectLibW (HANDLE hProcess,
   LPCWSTR lpszLibFile) {

   return(InjectLibWorA(hProcess, (LPBYTE) lpszLibFile,
      TRUE));
}


//////////////////////// End Of File /////////////////////////
```

INJLIB.H
```
/************************************************************
Module name: InjLib.H
Notices: Copyright (c) 1995 Jeffrey Richter
************************************************************/


BOOL WINAPI InjectLibA (HANDLE hProcess, LPCSTR lpszLibFile);
BOOL WINAPI InjectLibW (HANDLE hProcess, LPCWSTR lpszLibFile);


#ifdef UNICODE
#define InjectLib InjectLibW
#else
#define InjectLib InjectLibA
#endif // !UNICODE


//////////////////////// End Of File /////////////////////////
```

Testing the *InjectLib* Function

Having written the *InjectLib* function, I needed to devise a way to test it. I describe how I did so in this section. There are two parts to testing *Inject-Lib*. First, I wrote an application, which I call TInjLib, to call the *InjectLib* function. Second, I wrote a DLL to be injected into a remote process. This DLL retrieves information that is specific to the application that contains the injected DLL. If I get back information that seems correct based on the process that I inject into, I know that the *InjectLib* function is working successfully.

The Inject Library Test Sample Application

The TINJLIB.EXE application, listed in Figure 16-7, shows how to call *InjectLib*. The source code files, resource files, and make file for the application are in the TINJLIB.16 directory on the companion disc. The program simply accepts a single command-line parameter that is the process ID of a running process. You can obtain a process's ID by using the PVIEW.EXE or PSTAT.EXE tool that ships with Visual C++ 2.0. With the ID, the program attempts to open a handle to this running process by calling *OpenProcess* and requesting the appropriate access rights:

```
hProcess = OpenProcess(
    PROCESS_CREATE_THREAD |        // For CreateRemoteThread
    PROCESS_QUERY_INFORMATION |    // For VirtualQueryEx
    PROCESS_VM_OPERATION |         // For VirtualProtectEx
    PROCESS_VM_READ |              // For ReadProcessMemory
    PROCESS_VM_WRITE,              // For WriteProcessMemory
    FALSE, dwProcessId);
```

If *OpenProcess* returns NULL, TInjLib cannot open a handle to the process. This will happen in a highly secure system or if you attempt to open a handle to a secure process. The Win32 subsystem and some other processes (such as WinLogon, ClipSrv, and EventLog) are so secure that an application cannot obtain a handle to any of them when requesting the above access flags.

If *OpenProcess* is successful, TInjLib creates a buffer with the full pathname of the DLL that you want to inject and calls *InjectLib*. When *InjectLib* returns, the program displays a message box indicating whether the DLL successfully loaded in the remote process; it then closes the handle to the process. That's all there is to it.

You may notice when examining the code that I make a special check to see whether the process ID passed on the command line is 0. If so, I set the process ID to TINJLIB.EXE's own process ID by calling *Get-CurrentProcessId*. This way, when TInjLib calls *InjectLib*, TInjLib is injecting the DLL into its own address space. I do this to make debugging easier. As you can imagine, when bugs popped up it was sometimes difficult to determine whether the bugs were in the local process or in the remote process. Originally, I started debugging my code with two debuggers, one watching TInjLib and the other watching the remote process. This turned out to be terribly inconvenient. And then it dawned on me that TInjLib can also inject a DLL into itself—that is, into the same address space as the caller. This made it much easier to debug my code.

TInjLib.ico

```
TINJLIB.C
/*******************************************************
Module name: TInjLib.C
Notices: Copyright (c) 1995 Jeffrey Richter
*******************************************************/


#include "..\AdvWin32.H"       /* See Appendix B for details. */

#include <windows.h>
#pragma warning(disable: 4001)         /* Single-line comment */

#include <windowsx.h>

#include <stdio.h>
#include <tchar.h>

#include "InjLib.H"



//////////////////////////////////////////////////////////////////////



int WINAPI WinMain (HINSTANCE hinstExe, HINSTANCE hinstPrev,
    LPSTR lpszCmdLine, int nCmdShow) {

    DWORD dwProcessId = 0;
    HANDLE hProcess;
```

Figure 16-7.   *(continued)*
The TInjLib application.

Figure 16-7. *continued*

```
    if ((lpszCmdLine == NULL) || (*lpszCmdLine == 0)) {
        MessageBox(NULL,
            __TEXT("Usage: InjLib [ProcessID (in hex)]"),
            __TEXT("InjLib"), MB_ICONINFORMATION | MB_OK);
            return(0);
    } else {
        sscanf(lpszCmdLine, "%x", &dwProcessId);
    }

    if (dwProcessId == 0) {
        // A command-line argument of 0 causes everything to
        // take place in the local process; this makes things
        // easier for debugging.
        dwProcessId = GetCurrentProcessId();
    }

    hProcess = OpenProcess(
        PROCESS_CREATE_THREAD |         // For CreateRemoteThread
        PROCESS_QUERY_INFORMATION |     // For VirtualQueryEx
        PROCESS_VM_OPERATION |          // For VirtualProtectEx
        PROCESS_VM_READ |               // For ReadProcessMemory
        PROCESS_VM_WRITE,               // For WriteProcessMemory
        FALSE, dwProcessId);
    if (hProcess == NULL) {
        MessageBox(NULL, (GetLastError() == ERROR_ACCESS_DENIED) ?
            __TEXT("Insufficient access to process")
                : __TEXT("Invalid process Id"),
            __TEXT("Inject Library Tester"), MB_OK);
    } else {
        TCHAR szLibFile[MAX_PATH];
        GetModuleFileName(hinstExe, szLibFile, sizeof(szLibFile));
        _tcscpy(_tcsrchr(szLibFile, __TEXT('\\')) + 1,
            __TEXT("ImgWalk.DLL"));
        MessageBox(NULL, InjectLib(hProcess, szLibFile) ?
            __TEXT("Remote DLL Loaded")
                : __TEXT("Remote DLL failed load"),
            __TEXT("Inject Library Tester"), MB_OK);
        CloseHandle(hProcess);
    }

    return(0);
}


/////////////////////// End Of File ///////////////////////////
```

The Image Walk Dynamic-Link Library

IMGWALK.DLL, listed in Figure 16-8 beginning on page 875, is a DLL that, once injected into a process's address space, can report on all the DLLs that the process is using. The source code files, resource files, and make file for the DLL arc in the TINJLIB.16 directory on the companion disc. For example, if I first run Notepad and then run TInjLib, passing it Notepad's process ID, TInjLib injects the IMGWALK.DLL into Notepad's address space. Once there, ImgWalk determines which file images (EXEs and DLLs) are being used by Notepad and displays the following message box showing the results.

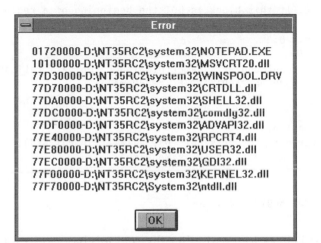

At first glance, it seems that there is practically no way to accomplish what ImgWalk does without using undocumented functions. A process's image information can be obtained by debugging the desired process. However, there are problems associated with creating a debugger—the biggest being that a debugger attached to a debuggee can never detach itself without terminating the debuggee. This is clearly visible in the way that terminating a debugger also terminates its debuggee. The *InjectLib* function does not have this problem—it attaches the DLL to a process and then *InjectLib* detaches the DLL from that process.

ImgWalk walks through a process's address space looking for mapped file images by repeatedly calling *VirtualQuery* to fill a MEMORY-_BASIC_INFORMATION structure. With each iteration of the loop,

ImgWalk checks to see whether there's a file pathname to concatenate with a string. This string appears in the message box.

```
while (VirtualQuery(lp, &mbi, sizeof(mbi)) == sizeof(mbi)) {
    if (mbi.State == MEM_FREE)
        mbi.AllocationBase = mbi.BaseAddress;

    if ((mbi.AllocationBase == hinstDll) ||
        (mbi.AllocationBase != mbi.BaseAddress) ||
        (mbi.AllocationBase == NULL)) {
        // Do not add the module name to the list
        // if any of the following is true:
        // 1. If this region contains this DLL
        // 2. If this block is NOT the beginning of a region
        // 3. If the address is NULL
        nLen = 0;
    } else {
        nLen = GetModuleFileName((HINSTANCE) mbi.AllocationBase,
            szModName, ARRAY_SIZE(szModName));
    }

    if (nLen > 0) {
        _stprintf(_tcschr(szBuf, 0), __TEXT("\n%08X-%s"),
            mbi.AllocationBase, szModName);
    }

    lp += mbi.RegionSize;
}
```

First I check to see whether the region's base address matches the base address of the injected DLL. If we have a match, I set *nLen* to 0 so that I do not show the injected library in the message box. If we don't have a match, I attempt to get the filename for the module loaded at the region's base address. If the *nLen* variable is greater than 0, the system recognizes that the address identifies a loaded module and the system fills the *szModName* buffer with the full pathname of the module. I then concatenate the module's HINSTANCE (base address) and its pathname with the *szBuf* string that will eventually be displayed in the message box. When the loop is finished, the DLL presents a message box with the final string as its contents.

IMGWALK.C

```
/**************************************************************
Module name: ImgWalk.C
Notices: Copyright (c) 1995 Jeffrey Richter
**************************************************************/


#include "..\AdvWin32.H"      /* See Appendix B for details. */

#include <windows.h>

#pragma warning(disable: 4001)        /* Single-line comment */

#include <stdio.h>
#include <tchar.h>


//////////////////////////////////////////////////////////////


BOOL WINAPI DllMain (HINSTANCE hinstDll, DWORD fdwReason,
   LPVOID lpvReserved) {

   TCHAR szBuf[MAX_PATH * 30], szModName[MAX_PATH];

   if (fdwReason == DLL_PROCESS_ATTACH) {
      LPBYTE lp = NULL;
      MEMORY_BASIC_INFORMATION mbi;
      int nLen;
      szBuf[0] = 0;
      szBuf[1] = 0;

      while (VirtualQuery(lp, &mbi, sizeof(mbi))
         == sizeof(mbi)) {

         if (mbi.State == MEM_FREE)
            mbi.AllocationBase = mbi.BaseAddress;

         if ((mbi.AllocationBase == hinstDll) ||
             (mbi.AllocationBase != mbi.BaseAddress) ||
             (mbi.AllocationBase == NULL)) {
```

Figure 16-8.   *(continued)*
Source code for IMGWALK.DLL.

Figure 16-8. *continued*

```
                // Do not add the module name to the list
                // if any of the following is true:
                // 1. If this region contains this DLL
                // 2. If this block is NOT the beginning of
                //    a region
                // 3. If the address is NULL
            nLen = 0;
         } else {
            nLen = GetModuleFileName((HINSTANCE)
               mbi.AllocationBase,
               szModName, ARRAY_SIZE(szModName));
         }

         if (nLen > 0) {
            _stprintf(_tcschr(szBuf, 0), __TEXT("\n%08X-%s"),
               mbi.AllocationBase, szModName);
         }

         lp += mbi.RegionSize;
      }

      MessageBox(NULL, &szBuf[1], NULL, MB_OK);
   }
   return(TRUE);
}


////////////////////// End Of File //////////////////////////
```

A Summary

The table on the facing page summarizes the pros and cons of the three library injection methods discussed in this chapter.

Whenever I discuss with other programmers these methods of injecting a library into another process's address space, I always get the following question: "Doesn't Windows NT prevent you from injecting a DLL into another process's address space because it's supposed to be a secure environment?" The answer is that of course Windows NT is a secure environment, but certain security features such as the ability to disable the installation of systemwide hooks are disabled by default. Also, as it turns out, certain processes by default do not allow the *CreateRemoteThread*

	AppInit_DLLs	Hooks	Remote Threads
Method works under Windows 95?	No	Yes	No
Method works under Windows NT?	Yes	Yes	Yes
Requires restarting the computer?	Yes	No	No
Requires the target process map USER32.DLL?	Yes	Yes	No
Requires the target process map KERNEL32.DLL?	Yes	Yes	Yes
Can the injected library be unloaded from the target process?	No	Yes	Yes
Is the library injected into every process that maps USER32.DLL?	Yes	No	No
Is the source code CPU platform independent?	Yes	Yes	99% Yes

function to create a thread in their address spaces. For example, the Win32 subsystem (CSRSS.EXE) and the Logon process (WINLOGON .EXE) have an access mask specified that prohibits another process from creating a thread in their address spaces by using the *CreateRemoteThread* function.

However, Win32 under Windows NT is much more robust than 16-bit Windows even with these defaults. Also, for backward compatibility, turning on many of the security features would mean breaking existing 16-bit Windows-based and ported Win32-based applications. Plus, many really cool programs such as Spy++ require the ability to set hooks and subclass windows created by other processes' threads.

MESSAGE CRACKERS

When Windows was introduced, there were only two programming languages that could be used for developing Windows-based applications: C and assembly language. And the only C compiler that could produce executable files for Windows was Microsoft's; no other compiler on the market supported the development of applications for Windows. Well, things have changed significantly over the past few years. Now you can develop Windows-based applications using Ada, assembly language, C, C++, COBOL, dBASE, FORTRAN, LISP, Modula-2, Pascal, REXX, and Smalltalk/V. And let's not forget Basic.

But even with all these languages that support Windows coming out of the woodwork, C is still the language used most often, with C++ slowly gaining popularity. When it came time to choose a language for presenting the sample code in this book, I narrowed down the choices to these four:

1. Straight C

2. C with message crackers

3. Straight C++

4. C++ using the Microsoft Foundation Classes

It was a tough decision.

Because I wanted the book to appeal to the broadest possible audience, I decided to rule out option 4. Since several companies produce C++ class libraries for Windows development, I didn't want to require one particular class library. Also, some class libraries do more for you than just put a wrapper around the Windows APIs, and I didn't want to introduce extraneous code or procedures into the code samples. I will say, however, that I personally love the Microsoft Foundation Classes and use them when I develop large applications of my own.

Option 3 didn't seem to offer much either. Even without a class library, developing Windows-based applications in C++ can be easier than using straight C, but because the programs in this book are relatively small, using C++ wouldn't have offered many advantages. Another big reason for not choosing option 3 or 4 is that most people are still doing development for Windows in C and haven't yet switched to C++.

Option 1 would have been a good choice because there would have been almost no learning curve for people trying to understand my programs, but I chose to go with option 2. When I go to conferences, I frequently ask people if they are using message crackers, and I usually get a "no" response. When I probe further, I discover that they don't even know what message crackers are or what they do. By using C with message crackers to present the sample code in this book, I get to introduce these little-known but useful macros to many people who might not know about them.

Message crackers are contained in the WINDOWSX.H file supplied with Visual C++ 2.0. You usually include this file immediately after the WINDOWS.H file. The WINDOWSX.H file is nothing more than a bunch of #*define* statements that create a set of macros for you to use. Microsoft designed the macros to provide the following advantages:

■ They reduce the amount of casting necessary in an application and make the casting that is required error free. One of the big problems with programming for Windows in C has been the amount of casting required. You hardly ever see a call to a Win32 API function that doesn't require some sort of cast. Casts should be avoided because they prevent the compiler from catching potential errors in your code. A cast tells the compiler, "I know I'm passing the wrong type here, but that's OK; I know what I'm doing." When you do so much casting, it's easy to make a mistake. The compiler should be doing as much work to help us as it possibly can. If you use these macros, you'll have much less casting to perform.

■ They make your code more readable.

■ They simplify porting between the 16-bit Windows API and the Win32 API.

■ They're easy to understand—they're just macros, after all.

■ They're easy to incorporate into existing code. You can leave old code alone and immediately start using the macros in new code. You don't have to retrofit an entire application.

■ They can be used in C and C++ code, although they're not necessary if you're using a class library.

■ If you need a feature that the macros don't support, you can easily write your own macros by following the model used in the header file.

■ If you use the macros, you don't need to reference or remember obscure Windows constructs. For example, many functions in Windows expect a long parameter where the value in the long's high-word means one thing and the value in its low word means something else. Before calling these functions, you must construct a long value out of the two individual values. This is usually done by using the MAKELONG macro from WINDEF.H. But I can't tell you how many times I've accidentally reversed the two values, causing an incorrect value to be passed to a function. The macros in WINDOWSX.H come to the rescue.

The macros contained in WINDOWSX.H are actually divided into three groups: message crackers, child control macros, and API macros.

Message Crackers

Message crackers make it easier to write window procedures. Typically, window procedures are implemented as one huge *switch* statement. In my travels, I have seen window procedure *switch* statements that contained well over 500 lines of code. We all know that implementing window procedures this way is a bad practice, but we do it anyway. I have been known to do it myself on occasion. Message crackers force you to break up your *switch* statements into smaller functions—one function per window message. This makes your code much more manageable.

Another problem with window procedures is that every message has *wParam* and *lParam* parameters, and depending on the message, these parameters have different meanings. In some cases, such as for a WM_COMMAND message, *wParam* contains two different values. The high-word of the *wParam* parameter is the notification code, and the low-word is the ID of the control. Or is it the other way around? I always forget. Even worse, in 16-bit Windows, the *lParam* parameter for a WM_COMMAND message contains the window handle and the notification code. If you use message crackers, you don't have to remember or look up any of this. These macros are called message crackers because they crack apart the parameters for any given message. If you want to process the WM_COMMAND message, you simply write a function that looks like this:

```
void Cls_OnCommand(HWND hwnd, int id, HWND hwndCtl,
    UINT codeNotify) {

    switch (id) {

        case ID_SOMELISTBOX:
            if (codeNotify != LBN_SELCHANGE)
                break;

            // Do LBN_SELCHANGE processing.
            break;

        case ID_SOMEBUTTON:
            break;
        :
        :

    }
}
```

Look how easy it is! The crackers look at the message's *wParam* and *lParam* parameters, break the parameters apart, and call your function. There is a WINDOWSX.H file for Win32 and a WINDOWSX.H file for 16-bit Windows. The WM_COMMAND cracker for 16-bit Windows cracks *wParam* and *lParam* differently from the Win32 version. No matter how the parameters are cracked, you still write just the one function. You instantly have code that will compile and work correctly for both 16-bit Windows and Win32!

To use message crackers, you need to make some changes to your window procedure's *switch* statement. Take a look at the window procedure below:

```
LRESULT WndProc (HWND hwnd, UINT uMsg,
    WPARAM wParam, LPARAM lParam) {

    switch (uMsg) {
        HANDLE_MSG(hwnd, WM_COMMAND, Cls_OnCommand);
        HANDLE_MSG(hwnd, WM_PAINT, Cls_OnPaint);
        HANDLE_MSG(hwnd, WM_DESTROY, Cls_OnDestroy);
        default:
            return(DefWindowProc(hwnd, uMsg, wParam, lParam));
    }
}
```

In both the 16-bit Windows and the Win32 version of WINDOWSX.H, the HANDLE_MSG macro is defined as follows:

```
#define HANDLE_MSG(hwnd, message, fn)    \
    case (message): \
        return HANDLE_##message((hwnd), (wParam), (lParam), (fn));
```

For a WM_COMMAND message, the preprocessor expands this line to read as follows:

```
case (WM_COMMAND):
    return HANDLE_WM_COMMAND((hwnd), (wParam), (lParam),
        (Cls_OnCommand));
```

The HANDLE_WM_* macros are also defined in WINDOWSX.H. These macros are actually message crackers. They crack the contents of the *wParam* and *lParam* parameters, perform all the necessary casting, and call the appropriate message function, such as the *Cls_OnCommand* function shown earlier. The macro for the 16-bit Windows version of HANDLE_WM_COMMAND is:

```
#define HANDLE_WM_COMMAND(hwnd, wParam, lParam, fn) \
    ((fn)((hwnd), (int)(wParam), (HWND)LOWORD(lParam),
    (UINT) HIWORD(lParam)), 0L)
```

The macro for the Win32 version is:

```
#define HANDLE_WM_COMMAND(hwnd, wParam, lParam, fn) \
    ( (fn) ((hwnd), (int) (LOWORD(wParam)), (HWND)(lParam),
    (UINT) HIWORD(wParam)), 0L)
```

When the preprocessor expands either of these macros, the result is a call to the *Cls_OnCommand* function with the contents of the *wParam* and *lParam* parameters broken down into their respective parts and cast appropriately.

When you are going to use message cracker macros to process a message, you should open the WINDOWSX.H file and search for the message you want to process. For example, if you search for WM-_COMMAND, you see the part of the file that contains these lines:

```
/* void Cls_OnCommand(HWND hwnd, int id, HWND hwndCtl,
    UINT codeNotify); */
#define HANDLE_WM_COMMAND(hwnd, wParam, lParam, fn) \
    ((fn)((hwnd), (int)LOWORD(wParam)), (HWND)(lParam),
    (UINT)HIWORD(wParam)), 0L)
#define FORWARD_WM_COMMAND(hwnd, id, hwndCtl, codeNotify, fn) \
    (void)(fn)((hwnd), WM_COMMAND,
    MAKEWPARAM((UINT)(id),(UINT)(codeNotify)),
    (LPARAM)(HWND)(hwndCtl))
```

The first line is a comment that shows you the prototype of the function you have to write. This prototype is the same whether you are looking at the 16-bit Windows version or the Win32 version of the WINDOWSX.H file. The next line is the HANDLE_WM_* macro, which we have already discussed. The last line is a message forwarder. Let's say that during your processing of the WM_COMMAND message you want to call the default window procedure to have it do some work for you. This function would look like this:

```
void Cls_OnCommand (HWND hwnd, int id, HWND hwndCtl,
  UINT codeNotify) {

  // Do some normal processing.

  // Do default processing.
  FORWARD_WM_COMMAND(hwnd, id, hwndCtl, codeNotify,
    DefWindowProc);
}
```

The FORWARD_WM_* macro takes the cracked message parameters and reconstructs them to their *wParam* and *lParam* equivalents. The macro then calls a function that you supply. In the example above, the macro calls the *DefWindowProc* function, but you could just as easily have used *SendMessage* or *PostMessage*. In fact, if you want to send (or post) a message to any window in the system, you can use a FORWARD-_WM_* macro to help combine the individual parameters. Like the HANDLE_WM_* macros, the FORWARD_WM_* macros are defined differently depending on whether you are compiling for 16-bit Windows or for Win32.

Child Control Macros

The child control macros make it easier to send messages to child controls. They are very similar to the FORWARD_WM_* macros. Each of the macros starts with the type of control you are sending the message to, followed by an underscore and the name of the message. For example, to send an LB_GETCOUNT message to a list box, you would use the following macro from WINDOWSX.H:

```
#define ListBox_GetCount(hwndCtl)
  ((int)(DWORD)SendMessage((hwndCtl), LB_GETCOUNT, 0, 0L))
```

Let me point out a couple of things about this macro. First, it takes only one parameter, *hwndCtl*, which is the window handle of the list box. Since the LB_GETCOUNT message ignores the *wParam* and *lParam* parameters, you don't need to be bothered with them at all. The macro will pass zeros in, as you can see on the preceding page.

Second, when *SendMessage* returns, the result is cast to an *int* to remove the necessity for you to supply your own cast. Normally you would write code like this:

```
int n = (int) SendMessage(hwndCtl, LB_GETCOUNT, 0, 0);
```

When this line is compiled for 16-bit Windows, the compiler warns you that you might lose significant digits. The reason for this is that you are attempting to put a DWORD value (returned from *SendMessage*) into an integer. It's much simpler to write:

```
int n = ListBox_GetCount(hwndCtl);
```

Also, I'm sure you'll agree that the line above is a little easier to read than the *SendMessage* line.

The one thing I don't like about the child control macros is that they all take the handle of the control window. Most of the time, the controls you need to send messages to are children of a dialog box. So you end up having to call *GetDlgItem* all the time, producing code like this:

```
int n = ListBox_GetCount(GetDlgItem(hDlg, ID_LISTBOX));
```

This code doesn't run any slower than it would if you had used *SendDlgItemMessage*, but your application does contain some extra code because of the additional call to *GetDlgItem*. If you need to send several messages to the same control, you may want to call *GetDlgItem* once, save the child window's handle, and then call all the macros you need, as shown in the following code:

```
HWND hwndCtl = GetDlgItem(hDlg, ID_LISTBOX);
int n = ListBox_GetCount(hwndCtl);
ListBox_AddString(hwndCtl, "Another string");
    :
    :
```

If you design your code in this way, your application runs faster because it doesn't repeatedly call *GetDlgItem*. *GetDlgItem* can be a slow function if your dialog box has many controls and the control you are looking for is toward the end of the z-order.

API Macros

The API macros exist to make some common operations a little simpler. For example, one common operation is to create a new font, select the font into a device context, and save the handle of the original font. This code looks something like this:

```
HFONT hfontOrig = (HFONT) SelectObject(hdc, (HGDIOBJ) hfontNew);
```

This statement requires two casts in order to get a warning-free compilation. One of the macros in WINDOWSX.H was designed for exactly this purpose:

```
#define SelectFont(hdc, hfont) \
   ((HFONT) SelectObject( (hdc), (HGDIOBJ) (HFONT) (hfont)))
```

If you use this macro, the line of code in your program becomes:

```
HFONT hfontOrig = SelectFont(hdc, hfontNew);
```

This code is easier to read and is far less subject to error.

Several more API macros are defined in WINDOWSX.H to help with commonly performed Windows tasks. I urge you to examine them and to use them.

THE BUILD ENVIRONMENT

In order to build the sample applications in this book, you must be concerned with compiler and linker switch settings. I have tried to isolate these details from the sample applications by putting almost all of these settings in a single header file, called ADVWIN32.H, that is included in all of the sample application source code files. Unfortunately, there are some settings I wasn't able to put in this header file; I was therefore forced to make some changes to each sample application's project make file. This appendix discusses why I chose the compiler and linker switches I did and how I went about setting them for the sample applications.

The ADVWIN32.H Header File

All the sample programs in this book include the ADVWIN32.H header file before including any other header file. I wrote the ADVWIN32.H header file, listed in Figure B-1 beginning on page 892, in order to make life a little easier for me. The file contains macros, linker directives, and other code that I wanted to be common across all the applications. Sometimes when I want to try different things out, all I need to do is modify the ADVWIN32.H file and rebuild all the sample applications. The ADVWIN32.H file is in the root directory on the companion disc.

The remainder of this appendix discusses each of the sections contained within the ADVWIN32.H header file. I explain the rationale for each section and also describe how and why you might want to change the section before rebuilding all the sample applications.

Warning Level 4

When I develop software, I always do my best to ensure that the code compiles both error and warning free. I also like to compile at the highest warning level possible. This way, the compiler is doing the most work for me and is examining even the most minute details of my code. For the Microsoft C/C++ compilers, this means that I built all the sample applications on the companion disc using warning level 4.

Unfortunately, Microsoft's Operating Systems group doesn't share my sentiments about compiling using warning level 4, and as a result, when I set the sample applications to compile at warning level 4 there are many lines in the Windows header files that cause the compiler to generate warnings. Fortunately, these warnings do not represent problems in the code—most are generated by unconventional uses of the C language. These uses rely on compiler extensions that almost all vendors of PC-compatible compilers implement.

The first part of the ADVWIN32.H header file explicitly tells the compiler to ignore some common warnings using the *#pragma warning* directive.

The STRICT Macro

All my sample applications are compiled taking advantage of the strict type-checking support available in the Windows header files. This support makes sure that I assign HWNDs to HWNDs and HDCs to HDCs and so forth. With STRICT defined, the compiler will issue a warning if, for example, I attempt to assign an HWND to an HDC.

In order to turn strict type-checking on, the compiler must have the STRICT macro defined prior to including the Windows header files.

Unicode

I have written all the sample applications so that they can be compiled as either ANSI or Unicode. By default, the applications compile using ANSI strings and characters, but by defining the UNICODE and _UNICODE macros, the applications compile using Unicode strings and characters. By defining the UNICODE macro in ADVWIN32.H, it is easy for me to control how I want the sample applications to build. For more information on Unicode, see Chapter 15.

The ARRAY_SIZE Macro

The ARRAY_SIZE macro is a useful macro that I tend to use in many programs I write. It simply returns the number of elements in an array. It does this by using the *sizeof* operator to first calculate the size of the entire array in bytes. It then divides this number by the number of bytes required for a single entry in the array. Here is the macro:

```
#define ARRAY_SIZE(Array)   \
   (sizeof(Array) / sizeof((Array)[0]))
```

The BEGINTHREADEX Macro

All the multithreaded samples in this book use the new *_beginthreadex* function, supplied in Microsoft's C run-time library, instead of Win32's *CreateThread* function. This is because the *_beginthreadex* function prepares the new thread so that it can use the C run-time library functions and also ensures that the per-thread C run-time library information is destroyed when the thread returns. (See Chapter 3 for more details.) Unfortunately, the *_beginthreadex* function is prototyped as follows:

```
unsigned long __cdecl _beginthreadex(void *lpsa, unsigned cbStack,
   unsigned (__stdcall *) (void *lpStartAddr), void *lpvThreadParm,
   unsigned fdwCreate, unsigned *lpIDThread);
```

Although the parameter values for *_beginthreadex* are identical to the parameter values for the Win32 *CreateThread* function, the data types of the parameters do not match. Here is the prototype for the *CreateThread* function:

```
HANDLE CreateThread (LPSECURITY_ATTRIBUTES lpsa, DWORD cbStack,
   LPTHREAD_START_ROUTINE lpStartAddr, LPVOID lpvThreadParm,
   DWORD fdwCreate, LPDWORD lpIDThread);
```

Microsoft did not use the Win32 data types when creating the *_beginthreadex* function's prototype because Microsoft's C run-time group does not want to have any dependencies on the Operating System group. I commend this decision; however, this makes using the *_beginthreadex* function more difficult in your code, especially if you define the STRICT macro when you compile.

There are really two problems with the way Microsoft prototyped the *_beginthreadex* function. First, some of the data types they used for the function do not match the primitive types used by the *CreateThread* function. For example, the Win32 data type LPDWORD is defined as follows:

```
typedef unsigned long DWORD;
```

This data type is used for *CreateThread*'s *cbStack* parameter as well as for its *fdwCreate* parameter. The problem is that *_beginthreadex* prototypes these two parameters as unsigned, which really means unsigned int. The compiler considers an unsigned int to be different from an unsigned long and generates a warning. Since the *_beginthreadex* function is not a part of the standard C run-time library and exists only as an alternative to calling the Win32 *CreateThread* function, I believe that Microsoft should have prototyped *_beginthreadex* this way so that warnings are not generated:

```
unsigned long __cdecl _beginthreadex(void *lpsa,
   unsigned long cbStack,
   unsigned (__stdcall *) (void *lpStartAddr), void *lpvThreadParm,
   unsigned long fdwCreate, unsigned long *lpIDThread);
```

The second problem is just a small variation of the first. The *_beginthreadex* function returns an unsigned long representing the handle of the newly created thread. An application will typically want to store this return value in a data variable of type HANDLE as follows:

```
HANDLE hThread = _beginthreadex(...);
```

The line of code above causes the compiler to generate another warning if you define STRICT when you compile your code. In order to avoid the compiler warning, you must rewrite the line above introducing a cast as follows:

```
HANDLE hThread = (HANDLE) _beginthreadex(...);
```

Again, this is very inconvenient. In order to make my life a little easier, I define a BEGINTHREADEX macro in ADVWIN32.H to perform all of this casting for me.

Linker Directives

One of my goals when creating the sample applications in the book was to avoid putting a lot of dependencies in the applications' project make files. For example, I could have used Visual C++'s Project Settings dialog box to add the STRICT, UNICODE, and _UNICODE macros to the project's settings, but that would have created a dependency on the project's make file. If you ever wanted to create the project's make file from scratch, you might forget to select certain options and some of the programs might not work properly.

In fact, this is what happened to me while I was developing some of the sample applications. Some of the sample DLLs require that certain linker switches be set in order for them to function correctly. Whenever I would create a new project make file for these DLLs, I always forgot to set one of the linker switches, the DLL functioned improperly, and I would have to start debugging the application and the DLL in order to find out why. As soon as I realized that the code was fine but that I had forgotten to set a linker switch, I would kick myself.

I knew that this was going to continue to be a problem for me as well as for readers of this book, so I set out on a mission to remove specific project settings from all the make files for the samples.

The real problem comes in with linker switches. Most of the compiler switches can be set using the *#pragma* directives in the source files. Setting linker switches in the source files is a little more difficult, but there is a way to do it.

When you run the linker, the linker looks in the OBJ files for a section called .drectve. The linker thinks that the strings in this section are command-line arguments to the linker. For example, if I want to tell the linker to link the application or the DLL as a Windows version 4.0 file, I can put the following lines of code in one of my application's source files:

```
#pragma data_seg(".drectve")
   static char szLinkDirectiveSubSystem[] = "-subsystem:Windows,4.0";
#pragma data_seg()
```

This tells the compiler that the OBJ file for this source file should have a .drectve section and that the string "-subsystem:Windows,4.0" should be in this section. When the linker links this OBJ file, it sees the "-subsystem:Windows,4.0" string in the .drectve section and treats this string as though it were a command-line option passed to the linker.

If you want to have multiple directives in the .drectve section, you would like to do something like this:

```
#pragma data_seg(".drectve")
   static char szLinkDirectiveSubSystem[] = "-subsystem:Windows,4.0";
   static char szLinkDirectiveShared[] = "-section:Shared,rws";
#pragma data_seg()
```

Unfortunately, there is a bug in the linker that causes it to read only the first string that appears in the .drectve section. In the example above, the linker will set the EXE or the DLL as a Windows version 4.0 image file but will not make the Shared section readable, writable, and shared. Microsoft says that they will fix this bug in the next release of the linker.

I trick the compiler into emitting the linker directives I want by using the following statement:

```
// Instruct the linker to make the Shared section
// readable, writable, and shared.
#pragma comment(lib, "msvcrt " "-section:Shared,rws")
```

When the comment *#pragma* is used this way, the system embeds library file information into the resultant OBJ file. Naturally, this library file information is embedded as linker directives that are inserted into the OBJ file's .drectve section. Unfortunately, the compiler takes whatever string I pass and prepends "-defaultlib:" to it. This means that I cannot simply use a line like this:

```
#pragma comment(lib, "-section:Shared,rws")
```

because the compiler would create a linker switch that looks like "-defaultlib:-section:Shared,rws". The linker will vomit when it sees this! So, to make this hack work, I need to use the first *#pragma* line above, which causes the compiler to emit two linker switches as a single string: "-defaultlib:msvcrt -section:Shared,rws". The biggest problem with this hack is that I am assuming that all my EXEs and DLLs link with the dynamic library version of the C run-time library instead of the static-link library version.

ADVWIN32.H

```
/************************************************************
Module name: AdvWin32.H
Notices: Copyright (c) 1995 Jeffrey Richter
************************************************************/


/* Disable ridiculous warnings so that the code          */
/* compiles cleanly using warning level 4.                */

/* nonstandard extension 'single-line comment' was used */
#pragma warning(disable: 4001)

// nonstandard extension used : nameless struct/union
#pragma warning(disable: 4201)
```

Figure B-1. *(continued)*
The ADVWIN32.H header file.

Figure B-1. *continued*

```
// nonstandard extension used : bit field types other than int
#pragma warning(disable: 4214)

// Note: Creating precompiled header
#pragma warning(disable: 4699)

// unreferenced inline function has been removed
#pragma warning(disable: 4514)

// unreferenced formal parameter
#pragma warning(disable: 4100)

// 'type' differs in indirection to slightly different base
// types from 'other type'
#pragma warning(disable: 4057)

// named type definition in parentheses
#pragma warning(disable: 4115)

// nonstandard extension used : benign typedef redefinition
#pragma warning(disable: 4209)

///////////////////////////////////////////////////////////////

// Force all EXEs/DLLs to use STRICT type checking.
#define STRICT

///////////////////////////////////////////////////////////////

// Force all EXEs/DLLs to be compiled for Unicode.
// Uncomment the line below to compile using Unicode strings
// #define UNICODE
#ifdef UNICODE
#define _UNICODE
#endif

///////////////////////////////////////////////////////////////

// Create an ARRAY_SIZE macro that returns the number of
// elements in an array. This is a handy macro that I use
// frequently throughout the sample applications.
#define ARRAY_SIZE(Array) \
   (sizeof(Array) / sizeof((Array)[0]))
```

(continued)

Figure B-1. *continued*

```
/////////////////////////////////////////////////////////////

// Create a BEGINTHREADEX macro that calls the C run-time's
// _beginthreadex function. The C run-time library doesn't
// want to have any reliance on Win32 data types such as
// HANDLE. This means that a Win32 programmer needs to cast
// the return value to a HANDLE. This is terribly inconvenient,
// so I have created this macro to perform the casting.
typedef unsigned (__stdcall *PTHREAD_START) (void *);

#define BEGINTHREADEX(lpsa, cbStack, lpStartAddr, \
    lpvThreadParm, fdwCreate, lpIDThread)            \
      ((HANDLE)_beginthreadex(                       \
          (void *) (lpsa),                           \
          (unsigned) (cbStack),                      \
          (PTHREAD_START) (lpStartAddr),             \
          (void *) (lpvThreadParm),                  \
          (unsigned) (fdwCreate),                    \
          (unsigned *) (lpIDThread)))


/////////////////////////////////////////////////////////////


// Compile all CONTEXT structures to use 32-bit members
// instead of 16-bit members.  Currently, the only sample
// application that requires this is TInjLib.16 in order
// for it to work correctly on the DEC Alpha AXP.
#define _PORTABLE_32BIT_CONTEXT


/////////////////////////////////////////////////////////////


// Force all EXEs and DLLs to be built for Windows 4.0.
// Comment out the one line below to create samples
// that run under Windows NT 3.1 or Win32s.
// NOTE: Windows NT 3.5 runs Win32 programs marked as 4.0.
#pragma comment(lib, "msvcrt " "-subsystem:Windows,4.0")


//////////////////////////// End Of File ////////////////////
```

Project Settings I Couldn't Set in the Source Files

There are a couple of project settings that I couldn't set in the source files. If you need to create new make files for any of my sample applications, you'll need to set these manually.

First, for the project's General settings, you must make sure that the Microsoft Foundation Classes combo box is set to Not Using MFC, as shown below. By default, every new project has this option set to Use MFC In A Shared DLL (mfc30(d).dll). If you fail to change this setting, the application will not link.

The only other change you *might* have to make is in the Output Directories group box. You have to make this change only if the project is a DLL or an EXE that uses one of my DLLs. (There are three sample applications in my book that do this: ModUse, PMRest, and TLSDyn.) You'll need to change the entries in the Output Directories group box because I have, hard-coded in these EXEs, a linker directive that tells the linker which directory it should look in when trying to locate the associated DLL's LIB file. I tell the linker where to look by embedding the following code in the EXE's source code file:

```
#define LIBNAME         "PMRstSub"

#if defined(_X86_)
   #if defined(_DEBUG)
      #pragma comment(lib, "Dbg_x86\\" LIBNAME)
   #else
      #pragma comment(lib, "Rel_x86\\" LIBNAME)
```

(continued)

```
    #endif
#elif defined(_MIPS_)
    #if defined(_DEBUG)
        #pragma comment(lib, "Dbg_MIPS\\" LIBNAME)
    #else
        #pragma comment(lib, "Rel_MIPS\\" LIBNAME)
    #endif
#elif defined(_ALPHA_)
    #if defined(_DEBUG)
        #pragma comment(lib, "Dbg_Alph\\" LIBNAME)
    #else
        #pragma comment(lib, "Rel_Alph\\" LIBNAME)
    #endif
#else
    #error Modification required for this CPU platform.
#endif
```

The code fragment above is from the PMRest sample, but the code for the other two samples is identical except for the first line, where I define the LIBNAME macro.

When you create a new project file for a DLL, you must set both fields in the Output Directories group box to the appropriate subdirectory as indicated by the code above. The DLL will build correctly if you do not do this, but the EXE file will not be able to locate the DLL's LIB file unless the linker is told to put it in the appropriate directory.

When you create a new project file for an EXE, you must also set both of these fields so that the linker can find the DLL's LIB file and so that the linker puts the EXE file in the same directory as the DLL. This way, when you run the EXE the system can locate the DLL file it needs.

INDEX

Italic page-number references indicate a figure, a listing, or a table.

About the author...

Jeffrey Richter was born in Philadelphia, Pa., and graduated in 1987 from Drexel University with a bachelor's degree in computer science. In 1990, Jeff wrote *Windows 3.0: A Developer's Guide* (M & T Books); and in 1992, he wrote the revised edition, *Windows 3.1: A Developer's Guide*. A third edition is due out in mid-1995. Jeff is also a contributing editor to *Microsoft Systems Journal*, for which he authors the Win32 Q & A column and has written a number of articles.

Jeff speaks regularly at industry conferences, including Software Development and COMDEX. In addition, he frequently conducts Windows NT and Windows 95 training seminars at many companies, including AT&T, DEC, Intel, Microsoft, and Pitney Bowes. He can be reached at *v-jeffrr@microsoft.com*.

Jeff now lives in Bellevue, Wash., where he is a frequent consultant to Microsoft. His code appears in Visual C++ and other applications produced by Microsoft's Personal Operating Systems group. He likes to eat teriyaki chicken bowls from Costco and top them off with Ben and Jerry's ice cream while watching *The Simpsons*. He has a passion for classic rock and jazz fusion bands.

The manuscript for this book was prepared and submitted to Microsoft Press in electronic form. Text files were prepared using Microsoft Word 2.0 for Windows. Pages were composed by Microsoft Press using Aldus PageMaker 5.0 for Windows, with text in New Baskerville and display type in Helvetica Bold. Composed pages were delivered to the printer as electronic prepress files.

Cover Graphic Designers
Hornall Anderson Design/
Rebecca Geisler

Interior Graphic Designer
Kim Eggleston

Interior Graphic Artists
David Holter & Michael Victor

Principal Typographer
John Sugg

Principal Proofreader/Copy Editor
Shawn Peck

Indexer
Foxon-Maddocks Associates

Follow the Windows® 95 Story!

For up-to-the minute changes in information about Windows 95, visit the WIN_NEWS forum, which you can find at the following locations:

On Marvel: *\\categories\computers and software \software\microsoft\windows95\winnews*

On CompuServe: *GO WINNEWS*

On the Internet: *ftp://ftp.microsoft.com/peropsys/ Win_News/http://www.microsoft.com*

On AOL: keyword *WINNEWS*

On Prodigy: jumpword *WINNEWS*

On Genie: *WINNEWS* file area on Windows RTC

You can also subscribe to Microsoft's electronic newsletter *WinNews*. To subscribe, send Internet e-mail to *enews@microsoft.nwnet.com* and put the words *SUBSCRIBE WINNEWS* in the text of the e-mail.

When Windows 95 is released, be sure to head to your bookstore for complete accounts of developing for and using Windows 95.

IMPORTANT—READ CAREFULLY BEFORE OPENING SOFTWARE PACKET(S). By opening the sealed packet(s) containing the software, you indicate your acceptance of the following Microsoft License Agreement.

MICROSOFT LICENSE AGREEMENT

(Book Companion Disks)

This is a legal agreement between you (either an individual or an entity) and Microsoft Corporation. By opening the sealed software packet(s) you are agreeing to be bound by the terms of this agreement. If you do not agree to the terms of this agreement, promptly return the unopened software packet(s) and any accompanying written materials to the place you obtained them for a full refund.

MICROSOFT SOFTWARE LICENSE

1. GRANT OF LICENSE. Microsoft grants to you the right to use one copy of the Microsoft software program included with this book (the "SOFTWARE") on a single terminal connected to a single computer. The SOFTWARE is in "use" on a computer when it is loaded into the temporary memory (i.e., RAM) or installed into the permanent memory (e.g., hard disk, CD-ROM, or other storage device) of that computer. You may not network the SOFTWARE or otherwise use it on more than one computer or computer terminal at the same time.

2. COPYRIGHT. The SOFTWARE is owned by Microsoft or its suppliers and is protected by United States copyright laws and international treaty provisions. Therefore, you must treat the SOFTWARE like any other copyrighted material (e.g., a book or musical recording) except that you may either (a) make one copy of the SOFTWARE solely for backup or archival purposes, or (b) transfer the SOFTWARE to a single hard disk provided you keep the original solely for backup or archival purposes. You may not copy the written materials accompanying the SOFTWARE.

3. OTHER RESTRICTIONS. You may not rent or lease the SOFTWARE, but you may transfer the SOFTWARE and accompanying written materials on a permanent basis provided you retain no copies and the recipient agrees to the terms of this Agreement. You may not reverse engineer, decompile, or disassemble the SOFTWARE. If the SOFTWARE is an update or has been updated, any transfer must include the most recent update and all prior versions.

4. DUAL MEDIA SOFTWARE. If the SOFTWARE package contains both 3.5" and 5.25" disks, then you may use only the disks appropriate for your single-user computer. You may not use the other disks on another computer or loan, rent, lease, or transfer them to another user except as part of the permanent transfer (as provided above) of all SOFTWARE and written materials.

5. SAMPLE CODE. If the SOFTWARE includes Sample Code, then Microsoft grants you a royalty-free right to reproduce and distribute the sample code of the SOFTWARE provided that you: (a) distribute the sample code only in conjunction with and as a part of your software product; (b) do not use Microsoft's or its authors' names, logos, or trademarks to market your software product; (c) include the copyright notice that appears on the SOFTWARE on your product label and as a part of the sign-on message for your software product; and (d) agree to indemnify, hold harmless, and defend Microsoft and its authors from and against any claims or lawsuits, including attorneys' fees, that arise or result from the use or distribution of your software product.

DISCLAIMER OF WARRANTY

The SOFTWARE (including instructions for its use) is provided "AS IS" WITHOUT WARRANTY OF ANY KIND. MICROSOFT FURTHER DISCLAIMS ALL IMPLIED WARRANTIES INCLUDING WITHOUT LIMITATION ANY IMPLIED WARRANTIES OF MERCHANTABILITY OR OF FITNESS FOR A PARTICULAR PURPOSE. THE ENTIRE RISK ARISING OUT OF THE USE OR PERFORMANCE OF THE SOFTWARE AND DOCUMENTATION REMAINS WITH YOU.

IN NO EVENT SHALL MICROSOFT, ITS AUTHORS, OR ANYONE ELSE INVOLVED IN THE CREATION, PRODUCTION, OR DELIVERY OF THE SOFTWARE BE LIABLE FOR ANY DAMAGES WHATSOEVER (INCLUDING, WITHOUT LIMITATION, DAMAGES FOR LOSS OF BUSINESS PROFITS, BUSINESS INTERRUPTION, LOSS OF BUSINESS INFORMATION, OR OTHER PECUNIARY LOSS) ARISING OUT OF THE USE OF OR INABILITY TO USE THE SOFTWARE OR DOCUMENTATION, EVEN IF MICROSOFT HAS BEEN ADVISED OF THE POSSIBILITY OF SUCH DAMAGES. BECAUSE SOME STATES/COUNTRIES DO NOT ALLOW THE EXCLUSION OR LIMITATION OF LIABILITY FOR CONSEQUENTIAL OR INCIDENTAL DAMAGES, THE ABOVE LIMITATION MAY NOT APPLY TO YOU.

U.S. GOVERNMENT RESTRICTED RIGHTS

The SOFTWARE and documentation are provided with RESTRICTED RIGHTS. Use, duplication, or disclosure by the Government is subject to restrictions as set forth in subparagraph (c)(1)(ii) of The Rights in Technical Data and Computer Software clause at DFARS 252.227-7013 or subparagraphs (c)(1) and (2) of the Commercial Computer Software — Restricted Rights 48 CFR 52.227-19, as applicable. Manufacturer is Microsoft Corporation, One Microsoft Way, Redmond, WA 98052-6399.

If you acquired this product in the United States, this Agreement is governed by the laws of the State of Washington.

Should you have any questions concerning this Agreement, or if you desire to contact Microsoft Press for any reason, please write: Microsoft Press, One Microsoft Way, Redmond, WA 98052-6399.

097-000-680